湖北统计年鉴

HUBEI STATISTICAL YEARBOOK

2017

（总第33期）

湖 北 省 统 计 局
国家统计局湖北调查总队 编

图书在版编目（C I P）数据

湖北统计年鉴. 2017：汉英对照 / 湖北省统计局，国家统计局湖北调查总队编. -- 北京 ：中国统计出版社，2017.8
ISBN 978-7-5037-8206-0

Ⅰ. ①湖… Ⅱ. ①湖… ②国… Ⅲ. ①统计资料－湖北－2017－年鉴－汉、英 Ⅳ. ①C832.63-54

中国版本图书馆 CIP 数据核字(2017)第 171447 号

湖北统计年鉴-2017

作　　者/ 湖北省统计局　国家统计局湖北调查总队
责任编辑/ 佘竞雄　李潇潇
责任校对/ 徐晓颖　胡艺
装帧设计/ 刘亚非
出版发行/ 中国统计出版社
地　　址/ 北京市丰台区西三环南路甲 6 号
邮政编码/ 100073
电　　话/ 邮购（010）63376909　书店（010）68783171
网　　址/ http://www.zgtjcbs.com
印　　刷/ 武汉临江彩印有限公司
经　　销/ 新华书店
开　　本/ 890mm×1240mm　1/16
字　　数/ 1200 千字
印　　张/ 39
版　　别/ 2017 年 8 月第 1 版
版　　次/ 2017 年 8 月第 1 次印刷
定　　价/ 380.00 元　Price:380.00(RMB)

本书附同版本 CD-ROM 一张，光盘内容以书面文字为准。
如有印装差错，由本社发行部调换。

编 者 说 明

一、《湖北统计年鉴—2017》是一本信息密集的资料工具书。通过大量数据，全面地分析、记载和反映了湖北省2016年经济、社会、科技、文化等方面的发展情况。具有信息量大、权威性强、适用性广等特点。

二、本年鉴包括综合、人口、从业人员和职工工资、固定资产投资、能源生产和消费、物价指数、人民生活、资源和环境、城市概况、农业、工业、建筑业、运输和邮电、国内贸易、对外经济和旅游、财政和金融、教育、科技和文化、体育、卫生、社会福利、湖北省开发区主要经济指标、武汉城市圈、鄂西生态文化旅游圈、长江经济带、县市概况、附录等24个部分。

三、2017年的湖北统计年鉴，篇章结构与《中国统计年鉴》保持一致，参照执行了国家统计局《省级统计年鉴指标体系目录》，采用了最新的国民经济行业分类标准和指标口径，并对英文注释和指标解释进行了全面修订。2017年湖北统计年鉴新增了长江经济带主要指标，对县域经济个别指标进行了删减。

四、本年鉴对过去发表的统计资料重新予以审核，凡与本年鉴资料有出入的，均以本年鉴为准。本年鉴中统计公报的数据为初步数，若与年鉴数据不一致，请以年鉴数据为准。

五、年鉴中指标的使用要结合文中的指标解释，以及注解合理使用，以免发生错误。

六、《湖北统计年鉴》公开出版以来，受到国内外读者的爱护与支持，对本年鉴的内容和编辑工作提出了许多宝贵意见，为此，我们特表谢意。由于水平有限，编辑工作中难免有疏误之处，竭诚欢迎读者批评指正。

COMPLIERS NOTES

I. *Statistical Yearbook of Hubei* 2017 is an information–intensive data reference book. Through a large amount of data, comprehensive analysis, records and reflects the Hubei province 2016 economy, society, science and technology, culture and other aspects of development. With a large amount of information, authoritative, wide applicability and so on.

II. The Yearbook includes comprehensive, population, practitioners and staff salaries, fixed assets investment, energy production and consumption, price index, the life of people and natural resources and the environment, city situation, agriculture, industry, construction, transportation, post and telecommunications, domestic trade, foreign economy and tourism, finance and banking, education, science and culture, sports, public health, social welfare, Hubei Province Development Zone of main economic norms, Wuhan city circle ,ecological cultural tourism circle of Western Hubei,Yangtze River Economic Zone, county profiles, Appendix 24 departments, city of part of the Department of city information, not including the city administer county.

III. In 2017 statistical yearbook of Hubei, discourse structure and "China Statistical Yearbook" remain the same, with reference to the implementation of the "provincial statistics index system directory". The statistic of yearbook adopted the lastest standard and diameter range. And the English version and the interpretation of indicators were revised thoroughy.In 2017, Hubei statistical yearbook added the main indicators of the Yangtze River economic belt, and cut the individual indicator of the country economy.

IV. The Yearbook of the past published statistical data to examine every and the almanac data discrepancies, refer to this yearbook prevail. The Yearbook of statistics data for the initial count, if the Yearbook text data are not consistent, please refer to the text data is accurate.

V. In the annals of indicators are used to combine the interpretation of indicators, as well as annotations and reasonable use, so as to avoid mistakes.

VI. *Statistical Yearbook of Hubei* published since, by domestic and foreign readers to care and support, the Yearbook content and editorial work put forward a lot of valuable advice, for this, we express our gratitude. Because the level is limited, in the editing work of unavoidable errors, we welcome suggestions and criticisms.

《湖北统计年鉴-2017》

编委会和编辑工作人员

Hubei Statistical Yearbook -2017
EDITORIAL BOARD AND STAFF

目　　录
CONTENTS

特载

SPECIAL LOAD

1 综 合

GENERAL SURVEY

2 人 口

POPULATION

3 就业人员和职工工资

EMPLOYMENT AND WAGES

4 固定资产投资

INVESTMENT IN FIXED ASSETS

5 对外经济贸易和旅游

FOREIGN ECONOMIC, TRADE AND TOURISM

6 能 源

ENERGY

7 财政和金融

GOVERNMENT FINANCE AND BANKING

8 价 格

PRICE

9 居民生活

PEPOLE'S LIVELIHOOD

10 城市概况

CITY OVERVIEW

11 资源和环境

RESOURCES AND ENVIRONMENT

12 农 业

AGRICULTURE

13 工　业

INDUSTRY

14 建筑业

CONSTRUCTION

15 交通运输、邮电

TRANSPORTATION, POSTAL AND TELECOMMUNICATIONS SERVICES

16 国内贸易

DOMESTIC TRADE

17 科技和教育

SCIENCE, TECHNOLOGY AND EDUCATION

18 卫生和社会服务

HEALTH AND SOCIAL SERVICES

19 文化和体育

CULTURE AND SPORTS

20 公共管理及其他

PUBLIC ADMINISTRATION AND OTHER

21 开发区主要经济指标

MAJOR ECONOMIC INDICATORS OF DEVELOPMENT ZONE

22 “两圈”“长江经济带”主要经济指标

MAJOR ECONOMIC INDICATORS OF "TWICE" AND "YANGTZE RIVER ECDNDMIC ZONE"

23 县域经济主要指标

ECONOMY OF CITIES AND COUNTIES

附录 全国分省主要指标

MAJOR INDICATORS BY REGION

2016年湖北省国民经济和社会发展统计公报

湖 北 省 统 计 局
国家统计局湖北调查总队

过去的一年，是湖北站在新起点上克难奋进的一年。面对经济下行压力和特大洪涝灾害双重考验，在党中央、国务院和省委省政府坚强领导下，全省上下认真贯彻习近平总书记系列重要讲话精神和治国理政新理念新思想新战略，坚持稳中求进工作总基调，化压力为动力，视大灾如大考，苦干实干，砥砺前行，实现了"十三五"良好开局。

一、综 合

2016年，全省完成生产总值32297.91亿元，增长8.1 %。其中：第一产业完成增加值3499.3亿元，增长3.9%；第二产业完成增加值14375.13亿元，增长7.8%；第三产业完成增加值14423.48亿元，增长9.5%。三次产业结构由2015年的11.2:45.7:43.1调整为10.8:44.5:44.7。在第三产业中，交通运输仓储和邮政业、批发和零售业、住宿和餐饮业、金融业、房地产业、营利性服务业及非营利性服务业增加值分别增长3.5%、5.7%、6.9%、12.4%、7.7%、18.4%和6.8%。

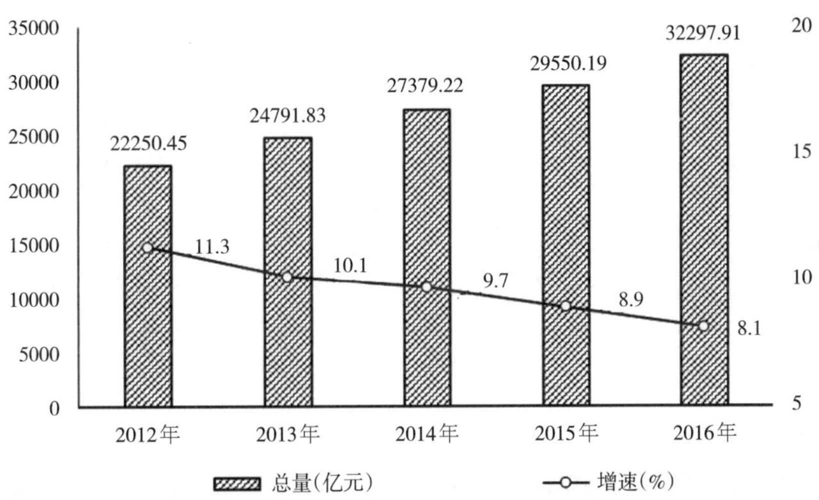

图1 2012–2016年湖北生产总值及其增长速度

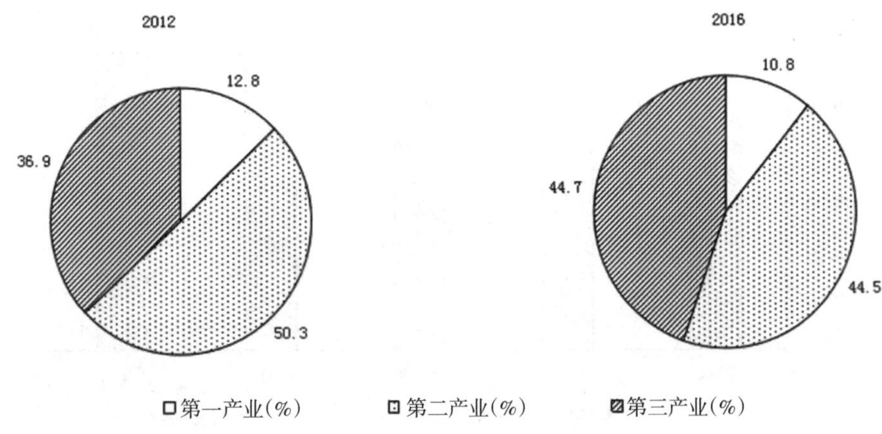

图2 2012年与2016年三次产业增加值占湖北生产总值比重

全省居民消费价格上涨2.2%。其中,农村上涨2.2%,城市上涨2.1%。分类别看,八大类商品价格呈“七涨一降”。其中食品烟酒上涨4.0%,居住、其他用品和服务价格均上涨2.8%,衣着价格上涨2.3%,教育文化和娱乐价格上涨2.2%,医疗保健价格上涨1.9%,生活用品及服务价格上涨0.4%;交通和通信价格下降2.8%。全省农业生产资料价格上涨0.3%。全省工业生产者出厂价格下降1.0%,工业生产者购进价格下降1.7%。

市场主体发展加快。全省新登记市场主体82.75万户,其中:新登记私营企业19.7万户,新登记个体工商户59.94万户。

就业保持稳定。年末全省城镇登记失业率为2.41%,比上年末下降0.23个百分点。

劳动生产率稳步提高。全省全员劳动生产率为8.86万元/人,比上年提高8.7%。

二、农　业

全年全省农林牧渔业增加值3780.79亿元,按可比价格计算,比上年增长4.0%。粮食种植面积4436.87千公顷,比上年减少29.17千公顷;棉花种植面积202.51千公顷,减少62.23千公顷;油料种植面积1452.91千公顷,减少71.28千公顷。粮食总产量2554.11万吨,比上年减少149.17万吨,下降5.5%;棉花总产量18.85万吨,减少10.91万吨,下降36.7%;油料产量329.75万吨,减少9.85万吨,下降2.9%。

畜牧、水产业保持稳定。全年全省生猪出栏4223.61万头,下降3.2%;水产品产量470.84万吨,增长3.3%。

表1　　2016年全省主要农产品产量　　单位:万吨

产品名称	产　量	比上年增长(%)
粮　食	2554.11	-5.5
棉　花	18.85	-36.7
油　料	329.75	-2.9
#花　生	71.73	5.6
油菜籽	241.63	-5.3
茶　叶	29.61	10.2
水　果(不含果用瓜)	649.72	5.5
蔬　菜	4001.70	3.9

三、工业和建筑业

工业生产保持稳定增长。全省全部工业增加值12255.46亿元,增长7.8%。年末全省规模以上工业企业达到16464家,比上年净增539家,增长3.4%。规模以上工业增加值增长8.0%。其中:国有及国有控股企业增长2.6%;集体企业下降1.5%;股份合作企业下降3.6%;外商及港澳台投资企业增长8.3%;其他经济类型企业增长7.7%。轻工业增长6.0%;重工业增长9.2%。

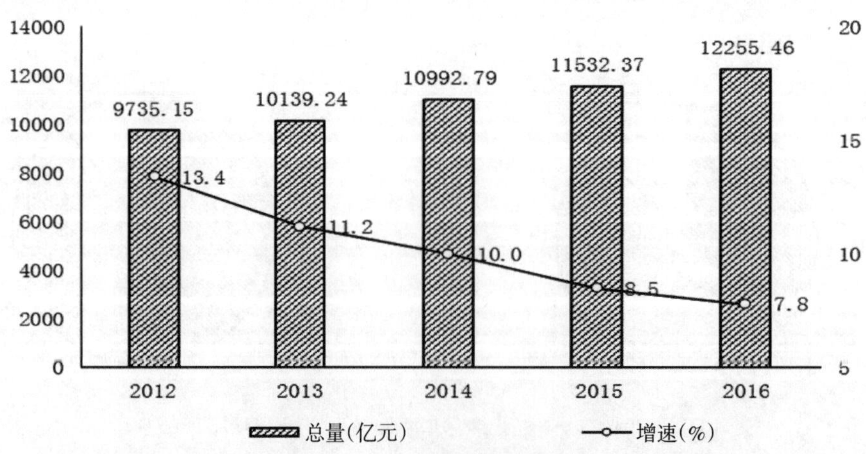

图3　2012-2016年工业增加值及其增长速度

制造业增长8.4%，快于规模以上工业0.4个百分点。高技术制造业增长10.7%，快于规模以上工业2.7个百分点，占规模以上工业增加值的比重达8.3%，对规模以上工业增长的贡献率达10.8%。

全年规模以上工业完成销售产值48725.2亿元，增长11.5%。产品销售率为99.5%，实现出口交货值2169.9亿元，增长15.0%。全省千亿元产业为17个，与上年持平。全年规模以上工业企业实现利润2441.35亿元，增长9.6%。

表2　　2016年主要工业产品产量

产品名称	单 位	产 量	比上年增长%
纱	万 吨	321.5	-0.3
布	亿 米	78.5	1.6
化学纤维	万 吨	27.5	0.7
卷 烟	亿 支	1221.0	-12.1
家用电冰箱	万 台	392.1	36.3
房间空气调节器	万 台	1206.4	-0.5
原 油	万 吨	58.1	-18.2
发电量	亿千瓦小时	2423.1	5.5
#水电	亿千瓦小时	1739.3	7.7
粗 钢	万 吨	2948.5	1.0
钢 材	万 吨	3563.8	3.7
十种有色金属	万 吨	87.5	-9.6
#精炼铜	万 吨	43.6	-14.0
水 泥	万 吨	11586.7	2.7
硫 酸	万 吨	742.7	-4.7
纯 碱	万 吨	164.8	3.3
烧 碱	万 吨	108.9	6.9
化肥(折100%)	万 吨	1156.1	-0.1
发电设备	万千瓦	68.0	-43.2
汽 车	万 辆	243.7	24.5
#轿车	万 辆	106.6	25.4
移动通信手持机	万 台	6220.7	13.6

建筑业发展步伐加快。全年全省资质以内建筑企业完成施工产值11862.40亿元，增长12.0%；实现利润509.65亿元，增长7.8%。新开工房屋建筑施工面积32702.23万平方米，增长4.3%。

四、固定资产投资

全省完成固定资产投资(不含农户)29503.88亿元，增长13.1%，其中房地产开发投资完成4296.38亿元，增长1.1%。商品房销售面积7427.16万平方米，增长18.9%，实现商品房销售额4994.05亿元，增长36.4%。按产业划分，全省一、二、三次产业投资分别为889.94亿元、12224.54亿元和16389.40亿元，分别增长41.8%、10.1%、14.2%。全省292个在建重点建设项目全年完成投资2702.86亿元，占固定资产投资的比重为9.2%。

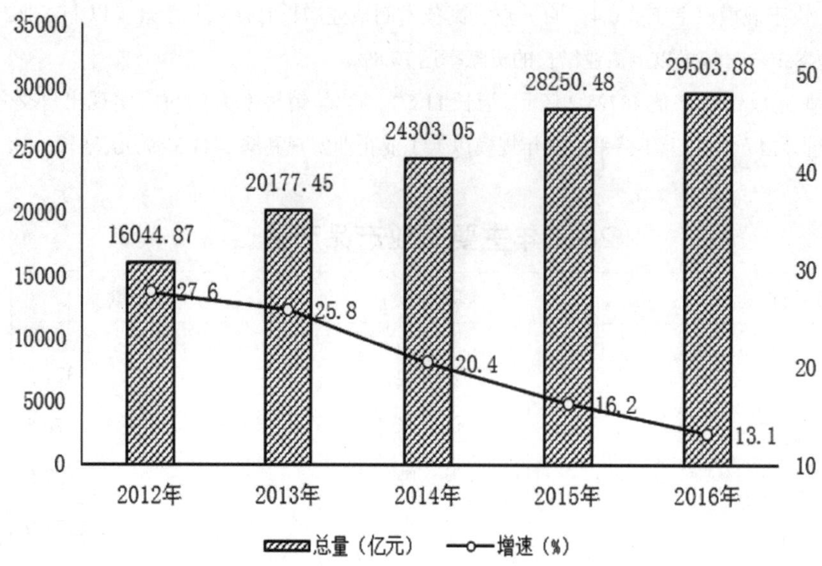

图4　2012-2016年固定资产投资(不含农户)及其增长速度

全省亿元以上新开工项目3996个,其中:第一、二和三产业亿元以上新开工项目分别为167个、2180个和1649个。亿元以上新开工项目完成投资8785.94亿元,增长27.1%。

五、国内贸易

全年全省实现社会消费品零售总额15649.22亿元,增长11.8%。分城乡看,城镇实现零售额13149.57亿元,增长11.7%;乡村实现零售额2499.65亿元,增长12.2%。其中,限额以上企业(单位)实现消费品零售额8568.81亿元,增长11.0%。

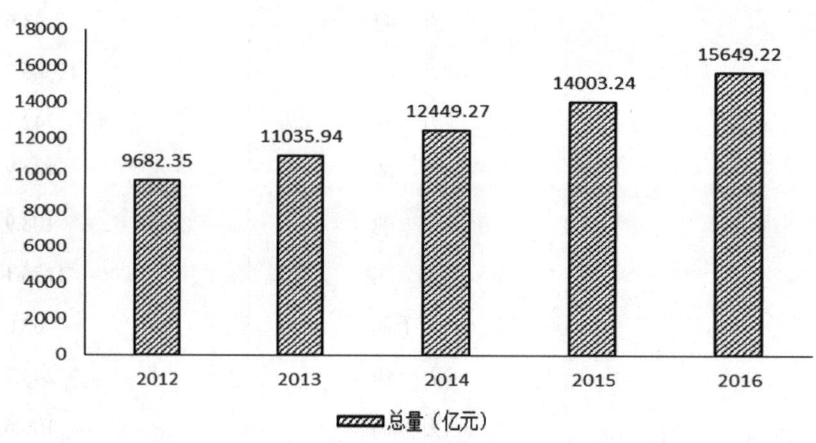

图5　2012-2016年社会消费品零售总额

2016年,我省网上零售额达到1121.2亿元,比上年增长22.7%,其中实物商品网上零售额827.7亿元,增长28.5%。

六、对外经济

全年全省实现外贸进出口总额2600.1亿元,下降8.3 %,其中:进口880.0亿元,下降13.6%;出口1720.1亿元,下降5.3%。新批外商直接投资项目235个。全年外商直接投资101.29亿美元,增长13.2%。

七、交通运输、邮电通信和旅游

全年全省完成货物周转量6159.90亿吨公里,比上年增长4.3%;旅客周转量1521.05亿人公里,增长2.0%;公路营运里程达260178.84公里,增长2.8%;高速公路里程达6204.29公里,与上年持平。

全省邮电业务总量1400.01亿元，增长44.5%。长途光缆线路总长度达到3.23万公里；局用交换机达到493.8万门；固定电话用户731.65万户；移动电话用户达到4683.75万户；全省电话普及率为92.02部／百人；计算机宽带互联网用户1131.88万户。

全省国内旅游人数5.73亿人次，增长12%；国内旅游收入4870亿元，增长13%。

八、财政和金融

全年全省完成财政总收入4974亿元，增长5.7%，其中地方一般公共预算收入3102.02亿元，增长7.3%。在地方一般公共预算收入中，税收收入2122.89亿元，增长7.7%。全年财政支出6453.07亿元，增长5.0%。

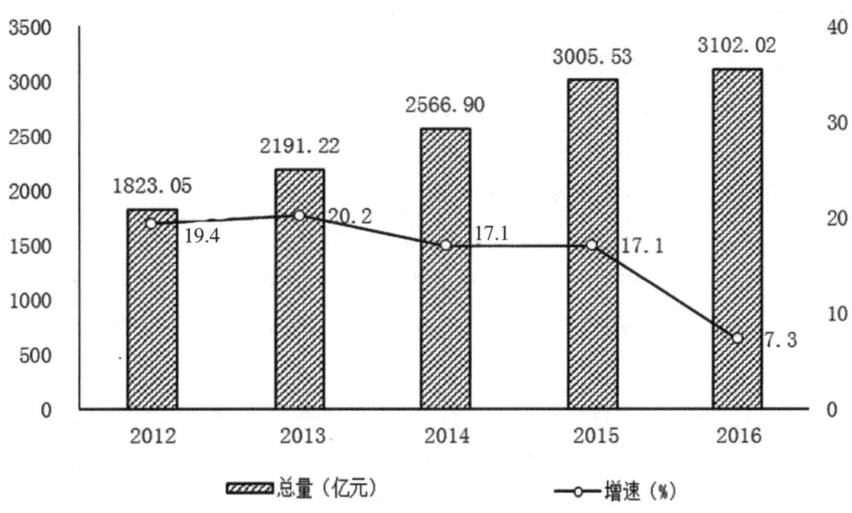

图6 2012-2016年地方一般公共预算收入及其增长速度

年末全省金融机构本外币各项存款余额47284.95亿元，比年初增加5939.07亿元。其中：住户存款22065.17亿元，增加2385.03亿元。金融机构各项贷款余额34530.72亿元，比年初增加5016.16亿元。其中：住户贷款9339.51亿元，增加1975.52亿元；非金融企业及机关团体贷款24050.61亿元，增加2771.61亿元。

全年实现保费收入1051.77亿元，增长24.67%。其中，财产险公司实现保费收入288.66亿元，增长12.5%；人身险公司实现保费收入763.11亿元，增长29.99%。支付各类赔款及给付372.36亿元，增长31.42%，其中，财产险公司赔款支出156.25亿元，增长22.91%；人身险公司赔付支出216.1亿元，增长38.33%。

九、教育和科学技术

2016年末，全省普通高等教育本专科招生39.83万人，在校生140.18万人，毕业生39.42万人；研究生招生4.08万人，在校研究生12.21万人，毕业生3.55万人；各类中等职业教育招生16.68万人，在校生45.48万人，毕业生13.84万人；普通高中招生27.71万人，在校生84.50万人，毕业生30.57万人；普通初中在校生141.49万人，小学在校生346.13万人，幼儿园在园幼儿169.95万人。

科学研究和技术开发取得新的成果。全年共登记重大科技成果2022项。其中，基础理论成果17项，应用技术成果1974项，软科学成果31项。全年共签订技术合同24248项，技术合同成交金额927.73亿元，合同金额比上年增长11.7%。

全省科学研究与实验发展(R & D)经费支出620亿元，增长10%，占全省生产总值的1.92%。全年共争取国家高技术产业发展项目6个，争取国家资金8.3亿元。

全省具备向社会出具检测报告的产品质量监督检验机构有123个，其中国家产品质量监督检验中心31个。累计有8757家企业通过ISO9000体系认证；企业获得强制性认证证书12278张。法定计量技术机构有192个，强制检定计量器具173万台件。

全省天气雷达观测站点有14个，卫星云图接受站点17个。地震遥测台网3个，地震台站47个。

十、文化、卫生和体育

2016年末，全省共有国有艺术表演团体87个，群艺馆、文化馆122个，公共图书馆113个，博物馆156个。电影放映管理机构96个，放映单位1558个。广播电台6座，电视台6座，广播电视台77座，有线电视用户1064.87万户。全年出版全国性和省级报纸13.13亿份，各类期刊2.03亿册，图书2.61亿册。

全省共有医疗卫生机构36248家，其中医院925家，基层医疗卫生机构34706家，专业公共卫生机构549家；全省共有卫生计生人员总数49.34万人，其中执业（助理）医师14.15万人，注册护士17.47万人；全省共有医疗卫生机构床位36.01万张，其中医院床位25.66万张，社区卫生服务机构床位1.46万张，卫生院床位7.29万张。

全年全省运动健儿在国际比赛中共获得冠军50项次、亚军32项次、季军25项次，其中奥运会项目最高水平比赛冠军12项次、亚军11项次、季军23项次；在各类全国比赛中，获冠军116项次、亚军102项次、第三名131项次，其中，全运会项目全国最高水平比赛中冠军12项次、亚军11项次、第三名23项次。全年销售体育彩票66.96亿元。

十一、人口、居民生活和社会保障

年末全省常住人口5885万人，其中：城镇3419.19万人，乡村2465.81万人。城镇化率达到58.1%。全年出生人口70.65万人，出生率为12.04‰；死亡人口40.9万人，死亡率为6.97‰，人口自然增长率为5.07‰。

居民收入稳定增长。2016年，湖北全体居民人均可支配收入21787元，增长8.8%，其中，城镇常住居民人均可支配收入29386元，增长8.6%；农村常住居民人均可支配收入12725元，增长7.4%。

社会保障进一步加强。年末全省参加城镇职工基本养老保险1354.40万人，其中：在职职工896.40万人，离退休人员457.90万人；参加城乡居民基本养老保险2219.70万人；参加城镇职工基本医疗保险960.99万人；参加城镇居民基本医疗保险1020.80万人；参加工伤保险651.08万人；参加生育保险511.85万人；参加失业保险人数541.88万人，全年累计领取失业保险金人数13.35万人。

全年全省城镇居民最低生活保障对象55.3万人，农村居民最低生活保障人数138.2万人，国家抚恤、补助各类优抚对象44.2万人。社会福利事业不断发展。年末全省各类社会福利收养床位33.2万张，城镇社区服务中心、站共计5112个。全年销售社会福利彩票101.38亿元。

十二、节能降耗、资源环境

全省继续大力推进节能降耗工作，单位GDP能耗继续保持下降态势，年初确定的3.4%的下降目标顺利完成。工业企业吨粗铜综合能耗比上年下降12.2%，吨钢综合能耗下降5.4%，单位烧碱综合能耗下降0.2%，吨水泥综合能耗下降4.8%，每千瓦时火力发电标准煤耗下降1.2%。

长江干流总体水质状况为优。监测的18个断面水质均达到Ⅱ～Ⅲ类，其中Ⅱ类占50%，Ⅲ类占50%。与上年相比，监测断面增加了3个，长江干流水质总体保持稳定。

全省累计已发现矿种149种，累计已查明资源储量的矿种92种。2016年我省新发现矿产地共计18处，其中特大型2处，大型1处，中型14处，小型1处。

全省自然保护区达79个，其中国家级自然保护区19个，省级自然保护区27个，自然保护区面积110.8万公顷。

注：本公报所列数据为快报数。

Hubei Province's National Economy and Society Development Statistical Communiqué 2016

Hubei Provincial Bureau of Statistics
Hubei Investigation Team of National Statistical Bureau

Last year was a year overcoming obstacles and endeavoring for Hubei. Facing dual test of economic downturn pressure and severe flood–waterlogging disaster, under the firm leadership of the Central Committee of the Communist Party of China (CPC), the State Council, the provincial Party committee and government, all the people of Hubei worked hard to implement the spirits of President Xi Jinping's important speeches, his new concept, idea and strategy of governing a state, adhered to the general keynote of making progress while maintaining stability, turned pressure into motivation, viewed severe disaster as final exam, worked hard through thick and thin, achieved a solid start for the thirteenth five year plan.

I. General Outlook

In 2016, Hubei's gross domestic product (GDP) was 3229.791 billion yuan, an increase of 8.1%. The output of primary industry was 349.93 billion yuan, grew by 3.9%; secondary industry, 1437.513 billion yuan and 7.8%; tertiary industry, 1442.348 billion yuan and 9.5%. Structure of the three industries has changed from 11.2:45.7:43.1 in 2015 to 10.8:44.5:44.7. In the tertiary industry, transport and storage and postal services, wholesale and retail, accommodation and catering, finance, real estate, profitable service and nonprofit services have risen by 3.5%、5.7%、6.9%、12.4%、7.7%、18.4% and 6.8%, respectively.

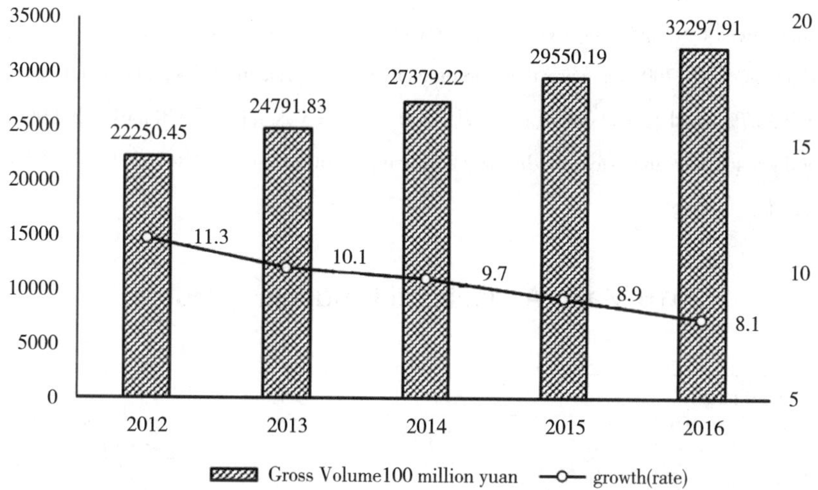

Figure I Hubei's GDP and its growth rate during 2012–2016

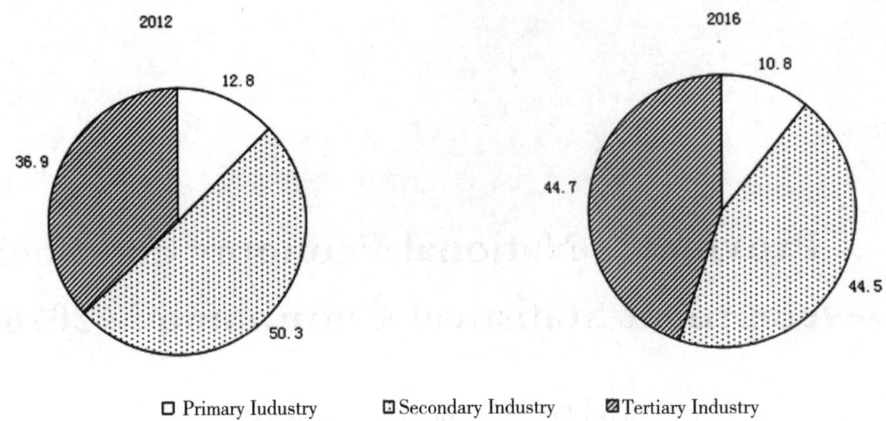

Figure II Proportion of Primary, Secondary and Tertiary Industry Added Value in Hubei's GDP in 2012 and 2016

The consumer price index increased by 2.2%. In city it rose 2.1% and in rural area, 2.2%. For the prices of the main eight kinds of commodities, the price of seven of them have risen, while one went down. In details, the price of food, cigarette and wine grew by 4.0%; residence, other commodities and service, 2.8%; clothing, 2.3%; educational, cultural and recreational, 2.2%; medical care, 1.9%; article of daily use and service, 0.4%; transportation and communication, minus 2.8%. Means of agricultural production's price increased by 0.3%. The PPI fell by 1.0%, while IPI decreased by 1.7%.

Development of market subject accelerated. Over the province, newly registered market players were 827, 500. Newly registered private enterprise contributed 197, 000 to the total number; while newly registered individual business accounted for another 599,400.

Employment rate remained steady. At the end of the year, the urban registered unemployment rate was 2.41%, decreased by 0.23%.

Our labor productivity rose in steady manner. The province's overall labor productivity was 8, 8600 yuan per person, increased by 8.7%.

II. Agriculture

This year, our province's total output value of agriculture, forestry, animal husbandry and fishery industry was 378.079 billion yuan, in comparable price, a 4.0% increase by last year. Grain acreage was 4,436,870 hectares, decreased by 29, 170 hectares; cotton plantation area was 202, 510 hectares, reduced by 62,230 hectares; oilseed acreage was 1,452,910 hectares, decreased by 71,280 hectares. The total grain output was 25,541,100 tons, 1,491,700 tons fewer than the previous year, decreasing 5.5%; total cotton output was 188,500 tons, decreased by 109,100 tons, fell 36.7%; total oilseed output was 3,297,500 tons, decreased by 98,500 tons, fell 2.9%.

Livestock breeding and aquaculture grew steadily. In this year, live pig output was 42,236,100, fell by 3.2%; aquatic product output was 4,708,400 tons, grew 3.3%.

Table 1: 2016 Major Agricultural Products of Hubei

Unit: 10,000 ton

product name	out put	Increased over 2015
Grain	2554.11	-5.5
Cotton	18.85	-36.7
Oil-bearing Crops	329.75	-2.9
#Peanuts	71.73	5.6
Rapeseed	241.63	-5.3
Tea	29.61	10.2
Fruits (melon not included)	649.72	5.5
Vegetables	4001.70	3.9

III. Industry and Construction

Industrial production maintained a steady growth. The overall output of industry was 1225,546 billion yuan, an increase of 7.8%. At the end of the year, Hubei's total number of above-scale industrial enterprises was 16,464; 539 more than previous year, grew by 3.4%. The above-scale industrial added value increased by 8.0%. In detail, State-owned and state-holding enterprises grew 2.6%; collective enterprises decreased 1.5%; joint-stock cooperative enterprises decreased 3.6%; foreign, Hong Kong and Macao investment enterprises increased 8.3%; other economic enterprises grew 7.7%. Light industrial grew 6.0%; heavy industrial grew 9.2%.

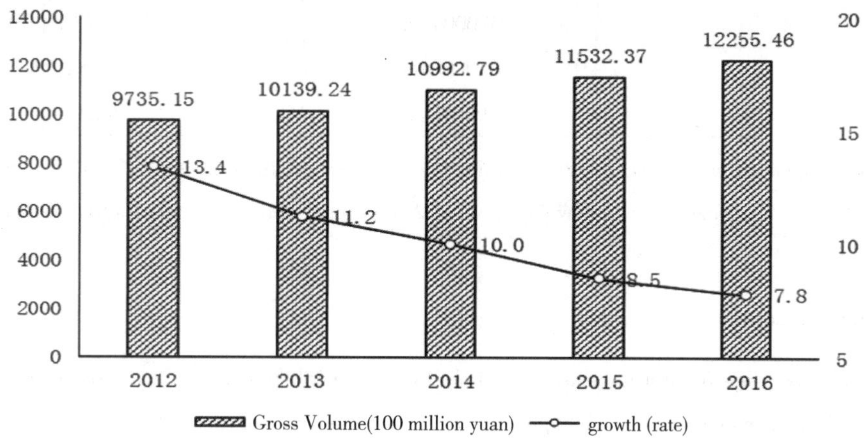

Figure III Hubei's industrial added value and its growth rate during 2011-2016

Manufacturing industry increased 8.4%, 0.4% faster than above-scale industry. High-tech manufacturing grew 10.7%, 2.7% faster than above-scale industry, took up 8.3% of above-scale industry, and contributed 10.8% to the growth of above-scale industry.

In 2016, sales value of above-scale industry was 4872.52 billion yuan, increased by 11.5%. 99.5% of the products were sold, value of export delivery was 216.99 billion yuan, grew 15.0%. Over the province, 17 industries outputted more than 100 billion yuan per year, the same with 2015. Profit of the above-scale industrial enterprises was 244.135 billion yuan, rose 9.6%.

Table 2: Output of Major Industrial Products 2016

name of the product	unit	out put	Increased over 2015
Yarn	10,000 tons	321.5	-0.3
Cloth	100 million meters	78.5	1.6
Chemical Fiber	10,000 tons	27.5	0.7
Cigarettes	100 million units	1221.0	-12.1
Household Friddge	10,000 units	392.1	36.3
Air Conditioner	10,000 units	1206.4	-0.5
Crude Oil	10,000 tons	58.1	-18.2
Power generation	100 million KWH	2423.1	5.5
#Hydropower	100 million KWH	1739.3	7.7
Crude Steel	10,000 tons	2948.5	1.0
Rolled Steel	10,000 tons	3563.8	3.7
Ten Kinds of Nonferrous Metal	10,000 tons	87.5	-9.6
#refined copper	10,000 tons	43.6	-14.0
Cement	10,000 tons	11586.7	2.7

name of the product	unit	out put	Increased over 2015
Sulfuric Acid	10,000 tons	742.7	-4.7
Sodium Carbonate	10,000 tons	164.8	3.3
Caustic Soda	10,000 tons	108.9	6.9
Chemical Fertilizer(100% equivalent)	10,000 tons	1156.1	-0.1
Power Generating Equipment	10,000 KW	68.0	-43.2
Automobile	10,000 units	243.7	24.5
#Car	10,000 units	106.6	25.4
Mobile Phones	10,000 units	6220.7	13.6

Development of construction industry accelerated. Qualified construction enterprises outputted 1186.24 billion yuan, grew 12.0%; their profit reached 50.965 billion yuan, increased by 7.8%. 327,022,300 square meters' new houses have been under construction, grew by 4.3%.

IV. Investment in Fixed Assets

The investment in fixed assets (rural households not included) was 2950.388 billion yuan, increased 13.1%. Real estate investment contributed 429.638 billion yuan to the total number, grew 1.1%. The total sold area of commodity house was 74,271,600 square meters, grew 18.9%. The total sales value of commodity house was 499.405 billion yuan, grew 36.4%. According to the industries, the provincial investment in primary, secondary and tertiary industries were 88.994, 1222.454 and 1638.94 billion yuan, respectively; accordingly grew by 41.8 %、10.1%、14.2 %. Over the province, 292 key projects under construction have totally invested 270.286 billion yuan, accounting for 9.2% of total fixed assets investment.

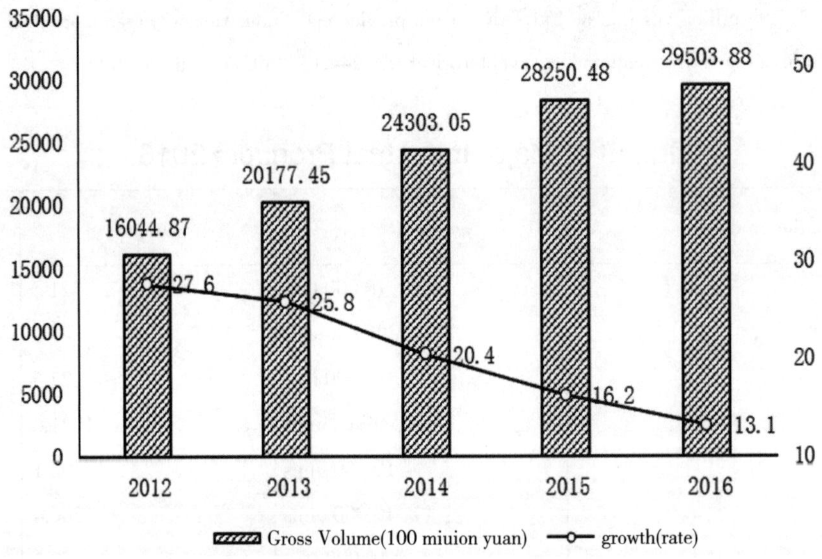

Figure IV fixed assets (rural households not included) and its growth rate during 2012–2016

There were 3996 newly–commenced projects in the province, primary, secondary and tertiary industries contributed 167, 2180 and 1649 projects respectively. The newly–commenced projects with more than 100 million yuan's total investment have invested 878.594 billion yuan, increased by 27.1%.

V. Domestic Trade

The social consumable total retail sales was 1564.922 billion yuan, grew 11.8%. In Urban areas, retail sales was 1314.957 billion yu–

an, increased 11.7%; in rural areas, retail sales was 249.965 billion yuan, grew 12.2%. In particular, retail sales of businesses above designated scale accumulated to 856.881 billion yuan, up by 11.0%.

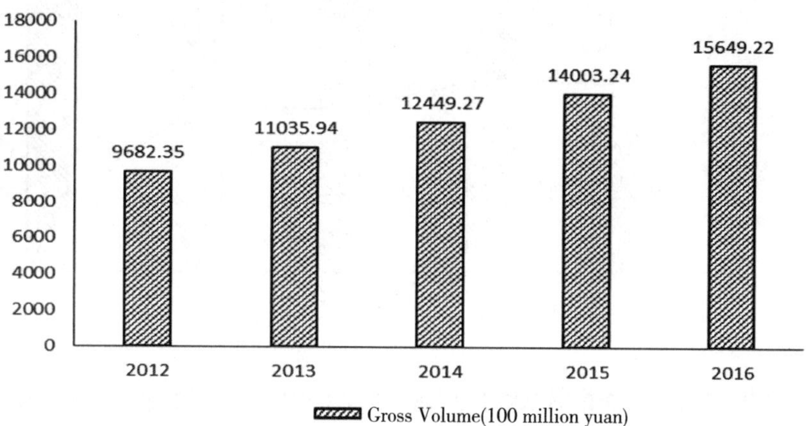

Figure V social consumable total retail sales during 2012–2016

In 2016, Hubei's on–line retail sales reached 112.12 billion yuan, a 22.7% increase from last year, physical commodity on–line retail sales was 82.77 billion yuan, increased by 28.5%.

VI. External Economy

The total foreign trade value was 260.01 billion yuan, fell by 8.3%. Import was 88.0 billion yuan, fell by 13.6%; export was 172.01 billion yuan, decreased 5.3%. 235 of foreign direct investment projects were approved. Total amount of FDI was 10.129 billion dollars, increased 13.2%.

VII. Transportation, Post, Telecommunications and Tourism

The provincial annual tonnage mileage was 615.99 billion ton kilometers, grew 4.3%; the volume of passenger transport was 152.105 billion passenger kilometers, grew 2.0%. Road operating mileage was 260,178.84 kilometers, increased by 2.8%; while highway operating mileage was 6,204.29 kilometers.

The annual income of post and telecommunications services was 140.001 billion yuan, up by 44.5%. Long distance optical cable lines reached a total length of 3,2300 kilometers; the capacity of office telephone exchanges reached 4.938 million lines; there were 7.3165 million fixed phone users and 46,8375 million mobile phone users; the provincial telephone penetration rate was 92.02 units per 100 people; broadband Internet users reached 11.3188 million.

The number of domestic tourists was 573 million person–times, grew by 12%; earnings from domestic tourism was 487 billion yuan, up by 13%.

VIII. Finance and Banking

The provincial annual general finance revenue was 497.4 billion yuan, a growth of 5.7%. In particular, the local public finance budget revenue was 310.202 billion yuan, grew 7.3%. In local public finance budget revenue, tax income accounted for 212.289 billion yuan, grew 7.7%. The annual fiscal expenditure was 645.307 billion yuan, up by 5%.

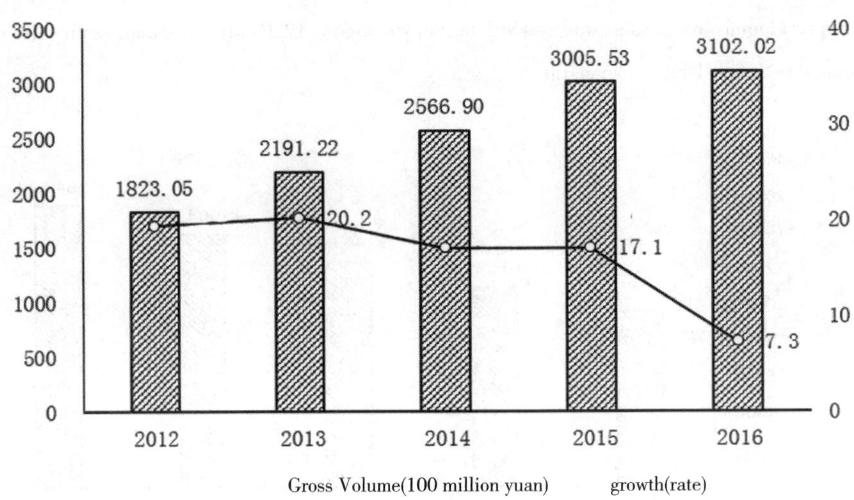

Figure VI Hubei's local public finance budget revenue and its growth rate during 2012-2016

At the end of 2016, the savings deposit in Renminbi and foreign currencies in all items of financial institutions totaled 4728.495 billion yuan, 593.907 billion yuan more than at the beginning of the year. Personal deposit was 2206.517 billion yuan, an increase of 238.503 billion yuan. Loans in all items of financial institutions reached 3453.072 billion yuan, 501.616 billion yuan more than that at the beginning of the year. In particular, households' loans were 933.951 billion yuan, an increase of 197.552 billion yuan; non-financial business and government institutions loans were 2405.061 billion yuan, increased 277.161 billion yuan.

The annual premium income was 105.177 billion yuan, grew 24.67%. Property insurance companies contributed 28.866 billion yuan to the total number, increased 12.5%; personal insurance companies' premium income was 76.311 billion yuan, grows 29.99%. Payment of various indemnities was 37.236 billion yuan, grew 31.42%. In particular, property insurance companies paid 15.625 billion yuan, increased 22.91%%; personal insurance companies paid 21.61 billion yuan, grows 38.33%.

IX. Education, Science and Technology

At the end of 2016, the total number of regular higher education enrolled is 398,300 undergraduate and specialized students, the number of students at school was 1.4018 million, and the number of graduates was 394,200. Postgraduate enrollment number was 40,800, in-school postgraduate student number was 122,100, and 35,500 graduated; number of enrollment for medium vocational education was 166,800, the number at school was 454,800, and the number graduated was 138,400, For regular high school the number of enrollment was 277,100, the number at school was 845,000, and the number graduated was 305,700. There were 1.4149 million middle school students, 3.4613 million pupils and 1.6995 million kindergarten infants.

Scientific research and technology development have made new achievements. There were 2022 registered major technical achievements. In particular, 17 were about basic theory, 1974 were about application and 31 are about soft science. 24248 technological contracts were signed, with 92.773 billion yuan's volume of transactions, up by11.7%.

The scientific research and experimental development (R&D) expenditure achieved 62 billion yuan, grew by 10%, occupying 1.92% of provincial gross domestic product. 6 national high technology and strategic emerging industry projects were brought in, with a national investment of 0.83 billion yuan.

There were 123 product quality supervision and inspection institutions that are capable of issuing product quality report and 31 of them are of national level. 8757 enterprises have received ISO9000 certification and 12278 China Compulsory Certifications were issued. The number of authorized technical institution of metrology was 192 and they compulsorily inspected 1.73 million measurement instruments.

The number of weather radar observation stations was 14. The number of satellite cloud images receiving stations was 17. There are together 3 seismic network and 47 seismic stations.

X. Culture, Public Health and Sports

At the end of 2016, in Hubei province, there were 87 state–owned art performance troupes, 122 community art centers and cultural centers, 113 public libraries and 156 museums. There were 96 film supervision institutions and 1558 showing units. There were 6 broadcasting stations, 6 television stations, 77 radio and television stations, and 10.65 million cable television subscribers. 1.313 billion copies of national and provincial newspapers, 203 million journals and 261 million books were published.

In Hubei Province, there were 36248 health institutions, including 925 hospitals, 34706 health care institutions at grass–root level and 549 specialized public health institutions. There were 493,400 medical technical personnel, there are 141,500 licensed (assistant) doctors and 174,700 registered nurses; the number of beds in health care institutions was 360,100, among which, 256,600 were hospital beds, 14,600 beds were in community health service centers, and 72,900 beds in health centers.

In international sports competitions, our athletes won the first, second and third place for 50, 32 and 25 times, respectively, in particular, in Olympic Games the numbers were 12, 11 and 23 times respectively; in all types of nationwide competitions, the numbers were 116, 102 and 131 times respectively, among which, in China National Sports Mass Meeting, they won 12, 11 and 23 times respectively. Annual sales value of sports lottery tickets was 6.696 billion yuan.

XI. Population, Living Conditions and Social Security

At the end of 2016, the provincial resident population was 58.85 million, including 34.1919 million in urban area and 24.6581 million in rural area. Our urbanization rate was 58.1%. The newly–born population was 706,500, a birth rate of 12.04‰; death population was 409,000, a death rate of 6.97‰, the natural population growth rate was 5.07‰.

Income residents increased steadily. In 2016, the Provincial residents' per capita disposable income was 21787 yuan, an increase of 8.8%, urban residents per capita disposable income was 29386 yuan, up by 8.6%; for rural residents, the number was 12725 yuan, grew by 7.4%.

Social security was further strengthened. At the end of the year, 13.544 million urban employees bought basic endowment insurances. Among them, 8.964 million were on–the–job and 4.579 million were retired; there were 22.197 million urban and rural residents bought basic endowment insurance; there were 9.6099 million urban employees bought basic medical care insurance; there were 10.208 million urban residents bought basic medical care insurance; 6.5108 million workers bought employment injury insurance; 5.1185 million bought maternity insurance; 5.4188 million bought unemployment insurance; the number of person receiving unemployment insurance was 133,500.

There were 553,000 urban minimal living standard protection objects and 1.382 million rural minimal living standard protection objects, 442,000 people were comforted and compensated by the government. Social welfare continued to develop. At the end of the year, social welfare institutions of various types provided 332,000 beds, 5112 social service centers were operation in urban area. The sales value of welfare lottery was 10.138 billion yuan.

XII. Energy–saving, Resources and Environment

The province continued to vigorously advance energy saving, our energy consumption per GDP maintained a trend of decline, succeed in achieving the goal of a 3.4% decrease decided at the beginning of this year. Comprehensive energy consumption of industrial enterprises for producing one ton of crude copper was 12.2% lower than last year, for crude steel the number was 5.4% lower, 0.2% lower for caustic soda, 4.8% lower for cement, 1.2% for standard coal consumption thermal used by power generation.

Water quality of the main stream of Yangtze River was good. 18 water quality monitoring sections showed that 100% achieved grade II~III, with grade II and III each take 50% respectively. 3 monitoring sections was newly added, the water quality of main stream of Yangtze River remained generally steady.

Inside the province, 149 types of mineral have been found. Accumulatively 92 kinds were identified as resource reserve. 18 ore fields, including 2 extra–large, 1 large, 14 middle and 1 small one were discovered in 2016's territorial resources and geological survey.

The province has 79 natural protection areas, including 19 of national level and 27 of provincial level, covering a total area of 1.108

million hectares.

Note:

I .*All figures in the Communiqué are preliminary statistics.*

1 综 合

General Survey

综 合
General Survey

从数字看2016年的湖北
Statistic about Hubei in 2016

湖 北 的 地 位
Position of Hubei in the Country

地区生产总值32297.91亿元	Gross Domestic Production: 32297.91 billion yuan	占全国的4.34%
#第三产业14263.45亿元	Tertiary Industry: 14263.45 billion yuan	占全国的3.71%
人均地区生产总值55038元	Per Capita Regional GDP:55038 yuan	相当于全国的101.96%
固定资产投资总额29503.88亿元	TotaL Investment in Fixed Assets: 29503.88 billion yuan	占全国的4.95%
社会消费品零售总额15649.22亿元	Total Retail Sales of Social Consumption: 15649.22 billion yuan	占全国的4.71%
进出口总额393.5亿美元	Total Imports and Exports: 393.5 billion US dollars	占全国的1.07%
#出口总额260.2亿美元	Total Exports: 260.2 billion US dollars	占全国的1.24%
实际外商直接投资101.29亿美元	Actual Foreign Direct Investment: 101.29 billion US dollars	占全国的8.04%
粮食产量2554.1万吨	Grain: 25.54 million tons	占全国的4.14%
钢产量2948.5万吨	Rolled Steel: 29.49 milliom tons	占全国的3.65%
发电量2423.1亿千瓦小时	Electricity: 2423.1 billion kwh	占全国的3.94%
城镇居民人均可支配收入29386元	Per Capita Disposable Income of Urban Residents: 29386 yuan	相当于全国的87.42%
农村居民人均可支配收入12725元	Per Capita Net Incomes of Rural Residents:12725 yuan	相当于全国的102.92%

湖 北 的 人 口
Population of Hubei

常住人口	Population of Permanent Residents	5885.00万人
从业人员	Employment	3633.00万人
#在岗职工人数	Staff and Workers	1030.95万人
出生人口	Birth Population	70.65万人
死亡人口	Death Population	40.90万人
城镇人口	Urban Population	3419.19万人
乡村人口	Rural Population	2465.81万人
人口密度	Density of Population	317人/平方公里

湖 北 的 经 济 发 展
Economic Development of Hubei

		79-2016年平均增长(%)
地区生产总值	Regional Gross Production	10.6
第一产业	Primary Industry	4.7
第二产业	Second Industry	12.6
第三产业	Tertiary Industry	12.5
固定资产投资	Investment in Fixed Assets	19.6
财政收入	Government Revenue	12.8
货物运输量	Cargo Transport Volume	7.6
社会消费品零售总额	Total Retail Sales of Social Consumption	15.8
出口总额	Total Exports	14.4

湖 北 的 一 天
One Day in Hubei

地区生产总值	Gross Domestic Product	88.25亿元
第一产业	First Industry	10.00亿元
第二产业	Second Industry	39.28亿元
第三产业	Tertiary Industry	38.97亿元
地方公共财政收入	Local Government Public Finance Income	8.48亿元
货物运输量	Freight Traffic	456.16万吨
竣工房屋面积	Floor Space of Building Completed	78.14万平方米
社会消费品零售总额	Total Retail Sales of Social Consumption	42.76亿元
出口总额	Total Exports	7123.74万美元
出版报纸	Newspapers Published	335.23万份
邮寄函件	Letters and Correspondents Delivered	17.26万件

1-1 土地面积与行政区划
LAND AREA AND ADMINISTRATIVE DIVISION

项目	单位	Item	unit	2000	2005	2010	2014	2015	2016
常住人口	(万人)	Population of the Whole Province	(10 000 persons)	5960	5710	5724	5816	5852	5885
土地面积	(万平方公里)	Land Area	(10 000 sq.km)	18.59	18.59	18.59	18.59	18.59	18.59
耕地面积	(千公顷)	Cultivated Area	(1000 hectares)	3283	3161.2	3323.9	3420.5	3436.2	3444.3
行政区划		Adinimisrtative Division							
省辖市	(个)	Municipality	(unit)	12	12	12	12	12	12
自治州	(个)	Autonomous	(unit)	1	1	1	1	1	1
林区	(个)	Forest Zone	(unit)	1	1	1	1	1	1
县级市	(个)	City	(unit)	24	24	24	24	24	24
省辖行政单位	(个)	Adinimistrative Units under the Jurisdiction of Province	(unit)	3	3	3	3	3	3
县	(个)	County	(unit)	41	39	40	39	39	39
乡政府	(个)	Local Government	(unit)	476	217	201	170	168	168
镇政府	(个)	Township Government	(unit)	853	737	742	761	761	759
办事处	(个)	Office	(unit)	145	163	211	302	304	307
村民委员会	(个)	Village Community	(unit)	32400	26678	26018	25606	25343	25063
村民小组	(个)	Village Groups	(unit)	259250	212587	209598	208966	208546	208050

1-2 市、州行政区划
ADMINISTRATIVE DIVISION OF MUNICIPALITIES AND PREFECTURE

单位:个 (2016年底)(by the End of 2016) (unit)

地区	Region	县级市 Cities	县 Counties	区 Districts	乡政府 Village Government	镇政府 Township Government	村民委员会 Village Community	村民小组 Village Groups
全 省	Total	24	39	39	168	759	25063	208050
武汉市	Wuhan			13	3	1	1895	16787
黄石市	Huangshi	1	1	4	1	27	800	7563
十堰市	Shiyan	1	4	3	34	72	1846	10063
荆州市	Jingzhou	3	3	2	13	89	2262	20181
宜昌市	Yichang	3	5	5	20	67	1388	8222
襄阳市	Xiangyang	3	3	3	4	74	2329	14837
鄂州市	Ezhou			3	3	18	324	4029
荆门市	Jingmen	1	2	2	2	50	1343	10001
孝感市	Xiaogan	3	3	1	23	72	2925	23345
黄冈市	Huanggang	2	7	1	16	99	4033	37411
咸宁市	Xianning	1	4	1	12	52	903	10005
恩施自治州	Enshi	2	6		34	49	2360	23072
随州市	Suizhou	1	1	1		37	852	8362
仙桃市	Xiantao	1				15	624	4455
天门市	Tianmen	1			1	21	759	6641
潜江市	Qianjiang	1				10	353	2744
神农架林区	Shennongjia				2	6	67	332

注:乡政府、镇政府、村民委员会、村民小组数只涉及农村生产经营单位数

Note:The number of village government, township government, village community and village groups only refers to the number of units run by village production operation.

1-3　全省法人、产业活动单位数(2016年)

指 标 名 称	Item	合计 Total
总 计	Total	783356
一、按地区分组	**Grouped by Region**	783356
武汉市	Wuhan	239952
黄石市	Huangshi	35606
十堰市	Shiyan	47741
宜昌市	Yichang	63592
襄阳市	Xiangyang	82264
鄂州市	Ezhou	16279
荆门市	Jingmen	33778
孝感市	Xiaogan	38932
荆州市	Jingzhou	43111
黄冈市	Huanggang	57336
咸宁市	Xianning	28432
随州市	Suizhou	21281
恩施州	Enshi	42775
仙桃市	Xiantao	10536
潜江市	Qianjiang	9080
天门市	Tianmen	10318
神农架	Shennongjia	2343
二、按国民经济行业门类分组	**Grouped by Sector**	783356
农、林、牧、渔业	Farming, Forestry, Animal husbandary and Fishery	75829
采矿业	Mining	4614
制造业	Manufacturing	88664
电力、热力、燃气及水生产和供应业	Power, Gas and Water Production and Supply	4822
建筑业	Construction	44807
批发和零售业	Transportaation, Storage and Post	207586
交通运输、仓储和邮政业	Information Transmission, Computer Service and software	21776
住宿和餐饮业	Wholesale and Retail Sale	14747
信息传输、软件和信息技术服务业	Hotel and Catering	25832
金融业	Banking	4750
房地产业	Real Estate	26387
租赁和商务服务业	Leasing and Commerical Service	85194
科学研究和技术服务业	Scietific Research, Polytechnical Service and Geological Prospecting	34874
水利、环境和公共设施管理业	Water Conservancy, Environment and Public Facility Management	6823
居民服务、修理和其他服务业	Resident Service and Others	18537
教育	Education	21728
卫生和社会工作	Health Care, Social Security and Social Welfare	12794
文化、体育和娱乐业	Culture, Sports and Recreation	13358
公共管理、社会保障和社会组织	Public Management and Social Organization	70234

NUMBER OF CORPORATIONS, INDUSTRIAL ACTIVITIES UNITS(2016)

法人单位数(个) Corporation Units			产业活动单位数(个) Number of Economic Activities Units	
单产业法人单位 Single-Industry Corperation Units	多产业法人单位 Multi-Industry Corperation Units	规模、资质或限额以上单位 Unit of Scale, Qualification or Above	合计 Total	多产业法人所属的产业活动单位 Economic Activities Units under Multi-Industry Corperation Units
755127	28229	39310	891826	136699
755127	28229	39310	891826	136699
235059	4893	9316	257785	22726
34304	1302	1841	40620	6316
45441	2300	2159	56382	10941
60951	2641	4036	73300	12349
79913	2351	4742	91678	11765
15837	442	878	18501	2664
32138	1640	2248	39643	7505
36898	2034	2207	46801	9903
40747	2364	2861	51409	10662
54543	2793	2925	70328	15785
27484	948	1618	32327	4843
20290	991	1297	25791	5501
41130	1645	1399	48798	7668
9999	537	731	12418	2419
8754	326	467	10902	2148
9372	946	531	12377	3005
2267	76	54	2766	499
755127	28229	39310	891826	136699
75576	253		77673	2097
4474	140	578	4907	433
87075	1589	15334	90728	3653
4539	283	347	6641	2102
43609	1198	3881	47539	3930
204209	3377	8030	232400	28191
20837	939	1229	27352	6515
14310	437	2423	18967	4657
25550	282	397	29418	3868
4117	633		15059	10942
25185	1202	4595	28684	3499
84099	1095	861	90310	6211
34116	758	579	37250	3134
6564	259	230	8078	1514
18290	247	179	19907	1617
19343	2385	198	25457	6114
11632	1162	191	32222	20590
13145	213	258	14336	1191
58457	11777		84898	26441

1-3 续表1 continued

指标名称	Item	合计 Total
总计	Total	783356
三、按登记注册类型分组	**Grouped by Type of Registration**	**783356**
内资	Inner Funded	779022
国有	State-owned	55915
集体	Collective-owned	9136
股份合作	Share Holding Cooperative	1331
联营	Joint Funded	899
国有联营	State Joint owned	184
集体联营	Collective Joint-owned	388
国有与集体联营	State - owned and Collective Joint-owned	89
其他联营	Other Joint-owned	238
有限责任公司	Co. Ltd	115597
国有独资公司	State-owned Solely Funded Co.	1609
其他有限责任公司	Other Co. Ltd	113988
股份有限公司	Share Holding Co.Ltd.	5346
私营	Private - owned Enterprises	447466
私营独资	Private Solely Funded Enterprises	87180
私营合伙	Private Partnership Enterprises	11307
私营有限责任公司	Private Co. Ltd	343752
私营股份有限公司	Private Share Holding Co.Ltd.	5227
其他内资	Others	143332
港澳台商投资	Hongkong, Macao and Taiwan Funded Enterprises	1736
与港澳台商合资经营	Joint Venture with Hongkong, Macao and Taiwan	571
与港澳台商合作经营	Cooperate with Hongkong, Macao and Taiwan Funded	45
港澳台商独资	Enterprises Solely Funded by Hongkong, Macao and Taiwan	1021
港澳台商投资股份有限公司	Share Holding Co.Ltd. with Hongkong, Macao and Taiwan Investment	64
其他港、澳、台商投资	Other Hongkong, Macao and Taiwan Investment	35
外商投资	Foreign Funded Enterprises	2598
中外合资经营	Sino - Foreign Joint Funded Enterprises	681
中外合作经营	Sino - Foreign Cooperative Funded Enterprises	36
外资企业	Foreign Solely Funded Enterprises	971
外商投资股份有限公司	Foreign Funded Share Holding Co.Ltd.	156
其他外商投资	Other Foreign Investment	754
四、按机构类型分组	**Grouped by Type**	**783356**
企业	Enterprise	609683
事业单位	Public Institution	41443
机关	Government Agency	9810
社会团体	Mass Organization	13280
民办非企业单位	Private Non Enterprise Unit	12996
基金会	Foundation	75
居委会	Neighborhood Committee	4209
村委会	Village Committee	26403
农民专业合作社	Farmer Specialized Cooperative	53988
其他组织机构	Others	11469

注：规模、资质或限额以上单位不包括省属重点服务业和投资专业法人单位

法人单位数(个) Corporation Units			产业活动单位数(个) Number of Economic Activities Units	
单产业法人单位 Single-Industry Corperation Units	多产业法人单位 Multi-Industry Corperation Units	规模、资质或限额以上单位 Unit of Scale, Qualification or Above	合计 Total	多产业法人所属的产业活动单位 Economic Activities Units under Multi-Industry Corperation Units
755127	28229	39310	891826	136699
755127	28229	39310	891826	136699
751085	27937	38093	884771	133686
48646	7269	841	86756	38110
8583	553	358	17725	9142
1238	93	45	2214	976
859	40	12	1576	717
173	11		408	235
368	20	4	649	281
85	4	5	165	80
233	5	3	354	121
112118	3479	15341	127056	14938
1436	173	489	2461	1025
110682	3306	14852	124595	13913
4619	727	1507	12890	8271
441185	6281	19428	468842	27657
86769	411	1151	91531	4762
11207	100	118	12036	829
338180	5572	17309	359079	20899
5029	198	850	6196	1167
133837	9495	561	167712	33875
1614	122	621	3080	1466
531	40	245	780	249
42	3	13	66	24
950	71	330	1963	1013
56	8	25	170	114
35	0	8	101	66
2428	170	596	3975	1547
630	51	307	811	181
33	3	10	45	12
881	90	248	1746	865
139	17	20	559	420
745	9	11	814	69
755127	28229	39310	891826	136699
597386	12297	38996	671953	74567
36966	4477	46	62271	25305
7532	2278		14763	7231
13141	139		14941	1800
12755	241	139	12755	
75			85	10
3546	663		4317	771
18497	7906		27816	9319
53906	82	10	54281	375
11323	146	119	28644	17321

1-4 国民经济和社会发展总量与速度指标

指标	Item	总量指标		
		1978	1990	2000
人口与就业	**Population and Employment**			
人口 (万人)	**Population (10 000 persons)**			
年末人口	Population at Year-end	4574.91	5439.29	5950.89
城镇人口	Urban	690.23	1551.51	2408.49
乡村人口	Rural	3884.68	3887.78	3542.40
就业 (万人)	**Employment (10 000 persons)**			
就业人数	Employment	1910.37	3040.40	3384.90
职工人数	Staff and Workers	457.34	698.55	677.96
#国有单位	State-owned Units	371.56	524.12	506.11
宏观经济	Marcoeconomy			
国民核算 (亿元)	**National Accounting (100 million yuan)**			
地区生产总值	Gross Domestic Products	151.00	824.38	3545.39
第一产业	First Industry	61.11	289.45	662.30
第二产业	Second Industry	63.71	313.39	1437.38
第三产业	Tertiary Industry	26.18	221.54	1445.71
支出法地区生产总值	Gross Domestic Expenditures			
#最终消费	Final Consumption Expenditures	81.70	535.49	2030.07
居民消费	Resident Consumption	74.70	434.62	1594.08
政府消费	Government Consumption Expenditures	7.00	100.87	436.00
资本形成总额	Gross Capital Formation	43.11	261.95	1882.47
固定资本形成	Fixed Capital Formation	31.40	147.13	1451.85
存货增加	Changes in Stock	11.71	114.82	430.62
固定资产投资 (亿元)	**Investment in Fixed Assets (100 million yuan)**			
固定资产投资总额	Investment in Fixed Assets	33.58	144.44	1421.55
#国有单位	State-Owned Units	33.19	100.35	857.01
集体单位	Collective-owned Units	0.39	15.59	128.32
#房地产开发	Real Estate Development		5.94	134.63
财政 (亿元)	**Public Finance (100 million yuan)**			
地方一般公共预算收入	Local Public Financial Revenue	31.38	77.85	214.35
地方一般公共预算支出	Local Public Financial Expenditures	29.98	84.82	368.77
物价(上年=100)	**Price (preceding year = 100)**			
商品零售价格总指数	General Retail Price Index	100.50	102.90	97.80
居民消费价格指数	General Consumer Price Index	100.30	104.20	99.00
利用外资 (亿美元)	**Utilization of Foreign Capital (100 million dollars)**			
实际外商直接投资	Actual Foreign Direct Investment		0.29	9.44
产 业	**Industry**			
农业	**Agriculture**			
乡村从业人员 (万人)	Rural Employment (10 000 persons)	1525.14	1791.30	1781.70
农林牧渔业总产值 (亿元)	Gross Output Value of Farming, Forestry, Animal Husbandry and Fishery (100 million yuan)	84.46	402.23	1125.64
主要农产品产量 (万吨)	Output of Major Farm Products (10 000 tons)			
粮食	Grain	1725.63	2475.03	2218.49
棉花	Cotton	36.67	51.73	30.43
油料	Oil-Bearing Crops	23.71	95.75	269.98
糖料	Sugar Crops	8.73	34.66	101.66
蚕茧	Silkworm Cocoons	0.47	0.79	1.22
肉类产量	Output of Meat	64.00	146.85	271.19
水产品	Aquatic Products	11.00	70.98	234.34

注：1.人口数除1982年、1990年、2000年、2010年是以人口普查为基数推算外，1982年及以后为人口抽样调查推算数。
2.2000年以前数据是总人口数，2001年以后数据为常住人口数。
3.2016年，固定资产投资总额对2015年基数进行调整，且不再包含农户投资。

AGGREGATE INDICATORS OF NATIONAL ECNONOMIC AND SOCIAL DEVELOPMENT, THEIR INDICES AND GROWTH RATES

Aggregate Data			速度指标 Indices and Growth Rates								
			2016年比下列各年增长(%) Increases					年平均增长(%) Average Annual Growth Rate			
2010	2015	2016	1978	1990	2000	2010	2015	1979~2016	1991~2016	2001~2016	2011~2016
5723.77	5851.50	5885.00	28.6	8.2	−1.1	2.8	0.6	0.7	0.3	−0.1	0.5
2844.95	3326.58	3419.19	395.4	120.4	42.0	20.2	2.8	4.3	3.1	2.2	3.1
2878.82	2524.92	2465.81	−36.5	−36.6	−30.4	−14.3	−2.3	−1.2	−1.7	−2.2	−2.5
3645.00	3658.00	3633.00	90.2	19.5	7.3	−0.3	−0.7	1.7	0.7	0.4	−0.1
685.21	980.01	1030.95	125.4	47.6	52.1	50.5	5.2	2.2	1.5	2.7	7.0
277.60	260.27	258.17	−30.5	−50.7	−49.0	−7.0	−0.8	−1.0	−2.7	−4.1	−1.2
15967.61	29550.19	32297.91	4558.9	1476.8	461.50	80.1	8.1	10.6	11.2	11.4	10.3
2147.00	3309.84	3659.33	473.4	200.3	104.34	30.0	3.9	4.7	4.3	4.6	4.5
7767.24	13503.56	14375.13	8973.8	2549.2	638.63	90.9	7.8	12.6	13.4	13.9	11.4
6053.37	12736.79	14263.45	8657.4	1873.0	475.93	84.5	9.5	12.5	12.2	11.6	10.7
7389.80	13799.70	15279.99	3501.4	1024.3	399.8	75.9	9.0	9.9	9.8	10.6	3.6
5136.78	10167.87	11379.23	2742.1	878.3	374.0	88.5	10.3	9.2	9.2	10.2	4.0
2253.02	3631.83	3900.76	11130.4	1697.7	487.8	46.5	5.3	13.2	11.8	11.7	2.4
8511.17	17418.40	18383.27	8793.6	2811.5	567.4	98.4	5.5	12.5	13.8	12.6	4.4
8200.40	16757.35	18112.84	4775.7	1867.6	245.5	102.2	7.9	10.8	12.1	8.1	4.5
310.77	661.05	270.43	276.2	−18.2	−69.2	−12.0	−57.7	3.5	−0.8	−7.1	−0.8
10802.69	29191.06	29503.88	87761.5	20326.4	1975.5	173.1	13.1	19.6	23.6	21.7	21.2
3768.95	6983.99	8021.33	24067.9	7893.4	836.0	112.8	25.6	15.4	18.9	14.3	11.7
602.80	754.53	677.42	173597.4	4245.2	427.9	12.4	−5.2	15.8	17.9	12.7	6.1
1618.24	4249.23	4296.38		72229.6	3091.3	165.5	1.1			26.4	21.7
1011.20	3005.53	3102.06	9785.5	3884.7	1347.2	206.8	3.2	12.8	15.2	18.2	20.5
2501.40	6132.84	6422.98	21324.2	7472.5	1641.7	156.8	4.7	15.2	18.1	19.6	17.0
103.10	100.50	100.80	0.3	−2.0	3.1	−2.2	0.3		−0.1	0.2	−0.4
102.90	101.50	102.20	1.9	−1.9	3.2	−0.7	0.7		−0.1	0.2	−0.1
40.50	89.48	101.29		34827.6	973.0	150.1	13.2		25.3	16.0	16.5
2154.44	2300.88	2290.90	50.2	27.9	28.6	6.3	−0.4	1.1	1.0	1.6	1.0
3501.99	5728.56	6278.35	7333.5	1460.9	457.8	79.3	9.6	12.0	11.1	11.3	10.2
2315.80	2703.28	2554.11	48.0	3.2	15.1	10.3	−5.5	1.0	0.1	0.9	1.6
47.18	29.83	18.85	−48.6	−63.6	−38.1	−60.0	−36.8	−1.7	−3.8	−2.9	−14.2
311.80	339.60	329.75	1290.8	244.4	22.1	5.8	−2.9	7.2	4.9	1.3	0.9
32.36	32.03	37.51	329.7	8.2	−63.1	15.9	17.1	3.9	0.3	−6.0	2.5
0.71	0.67	0.63	34.0	−20.3	−48.4	−11.3	−6.0	0.8	−0.9	−4.0	−2.0
379.42	431.93	424.18	562.8	188.9	56.4	11.8	−1.8	5.1	4.2	2.8	1.9
353.09	455.80	470.84	4180.4	563.3	100.9	33.3	3.3	10.4	7.5	4.5	4.9

Note: a)Data of 1982,1990,2000.and 2010 are based on population census Data of other years are based on sampling survey
b)Data before 2000 refer to total population. Data after 2001 refer to permanent residents
c)Since 2016,the basic number of 2015 is adjusted and famer investment is no longer included in the social fixed assets investment.

1-4 续表 1 continued

指 标		Item		总量指标 1978	1990	2000
工业		**Industry**				
主要工业产品产量	(万吨)	Output of Major Industrial Products	(10000 tons)			
粗 钢		Steel		307.97	629.25	895.92
成品钢材		Rolled-Steel		184.63	533.07	811.10
发电量	(亿千瓦小时)	Electricity	(100 million kWh)	91.64	340.39	538.11
原煤		Coal		644.01	924.26	389.34
农用化肥(折100%)		Chemical Furtilizers		27.62	132.07	221.11
化学农药		Chemical Pesicide		2.97	1.07	5.18
水泥		Cement		328.65	987.00	2460.92
化学纤维		Chemical Fiber		0.48	2.48	9.82
布	(亿米)	Cloth	(100 million meter)	6.70	14.09	17.15
汽车	(万辆)	Automobile	(10000 Units)	0.80	11.38	19.57
建筑业		**Construction**				
建筑业企业职工平均人数	(万人)	Average Number of Employed Persons	(10000 persons)	25.94	41.88	82.76
建筑业总产值	(亿元)	Gross Output Value	(100 million yuan)	11.11	49.30	454.35
施工房屋面积	(万平方米)	Floor Space of Building Under Construction	(10 000 sq.m)	596.00	1684.90	6256.50
竣工房屋面积	(万平方米)	Floor Space of Building Completed	(10 000 sq.m)	297.40	785.90	3150.10
交通运输		**Transportation**				
货运量	(万吨)	Freight Traffic	(10 000 tons)	10199.08	10916.10	9345.19
#铁路		Railway		3342.00	3901.00	3857.00
公路		Highway		3382.00	2941.00	2228.00
水运		Waterway		3096.00	3784.00	3255.00
客运量	(万人)	Passenger Capacity	(10000 persons)	12009.20	32145.93	31593.00
#铁路		Railway		2854.00	2107.00	3469.00
公路		Highway		7429.00	27333.00	27184.00
水运		Waterway		1722.00	2693.00	679.00
港口货物吞吐量	(万吨)	Volume of Freight Handled at Seaports	(10 000 tons)			4113.46
邮电通信业		**Postal Telecommunication Services**				
邮电业务总量	(亿元)	Total Business Revenue	(100 million yuan)	0.56	4.80	116.60
函件	(亿件)	Number of Letters Delivered	(100 million pieces)	1.18	2.39	3.62
年末移动电话用户	(万户)	Number of Local Telephone Users	(10 000 units)			
国际互联网用户	(万户)	Internet Users	(10 000 units)			
农村电话用户	(万户)	Rural Telephone Users	(10 000 units)	4.13	7.07	180.00
国内商业		**Domestic Commerce**				
社会消费品零售总额	(亿元)	Total Retail Sales of Consumer Goods	(100 million yuan)	59.84	326.36	1789.35
对外经济贸易和旅游		**Foreign Trade and Tourism**				
进出口总额	(亿美元)	Total Imports and Exports	(100 million ollars)	1.73	11.90	32.10
进口		Imports		0.14	1.18	12.79
出口		Exports		1.59	10.72	19.31
入境旅游人数	(万人次)	Number of Tourists Received	(10 000 persons)	1.01	15.57	45.08
金融保险	**(亿元)**	**Banking and Insurance**	**(100 million yuan)**			
金融机构存款		Deposits of Banking System		42.16	406.56	3037.22
金融机构贷款		Loans of Banking System		96.78	732.77	3147.77
国内保险保费收入		Domestic Premium			6.19	60.53

Aggregate Data			速 度 指 标 Indices and Growth Rates								
			2016年比下列各年增长(%) Increases					年平均增长(%) Average Annual Growth Rate			
2010	2015	2016	1978	1990	2000	2010	2015	1979~2016	1991~2016	2001~2016	2011~2016
2498.67	2919.77	2948.48	857.4	368.6	229.1	18.0	1.0	6.1	6.1	7.7	2.8
2894.72	3421.22	3563.79	1830.2	568.5	339.4	23.1	4.2	8.1	7.6	9.7	3.5
2028.67	2301.43	2423.14	2544.2	611.9	350.3	19.4	5.3	9.0	7.8	9.9	3.0
1291.71	698.09	547.42	–15.0	–40.8	40.6	–57.6	–21.6	–0.4	–2.0	2.2	–13.3
899.08	1408.13	1156.05	4085.6	775.3	422.8	28.6	–17.9	10.3	8.7	10.9	4.3
19.71	25.39	27.81	836.4	2499.1	436.9	41.1	9.5	6.1	13.3	11.1	5.9
8982.87	11288.92	11586.66	3425.5	1073.9	370.8	29.0	2.6	9.8	9.9	10.2	4.3
11.66	35.35	27.49	5627.1	1008.5	179.9	135.8	–22.2	11.2	9.7	6.6	15.4
46.38	79.85	78.49	1071.5	457.1	357.7	69.2	–1.7	6.7	6.8	10.0	9.2
172.29	196.85	243.69	30361.3	2041.4	1145.2	41.4	23.8	16.2	12.5	17.1	5.9
170.71	232.85	269.17	937.7	542.7	225.2	57.7	15.6	6.4	7.4	7.6	7.9
4344.39	10591.71	11862.40	106672.3	23961.7	2510.9	173.1	12.0	20.1	23.5	22.6	18.2
25046.72	62195.32	72759.57	12108.0	4218.3	1062.9	190.5	17.0	13.5	15.6	16.6	19.5
12813.44	26825.20	28599.93	9516.7	3539.1	807.9	123.2	6.6	12.8	14.8	14.8	14.3
97006.94	156356.93	165124.84	1519.0	1412.7	1667.0	70.2	5.6	7.6	11.0	19.7	9.3
10145.60	6579.00	6744.20	101.8	72.9	74.9	–33.5	2.5	1.9	2.1	3.6	–6.6
71020.00	115800.30	122654.50	3526.7	4070.5	5405.2	72.7	5.9	9.9	15.4	28.5	9.5
15832.00	33968.00	35715.80	1053.6	843.9	997.3	125.6	5.1	6.6	9.0	16.2	14.5
105415.50	104693.75	105813.14	781.1	229.2	234.9	0.4	1.1	5.9	4.7	7.8	0.1
7281.30	15083.90	15855.30	455.5	652.5	357.1	117.8	5.1	4.6	8.1	10.0	13.8
96873.00	87953.26	88220.89	1087.5	222.8	224.5	–8.9	0.3	6.7	4.6	7.6	–1.5
375.80	574.46	572.22	–66.8	–78.8	–15.7	52.3	–0.4	–2.9	–5.8	–1.1	7.3
18782.67	32949.52	35191.90			755.5	87.4	6.8			14.4	11.0
1028.09	962.66	1400.01	249901.8	29066.9	1100.7	36.2	45.4	22.9	24.4	16.8	5.3
1.00	0.68	0.63	–46.5	–73.6	–82.5	–36.8	–7.1	–1.6	–5.0	–10.3	–7.4
3454.70	4650.60	4683.75				35.6	0.7				5.2
459.40	983.50	1131.88				146.4	15.1				16.2
355.70	240.00	199.90	4740.2	2727.4	11.1	–43.8	–16.7	10.7	13.7	0.7	–9.2
7013.90	14003.24	15649.22	26051.8	4695.1	774.6	123.1	11.8	15.8	16.1	14.5	14.3
259.07	455.86	393.98	22673.4	3210.8	1127.4	52.1	–13.6	15.4	14.4	17.0	7.2
114.65	163.72	133.25	95078.6	11192.4	941.8	16.2	–18.6	19.8	19.9	15.8	2.5
144.42	292.13	260.73	16298.1	2332.2	1250.2	80.5	–10.7	14.4	13.1	17.7	10.3
181.74	311.76	337.56	33321.8	2068.0	648.8	85.7	8.3	16.5	12.6	13.4	10.9
21568.31	40896.52	47284.95	112055.9	11530.5	1456.8	119.2	15.6	20.3	20.1	18.7	14.0
14136.58	28338.90	34530.72	35579.6	4612.4	997.0	144.3	21.8	16.7	16.0	16.1	16.0
500.33	843.63	1051.00		16879.0	1636.3	110.1	24.6		21.8	19.5	13.2

1–4 续表 2 continued

指 标		Item		1978	1990
教育、科技、文化		**Education, Science and Technology,Culture and**			
教育		**Education**			
高等学校本专科在校学生	(万人)	Students Enrollment in Institutions of Higher Eduction	(10 000persons)	4.94	13.04
中等专业学校在校学生	(万人)	Students Enrollment in Specialized Secondary Schools	(10 000persons)	5.36	1458.00
普通中学在校学生	(万人)	Students Enrollment in Regular Secondary Schools	(10 000persons)	372.38	211.56
小学在校学生	(万人)	Students Enrollment in Primary Schools	(10 000persons)	765.73	623.06
文化		**Culture**			
图书出版量	(亿册)	Books Published	(100 million copies)	1.62	4.02
杂志出版量	(亿册)	Magazines Issued	(100 million copies)	0.09	0.73
报纸出版量	(亿份)	Newspaper Issued	(100 million copies)	1.97	6.24
家庭、生活、环境		**Family, People's Livelihood and Environment**			
家庭		**Family**			
城镇居民平均每户家庭人口	(人)	Average Household size in Urban Areas	(person)	4.32	3.47
农村居民平均每户常住人口	(人)	Average Household size in Rural Areas	(person)	6.02	4.67
居住		**Housing**			
城镇居民人均住房建筑面积	(平方米)	Per Capita Net Floor Space of Urban Residents	(sq.m)		9.80
农村居民人均住房面积	(平方米)	Per Capita Net Floor Space of Rural Residents	(sq.m)		25.73
生活		**People's Livelihood**			
城镇居民人均可支配收入	(元)	Per Capita Annual Disposbale Income of Urban Residents	(yuan)	325.00	1427.20
农村居民人均可支配收入	(元)	Per Capita Annual Disposbale Income of Rural Residents	(yuan)	110.52	670.80
居民储蓄存款余额	(亿元)	Saving Deposit	(100 million yuan)	6.96	244.38
工资		**Wages**			
工资总额	(亿元)	Total Wages of Staff and Workers	(100 million yuan)	25.89	131.24
职工平均工资	(元)	Average Wages of Staff and Workers	(yuan)	581.00	1903.00
卫生		**Health Care**			
卫生机构数	(个)	Number of Health Care Organizations	(unit)	5940	10472
#医院		Hospitals		1817	2024
床位数	(万张)	Number of Hospital Beds	(10 000 units)	11.52	16.34
#医院		Hospitals		10.34	13.16
卫生技术人员数	(万人)	Number of Medical Technical Personels	(10 000 persons)	14.06	20.92
#职业(助理)医师		Professional(assitant)Doctors		5.82	8.68
环境		**Environment**			
污染治理项目本年完成投资	(亿元)	Investment for the Pollusion Treatment projects Completed	(100 million yuan)		1.81
本年施工污染治理项目数	(个)	Number of Pullution Treatment Project Under Construction	(unit)		1545
工业废水排放量	(亿吨)	Volume of Industrial Waste Water Discharged	(100 million tons)		16.23

总量指标 Aggregate Data				速 度 指 标 Indices and Growth Rates								
				2016年比下列各年增长(%) increases					年平均增长(%) Average Annual Growth Rate			
2000	2010	2015	2016	1978	1990	2000	2010	2015	1979~ 2016	1991~ 2016	2001~ 2016	2011~ 2016
34.66	129.69	140.87	139.99	2733.8	973.5	303.9	7.9	-0.6	9.2	9.6	9.1	1.3
27.86	90.38	36.49	37.56	600.7	-97.4	34.8	-58.4	2.9	5.3	-13.1	1.9	-13.6
350.93	341.83	224.13	225.99	-39.3	6.8	-35.6	-33.9	0.8	-1.3	0.3	-2.7	-6.7
667.74	365.55	335.81	346.13	-54.8	-44.4	-48.2	-5.3	3.1	-2.1	-2.2	-4.0	-0.9
2.88	2.75	2.63	2.70	66.7	-32.8	-6.2	-1.8	2.7	1.4	-1.5	-0.4	-0.3
2.20	3.01	2.51	1.85	1955.6	153.4	-15.9	-38.5	-26.3	8.3	3.6	-1.1	-7.8
13.42	18.17	15.39	12.27	522.8	96.6	-8.6	-32.5	-20.3	4.9	2.6	-0.6	-6.3
3.14	2.93	2.85	2.86	-33.8	-17.6	-9.0	-2.4	0.3	-1.1	-0.7	-0.6	-0.4
4.11	3.98	2.88	2.89	-52.0	-38.2	-29.7	-27.4	0.3	-1.9	-1.8	-2.2	-5.2
13.90	33.20	43.18	44.45		353.6	219.8	33.9	3.0		6.0	7.5	5.0
30.11	40.99	55.61	57.67		124.2	91.5	40.7	3.7		3.2	4.1	5.9
5524.50	16058.37	27051.47	29385.80	8941.8	1959.0	431.9	83.0	8.6	12.6	12.3	11.0	10.6
2268.50	5832.27	11843.89	12724.97	11413.7	1797.0	460.9	118.2	7.4	13.3	12.0	11.4	13.9
1908.80	9851.00	19566.1	22065.2	316928.3	8929.0	1056.0	124.0	12.8	23.6	18.9	16.5	14.4
405.34	1870.51	4582.41	5212.80	20034.4	3872.0	1186.0	178.7	13.8	15.0	15.2	17.3	18.6
7565.00	28092.00	47320.00	51415.00	8749.4	2601.8	579.6	83.0	8.7	12.5	13.5	12.7	10.6
11065	10305	36173	36261	510.5	246.3	227.7	251.9	0.2	4.9	4.9	7.7	23.3
2041	603	869	928	-48.9	-54.2	-54.5	53.9	6.8	-1.8	-3.0	-4.8	7.4
14.96	20.07	34.38	36.16	213.9	121.3	141.7	80.2	5.2	3.1	3.1	5.7	10.3
12.99	13.51	24.66	25.73	148.8	95.5	98.1	90.5	4.3	2.4	2.6	4.4	11.3
23.88	25.16	36.76	38.54	174.1	84.2	61.4	53.2	4.8	2.7	2.4	3.0	7.4
10.30	9.95	13.60	14.24	144.7	64.1	38.3	43.1	4.7	2.4	1.9	2.0	6.2
8.52	27.74	15.79	16.91		834.3	98.5	-39.0	7.1		9.0	4.4	-7.9
851	226	199	302		-80.5	-64.5	33.6	51.8		-6.1	-6.3	5.0
10.67	9.46	8.08	4.91		-69.7	-54.0	-48.1	-39.2		-4.5	-4.7	-10.4

1-5 国民经济和社会发展结构指标
STRUCTURAL INDICATORS ON NATIONAL ECONOMIC AND SOCIAL DEVELOPMENT

单位:% (%)

指 标	Item	1978	2000	2005	2010	2014	2015	2016
人口与就业	**Population and Employment**							
人 口	**Population**							
城乡结构	Urban and Rural Structure							
城镇	Urban	14.6	40.2	43.2	49.7	55.7	56.9	58.1
乡村	Rural	85.4	59.8	56.8	50.3	44.3	43.1	41.9
性别结构	Sexual Structure							
男	Male	51.3	52.1	51.8	51.4	51.2	52.0	52.0
女	Female	48.7	47.9	48.2	48.6	48.8	48.0	48.0
就 业	**Employment**							
产业结构	Industrial Structure							
第一产业	First Industry	77.0	48.0	47.7	46.4	40.3	38.4	36.8
第二产业	Second Industry	14.1	20.8	20.5	20.7	22.6	22.8	23.0
第三产业	Tertiary Industry	8.9	31.2	31.8	32.9	37.1	38.8	40.1
经济类型结构	Structrues by Ownership							
城镇单位从业人员	Staff and Workers Employed in Urban Units							
国有单位	State-Owned	81.2	74.7	62.1	40.4	26.3	26.9	25.5
城镇集体单位	Collective-Owned	18.8	14.3	8.0	3.1	1.5	1.3	1.2
其他单位	Others		11.0	29.9	56.5	72.2	71.8	73.3
宏观经济	**Macroeconomy**							
国民核算	**National Accounting**							
地区生产总值产业结构	Industrial Structure							
第一产业	First Industry	40.5	18.7	16.4	13.4	11.6	11.2	11.3
第二产业	Second Industry	42.2	40.5	43.3	48.7	46.9	45.7	44.5
第三产业	Tertiary Industry	17.3	40.8	40.3	37.9	41.5	43.1	44.2
地区生产总值支出结构	Domestic Expenditures							
最终消费	Total Consumption	54.0	54.0	55.9	45.7	43.7	44.2	45.5
居民消费	Residents Consumption	49.4	42.4	42.7	31.7	31.8	32.6	33.9
政府消费	Government Consumption Expenditures	4.6	11.6	13.2	13.9	12.0	11.6	11.6
资本形成总额	Gross Capital Formation	28.5	50.0	45.1	52.6	56.1	55.8	54.8
固定资本	Fixed Capital Formation	20.8	38.6	43.0	50.7	53.8	53.7	54.0
存货增加	Changes in Stock	7.7	11.4	2.1	1.9	2.3	2.1	0.8
净出口	Net Exports	17.4	-4.0	-1.0	1.7	0.2	0.0	-0.3
投 资	**Investment**							
经济类型结构	Structrues by Ownership							
国有经济	State-Owned	98.8	60.3	38.7	34.9	23.3	23.9	27.2
集体经济	Collective-Owned	1.2	9.0	2.8	5.6	3.3	2.6	2.3
其他	Others		30.7	58.5	59.5	73.4	73.5	70.5
资金来源结构	Structure of Funded Sources							
国家预算资金	State Budget	77.2	10.0	9.0	8.0	4.4	4.6	6.2
国内贷款	Domestic Loans	0.4	17.2	16.7	16.4	11.5	10.0	10.4
利用外资	Foreign Investment		2.0	2.5	1.4	0.3	0.2	0.2
自筹资金	Fundraising	18.0	54.9	52.7	62.1	74.9	77.0	69.9
其他投资	Others	4.3	15.9	19.1	12.2	8.8	8.2	13.3

1-5 续表 1 continued

指 标	Item	1978	2000	2005	2010	2014	2015	2016
财 政	**Finance**							
地方公共支出结构	Local Public Financial Expenditure Structure							
#一般公共服务	#General Public Service				12.6	12.1	10.1	10.0
教育	Education				14.7	15.7	14.9	16.3
社会保障和就业	Social Security and Employment				14.7	14.5	14.0	15.2
利用外资	**Foreign Investment**							
实际外商直接投资结构	Actual Foreign Direct Investment							
合资经营企业	Joint Venture		63.4	40.8	35.3	38.0	36.8	35.5
合作经营企业	Cooperation		3.0	4.8	1.6	0.1	0.5	0.7
独资经营企业	Sole Proprietorship Business		33.6	34.5	63.1	55.6	61.3	54.2
外商投资股份制企业	Joint-stock Enterprises with Foreign Investment			0.9		4.5	1.0	5.6
产业经济	**Industrial Economy**							
农 业	**Agriculture**							
农林牧渔业产值结构	Agricultural Output Value Structure							
农业	Agriculture	77.3	54.7	52.5	54.9	50.6	48.5	46.5
林业	Forestry	4.9	3.6	2.1	1.9	2.9	3.2	3.2
牧业	Animal Husbandry	12.8	30.1	30.7	26.4	26.2	26.2	27.3
渔业	Fishery	0.8	11.6	13.3	13.1	15.5	16.1	16.4
农林牧渔服务业	Agriculture,Animal Husbandry and Fishery service			1.4	3.8	4.8	6.0	6.5
工 业	**Industry**							
工业产值按经济类型分	Industrial Output by Type							
#国有企业	#State-owned Enterprises	77.3	35.3	25.3	21.0	7.5	6.1	5.1
集体企业	Collective Enterprises	22.7	18.4	1.8	0.9	0.3	0.3	0.2
港澳台商投资企业	Hong Kong, Macao And Taiwan Invested Enterprises		4.2	4.3	5.1	4.9	4.5	4.2
外商投资企业	Foreign-invested Enterprises		6.8	18.3	15.0	10.9	10.1	10.6
工业产值按轻重分	Industrial Output Divided by Weight							
轻工业	Light Industry	47.1	38.4	24.8	27.5	35.4	36.7	37.0
重工业	Heavy Industry	52.9	61.6	75.2	72.5	64.6	63.3	63.0
建筑业	**Building Industry**							
建筑业总产值结构	Gross Output Value Structure							
国有经济	State-owned Economy	88.6	58.6	57.6	52.6	47.3	44.3	46.8
地方	Local	42.8	23.5	19.9	9.5	9.2	10.1	9.0
中央	Central	45.6	35.1	37.7	43.1	38.1	34.2	37.8
其它经济	Other Economic		14.3	37.3	45.9	52.0	55.0	53.2
运输业	**Transport**							
货运量结构	Cargo Structures							
铁路	Railway	32.8	41.3	17.0	10.5	5.0	4.2	4.1
公路	Highway	33.2	23.8	67.1	73.2	75.1	74.1	74.3
水运	Water Transport	30.3	34.8	15.9	16.3	19.9	21.7	21.6

1–5 续表 2 continued

指 标	Item	1978	2000	2005	2014	2015	2016
国内商业	**Domestic Trade**						
社会消费品零售总额结构	Total Retail Sales of Consumer Goods						
#批发零售贸易业	Wholesale and Retail Sale	85.1	61.9	81.5	85.3	86.8	86.5
住宿及餐饮业	Hotel and Catering	2.8	10.8	13.1	10.7	10.2	10.3
其他	Others	12.1	27.3	5.4	4.0	3.0	3.2
对外经济贸易和国际旅游	**Foreign Trade and Tourism**						
进出口总额	Total Imports and Exports						
#出口	Exports	8.1	39.8	51.1	61.9	64.1	66.2
进口	Imports	91.9	60.2	48.9	38.1	35.9	33.8
海外旅游人数结构	Structure of Tourists						
外国人	Foreigners	47.3	79.3	75.9	77.0	76.9	75.4
港澳台同胞	Compatriots from Hongkong, Macao and Taiwan	52.7	20.7	24.1	23.0	23.1	24.6
教育、科技、文化	**Education,Science and Culture**						
教 育	**Education**						
在校学生结构	Structure of Students Enrollment						
大学生	College and University Students	0.4	3.3	10.4	19.4	18.9	18.5
中学生	Secondary School Students	32.6	33.3	45.7	36.5	36.1	35.8
小学生	Primary School Students	67.0	63.4	43.9	43.9	45.0	45.7
专任教师结构	Full-Time Teacher by Type						
大学	College and Universities	2.9	11.9	17.5	16.3	16.4	16.4
中学	Secondary Schools	39.6	38.9	44.5	44.0	44.4	44.0
小学	Primary Schools	57.5	49.2	38.0	39.2	39.2	39.6
科 技	**Science and Technology**						
R&D经费支出结构	Expenditure On R&D						
基础研究	Basic Research			4.6	3.6	4.1	4.3
实验研究	Applied Research			20.0	13.5	12.6	12.3
试验发展	Expenditure Development			71.3	82.2	83.3	83.4
生活、环境	**People's Livelihood and Environment**						
生 活	**People's Livelihood**						
城镇居民消费结构	Consumption Structutre of Urban Residents						
食品	Food		38.3	39.0	32.1	32.0	31.4
衣着	Clothing		11.4	12.0	9.2	8.4	7.8
居住	Residence		14.1	10.2	21.7	20.8	20.8
其他	Others		36.2	38.8	37.1	38.8	40.0
农村居民消费结构	Consumption Structutre of Rural Residents						
食品	Food	70.8	53.2	49.1	34.7	30.1	30.1
衣着	Clothing	12.0	4.8	5.1	6.3	5.6	5.2
居住	Residence	8.9	11.5	12.8	24.8	21.9	22.0
其他	Others	8.3	30.5	33.0	34.2	42.4	42.7

1-6 湖北国民经济占全国的比重(2016)
PERCENTAGE OF HUBEI´S NATIONAL ECONOMY IN THE COUNTRY(2016)

指 标		Item		全 国 Country	湖北 Hubei	湖北占全国的比重(%) Percentage to the Country
土地面积	(万平方公里)	Ground space	(10 000 sq.km.)	960.00	18.59	1.94
年末常住人口	(万人)	Population	(Year-end)	138271	5885	4.26
地区生产总值	(亿元)	Local Gross Production	(100 million yuan)	744127.2	32297.9	4.34
第一产业		First Industry		63670.7	3659.3	5.75
第二产业		Second Industry		296236.0	14375.1	4.85
第三产业		Tertiary Industry		384220.5	14263.5	3.71
人均地区生产总值	(元)	Local Gross Production Per Capita	(yuan)	53980	55038	相当于全国101.96%
投资	(亿元)	Investment	(100 million yuan)			
#固定资产投资		Investment in Fixed Assets		596500.75	29503.88	4.95
#房地产开发		Development of Real Estate		102580.6	4296.4	4.19
地方公共财政收入	(亿元)	Local Public Financial Revenue		87194.8	3102.0	3.56
社会消费品零售总额	(亿元)	Total Retail Sales of Social Consumption	(100 million yuan)	332316.3	15649.2	4.71
进出口总额	(亿美元)	Total Imports and Exports	(100 million dollars)	36855.7	393.5	1.07
#出口		Exports		20981.5	260.2	1.24
实际外商直接投资	(亿美元)	Actual Foreign Direct Investment	(100 million dollars)	1260.0	101.29	8.04
普通高等学校本专科在校生	(万人)	Students Enrollment in Institutions of Higher Eductioan	(10 000 persons)	2695.8	139.99	5.19
医院卫生院床位数	(万张)	Number of Hospital Beds	(10 000 units)	741.0	36.16	4.88
卫生技术人员	(万人)	Number of Medical Technical Personnels	(10 000 persons)	845.4	38.54	4.56
#执业(助理)医师		Professional (assistant) Doctors		319.1	14.24	4.46
在岗职工平均工资	(元)	Average Wages of Employee		68993	51415	相当于全国74.5%
城镇居民人均可支配收入	(元)	Per Capita Disposable Income of Urban Residents	(yuan)	33616.2	29385.8	相当于全国87.42%
农村居民人均可支配收入	(元)	Per Capita Net Incomes of Rural Residents	(yuan)	12363.4	12725.0	相当于全国102.92%
工农业主要产品产量	(万吨)	Output of Major Products in Argriculture and Industry				
粮食		Grain		61625.0	2554.1	4.14
棉花		Cotton		530.0	18.8	3.55
油料		Oil-Bearing Crops		3629.5	329.8	9.09
粗钢		Crude steel		80836.6	2948.5	3.65
钢材		Steel		113801.2	3563.8	3.13
发电量	(亿千瓦小时)	Electricity	(100 million kWh)	61424.9	2431.1	3.94
原煤		Coal		341060.4	593.9	0.17
农用化肥(折100%)		Chemical Furtilizer		7128.6	1164.9	16.34
水泥		Cement		241352.6	11600.5	4.81
化学纤维		Chemical Fiber		4943.7	27.49	0.56
布	(亿米)	Cloth	(100 million meter)	906.8	82.2	9.06
汽车	(万辆)	Moter Vehicles	(10 000 units)	2811.9	243.5	8.66

1-7 全省人均国民经济主要指标

指 标		Item		1990
地区生产总值	(元)	Gross Domestic Product	(yuan)	1541.00
第一产业		First Industry		541.00
第二产业		Second Industry		586.00
第三产业		Tertiary Industry		414.00
地方公共财政预算收入	(元)	Government Revenue	(yuan)	145.54
地方财政支出	(元)	Government Expenditure	(yuan)	158.57
固定资产投资额	(元)	Investment in Fixed Assets	(yuan)	270.00
社会消费品零售额	(元)	Total Retail Sales of Consumer Goods	(yuan)	610.00
进出口总额	(美元)	Total Imports and Exports	(US.dollars)	22.24
#出口		Exports	(US.dollars)	20.04
农村居民可支配收入	(元)	Net Income of Rural Residents	(yuan)	671.00
城镇居民可支配收入	(元)	Disposable Income of Urban Residents	(yuan)	1427.00
居民储蓄存款	(元)	Outstanding Amount of Saving Deposits of Urabn And Rural Residents	(yuan)	455.00
在校大学生数	(人/万人)	Number of Students Enrollment in Institutions of Higher Education	(person/10 000 persons)	24.38
医院病床数	(张/万人)	Hospital Beds	(bed/10000 persons)	24.50
卫生技术人员数	(人/万人)	Number of Medical Technical Personnels	(person/10000 persons)	39.11
#职业(助理)医师		Professional (assitant) Doctors		16.22
主要工农业产品产量	(千克)	Output of Major Industrial and Agricultural Products	(kg)	
粮 食		Grain		467.10
棉 花		Cotton		9.76
油 料		Oil-Bearing Crops		18.07
钢 材		Steel		100.60
原 煤		Coal		174.43
发电量	(千瓦小时)	Electricity	(kWh)	639.62

MAJOR PER CAPITA INDICATORS OF HUBEI´S

2000	2005	2010	2013	2014	2015	2016
6293.00	11554.00	27906.00	42825.76	47144.59	50653.85	55038.40
1164.00	1897.00	3766.67	5234.53	5470.32	5673.61	6235.8
2525.00	4926.00	13626.74	20360.41	22130.69	23147.31	24496.45
2540.00	4607.00	10619.95	17230.82	19543.57	21832.94	24306.14
376.61	658.36	1767.30	3785.14	4419.97	5151.97	5286.18
1647.93	1368.21	4371.64	7551.65	8624.80	10446.47	10945.31
2498.00	4970.00	18879.60	35850.60	43050.83	50038.24	50277.14
3144.00	5197.00	11743.40	18804.46	21436.54	24003.84	26667.61
56.40	159.40	452.77	628.61	741.52	781.42	671.38
33.93	78.02	252.40	394.51	458.82	500.78	444.31
2268.00	3099.00	5832.27	8866.95	10849.06	11843.89	12724.97
5524.00	8786.00	16058.37	22906.40	24852.28	27051.47	29385.8
3209.00	7929.00	17211.00	27591.00	29698.80	33539.49	37600.94
60.89	177.54	226.66	245.53	264.00	241.48	238.55
21.80	23.10	35.08	49.70	54.81	58.93	61.62
41.96	37.69	43.97	53.83	58.51	63.01	65.68
17.40	14.90	16.93	20.63	21.94	23.20	24.27
372.92	382.00	404.73	432.08	444.97	463.39	435.24
5.12	6.26	8.30	7.94	6.20	5.11	3.21
45.38	51.50	54.50	57.55	58.80	58.21	56.19
136.34	278.04	505.90	464.30	590.45	586.45	607.30
64.45	83.80	225.75	147.85	153.32	130.00	93.29
904.54	2204.00	3545.46	3660.08	4037.56	3944.98	4129.24

1-8 湖北的一天
ONE DAY IN HUBEI

指 标		Item		2000	2005	2010	2014	2015	2016
每天创造的财富		**Daily Production**							
地区生产总值	(亿元)	Gross Domestic Products	(100 million yuan)	9.71	17.86	43.75	75.01	80.96	88.25
第一产业		First Industry		1.81	2.96	5.88	8.70	9.07	10.00
第二产业		Second Industry		3.94	7.70	21.28	35.21	37.00	39.28
第三产业		Tertiary Industry		3.96	7.20	16.58	31.10	34.90	38.97
地方公共财政预算收入	(亿元)	Government Revenue	(100 million yuan)	0.59	1.03	2.77	7.03	8.23	8.48
粮食	(万吨)	Grain	(10 000 tons)	6.08	5.97	6.34	7.08	7.41	6.98
肉类产量	(吨)	Meat	(tons)	7430.00	9387.00	10395.07	12066.85	11833.70	11589.62
水产品	(吨)	Aquatic Products	(tons)	6420.00	8718.00	9673.70	11871.23	12487.67	12864.48
粗 钢	(万吨)	Steel	(10 000 tons)	2.45	4.31	6.85	8.37	8.00	8.06
成品钢材	(万吨)	Rolled-Steel	(10 000 tons)	2.22	4.34	7.93	9.39	9.37	9.74
发电量	(亿千瓦小时)	Electricity	(100 million kWh)	1.47	3.44	5.56	6.42	6.31	6.62
水泥	(万吨)	Cement	(10 000 tons)	6.74	12.36	24.61	31.97	30.93	31.66
布	(万米)	Cloth	(10 000 meters)	470.00	573.00	1270.69	2257.53	2187.67	2144.54
每天消费量		**Daily Consumption**							
最终消费	(亿元)	Final Consumption	(100 million yuan)	5.56	9.99	20.25	34.42	37.81	41.75
居民消费	(亿元)	Resident Consumption	(100 million yuan)	4.37	7.63	14.07	25.00	27.86	31.09
城镇居民每人消费性支出	(元)	Per Capita Living Expenditure of Urban Residents	(yuan)	12.72	18.46	31.37	45.70	49.84	54.75
#食品消费		Food Consumption		4.88	7.19	12.14	14.77	15.97	17.20
农村居民每人生活消费支出	(元)	Per Capita Living Expenditure of Rural Residents	(yuan)	4.26	6.66	11.21	23.78	26.86	29.89
#食品消费		Food Consumption		2.27	3.27	4.83	7.46	8.09	9.00
政府消费	(亿元)	Government Consumption Expenditure	(100 million yuan)	1.19	2.36	6.17	9.42	9.95	10.66
社会消费品零售总额	(亿元)	Total Retail Sales of Consumer Goods	(100 million yuan)	4.90	8.12	18.41	34.11	38.37	42.76
每天其他经济活动		**Other Daily Economic Acitivities**							
货物运输量	(万吨)	Freight Traffic	(10 000 tons)	25.60	136.78	265.77	423.93	439.43	451.16
旅客运输量	(万人)	Passenger Traffic	(10 000 persons)	86.56	195.61	288.81	284.03	286.83	289.11
竣工房屋面积	(万平方米)	Floor Space of Housing Completed	(10 000 sq.m)	8.63	18.90	35.11	68.13	73.49	78.14
出版报纸	(万份)	Newspapers Published	(10 000 pieces)	367.67	536.16	497.80	523.47	423.39	335.23
函件	(万件)	Letters Delivered	(10 000 pieces)	99.00	41.64	27.40	18.29	18.63	17.26
进出口总额	(万美元)	Total Imports and Exports	(10 000 USD)	879.45	2490.96	7097.81	11798.36	12489.32	10764.37
#出口		Exports		529.04	1219.18	3956.71	7300.22	8003.84	7123.74
实际外商直接投资	(万美元)	Actual Foreign Direct Investment	(10 000 USD)	258.63	598.63	1109.59	2172.03	2451.51	2767.46
每天人口变动和婚姻		**Daily Population Changes and Marriages**							
出生人数	(人)	Birth	(persons)	1582	1441	1625	1887	1716	1930
死亡人数	(人)	Death	(persons)	979	940	944	1107	932	1117
结婚对数	(对)	Marriage	(couple)	969	1080	1564	1704	1570	1404
离婚对数	(对)	Divorce	(couple)	58	146	244	366	396	438

1-9 地区生产总值
GROSS DOMESTIC PRODUCT

本表按当年价格计算 (At current price)

年份 Year	地区生产总值(亿元) Total Output (100 million yuan)	第一产业 Primary Industry	第二产业 Secondary Industry	工业 Industry	建筑业 Contruction	第三产业 Tertiary Industry	#金融业 Banking	#房地产业 Real Estate	人均地区生产总值(元) Per Capita GDP (yuan)	人均地区生产总值(美元) Per Capita GDP (USD)
1952	24.51	13.90	3.83	3.17	0.66	6.78			90.13	34.44
1955	34.05	18.14	7.45	6.25	1.20	8.46			117.88	47.88
1957	48.86	24.33	11.59	9.03	2.56	12.94			162.17	65.87
1962	52.13	29.30	10.63	9.10	1.53	12.20			161.47	65.59
1965	72.43	37.74	21.16	17.36	3.80	13.53			209.26	85.00
1970	88.15	44.41	26.90	21.79	5.11	16.84			221.78	90.09
1975	120.10	53.71	45.48	32.68	12.80	20.91			274.30	139.50
1978	151.00	61.11	63.71	52.17	11.54	26.18	4.54	1.42	332.03	210.53
1980	199.38	71.22	91.67	75.63	16.04	36.49	5.51	2.83	427.98	279.67
1985	396.26	144.44	174.35	152.88	21.47	77.47	10.71	4.61	800.69	272.66
1986	442.04	163.61	187.96	164.93	23.03	90.47	13.68	5.97	881.61	255.33
1987	517.77	183.99	224.53	197.66	26.87	109.25	17.09	7.39	1018.42	273.61
1988	626.52	214.66	271.25	244.17	27.08	140.61	20.82	8.88	1215.93	326.68
1989	717.08	239.07	300.46	276.47	23.99	177.55	28.14	9.18	1373.22	364.72
1990	824.38	289.45	313.39	284.15	29.24	221.54	33.77	11.36	1541.17	322.20
1991	913.38	279.30	359.86	327.50	32.36	274.22	40.30	13.61	1668.03	313.34
1992	1088.39	303.00	444.61	402.59	42.02	340.78	48.07	17.22	1962.45	355.86
1993	1325.83	346.39	537.60	475.44	62.16	441.84	52.22	25.63	2360.53	409.67
1994	1700.92	501.44	657.63	580.80	76.83	541.85	56.83	37.85	2991.33	347.07
1995	2109.38	619.77	780.18	680.92	99.26	709.43	60.86	42.07	3671.41	439.64
1996	2499.77	716.34	923.68	805.53	118.15	859.75	65.37	62.23	4310.98	811.22
1997	2856.47	767.92	1071.86	929.91	141.95	1016.69	69.68	69.65	4883.80	589.13
1998	3114.02	778.22	1199.08	1041.20	157.88	1136.72	74.14	81.78	5287.03	638.60
1999	3229.29	653.99	1314.44	1139.52	174.92	1260.86	78.81	85.01	5452.46	658.65
2000	3545.39	662.30	1437.38	1243.24	194.14	1445.71	81.49	99.40	6293.41	760.22
2001	3880.53	692.17	1574.39	1360.10	214.29	1613.97	88.48	122.49	6866.99	829.65
2002	4212.82	707.00	1709.89	1473.00	236.89	1795.93	96.95	145.17	7436.58	898.46
2003	4757.45	798.35	1956.02	1682.16	273.86	2003.08	107.31	176.80	8378.01	1012.20
2004	5633.24	1020.09	2320.60	1987.50	333.10	2292.55	118.85	204.80	9897.64	1195.83
2005	6590.19	1082.13	2852.12	2478.66	373.46	2655.94	127.32	217.17	11554.00	1410.45
2006	7617.47	1140.41	3365.08	2929.19	435.89	3111.98	174.99	294.73	13360.00	1710.91
2007	9333.40	1378.00	4143.06	3588.00	555.06	3812.34	337.27	409.65	16386.00	2178.55
2008	11328.92	1780.00	5082.07	4391.23	690.84	4466.85	393.05	526.88	19858.00	2859.57
2009	12961.10	1795.90	6038.08	5183.68	854.40	5127.12	479.11	546.11	22677.00	3317.24
2010	15967.61	2147.00	7767.24	6726.53	1040.71	6053.37	561.27	564.41	27906.00	4122.31
2011	19632.26	2569.30	9815.94	8538.04	1277.90	7247.02	674.57	634.67	34197.27	5294.68
2012	22250.45	2848.77	11193.10	9735.15	1457.95	8208.58	870.36	692.82	38572.33	6110.47
2013	24791.83	3030.27	11786.64	10139.24	1705.95	9974.92	1179.55	972.40	42825.76	6914.96
2014	27379.22	3176.89	12852.40	10992.79	1925.09	11349.93	1372.61	1062.71	47144.60	7674.77
2015	29550.19	3309.84	13503.56	11532.37	2039.88	12736.79	1853.12	1136.72	50653.85	8132.72
2016	32297.91	3659.33	14375.13	12255.46	2192.97	14263.45	2318.87	1291.35	55038.40	8286.05

注：从2013年起施行新的三次产业划分方法。
Note: The new classification of three industries has been implemented from 2013.

1-10 地区生产总值指数
INDICES OF GROSS DOMESTIC PRODUCT

按可比价计算,上年=100 (In comparable price, preceding year=100)

年 份 Year	地区生产总值(%) Total Output (%)	第一产业 Primary Industry	第二产业 Secondary Industry			第三产业 Tertiary Industry			人均地区生产总值(%) Per Capita GDP (%)
				工业 Industry	建筑业 Contruction		#金融业 Banking	#房地产业 Real Estate	
1953	114.0	107.4	129.4	141.0	93.3	122.7			111.6
1955	127.1	135.5	104.9	100.2	139.2	127.1			124.8
1957	107.4	106.4	115.3	109.5	146.0	102.6			104.8
1962	100.9	112.3	84.0	92.7	50.5	94.0			99.0
1965	118.1	111.5	132.5	124.5	196.4	114.9			115.4
1970	126.9	112.2	161.2	151.2	222.0	111.3			123.4
1975	111.4	94.5	139.0	135.2	152.5	116.0			110.0
1978	113.5	103.4	128.4	131.9	112.2	107.4			112.2
1980	106.4	86.9	123.5	126.7	107.0	111.0	96.3	160.6	105.1
1985	116.2	108.3	124.7	124.7	124.3	112.4	112.4	112.3	114.8
1986	105.5	103.3	105.2	103.9	116.8	110.2	120.5	122.2	104.1
1987	108.4	103.1	111.3	112.9	99.0	110.7	114.5	113.4	106.9
1988	107.8	94.9	113.7	115.1	101.5	114.3	107.0	105.6	106.4
1989	104.5	105.2	102.1	104.2	81.3	109.3	121.8	93.2	103.1
1990	105.0	107.5	99.0	99.5	92.8	114.8	108.9	109.7	102.5
1991	106.6	95.1	111.1	111.6	106.1	115.4	114.4	114.7	104.2
1992	114.1	108.2	116.6	117.5	107.5	116.9	111.5	117.8	112.6
1993	113.0	105.8	116.7	116.1	123.3	115.2	112.0	119.4	111.6
1994	113.7	107.1	118.8	118.9	117.6	112.4	107.7	127.3	112.3
1995	113.2	108.9	116.1	115.9	118.5	112.5	107.3	121.0	112.0
1996	111.6	104.5	115.5	115.4	116.6	111.3	107.3	116.5	110.5
1997	111.9	106.9	113.4	113.5	112.3	113.5	103.4	110.3	110.9
1998	108.6	99.4	111.2	110.9	113.9	111.5	107.0	117.9	107.9
1999	107.8	101.9	108.2	108.2	107.5	111.0	103.7	106.1	107.2
2000	108.6	102.5	109.1	109.0	110.7	111.5	105.6	116.8	114.2
2001	108.9	102.5	109.9	110.1	108.5	110.8	107.4	122.1	108.5
2002	109.2	102.0	110.1	110.1	110.5	111.4	108.4	114.5	108.9
2003	109.7	105.8	110.2	110.2	110.6	110.8	110.1	119.0	109.5
2004	111.2	106.5	113.6	113.5	114.4	110.6	106.3	114.4	111.0
2005	112.1	104.0	115.2	116.0	109.9	111.8	104.4	103.5	111.8
2006	113.2	105.1	116.0	116.3	115.3	113.5	135.0	129.4	113.2
2007	114.6	104.7	116.7	115.7	123.3	115.9	167.3	132.0	114.7
2008	113.4	106.0	116.6	116.9	114.8	112.4	110.8	115.1	113.2
2009	113.5	105.2	116.8	115.7	123.7	112.3	122.8	111.1	113.3
2010	114.8	104.6	120.2	121.3	112.9	111.3	110.3	103.1	114.7
2011	113.8	104.4	117.9	119.1	110.1	112.0	112.8	104.4	113.5
2012	111.3	104.7	113.2	113.4	111.5	110.8	126.1	105.0	110.7
2013	110.1	104.5	111.3	111.2	111.9	110.1	115.6	110.2	109.7
2014	109.7	104.8	110.1	110.0	110.9	110.5	114.7	106.6	109.3
2015	108.9	104.5	108.3	108.5	106.9	110.7	130.7	106.5	108.4
2016	108.1	103.9	107.8	107.8	107.8	109.5	123.6	107.7	107.5

1-11 地区生产总值指数

INDICES OF GROSS DOMESTIC PRODUCT

按可比价计算，1952=100 (In comparable price, 1952 = 100)

年 份 Year	地区生产总值(%) Total Output (%)	第一产业 Primary Industry	第二产业 Secondary Industry	工业 Industry	建筑业 Contruction	第三产业 Tertiary Industry	#金融业 Banking	#房地产业 Real Estate	人均地区生产总值(%) Per Capita GDP (%)
1953	114.0	107.4	129.4	141.0	93.3	122.7			111.6
1955	121.5	115.8	152.4	168.5	102.2	118.3			114.4
1957	169.6	143.9	280.1	295.3	233.2	172.1			153.0
1962	141.7	130.2	223.9	258.0	116.1	124.2			119.3
1965	205.6	161.5	490.4	538.5	338.9	161.1			161.5
1970	242.6	158.7	705.6	745.9	580.5	202.3			166.0
1975	320.2	185.3	1126.3	1165.1	995.9	259.1			198.9
1978	399.0	204.6	1616.5	1857.1	926.0	314.2			238.6
1980	490.8	211.4	2257.6	2637.6	1173.5	398.9	110.3	181.0	286.5
1985	871.1	342.0	4111.1	5128.2	1383.1	797.9	202.1	277.9	478.7
1986	919.1	353.1	4326.3	5327.6	1615.8	879.3	243.5	339.6	498.5
1987	996.7	364.1	4816.5	6017.4	1599.1	973.3	278.8	385.1	533.1
1988	1074.3	345.4	5475.9	6925.0	1623.7	1112.1	298.3	406.7	567.0
1989	1122.7	363.3	5592.5	7218.5	1319.6	1215.1	363.4	379.1	584.7
1990	1178.9	390.6	5536.7	7181.9	1224.3	1394.6	395.7	415.8	599.3
1991	1257.2	371.2	6151.9	8018.2	1298.9	1609.6	452.7	477.0	624.3
1992	1434.3	401.6	7175.3	9419.0	1396.0	1881.8	504.7	561.8	703.3
1993	1621.2	424.7	8372.8	10939.2	1720.9	2166.9	565.3	670.8	784.9
1994	1843.3	454.7	9948.0	13008.9	2024.1	2435.8	608.7	854.0	881.6
1995	2086.5	495.2	11547.9	15073.3	2398.9	2740.9	653.4	1033.2	987.5
1996	2327.5	517.4	13342.9	17402.1	2796.6	3050.0	701.2	1204.1	1091.5
1997	2604.6	553.0	15131.7	19753.3	3139.6	3461.5	725.3	1328.7	1211.0
1998	2829.4	549.4	16822.5	21912.2	3576.3	3858.8	776.3	1566.2	1306.3
1999	3048.8	560.1	18195.4	23713.5	3845.1	4285.0	805.2	1661.6	1399.9
2000	3310.6	574.1	19858.1	25847.7	4254.6	4777.6	850.3	1941.2	1598.1
2001	3604.0	588.5	21828.1	28458.3	4618.0	5291.6	913.2	2370.0	1734.3
2002	3936.2	600.2	24038.5	31332.6	5104.3	5892.2	990.1	2713.0	1889.5
2003	4318.6	634.9	26494.8	34517.7	5643.2	6525.7	1090.1	3229.7	2068.1
2004	4802.5	676.2	30099.5	39171.3	6456.0	7218.6	1158.5	3696.0	2294.6
2005	5383.6	703.2	34674.7	45438.7	7095.2	8070.4	1209.5	3825.4	2565.4
2006	6094.2	739.1	40222.6	52845.2	8180.7	9159.9	1632.8	4948.5	2904.0
2007	6984.0	773.8	46939.8	61141.9	10086.8	10616.3	2731.6	6532.1	3330.9
2008	7919.8	820.3	54731.8	71474.9	11579.7	11932.8	3026.7	7518.4	3770.6
2009	8989.0	862.9	63926.7	82696.4	14324.1	13400.5	3716.7	8353.0	4272.1
2010	10319.4	902.6	76839.9	100310.7	16171.9	14914.8	4099.5	8611.9	4900.1
2011	11746.5	942.3	90571.2	119440.0	17810.1	16701.5	4623.8	8994.3	5561.6
2012	13073.9	986.6	102526.6	135444.9	19858.3	18505.3	5830.7	9444.0	6156.7
2013	14394.4	1031.0	114112.1	150614.7	22221.4	20542.7	6740.3	10407.3	6753.9
2014	15790.7	1080.5	125637.4	165676.2	24643.5	22699.7	7731.1	11094.2	7382.0
2015	17196.0	1129.1	136065.3	179758.6	26343.9	25128.6	10104.6	11815.3	8002.1
2016	18588.9	1173.1	146678.4	193779.8	28398.7	27515.8	11357.6	12725.1	8602.3

注：金融业、房地产业指数以1978年为100。
Note: The indices of banking and real estate are 1978=100

1-12 地区生产总值构成
COMPOSITION OF GROSS DOMESTIC PRODUCT

本表按当年价格计算 (At current prices)

年 份 Year	地区生产总值(%) Total Output (%)	第一产业 Primary Industry	第二产业 Secondary Industry	工业 Industry	建筑业 Contruction	第三产业 Tertiary Industry	#金融业 Banking	#房地产业 Real Estate
1952	100	56.7	15.6	12.9	2.7	27.7		
1955	100	53.3	21.9	18.4	3.5	24.8		
1957	100	49.8	23.7	18.5	5.2	26.5		
1962	100	56.2	20.4	17.5	2.9	23.4		
1965	100	52.1	29.2	24.0	5.2	18.7		
1970	100	50.4	30.5	24.7	5.8	19.1		
1975	100	44.7	37.9	27.2	10.7	17.4		
1978	100	40.5	42.2	34.5	7.6	17.3	3.0	0.9
1980	100	35.7	46.0	37.9	8.0	18.3	2.8	1.4
1985	100	36.5	44.0	38.6	5.4	19.6	2.7	1.2
1986	100	37.0	42.5	37.3	5.2	20.5	3.1	1.4
1987	100	35.5	43.4	38.2	5.2	21.1	3.3	1.4
1988	100	34.3	43.3	39.0	4.3	22.4	3.3	1.4
1989	100	33.3	41.9	38.6	3.3	24.8	3.9	1.3
1990	100	35.1	38.0	34.5	3.5	26.9	4.1	1.4
1991	100	30.6	39.4	35.9	3.5	30.0	4.4	1.5
1992	100	27.8	40.9	37.0	3.9	31.3	4.4	1.6
1993	100	26.1	40.5	35.9	4.7	33.3	3.9	1.9
1994	100	29.5	38.7	34.1	4.5	31.9	3.3	2.2
1995	100	29.4	37.0	32.3	4.7	33.6	2.9	2.0
1996	100	28.7	37.0	32.2	4.7	34.4	2.6	2.5
1997	100	26.9	37.5	32.6	5.0	35.6	2.4	2.4
1998	100	25.0	38.5	33.4	5.1	36.5	2.4	2.6
1999	100	20.3	40.7	35.3	5.4	39.0	2.4	2.6
2000	100	18.7	40.5	35.1	5.5	40.8	2.3	2.8
2001	100	17.8	40.6	35.0	5.5	41.6	2.3	3.2
2002	100	16.8	40.6	35.0	5.6	42.6	2.3	3.4
2003	100	16.8	41.1	35.4	5.8	42.1	2.3	3.7
2004	100	18.1	41.2	35.3	5.9	40.7	2.1	3.6
2005	100	16.4	43.3	37.6	5.7	40.3	1.9	3.3
2006	100	15.0	44.2	38.5	5.7	40.8	2.3	3.9
2007	100	14.8	44.4	38.4	6.0	40.8	3.6	4.4
2008	100	15.7	44.9	38.8	6.1	39.4	3.5	4.7
2009	100	13.8	46.6	40.0	6.6	39.6	3.7	4.2
2010	100	13.5	48.6	42.1	6.5	37.9	3.5	3.5
2011	100	13.1	50.0	43.5	6.5	36.9	3.4	3.2
2012	100	12.8	50.3	43.8	6.5	36.9	3.9	3.1
2013	100	12.2	47.6	40.9	6.7	40.2	4.8	3.9
2014	100	11.6	46.9	40.2	6.7	41.5	5.0	3.9
2015	100	11.2	45.7	39.0	6.9	43.1	6.3	3.8
2016	100	11.3	44.5	37.9	6.8	44.2	7.2	4.0

注:2013年产业结构根据三经普数据进行了调整。
Note:The data of 2013 has been adjusted basing on the files of the 3rd national economics census.

1-13 按支出法计算的地区生产总值
GROSS DOMESTIC PRODUCT BY EXPENDITURE APPROACH

本表按当年价格计算 (At current prices)

年份 Year	地区生产总值(亿元) Gross Domestic Product (100 million yuan)	最终消费 Final Consumption Expenditure	居民消费 Residents Consumption Expenditure	政府消费 Government Consumption Expenditure	资本形成总额 Gross Capital Formation	固定资本形成 Fixed Capital Formation	存货增加 Changes in Inventories	货物和服务净流出 Net Export of Goods and Services
1978	151.20	81.70	74.70	7.00	43.12	31.40	11.72	26.38
1980	200.19	107.79	93.51	14.28	40.10	33.19	6.91	52.30
1985	386.76	240.02	203.23	36.79	135.43	96.71	38.72	11.31
1989	718.07	478.66	398.09	80.57	201.39	115.50	85.89	38.02
1990	818.89	535.49	434.62	100.87	261.95	147.13	114.82	21.45
1991	913.22	597.42	475.85	121.57	281.92	176.32	105.60	33.88
1992	1089.68	689.93	546.61	143.32	355.46	235.63	119.83	44.29
1993	1423.92	876.16	694.49	181.67	512.31	377.95	134.36	35.45
1994	1858.89	1043.25	845.14	198.10	740.13	571.68	168.45	75.51
1995	2364.45	1305.21	1095.97	209.20	973.63	778.25	195.38	85.61
1996	2720.28	1599.74	1346.76	253.00	1191.75	985.03	206.72	-71.21
1997	3107.91	1720.23	1438.12	282.10	1466.81	1102.10	364.71	-79.13
1998	3344.45	1859.97	1518.92	341.10	1614.60	1238.90	375.70	-130.12
1999	3504.01	1887.86	1507.12	380.70	1754.79	1320.10	434.69	-138.64
2000	3760.48	2030.07	1594.08	436.00	1882.47	1451.85	430.62	-152.06
2001	4102.08	2262.67	1767.38	495.30	1884.57	1610.93	273.64	-45.16
2002	4416.88	2499.95	1951.54	548.41	1905.92	1699.78	206.14	11.01
2003	4910.53	2819.24	2188.05	631.20	2037.19	1875.78	161.41	54.10
2004	5633.30	3174.18	2452.62	721.56	2538.77	2325.87	212.90	-79.65
2005	6520.14	3645.71	2785.42	860.29	2943.58	2804.01	139.57	-69.15
2006	7972.33	4245.68	3124.37	1121.31	3634.13	3555.21	78.92	92.52
2007	9550.04	4999.66	3709.69	1289.97	4450.25	4371.14	79.11	100.13
2008	11728.64	5892.03	4225.38	1666.65	5716.36	5368.99	347.37	120.25
2009	13240.42	6325.15	4456.31	1868.84	6827.00	6612.85	214.15	88.27
2010	16182.27	7389.80	5136.78	2253.02	8511.17	8200.40	310.77	281.30
2011	20167.28	8931.48	6241.95	2689.53	11027.27	10597.82	429.45	208.53
2012	22659.38	9982.79	7085.46	2897.33	12554.67	12064.75	489.92	121.92
2013	25431.66	11161.21	8053.82	3107.39	14245.35	13701.86	543.49	25.10
2014	28728.18	12562.76	9124.48	3438.28	16109.59	15442.86	666.73	55.83
2015	31226.44	13799.70	10167.87	3631.83	17418.40	16757.35	661.05	8.34
2016	33560.02	15279.99	11379.23	3900.76	18383.27	18112.84	270.43	-103.24

1-14 按支出法计算的地区生产总值指数
INDICES OF GROSS DOMESTIC PRODUCT BY EXPENDITURE APPROACH

按可比价计算 1952=100 (In comparable price, 1952=100)

年 份 Year	地区生产总值(%) Gross Domestic Product(%)	最终消费 Final Consumption Expenditure	居民消费 Residents Consumption Expenditure	政府消费 Government Consumption Expenditure	资本形成总额 Gross Capital Formation	固定资本形成 Fixed Capital Formation	存货增加 Changes in Inventories
1952	100.0	100.0	100.0	100.0	100.0	100.0	100.0
1978	488.3	313.7	308.9	369.3	820.0	1396.6	388.5
1980	605.4	388.8	363.4	706.7	663.9	1270.1	209.7
1985	1007.5	736.7	674.8	1492.5	1962.9	3155.5	1067.1
1990	1337.5	1004.9	897.4	2307.0	2504.8	3460.7	1786.7
1991	1344.2	970.7	850.8	2403.9	2595.0	3955.5	1604.4
1992	1471.9	1023.1	870.3	2819.7	2979.1	4806.0	1670.2
1993	1764.8	1242.1	1045.3	3550.0	3598.7	6218.9	1747.0
1994	2075.4	1379.9	1174.9	3802.1	4530.8	8246.3	1920.0
1995	2339.0	1508.3	1302.9	3950.4	5432.4	9945.0	2261.8
1996	2619.7	1702.8	1467.1	4507.4	6475.4	12520.8	2257.2
1997	2902.6	1776.1	1541.9	4584.0	8120.2	14486.6	3634.1
1998	3140.6	1985.6	1697.7	5418.3	9257.0	16775.4	3961.2
1999	3357.3	2130.6	1765.6	6431.5	10099.4	17966.5	4543.5
2000	3629.3	2260.5	1852.1	7055.4	10927.6	19709.2	4738.9
2001	3930.5	2513.7	2042.9	8057.2	10807.4	21542.2	3028.2
2002	4276.4	2795.3	2281.9	8814.6	11099.2	23093.2	2313.5
2003	4618.5	3072.0	2494.1	9890.0	11443.2	24594.3	1753.6
2004	5052.7	3336.2	2683.6	11086.7	13422.9	28775.3	2121.9
2005	5709.6	3726.5	2976.1	12672.1	15288.7	34041.2	1398.3
2006	6531.8	4326.5	3318.4	16600.0	18315.8	42245.1	465.6
2007	7446.3	4785.1	3680.1	18226.8	21667.6	20102.7	450.2
2008	8399.4	5282.8	3952.4	21653.4	25026.1	22575.3	1848.5
2009	9356.9	5689.6	4177.7	24381.7	30606.9	28151.4	1144.2
2010	11014.0	6423.5	4658.1	28307.2	36758.9	33669.1	1660.3
2011	12886.4	7310.0	5319.6	31902.2	44662.1	40806.9	2148.4
2012	14162.2	7931.3	5862.2	33401.6	50021.5	45662.9	2440.6
2013	15706.9	8653.0	6507.0	34904.7	56574.3	51690.4	2723.7
2014	17513.2	9561.6	7235.8	37871.6	63476.4	57738.2	3391.0
2015	19001.8	10364.8	7959.4	39386.5	69125.8	63107.9	3455.4
2016	20274.9	11297.6	8779.2	41474.0	72927.7	68093.4	1461.6

1-15 三次产业贡献率
CONTRIBUTING RATE OF THE THREE INDUSTRIES

单位：% 本表按可比价格计算 (In comparable price) (%)

年 份 Year	地区生产总值 Gross Domestic Product	第一产业 Primary Industry	第二产业 Second Industry	#工 业 Industry	第三产业 Tertiary Industry
1990	100	42.68	-9.84	-4.64	67.16
1991	100	-25.9	65.6	62.7	60.3
1992	100	18.0	48.2	46.4	33.8
1993	100	13.0	53.5	47.7	33.5
1994	100	14.2	59.2	54.7	26.6
1995	100	17.5	54.9	49.8	27.6
1996	100	9.6	62.2	56.7	28.2
1997	100	13.5	53.9	49.8	32.6
1998	100	-1.6	62.8	56.4	38.8
1999	100	5.1	52.2	48.2	42.7
2000	100	5.6	53.0	47.9	41.3
2001	100	5.3	45.2	40.0	49.5
2002	100	3.8	45.1	38.9	51.1
2003	100	9.8	43.4	37.4	46.8
2004	100	9.2	50.4	43.2	40.5
2005	100	6.5	53.5	48.8	40.0
2006	100	6.3	52.4	46.6	41.3
2007	100	4.9	50.9	41.8	44.2
2008	100	6.2	56.0	49.2	37.8
2009	100	5.1	57.9	47.0	37.0
2010	100	3.7	66.1	60.3	30.2
2011	100	4.3	62.9	58.1	32.8
2012	100	5.1	59.1	52.6	35.8
2013	100	5.1	55.3	48.1	39.6
2014	100	5.3	52.1	45.1	42.6
2015	100	5.3	46.8	42.0	47.9
2016	100	5.4	44.0	37.5	50.6

注：产业贡献率指各产业增加值增量与GDP增量之比。

Note: Contribution share of the three components to the increase of the GDP refers to the proportion of the increment of the each component of GDP expenditure approach to the increment of GDP.

1-16 三次产业拉动率
CONTRIBUTION OF THE THREE STRATA OF INDUSTRY TO GDP GROWTH

单位:百分点 本表按可比价格计算(In comparable price) (percentage point)

年 份 Year	地区生产总值 Gross Domestic Product	第一产业 Primary Industry	第二产业 Second Industry	#工 业 Industry	第三产业 Tertiary Industry
1990	5.00	2.1	-0.5	-0.2	3.4
1991	6.6	-1.7	4.3	4.1	4.0
1992	14.1	2.5	6.8	6.5	4.8
1993	13.0	1.7	7.0	6.2	4.4
1994	13.7	1.9	8.1	7.5	3.6
1995	13.2	2.3	7.3	6.6	3.6
1996	11.6	1.1	7.2	6.6	3.3
1997	11.9	1.6	6.4	5.9	3.9
1998	8.6	-0.1	5.4	4.8	3.3
1999	7.8	0.4	4.1	3.8	3.3
2000	8.6	0.5	4.6	4.1	3.6
2001	8.6	0.5	3.9	3.4	4.3
2002	9.2	0.4	4.1	3.6	4.7
2003	9.7	0.9	4.2	3.6	4.5
2004	11.2	1.0	5.6	4.8	4.5
2005	12.1	0.8	6.5	5.9	4.8
2006	13.2	0.8	6.9	6.1	5.5
2007	14.6	0.7	7.4	6.1	6.5
2008	13.4	0.8	7.5	6.6	5.1
2009	13.5	0.7	7.8	6.3	5.0
2010	14.8	0.5	9.8	8.9	4.5
2011	13.8	0.6	8.7	8.0	4.5
2012	11.3	0.6	6.7	5.9	4.0
2013	10.1	0.5	5.6	4.8	4.0
2014	9.7	0.5	5.1	4.4	4.1
2015	8.9	0.5	4.2	3.7	4.2
2016	8.1	0.4	3.6	3.0	4.1

注:三次产业对生产总值增长的拉动指GDP增长速度与各产业贡献率之乘积。
Note:Contribution of the three components to GDP growth refers to the growth rate of GDP multiplied by the contribution share of the three components.

1-17 三大需求贡献率
CONTRIBUTING RATE OF THE THREE REQUIREMENTS

单位:% 本表按可比价格计算 (In comparable price) (%)

年 份 Year	地区生产总值 Gross Domestic Product	最终消费支出 Final Consumption Expenditure	资本形成总额 Gross Capital Formation	货物和服务净流出 Net Outflow of Goods and Services
1990	100.0	59.4	111.8	-71.3
1991	100.0	-464.2	238.4	325.8
1992	100.0	35.7	51.8	12.5
1993	100.0	65.2	36.3	-1.5
1994	100.0	38.8	51.3	10.0
1995	100.0	42.5	58.3	-0.8
1996	100.0	60.2	63.5	-23.7
1997	100.0	22.7	99.2	-21.8
1998	100.0	76.6	81.1	-57.6
1999	100.0	58.2	65.9	-24.1
2000	100.0	41.6	51.7	6.8
2001	100.0	72.3	-6.4	34.1
2002	100.0	70.3	13.9	15.8
2003	100.0	70.5	17.0	12.5
2004	100.0	52.6	76.1	-28.6
2005	100.0	50.7	49.0	0.3
2006	100.0	44.3	43.9	11.9
2007	100.0	40.8	58.7	0.5
2008	100.0	35.5	64.4	0.1
2009	100.0	27.4	74.0	-1.4
2010	100.0	27.8	61.6	10.6
2011	100.0	36.9	66.3	-3.2
2012	100.0	38.2	66.2	-4.4
2013	100.0	36.7	67.2	-3.9
2014	100.0	39.0	60.0	1.0
2015	100.0	42.0	60.0	-2.0
2016	100.0	59.8	45.6	-5.4

注:贡献率指三大需求增量与支出法地区生产总值增量之比。
Note:Contribution share of the three components to the increase of the GDP refers to the proportion of the increment of the each component of GDP expenditure approach to the increment of GDP.

1-18 三大需求拉动率
CONTRIBUTION OF THE THREE COMPONENTS OF GDP TO THE GROWTH OF GDP

单位:百分点　　本表按可比价格计算 (In comparable price)　　(percentage point)

年 份 Year	地区生产总值 Gross Domestic Product	最终消费支出 Final Consumption Expenditure	资本形成总额 Gross Capital Formation	货物和服务净流出 Net Outflow of Goods and Services
1990	5.0	3.0	5.6	–3.6
1991	6.6	–30.6	15.7	21.5
1992	14.1	5.0	7.3	1.8
1993	13.0	8.5	4.7	–0.2
1994	13.7	5.3	7.0	1.4
1995	13.2	5.6	7.7	–0.1
1996	11.6	7.0	7.4	–2.7
1997	11.9	2.7	11.8	–2.6
1998	8.6	6.6	7.0	–5.0
1999	7.8	4.5	5.1	–1.9
2000	8.6	3.6	4.4	0.6
2001	8.9	6.4	–0.6	3.0
2002	9.2	6.5	1.3	1.5
2003	9.7	6.8	1.6	1.2
2004	11.2	5.9	8.5	–3.2
2005	12.1	6.1	5.9	0.1
2006	13.2	5.8	5.8	1.6
2007	14.6	6.0	8.6	0.1
2008	13.4	4.8	8.6	
2009	13.5	3.7	10.0	–0.2
2010	14.8	4.1	9.1	1.6
2011	13.8	5.1	9.1	–0.4
2012	11.3	4.3	7.5	–0.5
2013	10.9	4.0	7.3	–0.4
2014	11.5	4.5	6.9	0.1
2015	8.5	3.6	5.1	–0.2
2016	6.7	4.0	3.1	–0.4

注:1.三大需求指支出法地区生产总值的三大构成项目,即最终消费支出、资本形成总额、货物和服务净流出。
2.三大需求对国内生产总值增长的拉动指地区生产总值增长速度与三大需求贡献率的乘积。

Notes: a)Three components of GDP by exoenditure approach are final consumption expenditure, gross capital formation and net exports of goods and services.
b)Contribution of the three components to GDP growth refers to the growth refers to the growth rate of GDP multiplied by the contribution share of the three components.

1-19 市、州生产总值(2016)
GROSS DOMESTIC PRODUCT OF CITIES AND PREFECTURES(2016)

单位:亿元 (100 million yuan)

地　区	Regions	地区生产总值 Gross Domestic Product	第一产业 Primary Industry	第二产业 Secondary Industry	第三产业 Tertiary Industry
武　汉	Wuhan	11912.61	390.62	5227.05	6294.94
黄　石	Huangshi	1305.55	114.07	721.47	470.01
十　堰	Shiyan	1429.15	173.40	681.59	574.16
宜　昌	Yichang	3709.36	398.89	2122.74	1187.73
襄　阳	Xiangyang	3694.51	430.90	2046.77	1216.84
鄂　州	Ezhou	797.82	97.21	434.58	266.03
荆　门	Jingmen	1521.00	213.15	789.51	518.34
孝　感	Xiaogan	1576.69	281.52	756.40	538.77
荆　州	Jingzhou	1726.75	382.72	736.39	607.64
黄　冈	Huanggang	1726.17	395.30	654.05	676.82
咸　宁	Xianning	1107.93	184.34	527.81	395.78
随　州	Suizhou	852.18	140.54	398.44	313.20
恩施州	Enshi	735.70	152.52	264.73	318.45
仙　桃	Xiantao	647.55	87.94	342.94	216.67
潜　江	Qianjiang	602.19	72.21	310.24	219.74
天　门	Tianmen	471.27	74.75	238.98	157.54
神农架	Shennongjia	23.06	2.19	8.12	12.75

1-20 市、州生产总值指数(2016)
INDICES OF GROSS DOMESTIC PRODUCT OF CITIES AND PREFECTURES(2016)

(上年=100,单位:%) (preceding year = 100,%)

地　区	Regions	地区生产总值 Gross Domestic Product	第一产业 Primary Industry	第二产业 Secondary Industry	第三产业 Tertiary Industry
武　汉	Wuhan	107.8	103.4	105.7	109.9
黄　石	Huangshi	107.2	103.9	107.5	107.6
十　堰	Shiyan	108.9	104.0	109.6	109.6
宜　昌	Yichang	108.8	103.9	108.8	110.4
襄　阳	Xiangyang	108.5	103.8	109.0	109.4
鄂　州	Ezhou	108.0	103.9	107.5	110.6
荆　门	Jingmen	108.5	103.9	108.8	110.1
孝　感	Xiaogan	107.9	104.0	108.1	109.5
荆　州	Jingzhou	107.3	103.8	106.3	110.9
黄　冈	Huanggang	107.6	103.8	106.4	111.2
咸　宁	Xianning	107.6	104.0	106.4	111.1
随　州	Suizhou	108.0	104.0	107.7	110.3
恩施州	Enshi	107.9	104.2	108.2	109.5
仙　桃	Xiantao	108.2	104.1	108.8	109.0
潜　江	Qianjiang	108.1	103.9	108.5	109.0
天　门	Tianmen	108.0	102.6	108.9	109.7
神农架	Shennongjia	108.3	101.4	104.4	112.1

1-21 市、州支出法生产总值(2016)
GROSS DOMESTIC PRODUCT BY EXPENDITURE APPROACH OF CITIES AND PREFECTURES(2016)

单位:亿元 (100 million yuan)

地 区	Regions	支出法地区生产总值 Total Gross Domestic Product by Expenditure	最终消费支出 Final Consumption Expenditure	资本形成总额 Gross Capital Formation	货物和服务净流出 Net Export of Goods and Services
武 汉	Wuhan	11912.61	5525.36	6451.95	-64.70
黄 石	Huangshi	1305.58	513.48	778.95	13.15
十 堰	Shiyan	2262.74	632.21	1542.21	88.32
宜 昌	Yichang	3709.37	1680.34	1917.75	111.28
襄 阳	Xiangyang	3694.50	1706.60	1943.60	44.30
鄂 州	Ezhou	797.82	367.99	423.56	6.27
荆 门	Jingmen	1521.00	673.99	833.07	13.94
孝 感	Xiaogan	1617.67	698.31	904.72	14.64
荆 州	Jingzhou	1726.75	765.58	1267.76	-306.59
黄 冈	Huanggang	1726.17	882.72	843.45	
咸 宁	Xianning	1258.28	482.19	765.89	10.20
随 州	Suizhou	851.05	371.57	473.31	6.17
恩施州	Enshi	735.70	646.23	608.50	-519.03
仙 桃	Xiantao	647.55	189.67	400.14	57.74
潜 江	Qianjiang	602.19	166.80	422.74	12.65
天 门	Tianmen	471.27	247.29	217.44	6.54
神农架	Shennongjia	23.06	12.23	12.44	-1.61

1-22 市、州民营经济增加值(2016)
VALUE ADDED OF PRIVATE ECONOMY(2016)

地 区	Regions	增加值(亿元) Value-Added (100 million yuan)		占GDP比重(%) Percentage(%)	
		2015	2016	2015	2016
全 省	Total	16228.96	17801.65	54.9	55.1
武 汉	Wuhan	4620.40	5070.60	42.4	42.5
黄 石	Huangshi	683.24	732.16	55.6	56.1
十 堰	Shiyan	600.93	645.97	46.2	45.2
宜 昌	Yichang	2042.38	2247.89	60.3	60.6
襄 阳	Xiangyang	1764.84	1940.00	52.2	52.5
鄂 州	Ezhou	461.34	509.61	63.2	63.9
荆 门	Jingmen	822.74	918.27	59.3	60.4
孝 感	Xiaogan	939.30	1018.32	64.5	64.6
荆 州	Jingzhou	750.08	816.45	47.2	47.3
黄 冈	Huanggang	1057.13	1177.99	66.5	68.2
咸 宁	Xianning	766.80	828.16	74.4	74.7
随 州	Suizhou	557.58	609.19	71.0	71.5
恩施州	Enshi	292.40	322.68	43.6	43.9
仙 桃	Xiantao	433.34	470.19	72.5	72.6
潜 江	Qianjiang	388.09	430.88	69.6	71.6
天 门	Tianmen	298.77	325.00	67.9	69.0
神农架	Shennongjia	8.41	9.37	40.1	40.6

主要统计指标解释

平均增长速度 计算平均增长速度有两种方法:一种是习惯上经常使用的“水平法”,又称几何平均法,是以间隔期最后一年的水平同基期水平对比来计算平均每年增长(或下降)速度;另一种是“累计法”,又称代数平均法或方程法,是以间隔期内各年水平的总和同基期水平对比来计算平均每年增长(或下降)速度。在一般正常情况下,两种方法计算的平均每年增长速度比较接近;但在经济发展不平衡、出现大起大落时,两种方法计算的结果差别较大。

国民经济行业分类 自2003年定期报表开始使用新的《国民经济行业分类》(GB/T4754-2002)该分类是由国家统计局组织修订,经国家质量监督检验检疫总局批准,于2002年5月10日发布实施。这次修订是在1994年分类标准的基础上,参照联合国《全部经济活动的国际标准产业分类》(ISIC/Rev.3)进行的。修订后的《国民经济行业分类》(GB/T4754-2002)共有门类20个,大类95个,中类396个,小类913个。新增门类4个,大类增加3个,中类增加28个,小类增加67个。

企业(单位)登记注册类型 是以在工商行政管理机关登记注册的各类企业为划分对象,以工商行政管理部门对企业登记注册的类型为依据,将企业登记注册类型分为内资企业、港澳台商投资企业和外商投资企业三大类。内资企业包括国有企业、集体企业、股份合作企业、联营企业、有限责任公司、股份有限公司、私营公司和其他企业;港澳台商投资企业和外商投资企业分别包括合资经营企业、合作经营企业、独资经营企业和股份有限公司。对不在工商行政管理部门进行登记注册的行政机关、事业单位和社会团体,主要按其经费来源和管理方式进行划分。

国有企业 指企业全部资产归国家所有,并按《中华人民共和国企业法人登记管理条例》规定登记注册的非公司制的经济组织。不包括有限责任公司中的国有独资公司。

集体企业 指企业资产归集体所有,并按《中华人民共和国企业法人登记管理条例》规定登记注册的经济组织。

股份合作企业 指以合作制为基础,由企业职工共同出资入股,吸收一定比例的社会资产投资组建,实行自主经营,自负盈亏,共同劳动,民主管理,按劳分配与按股分红相结合的一种集体经济组织。

联营企业 指两个及两个以上相同或不同所有制性质的企业法人或事业单位法人,按自愿、平等、互利的原则,共同投资组成的经济组织。联营企业包括国有联营企业、集体联营企业、国有与集体联营企业和其他联营企业。

有限责任公司 指根据《中华人民共和国公司登记管理条例》规定登记注册,由两个以上、五十个以下的股东共同出资,每个股东以其所认缴的出资额对公司承担有限责任,公司以其全部资产对其债务承担责任的经济组织。有限责任公司包括国有独资公司以及其他有限责任公司。

股份有限公司 指根据《中华人民共和国公司登记管理条例》规定登记注册,其全部注册资本由等额股份构成并通过发行股票筹集资本,股东以其认购的股份对公司承担有限责任,公司以其全部资产对其债务承担责任的经济组织。

私营企业 指由自然人投资设立或由自然人控股,以雇佣劳动为基础的营利性经济组织。包括按照《公司法》、《合伙企业法》、《私营企业暂行条例》规定登记注册的私营有限责任公司、私营股份有限公司、私营合伙企业和私营独资企业。

其他企业 指上述企业之外的其他内资经济组织。

与港澳台商合资经营企业 指港澳台地区投资者与内地企业依照《中华人民共和国中外合资经营企业法》及有关法律的规定,按合同规定的比例投资设立、分享利润和分担风险的企业。

与港澳台商合作经营企业 指港澳台地区投资者与内地企业依照《中华人民共和国中外合作经营企业法》及有关法律的规定,依照合作合同的约定进行投资或提供条件设立、分配利润和分担风险的企业。

港澳台商独资经营企业 指依照《中华人民共和国外资企业法》及有关法律的规定,在内地由港澳台地区投资者全额投资设立的企业。

港澳台商投资股份有限公司 指根据国家有关规定,经原外经贸部依法批准设立,其中港、澳、台商的股本占公司注册资本的比例达25% 以上的股份有限公司。凡其中港、澳、台商的股本占公司注册资本的比例小于25%的,属于内资企业中的股份有限公司。

中外合资经营企业 指外国企业或外国人与中国内地企业依照《中华人民共和国中外合资经营企业法》及有关法律的规定,按合同规定的比例投资设立、分享利润和分担风险的企业。

中外合作经营企业 指外国企业或外国人与中国内地企业依照《中华人民共和国中外合作经营企业法》及有关法律的规定,依照合作合同的约定进行投资或提供条件设立、分配利润和分担风险的企业。

外资企业 指依照《中华人民共和国外资企业法》及有关法律的规定,在中国内地由外国投资者全额投资设立的企业。

外商投资股份有限公司 指根据国家有关规定,经原外经贸部依法批准设立,其中外资的股本占公司注册资本的比例达25% 以上的股份有限公司。凡其中外资股本占公司注册资本的比例小于25%的,属于内资企业中的股份有限公司。

行政机关、事业单位和社会团体 参照企业登记注册类型,主要按其经费来源和管理方式划分。具体规定如下:

⑴行政机关:包括国家机关和政党机关,原则上均列为“国有”。但有特殊规定的,如供销社等,则列为“集体”。

⑵事业单位:包括经国家机构编制部门和有关业务主管部门批准成立的各类事业单位,不包括实行企业化管理的事业单位。事业单位的划分办法如下:

①由国家财政预算拨款或列入财政预算外资金管理以及经费主要来源于国有主管部门或国有上级单位的事业单位,列为“国有”。

②经费主要来源于集体单位的事业单位,列为“集体”。

③公民个人(或个人合伙)开办的事业单位,列为“私营”。

④上述以外的其他事业单位,如果其经费来源不明确,按管理方式进行归类。

⑶社会团体:包括经民政部门批准成立以及未纳入社会团体管理条例范围的工会、妇联等各类社会团体。社会团体的划分办法如下:

①未纳入民政部社会团体管理条例范围的工会、妇联、共青团、青联、工商联、科协、侨联等社会团体,国家拨款设立的基金会或基金管理组织以及经费主要来源于国有业务主管部门或国有上级单位的社会团体,列为“国有”。

②经费主要来源于集体单位的社会团体,列为“集体”。

③公民个人(或个人合伙)开办的社会团体,划为“私营”。

④上述以外的其他社会团体,如果其经费来源不明确,改按管理方式进行归类。

地区生产总值(GDP) 指按市场价格计算的一个地区所有常住单位在一定时期内生产活动的最终成果。地区生产总值有三种表现形态,即价值形态、收入形态和产品形态。从价值形态看,它是所有常住单位在一定时期内生产的全部货物和服务价值超过同期投入的全部非固定资产货物和服务价值的差额,即所有常住单位的增加值之和;从收入形态看,它是所有常住单位在一定时期内创造并分配给常住单位和非常住单位的初次收入之和;从产品形态看,它是所有常住单位在一定时期内最终使用的货物和服务价值减去货物和服务流进价值。在实际核算中,地区生产总值有三种计算方法,即生产法、收入法和支出法。三种方法分别从不同的方面反映地区生产总值及其构成。

国民总收入(GNI) 即国民生产总值,指一个国家(或地区)所有常住单位在一定时期内收入初次分配的最终结果。一国常住单位从事生产活动所创造的增加值在初次分配中主要分配给该国的常住单位,但也有一部分以生产税及进口税(扣除生产和进口补贴)、劳动者报酬和财产收入等形式分配给非常住单位;同时,国外生产所创造的增加值也有一部分以生产税及进口税(扣除生产和进口补贴)、劳动者报酬和财产收入等形式分配给该国的常住单位,从而产生了国民总收入的概念。它等于国内生产总值加上来自国外的净要素收入。与国内生产总值不同,国民总收入是个收入概念,而国内生产总值是个生产概念。

三次产业 三产业的划分是世界上较为常用的产业结构分类,但各国的划分不尽一致。我国的三次产业划分是:

第一产业是指农、林、牧、渔业。

第二产业是指采矿业,制造业,电力、煤气及水的生产和供应业,建筑业。

第三产业是指除第一、二产业以外的其他行业。

劳动者报酬 指劳动者因从事生产活动所获得的全部报酬。包括劳动者获得的各种形式的工资、奖金和津贴,既包括货币形式的,也包括实物形式的,还包括劳动者所享受的公费医疗和医药卫生费、上下班交通补贴、单位支付的社会保险费、住房公积金等。对于个体经济来说,其所有者所获得的劳动报酬和经营利润不易区分,这两部分统一作为劳动者报酬处理。

生产税净额 指生产税减生产补贴后的余额。生产税指政府对生产单位从事生产、销售和经营活动以及因从事生产活动使用某些生产要素(如固定资产、土地、劳动力)所征收的各种税、附加费和规费。生产补贴与生产税相反,指政府对生产单位的单方面转移支出,因此视为负生产税,包括政策亏损补贴、价格补贴等。

固定资产折旧 指一定时期内为弥补固定资产损耗按照规定的固定资产折旧率提取的固定资产折旧,或按国民经济核算统一规定的折旧率虚拟计算的固定资产折旧。它反映了固定资产在当期生产中的转移价值。各类企业和企业化管理的事业单位的固定资产折旧是指实际计提的折旧费;不计提折旧的政府机关、非企业化管理的事业单位和居民住房的固定资产折旧是按照统一规定的折旧率和固定资产原值计算的虚拟折旧。原则上,固定资产折旧应按固定资产当期的重置价值计算,但是目前我国尚不具备对全社会固定资产进行重估价的基础,所以暂时只能采用上述办法。

营业盈余 指常住单位创造的增加值扣除劳动者报酬、生产税净额和固定资产折旧后的余额。它相当于企业的营业利润加上生产补贴,但要扣除从利润中开支的工资和福利等。

支出法地区生产总值 是从最终使用的角度反映一个地区一定时期内生产活动最终成果的一种方法,包括最终消费支出、资本形成总额及货物和服务净流出三部分。计算公式为:

支出法国内生产总值=最终消费支出+资本形成总额+货物和服务净流出

最终消费支出 指常住单位为满足物质、文化和精神生活的需要,从本国经济领土和国外购买的货物和服务的支出。它不包括非常住单位在本国经济领土内的消费支出。最终消费支出分为居民消费支出和政府消费支出。

居民消费支出 指常住住户在一定时期内对于货物和服务的全部最终消费支出。居民消费支出除了直接以货币形式购买的货物和服务的消费支出外,还包括以其他方式获得的货物和服务的消费支出,即所谓的虚拟消费支出。居民虚拟消费支出包括如下几种类型:单位以实物报酬及实物转移的形式提供给劳动者的货物和服务;住户生产并由本住户消费了的货物和服务,其中的服务仅指住户的自有住房服务和付酬的家庭雇员提供的家庭和个人服务;金融机构提供的金融媒介服务;保险公司提供的保险服务。

政府消费支出 指政府部门为全社会提供的公共服务的消费支出和免费或以较低的价格向居民住户提供的货物和服务的净支出,前者等于政府服务的产出价值减去政府单位所获得的经营收入的价值,后者等于政府部门免费或以较低价格向居民住户提供的货物和服务的市场价值减去向住户收取的价值。

资本形成总额 指常住单位在一定时期内获得减去处置的固定资产和存货的净额,包括固定资本形成总额和存货增加两部分。

固定资本形成总额 指生产者在一定时期内获得的固定资产减处置的固定资产的价值总额。固定资产是通过生产活动生产出来的,且其使用年限在一年以上、单位价值在规定标准以上的资产,不包括自然资产。可分为有形固定资本形成总额和无形固定资本形成总额。有形固定资本形成总额包括一定时期内完成的建筑工程、安装工程和设备工器具购置(减处置)价值,以及土地改良、新增役、种、奶、毛、娱乐用牲畜和新增经济林木价值。无形固定资本形成总额包括矿藏的勘探、计算机软件等获得减处置。

存货增加 指常住单位在一定时期内存货实物量变动的市场价值,即期末价值减期初价值的差额,再扣除当期由于价格变动而产生的持有收益。存货增加可以是正值,也可以是负值,正值表示存货上升,负值表示存货下降。存货包括生产单位购进的原材料、燃料和储备物资等存货,以及生产单位生产的产成品、在制品和半成品等存货。

货物和服务净流出 指货物和服务流出减货物和服务流进的差额。流出包括常住单位向非常住单位出售或无偿转让的各种货物和服务的价值;流进包括常住单位从非常住单位购买或无偿得到的各种货物和服务的价值。由于服务活动的提供与使用同时发生,一般把常住单位从非常住单位得到的服务作为流进,非常住单位从常住单位得到的服务作为流出。

Explanatory Notes on Main Statistical Indicators

Average Annual Growth Rate Two methods for calculating average annual growth rate are applied, one is often called level approach, or the method of calculating geometric average, which is derived by comparing the level of the last year of the interval with that of the beginning year; the other is called accumulative approach or algebraic average or equation method, which is derived by the summation of the actual figure of each year in the interval divided by the figure in the base year. Usually the results calculated by the two methods are fairly close, but they differed sharply when uneven economic development occurred with striking fluctuations in growth.

Industrial Classification of the National Economy The new Industrial Classification of the National Economy (GB/T 4754–2002) is introduced starting from the compilation of 2003 annual statistics. The new revision was based on the 1994 classification and organized by the National Bureau of Statistics taking into consideration of the International Standards of the Industrial Classification of All Economic Activities (ISIC/Rev.3) of the United Nations, and the new Classification was promulgated by the National Administration of Quality Supervision, Inspection and Quarantine on May 10, 2002. The revised version of the Industrial Classification of the National Economy (GB/T 4754–2002) is composed of 20 major divisions, 95 divisions, 396 major groups and 913 groups, including 4 new major divisions, 3 new divisions, 28 major groups and 67 groups.

Registration Status of Enterprises Enterprises are classified into 3 categories, namely domestic–funded enterprises, enterprises with investment from Hong Kong, Macau and Taiwan, and enterprises with foreign investment, in the light of the registration status of an enterprise in industrial and commercial administration agencies. Domestic–funded enterprises include state–owned enterprises, collective–owned enterprises, cooperative enterprises, joint ownership enterprises, limited liability corporations, share–holding corporations Ltd., private enterprises and other enterprises. Included in the enterprises with investment from Hong Kong, Macau and Taiwan and enterprises with foreign investment are joint–venture enterprises, cooperative enterprises, sole investment enterprises and share–holding corporations Ltd. For government agencies, institutions and social organizations which are not requested to be registered in industrial and commercial administration agencies, they are classified mainly by their sources of funds and way of management.

State–owned Enterprises refer to non–corporation economic units where the entire assets are owned by the state and which have registered in accordance with the Regulation of the People's Republic of China on the Management of Registration of Corporate Enterprises. Excluded from this category are sole state–funded corporations in the limited liability corporations.

Collective–owned Enterprises refer to economic units where the assets are owned collectively and which have registered in accordance with the Regulation of the People's Republic of China on the Management of Registration of Corporate Enterprises.

Cooperative Enterprises refer to a form of collective economic units (enterprises) where capitals come mainly from employees as their shares, with certain proportion of capital from the outside, where production is organized on the basis of independent operation, independent accounting for profits and losses, joint work, democratic management, and a distribution system that integrates remuneration according to work with dividend according to capital share.

Joint Ownership Enterprises refer to economic units established by two or more corporate enterprises or corporate institutions of the same or different ownership, through joint investment on the basis of equality, voluntary participation and mutual benefits. They include state joint ownership enterprises, collective joint ownership enterprises, joint state–collective enterprises, other joint ownership enterprises.

Limited Liability Corporations refer to economic units established with investment from 2–50 investors and registered in accordance with the Regulation of the People's Republic of China on the Management of Registration of Corporations, each investor bearing limited liability to the corporation depending on its share of investment, and the corporation bearing liability to its debt to the maximum of its total assets. Limited liability corporations include exclusive state–funded limited liability corporations and other limited liability corporations.

Share–holding Corporations Ltd. refer to economic units registered in accordance with the Regulation of the People's Republic of China on the Management of Registration of Corporations, with total registered capitals divided into equal shares and raised through issuing stocks. Each investor bears limited liability to the corporation depending on the holding of shares, and the corporation bears liability to its debt to the maximum of its total assets.

Private Enterprises refer to profit–making economic units invested and established by natural persons, or controlled by natural persons using employed labour. Included in this category are private limited liability corporations, private share–holding corporations Ltd., private partnership enterprises and private–funded enterprises registered in accordance with the Corporation Law, Partnership Enterprises Law and Interim Regulations on Private Enterprises .

Other Domestic–funded Enterprises refer to domestic–funded economic units other than those mentioned above.

Cooperative Enterprises with Funds from Hong Kong Macau and Taiwan established by investors from Hong Kong, Macau and Taiwan with enterprises in the mainland of China in accordance with the Law of the People's Republic of China on Sino–foreign Cooperative Enterprises and other relevant laws, where the investment or provision of facilities, and the share of profits and risks is stipulated in the cooperative contract.

Enterprises with Sole (exclusive) Investment from Hong Kong, Macau and Taiwan refer to enterprises established in the mainland of China with exclusive investment from investors from Hong Kong, Macau and Taiwan in accordance with the Law of the People's Republic of China on Foreign–Funded Enterprises and other relevant laws.

Share–holding Corporations Ltd. with Investment from Hong Kong, Macau and Taiwan refer to share–holding corporations Ltd. established with the approval from the former Ministry of Foreign Trade and Economic Relations in line with relevant state regulations, where the share of investment from Hong Kong, Macau or Taiwan businessmen exceeds 25% of the total registered capital of the corporation. In case the share of investment from Hong Kong, Macau or Taiwan is less than 25% of the total registered capital, the enterprise is to be classified as domestic–funded share–holding corporation Ltd.

Joint–venture Enterprises with Foreign Investment refer to enterprises jointly established by foreign enterprises or foreigners with enterprises in the mainland of China in accordance with the Law of the People's Republic of China on Sino–foreign Joint Venture Enterprises and other relevant laws, where the share of investment, profits and risks is stipulated in the contract.

Cooperation Enterprises with Foreign Investment refer to enterprises jointly established by foreign enterprises or foreigners with enterprises in the mainland of China in accordance with the Law of the People's Republic of China on Sino–foreign Cooperative Enterprises and other relevant laws, where the investment or provision of facilities, and the share of profits and risks is stipulated in the cooperative contract.

Enterprises with Sole (exclusive) Foreign Investment refer to enterprises established in the mainland of China with exclusive investment from foreign investors in accordance with the Law of the People's Republic of China on Foreign–Funded Enterprises and other relevant laws.

Share–holding Corporations Ltd. with Foreign Investment refer to share–holding corporations Ltd. established with the approval from the Ministry of Foreign Trade and Economic Relations in line with relevant state regulations, where the share of investment from foreign investors exceeds 25% of the total registered capital of the corporation. In case the share of foreign investment is less than 25% of the total registered capital, the enterprise is to be classified as domestic–funded share–holding corporation Ltd.

Government Agencies, Institutions and Social Organizations are classified into following categories by source of funds and way of management taking reference of the registration status of enterprises:

(1) Government agencies: include state and party agencies, classified in principle as state–owned. There are exceptions, such as sup–

ply and marketing cooperatives which are classified as collective-owned.

(2) Institutions: include institutions of various types established with the approval by organization and staffing departments of the government, but exclude institutions where enterprise management system is introduced. Institutions are further classified as follows:

(a) Institutions whose main budget is listed in the government budget appropriations or extra-budget funds, or allocated from the budget of their competent government agencies. Such institutions are classified as state-owned.

(b) Institutions whose budget mainly comes from collective units. Such institutions are classified as collective-owned.

(c) Institutions other than those mentioned above whose source of budget is not clear. Such institutions are classified by way of management.

(3) Social organizations: include social organizations established with the approval from the Ministry of Civil Affairs, and organizations that are not covered by social organization management regulations such as trade unions, womens federations etc.. Social organizations are further classified as follows:

(a) Social organizations that are not covered by social organization management regulations of the Ministry of Civil Affairs such as trade unions, womens federations, communist youth leagues, youth associations, industrial and commerce associations, scientists associations, overseas Chinese associations, etc., foundations and fund management organizations established with funds from the state, and social organizations whose funds mainly come from the budget of their competent government agencies. Such institutions are classified as state-owned.

(b) Social organizations whose budget mainly comes from collective units. Such institutions are classified as collective-owned.

(c) Social organizations established by individual or a group of citizens, which are classified as private.

(d) Social organizations other than those mentioned above whose source of budget is not clear. Such organizations are classified by way of management.

Gross Domestic Product (GDP) refers to the final products at market prices produced by all resident units in a country (or a region) during a certain period of time. Gross domestic product is expressed in three different forms, i.e. value, income, and products respectively. GDP in its value form refers to the total value of all goods and services produced by all resident units during a certain period of time, minus the total value of input of goods and services of the nature of non-fixed assets; in other term, it is the sum of the value-added of all resident units. GDP in the form of income includes the income created by all resident units and distributed to resident and non-resident units. GDP in the form of products refers to the value of all goods and services for final consumption by all resident units minus the net exports of goods and services during a given period of time. In the practice of national accounting, gross domestic product is calculated with three approaches, i.e. production approach, income approach and expenditure approach, which reflect gross domestic product and its composition from different aspects.

Gross National Income (GNI) also known as gross national product, refers to the final result of the primary distribution of the income created by all the resident units of a country (or a region) during a certain period of time. The value-added created by the resident units of a country engaged in production activities is distributed, during the primary distribution, mainly to the resident units of that country, while part of it is distributed to the non-resident units in the form of production tax and import duties (minus subsidies to production and import), remuneration for the labourers and property income. At the meantime, a part of the value-added created abroad is distributed to the resident units of the country in the form of production tax and import duties (minus subsidies to production and import), remuneration for the labourers and property income. The concept of gross national income is thus developed, which equals to the gross domestic product plus the net factor income from abroad. Unlike the gross domestic product which is a concept of production, the gross national income is a concept of income.

Three Industries Classification of economic activities into three branches of industries is a common practice in the world, although the grouping varies to some extent form country to country. In China economic activities are categorized into following industries:

Primary industry: refers to agriculture, forestry, animal husbandry and fishery.

Secondary industry: refers to mining and quarrying, manufacturing, production and supply of electricity, water and gas, and construction.

Tertiary industry: refers to all other economic activities not included in primary or secondary industry.

Labourers Remuneration refers to the whole payment of various forms earned by the labourers from the productive activities they are engaged in. It includes wages, bonuses and allowances the labourers earned in monetary form and in kind. It also includes the free medical services provided to the labourers and the medicine expenses, traffic subsidies and social insurance, housing fund paid by the employers. As the individual economy is concerned, since the labourers remuneration is not easily distinguished from the operating profit, both are treated as labourers remuneration.

Net Taxes on Production refers to the difference of the taxes on production minus the subsidies on production. The taxes on production refers to the various taxes, extra charges and fees levied on the production units on their production, sale and business activities as well as on the use of some factors of production, such as fixed assets, land and labour force in the production activities they are engaged in. In contrast to the taxes on production, the subsidies on production refer to the unilateral government transfer to the production units and are therefore regarded as negative taxes on production. They include subsidies on the loss due to implementation of government policies, price subsidies, etc.

Depreciation of Fixed Assets refers to the depreciation of fixed assets of a given period, drawn in accordance with the stipulated depreciation rate for the purpose of compensating the wear loss of the fixed assets or the depreciation of fixed assets calculated in a fictitious way in accordance with the stipulated unified depreciation rate in the national economic accounting system. It reflects the value of transfer of the fixed assets in the production of the current period. The depreciation of fixed assets in various enterprises and institutions managed as enterprises refers to the depreciation expenses actually drawn. In government agencies and institutions not managed as enterprises which do not draw the depreciation expenses, as well as for the houses of residents, the depreciation of fixed assets is the imputed depreciation, which is calculated in accordance with the stipulated unified depreciation rate. In principle, the depreciation of fixed assets should be calculated on the basis of the re-purchased value of the fixed assets. However, there is no actual condition to re-evaluate all the fixed assets in China. Therefore, the above-mentioned methods are temporarily adopted at present.

Operating Surplus refers to the balance of the value added created by the resident units deducting the labourers remuneration, net taxes on production and the depreciation of fixed assets. It is equivalent to the business profit of the enterprises plus subsidies on production, but the wages and welfare expenses paid from the profits should be deducted.

GDP by Expenditure Approach refers to the method of measuring the final results of production activities of a country (region) during a given period from the perspective of final use. It includes final consumption expenditure, total capital formation and net export of goods and services, i.e.:

GDP by expenditure approach = final consumption expenditure + total capital formation + net export of goods and services

Final ConsumptionExpenditure refers to the total expenditure of resident units for purchases of goods and services from domestic economic territory and abroad to meet the requirements of material, cultural and spiritual life. It excludes the expenditure of non-resident units on consumption in the economic territory of the country. The final consumption expenditure is broken down into household consumption expenditure and government consumption expenditure.

Households ConsumptionExpenditure refers to the total expenditure of resident households on the final consumption of goods and services. In addition to the consumption of goods and services bought by the households directly with money, the households consumption expenditure also includes expenditure on goods and services obtained by the households in other ways, i.e. the so-called imputed consumption expenditure, which includes the following: (a) the goods and services provided to the households by the employer in the form of payment in kind and transfer in kind; (b) goods and services produced and consumed by the households themselves, in which the services refer only to the owner–occupied housing and domestic and individual services provided by the paid household workers; (c) financial intermediate services provided by financial institutions; (d) insurance services provided by insurance companies.

Government ConsumptionExpenditure refers to the expenditure on the consumption of the public services provided by the government to the whole society and the net expenditure on the goods and services provided by the government to the households free of charge or at low prices. The former equals to the output value of the government services minus the value of operating income obtained by the government departments. The latter equals to the market value of the goods and services provided by the government free of charge or at low prices to the households minus the value received by the government from the households.

Total Capital Formation refers to the fixed assets acquired minus those disposed of and the net value of inventory, including the total fixed capital formation and the increase in inventory.

Total Fixed Capital Formation refers to the value of fixed assets acquired minus those disposed of during a given period. Fixed assets are the assets produced through production activities with specified unit value which could be used for over one year, excluding natural assets. Total fixed capital formation can be categorized into total tangible capital formation and total intangible capital formation. The total tangible capital formation include the value of the construction projects, installation projects completed and the equipment, apparatus and instruments purchased as well as the value of land improved, the value of draught animals, breeding stock, animals for milk, wool and for recreational purpose, and the newly increased forest with economic value during a given period. The total intangible capital formation includes the prospecting of minerals, the acquisition of computer software minus the disposal of them.

Increase in Inventory refers to the market value of the change in inventory of resident units during a given period, i.e. the difference of value between the beginning and the end of the period minus the current gains due to the change in prices. The increase in inventory can be positive or negative. A positive value indicates the increase in inventory while a negative value indicates the decrease in stock. The inventory includes the raw materials, fuels and reserve materials purchased by the production units as well as the inventory of finished products, semi–finished products, work–in–progress, etc.

Outflow of Goods and Services refers to the difference of the exports of goods and services minus the imports of goods and services. The imports include the value of various goods and services sold or gratuitously transferred by the resident units to the non–resident units. The imports include the value of various goods and services purchased or gratuitously acquired by the resident units from the non–resident units. Because the provision of services and the use of them happen simultaneously, the acquisition of services by the resident units from abroad is usually treated as import while the acquisition of services by non–resident units in this country is usually treated as export. The export and import of goods are calculated at FOB.

2 人口

Population

2-1 人 口 数
POPULATION

单位:万人 (年底数)(number at year-end) (10 000 persons)

年份 Year	户籍人口 Total Population	男 Male	女 Female	常住人口 Total Population	男 Male	女 Female
1952	2745.0	1414.6	1330.4			
1957	3062.4	1579.7	1482.7			
1965	3504.5	1793.4	1711.2			
1975	4408.2	2261.6	2146.5			
1980	4684.5	2401.7	2282.7			
1985	4931.0	2540.0	2391.0	4980.8	2565.8	2414.0
1986	4989.0	2573.4	2415.6	5047.8	2602.8	2444.1
1987	5058.1	2608.7	2449.4	5120.3	2639.8	2479.5
1988	5144.2	2652.1	2492.1	5184.9	2673.1	2511.8
1989	5223.9	2694.6	2529.3	5258.8	2712.6	2546.3
1990	5373.5	2771.5	2602.0	5439.3	2805.5	2633.8
1991	5446.8	2805.4	2641.4	5512.3	2839.2	2673.2
1992	5513.6	2841.3	2672.4	5579.9	2862.2	2717.6
1993	5590.5	2880.8	2709.6	5653.5	2913.3	2740.2
1994	5656.8	2915.6	2741.2	5718.8	2947.5	2771.3
1995	5727.1	2952.2	2775.0	5772.1	2959.6	2812.5
1996	5776.3	2979.6	2796.8	5825.1	3004.8	2820.3
1997	5838.8	3014.1	2824.8	5872.6	3016.6	2856.0
1998	5890.6	3039.9	2850.7	5907.2	3032.7	2874.6
1999	5942.5	3061.8	2880.7	5938.0	3031.9	2906.1
2000	5936.0	3066.1	2869.9	5646.0	2939.3	2706.7
2001	5956.6	3073.2	2883.4	5658.0	2919.1	2738.9
2002	5978.2	3086.2	2892.0	5672.0	2928.1	2743.9
2003	6000.5	3109.9	2890.6	5685.0	2946.3	2738.7
2004	6001.3	3107.8	2893.5	5698.0	2950.7	2747.3
2005	5984.1	3102.4	2881.7	5710.0	2960.2	2749.8
2006	6038.3	3129.7	2908.7	5693.0	2950.6	2742.4
2007	6084.9	3154.0	2930.9	5699.0	2953.9	2745.1
2008	6110.8	3167.5	2943.3	5711.0	2960.2	2750.8
2009	6141.9	3185.5	2956.4	5720.0	2966.6	2753.4
2010	6176.0	3202.0	2974.0	5723.8	2939.3	2784.5
2011	6164.1	3194.0	2970.1	5758.0	2956.1	2802.0
2012	6165.4	3193.9	2971.4	5779.0	2963.9	2815.1
2013	6170.6	3199.5	2971.1	5799.0	2972.0	2827.0
2014	6162.3	3198.1	2964.2	5816.0	2980.3	2835.7
2015	6138.9	3190.1	2948.8	5851.5	2984.5	2867.0
2016	6156.8	3200.4	2956.3	5885.0	2997.2	2887.8

2-2 人口城乡构成
COMPOSITION OF URBAN AND RURAL POPULATION

单位:万人 (年底数)(number at year-end) (10 000 persons)

年份 Year	Total Population	城镇人口 Urban Population	乡村人口 Rural Population
1952	2745.00	271.41	2416.17
1957	3062.41	411.69	2650.72
1965	3504.54	485.06	3019.48
1975	4408.15	626.22	3781.93
1980	4684.45	786.49	3897.96
1985	4980.81	1464.65	3516.16
1986	5047.83	1187.23	3860.60
1987	5120.27	1288.61	3831.66
1988	5184.94	1389.99	3794.95
1989	5258.83	1491.37	3767.46
1990	5439.29	1551.51	3887.78
1991	5512.33	1433.06	4079.27
1992	5579.85	1637.68	3942.17
1993	5653.48	1731.66	3921.82
1994	5718.81	1604.13	4114.68
1995	5772.07	1800.89	3971.18
1996	5825.13	1965.40	3859.73
1997	5872.60	1834.60	4038.00
1998	5907.23	1884.41	4022.82
1999	5938.03	1990.17	3947.86
2000	5646.00	2285.11	3360.89
2001	5658.00	2308.50	3349.50
2002	5672.00	2348.20	3323.80
2003	5685.00	2387.70	3297.30
2004	5698.00	2427.30	2466.70
2005	5710.00	2466.70	3243.30
2006	5693.00	2493.50	3199.50
2007	5699.00	2524.70	3174.30
2008	5711.00	2581.40	3129.60
2009	5720.00	2631.20	3088.80
2010	5723.77	2844.51	2879.26
2011	5758.00	2984.32	2773.68
2012	5779.00	3091.77	2687.23
2013	5799.00	3161.03	2637.97
2014	5816.00	3237.80	2578.20
2015	5851.50	3326.58	2524.92
2016	5885.00	3419.19	2465.81

注:1981年及以前数据为户籍统计数;1982、1990、2000、2010年数据为当年人口普查时点数据;其余年份数据为年度人口抽样调查推算数据(下相关表同)。

2-3 人口自然变动
NATURAL CHANGE OF POLULATION

年 份 Year	人口变动数(万人) Number of Population Changed (10 000 persons)			变动系数(‰) Growth Rates		
	出生数 Number of Birth	死亡数 Number of Death	自然增长数 Number of Nature Growth	出生率 Birth Rate	死亡率 Death Rate	自然增长率 Natural Growth Rate
1965	121.48	34.75	86.73	35.10	10.04	25.06
1975	90.80	34.52	56.28	20.74	7.88	12.86
1980	94.84	32.59	62.25	20.36	7.00	13.36
1985	97.83	37.37	60.46	19.95	7.62	12.33
1986	107.09	39.45	67.64	21.01	7.74	13.27
1987	108.56	36.12	72.44	21.43	7.13	14.30
1988	97.62	32.95	64.67	19.08	6.44	12.64
1989	110.13	36.24	73.89	21.09	6.94	14.15
1990	114.40	38.66	75.74	21.60	7.30	14.30
1991	113.34	40.30	73.04	20.70	7.36	13.34
1992	105.60	38.08	67.52	19.05	6.87	12.18
1993	112.55	38.92	73.63	20.04	6.93	13.11
1994	103.31	37.98	65.33	18.17	6.68	11.49
1995	92.96	39.70	53.26	16.18	6.91	9.27
1996	93.24	40.18	53.06	16.08	6.93	9.15
1997	86.62	39.13	47.49	14.81	6.69	8.12
1998	74.09	39.46	34.63	12.58	6.70	5.88
1999	68.52	37.73	30.79	11.57	6.37	5.20
2000	57.76	35.75	22.01	9.71	6.01	3.70
2001	50.84	36.27	14.57	8.51	6.07	2.44
2002	50.10	36.90	13.20	8.38	6.17	2.21
2003	49.50	35.60	13.90	8.26	5.94	2.32
2004	50.66	36.23	14.43	8.43	6.03	2.40
2005	52.60	34.30	18.30	8.74	5.69	3.05
2006	54.80	35.90	18.90	9.08	5.95	3.13
2007	55.69	36.12	19.57	9.19	5.96	3.23
2008	55.98	39.51	16.47	9.21	6.50	2.71
2009	57.80	36.58	21.22	9.48	6.00	3.48
2010	59.30	34.46	24.84	10.36	6.02	4.34
2011	59.67	34.52	25.15	10.39	6.01	4.38
2012	63.45	35.30	28.15	11.00	6.12	4.88
2013	64.14	35.60	28.54	11.08	6.15	4.93
2014	68.88	40.42	28.46	11.86	6.96	4.90
2015	62.65	34.01	28.64	10.74	5.83	4.91
2016	70.65	40.90	29.75	12.04	6.97	5.07

2-4 分市、州、县年底人口数(2016)
POPULATION OF CITIES, TOWNS, AND

单位: 万人 (10 000 persons)

地 区	Region	户籍人口 (万人) Total Population	常住人口 (万人) Population of Permnant Residents	地 区	Region	户籍人口 (万人) Total Population	常住人口 (万人) Population of Permnant Residents
全 省	**Province**	**6156.76**	**5885.00**	丹江口市	Danjiangkou	46.49	44.57
武汉市	**Wuhan**	**833.85**	**1076.62**	**宜昌市**	**Yichang**	**394.31**	**413.00**
江岸区	Jiang'an	72.62	96.19	西陵区	Xiling	41.64	54.11
江汉区	Jianghan	48.62	73.00	伍家岗区	Wujiagang	17.30	22.86
硚口区	Qiaokou	52.46	86.76	点军区	Dianjun	10.49	10.59
汉阳区	Hanyang	59.58	64.89	猇亭区	Xiaoting	5.08	6.46
武昌区	Wuchang	107.77	127.78	夷陵区	Yiling	52.27	52.53
青山区	Qingshan	42.88	52.71	远安县	Yuan'an	19.25	18.78
洪山区	Hongshan	92.89	160.61	兴山县	Xingshan	16.88	17.13
东西湖区	Dongxihu	29.65	53.88	秭归县	Zigui	37.53	36.23
汉南区	Hannan	11.39	13.16	长阳县	Changyang	39.66	39.00
蔡甸区	Caidian	45.99	71.99	五峰县	Wufeng	19.99	19.03
江夏区	Jiangxia	59.83	89.46	宜都市	Yidu	39.19	39.07
黄陂区	Huangpi	113.28	96.71	当阳市	Dangyang	47.19	46.93
新洲区	Xinzhou	96.88	89.48	枝江市	Zhijiang	47.85	50.28
黄石市	**Huangshi**	**269.90**	**246.55**	**襄阳市**	**Xiangyang**	**594.25**	**563.90**
黄石港区	Huangshigang	20.67	23.79	襄城区	Xiangcheng	46.18	50.17
西塞山区	Xisai mountainous	21.39	24.68	樊城区	Fancheng	80.35	89.98
下陆区	Xialu	15.55	18.30	襄州区	Xiangzhou	99.79	91.89
铁山区	Tieshan	5.11	5.83	南漳县	Nanzhang	58.12	54.29
大冶市	Daye	98.01	90.89	谷城县	Gucheng	60.16	52.03
阳新县	Yangxin	109.17	83.06	保康县	Baokang	26.90	25.48
十堰市		**347.52**	**340.90**	老河口市	Laohekou	52.19	47.89
茅箭区	Maojian	29.28	42.12	枣阳市	Zaoyang	114.06	99.77
张湾区	Zhangwan	26.22	38.89	宜城市	Yicheng	56.49	52.40
郧阳区	Yunyang	63.19	56.79	**鄂州市**	**Ezhou**	**111.19**	**106.85**
郧西县	Yunxi	51.87	45.56	梁子湖区	Liangzihu	18.97	14.48
竹山县	Zhushan	46.52	41.70	华容区	Huarong	26.49	24.47
竹溪县	Zhuxi	36.09	31.39	鄂城区	Ercheng	65.74	67.90
房 县	Fang	47.85	39.88				

2-4 续表 Continued

单位: 万人 (10 000 persons)

地 区	Regions	户籍人口 Total Population	常住人口 Permnant Population	地 区	Regions	户籍人口 Total Population	常住人口 Permnant Population
荆门市	**Jingmen**	**299.64**	**290.13**	蕲春县	Hanchun	101.85	78.03
东宝区	Dongbao	36.93	37.14	黄梅县	Huangmei	104.70	86.88
掇刀区	Zhuodao	29.91	31.45	麻城市	Macheng	116.95	88.08
京山县	Jingshan	64.59	62.80	武穴市	Wuxue	82.29	65.55
沙洋县	Shayang	62.33	57.25	**咸宁市**	**Xianning**	**303.59**	**252.60**
钟祥市	Zhongxiang	105.88	101.49	咸安区	Xian'an	62.20	52.66
孝感市	**Xiaogan**	**523.21**	**490.43**	嘉鱼县	Jiayu	37.20	31.66
孝南区	Xiaonan	95.80	92.67	通城县	Tongcheng	52.32	41.40
孝昌县	Xiaochang	67.74	59.80	崇阳县	Congyang	50.73	40.54
大悟县	Dawu	63.48	62.32	通山县	Tongshan	47.70	37.40
云梦县	Yunmeng	58.29	53.54	赤壁市	Chibi	53.45	48.94
应城市	Yingcheng	66.59	60.43	**随州市**	**Suizhou**	**252.15**	**220.18**
安陆市	Anlu	62.04	58.20	曾都区	Zengdu	65.57	63.38
汉川市	Hanchuan	109.27	103.47	随县	Sui	93.43	79.90
荆州市	**Jingzhou**	**646.35**	**569.79**	广水市	Guangshui	93.14	76.90
沙市区	Shashi	53.74	65.69	**恩施州**	**Enshi Prefecture**	**404.01**	**334.60**
荆州区	Jingzhou	54.90	57.78	恩施市	Enshi	80.85	77.33
公安县	Gong'an	101.32	87.89	利川市	Jianli	92.03	66.60
监利县	Jianli	156.60	106.64	建始县	Jianshi	51.46	41.84
江陵县	Jianglin	39.54	33.11	巴东县	Badong	49.27	42.71
石首市	Shishou	63.01	57.04	宣恩县	Xuan'en	36.11	30.44
洪湖市	Honghu	93.19	84.78	咸丰县	Xianfeng	38.73	30.66
松滋市	Songzi	84.05	76.86	来凤县	Laifeng	33.29	24.70
黄冈市	**Huanggang**	**746.87**	**632.10**	鹤峰县	Hefeng	22.27	20.32
黄州区	Huangzhou	35.13	38.86	**省直管单位**	**Jurisdictional**		
团风县	Tuanfeng	37.53	34.42	仙桃市	Xiantao	156.35	114.80
红安县	Hong'an	66.07	60.74	潜江市	Qianjiang	102.33	96.20
罗田县	Luotian	60.07	55.20	天门市	Tianmen	163.36	128.66
英山县	Yingshan	40.49	36.27	**神农架林区**	**Shennongjian**	**7.89**	**7.69**
浠水县	Xishui	101.77	88.07				

主要统计指标解释

人口数 指一定时点、一定地区范围内有生命的个人总和。

年度统计的年末人口数指每年12月31日24时的人口数。

城镇人口和乡村人口 城镇人口是指居住在城镇范围内的全部常住人口；乡村人口是除上述人口以外的全部人口。

出生率(又称粗出生率) 指在一定时期内(通常为一年)一定地区的出生人数与同期内平均人数(或期中人数)之比，用千分率表示。本资料中的出生率指年出生率，其计算公式为：

$$出生率=\frac{年出生人数}{年平均人数}\times 1000‰$$

式中：出生人数指活产婴儿，即胎儿脱离母体时(不管怀孕月数)，有过呼吸或其他生命现象。年平均人数指年初、年底人口数的平均数，也可用年中人口数代替。

死亡率(又称粗死亡率) 指在一定时期内(通常为一年)一定地区的死亡人数与同期内平均人数(或期中人数)之比，用千分率表示。本资料中的死亡率指年死亡率，其计算公式为：

$$死亡率=\frac{年死亡人数}{年平均人数}\times 1000‰$$

人口自然增长率 指在一定时期内(通常为一年)人口自然增加数(出生人数减死亡人数)与该时期内平均人数(或期中人数)之比，用千分率表示。计算公式为：

$$人口自然增长率=\frac{本年出生人数-本年死亡人数}{年平均人数}\times 1000‰$$

$$=人口出生率-人口死亡率$$

Explanatory Notes on Main Statistical Indicators

Total Population refers to the total number of people alive at a certain point of time within a given area.

The annual statistics on total population is taken at midnight, the 31st of December.

Urban Population and Rural Population Urban population refer to all people residing in cities and towns, while rural population refer to population other than urban population.

Birth Rate (or Crude Birth Rate) refers to the ratio of the number of births to the average population (or mid-period population) during a certain period of time (usually a year), expressed in ‰. Birth rate in the chapter refers to annual birth rate. The following formula is used:

Birth Rate = (Number of Births/Average Number of Population) × 1000‰

Number of births in the formula refers to live births, i.e. when a baby has breathed or showed any vital phenomena regardless of the length of pregnancy.

Annual average number of population is the average of the number of population at the beginning of the year and that at the end of the year. Sometimes it is substituted by the mid–year population.

Death Rate (or Crude Death Rate) refers to the ratio of the number of deaths to the average population (or mid–period population) during a certain period of time (usually a year), expressed in ‰. Death rate in the chapter refers to annual death rate. The following formula is used:

Death Rate= (Number of Deaths/Annual Average Number of Population) × 1000‰

Natural Growth Rate of Population refers to the ratio of natural increase in population (number of births minus number of deaths) in a certain period of time (usually a year) to the average population (or mid–period population) of the same period, expressed in ‰. The following formula is applied:

Natural Growth Rate of Population = [(Number of Births–Number of Deaths)/Average Number of Population] × 1000‰

Natural Growth Rate of Population = Birth Rate–Death Rate

3 就业人员和职工工资

Employment and Wages

3-1 全社会从业人员
NUMBER OF EMPLOYED PERSONS

单位：万人 (10 000 person)

年份 Year	合计 Total	按城乡分 Grouped by Areas		按产业分 Grouped by Industries		
		城镇 Urban	乡村 Rural	第一产业 Primary Industry	第二产业 Secondary Industry	第三产业 Tertiary Industry
1952	1020.30	141.60	878.70			
1965	1404.20	222.70	1181.60			
1970	1618.50	278.00	1340.80			
1975	1802.50	381.70	1420.80			
1978	1910.40	458.00	1452.30	1470.60	269.00	170.80
1980	1986.90	507.20	1479.70	1453.70	286.30	247.00
1985	2238.10	637.60	1600.50	1383.30	485.40	369.50
1990	3040.40	890.80	2149.60	1859.80	628.50	552.10
1991	3082.70	909.40	2173.30	1897.40	623.00	562.30
1992	3118.60	923.10	2195.50	1869.00	650.90	598.70
1993	3157.60	940.90	2216.70	1818.80	684.60	654.20
1994	3196.90	980.10	2216.80	1760.50	717.10	719.30
1995	3232.50	1015.00	2217.50	1697.00	743.50	792.00
1996	3275.50	1050.80	2224.70	1677.10	746.80	851.60
1997	3311.20	1070.50	2240.70	1663.20	752.00	896.00
1998	3328.20	1093.60	2234.60	1612.50	705.60	1010.10
1999	3358.10	1110.50	2247.60	1612.60	697.80	1047.70
2000	3384.90	1123.80	2261.10	1625.10	702.40	1057.40
2001	3414.50	1148.70	2265.80	1639.00	706.80	1068.70
2002	3443.00	1177.00	2266.00	1652.60	704.10	1086.30
2003	3476.00	1211.00	2265.00	1661.50	712.60	1101.90
2004	3507.00	1245.00	2262.00	1672.90	720.30	1113.80
2005	3537.00	1271.00	2266.00	1687.30	725.00	1124.70
2006	3564.00	1297.00	2267.00	1694.70	732.40	1136.90
2007	3584.00	1322.00	2262.00	1697.00	740.10	1146.90
2008	3607.00	1337.00	2270.00	1707.91	730.42	1168.67
2009	3622.00	1357.00	2265.00	1702.30	736.60	1183.10
2010	3645.00	1382.60	2262.40	1691.10	754.70	1199.20
2011	3672.00	1413.00	2259.00	1678.10	771.12	1222.78
2012	3687.00	1430.60	2256.40	1638.90	781.60	1266.50
2013	3692.00	1438.00	2254.00	1582.00	793.80	1316.20
2014	3687.50	1437.60	2249.90	1487.00	834.30	1366.20
2015	3658.00	1935.00	1723.00	1404.00	834.00	1420.00
2016	3633.00	2074.00	1559.00	1338.00	837.00	1458.00

注：因2015年开展全国1%人口抽样调查，根据调查结果对部分数据进行修正，使2015年全省全社会从业人员数据产生较大波动。

3-2 分行业城镇单位从业人员数(2016)
NUMBER OF EMPLOYEES IN URBAN UNITS BY SECTOR (2016)

单位：人 (person)

行业	Sector	城镇全部单位 All the Units In Urban Area	国有经济单位 State Owned Units	城镇集体单位 Urban Collective Owned Units	其他经济单位 Other Units	城镇私营单位 Urban Private Units
总计	**Total**	**10875262**	**2773961**	**130450**	**4288752**	**3682099**
农、林、牧、渔业	Farming,Forest,Herd, ishery	151984	99928	819	2252	48985
采矿业	Mining and Quarrying	164357	10745	2604	51582	99426
制造业	Manufacturing	3446677	128041	21628	1710928	1586080
电力、燃气及水的生产和供应业	Power, Gas and water production and supply	188215	109155	1101	53536	24423
建筑业	Construction	2144585	77479	35495	1290611	741000
批发和零售业	Wholesale and Retail sale	923764	38828	17171	341231	526534
交通运输、仓储和邮政业	Transportation, storage and post	441775	194290	3792	151598	92095
住宿和餐饮业	Hotel and Catering	256361	7612	1083	84853	162813
信息传输、软件和信息技术服务业	Information Transmission, Software and Computer Services	149783	15249	101	107924	26509
金融业	Banking	216136	77417	11850	120431	6438
房地产业	Real Estate	244808	9512	1056	138409	95831
租赁和商务服务业	Leasing and Commerical Services	208157	32033	3557	69546	103021
科学研究、技术服务业	Scietific Research, polytechnical	183188	87274	2361	68854	24699
水利、环境和公共设施管理业	Water Conservance, Environment and Public Facilities Management	124462	93373	6674	13990	10425
居民服务、修理和其他服务业	Resident Service and Others	62170	4940	389	9014	47827
教育	Education	770972	689309	5492	34613	41558
卫生和社会工作	Health, Social Security and	447437	396562	14614	23618	12643
文化、体育和娱乐业	Culture, Sports and Entertainment	96324	49259	562	14711	31792
公共管理、社会保障和社会组织	Public management, social security and social organization	654107	652955	101	1051	

注:城镇全部单位统计范围含城镇私营单位。(后表未经特别注明均同此口径)

Note: All Statistics of Units in Urban Areas of 2010 including all the private run unit.
(The following tables if without specific notes are considered the same standard with this one.)

3-3 分行业在岗职工人数(2016)
NUMBER OF STAFF AND WORKERS BY SECTOR(2016)

单位：人 (person)

行业	Sector	城镇全部单位 All the Units In Urban Area	国有经济单位 State Owned Units	城镇集体单位 Urban Collective Owned Units	其他经济单位 Other Units	城镇私营单位 Urban Private Units
总计	**Total**	**10309547**	**2581740**	**120468**	**3925240**	**3682099**
农、林、牧、渔业	Farming, Forest, Herd, Fishery	125179	73314	762	2118	48985
采矿业	Mining and Quarrying	159071	8374	2529	48742	99426
制造业	Manufacturing	3398246	120780	21124	1670262	1586080
电力、燃气及水的生产和供应业	Power, Gas and water production and supply	185262	107041	1096	52702	24423
建筑业	Construction	1890091	64205	33521	1051365	741000
批发和零售业	Wholesale and Retail sale	907487	37431	14692	328830	526534
交通运输、仓储和邮政业	Transportation, storage and post	427833	187205	3570	144963	92095
住宿和餐饮业	Hotel and Catering	253771	7274	1005	82679	162813
信息传输、软件和信息技术服务业	Information Transmission, Software and Computer Services	145750	14588	79	104574	26509
金融业	Banking	172136	67893	11544	86261	6438
房地产业	Real Estate	237025	8234	933	132027	95831
租赁和商务服务业	Leasing and Commerical Services	204180	31334	3335	66490	103021
科学研究、技术服务业	Scietific Research, polytechnical	172498	82680	2231	62888	24699
水利、环境和公共设施 管理业	Water Conservance, Environment and Public Facilities Management	102854	76293	3888	12248	10425
居民服务、修理和其他服务业	Resident Service and Others	61131	4335	320	8649	47827
教育	Education	733623	653829	5241	32995	41558
卫生和社会工作	Health, Social Security and	426014	376293	14008	23070	12643
文化、体育和娱乐业	Culture, Sports and Entertainment	92546	46851	500	13403	31792
公共管理、社会保障和社会组织	Public management, social security and social organization	614850	613786	90	974	

3-4 分行业在岗女职工人数(2016)
NUMBER OF FEMALE STAFF AND WORKERS BY SECTOR(2016)

单位：人 (person)

行业	Sector	城镇全部单位(不含私营单位) All the Units In Urban Area	国有经济单位 State Owned Units	城镇集体单位 Urban Collective Owned Units	其他经济单位 Urban Private Units
总计	**Total**	**2458351**	**1051169**	**44083**	**1363099**
农、林、牧、渔业	Farming, Forest, Herd, Fishery	36716	35673	201	842
采矿业	Mining and Quarrying	20916	4807	333	15776
制造业	Manufacturing	691497	28470	8095	654932
电力、燃气及水的生产和供应业	Power, Gas and water production and supply	47795	31173	392	16230
建筑业	Construction	158443	11960	4903	141580
批发和零售业	Wholesale and Retail sale	211406	11565	9990	189851
交通运输、仓储和邮政业	Transportation, storage and post	96522	55655	907	39960
住宿和餐饮业	Hotel and Catering	56527	4174	707	51646
信息传输、软件和信息技术服务业	Information Transmission, Software and Computer Services	45291	4792	65	40434
金融业	Banking	109643	38366	5056	66221
房地产业	Real Estate	56135	3172	438	52525
租赁和商务服务业	Leasing and Commerical Services	35243	9647	1079	24517
科学研究、技术服务业	Scietific Research, polytechnical	41886	24640	453	16793
水利、环境和公共设施管理业	Water Conservance, Environment and Public Facilities Management	43922	35011	2973	5938
居民服务、修理和其他服务业	Resident Service and Others	6960	1698	156	5106
教育	Education	327288	307293	2806	17189
卫生和社会工作	Health, Social Security and	254507	232900	5252	16355
文化、体育和娱乐业	Culture, Sports and Entertainment	27062	19778	246	7038
公共管理、社会保障和社会组织	Public Management、social security and Social Organization	190592	190395	31	166

3-5 城镇登记失业人数及失业率
NUMBER OF URBAN UNEMPLOYED PERSONS AND UNEMPLOYMENT RATE

单位：万人 (10 000 person)

年份 Year	年末城镇登记失业人数 The Number of Unemployeed in Urban Areas by the End of Year	年末城镇登记失业率(%) Year End Unemployment registered Rate %
1978	20.03	4.19
1980	15.54	2.97
1990	12.66	1.72
1991	14.20	1.88
1992	16.89	2.17
1993	17.96	2.20
1994	21.06	2.90
1995	24.45	3.10
1996	28.25	3.50
1997	29.83	3.50
1998	31.33	3.30
1999	33.10	3.30
2000	36.64	3.50
2001	42.15	4.00
2002	44.66	4.30
2003	49.34	4.30
2004	49.37	4.20
2005	52.60	4.33
2006	52.56	4.22
2007	46.72	4.21
2008	55.07	4.20
2009	55.25	4.21
2010	55.65	4.18
2011	55.11	4.10
2012	42.26	3.83
2013	40.26	3.49
2014	37.88	3.10
2015	33.43	2.64
2016	32.91	2.41

3-6 职工平均工资及指数

年份 Year	平均货币工资(元) Average Money Wages (yuan)					指数(上年=100) Indices(preceding year=100)	
	合计 Total	国有经济单位 State Owned Units	城镇集体经济单位 Urban Collective Owned	其他经济单位 Other Units	城镇私营单位 Urban private units	货币工资 Money Wages	国有经济单位 State Owned Units
1978	581	592	532			104.5	104.5
1980	719	744	619			116.0	115.9
1990	1903	2045	1467	2259		111.7	107.6
1992	2370	2532	1837	2575		113.9	114.4
1993	2933	3141	2183	3248		123.8	124.1
1994	4050	4348	2845	4352		138.1	138.4
1995	4685	4991	3308	5093		115.7	114.8
1996	5099	5411	3590	5754		108.8	108.4
1997	5401	5741	3731	5740		105.9	106.1
1998	6436	6783	4748	6166		108.7	109.1
1999	6991	7381	5001	6681		108.6	108.8
2000	7565	7989	5090	7327		108.2	108.2
2001	8619	9133	5677	8035		113.9	114.3
2002	9611	10403	6534	8180		111.5	113.9
2003	10692	11806	7137	8698		111.2	113.5
2004	11855	13096	7608	10270		110.9	110.9
2005	13330	14774	8663	11572		112.4	112.8
2006	15172	17078	9848	13098		113.8	115.6
2007	17397	21971	12921	16829		114.7	128.7
2008	19597	24756	14840	20293		112.6	112.7
2009	23709	30032	19181	23528	15615	121.0	121.3
2010	28092	35981	24429	28799	18626	118.5	119.8
2011	32050	40345	26988	34354	20788	114.1	112.1
2012	35179	43438	33551	38675	23037	109.8	107.7
2013	38720	46126	34181	43975	25898	110.1	106.2
2014	43217	55071	37599	48163	28534	111.6	119.4
2015	47320	60615	41152	52060	31051	109.5	110.1
2016	51415	68983	44154	56461	34167	108.7	113.8

注：1998年以后为在岗职工平均工资。2007年以后统计范围含城镇全部私营单位。

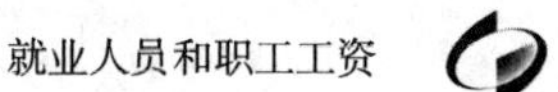

AVERAGE WAGES AND INDICES OF STAFF AND WORKERS

指数(上年=100) Indices(preceding year=100)							
城镇集体经济单位 Urban Collective Owned	其他经济单位 OtherUnits	城镇私营单位 Urban private units	实际工资 Real Wages	国有经济单位 State Owned Units	城镇集体经济单位 Urban Collective Owned	其他经济单位 OtherUnits	城镇私营单位 Urban private units
106.4			104.2	103.9	106.1		
116.4			108.6	108.5	109.0		
107.1	107.1		107.8	108.3	104.4	103.9	
110.5	109.0		103.1	103.5	100.0	98.7	
118.8	126.1		106.6	106.8	102.3	108.6	
130.3	134.0		108.7	109.0	102.6	105.5	
116.3	117.0		96.3	95.6	96.8	97.4	
108.5	113.0		95.1	94.0	95.3	99.9	
103.9	99.8		97.6	96.6	95.9	96.6	
109.2	99.1		110.2	110.2	110.8	100.5	
105.3	108.4		110.0	111.0	107.4	110.6	
101.8	109.7		109.3	109.3	102.7	110.8	
111.5	109.7		113.6	114.0	111.2	109.3	
115.1	101.8		112.0	114.4	115.6	102.2	
109.2	106.3		108.8	111.1	106.8	104.0	
106.6	118.1		105.7	105.7	101.6	112.6	
113.9	112.7		109.2	109.6	110.7	109.5	
113.7	113.2		112.0	113.8	111.9	111.4	
131.2	128.5		109.4	122.8	125.2	122.6	
114.9	120.6		106.0	106.0	108.0	113.4	
129.3	115.9		121.8	122.2	130.2	116.8	
127.4	122.4	119.3	115.1	116.4	123.8	119.0	115.9
110.5	119.3	111.6	107.8	106.0	104.4	112.8	105.5
124.3	112.6	110.8	106.7	104.6	120.8	109.4	107.7
101.9	113.7	112.4	107.1	103.3	99.1	110.6	109.4
110.0	109.5	110.2	109.4	117.1	107.8	107.4	108.0
109.4	108.1	108.8	107.9	108.4	107.8	106.5	107.2
107.3	108.5	110.0	106.3	111.4	105.0	106.1	107.7

Notes:Data after 1998 refers to average wages and indices of employed staff and workers.Statistics of 2007 involves all the private run units in urban areas.

3-7 分行业在岗职工平均工资(2016)
AVERAGE WAGES OF STAFF AND WORKER BY SECTOR(2016)

单位：元 (yuan)

行业	Sector	城镇全部单位 All the Units In Urban Area	国有经济单位 State Owned Units	城镇集体单位 Urban Collective Owned Units	其他经济单位 Other Units	城镇私营单位 Urban Private Units
总计	**Total**	51415	68983	44154	56461	34167
农、林、牧、渔业	Farming, Forest, Herd, Fishery	31462	34486	32304	29297	26956
采矿业	Mining and Quarrying	44234	55603	47614	55006	37935
制造业	Manufacturing	44912	78616	41438	52663	34037
电力、燃气及水的生产和供应业	Power, Gas and water production and supply	78367	86604	35910	82348	32936
建筑业	Construction	47121	50802	36753	55003	37157
批发和零售业	Wholesale and Retail sale	38638	61350	32409	47420	31260
交通运输、仓储和邮政业	Transportation, storage and post	58401	75318	32777	53277	33129
住宿和餐饮业	Hotel and Catering	32935	37143	39651	38464	29900
信息传输、软件和信息技术服务业	Information Transmission, Software and Computer Services	79113	56138	25257	92167	40709
金融业	Banking	105795	101851	73537	118086	39226
房地产业	Real Estate	49162	53464	41181	56659	38739
租赁和商务服务业	Leasing and Commerical Services	41188	43197	45856	53170	33088
科学研究、技术服务业	Scietific Research, polytechnical	76217	67947	43620	104121	36296
水利、环境和公共设施管理业	Water Conservance, Environment and Public Facilities Management	47352	49397	39417	53560	28918
居民服务、修理和其他服务业	Resident Service and Others	32677	55830	48732	39588	29222
教育	Education	65394	68412	55854	48508	32628
卫生和社会工作	Health, Social Security and	69773	72252	54836	58098	33174
文化、体育和娱乐业	Culture, Sports and Entertainment	51001	62937	43723	63594	29014
公共管理、社会保障和社会组织	Public Management、social security and Social Organization	68788	68831	49400	43913	

主要统计指标解释

经济活动人口 指在16周岁及以上，有劳动能力，参加或要求参加社会经济活动的人口。包括就业人员和失业人员。

就业人员 指在16周岁及以上，从事一定社会劳动并取得劳动报酬或经营收入的人员。这一指标反映了一定时期内全部劳动力资源的实际利用情况，是研究我国基本国情国力的重要指标。

单位就业人员指报告期末最后一日24时在各类单位工作，并取得工资或其他形式劳动报酬的人员数。该指标为时点指标，不包括最后一日当天及以前已经与单位解除劳动合同关系的人员，是在岗职工、劳务派遣人员及其他从业人员之和。从业人员不包括：

1.离开本单位仍保留劳动关系，并定期领取生活费的人员；

2.利用课余时间打工的学生及在本单位实习的各类在校学生；

3.本单位因劳务外包而使用的人员。

在岗职工 指在本单位工作且与本单位签订劳动合同，并由单位支付各项工资和社会保险、住房公积金的人员，以及上述人员中由于学习、病伤、产假等原因暂未工作仍由单位支付工资的人员。在岗职工还包括：

1.应订立劳动合同而未订立劳动合同人员（如使用的农村户籍人员）；

2.处于试用期人员；

3.编制外招用的人员，如临时人员；

4.派往外单位工作，但工资仍由本单位发放的人员（如挂职锻炼、外派工作等情况）。

在岗职工平均工资指单位在岗职工在一定时期内平均每人所得的货币工资。它表明一定时期在岗职工工资收入的高低程度，是反映在岗职工工资水平的主要指标。计算公式为:

$$\text{平均工资}=\frac{\text{报告期实际支付的全部在岗职工工资总额}}{\text{报告期全部在岗职工平均人数}}$$

平均工资指数 指报告期在岗职工平均工资与基期平均工资的比率，是反映不同时期在岗职工货币工资水平变动情况的相对数。计算公式为:

$$\text{平均工资指数}=\frac{\text{报告期在岗职工平均工资}}{\text{基期在岗职工平均工资}}\times 100\%$$

平均实际工资指数在岗职工平均实际工资指扣除物价变动因素后的在岗职工平均工资。在岗职工平均实际工资指数是反映实际工资变动情况的相对数，表明职工实际工资水平提高或降低的程度。计算公式为:

$$\text{平均实际工资指数}=\frac{\text{报告期职工平均工资指数}}{\text{报告期城镇居民消费价格指数}}\times 100\%$$

城镇登记失业人员 指有非农业户口，在一定的劳动年龄内(16周岁至退休年龄)，有劳动能力，无业而要求就业，并在当地就业服务机构进行求职登记的人员。

城镇登记失业率 城镇登记失业人员与城镇单位就业人员(扣除使用的农村劳动力、聘用的离退休人员、港澳台及外方人员)、城镇单位中的不在岗职工、城镇私营业主、个体户主、城镇私营企业和个体就业人员、城镇登记失业人员之和的比。

$$\text{城镇登记失业率}=\frac{\text{城镇登记失业人数}}{(\text{城镇单位就业人员}-\text{使用的农村劳动力}-\text{聘用的离退休人员}-\text{聘用的港澳台及外方人员})}\times 100\%$$

Explanatory Notes on Main Statistical Indicators

Economically Active Population refers to the population aged 16 and over who are capable to work, are participating in or willing to participate in economic activities, including employed persons and unemployed persons.

Employed Persons refer to the persons aged 16 and over who are engaged in social working and receive remuneration payment or earn business income. This indicator reflects the actual utilization of total labour force during a certain period of time and is often used for the research on China's economic situation and national power.

Persons Employed in Various Units refer to all the persons working in government agencies of various levels, political and party organizations, social organizations, enterprises and institutions, and receiving wages or other forms of payment. They include fully–employed staff and workers, re–employed retirees, teachers in schools run by the local people, foreigners and Chinese compatriots from Hong Kong, Macao, and Taiwan working in various units, part–time employees, employees of other units working temporarily at current posts, and employees holding the second job, but exclude staff and workers who have left their working units while keeping their labour contract (employment relation) unchanged. This indicator reflects the total number of laborers actually engaged in production or other operations in various units.

Persons Employed in Private Enterprises and Self–Employed Individuals in Urban Areas Persons employed in private enterprises refer to the persons employed in the private enterprises which have been registered at the departments of industrial and commercial administration and are situated at a county town (i.e. a town where the county government is located) for business operation or at urban areas with the level higher than a county town. The self–employed individuals in urban areas refer to persons who hold the certificates of residence in urban areas or have resided in the urban areas for a long time and have been registered at the departments of industrial and commercial administration and approved to be engaged in individual industrial or commercial business, including self–employed persons as well as helpers and hired labourers who work in the individual households engaged in industrial or commercial business.

Registered Urban Unemployed Persons refer to the persons with non–agricultural household registration at certain working ages (16–50 years for male and 16–45 years for females), who are capable of work, unemployed and willing to work, and have been registered at the local employment service agencies to apply for a job.

Registered Urban Unemployment Rate refers to the ratio of the number of the registered unemployed persons to the sum of the number of persons employed in various units (minus the rural labour force, retirees, and Hong Kong, Macao, Taiwan or foreign employees they employ) laid–off workers in urban units, owners and employees in urban private enterprises, urban self–employed individuals and the registered urban unemployed persons. The formula is as follows:

Registered urban unemployment rate = number of registered urban unemployed persons ÷ (number of persons employed in urban units – rural labour force employed retirees employed – Hong Kong, Macao, Taiwan or foreign employees employ + laid–off workers + owners and employees in urban private enterprises + self–employed individuals in urban areas + registered urban unemployed persons) × 100%.

Staff and Workers refer to persons working in, and receive payment from units of state ownership, collective ownership, joint ownership, share holding ownership, foreign ownership, and ownership by entrepreneurs from Hong Kong, Macao, and Taiwan, and other types of ownership and their affiliated units. They do not include 1) persons employed in township enterprises, 2) persons employed in private enterprises, 3) urban self–employed persons, 4) retirees, 5) re–employed retirees, 6) teachers in the schools run by the local people, 7) foreigners and persons from Hong Kong, Macao and Taiwan who work in urban units, and 8) other persons not to be included by relevant regulations. (Data of 1998 and afterward refer to fully employed staff and workers. Other related statistics such as total wage bill and average wage are adjusted since 1998 accordingly).

State-owned Units refer to economic units whose assets are owned by the state. Included are non-corporation units registered according to Regulation of the PeopleRepublic of China on the Registration of Enterprises and Corporations, state organs, institutions and social organizations at the central and local levels.

Collective-Owned Units refer to economic units registered according to Regulation of the People Republic of China on the Registration of Enterprises and Corporations where the means of production are collectively owned.

Units of Other Types of Ownership refer to units registered with other types of ownership, including cooperative units, joint ownership units, limited companies, share holding corporations, units invested by entrepreneurs from Hong Kong, Macao, and Taiwan, and foreign-invested units.

Fully Employed Staff and Workers refer to persons who work in, and receive wages from their working units, as well as persons who have their work posts, but are temporarily absent from work for reasons of study or on sick, injury or maternal leave and still receive wages from their working units.

Total Wages Bill refer to the total remuneration payment to staff and workers in various units during a certain period of time. The calculation of total wages is based on the total remuneration payment to the staff and workers. Therefore, all the wages and salaries and other payments to staff and workers are included in the total wages regardless of their sources, category, and forms (in kind or cash). (Total wages of staff and workers in this yearbook include only total wages of fully employed staff and workers, excluding the living allowances distributed to those who have left their working units while keeping their labour contract/employment relation unchanged).

Average Wage refers to the average wage in money terms per person during a certain period of time for staff and workers in enterprises, institutions, and government agencies, which reflects the general level of wage income during a certain period of time and is calculated as follows:

Average Wage = Total Wages of Staff and Workers at Reference Time /Average Number of Staff and Workers at Reference Time.

Average Wage Indices refers to the ratio of average wage of staff and workers in the report period to that in the base period, which reflects the change of wage of staff and workers at the different period. It is calculated as follows:

Average Wage Indices = Average Wage of Staff and Workers at Reference Time / Average Wage of Staff and Workers at Base Period x 100%

Average Real Wage Indices average real wage of staff and workers refers to the average wage of staff and workers after removing the effects of the price changes and average real wage indices of staff and workers refers to the change of real wage, which reflects the relative increasing or decreasing level of real wage of staff and workers, which is calculated as follows:

Average Real Wage Indices = Average Wage Indices of Staff and Workers at the Reference Time / Urban Consumer Price Indices at Reference Time × 100%

4 固定资产投资

Investment In Fixed Assets

固定资产投资

INVESTMENT IN FIXED ASSETS

2016

固定资产投资	Urban Investment	29503.88	亿元
#房地产开发	Real Estate Development	4296.38	亿元
#国有经济	State-Owned	8021.33	亿元
集体经济	Collective-Owned	677.42	亿元
房屋施工面积	Floor Space of Building Under Construction	44198.73	万平方米
房屋竣工面积	Floor Space of Building Completed	8878.64	万平方米

固定资产投资完成额（亿元）

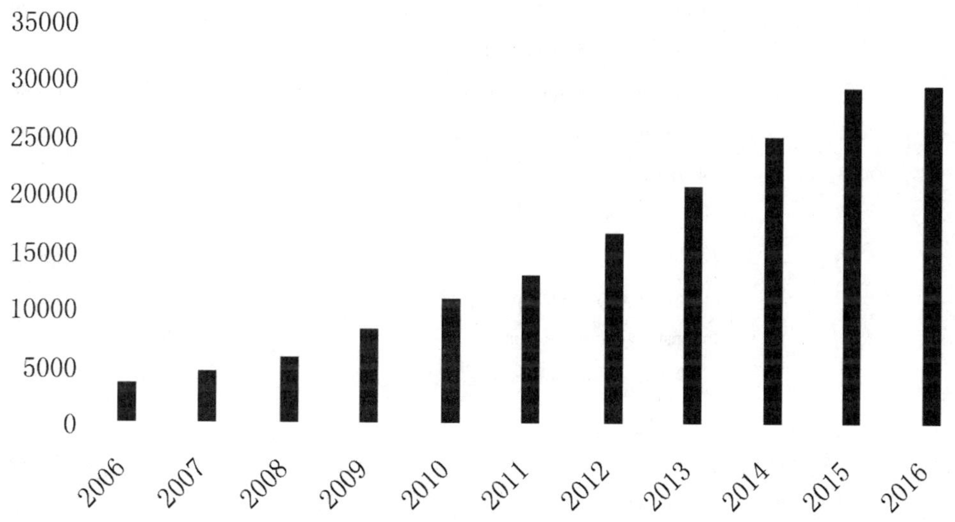

附:固定资产投资完成额构成(%)

		2006	2007	2009	2010	2011	2012	2013	2014	2015	2016
国有投资	State-Owned	41.2	39.9	38.1	34.9	29.1	25.8	24.4	23.3	23.9	27.2
集体投资	Collective-Owned	3.1	3.4	5.0	5.6	5.1	4.4	4.0	3.3	2.6	2.3
私营个体投资	Individuals	17.8	19.9	21.6	23.2	25.6	28.6	32.6	34.8	35.6	31.8
外商港澳台商投资	Foreign, HK, Macao and Taiwan	6.9	6.8	4.9	4.2	4.5	4.1	3.1	2.7	2.9	2.7
其他	Others	31.0	30.0	30.4	32.1	35.7	37.1	35.9	35.9	35.0	36.0

注:从2011年起固定资产投资统计口径调整为计划总投资500万元及以上项目,取消城镇农村公布口径,其他年份未做相应调整。2016年对2015年基数进行了调整。从2016年起,固定资产投资不包含农户投资。

Note:Since 2011, the fixed assets investment accounts for investment over 5 million yuan, canceling town and countryside. Other years' statistics do not correspond to this adjustment.The basic number of 2015 is adjusted in 2016. Since 2016,farmer investment isn't induded in the fixed assets investment.

4-1 固定资产投资主要指标

指 标	Item	1990	2000	2005
投资总额(亿元)	**Total Investment (100 million yuan)**	144.44	**1421.55**	**2834.75**
按经济类型分	**Grouped by Ownership**			
国有经济	State-owned Units	100.35	857.01	1095.71
集体经济	Collective-owned Units	15.59	128.32	79.47
#农村	Rural Area	9.59	98.95	26.55
私营个体经济	Individuals	28.50	221.43	554.27
#农村	Rural Area	23.62	106.65	135.95
联营经济	Joint-ownership Economic Units		3.94	19.56
股份制经济	Share Holding Co.Ltd.		86.29	232.34
有限责任公司	Limited Liability Corporations		53.33	557.21
港澳台投资经济	Economic Units Funded by Hongkong, Macao and Taiwan		36.57	92.68
外商投资经济	Foreign Funded Enterprise Units		23.90	116.23
其他经济	Others		10.76	87.28
按资金来源分	**Grouped by Source of Finance**			
国家预算内资金	State Budgetary Apporpriations	11.38	141.48	255.76
国内贷款	Domestic Loans	22.22	243.90	474.21
利用外资	Foreign Investment	4.79	28.28	71.34
自筹资金	Fund Raising	92.96	781.50	1492.66
其他资金来源	Others	13.09	226.39	540.78
按构成分	**Grouped by Usage of Funds**			
建筑安装工程	Construction Installation	92.64	814.66	1696.80
设备工器具购置	Purchase of Equipments and Instruments	41.02	371.56	642.86
其他费用	Others	10.78	235.33	495.09
按产业分	**Grouped by Industry**			
#住宅	Residential Housing	39.61	290.24	510.04
第一产业	Primary Industry	12.16	103.05	92.88
第二产业	Second Industry	67.41	521.58	1086.34
第三产业	Tertiary Industry	64.87	796.92	1655.53
房屋建筑面积(万平方米)	**Floor Space of Building** (10000 sq.m)			
施工面积	Floor Space under Construction	5103.48	9920.42	12572.00
#住宅	Residential Housing	3507.53	6831.02	8401.20
竣工面积	Floor Space Completed	4169.12	7508.96	7863.85
#住宅	Residential Housing	3058.40	5417.38	5627.67
商品房销售面积(万平方米)	**Floor Space of Commercial House (sq.m)**	130.53	**612.05**	**1708.02**

注:2006年投资总额(城镇投资)不含城镇工矿区私人建房投资(下同)。由于方法制度调整,按可比口径计算,2005年扣除城镇工矿区私人建房投资基数应为2788.92亿元;从2011年起固定资产投资统计口径调整为计划总投资500万元及以上项目,取消城镇农村公布口径,其他年份未做相应调整。从2012年起,三次产业采用新的划分标准。

MAJOR INDICATORS OF INVESTMENT IN FIXED ASSETS

2008	2009	2010	2011	2013	2014	2015	2016
5798.56	**8211.85**	**10802.69**	**12935.02**	**20753.91**	**25001.77**	**29191.06**	**29503.88**
2273.83	3124.90	3768.95	3764.22	5068.42	5829.79	6983.99	8021.33
253.32	411.18	602.80	660.59	826.51	820.75	754.53	677.42
65.02	77.50	99.23	137.69	137.45	117.04	143.42	—
1201.53	1771.61	2510.61	3307.47	6763.68	8708.83	10386.49	9386.11
190.19	240.48	301.05	365.51	576.46	698.73	940.57	—
15.05	11.32	19.89	22.49	38.96	11.84	13.38	64.03
462.81	659.79	896.87	987.66	1487.62	1238.81	1125.37	983.55
1109.43	1648.26	2221.99	3056.98	4692.14	6026.42	6634.45	8614.44
160.62	202.38	207.81	253.89	245.87	343.93	393.90	443.65
178.60	200.79	245.92	328.55	397.02	333.45	459.38	344.86
143.37	181.62	327.85	553.17	1233.69	1687.95	2439.57	968.49
570.17	711.98	868.46	663.18	886.58	1107.45	1339.03	1829.24
894.57	1432.98	1768.79	1707.46	2720.19	2874.92	2907.66	3068.40
57.02	68.33	147.03	189.26	66.82	78.99	46.86	59.01
3677.00	4956.65	6703.61	8800.61	14823.15	18732.35	22470.65	20623.21
599.80	1041.91	1314.80	1574.51	2257.17	2208.06	2426.86	3924.02
3568.96	5025.62	6701.91	8056.53	14312.25	18185.42	21826.03	22876.58
1245.73	1753.28	2308.73	2812.91	3856.68	4292.85	4845.70	4124.21
983.87	1432.95	1792.05	2065.58	2584.98	2523.50	2519.33	2503.08
901.26	1127.28	1417.95	1750.16	2907.29	3461.65	3853.52	3434.85
231.25	321.59	393.00	440.91	590.61	799.35	997.94	889.94
2344.36	3097.68	4169.92	5526.40	9187.25	10733.09	12146.51	12224.54
3222.95	4792.58	6239.77	6967.71	10976.04	13469.32	16046.61	16389.40
16417.07	20142.81	25284.83	31388.88	51939.51	58064.39	58095.72	44198.73
9896.66	11762.06	14486.90	16337.96	23443.19	27199.41	29006.34	24286.60
7551.82	9772.28	11802.18	14585.68	18828.87	21175.37	22992.18	8878.64
4679.96	5556.71	6785.61	7375.38	8006.06	8702.01	9381.09	3582.22
1941.62	**2718.30**	**3508.61**	**4187.62**	**5298.54**	**5601.98**	**6244.55**	**7427.16**

Note: In 2006 the investment (town investment) does not contain town private house industrial investment.(same below) Because of method adjustment, according to comparable caliber, 2005's investment base should be 278.892 billion yuan deducting industrial town private house. Since 2011, the fixed as-sets investment accounts for investment over 5 million yuan, canceling town and countryside. Other years' statistics do not correspond to this adjustment. Since 2012, the division of three industries emploies a new standard.

4-2 固定资产投资额
INVESTMENT IN FIXED ASSETS

单位:亿元 (100 million yuan)

年 份 Year	投资额 Investment	#房地产开发 Real Estate Development	#国有经济 State Owned Units	#集体经济 Collective Owned Units	#私营个体 Individuals
"六五"时期 Period of the Six-Year Plan	315.82		207.57	49.41	58.84
1985	102.91		61.66	17.44	23.81
"七五"时期 Peroid of the Seven-Year Plan	680.12	5.94	435.32	94.17	150.64
1986	111.44		66.42	15.89	29.13
1987	140.08		85.32	22.31	32.46
1988	160.46		102.21	24.60	33.64
1989	123.70		81.02	15.78	26.91
1990	144.44	5.94	100.35	15.59	28.50
"八五"时期 Peroid of the Eight-Year Plan	2211.67	253.77	1467.69	190.04	261.87
1991	168.19	7.88	119.07	19.49	29.63
1992	240.73	12.55	182.86	22.52	35.35
1993	383.18	37.01	275.84	30.62	40.37
1994	593.07	76.20	401.16	44.83	56.62
1995	826.50	121.13	518.76	72.58	99.90
"九五"时期 Peroid of the Nine-Year Plan	6022.80	334.60	3425.23	573.74	943.77
1996	984.38	118.40	593.32	96.50	124.78
1997	1083.60	126.47	567.60	107.12	160.56
1998	1231.10	131.23	661.94	116.92	194.52
1999	1302.17	123.87	745.36	124.88	242.48
2000	1421.55	134.63	857.01	128.32	221.43
"十五"时期 Peroid of the Ten-Year Plan	10321.69	1354.15	4817.55	541.41	1806.78
2001	1551.75	151.24	918.21	126.41	249.59
2002	1695.22	178.64	963.18	121.42	263.00
2003	1883.59	239.04	888.72	109.05	303.90
2004	2356.38	337.28	951.73	105.06	436.02
2005	2834.75	447.95	1095.71	79.47	554.27
"十一五"时期 Peroid of the Eleven-Year Plan	32919.93	4999.84	12449.99	1533.63	7020.48
2006	3572.69	564.76	1473.70	110.67	636.25
2007	4534.14	723.73	1808.61	155.66	900.48
2008	5798.56	892.67	2273.83	253.32	1201.53
2009	8211.85	1200.44	3124.90	411.18	1771.61
2010	10802.69	1618.24	3768.95	602.80	2510.61
"十二五"时期 Peroid of the Twelve-Year Plan	104385.93	16124.98	25912.37	3796.30	33879.07
2011	12935.02	2066.48	3764.22	660.59	3307.47
2012	16504.17	2539.46	4265.95	733.92	4712.60
2013	20753.91	3286.02	5068.42	826.51	6763.68
2014	25001.77	3983.79	5829.79	820.75	8708.83
2015	29191.06	4249.23	6983.99	754.53	10386.49
"十三五"时期 Peroid of the Thirteen-Year Plan					
2016	29503.88	4296.38	8021.33	677.42	9386.11

注:房地产开发投资统计制度从1990年开始建立。从2011年起固定资产投资统计口径调整为计划总投资500万元及以上项目,取消城镇农村公布口径,其他年份未做相应调整。

Note: The statistical system of real estate development investment is established in 1990. Since 2011, the fixed assets investment accounts for investment over 5 million yuan, canceling town and countryside. Other years' statistics do not correspond to this adjustment.

4-3 按登记注册类型分固定资产投资
INVESTMENT IN FIXED ASSETS BY TYPE OF REGISTRATION

单位：亿元 (100 million yuan)

指　标	Item	2013	2014	2015	2016
总　计	**Total**	**20753.91**	**25001.77**	**29191.06**	**29503.88**
内资企业	Domestic Funded Enterprises	19497.88	23594.86	27369.80	28688.49
国有企业	State-owned Enterprises	4871.98	5548.96	6604.96	6466.89
集体企业	Collective-owned Enterprises	677.53	707.76	655.99	363.14
股份合作企业	Share Holding Cooperative Enterprises	131.21	89.71	86.11	300.13
联营企业	Joint Owned Enterprise	78.13	44.09	56.73	80.26
国有联营	State Joint ownership	21.40	8.98	30.92	2.09
集体联营	Collective Joint Ownership	17.77	23.27	12.43	14.15
国有与集体联营	Joint State-Collective	21.23	4.50	7.61	13.84
其他联营企业	Other Joint Owned Enterprise	17.73	7.34	5.77	50.19
有限责任公司	Co. Ltd	4867.18	6298.27	6982.56	10166.79
国有独资公司	Solely State Funded Co.	175.04	271.85	348.11	1552.35
其他有限责任公司	Other Co. Ltd	4692.14	6026.42	6634.45	8614.44
股份有限公司	Share Holding Co.Ltd.	1487.62	1238.81	1125.37	983.55
私营企业	Private - owned enterprises	6150.55	7979.30	9418.51	9359.24
其他企业	Others	1233.69	1687.96	2439.57	968.49
港、澳、台商投资企业	Hongkong, Macao and Taiwan Funded	245.87	343.93	393.90	443.65
合资经营企业	Joint Funded Enterprises	63.81	102.28	108.68	139.14
合作经营企业	Cooperative Operation Enterprises	1.12	7.56	6.51	22.41
独资经营企业	Solely Funded Enterprises	142.00	187.34	257.15	267.09
股份有限公司	Share Holding Co.Ltd.	35.62	44.38	18.44	6.06
外商投资企业	Foreign Invested Enterprises	397.02	333.45	459.38	344.87
合资经营企业	Joint Funded Enterprises	227.87	104.57	215.16	233.40
合作经营企业	Cooperative Operation Enterprises	8.06	10.60	1.34	
独资企业	Solely Funded Enterprises	116.11	154.10	167.97	68.90
股份有限公司	Share Holding Co.Ltd.	34.38	35.93	42.41	19.89
个体经营	Individual Investment	613.13	729.53	967.98	26.87
个体户	Individual Self-Employed	595.47	717.82	954.25	21.36
个人合伙	Individual Pattenership	17.66	11.71	13.73	5.51

注：从2011年起固定资产投资统计口径调整为计划总投资500万元及以上项目，取消城镇农村公布口径，其他年份未做相应调整。
Note:Since 2011, the fixed assets investment accounts for investment over 5 million yuan, canceling town and countryside. Other years' statistics do not correspond to this adjustment.

4-4 按构成分固定资产投资(不含农户) (2016)
URBAN INVESTMENT IN FIXED ASSETS BY USAGE OF FUNDS(2016)

单位: 亿元 (100 million yuan)

行业	Sector	投资额 Investment	建筑工程 Construction	安装工程 Installation	设备工器具购置 Purchases of Equipments and Instruments	其他 Others
总 计	**Total**	**29503.88**	**20091.66**	**2784.92**	**4124.21**	**2503.08**
农、林、牧、渔业	Farming, Forestry, Animal Husbandry and Fishery	1086.49	692.56	105.84	164.27	123.83
农业	Farming	477.71	292.84	51.63	75.19	58.05
林业	Forestry	108.85	65.90	9.17	15.76	18.03
畜牧业	Animal Husbandry	211.26	141.13	20.18	33.83	16.12
渔业	Fishery	92.11	61.77	9.48	12.33	8.53
农、林、牧、渔服务业	Farming, Forestry, Animal Husbandry and Fishery Services	196.56	130.92	15.38	27.16	23.10
采矿业	Mining	329.40	178.93	50.04	82.72	17.72
制造业	Manufacturing	10522.40	6193.45	1074.37	2657.87	596.72
农副食品加工业	Food Processing	870.93	538.31	95.22	184.33	53.06
食品制造业	Food Production	315.38	205.44	31.62	62.69	15.63
酒、饮料和精制茶制造业	Beverage Production	336.68	213.53	35.21	61.86	26.07
烟草制品业	Tobacco Processing	8.84	5.59	0.10	3.03	0.13
纺织业	Textile Industry	411.72	192.50	43.61	150.52	25.09
纺织服装、服饰业	Textile Wearing Apparel and Accessaries	329.29	202.80	31.51	75.99	18.98
皮革、毛皮、羽毛及其制品和制鞋业	Leather, Fur, Feather and Related Products	89.00	35.30	13.87	36.44	3.39
木材加工和木、竹、藤、棕、草制品业	Timber Processing and Wood, Bamboo, Rattan, Palm and Straw Products	152.29	92.15	15.50	33.77	10.87
家具制造业	Furniture Manufacturing	170.34	109.46	14.01	36.33	10.54
造纸和纸制品业	Papermaking and Paper Products	261.06	147.19	18.95	77.28	17.64
印刷和记录媒介复制业	Printing and Record Processing	83.67	47.69	8.16	23.79	4.03
文教、工美、体育和娱乐用品制造业	Stationery, Education, Art, Sport and Entertainment Products	130.87	74.42	33.59	16.99	5.87
石油加工、炼焦和核燃料加工业	Petroleum Processing, Coking Products and Nuclear Fuel Processing	36.26	17.10	5.64	12.20	1.32
化学原料和化学制品制造业	Raw Chemical Material and Chemical Products	794.68	398.32	96.38	254.36	45.63
医药制造业	Medical and Pharmaceutical Products	389.39	260.52	36.80	70.22	21.85
化学纤维制造业	Chemical Fibres	23.83	10.58	2.79	8.72	1.74
橡胶和塑料制品业	Rubber Products and Plastic Products	357.44	209.13	31.03	94.73	22.55
非金属矿物制品业	Non-metal Material Products	1058.57	600.90	104.91	293.87	58.88
黑色金属冶炼和压延加工业	Smelting and Processing of Ferrous Metals	172.29	92.58	24.63	45.86	9.22
有色金属冶炼和压延加工业	Smelting and Processing of Non-ferrous Metals	124.80	65.21	11.74	41.00	6.85
金属制品业	Metal Products	372.49	231.12	39.67	81.67	20.03
通用设备制造业	General Machinery Manufacturing	557.70	324.74	58.31	142.89	31.76
专用设备制造业	Special Purpose Equipment Manufacturing	584.25	354.70	64.84	133.02	31.68
汽车制造业	Automobile Manufacturing	1325.78	822.95	110.77	333.06	58.99
铁路、船舶、航空航天和其他运输设备制造业	Realway, Ship, Aircraft and Other Transport Equipment Manufacturing	122.69	66.29	16.75	34.47	5.17
电气机械和器材制造业	Electric Machinery and Equipment	637.26	412.97	54.34	133.97	35.97
计算机、通信和其他电子设备制造业	Computers, Communication Equipment and Other Electronic Equipment Manufacturing	571.96	314.01	49.75	175.98	32.22
仪器仪表制造业	Measuring Instruments Manufacturing	89.85	57.14	9.13	17.11	6.47
其他制造业	Other Equipment	50.95	39.20	2.16	5.76	3.83
废弃资源综合利用业	Recycling and Disposal of Waste	62.98	33.79	10.57	10.78	7.84
金属制品、机械和设备修理业	Repairing of Metal and Mechanical Equipment	29.17	17.81	2.79	5.16	3.41
电力、热力、燃气及水生产和供应业	Electric Power, Gas and Water Production and Supply	934.69	544.46	130.80	216.25	43.18
电力、热力生产和供应业	Electric Power and and Heat Power Production and Supply	614.46	312.60	98.49	173.49	29.87
燃气生产和供应业	Gas Production and Supply	81.35	49.19	10.22	17.65	4.29
水的生产和供应业	Water Production and Supply	238.88	182.66	22.10	25.11	9.01

注:从2011年起固定资产投资统计口径调整为计划总投资500万元及以上项目,取消城镇农村公布口径,其他年份未做相应调整。从2012年起执行新的国民经济行业代码(GB/T4754-2011)。

Note:Since 2011, the fixed assets investment accounts for investment over 5 million yuan, canceling town and countryside. Other years' statistics do not correspond to this adjustment.Since 2012,a new national economy industry code(GB/T4754-2011)is implemented.

4-4 续表 continued

单位：亿元 (100 million yuan)

行 业	Sector	投资额 Investment	建筑工程 Construction	安装工程 Installation	设备工器具购置 Purchases of Equipments and Instruments	其他 Others
建筑业	Construction	475.46	361.20	26.89	59.11	28.26
交通运输、仓储和邮政业	Transportation, Storage and Post	2794.23	2196.82	196.94	200.77	199.71
铁路运输业	Railway Transportation	246.00	221.99	5.14	6.05	12.82
道路运输业	Road Transportation	1822.89	1461.94	143.51	72.63	144.81
水上运输业	Waterway Transportation	131.68	89.15	8.60	21.90	12.02
航空运输业	Air Transportation	135.08	89.92	1.43	38.73	4.99
管道运输业	Pipeline Transportation	1.10	0.84	0.05	0.03	0.18
装卸搬运和运输代理业	Load, Unload, and Agency	67.34	39.32	7.26	13.36	7.40
仓储业	Transportation Storage	387.90	292.21	30.72	47.52	17.44
邮政业	Post	2.25	1.44	0.23	0.55	0.04
信息传输、软件和信息技术服务业	Information Transmission, Software and Information Technology Service	150.75	74.04	23.57	46.31	6.82
电信、广播电视和卫星传输服务	Telecom, Radio Tv and Satellite	65.68	23.11	16.41	24.34	1.82
互联网和相关服务	Internet and Related	29.95	15.94	1.12	12.64	0.25
软件和信息技术服务业	Software and Information Technology	55.11	34.98	6.05	9.33	4.75
批发和零售业	Wholesale and Retail	725.27	494.62	56.92	109.89	63.83
住宿和餐饮业	Hotel and Catering Service	286.04	204.19	35.34	29.58	16.93
金融业	Finance	33.00	18.65	2.57	9.48	2.30
货币金融服务	Monetary Financial Service	15.52	7.62	0.82	6.13	0.95
资本市场服务	Monetary Financial Service	16.23	10.08	1.61	3.26	1.28
保险业	Insurance	0.27	0.11	0.08	0.05	0.03
其他金融业	Other Financial Acitivities	0.98	0.84	0.06	0.04	0.04
房地产业	Real Estate	6063.74	4402.13	593.16	137.20	931.24
租赁和商务服务业	Leasing and Commercial Service	806.37	610.47	67.40	64.15	64.36
租赁业	Leasing Service	28.48	22.57	0.50	4.08	1.33
商务服务业	Commercial Service	777.89	587.89	66.90	60.06	63.03
科学研究和技术服务业	Scientific Research and Technical Services	151.87	107.78	12.10	21.34	10.65
水利、环境和公共设施管理业	Water Conservancy, Environment and Public Facility Management	3735.20	2978.94	299.62	166.75	289.89
水利管理业	Water Conservancy Management	513.25	428.67	28.35	24.59	31.63
生态保护和环境治理业	Environment Management	197.75	126.65	51.19	9.85	10.07
公共设施管理业	Public Facility Management	3024.20	2423.62	220.08	132.31	248.19
居民服务、修理和其他服务业	Resident Service and Others	139.16	100.33	13.29	14.43	11.11
教育	Education	366.66	276.47	25.82	43.17	21.20
卫生和社会工作	Health Care and Social Work	269.46	184.18	21.25	46.13	17.90
卫生	Health Care	197.91	131.95	15.97	38.99	10.99
社会工作	Social Work	71.55	52.23	5.28	7.14	6.91
文化、体育和娱乐业	Culture, Sports and Recreation	323.91	230.81	30.95	22.09	40.05
新闻和出版业	News and Publication					
广播、电视、电影和影视录音制作业	Radio, Television, Film and Recording	19.75	4.77	1.56	3.42	10.00
文化艺术业	Culture and Arts	127.64	97.06	11.42	6.30	12.87
体育	Sports	65.38	52.74	3.08	3.03	6.54
娱乐业	Receation	111.13	76.24	14.88	9.36	10.65
公共管理、社会保障和社会组织	Public Management and Social Organizations	309.77	241.64	18.03	32.70	17.40

4–5 按建设性质分固定资产投资(不含农户) (2016)

URBAN INVESTMENT IN FIXED ASSETS BY TYPE OF CONSTRUCTION(2016)

单位：亿元　　(100 million yuan)

行　业	Sector	投资额 Investment	#新 建 New Construction	#扩 建 Expension	#改 建 Replacement
总　计	**Total**	**29503.88**	**22699.53**	**2931.03**	**3206.50**
农、林、牧、渔业	Farming, Forestry, Animal Husbandry and Fishery	1086.49	895.40	112.77	68.36
农业	Farming	477.71	401.10	54.06	21.42
林业	Forestry	108.85	84.58	13.23	8.24
畜牧业	Animal Husbandry	211.26	172.54	22.68	15.86
渔业	Fishery	92.11	75.88	7.99	8.23
农、林、牧、渔服务业	Farming, Forestry, Animal Husbandry and Fishery Services	196.56	161.30	14.81	14.60
采矿业	Mining and Qarrying	329.40	169.62	75.40	80.41
制造业	Manufacturing	10522.40	6776.46	1415.09	2027.73
农副食品加工业	Food Processing	870.93	549.30	148.32	160.99
食品制造业	Food Production	315.38	210.42	48.67	52.97
酒、饮料和精制茶制造业	Beverage Production	336.68	212.32	66.25	47.77
烟草制品业	Tobacco Processing	8.84	4.21		0.48
纺织业	Textile Industry	411.72	167.90	91.16	137.18
纺织服装、服饰业	Textile Wearing Apparel and Accessaries	329.29	212.69	46.83	63.44
皮革、毛皮、羽毛及其制品和制鞋业	Leather, Fur, Feather and Related Products	89.00	54.90	13.64	12.75
木材加工和木、竹、藤、棕、草制品业	Timber Processing and Wood, Bamboo, Rattan, Palm and Sraw Works	152.29	79.22	25.92	39.16
家具制造业	Furniture Manufacturing	170.34	127.43	21.53	19.11
造纸和纸制品业	Papermaking and Paper Products	261.06	171.81	55.96	31.68
印刷和记录媒介复制业	Printing and Record Processing	83.67	51.96	10.93	17.16
文教、工美、体育和娱乐用品制造业	Stationery, Education, Art, Sport and Entertainment Products	130.87	114.82	7.56	8.18
石油加工、炼焦和核燃料加工业	Petroleum Processing,Coking products and Nuclear Fuel Processing	36.26	30.06	4.43	1.20
化学原料和化学制品制造业	Raw Chemical Material and Chemical Products	794.68	445.88	117.59	205.96
医药制造业	Medical and pharmaceutical Products	389.39	297.82	26.79	48.78
化学纤维制造业	Chemical Fibers	23.83	17.60	2.20	3.50
橡胶和塑料制品业	Rubber Products and Plastic Products	357.44	208.26	71.55	70.53
非金属矿物制品业	Nonmetal Material Products	1058.57	643.44	176.14	217.68
黑色金属冶炼和压延加工业	Smelting and Processing of ferrous Metals	172.29	101.98	4.42	63.48
有色金属冶炼和压延加工业	Smelting and Processing of Nonferrous Metals	124.80	70.61	17.49	33.80
金属制品业	Metal Products	372.49	235.33	65.86	62.04
通用设备制造业	Ordinaryly Machinery Manufacturing	557.70	345.44	83.68	107.90
专用设备制造业	Special Purpose Equipment Manufacturing	584.25	399.26	54.34	110.55
汽车制造业	Automobile Manufacturing	1325.78	857.61	133.33	279.84
铁路、船舶、航空航天和其他运输设备制造业	Realway, Ship, Aircraft and Other Transport Equipment Manufacturing	122.69	100.62	1.68	16.56
电气机械和器材制造业	Electric Machinery and Equipment	637.26	434.24	48.34	121.82
计算机、通信和其他电子设备制造业	Computers, Communication Equipment and Other Electronic Equipment Manufacturing	571.96	468.87	39.93	56.21
仪器仪表制造业	Measuring Instruments Manufacturing	89.85	53.86	17.68	17.29
其他制造业	Other Equipment	50.95	37.85	3.01	9.75
废弃资源综合利用业	Recycling and Disposal of Waste	62.98	49.42	6.79	6.62
金属制品、机械和设备修理业	Repairing of Metal and Mechanical Equipment	29.17	21.32	3.08	3.35
电力、热力、燃气及水生产和供应业	Electric Power, Gas and Water Production and Supply	934.69	644.31	136.52	147.30
电力、热力生产和供应业	Electric Power, Steam and Hot Water Production and Supply	614.46	409.59	112.20	89.12
燃气生产和供应业	Gas Production and Supply	81.35	52.51	6.91	19.71
水的生产和供应业	Tap Water Production and Supply	238.88	182.22	17.41	38.46

注：从2011年起固定资产投资统计口径调整为计划总投资500万元及以上项目，取消城镇农村公布口径，其他年份未做相应调整。从2012年起执行新的国民经济行业代码(GB/T4754-2011)。

Note:Since 2011, the fixed assets investment accounts for investment over 5 million yuan, canceling town and countryside. Other years' statistics do not correspond to this adjustment.Since 2012,a new national econmy industry code(GB/T4754-2011) is implemanted.

4-5 续表 continued

单位:亿元 (100 million yuan)

行 业	Sector	投资额 Investment	#新 建 New Construction	#扩 建 Expension	#改 建 Replacement
建筑业	Construction	475.46	391.42	16.87	36.34
交通运输、仓储和邮政业	Transportation, storage and Post	2794.23	2233.65	307.79	212.22
铁路运输业	Railway Transportation	246.00	233.77	2.94	9.29
道路运输业	Road Transportation	1822.89	1462.96	154.56	181.49
水上运输业	Waterway Transportation	131.68	109.33	11.62	8.83
航空运输业	Air Transportation	135.08	56.08	66.40	
管道运输业	Pipeline Transportation	1.10	1.10		
装卸搬运和运输代理业	Load, Unload, and Agency	67.34	54.17	10.26	1.98
仓储业	Transportation Storage	387.90	314.62	61.90	10.36
邮政业	Post	2.25	1.62	0.10	0.28
信息传输、软件和信息技术服务业	Information Transmission, Software and Information Technology Service	150.75	107.26	14.42	23.85
电信、广播电视和卫星传输服务	Telecom, Radio Tv and Satellite	65.68	37.16	13.49	10.29
互联网和相关服务	Internet and Related	29.95	17.89	0.57	11.49
软件和信息技术服务业	Software and Information Technology	55.11	52.22	0.36	2.07
批发和零售业	Wholesale and Retail Trade	725.27	574.79	73.49	52.77
住宿和餐饮业	Hotel and Catering Services	286.04	232.18	28.04	22.65
金融业	Finance	33.00	22.88	2.03	3.85
货币金融服务	Monetary Financial Service	15.52	8.93	1.56	0.79
资本市场服务	Capital Markets Service	16.23	13.39		2.84
保险业	Insurance	0.27		0.27	
其他金融业	Other Financial Acitivities	0.98	0.56	0.20	0.22
房地产业	Real Estate Trade	6063.74	5836.67	105.76	58.35
租赁和商务服务业	Leasing and Commercial Service	806.37	720.30	60.94	14.43
租赁业	Leasing Service	28.48	18.99	6.07	1.59
商务服务业	Commercial Service	777.89	701.31	54.87	12.83
科学研究和技术服务业	Scientific Research, Polytechnical Services	151.87	126.97	7.37	9.84
水利、环境和公共设施管理业	Water Conservancy, Environment and Public Facility Management	3735.20	2841.09	455.19	361.01
水利管理业	Water Conservancy Management	513.25	377.16	48.84	70.96
生态保护和环境治理业	Environment Management	197.75	170.22	7.68	17.97
公共设施管理业	Public Facility Management	3024.20	2293.70	398.67	272.08
居民服务、修理和其他服务业	Resident Service and Others	139.16	123.02	5.86	7.32
教育	Education	366.66	264.33	43.84	30.08
卫生和社会工作	Health Care and Social Work	269.46	203.66	24.09	12.45
卫生	Health Care	197.91	141.22	18.62	10.23
社会工作	Social Work	71.55	62.44	5.47	2.22
文化、体育和娱乐业	Culture, Sports and Recreation	323.91	277.87	19.84	19.72
新闻和出版业	News and Publication				
广播、电视、电影和影视录音制作业	Radio, Television, Film and Recording	19.75	5.88	0.83	11.23
文化艺术业	Culture and Arts	127.64	107.41	10.92	6.59
体育	Sports	65.38	59.67	3.80	1.62
娱乐业	Receation	111.13	104.91	4.28	0.28
公共管理、社会保障和社会组织	Public Management and Social Organizations	309.77	257.66	25.71	17.82

4-6 按控股情况分固定资产投资(不含农户)(2016)
URBAN INVESTMENT IN FIXED ASSETS BY THE SITUATION OF CONTROLLING SHARE HOLDING(2016)

单位:亿元 (100 million yuan)

行业	Sector	投资额 Investment	国有控股 State Share Holding	集体控股 Collective Share Holding	私人控股 Private Share Holding	港澳台商控股 Hongkong, Macao and Taiwan Share Holding	外商控股 Foreign Sgare Holding
总 计	**Total**	**29503.88**	**10264.15**	**1137.96**	**14560.21**	**436.14**	**223.53**
农、林、牧、渔业	Farming, Forestry, Animal Husbandry and Fishery	1086.49	162.79	35.97	727.14	2.52	1.51
农业	Farming	477.71	42.27	13.23	348.55	0.47	0.29
林业	Forestry	108.85	23.17	6.16	60.78		0.56
畜牧业	Animal Husbandry	211.26	13.27	5.13	163.90	2.05	0.66
渔业	Fishery	92.11	12.77	4.81	62.54		
农、林、牧、渔服务业	Farming, Forestry, Animal Husbandry and Fishery Services	196.56	71.30	6.64	91.37		
采矿业	Mining and Qarrying	329.40	27.63	30.29	212.33		0.79
制造业	Manufacturing	10522.40	887.05	278.23	7974.88	188.15	140.63
农副食品加工业	Food Processing	870.93	49.74	16.16	708.87	1.88	3.80
食品制造业	Food Production	315.38	10.17	3.94	273.99	2.72	3.86
酒、饮料和精制茶制造业	Beverage Production	336.68	9.55	9.70	256.67	27.90	5.77
烟草制品业	Tobacco Processing	8.84	8.09		0.76		
纺织业	Textile Industry	411.72	14.85	18.31	329.36	9.56	2.10
纺织服装、服饰业	Textile Wearing Apparel and Accessaries	329.29	13.90	3.79	266.66	11.35	9.92
皮革、毛皮、羽毛及其制品和制鞋业	Leather, Fur, Feather and Related Products	89.00		0.07	82.35	1.17	0.95
木材加工和木、竹、藤、棕、草制品业	Timber Processing and Wwood, Bamboo,Rattan, Palm and Sraw Works	152.29	2.13	15.68	113.55	0.28	
家具制造业	Furniture Manufacturing	170.34	0.02	1.25	149.83		0.21
造纸和纸制品业	Papermaking and Paper Products	261.06	20.43	2.16	197.00	33.45	
印刷和记录媒介复制业	Printing and Record Processing	83.67	2.29	3.01	62.79		
文教、工美、体育和娱乐用品制造业	Stationery, Education, Art, Sport and Entertainment Products	130.87	2.79	3.51	116.44	3.35	
石油加工、炼焦和核燃料加工业	Petroleum Processing, Coking Products and Nuclear Fuel Processing	36.26	8.16	0.06	21.83		
化学原料和化学制品制造业	Raw Chemical Material and Chemical Products	794.68	50.88	48.95	591.46	15.13	3.89
医药制造业	Medical and pharmaceutical Products	389.39	24.15	9.74	304.03	20.83	3.89
化学纤维制造业	Chemical Fibers	23.83	0.44		20.17	2.18	1.03
橡胶和塑料制品业	Rubber Products and Plastic Products	357.44	4.65	4.44	303.04	2.54	3.70
非金属矿物制品业	Nonmetal Material Products	1058.57	46.43	8.36	892.47	8.03	2.49
黑色金属冶炼和压延加工业	Smelting and Processing of ferrous Metals	172.29	30.15	0.76	118.85	2.42	
有色金属冶炼和压延加工业	Smelting and Processing of Nonferrous Metals	124.80	3.35	2.68	113.05		
金属制品业	Metal Products	372.49	13.98	2.63	309.06	1.59	1.98
通用设备制造业	Ordinaryly Machinery Manufacturing	557.70	67.98	6.97	393.92	6.31	9.33
专用设备制造业	Special Purpose Equipment Manufacturing	584.25	37.44	13.00	462.58	0.93	4.20
汽车制造业	Automobile Manufacturing	1325.78	156.10	10.05	915.92	12.65	58.37
铁路、船舶、航空航天和其他运输设备制造业	Realway, Ship, Aircraft and Other Transport Equipment Manufacturing	122.69	13.21	6.14	71.31		5.66
电气机械和器材制造业	Electric Machinery and Equipment	637.26	62.28	31.11	478.29	4.62	11.75
计算机、通信和其他电子设备制造业	Computers, Communication Equipment and Other Electronic Equipment Manufacturing	571.96	202.14	44.61	248.01	18.88	6.78
仪器仪表制造业	Measuring Instruments Manufacturing	89.85	4.95		76.44		0.95
其他制造业	Other Equipment	50.95	16.53	0.26	32.29	0.29	
废弃资源综合利用业	Recycling and Disposal of Waste	62.98	10.26	2.73	44.34		
金属制品、机械和设备修理业	Repairing of Metal and Mechanical Equipment	29.17		8.19	19.54	0.09	
电力、热力、燃气及水生产和供应业	Electric Power, Gas and Water Production and Supply	934.69	526.59	43.03	263.94	43.01	2.98
电力、热力生产和供应业	Electric Power, Steam and Hot Water Production and Supply	614.46	339.10	22.32	183.23	41.08	0.98
燃气生产和供应业	Gas Production and Supply	81.35	18.38	6.60	50.80	1.93	
水的生产和供应业	Tap Water Production and Supply	238.88	169.11	14.10	29.91		2.00

注:从2011年起固定资产投资统计口径调整为计划总投资500万元及以上项目,取消城镇农村公布口径,其他年份未做相应调整。从2012年起执行新的国民经济行业代码(GB/T4754-2011)。

Note:Since 2011, the fixed assets investment accounts for investment over 5 million yuan, canceling town and countryside. Other years' statistics do not correspond to this adjustment.Since 2012,a new national econmy industry code(GB/T4754-2011) is implemanted.

4-6 续表 continued

单位:亿元 (100 million yuan)

行　　业	Sector	投资额 Investment	国有控股 State Share Holding	集体控股 Collective Share Holding	私人控股 Private Share Holding	港澳台商控股 Hongkong, Macao and Taiwan Share Holding	外商控股 Foreign Sgare Holding
建筑业	Construction	475.46	332.15	13.54	69.39	0.24	4.33
交通运输、仓储和邮政业	Transportation, storage and Post	2794.23	2121.92	47.92	466.76	23.46	9.64
铁路运输业	Railway Transportation	246.00	233.81		8.13		
道路运输业	Road Transportation	1822.89	1601.11	29.96	146.70		3.54
水上运输业	Waterway Transportation	131.68	83.28	0.43	42.32		0.09
航空运输业	Air Transportation	135.08	131.45		3.08		
管道运输业	Pipeline Transportation	1.10	0.51				
装卸搬运和运输代理业	Load, Unload, and Agency	67.34	13.11	0.95	48.10		3.00
仓储业	Transportation Storage	387.90	57.74	16.59	217.80	23.46	3.00
邮政业	Post	2.25	0.91		0.63		
信息传输、软件和信息技术服务业	Information Transmission, Software and Information Technology Service	150.75	70.39	22.46	44.40	7.88	1.53
电信、广播电视和卫星传输服务	Telecom, Radio Tv and Satellite	65.68	29.90	22.46	3.48	7.88	1.53
互联网和相关服务	Internet and Related	29.95	23.10		6.64		
软件和信息技术服务业	Software and Information Technology	55.11	17.40		34.28		
批发和零售业	Wholesale and Retail Trade	725.27	77.75	49.11	532.88	6.31	0.52
住宿和餐饮业	Hotel and Catering Services	286.04	27.30	15.34	213.75		
金融业	Finance	33.00	15.28	0.08	12.65		
货币金融服务	Monetary Financial Service	15.52	12.10	0.08	3.07		
资本市场服务	Capital Markets Service	16.23	2.84		8.87		
保险业	Insurance	0.27			0.27		
其他金融业	Other Financial Acitivities	0.98	0.34		0.44		
房地产业	Real Estate Trade	6063.74	1899.62	262.35	2750.36	152.95	61.41
租赁和商务服务业	Leasing and Commercial Service	806.37	237.01	85.40	439.13	5.51	
租赁业	Leasing Service	28.48	15.61	0.29	11.69		
商务服务业	Commercial Service	777.89	221.39	85.12	427.44	5.51	
科学研究和技术服务业	Scientific Research, Polytechnical Services	151.87	67.07	1.56	70.93		
水利、环境和公共设施管理业	Water Conservancy, Environment and Public Facility Management	3735.20	2868.71	169.85	496.79	0.47	
水利管理业	Water Conservancy Management	513.25	461.61	19.75	12.91		
生态保护和环境治理业	Environment Management	197.75	158.70	12.26	17.35		
公共设施管理业	Public Facility Management	3024.20	2248.41	137.84	466.53	0.47	
居民服务、修理和其他服务业	Resident Service and Others	139.16	88.48	3.60	34.47	1.20	
教育	Education	366.66	237.50	22.42	79.94		
卫生和社会工作	Health Care and Social Work	269.46	198.18	12.31	42.00	4.44	0.20
卫生	Health Care	197.91	160.52	5.69	24.62	4.44	
社会工作	Social Work	71.55	37.66	6.62	17.38		0.20
文化、体育和娱乐业	Culture, Sports and Recreation	323.91	163.63	22.92	121.01		
新闻和出版业	News and Publication						
广播、电视、电影和影视录音制作业	Radio, Television, Film and Recording	19.75	14.48		5.27		
文化艺术业	Culture and Arts	127.64	83.01	15.52	23.12		
体育	Sports	65.38	37.38	0.70	19.94		
娱乐业	Receation	111.13	28.76	6.71	72.68		
公共管理、社会保障和社会组织	Public Management and Social Organizations	309.77	255.10	21.57	7.45		

4-7 按行业分施工投产项目个数(2016)
NUMBER OF URBAN PROJECTS UNDER CONSTRUCTION AND PUT INTO PRODUCTION BY SECTOR(2016)

行业	Sector	施工项目(个) Number of Projects under Construction (unit)	#新开工 Newly Started	全部建成投产项目(个) Completion and Put into Production of All Projects (unit)	项目建成投产率(%) Rate of Completion and Put into Production (%)
总计	**Total**	**29367**	**21863**	**20122**	**68.5**
农、林、牧、渔业	Farming, Forestry, Animal Husbandry and Fishery	2147	1714	1502	70.0
农业	Farming	788	612	536	68.0
林业	Forestry	182	129	128	70.3
畜牧业	Animal Husbandry	501	425	340	67.9
渔业	Fishery	176	143	125	71.0
农、林、牧、渔服务业	Farming, Forestry, Animal Husbandry and Fishery Services	500	405	373	74.6
采矿业	Mining and Qarrying	378	258	272	72.0
制造业	Manufacturing	10248	7347	7229	70.5
农副食品加工业	Food Processing	1149	882	803	69.9
食品制造业	Food Production	313	225	221	70.6
酒、饮料和精制茶制造业	Beverage Production	365	254	245	67.1
烟草制品业	Tobacco Processing	7	4	3	42.9
纺织业	Textile Industry	397	302	304	76.6
纺织服装、服饰业	Textile Wearing Apparel and Accessaries	365	272	269	73.7
皮革、毛皮、羽毛及其制品和制鞋业	Leather, Fur, Feather and Related Products	118	91	88	74.6
木材加工和木、竹、藤、棕、草制品业	Timber Processing and Wwood, Bamboo, Rattan, Palm and Sraw Works	220	169	159	72.3
家具制造业	Furniture Manufacturing	166	116	113	68.1
造纸和纸制品业	Papermaking and Paper Products	181	127	127	70.2
印刷和记录媒介复制业	Printing and Record Processing	109	81	91	83.5
文教、工美、体育和娱乐用品制造业	Stationery, Education, Art, Sport and Entertainment Products	92	71	61	66.3
石油加工、炼焦和核燃料加工业	Petroleum Processing, Coking Products and Nuclear Fuel Processing	38	18	22	57.9
化学原料和化学制品制造业	Raw Chemical Material and Chemical Products	812	601	580	71.4
医药制造业	Medical and pharmaceutical Products	324	217	176	54.3
化学纤维制造业	Chemical Fibers	31	21	22	71.0
橡胶和塑料制品业	Rubber Products and Plastic Products	400	297	292	73.0
非金属矿物制品业	Nonmetal Material Products	1364	1064	953	69.9
黑色金属冶炼和压延加工业	Smelting and Processing of ferrous Metals	143	104	105	73.4
有色金属冶炼和压延加工业	Smelting and Processing of Nonferrous Metals	107	80	65	60.7
金属制品业	Metal Products	402	300	278	69.2
通用设备制造业	Ordinaryly Machinery Manufacturing	599	404	466	77.8
专用设备制造业	Special Purpose Equipment Manufacturing	535	373	385	72.0
汽车制造业	Automobile Manufacturing	1009	648	766	75.9
铁路、船舶、航空航天和其他运输设备制造业	Realway, Ship, Aircraft and Other Transport Equipment Manufacturing	70	48	51	72.9
电气机械和器材制造业	Electric Machinery and Equipment	451	286	295	65.4
计算机、通信和其他电子设备制造业	Computers, Communication Equipment and Other Electronic Equipment Manufacturing	283	160	158	55.8
仪器仪表制造业	Measuring Instruments Manufacturing	80	54	53	66.3
其他制造业	Other Equipment	37	25	24	64.9
废弃资源综合利用业	Recycling and Disposal of Waste	53	34	31	58.5
金属制品、机械和设备修理业	Repairing of Metal and Mechanical Equipment	28	19	23	82.1
电力、热力、燃气及水生产和供应业	Electric Power, Gas and Water Production and Supply	1001	732	626	62.5
电力、热力生产和供应业	Electric Power, Steam and Hot Water Production and Supply	541	373	331	61.2
燃气生产和供应业	Gas Production and Supply	116	98	73	62.9
水的生产和供应业	Tap Water Production and Supply	344	261	222	64.5

注:从2011年起固定资产投资统计口径调整为计划总投资500万元及以上项目,取消城镇农村公布口径,其他年份未做相应调整。从2012年起执行新的国民经济行业代码(GB/T4754-2011)。

Note:Since 2011, the fixed assets investment accounts for investment over 5 million yuan, canceling town and countryside. Other years' statistics do not correspond to this adjustment.Since 2012,a new national econmy industry code(GB/T4754-2011) is implemanted.

4-7 续表 continued

行 业	Sector	施工项目(个) Number of Projects under Construction (unit)	#新开工 Newly Started	全部建成投产项目(个) Completion and Put into Production of All Projects (unit)	项目建成投产率(%) Rate of Completion and Put into Production (%)
建筑业	Construction	746	654	568	76.1
交通运输、仓储和邮政业	Transportation, storage and Post	2721	1999	1772	65.1
铁路运输业	Railway Transportation	42	13	15	35.7
道路运输业	Road Transportation	2222	1674	1472	66.2
水上运输业	Waterway Transportation	79	45	47	59.5
航空运输业	Air Transportation	11	7	4	36.4
管道运输业	Pipeline Transportation	7	6	4	57.1
装卸搬运和运输代理业	Load, Unload, and Agency	77	57	50	64.9
仓储业	Transportation Storage	274	189	172	62.8
邮政业	Post	9	8	8	88.9
信息传输、软件和信息技术服务业	Information Transmission, Software and Information Technology Service	184	149	129	70.1
电信、广播电视和卫星传输服务	Telecom, Radio Tv and Satellite	105	89	79	75.2
互联网和相关服务	Internet and Related	28	23	20	71.4
软件和信息技术服务业	Software and Information Technology	51	37	30	58.8
批发和零售业	Wholesale and Retail Trade	954	717	709	74.3
住宿和餐饮业	Hotel and Catering Services	535	407	401	75.0
金融业	Finance	55	38	44	80.0
货币金融服务	Monetary Financial Service	43	31	37	86.0
资本市场服务	Capital Markets Service	7	3	3	42.9
保险业	Insurance	1	1	1	100.0
其他金融业	Other Financial Acitivities	4	3	3	75.0
房地产业	Real Estate Trade	1711	1188	1014	59.3
租赁和商务服务业	Leasing and Commercial Service	492	335	271	55.1
租赁业	Leasing Service	22	17	16	72.7
商务服务业	Commercial Service	470	318	255	54.3
科学研究和技术服务业	Scientific Research, Polytechnical Services	266	201	183	68.8
水利、环境和公共设施管理业	Water Conservancy, Environment and Public Facility Management	4868	3740	3127	64.2
水利管理业	Water Conservancy Management	1133	895	776	68.5
生态保护和环境治理业	Environment Management	250	193	153	61.2
公共设施管理业	Public Facility Management	3485	2652	2198	63.1
居民服务、修理和其他服务业	Resident Service and Others	309	240	243	78.6
教育	Education	954	766	720	75.5
卫生和社会工作	Health Care and Social Work	562	421	439	78.1
卫生	Health Care	360	254	299	83.1
社会工作	Social Work	202	167	140	69.3
文化、体育和娱乐业	Culture, Sports and Recreation	449	334	279	62.1
新闻和出版业	News and Publication				
广播、电视、电影和影视录音制作业	Radio, Television, Film and Recording	26	24	23	88.5
文化艺术业	Culture and Arts	214	154	127	59.3
体育	Sports	102	80	61	59.8
娱乐业	Receation	107	76	68	63.6
公共管理、社会保障和社会组织	Public Management and Social Organizations	787	623	594	75.5

4-8 按资金来源和构成分固定资产投资
INVESTMENT IN FIXED ASSETS BY SOURCE OF FUNDS AND USE OF FUNDS

年 份 Year	按资金来源分 Grouped by Source of Finance					按构成分 Grouped by Use of Funds		
	国家预算内资金 State Budgetary Appropriations	国内贷款 Domestic Loans	利用外资 Foreign Investment	自筹资金 Fund Raising	其他资金来源 Others	建筑安装工程 Construction Installation	设备工器具购置 Purchases of Equipment and Instruments	其他费用 Others
投资额(亿元) Investment(100 million yuan)								
1990	11.38	22.22	4.79	92.96	13.09	92.64	41.02	10.78
1995	58.40	173.47	88.71	422.92	83.00	454.40	248.51	123.59
1998	85.18	225.95	33.86	703.44	182.66	695.55	323.47	212.08
1999	108.18	207.61	36.57	730.92	218.89	771.24	329.26	201.67
2000	141.48	243.90	28.28	781.50	226.39	814.66	371.56	235.33
2001	174.03	241.96	29.89	874.60	231.27	890.60	419.20	241.95
2002	200.95	280.11	63.22	717.24	433.69	974.73	418.55	301.94
2003	150.20	291.60	57.41	786.40	597.98	1059.98	463.23	360.38
2004	197.03	383.78	64.74	1182.36	528.47	1409.25	537.25	409.88
2005	255.76	474.21	71.34	1492.66	540.78	1696.80	642.86	495.09
2006	378.79	708.39	79.32	1902.71	503.48	2252.72	717.10	602.87
2007	472.98	790.84	88.37	2470.28	711.66	2857.31	896.36	780.47
2008	570.17	894.57	57.02	3677.00	599.80	3568.96	1245.73	983.87
2009	711.93	1432.89	68.32	4956.88	1041.83	5025.62	1753.28	1432.95
2010	868.46	1768.79	147.03	6703.61	1314.80	6701.91	2308.73	1792.05
2011	663.18	1707.46	189.26	8800.61	1574.51	8056.52	2812.91	2065.59
2012	784.27	1964.14	131.64	11812.15	1811.96	11054.16	3162.99	2287.02
2013	886.58	2720.19	66.82	14823.15	2257.17	14312.25	3856.68	2584.98
2014	1107.45	2874.92	78.99	18732.35	2208.06	18185.42	4292.85	2523.50
2015	1339.03	2907.66	46.86	22470.65	2426.86	21826.03	4845.70	2519.33
2016	1829.24	3068.40	59.01	20623.21	3924.02	22876.58	4124.21	2503.08
构成(%) Composition (%)								
1990	7.9	15.4	3.3	64.4	9.0	64.1	28.4	7.5
1995	7.1	21.0	10.7	51.2	10.0	58.6	30.3	11.1
1998	6.9	18.4	2.8	57.1	14.8	70.2	18.4	11.4
1999	8.3	15.9	2.8	56.1	16.9	63.4	26.5	10.1
2000	10.0	17.2	2.0	55.0	15.8	64.3	23.9	11.8
2001	11.2	15.6	1.9	56.4	14.9	64.8	24.3	10.9
2002	11.9	16.5	3.7	42.3	25.6	64.4	23.6	12.1
2003	8.0	15.5	3.0	41.8	31.7	60.9	23.4	15.7
2004	8.4	16.3	2.7	50.2	22.4	63.9	20.8	15.3
2005	9.0	16.7	2.5	52.7	19.1	59.9	22.7	17.4
2006	10.6	19.8	2.2	53.3	14.1	63.1	20.1	16.8
2007	12.6	19.7	1.3	81.1	13.2	78.7	27.5	21.7
2008	9.8	15.4	1.0	63.4	10.4	61.5	21.5	17.0
2009	8.7	17.4	0.8	60.4	12.7	61.2	21.4	17.4
2010	8.1	16.4	1.4	62.1	12.0	62.0	21.4	16.6
2011	5.1	13.2	1.5	68.0	12.2	62.3	21.7	16.0
2012	4.8	11.9	0.8	71.6	11.0	67.0	19.2	13.9
2013	4.3	13.1	0.3	71.4	10.9	69.0	18.6	12.4
2014	4.4	11.5	0.3	74.9	8.9	72.7	17.2	10.1
2015	4.6	10.0	0.2	77.0	8.3	74.8	16.6	8.6
2016	6.2	10.4	0.2	69.9	13.3	77.5	14.0	8.5

注:从2011年起固定资产投资统计口径调整为计划总投资500万元及以上项目,取消城镇农村公布口径,其他年份未做相应调整。

Note:Since 2011,the fixed assets investment statistical adjustment plan for a total investment of 5 million yuan RMB and the above project, cancel the town and countryside,other years did not do corresponding adjustment.

4-9 国有单位固定资产投资
INVESTMENT IN FIXED ASSETS BY STATE OWNED UNITS

指　标	Item	2014		2015		2016	
		合计 Total	*房地产开发 Real Estate Development	合计 Total	*房地产开发 Real Estate Development	合计 Total	*房地产开发 Real Estate Development
建设项目	**Number of Construction Projects**						
施工项目(个)	Projects under Construction (unit)	8747		8910		10868	
全部建成投产项目(个)	Total Projects Completed Put into Operation	5461		5905		7183	
建成项目投产率(%)	Rate of Projects Completed Put into Operation %	62.4		66.3		66.1	
建设周期(年)	Construction Cycle (year)	1.60		1.51		1.51	
资金来源(亿元)	**Tatal Financial Allocation and Loans(100 million yuan)**	**5961.19**	**162.88**	**6904.50**	**201.15**	**7432.42**	**253.77**
国家预算内资金	State Appropriation	959.15		1159.51		1657.05	
国内贷款	Domestic Loans	810.50	48.90	782.99	52.69	837.10	99.37
利用外资	Foreign Investment	25.57		7.51		8.41	
自筹资金	Fund Raising	3882.26	66.29	4636.95	95.79	3952.78	95.29
其他资金	Others	283.71	47.69	306.54	52.67	977.09	59.11
投资总额(亿元)	**Total Value of Investment (100 million yuan)**	**5829.79**	**126.28**	**6983.99**	**174.68**	**8021.33**	**192.94**
按构成分	Grouped by Use of Funds						
*建筑工程	Construction Projects	4312.42	89.15	5330.32	120.17	6338.52	141.40
安装工程	Installation Projects	349.58	16.22	423.67	14.66	620.22	8.62
设备工具器具购置	Purchase of Equipment, Tools and Instruments	655.97	3.57	702.53	1.54	477.16	2.02
按产业分	Grouped by Industry						
第一产业	Primary Industry	40.73		62.76		85.28	
第二产业	Second Industry	1117.12		1177.53		1001.03	
第三产业	Tertiary Industry	4671.94	126.28	5743.70	174.68	6935.01	192.94
*住宅	Residential Housing	188.42	82.92	244.67	149.50	411.39	146.35
按建设性质分	Grouped by Type of Construction						
*新建	New Construction	3836.47	126.28	4367.02	174.68	6210.12	192.94
扩建	Expension	851.17		1285.59		723.95	
改建	Replacement	808.71		964.64		654.21	
房屋建筑面积(万平方米)	**Floor Space of Building (10000 sq.m)**						
施工面积	Floor Space Under Construction	5872.98	1107.98	4793.87	1302.81	5375.97	1350.12
*住宅	Residential Buildings	2199.38	875.67	1935.21	1061.57	2809.08	1049.23
竣工面积	Floor Spaace Completed	2045.37	165.04	1924.06	132.57	1633.02	157.71
*住宅	Residential Buildings	546.44	146.85	511.83	108.92	1008.21	125.13

注：建设周期按项目个数计算；本表资金来源均为资金到位数。从2012年起，三次产业采用新的划分标准。
Note: The constructive period is counted by the numbers of project.The sources of capital in this table are the number of achieved funds.Since 2012, the division of three industries emploies a new standard.

4-10 房地产开发投资主要指标

指　标	Item	1990	1995	2000
企业个数(个)	**Number of Enterprises (unit)**	**129**	**571**	**1052**
内资	Inner Funded	129	404	848
#国有	State - owned	129	292	380
集体	Collective-owned		51	105
港澳台投资	Funded by Enterprises from Hongkong, Macao and Taiwan		68	149
外商投资	Foreign Funded		99	55
投资完成额(亿元)	**Investment Completed This Year**	**5.94**	**121.13**	**134.63**
按构成分	Grouped by Use of Funds			
#建筑安装工程	Construction Projects	5.45	89.56	99.59
设备工器具购置	Installation Projects		4.47	2.83
按工程用途分	Grouped by Use of Projects			
#住宅	Residential Houses	4.70	61.78	93.15
#经济适用房屋	Economical Houses		7.44	23.53
资金来源	Grouped by Source of Finance	5.94	138.88	117.88
国内贷款	Domestic Loans	1.21	39.01	18.08
利用外资	Foreign Investments		16.35	1.15
自筹投资	Fund Raising	3.72	41.26	47.27
其他投资	Others	1.01	42.26	51.38
房屋建筑面积(万平方米)	**Floor Space of Building (10000 sq.m)**			
施工面积	Floor Space Under Construction	390.11	2049.30	2102.86
#住宅	Residential Buildings	325.82	1299.03	1673.84
竣工面积	Floor Spaace Completed	183.91	518.88	843.55
#住宅	Residential Buildings	156.77	427.19	733.27
土地开发及购置(万平方米)	**Land Development and Purchase (10000sq.m)**			
本年土地开发面积	Area of Land development This Year		903.00	469.28
本年土地购置面积	Area of Land Purchased This Year		719.00	838.12
商品房销售情况	**Selling of Commercial Houses**			
房屋销售面积(万平方米)	Floor Psace of Selling Houses (10000sq.m)	130.53	240.00	612.05
#住宅	Residential Buildings	112.67	211.00	571.04
#经济适用房	Economic Houses		40.00	172.99
商品房销售额(亿元)	Sales Value of Commercial House	6.93	31.00	83.74
#住宅				

注：本表资金来源均为资金到位数；从2010年起本年土地开发面积指标取消；从2011年起经济适用房分组指标取消。

MAJOR INDICATORS OF INVESTMENT IN REAL ESTATE DEVELOPMENT

2005	2010	2011	2013	2014	2015	2016
1990	3556	3648	4267	4214	4212	4280
1782	3395	3505	4140	4101	4107	4173
228	187	189	194	140	134	74
74	66	66	57	19	14	15
129	106	96	87	81	78	83
79	55	47	40	32	27	24
447.95	1618.24	2066.48	3286.02	3983.79	4249.23	4296.38
315.15	1059.26	1407.17	2426.17	3092.49	3243.50	3377.98
4.68	29.07	36.29	75.79	67.78	68.09	75.45
317.65	1040.25	1334.42	2251.56	2755.42	3020.54	3012.35
13.49	40.33					
513.44	2219.50	2864.05	4224.48	4322.24	4880.42	5696.35
100.41	415.43	462.25	796.57	737.54	777.89	1031.66
1.82	97.29	39.03		19.63	0.90	0.80
186.95	784.39	1195.28	1735.33	1971.63	2357.67	2175.22
224.26	922.40	1167.49	1692.58	1593.44	1743.96	2488.67
4804.35	11589.44	13922.07	21865.81	26321.99	28296.28	29879.88
4012.13	9172.43	11013.30	16640.27	19610.09	20906.65	21803.01
1627.03	2541.21	3221.05	3040.84	3431.18	2785.17	3127.49
1411.67	2129.33	2728.39	2547.39	2812.35	2193.44	2348.38
941.26						
1530.64	1422.06	1582.27	1894.68	1244.99	729.91	648.64
1708.02	3508.61	4187.62	5298.54	5601.98	6244.55	7427.16
1549.19	3236.88	3788.68	4765.68	5002.60	5647.72	6789.21
111.31	99.48					
386.57	1313.20	1878.73	2790.32	3088.31	3661.37	4994.05
335.19	1134.94	1569.32	2310.04	2543.76	3198.53	4383.81

Note: The source of capital in this table are the number of achieved funds; From 2010 the land development indicators of this year had been canceled. From 2011 the group index of affordable housing had been canceled.

4-11 按登记注册类型分房地产开发投资(2016)

单位:亿元

项 目	Item	总计 Total	内资 Inner Funded	国有 State - owned	集体 Collective -owned	股份合作 Share Holding Cooperation	联营 Joint- Owned	国有独资公司 Solely co.	其他有限责任公司 Responsibility Co. Ltd
企业个数(个)	**Number of Enterprises (unit)**	**4280**	**4173**	**74**	**15**	**3**		**63**	**1856**
#亏损企业个数	Loss- Making Enterprises	1951	1908	17	5			23	895
本年完成投资	**Investment Completed** This Year	**4296.38**	**4107.58**	**39.56**	**17.77**	**0.42**		**153.37**	**2395.30**
按构成分	Grouped by Use of Funds								
建筑工程	Construction Projects	2912.41	2758.55	20.87	13.816	0.34		120.53	1556.77
安装工程	Installation Projects	465.57	446.22	2.50	1.152	0.08		6.12	220.69
设备工器具购置	Purchase of Equipment, Tools and Instruments	75.45	72.21	0.21	0.738			1.80	37.05
其他费用	Other Funds	842.96	830.61	15.98	2.0688			24.92	580.78
#土地购置费	Purchase of Land	570.12	561.10	5.02	0.678			22.56	377.38
按构成用途分	Grouped by Use of Projects								
住宅	Residential Buildings	3012.35	2890.53	20.74	10.70	0.32		125.61	1624.84
#经济适用房	Economical Houses								
别墅、高档公寓	Villa, Top Grade Flat	78.88	76.44		1.45			4.82	42.90
办公楼	Office Building	223.90	205.53	5.4342	0.244			7.10	123.45
商业营业用房	Business Buildings	547.69	526.24	1.6365	4.2535	0.10		10.92	292.68
其他	Others	512.44	485.28	11.7522	2.5815			9.74	354.32
本年新增固定资产	**Newly Increased Fixed Assets This Year**	**1256.81**	**1212.43**	**17.28**	**10.95**	**0.13**		**53.04**	**642.01**
资金来源	**Finance Sources**	5696.35	5397.09	63.74	17.97	0.32		190.03	2996.35
国内贷款	Domestic Loans	1031.66	991.89	17.22	2.08			82.15	570.66
利用外资	Foreign Investments	0.80	0.10						
自筹资金	Fund Raising	2175.22	2096.45	26.06	4.61	0.14		69.22	1082.46
#自有资金	Self Owned	802.90	762.62	18.96				12.91	449.73
其他资金来源	Others	2488.67	2308.65	20.45	11.28	0.18		38.66	1343.22
#定金及预收款	Funds Ordered and Pre-received	1317.15	1209.43	9.77	4.08	0.08		20.66	704.52
土地开发(万平方米)	**Land Development (10000 sq.m)**								
待开发土地面积	Area of Land to be Developed	1091.48	1042.08			1.00		14.51	427.55
本年购置土地面积	Area of Land Purchased This Year	648.64	646.92		4.61	1.00			351.19
本年土地成交价款	Value of Land Transaction	214.93	213.86		2.62	0.05			133.98

注:本表资金来源均为资金到位数,从2010年起土地开发投资额和本年土地开发面积指标取消。

INVESTMENT IN REAL ESTATE DEVELOPMENT BY TYPE OF REGISTRATION(2016)

(100 million yuan)

股份有限公司 Share Holding Co.Ltd.	私营 Private	其他 Others	港澳台商投资 Hongkong, Macao and Taiwan Funded	合资经营 Joint Venture Corperation	合作经营 Cooperative Corperation	独资 Solely Funded	股份有限公司 Share Holding Co.Ltd.	外商投资 Foreign nvestment	合资经营 Joint Venture Corperation	合作经营 Cooperative Corperation	独资 Solely Funded	股份有限公司 Share Holding Co.Ltd.
197	**1954**	**11**	**83**	**34**	**3**	**42**	**3**	**24**	**15**		**6**	**1**
70	897	1	30	12	1	16		13	9		3	
290.90	**1208.56**	**1.69**	**141.42**	**26.59**	**9.32**	**105.17**		**47.38**	**19.77**		**15.36**	**2.70**
180.52	864.15	1.55	120.06	20.59	8.58	90.61		33.81	14.34		12.57	2.70
78.88	136.80		11.68	1.32		10.31		7.66	1.17		1.14	
13.36	19.04		2.98	0.48		2.50		0.26	0.26			
18.14	188.57	0.14	6.70	4.20	0.74	1.76		5.65	3.99		1.66	
15.09	140.23	0.14	4.08	4.06		0.02		4.94	3.34		1.60	
203.55	903.13	1.64	84.49	23.40	9.17	51.61		37.33	13.66		11.52	2.70
8.47	18.03	0.77	2.44	1.85		0.58						
38.82	30.48		14.13	2.16		11.97		4.23	3.35		0.88	
37.48	179.12	0.05	19.02	0.43		18.56		2.43	0.53		1.80	
11.05	95.84		23.77	0.59	0.15	23.03		3.39	2.23		1.16	
65.85	**422.40**	**0.77**	**44.38**	**7.32**		**36.14**						
584.38	1542.48	1.83	237.25	44.08	31.32	160.97		62.01	19.23		21.99	2.08
155.71	164.07		29.37		4.40	24.97		10.41	2.06		8.35	
	0.10		0.20		0.20			0.50	0.50			
163.64	749.14	1.18	73.75	13.95	0.20	59.45		5.01	5.01			
50.67	229.97	0.37	39.93	8.49		31.44		0.34	0.34			
265.03	629.18	0.65	133.93	30.14	26.52	76.55		46.09	11.66		13.64	2.08
121.19	348.67	0.47	81.69	7.07	8.97	65.31		26.04	5.10		1.16	1.07
26.56	572.46		40.03	3.06	36.97			9.37	1.71		7.66	
25.51	264.61							1.71	1.71			
3.95	73.26							1.07	1.07			

Note: The sources of capital in this table are the number of achieved funds.From 2010,the indicators of investment and area of land development had been canceled.

4-12 市、州固定资产投资
INVESTMENT IN FIXED ASSETS IN CITIES AND PREFECTURES

单位：亿元 (100 million yuan)

市、州	Cities and Prefectures	2007	2008	2009	2010	2011	2013	2014	2015	2016
全省	**Total**	**4534.14**	**5798.56**	**8211.85**	**10802.69**	**12935.02**	**20753.91**	**25001.77**	**29191.06**	**29503.88**
武汉市	Wuhan Municipality	1732.79	2222.91	3001.10	3752.92	4263.24	6001.96	7002.85	7725.26	7039.79
黄石市	Huangshi Municipality	179.85	232.90	343.05	474.06	597.45	963.50	1168.46	1380.02	1350.83
十堰市	Shiyan Municipality	141.66	185.44	278.35	406.31	522.37	904.32	1101.51	1307.25	1323.81
宜昌市	Yichang Municipality	390.36	523.46	750.27	949.51	1189.92	2106.96	2570.41	3085.35	3191.15
襄阳市	Xiangyang Municipality	265.80	373.77	574.79	835.32	1134.74	2086.64	2553.46	3071.94	3188.64
鄂州市	Ezhou Municipality	105.01	150.01	220.60	298.64	336.85	571.69	698.04	823.69	853.26
荆门市	Jingmen Municipality	153.25	210.08	317.18	448.62	590.63	1014.64	1232.55	1456.93	1531.46
孝感市	Xiaogan Municipality	195.93	270.83	397.26	570.70	729.24	1260.82	1536.96	1824.92	1899.43
荆州市	Jingzhou Municipality	210.75	291.46	435.16	600.93	771.42	1355.60	1651.63	1950.49	2001.67
黄冈市	Huanggang Municipality	258.50	370.85	553.29	736.06	823.71	1416.02	1717.39	2027.25	2041.65
咸宁市	Xianning Municipality	138.38	200.83	301.58	436.29	563.08	971.84	1170.85	1372.52	1438.29
随州市	Suizhou Municipality	101.92	147.07	208.70	291.18	384.48	654.60	799.33	959.66	974.27
恩施自治州	Enshi Prefecture	116.09	139.37	182.21	244.38	314.27	510.40	613.95	726.10	719.40
仙桃市	Xiantao Municipality	64.29	85.24	120.05	167.46	178.11	314.99	384.55	461.60	483.93
潜江市	Qianjiang Municipality	72.37	88.32	123.96	172.92	175.54	305.88	372.25	438.90	462.32
天门市	Tianmen Municipality	67.28	86.07	116.51	153.62	156.07	272.18	330.65	392.11	402.68
神农架林区	Shennongjia Forest Zone	5.63	7.50	10.65	14.15	15.77	25.56	31.06	36.38	37.08

注：2006年固定资产投资(城镇投资)不含城镇工矿区私人建房投资(下同)。由于方法制度调整,按可比口径计算,2005年扣除城镇工矿区私人建房投资基数应为2788.92亿元,各市、州固定资产投资未做调整。从2011年起固定资产投资统计口径调整为计划总投资500万元及以上项目,取消城镇农村公布口径,其他年份未做相应调整。

Note: in 2006 the investment (town investment) does not contain town private house industrial investment (the same below). Because method system adjustment, the comparable caliber calculation, 2005 deduct industrial town private house should be 278.892 billion yuan investment base; Since 2011, the fixed assets investment statistical adjustment plan for a total investment of 5 million yuan RMB and the above project, cancel the town and country-side,other years did not corresponding adjustment.

4-13 市、州国有单位固定资产投资
INVESTMENT IN FIXED ASSETS BY STATE OWNED UNITS IN CITIES AND PREFECTURES

单位：亿元 (100 million yuan)

市、州	Cities and Prefectures	2008	2009	2010	2011	2012	2013	2014	2015	2016
全省	**Total**	**2273.83**	**3124.16**	**3768.95**	**3764.22**	**4265.95**	**5068.42**	**5829.79**	**6983.99**	**8021.33**
武汉市	Wuhan	1072.32	1312.11	1655.04	1703.62	1676.10	1717.62	1883.46	2126.13	1857.10
黄石市	Huangshi	57.71	106.17	166.26	126.63	166.27	220.15	227.18	304.88	294.04
十堰市	Shiyan	76.53	136.88	176.18	226.42	344.22	454.68	479.50	610.17	630.80
宜昌市	Yichang	200.93	281.88	279.98	246.92	368.67	474.67	546.80	702.34	720.26
襄阳市	Xiangyang	96.61	111.61	144.10	202.59	300.18	323.20	368.97	523.17	667.65
鄂州市	Ezhou	62.67	112.80	107.33	63.70	102.35	76.26	154.37	177.88	335.64
荆门市	Jingmen	37.64	69.84	113.69	121.27	166.31	203.16	227.23	241.68	352.31
孝感市	Xiaogan	74.62	111.71	119.95	136.08	121.02	214.72	281.76	340.04	505.71
荆州市	Jingzhou	67.44	130.57	144.46	164.24	191.88	291.50	339.64	430.71	519.51
黄冈市	Huanggang	116.76	199.84	236.10	194.99	271.21	399.09	450.68	521.45	568.20
咸宁市	Xianning	59.27	103.42	129.30	155.54	184.16	238.80	291.23	313.67	460.09
随州市	Suizhou	37.99	70.68	77.94	77.30	73.57	124.28	140.37	158.34	191.09
恩施自治州	Enshi	57.47	88.85	111.07	110.16	149.84	193.99	233.63	319.55	412.27
仙桃市	Xiantao	6.54	26.99	12.79	14.48	16.52	25.56	35.45	34.51	63.15
潜江市	Qianjiang	38.82	53.64	68.65	51.62	63.30	60.47	85.85	106.91	55.46
天门市	Tianmen	28.47	30.47	46.30	25.51	15.31	30.16	17.78	15.16	16.31
神农架林区	Shennongjia	4.89	8.69	10.20	13.36	14.79	17.69	18.36	19.09	21.63

4-14 市、州按经济类型分的固定资产投资(2016)
INVESTMENT IN FIXED ASSETS BY OWNERSHIP IN CITIES AND PREFECTURES(2016)

单位：亿元 (100 million yuan)

市、州	Cities and Prefectures	合 计 Total	国有经济单位 State Owned Units	集体经济单位 Collective Owned Units	城乡私人 Private Owned Units	其他经济单位 Others
全省	**Total**	**29503.88**	**8021.33**	**677.42**	**9386.11**	**11419.02**
武汉市	Wuhan	7039.79	1857.10	92.88	1103.27	3986.54
黄石市	Huangshi	1350.83	294.04	36.41	474.02	546.36
十堰市	Shiyan	1323.81	630.80	5.87	379.03	308.11
宜昌市	Yichang	3191.15	720.26	34.65	949.65	1486.58
襄阳市	Xiangyang	3188.64	667.65	47.40	1240.07	1233.53
鄂州市	Ezhou	853.26	335.64	4.69	269.74	243.20
荆门市	Jingmen	1531.46	352.31	56.78	838.82	283.55
孝感市	Xiaogan	1899.43	505.71	65.14	824.82	503.76
荆州市	Jingzhou	2001.67	519.51	84.50	578.39	819.27
黄冈市	Huanggang	2041.65	568.20	81.65	896.03	495.77
咸宁市	Xianning	1438.29	460.09	45.88	539.02	393.30
随州市	Suizhou	974.27	191.09	51.99	362.71	368.48
恩施自治州	Enshi	719.40	412.27	2.56	210.96	93.61
仙桃市	Xiantao	483.93	63.15	29.39	227.53	163.87
潜江市	Qianjiang	462.32	55.46	11.06	165.94	229.87
天门市	Tianmen	402.68	16.31	11.34	210.12	164.92
神农架林区	Shennongjia	37.08	21.63	0.22	6.18	9.05

4-15 市、州基本建设投资
INVESTMENT IN INFRASTRUCTION CONSTRUCTION IN CITIES AND PREFECTURES

单位：亿元 (100 million yuan)

市、州	Cities and Prefectures	2008	2009	2010	2011	2012	2013	2014	2015	2016
全省	**Total**	**3393.06**	**4955.85**	**6504.20**	**8037.32**	**10715.01**	**13511.09**	**16140.94**	**18842.05**	**21717.26**
武汉市	Wuhan	1132.30	1511.96	1873.82	2312.36	2851.17	3438.78	3676.30	4032.80	4020.99
黄石市	Huangshi	135.11	214.79	295.51	368.95	550.46	718.40	822.00	1016.18	1104.84
十堰市	Shiyan	99.94	165.87	266.99	335.23	468.50	641.53	808.56	968.72	1105.28
宜昌市	Yichang	371.91	547.86	680.30	854.05	1092.25	1527.28	2028.62	2447.93	2746.87
襄阳市	Xiangyang	210.13	310.74	428.23	651.27	980.84	1287.08	1707.23	2205.65	2492.65
鄂州市	Ezhou	84.44	125.34	200.98	266.48	369.63	484.67	608.46	715.97	783.42
荆门市	Jingmen	122.10	207.60	278.03	336.03	519.00	578.07	683.41	858.27	1048.73
孝感市	Xiaogan	149.33	226.40	338.58	425.55	619.60	824.23	985.19	1156.36	1490.20
荆州市	Jingzhou	173.44	290.16	390.92	534.24	750.55	947.60	1181.00	1418.68	1662.99
黄冈市	Huanggang	245.58	413.73	547.27	567.38	787.85	976.36	1172.58	1337.48	1518.38
咸宁市	Xianning	117.42	175.98	287.62	395.79	526.46	601.17	718.79	852.52	925.49
随州市	Suizhou	96.23	152.87	206.41	257.42	406.04	466.65	571.49	638.12	717.28
恩施自治州	Enshi	90.74	122.32	158.37	214.65	292.50	365.62	435.87	523.94	558.18
仙桃市	Xiantao	52.62	89.47	135.29	145.69	159.09	238.72	172.70	89.31	344.56
潜江市	Qianjiang	39.40	36.41	66.68	97.11	150.18	167.45	216.79	194.22	310.24
天门市	Tianmen	56.79	75.96	101.33	80.24	130.98	210.89	279.01	326.66	342.75
神农架林区	Shennongjia	7.25	10.40	13.80	15.37	19.56	22.71	27.92	32.19	33.23

4-16 市、州技术改造投资
INVESTMENT IN TECHNOLOGY TRANFER IN CITES AND PREFECTURES

单位：亿元 (100 million yuan)

市、州	Cities and Prefectures	2008	2009	2010	2011	2012	2013	2014	2015	2016
全省	**Total**	**1033.28**	**1301.07**	**1609.33**	**1696.12**	**2032.15**	**2333.72**	**3344.93**	**4245.94**	**2503.14**
武汉市	Wuhan	406.15	410.32	419.75	374.97	331.50	249.30	569.55	705.43	288.26
黄石市	Huangshi	48.91	64.46	83.45	128.33	93.12	119.49	194.68	198.26	73.91
十堰市	Shiyan	31.67	46.87	54.38	35.19	62.66	84.19	123.08	146.74	76.13
宜昌市	Yichang	65.62	86.65	105.96	114.68	257.85	235.32	233.95	224.80	135.48
襄阳市	Xiangyang	70.35	137.43	205.46	229.29	258.40	275.00	313.97	323.38	279.40
鄂州市	Ezhou	38.90	64.77	65.08	31.83	44.37	58.08	58.08	66.29	28.70
荆门市	Jingmen	52.92	60.57	100.51	159.65	165.63	221.70	269.47	272.33	243.14
孝感市	Xiaogan	55.47	79.35	105.82	158.31	190.66	255.04	329.83	403.50	217.55
荆州市	Jingzhou	61.98	75.23	121.84	113.04	131.57	129.36	213.49	257.78	123.89
黄冈市	Huanggang	56.74	61.45	68.45	96.79	142.12	213.75	279.96	388.97	182.36
咸宁市	Xianning	38.68	61.43	62.46	61.96	113.14	177.29	275.99	414.31	416.85
随州市	Suizhou	11.45	12.02	28.86	54.64	45.95	117.72	135.14	225.14	185.84
恩施自治州	Enshi	17.30	21.62	31.96	29.72	37.42	35.71	33.11	30.36	9.90
仙桃市	Xiantao	8.82	4.75	9.10	4.80	54.92	28.60	166.67	328.05	93.94
潜江市	Qianjiang	43.17	81.01	94.07	59.74	73.14	107.68	120.32	223.57	123.92
天门市	Tianmen	21.00	29.68	36.60	34.57	29.69	22.96	5.55	21.55	24.94
神农架林区	Shennongjia	0.05	0.02	0.05			2.35	2.03	3.16	2.78

4-17 市、州房地产开发投资
INVESTMENT IN REAL ESTATE DEVELOPMENT IN CITIES AND PREFECTURES

单位：亿元 (100 million yuan)

市、州	Cities and Prefectures	2008	2009	2010	2011	2012	2013	2014	2015	2016
全省	**Total**	892.67	1200.44	1618.24	2066.48	2539.46	3286.02	3983.79	4249.23	4296.38
武汉市	Wuhan	560.36	778.59	1017.40	1282.25	1574.86	1905.60	2353.63	2581.79	2517.44
黄石市	Huangshi	21.53	25.30	38.36	42.51	56.04	84.68	115.77	130.14	132.37
十堰市	Shiyan	28.99	35.73	41.08	52.00	76.64	101.11	90.80	83.01	87.28
宜昌市	Yichang	56.68	79.33	105.78	135.97	176.59	203.18	194.60	241.89	244.18
襄阳市	Xiangyang	46.21	55.39	106.52	144.97	186.19	301.94	330.94	334.58	340.76
鄂州市	Ezhou	10.79	8.11	11.49	18.82	11.65	22.78	20.39	21.09	22.88
荆门市	Jingmen	16.84	27.19	38.83	55.65	64.31	87.79	123.98	118.11	100.39
孝感市	Xiaogan	28.57	32.40	49.60	56.40	74.95	111.13	136.35	171.58	160.02
荆州市	Jingzhou	26.59	32.87	35.53	55.80	54.89	76.79	134.17	113.33	151.53
黄冈市	Huanggang	27.38	37.33	43.84	62.15	78.57	132.73	174.27	200.05	265.73
咸宁市	Xianning	25.35	39.55	59.57	65.46	84.96	112.06	109.14	59.94	56.99
随州市	Suizhou	15.96	17.05	21.66	24.68	19.79	29.23	33.98	28.77	24.05
恩施自治州	Enshi	16.48	16.97	25.65	35.47	40.28	57.06	91.54	100.99	130.75
仙桃市	Xiantao	3.92	4.79	7.75	16.34	15.66	26.62	24.80	22.66	19.23
潜江市	Qianjiang	2.76	3.57	6.39	5.75	9.15	18.11	22.58	15.60	21.06
天门市	Tianmen	4.27	6.27	8.77	12.26	14.93	15.24	26.84	25.68	21.73
神农架林区	Shennongjia									

4-18 按国民经济行业分的基本建设投资
ACCORDING TO THE NATIONAL ECONOMIC CONSTRUCTION OF BASIC INDUSTRY INVESTMENT

单位：亿元 (100 million yuan)

行业	sector	全省		#地方	
		2015	2016	2015	2016
总 计	**Total**	**18842.05**	**21717.26**	**18449.16**	**21214.61**
农、林、牧、渔业	Farming, Forestry, Animal Husbandry and Fishery	829.39	1016.78	829.39	1010.64
农业	Farming	318.27	456.28	318.27	455.27
林业	Forestry	89.92	100.61	89.92	100.61
畜牧业	Animal Husbandry	160.03	195.22	160.03	192.58
渔业	Fishery	61.94	83.89	61.94	83.55
农、林、牧、渔服务业	Farming, Forestry, Animal Husbandry and Fishery Services	199.22	180.78	199.22	178.64
采矿业	Mining and Qarrying	309.87	245.43	233.97	238.97
制造业	Manufacturing	7192.19	8346.63	7109.09	8240.01
农副食品加工业	Food Processing	686.26	701.54	686.26	700.90
食品制造业	Food Production	192.49	260.10	192.49	259.62
酒、饮料和精制茶制造业	Beverage Production	183.80	287.37	183.80	287.37
烟草制品业	Tobacco Processing	23.04	7.07	23.04	7.07
纺织业	Textile Industry	211.97	267.77	211.97	267.53
纺织服装、服饰业	Textile Wearing Apparel and Accessaries	232.20	260.10	232.20	260.10
皮革、毛皮、羽毛及其制品和制鞋业	Leather, Fur, Feather and Related Products	54.01	68.82	54.01	68.82
木材加工和木、竹、藤、棕、草制品业	Timber Processing and Wwood, Bamboo,Rattan, Palm and Sraw Works	110.59	111.76	110.59	111.76
家具制造业	Furniture Manufacturing	126.88	149.96	126.88	149.96
造纸和纸制品业	Papermaking and Paper Products	135.73	227.97	135.73	227.97
印刷和记录媒介复制业	Printing and Record Processing	71.43	62.90	71.43	62.78
文教、工美、体育和娱乐用品制造业	Stationery, Education, Art, Sport and Entertainment Products	103.91	122.38	103.91	122.38
石油加工、炼焦和核燃料加工业	Petroleum Processing, Coking Products and Nuclear Fuel Processing	44.00	34.79	41.35	28.93
化学原料和化学制品制造业	Raw Chemical Material and Chemical Products	336.98	584.51	336.98	580.95
医药制造业	Medical and pharmaceutical Products	287.20	337.77	287.20	337.77
化学纤维制造业	Chemical Fibers	5.89	19.79	5.89	19.79
橡胶和塑料制品业	Rubber Products and Plastic Products	209.45	280.98	209.04	277.64
非金属矿物制品业	Nonmetal Material Products	674.14	831.36	674.14	810.60
黑色金属冶炼和压延加工业	Smelting and Processing of ferrous Metals	133.93	107.21	131.59	107.21
有色金属冶炼和压延加工业	Smelting and Processing of Nonferrous Metals	67.68	90.15	67.68	87.46
金属制品业	Metal Products	297.79	308.25	295.14	301.56
通用设备制造业	Ordinaryly Machinery Manufacturing	388.86	435.91	375.32	431.99
专用设备制造业	Special Purpose Equipment Manufacturing	555.10	464.47	537.66	462.48
汽车制造业	Automobile Manufacturing	879.06	1009.43	855.97	983.64
铁路、船舶、航空航天和其他运输设备制造业	Realway, Ship, Aircraft and Other Transport Equipment Manufacturing	121.09	102.75	112.84	92.44
电气机械和器材制造业	Electric Machinery and Equipment	476.83	507.24	476.83	506.22
计算机、通信和其他电子设备制造业	Computers, Communication Equipment and Other Electronic Equipment Manufacturing	375.47	510.62	368.70	505.23
仪器仪表制造业	Measuring Instruments Manufacturing	87.01	72.17	82.03	72.17
其他制造业	Other Equipment	61.52	40.86	61.52	27.05
废弃资源综合利用业	Recycling and Disposal of Waste	47.08	56.21	47.08	56.21
金属制品、机械和设备修理业	Repairing of Metal and Mechanical Equipment	10.78	24.41	9.79	24.41
电力、热力、燃气及水生产和供应业	Electric Power, Gas and Water Production and Supply	514.61	784.56	490.71	702.66
电力、热力生产和供应业	Electric Power, Steam and Hot Water Production and Supply	320.03	523.21	299.50	445.94
燃气生产和供应业	Gas Production and Supply	55.10	61.41	53.22	60.54
水的生产和供应业	Tap Water Production and Supply	139.48	199.94	137.99	196.18

注：从2012年起执行新的国民经济行业代码（GB/T4754-2011）。
Note:Since 2012,a new national economy industry code(GB/T4754-2011)is implemented.

4-18 续表 continued

单位：亿元 (100 million yuan)

行业	sector	全省 2015	全省 2016	#地方 2015	#地方 2016
建筑业	Construction	141.13	415.68	139.49	395.29
交通运输、仓储和邮政业	Transportation, storage and Post	2328.42	2559.99	2276.96	2390.59
铁路运输业	Railway Transportation	61.35	236.71	29.45	72.09
道路运输业	Road Transportation	1600.69	1635.40	1585.35	1632.49
水上运输业	Waterway Transportation	160.71	120.95	160.71	120.95
航空运输业	Air Transportation	48.05	122.48	48.05	122.48
管道运输业	Pipeline Transportation	5.49	1.10	5.49	1.10
装卸搬运和运输代理业	Load, Unload, and Agency	94.91	64.57	94.91	64.57
仓储业	Transportation Storage	352.72	377.05	348.50	375.19
邮政业	Post	4.50	1.72	4.50	1.72
信息传输、软件和信息技术服务业	Information Transmission, Software and Information Technology Service	88.48	121.84	77.67	114.60
电信、广播电视和卫星传输服务	Telecom, Radio Tv and Satellite	48.49	50.80	37.84	43.72
互联网和相关服务	Internet and Related	5.73	18.46	5.73	18.30
软件和信息技术服务业	Software and Information Technology	34.26	52.58	34.10	52.58
批发和零售业	Wholesale and Retail Trade	761.26	660.39	758.16	659.88
住宿和餐饮业	Hotel and Catering Services	324.96	262.06	324.96	261.87
金融业	Finance	52.02	24.98	50.98	23.53
货币金融服务	Monetary Financial Service	17.10	10.56	16.06	9.45
资本市场服务	Capital Markets Service	31.30	13.39	31.30	13.39
保险业	Insurance	1.92	0.27	1.92	0.27
其他金融业	Other Financial Acitivities	1.70	0.76	1.70	0.42
房地产业	Real Estate Trade	1524.60	1708.46	1519.97	1681.07
租赁和商务服务业	Leasing and Commercial Service	685.32	787.63	681.40	784.30
租赁业	Leasing Service	16.91	25.06	16.91	22.04
商务服务业	Commercial Service	668.42	762.57	664.50	762.27
科学研究和技术服务业	Scientific Research, Polytechnical Services	129.46	138.85	112.11	131.24
水利、环境和公共设施管理业	Water Conservancy, Environment and Public Facility Management	2740.50	3366.82	2677.19	3333.50
水利管理业	Water Conservancy Management	323.44	442.21	298.92	441.26
生态保护和环境治理业	Environment Management	142.99	179.61	131.86	179.39
公共设施管理业	Public Facility Management	2274.08	2745.00	2246.41	2712.85
居民服务、修理和其他服务业	Resident Service and Others	121.76	129.90	121.47	129.90
教育	Education	241.75	322.23	217.26	312.88
卫生和社会工作	Health Care and Social Work	188.10	235.59	181.71	228.37
卫生	Health Care	147.96	167.00	141.57	160.33
社会工作	Social Work	40.14	68.59	40.14	68.04
文化、体育和娱乐业	Culture, Sports and Recreation	294.82	301.70	277.60	293.83
新闻和出版业	News and Publication	2.29		2.29	
广播、电视、电影和影视录音制作业	Radio, Television, Film and Recording	8.53	6.71	8.53	6.71
文化艺术业	Culture and Arts	126.71	121.06	126.16	120.68
体育	Sports	50.65	63.47	49.87	63.47
娱乐业	Receation	106.64	110.45	90.75	102.97
公共管理、社会保障和社会组织	Public Management and Social Organizations	373.40	287.77	369.08	281.46

4-19 按国民经济行业分的技术改造投资
ACCORDING TO THE NATIONAL ECONOMIC

单位：亿元 (100 million yuan)

行业	sector	全省		#地方	
		2015	2016	2015	2016
总　计	**Total**	**4245.94**	**2503.14**	**4149.02**	**2419.27**
农、林、牧、渔业	Farming, Forestry, Animal Husbandry and Fishery	74.07	37.41	74.07	37.41
农业	Farming	19.38	6.44	19.38	6.44
林业	Forestry	2.95	5.97	2.95	5.97
畜牧业	Animal Husbandry	9.90	11.58	9.90	11.58
渔业	Fishery	12.87	4.69	12.87	4.69
农、林、牧、渔服务业	Farming, Forestry, Animal Husbandry and Fishery Services	28.96	8.73	28.96	8.73
采矿业	Mining and Qarrying	137.60	72.74	137.60	71.21
制造业	Manufacturing	3257.19	1893.77	3198.05	1848.94
农副食品加工业	Food Processing	231.41	145.27	231.41	145.27
食品制造业	Food Production	100.00	48.63	100.00	48.63
酒、饮料和精制茶制造业	Beverage Production	104.59	45.74	104.59	45.74
烟草制品业	Tobacco Processing	10.89	0.48	10.89	0.48
纺织业	Textile Industry	210.39	128.96	206.16	128.96
纺织服装、服饰业	Textile Wearing Apparel and Accessaries	89.50	55.25	89.50	55.25
皮革、毛皮、羽毛及其制品和制鞋业	Leather, Fur, Feather and Related Products	31.87	12.75	31.87	12.75
木材加工和木、竹、藤、棕、草制品业	Timber Processing and Wwood, Bamboo,Rattan, Palm and Sraw Works	45.23	38.02	45.23	38.02
家具制造业	Furniture Manufacturing	24.24	18.60	24.24	18.60
造纸和纸制品业	Papermaking and Paper Products	56.82	27.55	56.82	27.55
印刷和记录媒介复制业	Printing and Record Processing	20.94	16.97	20.94	16.97
文教、工美、体育和娱乐用品制造业	Stationery, Education, Art, Sport and Entertainment Products	20.38	8.04	20.38	8.04
石油加工、炼焦和核燃料加工业	Petroleum Processing, Coking Products and Nuclear Fuel Processing	22.36	0.08	12.16	0.08
化学原料和化学制品制造业	Raw Chemical Material and Chemical Products	277.15	202.34	276.86	201.46
医药制造业	Medical and pharmaceutical Products	122.41	45.93	122.41	45.74
化学纤维制造业	Chemical Fibers	6.57	3.50	6.57	3.06
橡胶和塑料制品业	Rubber Products and Plastic Products	115.19	67.62	115.19	67.62
非金属矿物制品业	Nonmetal Material Products	341.37	200.02	341.37	200.02
黑色金属冶炼和压延加工业	Smelting and Processing of ferrous Metals	101.71	61.43	81.75	44.02
有色金属冶炼和压延加工业	Smelting and Processing of Nonferrous Metals	42.44	33.52	42.44	33.43
金属制品业	Metal Products	107.27	55.48	107.27	55.48
通用设备制造业	Ordinaryly Machinery Manufacturing	150.69	94.70	150.48	90.94
专用设备制造业	Special Purpose Equipment Manufacturing	116.68	104.03	116.68	104.03
汽车制造业	Automobile Manufacturing	464.43	257.50	446.12	237.84
铁路、船舶、航空航天和其他运输设备制造业	Realway, Ship, Aircraft and Other Transport Equipment Manufacturing	7.60	16.35	4.86	16.35
电气机械和器材制造业	Electric Machinery and Equipment	160.11	116.81	160.11	116.81
计算机、通信和其他电子设备制造业	Computers, Communication Equipment and Other Electronic Equipment Manufacturing	210.47	55.45	208.63	53.05
仪器仪表制造业	Measuring Instruments Manufacturing	25.10	17.00	25.10	17.00
其他制造业	Other Equipment	20.10	6.07	20.10	6.07
废弃资源综合利用业	Recycling and Disposal of Waste	17.76	6.34	16.40	6.34
金属制品、机械和设备修理业	Repairing of Metal and Mechanical Equipment	1.52	3.35	1.52	3.35
电力、热力、燃气及水生产和供应业	Electric Power, Gas and Water Production and Supply	220.38	107.49	202.84	90.82
电力、热力生产和供应业	Electric Power, Steam and Hot Water Production and Supply	181.88	66.56	164.35	49.89
燃气生产和供应业	Gas Production and Supply	8.05	19.14	8.05	19.14
水的生产和供应业	Tap Water Production and Supply	30.46	21.80	30.44	21.80

4-19 续表 continued

单位:亿元 (100 million yuan)

行业	sector	全省		#地方	
		2015	2016	2015	2016
建筑业	Construction	2.37	6.89	2.37	6.89
交通运输、仓储和邮政业	Transportation, storage and Post	138.69	101.42	120.34	92.42
铁路运输业	Railway Transportation	19.14	9.04	0.80	0.30
道路运输业	Road Transportation	104.75	81.09	104.75	81.09
水上运输业	Waterway Transportation	3.15	1.89	3.15	1.89
航空运输业	Air Transportation				
管道运输业	Pipeline Transportation				
装卸搬运和运输代理业	Load, Unload, and Agency	3.77	1.81	3.77	1.81
仓储业	Transportation Storage	6.59	7.31	6.59	7.05
邮政业	Post	1.28	0.28	1.28	0.28
信息传输、软件和信息技术服务业	Information Transmission, Software and Information Technology Service	33.04	17.65	32.66	6.18
电信、广播电视和卫星传输服务	Telecom, Radio Tv and Satellite	17.56	5.16	17.18	5.16
互联网和相关服务	Internet and Related	13.41	11.00	13.41	0.69
软件和信息技术服务业	Software and Information Technology	2.07	1.49	2.07	0.34
批发和零售业	Wholesale and Retail Trade	70.80	28.00	70.80	28.00
住宿和餐饮业	Hotel and Catering Services	13.55	15.17	13.55	15.17
金融业	Finance	2.29	3.06	1.82	3.06
货币金融服务	Monetary Financial Service	1.29		0.82	
资本市场服务	Monetary Financial Service	0.71	2.84	0.71	2.84
保险业	Insurance				
其他金融业	Other Financial Acitivities	0.29	0.22	0.29	0.22
房地产业	Real Estate Trade	33.50	8.73	33.10	8.37
租赁和商务服务业	Leasing and Commercial Service	7.02	5.45	7.02	5.45
租赁业	Leasing Service		1.20		1.20
商务服务业	Commercial Service	7.02	4.25	7.02	4.25
科学研究和技术服务业	Scientific Research, Polytechnical Services	6.23	5.98	6.23	5.98
水利、环境和公共设施管理业	Water Conservancy, Environment and Public Facility Management	175.34	171.26	174.91	171.26
水利管理业	Water Conservancy Management	72.34	28.47	72.34	28.47
生态保护和环境治理业	Environment Management	9.32	11.48	9.32	11.48
公共设施管理业	Public Facility Management	93.68	131.31	93.25	131.31
居民服务、修理和其他服务业	Resident Service and Others	8.13	5.67	8.13	5.67
教育	Education	18.07	5.73	18.07	5.73
卫生和社会工作	Health Care and Social Work	11.48	3.73	11.48	3.73
卫生	Health Care	10.39	2.94	10.39	2.94
社会工作	Social Work	1.09	0.78	1.09	0.78
文化、体育和娱乐业	Culture, Sports and Recreation	10.59	4.01	10.59	4.01
新闻和出版业	News and Publication	0.73		0.73	
广播、电视、电影和影视录音制作业	Radio, Television, Film and Recording	0.40	0.78	0.40	0.78
文化艺术业	Culture and Arts	1.21	2.90	1.21	2.90
体育	Sports	2.25	0.33	2.25	0.33
娱乐业	Receation	6.00		6.00	
公共管理、社会保障和社会组织	Public Management and Social Organizations	25.61	8.98	25.41	8.98

4-20 按构成分的固定资产投资
ACCORDING TO THE COMPOSITION OF FIXED ASSETS INVESTMENT

单位:亿元 (100 million yuan)

年 份 In copies	全省 建筑安装工程 Building installation	全省 设备工具器具购置 Equipment tools, equipment purchase	全省 其他费用 Other expenses	*地方 建筑安装工程 Building installation	*地方 设备工具器具购置 Equipment tools, equipment purchase	*地方 其他费用 expenses Other
1978	20.30	9.98	3.30	9.89	4.51	0.48
1980	23.85	9.76	1.89	14.01	4.55	0.97
"六五"时期	**216.19**	**83.11**	**16.52**	**155.63**	**59.71**	**7.43**
1985	67.53	28.67	6.71	54.64	23.00	3.39
"七五"时期	**434.43**	**195.59**	**50.10**	**352.24**	**152.75**	**32.96**
1990	92.64	41.02	10.78	73.58	29.31	7.11
"八五"时期	**1300.95**	**606.68**	**304.04**	**972.09**	**429.78**	**178.69**
1991	108.07	45.11	15.01	86.74	33.68	10.64
1992	149.34	68.03	23.36	119.61	51.46	15.94
1993	227.25	98.91	57.02	174.02	74.17	39.83
1994	361.89	146.12	85.06	261.27	99.72	49.60
1995	454.40	248.51	123.59	330.45	170.75	62.68
"九五"时期	**3392.01**	**1596.34**	**1034.45**	**2593.68**	**1108.81**	**598.32**
1996	510.52	307.89	165.97	392.06	218.14	82.28
1997	600.04	264.16	219.40	405.69	171.97	201.38
1998	695.55	323.47	212.08	556.36	230.59	101.48
1999	771.24	329.26	201.67	594.41	248.78	94.54
2000	814.66	371.56	235.33	645.16	239.33	118.64
"十五"时期	**6031.36**	**2481.09**	**1809.24**	**5317.08**	**1883.69**	**1216.75**
2001	890.60	419.20	241.95	739.97	276.93	124.89
2002	974.73	418.55	301.94	829.11	303.57	155.49
2003	1059.98	463.23	360.38	945.58	363.78	243.47
2004	1409.25	537.25	409.88	1282.71	416.98	307.87
2005	1696.80	642.86	495.09	1519.71	522.43	385.03
"十一五"时期	**20406.53**	**6921.20**	**5592.20**	**18649.08**	**5890.61**	**4859.93**
2006	2252.72	717.10	602.87	1918.63	601.90	477.07
2007	2857.31	896.36	780.47	2492.24	756.58	660.27
2008	3568.97	1245.73	983.86	3226.13	971.37	819.50
2009	5025.62	1753.28	1432.95	4683.30	1472.52	1243.52
2010	6701.91	2308.73	1792.05	6328.78	2088.24	1659.57
"十二五"时期	**73434.38**	**18971.13**	**11980.42**	**71272.16**	**18040.47**	**11545.96**
2011	8056.52	2812.91	2065.59	7626.28	2520.40	1950.61
2012	11054.16	3162.99	2287.02	10609.45	2942.10	2192.00
2013	14312.25	3856.68	2584.98	13934.73	3702.30	2508.97
2014	18185.42	4292.85	2523.50	17765.47	4160.35	2425.92
2015	21826.03	4845.70	2519.33	21336.23	4715.32	2468.46
"十三五"时期						
2016	22876.58	4124.21	2503.08	22349.47	3980.74	2421.55

4-21 按国民经济行业分的固定资产投资
ACCORDING TO THE NATIONAL ECONOMY OF FIXED ASSETS INVESTMENT

单位：亿元 (100 million yuan)

行业	sector	全省		#地方	
		2015	2016	2015	2016
总 计	**Total**	**29191.06**	**29503.88**	**28520.01**	**28751.75**
农、林、牧、渔业	Farming, Forestry, Animal Husbandry and Fishery	1238.63	1086.49	1238.63	1080.36
农业	Farming	650.49	477.71	650.49	476.69
林业	Forestry	93.73	108.85	93.73	108.85
畜牧业	Animal Husbandry	177.02	211.26	177.02	208.62
渔业	Fishery	76.69	92.11	76.69	91.77
农、林、牧、渔服务业	Farming, Forestry, Animal Husbandry and Fishery Services	240.70	196.56	240.70	194.43
采矿业	Mining and Qarrying	453.25	329.40	377.35	321.42
制造业	Manufacturing	10783.16	10522.40	10634.87	10368.19
农副食品加工业	Food Processing	935.56	870.93	935.56	870.29
食品制造业	Food Production	297.41	315.38	297.41	314.90
酒、饮料和精制茶制造业	Beverage Production	299.60	336.68	299.60	336.68
烟草制品业	Tobacco Processing	33.93	8.84	33.93	8.84
纺织业	Textile Industry	439.59	411.72	435.35	411.48
纺织服装、服饰业	Textile Wearing Apparel and Accessaries	331.25	329.29	331.25	329.29
皮革、毛皮、羽毛及其制品和制鞋业	Leather, Fur, Feather and Related Products	87.72	89.00	87.72	89.00
木材加工和木、竹、藤、棕、草制品业	Timber Processing and Wwood, Bamboo,Rattan, Palm and Sraw Works	156.43	152.29	156.43	152.02
家具制造业	Furniture Manufacturing	151.36	170.34	151.36	170.34
造纸和纸制品业	Papermaking and Paper Products	199.53	261.06	199.53	261.06
印刷和记录媒介复制业	Printing and Record Processing	95.95	83.67	95.95	82.82
文教、工美、体育和娱乐用品制造业	Stationery, Education, Art, Sport and Entertainment Products	124.29	130.87	124.29	130.87
石油加工、炼焦和核燃料加工业	Petroleum Processing, Coking Products and Nuclear Fuel Processing	67.95	36.26	55.12	30.41
化学原料和化学制品制造业	Raw Chemical Material and Chemical Products	631.75	794.68	631.46	790.23
医药制造业	Medical and pharmaceutical Products	420.98	389.39	420.98	389.20
化学纤维制造业	Chemical Fibers	14.50	23.83	14.50	23.39
橡胶和塑料制品业	Rubber Products and Plastic Products	344.45	357.44	344.04	354.09
非金属矿物制品业	Nonmetal Material Products	1054.28	1058.57	1054.28	1037.81
黑色金属冶炼和压延加工业	Smelting and Processing of ferrous Metals	238.26	172.29	215.95	154.88
有色金属冶炼和压延加工业	Smelting and Processing of Nonferrous Metals	125.32	124.80	125.32	122.02
金属制品业	Metal Products	417.73	372.49	415.08	365.79
通用设备制造业	Ordinaryly Machinery Manufacturing	566.23	557.70	551.44	549.88
专用设备制造业	Special Purpose Equipment Manufacturing	686.75	584.25	669.30	582.26
汽车制造业	Automobile Manufacturing	1399.79	1325.78	1354.10	1278.72
铁路、船舶、航空航天和其他运输设备制造业	Realway, Ship, Aircraft and Other Transport Equipment Manufacturing	136.07	122.69	124.78	112.37
电气机械和器材制造业	Electric Machinery and Equipment	651.86	637.26	651.86	636.24
计算机、通信和其他电子设备制造业	Computers, Communication Equipment and Other Electronic Equipment Manufacturing	594.86	571.96	586.13	564.16
仪器仪表制造业	Measuring Instruments Manufacturing	115.90	89.85	110.63	89.85
其他制造业	Other Equipment	83.48	50.95	83.48	37.13
废弃资源综合利用业	Recycling and Disposal of Waste	65.67	62.98	64.30	62.98
金属制品、机械和设备修理业	Repairing of Metal and Mechanical Equipment	14.73	29.17	13.75	29.17
电力、热力、燃气及水生产和供应业	Electric Power, Gas and Water Production and Supply	769.17	934.69	726.80	835.30
电力、热力生产和供应业	Electric Power, Steam and Hot Water Production and Supply	528.95	614.46	490.26	519.70
燃气生产和供应业	Gas Production and Supply	65.60	81.35	63.71	80.48
水的生产和供应业	Tap Water Production and Supply	174.62	238.88	172.83	235.13

4-21 续表 continued

单位: 亿元 (100 million yuan)

行业	sector	全省		#地方	
		2015	2016	2015	2016
建筑业	Construction	164.06	475.46	151.96	440.96
交通运输、仓储和邮政业	Transportation, storage and Post	2574.55	2794.23	2503.19	2613.63
铁路运输业	Railway Transportation	83.02	246.00	32.08	72.63
道路运输业	Road Transportation	1793.83	1822.89	1778.49	1818.78
水上运输业	Waterway Transportation	170.77	131.68	169.91	130.68
航空运输业	Air Transportation	48.26	135.08	48.26	135.08
管道运输业	Pipeline Transportation	5.49	1.10	5.49	1.10
装卸搬运和运输代理业	Load, Unload, and Agency	105.15	67.34	105.15	67.34
仓储业	Transportation Storage	362.18	387.90	357.97	385.78
邮政业	Post	5.85	2.25	5.85	2.25
信息传输、软件和信息技术服务业	Information Transmission, Software and Information Technology Service	156.88	150.75	142.19	131.42
电信、广播电视和卫星传输服务	Telecom, Radio Tv and Satellite	96.75	65.68	82.21	57.98
互联网和相关服务	Internet and Related	20.99	29.95	20.99	19.47
软件和信息技术服务业	Software and Information Technology	39.14	55.11	38.99	53.96
批发和零售业	Wholesale and Retail Trade	858.15	725.27	854.81	724.34
住宿和餐饮业	Hotel and Catering Services	353.51	286.04	353.51	285.86
金融业	Finance	60.82	33.00	59.31	31.20
货币金融服务	Monetary Financial Service	23.66	15.52	22.15	14.06
资本市场服务	Monetary Financial Service	32.01	16.23	32.01	16.23
保险业	Insurance	2.19	0.27	2.19	0.27
其他金融业	Other Financial Acitivities	2.96	0.98	2.96	0.64
房地产业	Real Estate Trade	6503.46	6063.74	6358.54	5908.31
租赁和商务服务业	Leasing and Commercial Service	700.14	806.37	696.22	803.05
租赁业	Leasing Service	22.23	28.48	22.23	25.46
商务服务业	Commercial Service	677.91	777.89	673.99	777.59
科学研究和技术服务业	Scientific Research, Polytechnical Services	144.24	151.87	122.78	143.42
水利、环境和公共设施管理业	Water Conservancy, Environment and Public Facility Management	3061.06	3735.20	2994.38	3698.77
水利管理业	Water Conservancy Management	438.27	513.25	413.76	512.21
生态保护和环境治理业	Environment Management	156.74	197.75	145.61	197.53
公共设施管理业	Public Facility Management	2466.05	3024.20	2435.01	2989.03
居民服务、修理和其他服务业	Resident Service and Others	134.09	139.16	133.80	139.16
教育	Education	280.81	366.66	245.50	345.83
卫生和社会工作	Health Care and Social Work	227.11	269.46	220.07	261.66
卫生	Health Care	181.43	197.91	174.40	191.16
社会工作	Social Work	45.67	71.55	45.67	70.50
文化、体育和娱乐业	Culture, Sports and Recreation	314.06	323.91	296.84	316.05
新闻和出版业	News and Publication	3.02		3.02	
广播、电视、电影和影视录音制作业	Radio, Television, Film and Recording	12.01	19.75	12.01	19.75
文化艺术业	Culture and Arts	131.88	127.64	131.33	127.27
体育	Sports	53.89	65.38	53.11	65.38
娱乐业	Receation	113.25	111.13	97.37	103.65
公共管理、社会保障和社会组织	Public Management and Social Organizations	413.92	309.77	409.24	302.84

4-22 按三次产业划分的固定资产投资
ACCORDING TO THE THREE INDUSTRIES OF FIXED ASSETS INVESTMENT

单位:亿元 (100 million yuan)

年 份 In copies	全省			*地方		
	第一产业 The first industry	第二产业 The second industry	第三产业 The third industry	第一产业 The first industry	第二产业 The second industry	第三产业 The third industry
1978	2.24	25.28	6.06	2.24	8.80	3.85
1980	2.11	22.75	10.64	2.03	9.98	7.52
六五时期	**24.77**	**155.02**	**136.03**	**24.05**	**83.83**	**114.89**
1985	8.37	47.42	47.12	8.09	31.48	41.46
七五时期	**49.76**	**335.53**	**294.83**	**47.24**	**245.00**	**245.71**
1990	12.16	67.41	64.87	11.61	46.30	52.09
八五时期	**78.98**	**1074.06**	**1058.63**	**73.97**	**674.84**	**831.75**
1991	12.48	77.95	77.76	12.12	55.25	63.69
1992	12.42	121.00	107.31	11.04	87.18	88.79
1993	11.89	170.93	200.36	10.10	114.05	163.87
1994	14.97	302.49	275.61	14.38	173.32	222.89
1995	27.22	401.69	397.59	26.11	220.95	316.82
九五时期	**272.08**	**2298.38**	**3452.34**	**271.69**	**1265.99**	**2763.13**
1996	29.76	451.28	503.34	29.73	272.79	389.96
1997	41.02	436.04	606.54	41.02	269.87	468.15
1998	59.48	450.16	721.46	59.48	234.94	594.01
1999	71.22	439.32	791.63	71.22	227.20	639.31
2000	70.60	521.58	829.37	70.24	261.19	671.70
十五时期	**416.79**	**3952.90**	**5969.82**	**414.74**	**2724.92**	**5277.86**
2001	77.48	590.01	902.08	77.33	323.55	740.91
2002	80.08	648.81	966.33	79.02	375.77	833.38
2003	88.80	714.81	1079.98	88.35	489.49	974.99
2004	77.55	912.93	1365.90	77.16	684.54	1245.86
2005	92.88	1086.34	1655.53	92.88	851.57	1482.72
十一五时期	**1202.88**	**12641.78**	**19075.27**	**1197.58**	**10748.83**	**17471.71**
2006	107.64	1317.12	2147.93	107.56	1044.17	1845.87
2007	149.40	1710.74	2674.00	148.72	1395.28	2365.09
2008	231.25	2346.32	3220.99	230.95	1859.42	2926.62
2009	321.59	3097.68	4792.58	319.58	2656.02	4442.25
2010	393.00	4169.92	6239.77	390.77	3793.94	5891.88
十二五时期	**3354.26**	**44874.29**	**56157.36**	**3351.93**	**43109.22**	**54397.45**
2011	440.91	5526.40	6967.71	440.51	5032.88	6623.90
2012	525.45	7281.04	8697.68	525.13	6891.67	8326.75
2013	590.61	9187.25	10976.04	589.28	8883.83	10672.89
2014	799.35	10733.09	13469.32	799.07	10432.00	13120.68
2015	997.94	12146.51	16046.61	997.94	11868.84	15653.23
十三五时期						
2016	889.94	12224.54	16389.40	885.93	11929.18	15936.64

4-23 全社会竣工房屋建筑面积及竣工率
THE FLOOR SPACE OF BUILDINGS COMPLETED ALL SOCIAL AND COMPLETION RATE

年 份 In copies	施工面积(万平方米) Construction area (million square meters)	#住宅 # residential	竣工面积(万平方米) Completion of (million square meters)	#住宅 # residential	竣工率(%) Completion rate (%)	#住宅 # residential
1978	1343.27	513.20	666.76	280.16	49.6	54.6
1980	1951.16	1004.17	1024.51	586.27	52.5	58.4
六五时期			**25700.97**	**19626.87**		
1985	8079.90	5965.71	6899.59	5434.20	85.4	91.1
七五时期			**29202.17**	**22387.23**		
1990	5103.48	3507.53	4169.12	3058.40	81.7	87.2
八五时期			**23403.26**	**16559.28**		
1991	5300.98	3652.67	4211.39	3157.13	79.4	86.4
1992	5954.84	4066.51	4621.87	3383.72	77.6	83.2
1993	5807.24	3540.57	4050.56	2798.42	69.8	79.0
1994	7158.68	4476.46	4916.24	3482.20	68.7	77.8
1995	8294.84	5304.79	5603.20	3737.81	67.6	70.5
九五时期			**35861.86**	**26378.48**		
1996	8749.65	5581.32	6073.43	4485.82	69.4	80.4
1997	8963.28	5976.86	6430.48	4790.34	71.7	80.1
1998	10485.86	7179.25	7897.96	5792.97	75.3	80.7
1999	10228.93	7219.06	7951.03	5891.97	77.7	81.6
2000	9920.42	6831.02	7508.96	5417.38	75.7	79.3
十五时期			**40164.49**	**29588.06**		
2001	10040.11	7273.21	7716.37	5850.27	76.9	80.4
2002	10301.00	7019.76	7796.76	5583.27	75.7	79.5
2003	10667.78	7276.62	7469.17	5457.42	70.0	75.0
2004	13152.08	9285.64	9318.34	7069.45	70.6	75.9
2005	12572.00	8401.20	7863.85	5627.67	62.6	67.0
十一五时期			**43810.54**	**26870.86**		
2006	12346.48	8039.75	7126.64	4812.39	57.7	59.9
2007	13686.34	8910.75	7557.62	5036.19	55.2	56.5
2008	16417.07	9896.66	7551.82	4679.96	46.0	47.3
2009	20142.81	11762.06	9772.28	5556.71	48.5	47.2
2010	25284.83	14486.90	11802.18	6785.61	46.7	46.8
十二五时期			**94158.28**	**41354.62**		
2011	31388.88	16337.96	14585.68	7375.38	46.5	45.1
2012	40103.56	19154.75	16576.18	7890.08	41.3	41.2
2013	51939.51	23443.19	18828.87	8006.06	36.3	34.2
2014	58064.39	27199.41	21175.37	8702.01	36.5	32.0
2015	58095.72	29006.34	22992.18	9381.09	39.6	32.3
十三五时期						
2016	44198.73	24286.60	8878.64	3582.22	20.1	14.7

注:2016年对2015年基数进行了调整。从2016年起,固定资产投资不包含农户投资。
Note: The basic number of 2015 is adjusted in 2016.Since 2016,farmer investment isn't included in the fixed assets investment.

主要统计指标解释

全社会固定资产投资 是以货币形式表现的在一定时期内全社会建造和购置固定资产的工作量以及与此有关的费用的总称。该指标是反映固定资产投资规模、结构和发展速度的综合性指标,又是观察工程进度和考核投资效果的重要依据。全社会固定资产投资按登记注册类型可分为国有、集体、个体、联营、股份制、外商、港澳台商、其他等。

固定资产投资 指各种登记注册类型的企业、事业、行政单位及个体户进行的计划总投资500万元及500万元以上的建设项目投资、房地产开发投资、城镇和工矿区私人建房投资。

房地产开发投资 指各种登记注册类型的房地产开发公司、商品房建设公司及其他房地产开发法人单位和附属于其他法人单位实际从事房地产开发或经营活动的单位统一开发的包括统代建、拆迁还建的住宅、厂房、仓库、饭店、宾馆、度假村、写字楼、办公楼等房屋建筑物和配套的服务设施,土地开发工程(如道路、给水、排水、供电、供热、通讯、平整场地等基础设施工程)的投资;不包括单纯的土地交易活动。

城镇和工矿区私人建房投资 包括市、县城、城关镇、工矿区所辖范围内的全部私人建房,不论其房主是否系本地的常住户口均应包括。

农村投资 包括在农村区域范围内进行固定资产投资活动的企业、事业、行政单位及农村个人投资。

固定资产投资的资金来源 根据固定资产投资的资金来源不同,分为国家预算内资金、国内贷款、利用外资、自筹资金和其他资金。

(1)国家预算内资金:分为财政拨款和财政安排的贷款两部分。包括中央财政的基本建设基金(分经营性基金和非经营性基金两部分)、专项支出(如煤代油专项等)、收回再贷、贴息资金,财政安排的挖潜改造和新产品试制支出、城建支出、商业部门简易建筑支出、不发达地区发展基金等资金中用于固定资产投资的资金;地方财政中由国家统筹安排的资金等。

(2)国内贷款:指报告期固定资产投资单位向银行及非银行金融机构借入的用于固定资产投资的各种国内借款,包括银行利用自有资金及吸收的存款发放的贷款、上级主管部门拨入的国内贷款、国家专项贷款(包括煤代油贷款、劳改煤矿专项贷款等)、地方财政专项资金安排的贷款、国内储备贷款、周转贷款等。

(3)利用外资:指报告期收到的用于固定资产建造和购置的国外资金(包括设备、材料、技术在内)。包括对外借款(外国政府、国际金融组织贷款、出口信贷、外国银行商业贷款、对外发行债券和股票)、外商直接投资及外商其他投资。不包括我国自有外汇资金(国家外汇、地方外汇、留成外汇、调剂外汇和中国银行自有资金发行的外汇贷款等)。计算利用外资时,需要折算成人民币,折算中所使用的外汇汇率按现汇计算,即按使用外汇时的汇率计算。

(4)自筹资金:指固定资产投资单位报告期收到的,由各地区、各部门及企、事业单位筹集用于固定资产投资的预算外资金,包括中央各部门、各级地方和企、事业单位的自筹资金。

(5)其他资金:指在报告期收到的除以上各种资金之外其他用于固定资产投资的资金,包括企业或金融机构通过发行各种债券筹集到的资金、群众集资、个人资金、无偿捐赠的资金及其他单位拨入的资金等。

固定资产投资按国民经济行业分 根据建设项目建成投产后的主要产品或主要用途及社会经济活动性质来确定国民经济行业。一般情况下,一个建设项目或一个企业、事业单位只能属于一种国民经济行业。

固定资产投资按隶属关系分 是按建设单位或企业、事业、行政单位的主管上级机关确定的。

(1)中央:是指中共中央、人大常委会和国务院各部、委、局、总公司以及直属机构直接领导的建设项目和企业、事业、行政单位。这些单位的固定资产投资计划由国务院各部门直接编制和下达,建设中所需物资、主要设备以及建设中的问题都由中央有关部门安排和解决。

(2)地方:是由省(自治区、直辖市)、地区(州、盟、省辖市)、县(旗、县级市)三级政府及业务主管部门直接领导和管理的建设项目、企业、事业、行政单位。地方项目还包括不隶属以上各级政府及主管部门的建设项目和企业、事业单位,如外商投资企业和无主管部门的企业等。

固定资产投资按建设性质分 根据整个建设项目情况来确定。建设项目的性质一般分为新建、扩建、改建和技术改造、迁建、恢复。房地产开发单位、农村投资、城镇工矿区私人建房投资不划分建设性质。

(1)新建:一般指从无到有"平地起家"开始建设的企业、事业和行政单位或建设项目。现有企业、事业、行政单位一般不属于新建。但如有的单位原有基础很小,经过建设后新增的固定资产价值超过该企、事业、行政单位原有固定资产价值(原值)三倍以上的也应作为新建。

(2)扩建:指在厂内或其他地点,为扩大原有产品的生产能力(或效益)或增加新的产品生产能力,而增建主要的生产车间(或主要工程)、分厂、独立的生产线。行政、事业单位在原单位增建业务用房(如学校增建教学用房、医院增建门诊部、病房等)也作为扩建。

现有企、事业单位为扩大原有主要产品生产能力或增加新的产品生产能力,增建一个或几个主要生产车间(或主要工程)、分厂,同时进行一些更新改造工程的,也应作为扩建。

(3)改建和技术改造:指现有企业、事业单位,对原有设施进行技术改造或更新(包括相应配套的辅助性生产、生活福利设施)的建设项目。现有企业、事业单位为适应市场变化的需要,而改变企业的主要产品种类(如军工企业转产民用品等) 的建设项目,应作为改建。原有产品生产作业线由于各工序(车间)之间能力不平衡,为填平补齐充分发挥原有生产能力而增建不增加本企业主要产品设计能力的车间,也应作为改建。技术改造是指企业、事业单位在现有基础上,用先进的技术代替落后的技术,用先进的工艺和装备代替落后的工艺和装备,以改变企业落后的技术经济面貌,实现以内涵为主的扩大再生产,达到提高产品质量、促进产品更新换代、节约能源、降低消耗、扩大生产规模、全面提高社会经济效益的目的。技术改造具体包括以下内容:机器设备和工具的更新改造;生产工艺改革、节约能源和原材料的改造;厂房建筑和公共设施的改造;劳动条件和生产环境的改造等。

固定资产投资按构成分 固定资产投资活动按其工作内容和实现方式分为建筑安装工程,设备、工具、器具购置,其他费用三个部分。

(1)建筑安装工程(建筑安装工作量):指各种房屋、建筑物的建造工程和各种设备、装置的安装工程。包括各种房屋建造工程;各种用途设备基础和各种工业窑炉的砌筑工程及金属结构工程;为施工而进行的各种准备工作和临时工程以及完工后的清理工作等;铁路、道路的铺设,矿井的开凿及石油管道的架设等;水利工程;防空地下建筑等特殊工程;列入房屋工程预算内的暖气、卫生、通风、照明、煤气等设备的价值及装设油饰工程;列入建筑工程预算内的各种管道(蒸汽、压缩空气、石油、给排水等管道)、电力、电讯电缆导线等的敷设工程;以及各种机械设备的安装工程;为测定安装工程质量,对设备进行的试运工作;房地产开发单位进行的商品房屋开发建设工程、土地开发工程。

在安装工程中,不包括被安装设备本身的价值。

(2)设备、工具、器具购置:指建设单位或企、事业单位购置或自制的,达到固定资产标准的设备、工具、器具的价值。新建单位及扩建单位的新建车间,按照设计或计划要求购置或自制的全部设备、工具、器具,不论是否达到固定资产标准均计入"设备、工具、器具购置"中。

(3)其他费用:指在固定资产建造和购置过程中发生的,除上述几项内容以外的各种应分摊计入固定资产的费用。

施工项目 指报告期内进行过建筑或安装施工活动的项目。凡是报告期内施过工的建设项目,不论施工时间长短,均作为施工项目统计。施工项目个数可以反映一定时期固定资产投资的实际规模,与同期全部建成投产项目个数相比,可以从建设速度的角度反映固定资产投资的效果。根据建设项目施工活动的不同性质,施工项目又分为:本年正式施工项目、本年收尾项目和以前年度全部停缓建项目。

全部建成投产项目 工业项目指设计文件规定形成生产能力的主体工程及其相应配套的辅助设施全部建成,经负荷试运转,证明具备生产设计规定合格产品的条件,并经过验收鉴定合格或达到竣工验收标准,与生产性工程配套的生活福利设施可以满足近期正常生产的需要,正式移交生产的建设项目。非工业项目指设计文件规定的主体工程和相应的配套工程全部建成,能够发挥设计规定的全部效益,经验收鉴定合格或达到竣工验收标准,正式移交使用的建设项目。

新增生产能力(或工程效益) 指通过固定资产投资活动而增加的设计能力(或工程效益),该指标是以实物形态表现的反映固定资产投资成果的指标,也是考核投资经济效果的重要依据之一。

房屋建筑面积 指房屋建筑物勒脚以上外墙外围的水平截面面积,包括房屋建筑物的有效面积和结构面积。该指标是从实物形态上反映建设规模和建设成果的重要指标之一,也是检查工程形象进度、计算工程造价、分析投资效果、研究施工任务和建筑材料之间平衡情况的重要依据。

住宅建筑面积 指施工和竣工房屋建筑面积中供居住用的房屋建筑面积。

施工面积 指报告期内施工的全部房屋建筑面积。包括本期新开工的面积和上期开工跨入本期继续施工的房屋面积,以及上期已停建在本期恢复施工的房屋面积。本期竣工和本期施工后又停缓建的房屋,其建筑面积仍计入本期房屋施工面积中。

竣工面积 指在报告期内房屋建筑按照设计要求已经全部完工,达到住人和使用条件,经验收鉴定合格(或达到竣工验收标准),正式移交使用单位的各栋房屋建筑面积的总和。

房屋建筑面积竣工率 指一定时期内房屋竣工面积占同期房屋施工面积的比率。是从房屋建筑施工速度的角度反映投资效果的指标。

新增固定资产 指报告期内已经完成建造和购置过程,并已交付生产或使用单位的固定资产价值。该指标是表示固定资产投资成果的价值指标,也是反映建设进度,计算固定资产投资效果的重要指标。

项目建设投产率 指一定时期内全部建成投产项目个数与同期施工项目个数的比率。该指标是从建设单位建设速度的角度反映投资效果的指标。

固定资产交付使用率 指一定时期新增固定资产与同期完成投资额的比率。该指标是反映固定资产动用速度,衡量建设过程中宏观投资效果的综合指标。由于新增固定资产是较长时期内形成的结果,而投资额则是当年完成的,因此,该指标一般适宜于反映较长时期内固定资产的动用情况。

商品房销售面积 指报告期内出售商品房屋的合同总面积(即双方签署的正式买卖合同中所确定的建筑面积)。由现房销售建筑面积和期房销售建筑面积两部分组成。

商品房销售额 指报告期内出售商品房屋的合同总价款(即双方签署的正式买卖合同中所确定的合同总价)。该指标与商品房销售面积同口径,由现房销售额和期房销售额两部分组成。

经济适用房 指根据地方经济适用房计划安排建设的政策性住宅。经济是指房屋建筑造价和销售价格低于一般商品住宅;适用是指适合中低收入家庭购买使用。经济适用房主要是由国家统一下达投资计划,房地产公司开发,对外销售;用地一般采用行政划拨或招标投标方式,免收土地出让金;对各种经批准的收费减半征收,开发利润不超过3%;销售价格实行政府指导价。该指标可以分析房地产投资结构,反映中低收入家庭商品住宅的供求平衡情况。

Explanatory Notes on Main Statistical Indicators

Total Investment in Fixed Assets in the Whole Country refers to the volume of activities in construction and purchases of fixed assets and related fees, expressed in monetary terms. It is a comprehensive indicator which shows the size, structure and growth of the investment in fixed assets, providing basis for observing the progress of construction projects and evaluating results of investment. Total investment in fixed assets in the whole country includes, by type of ownership, the investment by the state-owned units, collective units, individuals, joint ownership units, share-holding units, as well as investment by businessmen from foreign countries and from Hong Kong, Macao and Taiwan, and by other units.

Investment in Fixed Assets refers to construction projects involving a total planned investment of 500,000 yuan and over by enterprises and institutions of various types of ownership, by administrative units and by individuals, investment in real estate development, and housing investment by individuals in urban areas and in industrial and mining areas.

Investment in Real Estate Development refers to the investment by the real estate development companies, commercial buildings construction companies and other real estate development units of various types of ownership in the construction of house buildings, such as residential buildings, factory buildings, warehouses, hotels, guesthouses, holiday villages, office buildings, and the complementary service facilities and land development projects, such as roads, water supply, water drainage, power supply, heating, telecommunications, land leveling and other projects of infrastructure. It excludes the activities in pure land transactions.

Investment in Housing Construction in Urban Areas and in Industrial and Mining Areas refers to all private housing construction under the jurisdiction of cities, county towns and industrial and mining areas, no matter whether the owner of the house is registered as the permanent resident in the locality or not.

Investment in Rural Areas refers to investment in fixed assets by enterprises, institutions and individuals in rural areas.

Sources of Funds for Investment in Fixed Assets include fund from state budget, domestic loans, foreign investment, self-raised funds, and others depending on the source of investment.

(1) Fund from state budget consists of budgetary appropriation and loans from state budget. More specifically, it includes, from the budget of the central government, capital construction fund (operation fund and non–operational fund), special expenses (e.g. expenses on substituting petroleum with coal), loans from repayment, discount fund, expenses on innovation and trial production of new products, expenses on urban construction, expenses on temporary construction by trade departments, development fund for less developed areas, as well as local budgetary fund transferred from the central budget.

(2) Domestic loans refer to loans of various forms borrowed by investing units from banks and non–bank financial institutions during the reference period for the purpose of investment in fixed assets, including loans issued by banks from their self–owned funds and deposit, loans appropriated by higher responsible authorities, special loans by government (including loan for substituting petroleum with coal, special loan for reform–through–labour coal mines), loans arranged by local government from special funds, domestic reserve loan, and working loan, etc..

(3) Foreign Investment refers to foreign funds received during the reference period for the construction and purchase of investment in fixed assets (covering equipment, materials and technology), including foreign borrowings (loans from foreign governments and international financial institutions, export credit, commercial loans from foreign banks, issue of bonds and stocks overseas), foreign direct investment and other foreign investment. Excluded in this category are capitals in foreign exchanges owned by China (foreign exchanges owned by the central and local governments, foreign exchanges retained by enterprises, foreign exchanges by enterprises through regulating mechanism, loans in foreign exchanges issued by the Bank of China with its own fund, etc.). In calculating the utilization of foreign capitals, foreign currencies are converted into Chinese Renminbi applying the current exchange rate when the foreign capitals are actually used.

(4) Self–raised funds refer to extra–budgetary funds for investment in fixed assets received by investing units from central government ministries, local governments, enterprises and institutions, including their self–raised funds.

(5) Others refer to funds for investment in fixed assets received from the sources other than those listed above, including capitals raised through issuing bonds by enterprises or financial institutions, funds raised from individuals and through donations, and funds transferred from other units.

Investment in Fixed Assets by Sector The classification of construction projects by sector is determined by the major products or the purpose of the projects when they are put into production or use, and by the nature of their social economic activities. In general, one project or one enterprise or institution can only be classified into one sector.

Investment in Fixed Assets by Jurisdiction of Management refers to the classification of investment by the competent authorities under which investment is made by construction units, enterprises, institutions or administrative units.

(1) Central investment refers to the investment in projects or by enterprises, institutions or administrative units which are under the direct leadership and management of the CPC Central Committee, the NPC Standing Committee, the State Council and of the national commissions, ministries, agencies and state–owned large corporations. Various ministries and departments of the State Council prepare and implement plans for investment in fixed assets by those departments, and arrange and ensure the supply of materials and key equipment required for the projects.

(2) Local investment refers to the investment in projects or by enterprises, institutions or administrative units which are under the direct leadership and management of departments under the provincial, prefecture and county governments. Also included are projects by foreign–invested enterprises and enterprises without competent managing authorities.

Investment in Fixed Assets by Type of Construction The construction projects in general can be classified, by the type of construction, into new construction, expansion, reconstruction and technical transformation, moving and restoration. However, investment by type of construction is not applied to investment by real–estate development units, investment in rural areas and investment in housing by urban individuals.

(1) New construction in general refers to newly constructed enterprises, institutions, administrative agencies or independent projects from scratch. Construction in the existing enterprises, institutions or agencies is not considered as new construction. In case the assets of the existing unit is quite small, and the value of newly added fixed assets exceeds the original value of assets by three times, the expansion will be considered as new construction.

(2) Expansion refers to construction of new major production workshop, branch factory or independent production line within a facto–

ry or in other locations, for the purpose of increasing the production capacity (or improving efficiency) of the original products. Newly constructed houses for the operation of institutions and administrative organizations (such as the newly constructed buildings for teaching in schools, buildings for clinics or wards in hospitals, etc.) are also classified as expansion.

Also included in the expansion are investments by existing enterprises or institutions in building major production line(s) or branch factory(ies) along with some work on innovation, for the purpose of expending the production capacity of original products or producing new products.

(3) Reconstruction refers to construction projects by existing enterprises or institutions in innovation or technical transformation of the old facilities (including auxiliary production equipment and welfare facilities). Also considered as reconstruction is the construction of new workshops by the existing enterprises or institutions to change the variety of products to meet the market demand (such as the production of civil products by defence industries), or to bring the designed production capacity into full play through a more balanced production process on production lines. Technical transformation refers to replacement of old technology or equipment by new technology or equipment, in order to expand the reproduction through improvement of technology contents in production, to improve product quality, to promote new products, to save energy and reduce consumption and to improve overall social–economic efficiency. Contents of technical transformation include: updating of machinery, equipment and tools; reforming production process by using energy or materials saving technology; construction of factory workshops and transformation of public facilities; improvement of working conditions and environment, etc.

Investment in Fixed Assets by Structure By their contents, investment activities are classified into 3 categories, i.e. construction and installation, purchase of equipment and instrument, and other expenses.

(1) Construction and installation (work volume of construction and installation) refers to the construction of various houses and buildings and installation of various kinds of equipment and instruments. They include construction of various houses; equipment foundations, industrial kilns and stoves, and metal structure work; preparation works for project construction, and clearing up works post project construction; pavement of railways and roads, drilling of mines and putting up of oil pipes; construction of projects of water conservancy; construction of underground air–raid shelters and construction of other special projects; value of equipment for heating, sanitation, ventilation, lighting, gas, painting, etc. that are covered by the budget of housing projects; laying out of various pipelines (for steam, compressed air, petroleum, tap water and sewage) and lines for electric power and for communications; installation of various machinery equipment, testing operation for pre–testing the quality of installation projects, and land and other development work conducted by real estate developers for commercial housing. The value of equipment installed is not included in the value of installation projects.

(2) Purchase of equipment and instruments refers to the total value of equipment, tools, and instruments purchased or self–produced which come up to standards for fixed assets by the construction units or investing enterprises or institutions. Equipment, tools and instruments purchased or self–produced for new workshops by newly established or expanded units are categorized as "purchase of equipment and instruments" no matter whether they come up to the standards for fixed assets.

(3) Other expenses refer to expenses occurring during the construction or purchase of fixed assets other than those mentioned above.

Projects under Construction refer to projects with construction and installation activities undertaken in the reference period. All projects that have construction activities undertaken during the reference period are reported as projects under construction irrespective of the length of construction work. The number of projects under construction can reflect the actual size of investment in fixed assets during a given period, and when compared with the number of projects completed and put into use during the same period, it demonstrates the results of investment in fixed assets. Depending on the nature of construction activities, projects under construction can also be classified into projects under construction in current year, winding–up projects in current year and stopped or suspended projects in previous years (with preservation work in current year).

Projects Completed and Put into Use Industrial projects refer to the major projects and accessory facilities completed which result in forming production capacity and have been checked and accepted while the living and welfare facilities have been completed and can ensure normal production and formally put into production. Non–industrial projects refer to the major projects and accessory facilities completed which possess the designed capacity and have been checked, accepted and formally put into production.

Newly Increased Production Capacity(or Project Efficiency) refers to the increase of designed capacity (or project effi–

ciency) through investment in fixed assets, which reflects the accomplishment of investment in fixed assets in kind and serves as important basis for evaluating the economic efficiency of investment.

Floor Space of Buildings under Construction refers to total floor space of the horizontal section of outer walls above the plinth of the building, including the effective area and the area occupied by the structure. This indicator is one of the important indicators in physical terms to reflect the scale and accomplishment of the construction industry, and important basis for monitoring the progress, calculating the cost, analyzing the efficiency and studying the supply of building materials in relation with the construction projects.

Floor Space of Residential Buildings refers to the floor space of the residential buildings among the total space of buildings under construction or completed.

Floor Space under Construction refers to total floor space of all buildings under construction during the reference period, including floor space of newly started buildings during the reference period, floor space of construction extended from the previous period to the current period, and floor space of construction suspended during the previous period and resumed in the current period. Floor space of construction completed in the current period, and floor space of construction started and then suspended in the current period are also included in the floor space under construction of the current year.

Floor Space of Buildings Completed refers to the floor space of all buildings completed in the reference period, which have been appraised and accepted (or come up to the designed standards) and have been transferred to the owners for use.

Completion Rate of Floor Space of Buildings refers to the ratio of the floor space of buildings completed in certain period of time to the floor space of buildings under construction in the same period. This indicator reflects the investment result from the perspective of the speed of construction.

Newly Increased Fixed Assets refer to the newly increased value of fixed assets, constructed or purchased, that have been transferred to the investors. This is an indicator that demonstrates the results of investment in fixed assets in monetary terms, and an important indicator to reflect the speed of construction and to calculate the efficiency of investment.

Rate of Construction Projects Completed and Put into Use refers to the ratio of the number of construction projects completed and put into use in certain period of time to the number of projects under construction in the same period. This reflects the investment efficiency from the perspective of the speed of projects construction.

Rate of Projects of Fixed Assets Completed and Put into Operation refers to the ratio of the newly increased fixed assets to the total investment made in the same period. This is a comprehensive indicator reflecting the speed of the employment of fixed assets and the investment efficiency at the macro-level. As the newly increase fixed assets is the result of a long period while the investment is completed in the current year, this indicator is expected to be used to reflect the employment of fixed assets over a long period of time.

Area of Commercial Housing Sold refers to total contracted area of commercial housing (i.e. area of floor space as designated in the formal contracts signed by both sides) during the reference time. It constitutes floor space of completed housing and floor space of future housing.

Value of Commercial Housing Sold refer to total value of contracts (i.e. value of sales/purchase for selling/purchase of commercial housing as designated in the contracts signed by both sides) during the reference time. It has the same coverage as the area of commercial housing sold, constituting completed housing and floor space of future housing

Economically Affordable Housing refers to housing constructed according to the state plan for economically affordable housing. Houses of this category featured in low cost in construction and low prices, and therefore are affordable to mid-income or low income households. Economically affordable housing projects are developed by real estate companies under the state investment plan, with the land provided through government allocation or tendering procedures. Developers are exempted from land utilization fees and enjoy another 50% exemption of all other legitimate fees, while their profits are limited to less than 3%, and the completed houses are sold under the government-guided prices. This indicator helps to analyze the investment structure of the real estate industry and the demand and supply of housing for mid or low income households.

5 对外经济贸易和旅游

Foreign Economic, Trade and Tourism

5-1 对外经济主要指标
MAJOR INDICATORS OF FOREIGN TRADE AND ECONOMIC COOPERATION

单位:万美元 (USD 10 000)

指 标	Item	1995	2000	2005	2010	2013	2014	2015	2016
进出口总额	**Total Imports and Exports**	**340920**	**320249**	**905475**	**2593211**	**3638928**	**4306401**	**4558578**	**3939760**
进口总额	Total Imports	142484	127369	462607	1149031	1355160	1641821	1637232	1332470
出口总额	Total Exports	198435	192880	442868	1444180	2283768	2664580	2921346	2607290
合同外商直接投资项目(个)	**Contracted Projets of Foreign Direct Investment (uint)**	**881**	**331**	**520**	**306**	**297**	**301**	**274**	**235**
合同外商直接投资	**Contracted Value of Foreign Direct Investment**	**108847**	**106583**	**211023**	**278627**	**485467**	**629624**	**416112**	**334118**
实际外商直接投资	**Actual Value of Foreign Direct Investment**	**62253**	**94368**	**218475**	**405015**	**688847**	**792792**	**894801**	**1012889**
对外经济合作	**Economic and Technical Cooperation with Foreign** Countries								
合同金额	Contracted Value	7300	36706	35953	776945	1033540			
#对外承包工程	#Contracted Projects			27952	765547	1015084	1269954	1145362	1263523
对外劳务合作	Labor Services			5568	11398	12286			
完成营业额	Value of Business Fulfilled	4100	15815	31843	327164	538927			
#对外承包工程	#Contracted Projects			28852	319979	520733	579636	523369	511109
对外劳务合作	Labor Services			2601	7186	18194			

5-2 对外贸易进出口总额
TOTAL IMPORTS AND EXPORTS

单位:万美元 (USD 10 000)

年 份 Year	合 计 Total	进 口 Imports	出 口 Exports
1992	174533	58696	115837
1995	340920	142484	198435
1996	286287	133684	152603
1997	320668	128583	192084
1998	283189	112478	170711
1999	268107	116729	151378
2000	320249	127369	192880
2001	357720	178041	179679
2002	395314	185488	209826
2003	510930	245393	265537
2004	676581	338361	338219
2005	905475	462607	442868
2006	1176219	550157	626063
2007	1489647	669593	820054
2008	2070567	899676	1170891
2009	1725102	727222	997880
2010	2593211	1149031	1444180
2011	3358693	1405233	1953460
2012	3196409	1256525	1939884
2013	3638928	1355160	2283768
2014	4306401	1641821	2664580
2015	4558578	1637232	2921346
2016	3939760	1332470	2607290

注:根据海关统计有关文件规定2008年年终数据部分调整。

Note:According to the provisions of the relevant documents to customs statistics data portion of the 2008 year-end adjustments.

5-3 按贸易方式和经济类型分的进出口总额

单位:万美元

项 目	Item	2000		2005	
		进口 Imports	出口 Exports	进口 Imports	出口 Exports
总 计	**Total**	**127369**	**192880**	**462607**	**442868**
按贸易方式分	**Grouped by Type of Trade**				
一般贸易	General Trade	91576	138907	340768	350354
来料加工装配贸易	Processing and Assembling Trade	20136	13265	15428	22381
进料加工贸易	Raw Material Input Processing Trade	32803	14154	54328	71920
来料加工装配进口的设备	Processing and Assembling Import Equipment Provided With Material	6		18	
外商作为投资进口的设备	Goods as Invested for Import Equipments	8602		45087	
租赁贸易	Leasing Trade			114	
出料加工贸易	Raw Material Output Processing Trade				
易货贸易	Repalce Goods with Goods				
保税仓库进出境货物	Import and Export Goods of Protcetive Tariff Storage	105		8028	33
按经济类型分	**Grouped by Ownership**				
#国有企业	#State-Owned Enterprises	64805	140826	221963	213955
集体企业	Collective-Owned Enterprises	1255	9124	5719	20033
外商投资企业	Foreign-funded Enterprises	61691	42901	190170	130579
民营企业	Private-Owned Enterprises	111	240	45839	80397

TOTAL IMPORTS AND EXPORTS VOLUME BY TYPE OF TRADE AND OWNERSHIP

(USD 10 000)

2010		2013		2014		2015		2016	
进口 Imports	出口 Exports	进口 Imports	出口 Exports	进口 Imports	出口 Exports	进口 Imports	出口 Exports	进口 Imports	出口 Exports
1149031	**1444180**	**1355160**	**2283768**	**1641821**	**2664580**	**1637232**	**2921346**	**1332470**	**2607290**
841306	829994	1000601	1520152	1164862	1845637	1088411	1961768	1016458	1816526
28304	32269	18128	38854	14331	54818	11584	798372	11591	71337
210483	518911	281413	593316	430709	704313	487467	53984	177423	583486
348		230		38		29		15	
43809		13487		12775		8312		4626	
5	144	5	150	96	70		10	63	
320	212	729	532	822	729	913	607	766	349
20511	16794	32427	38794	9389	17789	1630	16982	45252	9537
513134	**472230**	**452200**	**527257**	**481941**	**545399**	**401246**	**574791**	**366613**	**469965**
4021	16161	2427	19933	1746	19684	1398	18099	1126	15948
534565	569501	665555	732420	682190	772107	556216	674909	462757	601574
93032	386177	190004	1002635	455332	1326652	679603	1653454	500974	1516962

5-4 进出口商品主要国别和地区
IMPORTS AND EXPORTS VALUE BY COUNTRIES AND REGIONS

单位:万美元 (USD 10 000)

国家(地区)	Countries (Regions)	2015			2016		
		进出口 Imports and Exports	进口 Imports	出口 Exports	进出口 Imports and Exports	进口 Imports	出口 Exports
亚 洲	**Asia**	**2687717**	**956719**	**1730999**	**2226572**	**762384**	**1464188**
#香港	#Hongkong	723497	78844	644653	466378	1296	465082
印度	India	179956	8760	171196	162382	11675	150706
日本	Japan	304607	205522	99085	304019	211595	92424
新加坡	Singapore	85489	28734	56755	68204	19856	48349
韩国	Korea, Rep.	209909	124842	85067	202018	126910	75108
台湾省	Taiwan Province	175970	122480	53490	185851	117095	68756
非 洲	**Afria**	**198382**	**74157**	**124225**	**149235**	**64812**	**84422**
#南非	#South Africa	59448	45158	14290	58555	46462	12092
欧 洲	**European**	**705112**	**233314**	**471798**	**648924**	**195804**	**453121**
#比利时	#Belgium						
英国	United Kingdom						
德国	Germany	136453	68803	67650	123748	57733	66015
法国	France	101523	78865	22658	77595	56654	20941
意大利	Italy						
荷兰	Netherland						
西班牙	Spanish						
芬兰	Finland						
拉丁美洲	**Latin America**	**325830**	**124259**	**201571**	**317376**	**117446**	**199929**
#巴西	#Brazil	82284	47393	34891	93431	35666	57765
智利	Chile						
北美洲	**North America**	**469525**	**142621**	**326905**	**466578**	**109458**	**357120**
#加拿大	#Canada						
美国	United States of America	425177	118461	306716	425413	85572	339841
大洋洲	**Occeania**	**173929**	**107386**	**66543**	**130666**	**82157**	**48509**
#澳大利亚	#Australia	150332	107185	43147	108343	79307	29036
附:东南亚国家联盟	**Association of Southeast-Asia Nations**	**637841**	**268060**	**369781**	**471742**	**136768**	**334974**
欧洲联盟	**European Union**	**612001**	**220188**	**391813**	**551733**	**185598**	**366136**
亚太经济合作组织	**Asia-Pacific Economic Cooperation**	**2883838**	**1098367**	**1785470**	**2582811**	**995132**	**1587679**

5-5 合同外商直接投资项目

NUMBER OF CONTRACTED PROJECTS OF FOREIGN DIRECT INVESTMENT

单位:个 (unit)

指 标	Item	1990	1995	2000	2005	2010	2012	2013	2014	2015	2016
合 计	**Total**	**99**	**881**	**331**	**520**	**306**	**271**	**297**	**301**	**274**	**235**
合资经营企业	Joint Venture	17	577	156	203	108	102	116	127	101	92
合作经营企业	Cooperative Operation	75	44	16	29	5	5	8	3	4	1
独资经营企业	Foreign Solely Funded Enterprises	7	260	158	285	193	164	173	169	168	139
外商投资股份制企业	Share Holding Enterprises With Foreign Investment			1	3				2	1	3

5-6 合同外商直接投资金额

VALUE OF CONTRACTED PROJECTS OF FOREIGN DIRECT INVESTMENT

单位:万美元 (USD 10 000)

指 标	Item	1990	1995	2000	2005	2010	2012	2013	2014	2015	2016
合 计	**Total**	**3947**	**108847**	**106583**	**211023**	**278627**	**363927**	**485467**	**629624**	**416112**	**334118**
合资经营企业	Joint Venture	1364	68923	27936	51010	132679	93573	135618	262121	78912	124301
合作经营企业	Cooperative Operation	2464	7899	48711	24480	3319	7315	15924	13424	11078	1171
独资经营企业	Foreign Solely Funded	119	32025	29936	132897	235498	252964	334151	345271	313337	195939
外商投资股份制企业	Share Holding Enterprises With Foreign Investment				2636	33519	10075	-226	8808	12785	12707

5-7 实际外商直接投资金额
ACTUAL VALUE OF FOREIGN DIRECT INVESTMENT

单位:万美元 (USD 10 000)

指 标	Item	1990	1995	2000	2004	2005	2010
合 计	**Total**	**2900**	**62253**	**94368**	**207126**	**218475**	**405015**
合资经营企业	Joint Venture	2492	40259	59879	130048	65472	132679
合作经营企业	Cooperative Operation	85	5012	2789	11741	5089	3319
独资经营企业	Foreign Solely Funded	323	16982	31700	62155	75305	235498
外商投资股份制企业	Share Holding With Foreign Investment					2739	33519

5-7 续表 continued

单位:万美元

指 标	Item	2011	2012	2013	2014	2015	2016
合 计	**Total**	**465503**	**566591**	**688847**	**792792**	**894801**	**1012889**
合资经营企业	Joint Venture	202268	257765	223950	300982	329123	359083
合作经营企业	Cooperative Operation	2992	647	3758	759	4261	7480
独资经营企业	Foreign Solely Funded	231847	298393	442107	440949	548452	548867
外商投资股份制企业	Share Holding Enterprises With Foreign Investment	28396	9786	19032	35969	9325	56625

5-8 按行业分外商直接投资(2016)
FOREIGN DIRECT INVESTMENT GROUPED BY SECTOR (2016)

行 业	Item	项目(个) Number of Projects (unit)	合同外资 (万美元) Contracted Foreign Capital (USD 10 000)	实际投资 (万美元) Actual Foreign Investment (USD 10 000)
总 计	**Total**	**235**	**334118**	**1012889**
农、林、牧、渔业	Farming, Forestry, Animal Husbandry and Fishery	13	113298	9364
采矿业	Mining and Quarrying	1	558	4480
制造业	Manufactruring	41	115548	547480
电力、燃气及水的生产和供应业	Power, Gas and Water Production and Supply	10	20354	42776
建筑业	Construction	2	1015	1250
交通运输、仓储和邮政业	Transportation, Storage and Post	10	25819	42218
信息传输、计算机服务和软件业	Information Transmmision, Computer Service and software	11	4064	200
批发和零售业	Wholesale and Retail sale	54	22210	76809
住宿和餐饮业	Hotel and Catering	8	1957	19567
金融业	Finance	2	3333	39048
房地产业	Real Estate	2	-23105	164097
租赁和商务服务业	Leasing and Commerical Service	44	31039	46081
科学研究、技术服务和地质勘查业	Scietific research, Polytechnical Service and Geological Prospecting	27	5274	13029
水利、环境和公共设施管理业	Water Conservancy, Environment and Public Facility Management	4	11646	745
居民服务和其他服务业	Resident Service and Others	2	30	4378
教育	Education			
卫生、社会保障和社会福利业	Health Care, Social Security and Social Welfare	1	400	
文化、体育和娱乐业	Culture, Sports and Recreation	3	678	1367

5-9 年末登记外商投资企业行业分布情况(2016)
SECTOR DISTRIBUTION REGISTERED OF FOREIGN-FUNDED ENTERPRISES AT THE YEAR-END(2016)

单位:个 (unit)

行 业	Item	企业数 Number of Enterprises
总 计	**Total**	**235**
农、林、牧、渔业	Farming, Forestry, Animal Husbandry and Fishery	13
采矿业	Mining and Quarrying	1
制造业	Manufactruring	41
电力、燃气及水的生产和供应业	Power, Gas and Water Production and Supply	10
建筑业	Construction	2
交通运输、仓储和邮政业	Transportation, Storage and Post	10
信息传输、计算机服务和软件业	Information Transmmision, Computer Service and software	11
批发和零售业	Wholesale and Retail sale	54
住宿和餐饮业	Hotel and Catering	8
金融业	Finance	2
房地产业	Real Estate	2
租赁和商务服务业	Leasing and Commerical Service	44
科学研究、技术服务和地质勘查业	Scietific research, Polytechnical Service and Geological Prospecting	27
水利、环境和公共设施管理业	Water Conservancy, Environment and Public Facility Management	4
居民服务和其他服务业	Resident Service and Others	2
教育	Education	
卫生、社会保障和社会福利业	Health Care, Social Security and Social Welfare	1
文化、体育和娱乐业	Culture, Sports and Recreation	3

5-10 对外承包工程和劳务合作
CONTRACTED PROJECTS AND LABOR SERVICES CO-OPERATION WITH FOREIGN COUNTRIES

年份 Year	Item	合同金额 (万美元) Contracted Value (USD 10 000)	实际完成营业额 (万美元) Value of Business Fulfilled (USD 10 000)	年末在外人数(人) Number of Persons Working Abroad at Year-end (person)
对外承包工程	**Contracted Projects**			
2003		17900	28552	1759
2004		28027	25334	2199
2005		27952	28852	2365
2006		56930	36266	2671
2007		183749	54416	5950
2008		318872	142456	9145
2009		526671	256368	10546
2010		765547	319978	17655
2011		631308	406741	13961
2012		726900	456194	16404
2013		1021254	520733	20801
2014		1269954	579636	31957
2015		1145362	523369	16406
2016		1263523	511109	20274
对外劳务合作	**Labor Cooperation**			
2003		823	1783	3136
2004		1565	1597	3583
2005		5568	2601	5143
2006		6331	4379	7602
2007		6520	5340	8704
2008		6016	6856	6239
2009		6208	6988	4602
2010		11398	7186	4717
2011		7965	8261	3425
2012		11045	9669	8258
2013		12286	18194	8296
2014				
2015				
2016				
对外设计咨询	**Design Consulting**			
2002		541	267	42
2003		507	650	28
2004		475	1517	72
2005		390	2433	91
2006		983	452	90
2007		5423	2511	461
2008		6531	2804	22

注:2009年起"对外设计咨询"指标数并入"对外承包工程"中;"年末在外人数(人)"修订为"劳务外派人数(人)"
Note:From 2009, "design and consultation," index number into the "International Contractors" in; "at the end of outer (person)" to "manning (person)".

5-11 湖北旅游主要指标
MAJOR INDICATORS OF HUBEI TOURISM

年 份 Year	旅游总收入 (亿元) Total Earnings of Tourism (100 million yuan)	国内旅游收入 (亿元) Earnings from Domestic Tourism (100 million yuan)	国内旅游人数 (万人次) Number of Domestic Tourists (10 000 persons-time)	外汇收入 (万美元) Foreign Exchange Earnings (USD 10 000)	入境旅游人数 (万人次) Number of Tourists Received (10 000 persons-time)
1982				299.60	2.00
1983				355.30	2.40
1984				731.30	5.40
1985				1008.60	8.50
1986	3.47	2.50	1262	1166.00	10.50
1987	3.67	2.40	1184	1545.00	12.20
1988	3.56	2.40	1208	1411.80	11.30
1989	3.99	3.10	1034	1085.50	8.20
1990	4.56	2.70	890	2263.20	15.60
1991	5.83	3.90	984	2350.00	17.00
1992	9.03	5.40	1071	4432.20	26.30
1993	13.26	9.50	1350	4588.90	23.10
1994	18.09	13.00	1500	6211.40	24.70
1995	24.00	18.00	1700	7316.90	27.10
1996	163.28	153.00	3152	12545.60	36.90
1997	193.92	180.00	3600	16977.50	58.00
1998	217.24	210.00	4044	8831.40	29.60
1999	247.11	238.50	4659	10498.50	30.50
2000	282.26	270.30	5478	14572.10	45.10
2001	353.66	337.20	6064	20075.20	66.80
2002	407.48	384.20	6670	28390.90	102.40
2003	342.77	331.60	5684	13626.90	40.50
2004	410.00	394.20	6849	19240.40	61.20
2005	473.15	450.80	7630	27636.30	82.60
2006	539.74	514.24	8459.78	32000.38	105.57
2007	640.87	609.40	10135.00	41264.00	131.81
2008	744.19	713.43	11678.00	44255.31	118.75
2009	1004.48	969.63	15065.18	51020.22	133.46
2010	1460.53	1409.48	20946.00	75116.49	181.74
2011	1992.89	1931.80	27154.87	94018.00	213.52
2012	2629.54	2553.55	34230.00	120296.72	264.72
2013	3205.61	3130.13	40621.04	121892.18	267.96
2014	3752.11	3675.98	46900.00	123851.30	277.07
2015	4308.76	4206.02	50668.24	167190.01	311.76
2016	4879.24	4764.18	56930.83	187238.97	337.56

5-12 接待入境旅游人数
NUMBER OF ENTRANCE TOURISTS

单位:人次 (person-times)

年 份 Year	总计 Total	外国人 Foreigners	港澳台同胞 Compatroits from Hongkong, Maco and Taiwan	#港澳同胞 #Compatroits from Hongkong, Macao	#台湾同胞 #Compatroits from Taiwan
1982	19775	15126	4649		
1983	24200	18903	5297		
1984	53800	40496	13304		
1985	84598	68103	16495		
1986	105300	83570	21730		
1987	122390	82029	40361		
1988	113051	78206	34845	19725	15120
1989	81781	49511	32270	13908	18362
1990	155734	36374	119360	11560	107800
1991	170121	53055	117066	12645	104421
1992	263401	72691	190323	14054	176269
1993	230883	84552	146331	28460	117871
1994	247212	133343	113869	56417	57452
1995	270890	172869	98021	42785	55236
1996	368877	243595	125282	58949	66333
1997	580223	359700	220523	64466	156057
1998	295643	209402	86241	30337	55904
1999	305408	224748	80660	30935	49725
2000	450805	357352	93453	42928	53162
2001	667818	542737	125081	48417	76664
2002	1024312	755718	268594	49113	219481
2003	405214	323151	82063	40294	41769
2004	611859	501873	109986	57086	52900
2005	825700	626805	198895	107141	91754
2006	1055752	857028	198724	110246	88478
2007	1318179	1077189	240990	140384	100606
2008	1187549	926625	260924	152631	108293
2009	1334634	1017620	317014	182616	134398
2010	1817416	1385457	431959	241430	190529
2011	2135247	1601129	534118	291487	242631
2012	2647163	1929571	717592	410921	306671
2013	2679623	2047316	632307	365184	267123
2014	2770689	2132562	638127	363810	274317
2015	3117592	2397892	719700	377115	342585
2016	3375628	2546454	829174	390797	438377

5-13 入境旅游外汇收入
FOREIGN EXCHANGE REVENUE OF ENTRANCE TOURISTS

年份 Year	外汇收入(万美元) Foreign Exchange Earnings (USD 10 000)	发展指数(1978年为100) Development Index (year1978=100)	同比 Comparision Percentage (±%)	人均天花费(美元) Expenditures Per Capita (USD)
1982	299.64	129.85	82.00	
1983	355.30	153.98	18.58	
1984	731.30	316.92	105.83	
1985	1008.58	327.69	37.92	
1986	1166.00	505.31	15.61	
1987	1545.00	669.56	32.50	
1988	1411.75	611.81	-8.62	
1989	1085.45	470.40	-23.11	
1990	2263.18	980.79	108.50	
1991	2350.00	1018.42	3.84	
1992	4432.16	1920.76	88.60	
1993	4588.88	1988.68	3.54	
1994	6211.42	2691.84	35.36	125.10
1995	7316.86	3170.90	17.80	155.70
1996	12545.60	5436.88	71.46	167.04
1997	16977.51	7357.53	35.33	168.52
1998	8831.43	3827.27	-47.98	162.87
1999	10498.49	4549.72	18.88	166.31
2000	14572.13	6315.12	38.80	166.58
2001	20075.16	8699.96	37.76	164.25
2002	28390.95	12303.77	41.42	160.57
2003	13626.93	5905.50	-52.00	160.57
2004	19240.41	8338.21	51.00	169.92
2005	27636.30	11976.73	43.64	170.14
2006	32000.38	13867.99	15.79	177.16
2007	41264.00	17882.56	28.95	181.68
2008	44255.31	19178.90	7.25	197.56
2009	51020.22	22110.60	15.29	193.43
2010	75116.49	32553.20	47.23	192.84
2011	94018.00	40744.53	25.16	195.36
2012	120296.72	52132.92	27.95	193.04
2013	121892.18	52824.35	1.33	194.44
2014	123851.30	53675.70	1.61	194.40
2015	167190.01	72458.19	34.99	230.65
2016	187238.97	81143.65	11.99	233.27

5-14 接待入境旅游者天数
NUMBER OF DAYS THE ENTRANCE TOURISTS STAYED IN HUBEI

单位：人天 (person/day)

年 份 Year	总计 Total	外国人 Foreigners	港澳台同胞 Compatroits from Hongkong, Maco and Taiwan	#港澳同胞 #Compatroits from Hongkong, Macao	#台湾同胞 #Compatroits from Taiwan
1981	22946	15282	7664		
1982	29016	24188	4828		
1983	29830	25298	4532		
1984	107600	37806	69794		
1985	143815	115774	28041		
1986	186379	139677	46702		
1987	167035	115219	51816		
1988	190486	132301	58185	35505	22680
1989	127891	79217	48674	20862	27812
1990	178737	49487	129250	11960	117290
1991	235595	74913	160682	17450	143232
1992	351591	101878	249713	18973	230740
1993	324350	142240	182110	49959	132151
1994	472467	231716	240751	117889	122862
1995	501038	317246	183792	86910	96882
1996	729968	477152	252816	131993	120823
1997	949661	591127	358534	111291	247243
1998	513569	366348	147221	61491	85730
1999	622037	478486	143551	57765	85786
2000	852455	676130	176325	81432	94893
2001	1208938	891787	317151	93376	223775
2002	1712230	1232818	479412	86427	392985
2003	799824	603001	196823	98230	98593
2004	1069442	849071	220371	118234	102137
2005	1513678	1135995	377683	194122	183561
2006	1824387	1502277	322110	176901	145209
2007	2342786	1926484	416302	233946	182356
2008	2217172	1734211	482961	243638	239323
2009	2640362	2025972	614390	338898	275492
2010	3750746	2868024	882722	481484	401238
2011	4596252	3494098	1102154	581193	520961
2012	5934359	4424239	1510060	822210	687850
2013	6009111	4581165	1427946	802642	625304
2014	6370867	4926991	1443876	805502	638374
2015	7248536	5634388	1614448	833216	781232
2016	8026469	6119616	1901053	906834	994219

注：2000年国家不再设“华侨”指标，“华侨”人数含在“外国人”中。
Note:The item of "overseas Chinese" is cancled by state since 2000, The number of "Overseas Chinese" is included in the number of "Foreigner".

5-15 湖北国内旅游接待人数及收入

TOATL NUMBER OF DOMESTIC TOURISTS AND EARNINGS FORM DOMESTIC TORUISM

年份 Year	接待人数(万人次) Number of Tourists Received (10 000person-times)	同比(±%) Comparision Percentage (±%)	旅游收入(亿元) Earnings (100 million yuan)	同比(±%) Comparision Percentage (±%)	人均天花费(元) Expenditures Per Capita a day (yuan) 全国 The Whole Nation	湖北 Hubei
1987	1184	-6.18	2.37	-6.0		
1988	1208	2.03	2.42	2.1		
1989	1034	-14.40	3.10	28.1		
1990	890	-13.92	2.67	-13.9		
1991	984	10.56	3.93	47.2		
1992	1071	8.84	5.36	36.4		
1993	1350	26.05	9.50	77.2		
1994	1500	11.11	13.00	36.8		
1995	1700	13.33	18.00	38.5		
1996	3152	85.41	152.95		256	485
1997	3600	14.21	180.00	17.7	328	500
1998	4044	12.33	210.03	16.7	344	519
1999	4659	15.21	238.50	13.6	394	511
2000	5478	17.58	270.31	13.3	427	493
2001	6064	10.70	337.18	24.7	450	556
2002	6670	9.99	384.24	14.0	441	576
2003	5684	-14.78	331.60	-13.7	395	583
2004	6849	20.50	394.22	18.9	550	576
2005	7630	11.40	450.76	14.3	436	591
2006	8460	10.88	514.24	14.1	447	607
2007	10135	19.80	609.40	18.5	482	601
2008	11678	15.2	713.43	17.1	511	610
2009	15065	29.0	969.63	35.9	535	644
2010	20946	39.0	1409.48	45.4	598	673
2011	27155	29.6	1931.80	37.1	731	711
2012	34230	26.1	2553.55	32.2	766	746
2013	40621	18.6	3130.13	22.6	806	771
2014	46900	15.5	3752.11	17.1	839	782
2015	50668	12.7	4206.02	14.3	857	830
2016	56931	12.4	4764.18	13.3	888	837

注：表中所列是人均花费(元)。
Note: The table is a list of per capita spending ($).

5-16 湖北旅游总收入
THE TOTAL EARNINGS OF HUBEI TOURISM

年份 Year	旅游总收入 Total Earnings of Tourism	
	绝对额(亿元) (100 million yuan)	同比(±%) Comparision Percentage (±%)
1997	193.92	18.8
1998	217.27	12.0
1999	247.11	13.7
2000	282.26	14.2
2001	353.64	24.9
2002	407.52	15.2
2003	342.77	-15.9
2004	410.00	19.6
2005	473.15	15.5
2006	539.74	14.1
2007	640.87	18.7
2008	744.19	16.1
2009	1004.48	35.0
2010	1460.53	45.4
2011	1992.89	36.5
2012	2629.54	32.0
2013	3205.61	21.9
2014	3752.11	17.1
2015	4308.76	14.8
2016	4879.24	13.2

主要统计指标解释

进出口总额 指实际进出我国国境的货物总金额。包括对外贸易实际进出口货物,来料加工装配进出口货物,国家间、联合国及国际组织无偿援助物资和赠送品,华侨、港澳台同胞和外籍华人捐赠品,租赁期满归承租人所有的租赁货物,进料加工进出口货物,边境地方贸易及边境地区小额贸易进出口货物(边民互市贸易除外),中外合资企业、中外合作经营企业、外商独资经营企业进出口货物和公用物品,到、离岸价格在规定限额以上的进出口货样和广告品(无商业价值、无使用价值和免费提供出口的除外),从保税仓库提取在中国境内销售的进口货物,以及其他进出口货物。该指标可以观察一个国家在对外贸易方面的总规模。我国规定出口货物按离岸价格统计,进口货物按到岸价格统计。

商品经营单位所在地进、出口额 指所在地海关注册登记的有进出口经营权的企业实际进、出口额。

商品目的地进口额和商品货源地出口额 目的地进口额指进口货物的消费、使用或最终抵运地的实际进口额;货源地出口额指出口货物的产地或原始发货地的实际出口额。

利用外资 指我国各级政府、部门、企业和其他经济组织通过对外借款、吸收外商直接投资以及用其他方式筹措的境外现汇、设备、技术等。

对外借款 指通过对外正式签订借款协议,从境外筹措的资金,包括外国政府贷款、国际金融组织贷款、外国银行商业贷款、出口信贷以及对外发行债券等。1996年及以前还包括对外发行股票。该指标是我国利用外资的重要部分。

外商直接投资 指外国企业和经济组织或个人(包括华侨、港澳台胞以及我国在境外注册的企业)按我国有关政策、法规,用现汇、实物、技术等在我国境内开办外商独资企业、与我国境内的企业或经济组织共同举办中外合资经营企业、合作经营企业或合作开发资源的投资(包括外商投资收益的再投资),以及经政府有关部门批准的项目投资总额内企业从境外借入的资金。

外商其他投资 指除对外借款和外商直接投资以外的各种利用外资的形式。包括企业在境内外股票市场公开发行的以外币计价的股票(目前主要是在香港证券市场发行的H股和在境内证券市场发行的B股)发行价总额,国际租赁进口设备的应付款,补偿贸易中外商提供的进口设备、技术、物料的价款,加工装配贸易中外商提供的进口设备、物料的价款。

对外直接投资 指我国国内投资者以现金、实物、无形资产等方式在国外及港澳台地区设立、购买国(境)外企业,并以控制该企业的经营管理权为核心的经济活动。

对外承包工程 指各对外承包公司以招标议标承包方式承揽的下列业务:(1)承包国外工程建设项目;(2)承包我国对外经援项目;(3)承包我国驻外机构的工程建设项目;(4)承包我国境内利用外资进行建设的工程项目;(5)与外国承包公司合营或联合承包工程项目时我国公司分包部分;(6)对外承包兼营的房屋开发业务。对外承包工程的营业额是以货币表现的本期内完成的对外承包工程的工作量,包括以前年度签订的合同和本年度新签订的合同在报告期内完成的工作量。

对外劳务合作 指以收取工资的形式向业主或承包商提供技术和劳动服务的活动。我国对外承包公司在境外开办的合营企业,中国公司同时又提供劳务的,其劳务部分也纳入劳务合作统计。劳务合作营业额按报告期内向雇主提交的结算数(包括工资、加班费和奖金等)统计。

对外设计咨询 指以服务成果向业主收费的技术服务项目。包括承担地形地貌测绘,地质资源勘探与普查,建设区域规划,提供设计文件、图纸、生产工艺技术资料和工程技术经济咨询,工程项目的可行性考察、研究和评估,进行技术指导和培训人员等;也包括承担国(境)内利用外资建设工程项目中的设计咨询项目内收取外币部分。

旅游者人数

(1)入境国际旅游者人数:指来中国参观、访问、旅行、探亲、访友、休养、考察、参加会议和从事经济、科技、文化、教育、宗教等活动的外国人、华侨、港澳同胞和台湾同胞的人数。不包括外国在我国的常驻机构,如使领馆、通讯社、企业办事处的工作人员;来我国常住的外国专家、留学生以及在岸逗留不过夜人员。

(2)出境居民人数:指大陆居民因公务活动或私人事务短期出境的人数。公务活动出境居民人数包括在国际交通工具上的中国服务员工,因私出境居民人数不包括在国际交通工具上的中国服务员工。

(3)国内旅游者人数:指我国大陆居民和在我国常住1年以上的外国人、华侨、港澳台同胞离开常住地在境内其他地方的旅游设施内至少停留一夜,最长不超过6个月的人数。

国际旅游(外汇)收入 指入境旅游的外国人、华侨、港澳同胞和台湾同胞在中国大陆旅游过程中发生的一切旅游支出,其对于国家来说就是国际旅游(外汇)收入。

国际旅行社 指经营对外招徕并接待外国人、华侨、港澳同胞和台湾同胞来中国、归国或回内地旅游业务的旅行社。

国内旅行社 指负责经营招徕、组团、接待国内旅客的旅游业务,以及不对外招徕,负责经营接待国际旅行社或其它涉外部门组织的外国人、华侨、港澳同胞和台湾同胞来中国、归国或回内地的旅游业务的旅行社。

星级饭店 指已评定星级的饭店。

Explanatory Notes on Main Statistical Indicators

Total Imports and Exports at Customs refer to the real value of commodities imported into and exported from the boundary of China. They include the actual imports and exports through foreign trade, imported and exported goods under the processing and assembling trades and materials, supplies and gifts as aid given gratis between governments and by the United Nations and other international organizations, and contributions donated by overseas Chinese, compatriots in Hong Kong and Macao and Chinese with foreign citizenship, leasing commodities owned by tenant at the expiration of leasing period, the imported and exported commodities processed with imported materials, commodities trading in border areas (excluding mutual exchange goods), the imported and exported commodities and articles for public use of the Sino-foreign joint ventures, cooperative enterprises and ventures exclusively with foreign own investment. Also included are import or export of samples and advertising goods for whose CIF or FOB value are beyond the permitted ceiling (excluding goods of no trading or use value and free commodities for export), imported goods sold in China from bonded warehouses and other imported or exported goods. The indicator of the total imports and exports at customs can be used to observe the total size of external trade in a country. In accordance with the stipulation of the Chinese government, imports are calculated at CIF, while exports are calculated at FOB.

Import Export Value by Location of China's Foreign Trade Managing Units refers to actual value of imports and exports carried out by corporations which have been registered by the local customhouse and are vested with right to run import export business.

Import Value of Commodities by the Places of their Destination and Export Value of Commodities by the Places of their Origin in China The former indicator refers to the value of import commodities of the places of their consumption, utilization or the places of their final destination. The latter indicator refers to the value of export commodities of the places of their origin or the places of the commodities dispatched.

Utilization of Foreign Capitals refers to remittance, equipment and technology financed from abroad, by loans, foreign direct investment and other forms undertaken by the Chinese governments at all levels, by various departments, enterprises and other economic units.

Foreign Borrowings refer to funds borrowed from abroad through formal signing of borrowing agreements with foreign institutions, including loans of foreign governments, loans of international financial institutions, commercial loans of foreign banks, export credit, and funds raised by Chinese bonds (and shares before 1996) issued abroad. It is an important part of China's utilization of foreign capitals.

Foreign Direct Investment refers to the investments inside China by foreign enterprises and economic organizations or individuals (including overseas Chinese, compatriots from Hong Kong, Macao and Taiwan, and Chinese enterprises registered abroad), following the relevant policies and laws of China, for the establishment of ventures exclusively with foreign own investment, Sino-foreign joint ventures and cooperative enterprises or for co-operative exploration of resources with enterprises or economic organizations in China. It includes the re investment of the foreign entrepreneurs with the profits gained from the investment and the funds that enterprises borrow from abroad in the total investment of projects which are approved by the relevant department of the government.

Overseas Direct Investment refers to enterprises set up or bought by domestic investors in foreign countries and in Hong Kong, Macao and Taiwan, and the economic activities centering on operation and management of those enterprises are under the control of domestic investors. The statistical scope covers various corporation type enterprises and non-corporation type enterprises receiving direct investment from domestic investment entities.

Other Investment by Foreign Entrepreneurs refers to all forms of utilization of foreign capitals other than foreign borrowings and foreign direct investment. It includes the total value of stock shares in foreign currencies issued by enterprises at domestic or foreign stock exchanges (now mainly consisting of H shares issued at Hong Kong Security Market and B shares issued at domestic security markets), rent payable for the imported equipment through international leasing arrangement, cost of imported equipment, technology and materials provided by foreign counterparts in compensation trade and processing and assembly trade.

Contracted Projects with Foreign Count riesrefer to projects undertaken by Chinese contractors (project contracting companies) through bidding process. They include: (1) overseas civil engineering construction projects financed by foreign investors; (2) overseas projects financed by the Chinese government through its foreign aid programs; (3) construction projects of Chinese diplomatic missions, trade offices and other institutions stationed abroad; (4) construction projects in China financed by foreign investment; (5) sub-contracted projects to be taken by Chinese contractors through a joint umbrella project with foreign contractor(s); (6) housing development projects. The business income from international contracted projects is the work volume of contracted projects completed during the reference period, expressed in monetary terms, including completed work on projects signed in previous years.

Service Cooperation with Foreign Countries refers to the activities of providing technology and labor services to employers or contractors in the forms of receiving salaries and wages. Labor services providing by contractual joint ventures of Chinese international contracting corporations should be included in the statistics of service co-operation with foreign countries. The business income of labor service cooperation is the income in the form of wages and salaries, overtime pay, bonuses and other remuneration received from the employers during the reference period.

Overseas Design and Consultation Service refers to projects with charges for technical services from overseas operators. It includes geographic and topographic mapping, geological resource prospecting and survey, planning of construction areas, provision of design documents, blueprints, materials on production process and techniques, as well as engineering, technical and economic consultation, and feasibility study, research and evaluation of projects. Also included under this category are the above-mentioned services of foreign-financed projects in China that are paid in foreign currencies.

Number of Tourists

(1) International tourists refer to foreigners, overseas Chinese, Chinese compatriots from Hong Kong, Macao and Taiwan coming to China for sight-seeing, visits, tours, family reunions, vacations, study tours, conferences and other activities of a business, scientific and technological, cultural, educational and religious nature. It does not include representatives and employees of resident institutions of foreign countries in China such as embassies, consulates, news agencies and offices of foreign companies and organizations, nor does it include long-term foreign experts or students residing in China, or persons in transition without spending a night in China.

(2) Chinese residents going abroad refer to Chinese residents going abroad for short terms for either public business or private purposes. Chinese employees working on international transport carriers are included in those going abroad for public business purpose, not in those for private purpose.

(3) Domestic tourists refer to residents of the mainland of China who stay for one night at least but no more than 6 months at tourist facilities in other places than their permanent residence within the territory of the mainland China, including foreigners, overseas Chinese and Chinese compatriots from Hong Kong, Macao and Taiwan who have resided in China for over one year.

Foreign Exchange Earnings from International Tourism refer to the total expenditures of foreigners, overseas Chinese, Chinese compatriots from Hong Kong, Macao and Taiwan during their stay in the mainland of China, which are earnings of foreign exchange from international tourism from the point of view from China.

International Travel Agencies refer to travel agencies engaged in the promotion, solicitation, organization and reception of tours to the mainland of China by foreigners, overseas Chinese, Chinese compatriots from Hong Kong, Macao and Taiwan.

Domestic Travel Agencies refer to travel agencies engaged in the promotion, solicitation, organization and reception of domestic tourists, and in the reception of foreigners, overseas Chinese, Chinese compatriots from Hong Kong, Macao and Taiwan organized by international travel agencies or other departments concerned, without their own promotion and solicitation programmes.

Star-Hotels refer to hotels rated with stars.

6 能源

Energy

6-1 工业能源生产量
OUTPUT OF ENERGY PRODUCTION OF INDUSTRY

产品		Item		2013	2014	2015	2016
一次能源生产量	（万吨标煤）	Primary Energy Output	(10 000 tons standardized coal)	5165.45	5708.76	5256.27	5490.13
原煤	（万吨）	Coal	(10 000 ton)	885.42	890.40	758.39	547.42
原油	（万吨）	Crude Oil	(10 000 ton)	80.08	79.00	71.00	58.09
天然气	（亿立方米）	Natural Gas	(100 million cu.m)	3.09	1.45	1.35	1.31
水电	（亿千瓦时）	Water and Electricity	(100 million KW/h)	1175.95	1375.80	1289.96	1379.30

说明：1.一次能源生产量为全部工业一次能源生产量；原煤、原油、天然气以及水电产量为规模以上工业生产量。
2.按照国家统计局统一部署和要求，2013年、2014年数据为根据第三次全国经济普查资料进行调整后的数据（下同）。
Note: 1.Primary energy production is the entire industrial primary energy production, raw coal, crude oil, natural gas and hydropower output are the above scale industrial production.
2.According to the requirements of the NBS, the data in 2013 and 2014 have been adjusted basing on the files of the third national economic census.

6-2 规模以上工业能源消费量
ENERGY CONSUMPTION OF INDUSTRY ABOVE DESIGNATED SIZE

产品		Item		2013	2014	2015	2016
能源消费量合计	（万吨标煤）	Total	（10000 tons standardized coal）	13310.45	13766.37	13827.77	13954.63
原煤	（万吨）	Coal	（10000 ton）	8270.13	7984.97	7724.61	7433.21
洗精煤	（万吨）	Cleaned Coal	（10000 ton）	1382.42	1346.53	1320.69	1253.29
其他洗煤	（万吨）	Other Washed Coal	（10000 ton）	13.04	11.16	7.78	23.86
煤制品	（万吨）	Moulded Coal	（10000 ton）	11.35	10.92	10.48	10.25
焦炭	（万吨）	Coke	（10000 ton）	1114.39	1124.40	1030.01	1095.31
其他焦化产品	（万吨）	Other Coked Products	（10000 ton）	1.34	1.93	4.05	1.68
焦炉煤气	（亿立方米）	Coke-oven Gas	（100 million cu.m）	38.59	38.23	37.80	35.69
高炉煤气	（亿立方米）	Bblast Furnace Gas	（100 million cu.m）	345.87	342.73	315.53	316.25
其他煤气	（亿立方米）	Other Gases	（100 million cu.m）	24.04	21.07	20.81	22.64
天然气	（亿立方米）	Natural Gas	（100 million cu.m）	18.10	17.42	23.20	25.69
原油	（万吨）	Crude Oil	（10000 ton）	1176.30	1290.47	1299.01	1239.61
汽油	（万吨）	Gasoline	（10000 ton）	13.48	12.09	11.11	12.08
煤油	（万吨）	Kerasene	（10000 ton）	1.08	1.34	1.00	1.14
柴油	（万吨）	Diesel Oil	（10000 ton）	49.72	58.52	54.59	48.76
燃料油	（万吨）	Fuel Oil	（10000 ton）	6.74	6.87	6.05	4.22
液化石油气	（万吨）	LPG	（10000 ton）	8.95	31.30	39.14	27.33
炼厂干气	（万吨）	Dry Gas	（10000 ton）	34.68	38.47	38.32	36.44
其他石油制品	（万吨）	Other Petroleum Products	（10000 ton）	176.62	280.52	385.07	638.38
热力	（万百万千焦）	Heat	（10 billion kilo-joule）	7744.13	7626.11	8313.48	7860.91
电力	（亿千瓦时）	Electricity	（100 million kW/h）	1281.29	1317.88	1311.13	1311.43
其他燃料	（万吨标准煤）	Other Fuels	（10000 tons standardized coal）	22.97	24.69	25.77	23.21

注：能源消费量包括加工转换投入量，且为当量值。
Note: The conversion of energy consumption, including processing input, and when the money is.

6-3 规模以上工业分行业能源消费量(2016)
ENERGY CONSUMPTION OF INDUSTRY ABOVE DESGINATED SIZE(2016)

行业	Item	原煤消费量(万吨) Coal Consumption (10000 tons)	汽油消费量(万吨) Gasoline Consumption (10000tons)	柴油消费量(万吨) Diesel Consumption (10000tons)	电力消费量(亿千瓦小时) Electricity Consumption (100million kw/h)
总消费量	**Total Consumption**	**7433.21**	**12.08**	**48.76**	**1311.43**
采矿业	**Mining**	**134.26**	**0.65**	**11.19**	**34.50**
煤炭开采和洗选业	Mining and Washing of Coal	73.19	0.05	0.13	1.90
石油和天然气开采业	Extraction of Petroleum and Natural Gas	12.69	0.18	0.64	8.04
黑色金属矿采选业	Mining and Processing of Ferrous Metal Ores	6.12	0.05	0.59	8.37
有色金属矿采选业	Mining and Processing of Non-Ferrous Metal Ores	0.00	0.01	0.06	2.93
非金属矿采选业	Mining and Processing of Non-metal Ores	28.84	0.23	4.26	11.94
开采辅助活动	Mining Auxiliary	11.00	0.13	5.51	1.19
其他采矿业	Mining of Other Ores	2.42	0.00	0.00	0.14
制造业	**Manufacturing**	**3658.10**	**11.18**	**36.50**	**1095.47**
农副食品加工业	Processing of Food from Agricultural Products	100.31	0.53	3.06	49.44
食品制造业	Manufacture of Foods	76.13	0.21	0.36	18.57
酒、饮料和精制茶制造业	Manufacture of Wine, Beverages and Tea	45.94	0.25	0.42	14.23
烟草制品业	Manufacture of Tobacco	1.05	0.00	0.00	1.30
纺织业	Manufacture of Textile	31.05	0.24	0.38	70.31
纺织服装、服饰业	Manufacture of Textile Wearing Apparel	5.23	0.15	0.50	8.24
皮革、毛皮、羽毛及其制品和制鞋业	Manufacture of Leather, Fur, Feather and Related and Footware	0.37	0.02	0.01	4.14
木材加工和木、竹、藤、棕、草制品业	Processing of Timber, Manufacture of Wood, Bamboo, Rattan, Palm, and Straw Products	4.42	0.06	0.39	11.19
家具制造业	Manufacture of Furniture	0.08	0.03	0.17	1.96
造纸和纸制品业	Manufacture of Paper and Paper Products	65.20	0.05	0.86	17.93
印刷和记录媒介复制业	Printing and Reproduction of Recording Media	2.04	0.15	0.11	4.98
文教、工美、体育和娱乐用品制造业	Manufacture of Articles for Culture, Education, Art, Sport and Entertainment	3.01	0.01	0.02	3.84
石油加工、炼焦和核燃料加工业	Processing of Petroleum, Coking and Nuclear Fuel	8.68	0.01	0.02	14.77
化学原料和化学制品制造业	Manufacture of Raw Chemical Materials and Chemical Products	1469.99	2.78	2.51	249.89
医药制造业	Manufacture of Medicines	96.25	0.20	2.08	23.53
化学纤维制造业	Manufacture of Chemical Fibres	22.17	0.00	0.13	3.68
橡胶和塑料制品业	Manufacture of Rubber and Plastics	11.20	0.68	1.20	28.44
非金属矿物制品业	Manufacture of Non-metal Mineral Products	989.09	0.56	9.60	136.16
黑色金属冶炼和压延加工业	Smelting an Processing of Ferrous Metals	537.87	0.15	2.07	192.37
有色金属冶炼和压延加工业	Smelting an Processing of Non-ferrous Metals	43.75	0.07	0.77	32.14
金属制品业	Manufacture of Metal Products	8.08	0.32	1.06	27.29
通用设备制造业	Manufacture of General Purpose Machinery	5.70	0.97	3.69	18.28
专用设备制造业	Manufacture of Special Purpose Machinery	3.19	0.56	1.89	14.29
汽车制造业	Manufacture of Automobile	120.30	2.26	3.42	88.27
铁路、船舶、航空航天和其他运输设备制造业	Manufacture of Realway, Ship, Aircraft and Other Transport Equipment	0.95	0.13	0.29	4.41
电气机械和器材制造业	Manufacture of Electrical Machinery and Equipment	2.99	0.32	0.30	32.84
计算机、通信和其他电子设备制造业	Manufacture of Computers, Communication Equipment and Other Electronic Equipment	1.83	0.14	0.03	15.87
仪器仪表制造业	Manufacture of Measuring Instruments	0.16	0.20	0.02	2.04
其他制造业	Manufacture of Other Products	0.39	0.01	0.00	2.96
废弃资源综合利用业	Recycling and Disposal of Waste	0.69	0.04	0.28	1.73
金属制品、机械和设备修理业	Repairing of Metal Products and Mechanical Equipment	0.00	0.10	0.85	0.40
电力、燃气及水生产和供应业	**Electric Power, Gas and Water Production and Supply**	**3640.85**	**0.24**	**1.07**	**181.46**
电力、热力生产和供应业	Production and Supply of Electric Power and Heat Power	3640.73	0.07	1.01	169.32
燃气生产和供应业	Production and Supply of Gas	0.00	0.06	0.02	4.21
水的生产和供应业	Production and Supply of Water	0.12	0.12	0.04	7.93

6-4 全社会综合能源平衡表(等价值)
BALANCE SHEET OF DOMESTIC ENERGY (EQIVALENCE PRICE)

单位: 万吨标准煤 (10000 tons standardized coal)

项 目	Item	2015	2016
一、可供量	**Quantity Available**	**16404**	**16850**
一次能源生产量	Primary Energy Production	5256	5490
外省(区、市)调入量	Engery moblized from other Province	13468	14041
进口量	Import Volume		
我轮、机在外国加油量	Volume of Fuel Charged Abroad		
本省(区、市)调出量(−)	Engery moblized to other Province	2542	2625
出口量(−)	Output Volume		
外轮、机在我国加油量(−)	Volume of Fuel Charged at Home		
年初年末库存差额	Storage Balance Difference between the Beginning and the End of the Year	222	−56
年初库存量	Storage Volume at the Beginning of the Year	749	748
年末库存量(−)	Storage Volume by the End of the Year	527	804
二、消费量	**Consumption**	**16404**	**16850**
消费量分组一	Consumption Group 1.	16404	16850
1.农.林.牧.渔业	Agriculture, Forestry, Animal Husbandary, Fishing	485	417
2.工 业	Industry	10404	10526
3.建筑业	Construction	428	367
4.交通运输.仓储和邮政业	Transport communication, Storage, Post Service	1600	1920
5.批发、零售业和住宿、餐饮业	Wholesale,Retail Sale, Hotel and Catering Industry	786	742
6.其他	Others	759	858
7.生活消费	Living Consumption	1942	2019
消费量分组二	Consumption Group 2.	16404	16850
1. 终端消费	Terminal Consumption	16234	16641
#工业	Industry	10234	10317
2. 加工转换损失	Loss in Processing	−126	−132
火力发电损失	Loss in Thermal Power Generation		
供热损失	Loss in Heating	241	237
洗选煤损失	Loss in Coal Seperation	3	2
炼焦损失	Loss in Coke Making	29	34
炼油及煤制油损失	Loss in Oil Refining	17	55
制气损失	Loss in Gas Drying		
天然气液化损失	Loss in Natural gas liquefaction	8	7
煤制品加工损失	Loss in Coal Products Processing		
回收能	Recuperated Energy	−424	−468
3. 损失量	Loss in Processing	296	341
三、平衡差额	**Balance**		

6-5 全社会煤炭平衡表
BALANCE SHEET OF DOMESTIC COAL CONSUMPTION

单位: 万吨 (10 000 tons)

项 目	Item	2015	2016
一、可供量	**Quantity Available**	**11766**	**11686**
生产量	Production Capacity	860	594
外省(区、市)调入量	Engery moblized from other Province	10605	11064
进口量	Import Volume		
本省(区、市)调出量(-)	Engery moblized to other Province		
出口量(-)	Output Volume		
年初年末库存差额	Storage Balance Difference between the Beginning and the End of the Year	301	28
年初库存量	Storage Volume at the Beginning of the Year	877	637
年末库存量(-)	Storage Volume by the End of the Year	576	610
二、消费量	**Consumption**	**11766**	**11686**
消费量分组一	Consumption Group 1.	11766	11686
1.农.林.牧.渔业	Agriculture, Forestry, Animal Husbandary, Fishing	217	205
2.工 业	Industry	10284	10316
3.建 筑 业	Construction	125	40
4.交通运输.仓储和邮政业	Transport communication, Storage, Post Service	68	55
5.批发、零售业和住宿、餐饮业	Wholesale,Retail Sale, Hotel and Catering Industry	264	239
6.其 他	Others	234	263
7.生活消费	Living Consumption	575	567
消费量分组二	Consumption Group 2.	11766	11686
1. 终端消费	Terminal Consumption	6348	6350
#工业	Industry	4866	4979
2. 用于加工转换	Coal Used for Processing	5418	5336
火力发电	Thermal Power Generation	3638	3624
供 热	Heating	465	445
洗煤损耗	Loss in Washing Coal	18	15
炼 焦	Coke Making	1297	1253
炼油及煤制油	Oil Refining and Coal Preparation		
制 气	Air Drying		
型煤加工损耗	Loss in Standardlized Coal Processing	0.01	
3. 损 失 量	Loss		
三、平衡差额	**Balance**		

6-6 全社会石油平衡表

BALANCE SHEET OF DOMESTIC PETROLEUM

单位: 万吨 (10 000 tons)

项 目	Item	2015	2016
一、可供量	**Quantity Available**	**2551**	**2529**
生产量	Production Capacity	71	58
外省(区、市)调入量	Engery moblized from other Province	2524	2522
进口量	Import Volume		
我轮、机在外国加油量	Volume of Fuel Charged Abroad		
本省(区、市)调出量(－)	Engery moblized to other Province	43	7
出口量(–)	Output Volume		
外轮、机在我国加油量(–)	Volume of Fuel Charged at Home		
年初年末库存差额	Storage Balance Difference between the Beginning and the End of the Year		–43
年初库存量	Storage Volume at the Beginning of the Year	41	167
年末库存量(–)	Storage Volume by the End of the Year	41	211
二、消费量	**Consumption**	**2551**	**2529**
消费量分组一	Consumption Group 1.	2551	2529
1.农.林.牧.渔业	Agriculture, Forestry, Animal Husbandary, Fishing	168	107
2.工 业	Industry	713	597
3.建筑业	Construction	175	174
4.交通运输.仓储和邮政业	Transport communication, Storage, Post Service	901	1112
5.批发、零售业和住宿、餐饮业	Wholesale,Retail Sale, Hotel and Catering Industry	168	125
6.其他	Others	107	114
7.生活消费	Living Consumption	319	300
消费量分组二	Consumption Group 2.	2551	2529
1. 终端消费	Terminal Consumption	2545	2481
#工业	Industry	707	548
2. 加工转换损失	Coal Used for Processing	6	49
火力发电	Thermal Power Generation	2	2
供 热	Heating	3	3
炼油损耗	Loss in Oil Refining	1	44
制 气	Gas Making		
3. 损失量	Loss		
三、平衡差额	**Balance**		0

6-7 全社会电力平衡表
BALANCE SHEET OF DOMESTIC ELECTRICITY

单位: 亿千瓦时 (100 million kw/h)

项 目	Item	2015	2016
一、可供量	**Quantity Available**	**1862**	**1971**
生产量	Production Capacity	2302	2479
火力发电	Thermal Power Generation	994	1017
水力发电、核发电、其它发电	Hydroelectricity Generation, Nuclearpower Generation, and others	1308	1463
外省(区、市)调入量	Engery moblized from other Province	336	308
进 口 量	Import Volume		
本省(区、市)调出量(-)	Engery moblized to other Province	775	815
出 口 量(-)	Output Volume		
二、消费量	**Consumption**	**1862**	**1971**
消费量分组一	Consumption Group 1.	1862	1971
1.农.林.牧.渔业	Agriculture, Forestry, Animal Husbandary, Fishing	22	30
2.工 业	Industry	1291	1323
3.建 筑 业	Construction	26	29
4.交通运输.仓储和邮政业	Transport communication, Storage, Post Service	42	47
5.批发、零售业和住宿、餐饮业	Wholesale,Retail Sale, Hotel and Catering Industry	86	93
6.其他	Others	116	135
7.生活消费	Living Consumption	279	315
消费量分组二	Consumption Group 2.	1862	1971
1. 终端消费	Terminal Consumption	1767	1862
#工业	Industry	1196	1214
2. 输配电损失量	Distribution Loss	95	109
三、平衡差额	**Balance**		

6-8 分市州单位GDP能耗降低率(2016)
UNIT GDP ENERGY CONSUMPTION OF SUB-CITY(2016)

地 区	Regions	2010年单位GDP能耗比2005年降低(±%) 2010year Unit GDP energy consumption lower than in 2005	2015年单位GDP能耗比2014年降低(±%) 2015year Unit GDP energy consumption lower than in 2014	2016年单位GDP能耗比2015年降低(±%) 2016year Unit GDP energy consumption lower than in 2015
全 省	**Total**	**-21.67**	**-7.66**	**-4.97**
武汉市	Wuhan	-21.85	-5.95	-4.59
黄石市	Huangshi	-21.71	-10.84	-6.44
十堰市	Shiyan	-20.13	-8.86	-7.30
宜昌市	Yichang	-20.87	-8.96	-7.17
襄阳市	Xiangyang	-21.40	-7.84	-4.77
鄂州市	Ezhou	-22.83	-8.51	-4.36
荆门市	Jingmen	-21.15	-8.35	-5.70
孝感市	Xiaogan	-22.55	-5.48	-4.76
荆州市	Jingzhou	-21.93	-5.31	-4.09
黄冈市	Huanggang	-22.02	-5.80	-4.50
咸宁市	Xianning	-22.10	-5.11	5.41
随州市	Suizhou	-20.04	-6.90	-4.23
恩施州	Enshi	-20.20	-4.88	-3.36
仙桃市	Xiantao	-20.03	-4.92	-4.87
潜江市	Qianjiang	-20.91	-8.43	-7.52
天门市	Tianmen	-20.99	-4.03	-4.87
神农架	Shennon-gjia	-19.35	-2.99	-8.42

主要统计指标解释

一次能源生产量 指一定时期内，一次能源生产量的总和。该指标是观察能源生产水平、规模、构成和发展速度的总量指标。一次能源生产量包括原煤、原油、天然气、水电、核能及其他动力能(如风能、地热能等)发电量，不包括低热值燃料生产量、生物质能、太阳能等的利用和由一次能源加工转换而成的二次能源产量。

能源消费总量 指一定区域内(国家或地区)国民经济各行业和居民家庭在一定时期消费的各种能源的总和。能源消费总量分为三部分，即终端能源消费量、能源加工转换损失量和能源损失量。

(1)终端能源消费量：指一定时期内地区各行业和居民生活消费的各种能源在扣除了用于加工转换二次能源消费量和损失量以后的数量。

(2)能源加工转换损失量：指一定时期内地区投入加工转换的各种能源数量之和与产出各种能源产品之和的差额。该指标是观察能源在加工转换过程中损失量变化的指标。

(3)能源损失量：指一定时期内，能源在输送、分配、储存过程中发生的损失和由客观原因造成的各种损失量，不包括各种气体能源放空、放散量。

单位国内生产总值能耗 指一定时期内，一个国家或地区每生产一个单位的国内生产总值所消耗的能源。计算公式为：

$$\text{单位国内生产总值能耗} = \frac{\text{能源消费总量}}{\text{国内生产总值}}$$

Explanatory Notes on Main Statistical Indicators

Primary Energy Production refers to the total production of primary energy by all energy producing enterprises in a given period of time. It is a comprehensive indicator to show the capacity, scale, composition and development of energy production. The production of primary energy includes that of coal, crude oil, natural gas, hydro-power and electricity generated by nuclear energy and other means such as wind power and geothermal power. However, it excludes the production of fuels of low calorific value, bio-energy, solar energy and the secondary energy converted from the primary energy.

Total Domestic Energy Consumption refers to the total consumption of energy of various kinds by material production sectors, non material production sectors and households in a given period of time. It is a comprehensive indicator to show the scale, composition and development of energy consumption. The total energy consumption includes that of coal, crude oil and their products, natural gas and electricity, However, it excludes the consumption of fuel of low calorific value, bio-energy and solar energy. Total domestic energy consumption can be divided into three parts: final energy consumption, loss during the process of energy conversion, and energy loss.

(1)Final Energy Consumption: It refers to the total energy consumption by material production sectors, non material production sectors and households in a given period of time, but excludes the consumption in conversion of the primary energy into the secondary energy and the loss in the process of energy conversion.

(2)Loss During the Process of Energy Conversion: It refers to the total input of various kinds of energy for conversion, minus the total output of various kinds of energy in a given period of time. It is an indicator to show the loss that occurs during the process of energy conversion.

(3)Energy Loss: It refers to the total of the loss of energy during the course of energy transport, distribution and storage and the loss caused by any objective reason in a given period of time. The loss of various kinds of gas due to gas discharges and stocktaking is excluded.

Energy Consumption per Unit of GDP refers to the energy consumption per unit of gross domestic production in a country or the gross region production in a region in the same reference period. The formula is:

Energy Consumption per Unit of GDP = Total Energy Consumption / Gross Domestic Production

7 财政和金融

Government Finance And Banking

财政和金融

GOVERNMENT FINANCE AND BANKING 2016

地方一般公共预算收入	Local Public Financial Revenue(100 million yuan)	3102.02	(亿元)
地方一般公共预算支出	Local Public Financial Expenditure(100 million yuan)	6453.07	(亿元)
金融机构(含外资)人民币存款年末余额	Balance of RMB Deposits of Financial Organizations (including Foreign Funded Enterprises) By the End of the year(100 million yuan)	47284.95	(亿元)
#住户存款	Household Deposit	22065.17	(亿元)
金融机构(含外资)人民币贷款年末余额	Balance of RMB Loans of Financial Organizations (including Foreign Funded Enterprises) By the End of the year(100 million yuan)	34530.72	(亿元)

一般公共预算收入与一般公共预算支出(亿元)

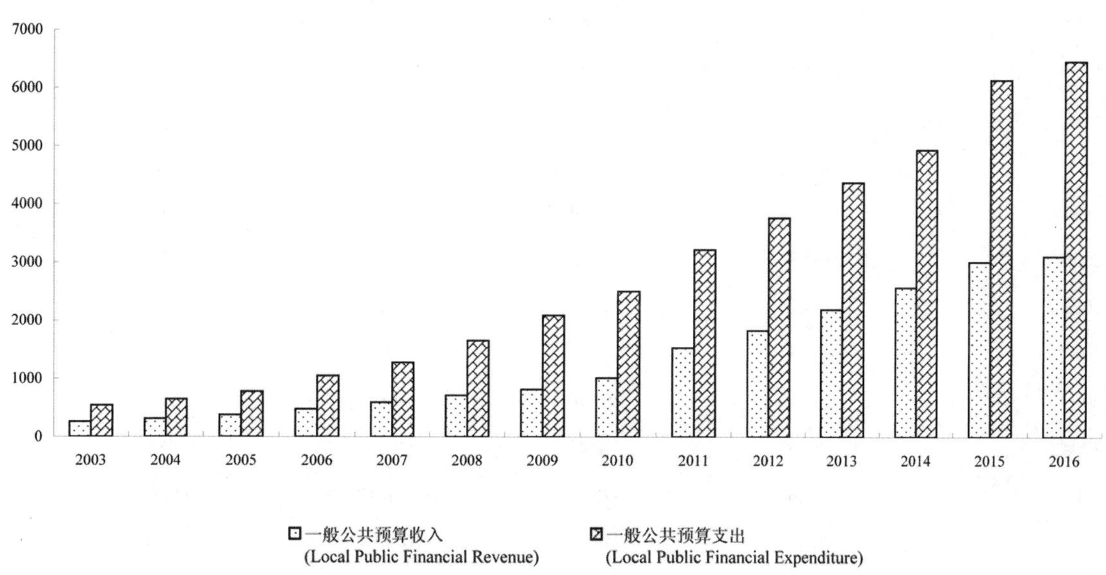

一般公共预算收入与一般公共预算支出(亿元)
Local Budgetary Revenue and Expenditure(100 million yuan)

年份(Year)	2003	2004	2005	2006	2007	2008	2009	2010	2011	2012	2013	2014	2015	2016
一般公共预算收入 (Local Public Financial Revenue)	260	311	376	476	590	711	815	1011	1527	1823	2191	2567	3006	3102
一般公共预算支出 (Local Public Financial Expenditure)	540	646	779	1047	1274	1650	2091	2501	3215	3760	4372	4934	6133	6423

7-1 历年地方财政收支额及指数
AMOVNT AND INDICES OF FINANCIAL REVENUE AND EXPENDITURE OVER THE YEARS

单位:亿元 (100 million yuan)

年份 Year	财政总收入 Total fiscal revenue	地方一般公共预算收入 Local Public Financial Revenue	地方一般公共预算支出 Local Public Financial Expenditure	指数(上年=100) Index (previous year=100)	
				收入 Revenue	支出 Expenditure
1952	3.81	3.81	1.96	100.0	100.0
1957	6.27	6.27	3.55	109.8	96.7
1965	11.26	11.26	6.85	97.4	105.2
1970	15.20	15.20	15.73	170.6	158.1
1975	24.05	24.05	17.52	139.5	103.9
1978	31.38	31.38	29.98	149.0	148.6
1980	34.01	34.01	26.53	107.6	94.5
1985	50.26	50.26	43.60	119.3	137.5
1990	77.85	77.85	84.82	100.8	106.1
1995	180.57	99.69	162.43	128.7	118.4
1996	216.68	124.51	197.44	124.9	121.6
1997	246.35	139.89	223.70	112.4	113.3
1998	284.44	168.95	280.12	120.8	125.2
1999	314.91	194.44	336.46	115.1	120.1
2000	343.98	214.35	368.77	110.2	109.6
2001	374.15	231.94	484.40	108.2	131.4
2002	435.50	243.44	511.39	105.0	105.6
2003	483.90	259.76	540.44	106.7	105.7
2004	589.65	310.45	646.29	119.5	119.6
2005	727.61	375.52	778.72	121.0	120.5
2006	901.17	476.08	1047.00	126.8	134.5
2007	1115.47	590.36	1274.27	124.0	121.7
2008	1338.75	710.85	1650.28	120.4	129.5
2009	1541.55	814.87	2090.92	114.6	126.7
2010	1918.94	1011.23	2501.40	124.1	119.7
2011	2639.81	1526.91	3214.74	151.0	128.5
2012	3115.63	1823.05	3759.79	119.4	117.0
2013	3566.89	2191.22	4371.65	120.2	116.3
2014	4096.00	2566.90	4934.15	117.1	112.9
2015	4705.00	3005.53	6132.84	117.1	124.3
2016	4974.00	3102.06	6422.98	107.3	104.7

7-2 财政收支
FINANCIAL REVENUE AND EXPENDITURE

单位:亿元 (100 million yuan)

指标	Item	2013	2014	2015	2016
地方一般公共预算收入	Local Public Financial Revenue	2191.22	2566.90	3005.53	3102.06
#税收收入	Revenue	1604.85	1856.53	2086.50	2122.93
#增值税	#Taxes on Value Added	225.68	254.92	285.48	563.33
营业税	Run Taxes	526.43	593.27	678.30	374.23
企业所得税	Enterprise Income Taxes	215.23	250.45	276.78	299.12
个人所得税	Individual Income Taxes	57.74	64.50	78.53	92.98
城市维护建设税	Taxes on City Maintenance and Construction	109.04	121.34	138.62	143.48
房产税	Real Estate Taxews	34.70	42.28	53.14	59.70
耕地占用税	Taxes on Use of Cultivated Land	80.39	99.66	116.42	115.60
地方一般公共预算支出	Local Public Financial Expenditure	4371.65	4934.15	6132.84	6422.98
1.一般公共服务	General Public Service	546.49	598.45	618.14	639.60
2.外交	Foreign Affairs				
3.国防	National Defence	4.12	4.18	4.25	3.55
4.公共安全	Public Security	227.04	259.05	295.24	352.73
5.教育	Education	690.63	773.35	913.05	1047.37
6.科学技术	Science and Technology	77.21	134.46	157.36	190.11
7.文化体育与传媒	Culture, Sports and Media	72.44	76.65	84.03	96.61
8.社会保障和就业	Social Security and Employment	605.70	717.63	858.70	978.82
9.医疗卫生与计划生育	Medical Care and family planning	322.08	410.31	515.25	588.90
10.节能环保	Environmental Protecction	109.72	103.78	145.84	145.64
11.城乡社区	Community Service in Urban and Rural Community	320.36	364.31	545.16	588.47
12.农林水	Water Affairs of Agriculture and Forestry	465.34	483.80	616.57	704.59
13.交通运输	Transportation	308.82	396.04	452.05	391.79
14.其他支出	Others	621.70	612.14	927.20	694.78

7-3 财政收入占地区生产总值的比重
FINANCIAL REVENUE AS PERCENTAGE TO GROSS DOMESTIC PRODUCT

年份 Year	地方一般公共预算收入(亿元) Local Public Financial Revenue (100 million yuan)	地区生产总值(亿元) Gross Domestic Product (100 million yuan)	一般公共预算收入占地区生产总值的比重(%) Percentage of Local Financial Revenue to GDP (%)
1980	26.53	199.38	13.31
1985	43.50	396.26	10.98
1986	58.04	442.04	13.13
1987	60.98	517.77	11.78
1988	68.66	626.52	10.96
1989	79.07	717.08	11.03
1990	84.82	824.38	10.29
1991	95.09	913.38	10.41
1992	94.14	1088.39	8.65
1993	115.07	1325.83	8.68
1994	77.46	1700.92	4.55
1995	99.69	2109.38	4.73
1996	124.51	2499.77	4.98
1997	139.89	2856.47	4.90
1998	168.95	3114.02	5.43
1999	194.44	3229.29	6.02
2000	214.35	3545.39	6.05
2001	231.94	3880.53	5.98
2002	243.44	4212.82	5.78
2003	259.76	4757.45	5.46
2004	310.45	5633.24	5.51
2005	375.52	6590.19	5.70
2006	476.08	7617.47	6.25
2007	590.36	9333.40	6.33
2008	710.85	11328.92	6.27
2009	814.87	12961.10	6.29
2010	1011.23	15967.61	6.33
2011	1526.91	19632.26	7.78
2012	1823.05	22250.45	8.19
2013	2191.22	24668.49	8.88
2014	2566.90	27379.22	9.38
2015	3005.53	29550.19	10.17
2016	3102.06	32297.91	9.60

7-4 市州一般公共预算收入
FINANCIAL REVENUE OF CITIES AND PREFECTURE

单位:亿元 (100 million yuan)

市州	Municipalities	2005	2007	2008	2009	2010	2011	2012	2013	2014	2015	2016
全 省	The Total	375.52	590.36	710.85	814.87	1011.23	1526.91	1823.05	2191.22	2566.90	3005.53	3102.06
省 级	Provinial	94.59	161.83	174.37	184.06	206.78	188.67	130.07	126.27	133.16	155.96	169.23
武汉市	Wuhan	138.82	221.68	277.32	316.07	390.19	673.26	828.58	978.52	1101.02	1245.63	1322.10
黄石市	Huangshi	11.96	19.71	24.09	26.03	34.10	53.84	65.64	78.36	89.38	100.53	105.47
十堰市	Shiyan	11.37	15.59	19.89	25.76	43.77	66.71	76.93	73.53	85.77	93.38	100.27
荆州市	Jingzhou	12.05	15.24	18.71	22.36	27.60	44.33	56.76	71.95	88.17	103.95	115.45
宜昌市	Yichang	22.53	35.57	44.27	54.94	70.24	113.98	153.25	206.31	271.51	339.10	300.04
襄阳市	Xiangyang	18.40	24.02	30.06	37.02	51.01	97.41	139.85	191.53	249.24	339.10	320.70
鄂州市	Ezhou	4.93	8.51	10.70	13.02	15.66	26.31	33.02	38.43	42.74	47.17	52.91
荆门市	Jingmen	9.34	12.06	14.92	18.14	23.25	39.39	50.69	59.84	69.82	80.43	91.73
孝感市	Xiaogan	10.78	16.63	21.46	26.97	34.20	51.58	69.50	89.05	107.22	122.77	129.23
黄冈市	Huanggang	13.14	19.93	26.21	32.17	38.98	51.61	62.92	79.98	96.04	112.82	119.52
咸宁市	Xianning	7.43	11.10	14.33	18.14	23.34	35.56	45.82	58.71	70.76	80.12	83.34
恩施自治州	Enshi	8.35	13.05	15.40	18.28	22.16	31.89	40.43	50.05	57.82	67.23	71.91
随州市	Suizhou	4.25	5.47	6.68	7.60	9.53	17.07	22.99	29.67	36.68	43.34	45.55
仙桃市	Xiantao	2.81	3.31	4.21	5.05	7.35	13.13	17.14	21.00	24.16	27.69	29.08
天门市	Tianmen	1.37	2.18	2.80	3.53	4.71	7.90	11.00	15.02	17.35	19.59	17.97
潜江市	Qianjiang	3.02	3.85	4.71	4.86	7.25	12.50	16.02	20.00	22.69	22.85	23.32
神农架林区	Shennongjia	0.42	0.60	0.73	0.87	1.10	1.77	2.44	3.00	3.37	3.86	4.25

7-5 市州一般公共预算支出
FINANCIAL EXPENDITURE OF CITIES AND PREFECTURES

单位:亿元 (100 million yuan)

市州	Municipalities	2005	2007	2008	2009	2010	2011	2012	2013	2014	2015	2016
全 省	The Total	778.70	1274.27	1650.28	2090.92	2501.40	3214.74	3759.79	4371.65	4934.15	6132.84	6422.98
省 级	Provinial	205.75	312.94	388.90	258.00	273.40	378.50	449.69	484.45	661.60	893.13	758.76
武汉市	Wuhan	176.88	307.23	377.88	503.64	583.55	765.04	885.55	1122.88	1175.10	1338.05	1524.68
黄石市	Huangshi	23.47	40.90	53.06	80.85	102.56	128.69	140.43	150.79	152.97	225.94	224.10
十堰市	Shiyan	33.42	54.24	73.97	118.50	146.98	185.09	207.75	231.42	258.87	307.65	323.70
荆州市	Jingzhou	39.51	65.80	90.41	130.35	163.15	197.18	226.83	255.92	276.29	346.48	384.71
宜昌市	Yichang	47.63	79.78	105.86	156.50	196.51	241.13	297.45	364.44	439.92	537.53	531.97
襄阳市	Xiangyang	49.19	71.52	96.64	148.16	184.92	248.14	313.97	364.87	437.93	584.50	624.12
鄂州市	Ezhou	10.38	17.85	23.97	35.67	43.01	56.66	62.69	70.87	75.65	86.80	100.24
荆门市	Jingmen	24.58	38.65	49.18	81.66	95.46	125.34	142.20	158.79	178.96	225.90	246.09
孝感市	Xiaogan	32.50	54.60	74.64	109.79	133.58	172.61	201.79	227.90	253.18	290.38	356.87
黄冈市	Huanggang	44.40	76.23	104.47	155.09	188.13	225.54	278.92	305.16	344.66	401.03	439.87
咸宁市	Xianning	21.41	37.87	56.50	84.97	100.02	127.07	143.03	158.14	176.97	190.85	216.15
恩施自治州	Enshi	32.12	54.89	71.04	102.25	129.79	160.14	179.69	216.69	216.32	332.59	320.24
随州市	Suizhou	14.11	23.10	31.73	46.11	57.23	72.32	85.55	100.04	103.70	153.10	148.32
仙桃市	Xiantao	8.29	13.30	17.03	26.25	32.91	42.34	47.71	50.08	59.56	69.30	74.58
天门市	Tianmen	6.22	10.79	15.14	23.44	28.27	38.51	41.84	46.53	54.36	64.73	67.96
潜江市	Qianjiang	6.99	11.43	15.36	23.03	28.60	37.68	42.01	46.80	51.27	64.11	63.54
神农架林区	Shennongjia	1.86	3.13	4.26	6.66	13.33	12.76	12.69	15.88	16.84	20.78	17.08

7-6 金融机构(含外资)人民币存款年末余额
BALANCE OF RMB DEPOSITS IN FINANCIAL ORGANIZATIONS (INCLUDING FOREIGN FUNDED ENTERPRISES) BY THE END

单位：亿元

指 标	Item	2016
各项存款	Deposits	47284.95
(一)境外存款	Domestic Deposits	47254.81
1.住户存款	Household Deposits	22065.17
(1)活期存款	Demand Deposits	8261.61
(2)定期及其他存款	Regular and Other Deposits	13803.57
2.非金融企业存款	Non Financial Enterprise Deposits	15229.03
(1)活期存款	Demand Deposits	8434.48
(2)定期及其他存款	Regular and Other Deposits	6794.54
3.广义政府存款	General Government Deposits	9001.04
(1)财政性存款	Public Financial Deposits	1244.94
(2)机关团体存款	Bank Deposits	7756.10
4.非银行业金融机构存款	Non Banking Financial Institutions Deposits	959.58
(二)境外存款	Offshore Deposits	30.14

注：本表采用数据为新口径数据。
Note: Data from this table are based on the new standard.

7-7 金融机构(含外资)人民币贷款年末余额
BALANCE OF RMB LOANS OF FINANCIAL ORGANIZTIONS (INCLUDING FOREIGN FUNDED ENTERPISES) BY THE END

单位：亿元 (100 million yuan)

指标	Item	2016
各项贷款	Loans	34530.72
(一)境内贷款	Domestil Loans	33390.26
1.住户贷款	Household Loans	9339.51
(1)短期贷款	Short-term Loans	1502.70
消费贷款	Consumer Loans	463.30
经营贷款	Operating Loans	1039.40
(2)中长期贷款	Medium-term and Long-term Loans	7836.82
消费贷款	Consumer Loans	6717.61
经营贷款	Operating Loans	1119.21
2.非金融企业及机关团体贷款	Non Financial Enterprise and Institution Loans	24050.61
(1)短期贷款	Short-term Loans	7002.87
(2)中长期贷款	Medium and Long Term Loans	14783.72
(3)票据融资	Bill Financing	1531.82
(4)融资租赁	Loans for Accomodation and Rent	667.73
(5)各项垫款	Money Advanced Payment for Others	64.46
3.非银行业金融机构贷款	Non Banking Financial Institution Loans	0.13
(二)境外贷款	Foreign Loans	1140.47

注：本表采用数据为新口径数据。
Note: Data from this table are based on the new standard.

7-8 保险业务主要指标
MAJOR INDICATORS OF INSURANCE BUSINESS

项　目	Item	2013	2014	2015	2016
一、保险密度 (元/人)	Density of Insurance (yuan/person)	1012.94	1204.00	1441.73	1787.19
二、保险深度 (%)	Depth of Insurance (%)	2.38	2.56	2.85	3.26
三、保费收入 (亿元)	Premium (100 million yuan)	587.40	700.23	843.63	1051.00
(一)财产保险	Property Insurnce	169.35	204.55	238.24	263.22
1.财产险	Property Insurnce	11.04	12.29	12.44	13.65
2.机动车辆保险	Machine Driving Cars Insurnce	128.98	161.27	193.35	219.76
3.责任险	Responsibility Insurance	6.63	7.84	9.47	10.75
4.信用保证险	Credit Guarantee Insurance	8.40	9.05	8.03	5.27
5.其它	Others	14.29	14.10	14.95	13.79
(二)人身保险	Life Insurance	418.07	495.67	605.38	788.54
1.人身意外伤害保险	Accident Insurance	15.79	18.52	22.01	30.13
团体保险	Group Insurance	8.06	9.35	10.36	11.69
个人保险	Individual Insurance	7.73	9.17	11.65	18.44
2.健康险	Healthy Insurance	39.47	55.64	87.97	128.41
团体保险	Group Insurance	14.69	21.24	25.80	30.75
个人保险	Individual Insurance	24.78	34.40	62.17	97.66
3.寿险	Personal Insurance	362.81	421.51	495.40	630.00
团体保险	Group Insurance	1.80	2.77	1.15	0.74
个人保险	Individual Insurance	361.01	418.74	494.25	629.27
四、各项赔款和给付 (亿元)	Claim and Payment (100 million yuan)	187.61	230.59	283.34	372.36
(一)财产保险	Property Insurnce	86.32	100.90	114.42	141.80
1.财产险	Property Insurnce	4.01	4.51	4.30	8.81
2.机动车辆保险	Machine Driving Cars Insurnce	71.60	83.82	97.27	114.11
3.责任险	Responsibility Insurance	3.00	3.69	4.13	5.35
4.信用保证险	Credit Guarantee Insurance	0.50	1.17	2.15	2.80
5.其它	Others	7.21	7.71	6.57	10.73
(二)人身保险	Life Insurance	101.28	129.69	168.92	230.55
1.人身意外伤害保险	Accident Insurance	3.93	4.67	5.97	6.98
团体保险	Group Insurance	1.61	2.03	3.01	3.67
个人保险	Individual Insurance	2.32	2.64	2.96	3.31
2.健康险	Healthy Insurance	14.43	26.73	32.33	38.41
团体保险	Group Insurance	7.49	18.54	22.00	24.69
个人保险	Individual Insurance	6.94	8.19	10.33	13.72
3.寿险	Personal Insurance	82.92	98.29	130.62	185.16
团体保险	Group Insurance	7.69	8.10	8.10	8.27
个人保险	Individual Insurance	75.23	90.19	122.52	176.89

注：本表采用数据均为保险业新口径数据。
Note: Data from this table are based on the new standard.

主要统计指标解释

财政总收入 指地方一般预算收入与上划中央税收收入之和。

公共财政收入 是指各级政府为履行职能,按照国家法律、法规规定收取的纳入一般预算管理的各项税收及非税收入总和。主要包括:

(1)各项税收:包括国内增值税、国内消费税、进口货物增值税和消费税、出口货物退增值税和消费税、营业税、企业所得税、个人所得税、资源税、城市维护建设税、房产税、印花税、城镇土地使用税、土地增值税、车船税、船舶吨税、车辆购置税、关税、耕地占用税、契税、烟叶税等。

(2)非税收入:包括专项收入、行政事业性收费、罚没收入和其他收入。

公共财政支出 国家财政将筹集起来的资金进行分配使用,以满足经济建设和各项事业的需要。主要包括:

(1)一般公共服务:指政府提供基本公共管理与服务的支出,包括人大事务、政协事务、政府办公厅(室)及相关机构事务、发展与改革事务、统计信息事务、财政事务、税收事务、审计事务、海关事务、人力资源事务、纪检监察事务、人口与计划生育事务、商贸事务、知识产权事务、工商行政管理事务、国土资源事务、海洋管理事务、测绘事务、地震事务、气象事务、民族事务、宗教事务、港澳台侨事务、档案事务、共产党事务、民主党派事务及工商联事务、群众团体事务、彩票事务等。

(2)外交:指政府外交事务支出,包括外交行政管理、驻外机构、对外援助、国际组织、对外合作与交流、边界勘界联检等方面的支出。

(3)国防:指政府用于国防方面的支出,包括用于现役部队、预备役部队、民兵、国防科研事业、专项工程、国防动员等方面的支出。

(4)公共安全:指政府维护社会公共安全方面的支出,包括武装警察、公安、国家安全、检察、法院、司法行政、监狱、劳教、国家保密、缉私警察等。

(5)教育:指政府教育事务支出,包括教育行政管理、学前教育、小学教育、初中教育、普通高中教育、普通高等教育、初等职业教育、中专教育、技校教育、职业高中教育、高等职业教育、广播电视教育、留学生教育、特殊教育、干部继续教育、教育机关服务等。

(6)科学技术:指用于科学技术方面的支出,包括科学技术管理事务、基础研究、应用研究、技术研究与开发、科技条件与服务、社会科学、科学技术普及、科技交流与合作等。

(7)文化教育与传媒:指政府在文化、文物、体育、广播影视、新闻出版等方面的支出。

(8)社会保障和就业:指政府在社会保障与就业方面的支出,包括社会保障和就业管理事务、民政管理事务、财政对社会保险基金的补助、补充全国社会保障基金、行政事业单位离退休、企业改革补助、就业补助、抚恤、退役安置、社会福利、残疾人事业、城市居民最低生活保障、其他城镇社会救济、农村社会救济、自然灾害生活救助、红十字事务等。

(9)医疗卫生:指政府医疗卫生方面的支出,包括医疗卫生管理事务支出、医疗服务支出、医疗保障支出、疾病预防控制支出、卫生监督支出、妇幼保健支出、农村卫生支出等。

(10)节能环保:指政府环境保护支出,包括环境保护管理事务支出、环境监测与监察支出、污染治理支出、自然生态保护支出、天然林保护工程支出、退耕还林支出、风沙荒漠治理支出、退牧还草支出、已垦草原退耕还草、能源节约利用、污染减排、可再生能源和资源综合利用等支出。

(11)城乡社区事务:指政府城乡社区事务支出,包括城乡社区管理事务支出、城乡社区规划与管理支出、城乡社区公共设施支出、城乡社区住宅支出、城乡社区环境卫生支出、建设市场管理与监督支出等。

(12)农林水事务:指政府农林水事务支出,包括农业支出、林业支出、水利支出、扶贫支出、农业综合开发支出等。

（13）交通运输：指政府交通运输和邮政业方面的支出，包括公路运输支出、水路运输支出、铁路运输支出、民用航空运输支出、邮政业支出等。

信贷资金 指金融机构以信用方式积聚和分配的货币资金。金融机构信贷资金的来源有各项存款、金融债券发行、应付及暂收款、对国际金融机构负债、流通中货币、各项准备、所有者权益和其他项目等；信贷资金的运用有各项贷款、有价证券及投资、应收及预付款、委托投资、金银占款、外汇占款、库存现金、财政借款及在国际金融机构中的资产等。

存款 指企业、机关、团体或居民根据资金必须收回的原则，把货币资金存入银行或其他信贷机构保管并取得一定利息的一种信用活动形式。根据存款对象或性质的不同可划分为企业存款、财政存款、机关团体存款、基本建设存款、储蓄存款、农村存款、委托存款、其他存款等科目。它是银行信贷资金的主要来源。

贷款 指银行或其他信贷机构根据资金必须归还的原则，按一定利率，为企业、个人等提供资金的一种信用活动形式。我国银行贷款分为短期贷款、中期流动资金贷款、中长期贷款、信托贷款、融资租赁、委托贷款、票据融资、各项垫款等。

保险公司 在中国境内的、经过保险监督管理部门批准设立，并依法登记注册的各类商业保险公司。

保险金额 指保险人承担赔偿或者给付保险金责任的最高限额。

保费 指投保人为取得保险人在约定范围内所承担赔偿责任而支付给保险人的费用。

赔款 指保险人根据保险合同的规定，向被保险人支付的赔偿保险责任损失的金额。

给付 包括死伤医疗给付和满期给付。死伤医疗给付是指保险人根据人寿保险及长期健康保险合同的规定，因被保险人在保险期内发生保险责任范围内的保险事故支付给被保险人(或受益人)的金额。满期给付是指被保险人生存期满，保险人按人寿保险合同规定支付给被保险人的满期保险金额。

Explanatory Notes on Main Statistical Indicators

Total income refers to the local fiscal revenue and the general budget tax revenue and central planning.Public Financial revenue is to perform its functions in accordance with national laws and regulations collected into the general budget of the revenue management and non-tax revenues combined. Public FinancialExpenditure refers to the distribution and use of the funds the government finances has risen, so as to meet the needs of economic construction and various causes. It includes the following main items:

(1) Expenditure for general public services: It refers to the spending on the basic public management and services which provided by governments, including the expense on affairs of People's Congress, affairs of People's Political Consultative Conference, affairs of government general office and relative institutions, affairs of development and reform, affairs of statistics, affairs of finance, affairs of taxation, affairs of audit, affairs of customs, affairs of human resources and social security, affairs of discipline inspection and supervision, affairs of population and family planning, affairs of commerce and trade, affairs of intellectual property, affairs of administration for industry and commerce, affairs of land and resources, affairs of oceanic administration, affairs of surveying and mapping, affairs of earthquake, ethnic affairs, religious affairs, affairs of Hong Kong, Macao, Taiwan, and Overseas Chinese, affairs of archives administration, affairs of Chinese Communist Party, affairs of democratic parties and federation of industry and commerce, affairs of mass organization, and affairs of lottery, etc.

(2) Expenditure for foreign affairs: It refers to the spending of government on foreign affairs, including the expense on administration of foreign affairs, missions overseas, external assistance, international organizations, foreign cooperation and communication, surveying and joint inspection on borderline, etc.

(3) Expenditure for national defence: It refers to the spending of government on national defence, including the expense on active force, reserve force, militia, scientific research on national defence, special projects, mobilization of national defence, etc.

(4) Expenditure for public security: It refers to the spending of government on maintaining social and public security, including the

expense on armed police force, public security, state security, prosecution, courts, justice, prison, labour education and rehabilitation, protection of state secrecy, anti-smuggling police, etc.

(5) Expenditure for education: It refers to the spending of government on education, including the expense on the administration of education, pre-primary education, primary education, secondary education, high school education, regular higher education, primary vocational education, secondary vocational education, technical school education, vocational high school education and higher vocational education, radio and television education, student abroad education, special education, on the job training of cadres, education authorities services, etc.

(6) Expenditure for science and technology: It refers to the spending of government on science and technology (S&T), including the expense on the administration of S&T, basic research, applied research, research and development, conditions and services of S&T, popularization of social science, science and technology, exchanges and cooperation of S&T, etc.

(7) Expenditure for culture, sport and media: It refers to the spending of government on culture, cultural heritage, sports, radio, film, television, press and publication, etc.

(8) Expenditure for social safety net and employment effort: It refers to the spending of government on social safety net and employment, including the expense on administration of social safety net and employment, civil affairs, budgetary subsidy on the social insurance funds, subsidy on National Social Security Fund, retirees of administrative units and institutions, subsidy on enterprise reform, subsidy on employment effort, pension, placement of ex-serviceman, social welfare, the handicapped undertakings, the system of cost of living allowances for urban residents, other urban social relief, rural social relief, living relief of natural disasters, affairs of Red Cross Society, etc.

(9) Expenditure for medical and health care: It refers to the spending of government on medical and health care, including the expense on administration of medical and health care, medical services, health care, disease prevention and control, health inspection and supervision, women and children's health, rural health care, etc.

(10) Expenditure for environment protection: It refers to the spending of government on environment protection, including the expense on administration of environment protection, environment monitoring and supervision, pollution control, natural ecology protection, project of virgin forests protection, reforesting farmland, controlling the sources of dust storms, returning pastureland to grassland, returning pastureland to grassland, returning cultivated land to grassland, energy conservation, emissions reduction, comprehensive utilization of renewable energy and resources, etc.

(11) Expenditure for urban and rural community affairs: It refers to the spending of government on urban and rural community affairs, including the expense on administration of urban and rural community, planning and management of urban and rural community, public facilities of urban and rural community, housing of urban and rural community, sanitation of urban and rural community, management and supervision on the construction market, etc.

(12) Expenditure for agriculture, forestry and water conservancy: It refers to the spending of government on agriculture, forestry and water conservancy, including the expense on agriculture, forestry, water conservancy, poverty alleviation, comprehensive agricultural development, etc.

(13) Expenditure for transportation: It refers to the spending of government on transportation and postal services, including the expense on road transportation, waterway transportation, railway transportation, civil aviation transportation, and postal services.

Credit Funds refer to the funds issued as loans by banking institutions. The sources of credit funds of the banking institutions included deposits, issue of financial bonds, account-payable and temporary gathering, liabilities to international financial institutions, currency in circulation, various reserves, owners' rights and interests and other items. The credit funds can be used in forms of loans, securities and investment, account receivable and advance payment, entrusted investment, gold, foreign exchange, cash on hand, government debt and assets in the international financial institutions.

Deposit is a form of credit by which enterprises, institutions, organizations or households can put money into banks and other credit institutions for safekeeping and interest earning under the principle of free withdrawal. According to different depositors, deposits are divided into enterprise deposits, treasury deposits, deposits of government agencies and organizations, capital construction deposits, savings deposits, rural saving deposits, entrusted deposits and other deposits. Deposits are major sources of the credit funds of banks.

Loan is a form of credit by which banks and other credit institutions provide funds at certain interest rate to enterprises and individuals in the light of the principle of unconditional repayment. Loans from Chinese banks include circulating capital loans, fixed assets loans, loans to urban and rural individuals engaged in industrial and commercial business and agricultural loans.

Insurance Companies refer to commercial insurance companies of various forms registered by law and established in China with the approval of insurance regulatory agencies.

Amount Insured refers to the maximum that the insurant will get for the claim of the case insured.

Premium is the fee paid by the insurant to the insurer to obtain the obligation of compensation from the insurance within the agreed terms.

Settled Claim is the compensation paid by the insurer to the insurant in accordance with the insurance contract.

Payment includes payment for death, injury or medical treatment and mature payment. Payment for death, injury or medical treatment refers to the money paid to the insurant (or the beneficiary) in accordance with the life or health insurance contract when the insurant encounters accidents within the insured period covered in the contract. Mature payment refers to the mature payment to the insurant in accordance with the life insurance contract at the end of the insured period.

8 价　格

Price

8-1 物 价 总 指 数 (2016)
GENERAL PRICE INDICES(2016)

基 期	Base Period	商品零售价格总指数 General Rtail Price Index	居民消费价格总指数 General Consumption Price Index
以1950年价格为100	The Price of 1950 Equals 100	664.0	1052.8
以1952年价格为100	The Price of 1952 Equals 100	588.8	926.1
以1957年价格为100	The Price of 1957 Equals 100	533.0	821.0
以1965年价格为100	The Price of 1965 Equals 100	477.7	722.2
以1970年价格为100	The Price of 1970 Equals 100	481.4	725.0
以1975年价格为100	The Price of 1975 Equals 100	482.1	718.0
以1978年价格为100	The Price of 1978 Equals 100	478.3	715.2
以1980年价格为100	The Price of 1980 Equals 100	450.9	653.1
以1985年价格为100	The Price of 1985 Equals 100	393.0	549.0
以1990年价格为100	The Price of 1990 Equals 100	243.8	346.3
以1995年价格为100	The Price of 1995 Equals 100	130.6	162.9
以2000年价格为100	The Price of 2000 Equals 100	133.1	151.6
以2005年价格为100	The Price of 2005 Equals 100	128.2	137.4
以2010年价格为100	The Price of 2010 Equals 100	112.7	118.4
以上年价格为100	The Price of Last Year Equals 100	100.8	102.2

8-2 各市、县物价指数(2016)
GENERAL PRICE INDICES(2016)

(上年=100) (preceding year = 100)

地 区	Region	居民消费价格指数 Consumer Price Index	商品零售价格指数 Retail Price Index	农业生产资料价格指数 Agricultural Production Material Price Index
湖北省	**Hubei**	**102.2**	**100.8**	**100.3**
武汉市	Wuhan	102.4	101.3	
黄石市	Huangshi	102.1	99.5	
十堰市	Shiyan	101.9	100.7	
竹山县	zhushan	101.8	101.5	100.2
宜昌市	Yichang	102.3	100.2	
宜都市	Yidu	102.3	100.9	99.7
襄阳市	Xiangyang	102.2	100.6	
老河口市	Laohekou	102.2	100.7	98.9
鄂州市	Ezhou	101.9	100.7	
荆门市	Jingmen	102.0	102.3	
孝感市	Xiaogan	102.2	101.5	
大悟县	Dawu	102.7	101.3	99.3
荆州市	Jingzhou	101.8	100.5	
洪湖市	Honghu	102.2	101.5	100.6
黄冈市	Huanggang	101.4	101.6	
浠水县	Xishui	102.4	100.8	100.4
麻城市	Macheng	102.3	100.2	100.0
咸宁市	Xianning	101.7	100.0	
崇阳县	Chongyang	102.5	100.7	102.9
随州市	Suizhou	101.9	100.3	
恩施市	Enshi	102.2	99.9	
天门市	Tianmen	102.0	101.0	98.9

8-3 全省居民消费、商品零售价格分类指数(2016)
RETAIL PRICE INDICES BY CATEGORY OF COMMODITIES(2016)

(上年=100) (preceding year=100)

类 别	Item	全 省 Provincial Indices	城 市 Urban Indices	农 村 Rural Indices
居民消费价格总指数	General Consumer Price Index	102.2	102.1	102.2
*服务项目价格指数	Service Price Index	103.0	103.0	103.0
一、食品烟酒	Food Tobacco and Alcohol	104.0	103.9	104.2
二、衣着	Clothing	102.3	102.2	102.5
三、居住	Residence	102.8	103.0	102.3
四、生活用品及服务	Daily Necessities and Services	100.4	100.5	100.2
五、交通和通信	Transportation and Communication	97.2	96.8	98.2
六、教育文化和娱乐	Education,Culture and Recreation	102.2	102.3	101.9
七、医疗保健	Medicine	101.9	101.7	102.3
八、其他用品和服务	Other Supplies and Services	102.8	103.4	101.5
商品零售价格总指数	General Price Index	100.8	100.7	100.9
一、食品	Foods	104.7	104.7	105.1
二、饮料、烟酒	Beverage, Tobacco and Liquor	101.3	101.4	100.6
三、服装、鞋帽	Garments, Shoes and Hats	101.9	101.9	101.9
四、纺织品	Texiles	101.1	101.0	101.3
五、家用电器及音像器材	Household Electric Appliance and Stereo	98.0	97.7	99.3
六、文化办公用品	Stationery and Business Articles	99.7	99.7	99.1
七、日用品	Daily Use Articles	100.7	100.9	100.2
八、体育娱乐用品	Sports and Receation Articles	101.5	101.7	100.8
九、交通、通信用品	Transportation and Communication Articles	95.3	95.3	95.2
十、家具	Furniture	100.6	100.8	99.6
十一、化妆品	Cosmetics	102.0	102.2	100.9
十二、金银珠宝	Gold, Silver and Pearls Jewelery	107.3	107.9	102.6
十三、中西药品及医疗保健用品	Chinese Traditional Medicine, Western Medicines and Health Care Appliances	103.4	103.5	103.1
十四、书报杂志及电子出版物	Books, Newspaper, Magzines and Electronic Publications	99.5	99.2	101.4
十五、燃料类	Fuels	96.4	96.5	96.2
十六、建筑材料及五金电料	Building and Decoration Materials	101.3	101.5	100.3
农业生产资料价格指数	General Price Index of Means of Agricultural	100.3		

8-4 工业生产者出厂价格指数
EX-FACTORY PRICE INDICES OF INDUSTRIAL PRODUCTS

分 类	Group Name	上年=100 preceding year=100	1990年=100 1990=100	
		2016	2015	2016
总指数	**General Indices**	**99.0**	**267.25**	**264.52**
一、按轻重工业分	Grouped by Light Industry and Heavy Industry			
1.轻工业	Light Industry	99.9	223.81	223.50
以农产品为原料	Using Farm Products as Raw Material	99.6	256.00	255.05
以非农产品为原料	Using Non-Farm Products as Raw Material	101.0	146.89	148.36
2.重工业	Heavy Industry	98.5	312.56	307.97
采 掘	Mining and Quarrying	97.7	602.35	588.74
原 料	Raw Material	99.0	447.47	442.97
加 工	Processing	98.4	188.71	185.78
二、按两大部类分	Grouped by Two Sectors			
1.生产资料	Means of Production	98.4	302.54	297.77
采 掘	Mining and Quarrying	97.7	601.86	588.26
原 料	Raw Material	98.9	366.96	363.02
加 工	Processing	98.3	196.78	193.51
2.生活资料	Consumer Goods	100.2	205.24	205.67
食 品	Foods	100.2	277.38	277.85
衣 着	Clothing	100.7	228.82	230.43
一般日用品	Daily Use Articles	101.4	193.53	196.32
耐用消费品	Durable Consumer Goods	99.1	63.06	62.46

8-5 原材料、燃料、动力购进价格指数
RAW MATERIAL, FUEL, POWER PURCHASE PRICE INDICES

分 类	Group Name	上年=100 preceding year=100	1990年=100 1990=100	
		2016	2015	2016
总指数	**General Index**	**98.32**	**385.03**	**378.55**
燃料、动力类	Fuel Powers	95.04	596.13	566.58
黑色金属材料类	Ferrous Metal	103.55	276.82	286.65
有色金属材料类	Non-ferrous Metal	98.62	294.46	290.38
化工原材料类	Chemical Materials	97.32	212.99	207.27
木材及纸浆类	Timber and Pulp	98.75	183.86	181.57
建筑材料及非金属矿类	Construction Materials and Non-Metal Mining Industry	98.10	307.22	301.38
其它工业原材料及半成品类	Other Industrial Raw Materials and Semi-Finished Products	97.36	185.05	180.16
农副产品类	Farm and Sideline Products	101.17	429.99	435.01
纺织原料类	Textile Raw Materials	99.74	193.36	192.86

8-6 固定资产投资价格指数
PRICE INDICES OF INVESTMENT IN FIXED ASSETS

分类	Name of Group	上年=100 preceding year=100	1990年=100 1990=100
		2016	2016
总指数	**Total Indices**	100.1	291.9
建筑安装工程	Construction and Installation	100.2	329.7
设备、工器具	Equipment and Devices	99.1	175.4
其他费用	Others	100.7	375.7

主要统计指标解释

居民消费价格指数 是反映一定时期内城乡居民所购买的生活消费品价格和服务项目价格变动趋势和程度的相对数，是对城市居民消费价格指数和农村居民消费价格指数进行综合汇总计算的结果。该指数可以观察和分析消费品的零售价格和服务价格变动对城乡居民实际生活费支出的影响程度。

城市居民消费价格指数 是反映一定时期内城市居民家庭所购买的生活消费品价格和服务项目价格变动趋势和程度的相对数。该指数可以观察和分析消费品的零售价格和服务项目价格变动对城镇职工货币工资的影响，作为研究职工生活和确定工资政策的依据。

农村居民消费价格指数 是反映一定时期内农村居民家庭所购买的生活消费品价格和服务项目价格变动趋势和程度的相对数。该指数可以观察农村消费品的零售价格和服务项目价格变动对农村居民生活消费支出的影响，直接反映农民生活水平的实际变化情况，为分析和研究农村居民生活问题提供依据。

商品零售价格指数 是反映一定时期内城乡商品零售价格变动趋势和程度的相对数。商品零售价格的变动直接影响到城乡居民的生活支出和国家的财政收入，影响居民购买力和市场供需的平衡，影响到消费与积累的比例关系。因此，该指数可以从一个侧面对上述经济活动进行观察和分析。

农业生产资料价格指数 指反映一定时期内农业生产资料价格变动趋势和程度的相对数。农业生产资料价格指数分为小农具、饲料、产品畜、役畜、半机械化农具、机械化农具、化学肥料、农药及农药械、农机用油、其他农业生产资料十大类。其编制目的是了解农业生产中物质资料投入价格的变动状况，服务于国民经济核算。1994年以前，农业生产资料价格指数仅仅是商品零售价格指数的一个类别，此后，从商品零售价格指数中分离出来，单独编制。

农产品生产者价格指数 是反映一定时期内，农产品生产者出售农产品价格水平变动趋势及幅度的相对数。该指数可以客观反映全国农产品生产价格水平和结构变动情况，满足农业与国民经济核算需要。其中某代表品生产价格指数是通过对全部有出售该产品行为的调查单位的个体指数进行几何平均求得的，类价格指数是通过对其所属的类(或代表品)的价格指数进行加权平均求得的。季度累计价格指数的计算方法与分季指数的计算方法相同。

工业生产者出厂价格指数 是反映一定时期内全部工业产品出厂价格总水平的变动趋势和程度的相对数，包括工业企业售给本企业以外所有单位的各种产品和直接售给居民用于生活消费的产品。该指数可以观察出厂价格变动对工业总产值及增加值的影响。

工业生产者购进价格指数 是反映工业企业作为生产投入，而从物资交易市场和能源、原材料生产企业购买原材料、燃料和动力产品时，所支付的价格水平变动趋势和程度的统计指标，是扣除工业企业物质消耗成本中的价格变动影响的重要依据。

目前，我国编制的原材料、燃料和动力购进价格指数所调查的产品包括燃料动力、黑色金属、有色金属、化工、建材等九大类的近1800种产品。

固定资产投资价格指数 是反映一定时期内固定资产投资品及项目的价格变动趋势和程度的相对数。固定资产投资额是由建筑安装工程投资完成额、设备工器具购置投资完成额和其他费用投资完成额三部分组成的。编制固定资产投资价格指数应首先分别编制上述三部分投资的价格指数，然后采用加权算术平均法求出固定资产投资价格总指数。

该指数可以准确地反映固定资产投资中涉及的各类投资品和取费项目价格变动趋势和变动幅度，消除按现价计算的固定资产投资指标中的价格变动因素，真实地反映固定资产投资的规模、速度、结构和效益，为国家科学地制定、检查固定资产投资计划并提高宏观调控水平，为完善国民经济核算体系提供科学的、可靠的依据。

房地产价格指数 是反映一定时期内房地产价格变动趋势和程度的相对数，包括新建住宅销售价格指数、二手住宅销售价格指数。

Explanatory Notes on Main Statistical Indicators

Consumer Price Indices reflect the trend and degree of changes in prices of consumer goods and services purchased by urban and rural households during a given period. It can be used to observe and analyze the impact of price changes in consumer goods and services on wages (in monetary terms) of urban and rural staff and workers, and provide basis for policy-making concerning the living cost and wages of staff and workers.

Urban Consumer Price Indices reflect the trend and degree of changes in prices of consumer goods and services purchased by urban households during a given period. It can be used to observe the impact of change in retail prices of consumer goods and service prices in urban areas on the wage of urban workers' money. It provides basis for analysis and research on condition of life in urban areas.

Rural Consumer Price Indices reflect the trend and degree of changes in prices of consumer goods and services purchased by rural households during a given period. It can be used to observe the impact of change in retail prices of consumer goods and service prices in rural areas on living expenditure of rural households, and to show the changes in the living standard of peasants. It provides basis for analysis and research on condition of life in rural areas.

Retail Price Indices reflect the trend and degree of change in retail prices of commodities during a given period. The change in retail prices of commodities directly affect the living expenditure of urban and rural residents, government revenue, purchasing power of residents and the equilibrium of market supply and demand, and the ratio of consumption to accumulation. Therefore, the retail price indices are useful to analyze the changes of the above economic activities.

Price Indices of Means of Agricultural Production reflect the trend and degree of changes in prices of means of agricultural production during a given period. Price indices of means of agricultural production are composed of 10 categories including small farm tools, feeds, domestic animals for meat, draught domestic animals, semi-mechanized farm machinery, mechanized farm machinery, chemical fertilizers, pesticides and spraying machinery, fuels for farm machinery and other means of agricultural production. Compilation of these indices helps to understand the changes in prices of input into agricultural production and facilitate the compilation of national account statistics. Before 1994, price indices of means of agricultural production was a sub-category in the in the retail price indices of commodities, and it has been compiled separately since 1994.

Indices of Producers' Prices for Farm Products reflect the trend and degree of changes in producers' prices received by farmers when they sell farm products during a given period. These indices depict the change in the level and structure of producers' prices of farm products of the country and meet the needs of agriculture statistics and national account statistics. The producers' price index of a given product is calculated through geometrical mean of individual indices of all surveyed units who sell such product, and the indices of a product category is obtained through weighted mean of price indices of all products in the category. Method for calculating accumulative quarterly indices is the same as for calculating the distinctive quarterly indices.

Producer Price Indices for Industrial Producers reflect the trend and degree of changes in general ex-factory prices of all industrial products during a given period, including sales of industrial products by an industrial enterprise to all units outside the enterprise, as well as sales of consumer goods to residents. It can be used to analyze the impact of ex-factory prices on gross output value and value-added of the industrial sector.

Purchasing Price Indices for Industrial Producers reflect changes in the level and degree of prices paid by industrial enterprises when they purchase production input such as raw materials, fuels and power from the market or from other energy or raw materials producing enterprises. These indices provide important basis for measuring the material consumption of industrial enterprises after removing influence of price changes.

At present, close to 1,800 products in 9 categories, including fuels and power, ferrous metals, non-ferrous metals, chemicals, building materials, are covered in China for the survey to produce indices of purchasing prices of raw materials, fuels and power.

Price Indices of Investment in Fixed Assets reflect the trend and degree of changes in prices of investment goods and projects in fixed assets during a given period. The investment in fixed assets consists of three components, namely the investment in construction and installation, the investment in purchases of equipment and instrument, and the investment in other items. Price indices of investment in fixed assets are calculated as the weighted arithmetic mean of the price indices of the three components of investment in fixed assets.

Removing the factor of price change in the aggregates of investment at current prices, this indicator shows the changes in the prices of commodities and fees involved in the investment of fixed assets, and can be used to observe the actual size, growth, structure, and efficiency of investment in fixed assets and provides reliable and scientific data for government planning, management, decision-making, and further improving the current national accounting system.

Price Indices for Real Estate reflect the trend and degree of changes in prices of real estate during a given period, including sales price indices of new houses, sales price indices of second-hand housing.

9 居民生活

People's Livelihood

9-1 居民生活水平情况
PEOPLE'S LIVING STANDARD

项 目	Item	单位	unit	2005	2010	2014	2015	2016
一、城乡就业	Employment							
每一农村劳动力负担人数	Average Person Supported by a Rural Laborer	人	person	1.34	1.27	1.41	1.41	1.41
每一城镇就业者负担人数	Average Person Supported by a Urban Laborer	人	person	1.96	2.01	1.79	1.86	1.88
城镇登记失业率	The Rate of Registered Unemployment	%	percentage	4.33	4.18	3.10	2.64	2.41
二、城乡居民收入	Revenue							
农村居民人均可支配收入	Net Income of Rural Residents Per Capita	元	yuan	3099.00	5832.00	10849.06	11843.89	12724.97
农村居民人均可支配收入指数(1990=100)	Indices of Net Income of Rural Residents Per Capita (1990=100)	%	percentage	461.80	869.24	1617.33	1765.63	1896.29
城镇居民人均可支配收入	Annual Disposable Income of Urban Residents	元	yuan	8786.00	16058.00	24852.28	27051.47	29385.80
城镇居民人均可支配收入指数(1990=100)	Indices of Net Annual Disposable Income of Urban Residents (1990=100)	%	percentage	615.80	1125.45	1741.33	1895.42	2058.43
国有职工平均工资	Average Wages of Staff and Workers in State-Owned Units	元	yuan	14774	35981	55071	60615	68983
三、城乡居民人平消费水平	Consumption Level							
农村居民	Rural Residents	元	yuan	2503	4758	8608	9542	10860
城镇居民	Urban Residents	元	yuan	8051	13576	21854	23561	25703
四、储 蓄	Savings							
城乡居民人平储蓄存款余额	Balance of Saving Deposits of Rural and Urban Residents Per Capita	元	yuan	7929	17216	30686	33539	37601
五、平均每人居住面积	Floor Area of Housing Per Capita							
城 市(大、中)	Municipalities (Large and Medium-sized)	平方米	sq.m	29.90	33.20	41.90	43.18	44.45
农 村	Rural Areas	平方米	sq.m	36.05	40.99	54.78	55.61	57.67
六、交 通	Transportations							
城镇每百户拥有汽车	Cars Ouned Per 100	辆	set		5.53	13.65	17.68	23.63
七、文 化	Culture							
每百人每天有报纸	Newspaper Owned Per 100 Persons Every Day	份	unit	8.89	8.70	9.01	7.23	5.71
每人每年有图书、杂志	Books and Magazines Owned Per Capita Annually	册	unit	8.99	9.90	9.52	8.82	7.77
八、教 育	Education							
学龄儿童入学率	Emrollment Ratio of School-Age Children	%	percentsge	99.65	99.96	99.99	99.99	100.00
每万人口有大学生数	Number of University Students Per 10000 Persons	人	person	167.91	226.58	244.10	240.75	258.96
九、卫 生	Health Care							
每千人有医院病床数	Number of Hospital-Beds Owned By Per 1000 Person	张	unit	2.31	3.26	5.47	5.87	6.14
每千人有医生	Number of Doctors Owned By Per 1000 Persons	人	person	1.49	1.62	2.19	2.32	2.42

注：平均每人居住面积中，城市(大、中)从2002年起为建筑面积，以前年份为居住面积。
Notes: Of Average Housing Areas, it refers to Construction Area of Municipalities (large and medium-sized)areas.since 2002, before2002, it refers to living areas.

9-2 居民消费水平
PEOPLE'S CONSUMPTION LEVEL

年份 year	居民消费 (亿元) People's Censurption (100 million yuan)	农村居民 rural residernts	城镇居民 wrban residernts	居民消费水平 (元) level of consumption	农村居民 rural residernts	城镇居民 wrban residernts
1982	126.75	90.67	36.08	266	227	462
1983	141.49	101.17	40.32	293	251	502
1984	172.19	120.41	51.78	352	300	592
1985	203.23	129.78	73.45	411	328	738
1986	247.13	158.31	88.82	493	402	825
1987	271.22	172.47	98.75	533	434	891
1988	328.82	204.21	124.61	638	509	1092
1989	398.09	255.09	143.00	762	630	1218
1990	434.62	273.27	161.35	813	659	1341
1991	475.85	286.08	189.77	869	674	1541
1992	546.61	301.60	245.01	986	706	1926
1993	694.49	357.10	337.35	1236	831	2554
1994	845.14	413.40	431.75	1486	964	3086
1995	1095.97	504.10	591.85	1908	1183	3989
1996	1346.76	594.80	751.99	2323	1396	4892
1997	1438.12	614.90	823.26	2459	1441	5208
1998	1518.92	610.20	908.68	2579	1427	5632
1999	1507.12	558.40	948.69	2545	1302	5802
2000	1594.08	559.10	1034.96	2680	1302	6250
2001	1767.38	585.40	1181.96	2962	1365	7042
2002	1951.54	606.80	1344.70	3263	1418	7899
2003	2188.05	637.70	1550.36	3853	1926	6547
2004	2452.62	700.80	1751.85	4309	2134	7277
2005	2785.42	815.32	1970.10	4883	2503	8051
2006	3124.37	906.15	2218.22	5480	2813	8944
2007	3709.69	1051.82	2657.87	6513	3300	10593
2008	4225.38	1217.95	3007.43	7406	3864	11780
2009	4456.31	1277.72	3178.59	7791	4137	12080
2010	5136.78	1419.65	3717.13	8977	4758	13576
2011	6241.95	1597.69	4644.26	10873	5653	15935
2012	7085.46	1830.83	5254.63	12283	6705	17296
2013	8053.82	2064.74	5989.08	13912	7755	19156
2014	9124.48	2292.06	6832.42	15762	8608	21854
2015	10167.87	2434.73	7733.14	17429	9542	23561
2016	11379.23	2709.89	8669.34	19391	10860	25703

9-3 居民消费水平指数
INDICES OF PEOPLE'S CONSUMPTION LEVEL

(1978年=100)

年 份 year	居民消费 (%) People's Censurption (%)	农村居民 rural residernts	城镇居民 wrban residernts	居民消费水平 (%) level of consumption(%)	农村居民 rural residernts	城镇居民 wrban residernts
1982	156.2	169.2	132.3	149.0	164.2	111.5
1983	172.2	186.6	145.4	162.1	179.7	119.0
1984	196.6	205.4	181.4	183.3	198.7	136.6
1985	218.4	212.2	233.3	201.1	208.2	154.2
1986	253.2	247.7	267.4	229.7	244.3	163.5
1987	263.0	255.1	282.4	235.4	249.4	167.4
1988	268.8	257.1	295.6	237.8	248.6	170.4
1989	278.8	273.6	292.7	243.0	262.6	163.9
1990	290.5	281.2	312.9	247.6	263.3	170.8
1991	275.4	257.6	314.1	229.3	235.7	167.6
1992	281.7	254.0	339.6	231.8	230.5	175.3
1993	338.3	276.9	460.8	274.7	250.1	229.1
1994	380.3	292.4	553.4	304.9	264.6	259.6
1995	421.7	303.5	653.0	334.8	276.3	288.9
1996	474.9	340.2	737.9	373.6	310.0	315.2
1997	499.1	342.9	802.9	389.3	311.8	333.1
1998	549.5	354.6	927.3	425.5	321.8	377.1
1999	571.5	356.0	989.4	440.0	322.1	397.1
2000	599.5	361.0	1062.6	459.8	326.0	420.9
2001	661.3	377.2	1206.1	505.8	341.3	471.0
2002	738.6	391.9	1394.3	564.0	355.3	537.0
2003	807.3	393.9	1578.3	614.7	359.2	595.0
2004	868.7	405.3	1726.7	659.6	372.5	640.2
2005	963.4	458.4	1899.3	729.5	425.0	692.7
2006	1074.2	502.9	2132.9	826.5	480.7	777.9
2007	1191.3	557.2	2365.4	917.4	538.4	853.4
2008	1279.5	599.5	2540.4	984.4	585.8	900.3
2009	1352.4	631.3	2690.3	1038.5	625.0	935.4
2010	1507.9	676.1	3045.4	1156.9	693.1	1017.7
2011	1722.0	710.6	3584.4	1316.6	768.6	1125.6
2012	1897.6	785.9	3946.4	1444.3	880.0	1188.6
2013	2106.3	863.7	4396.3	1597.4	991.8	1286.1
2014	2342.2	941.4	4919.5	1769.9	1107.8	1399.3
2015	2576.4	985.6	5500.0	1932.7	1209.7	1490.3
2016	2841.8	1077.3	6088.5	2120.2	1351.2	1605.1

注：2003年以前数据根据2004年第一次经济普查资料修订。
Notes: Data before 2003 is Gmended accordity to ecorymic survey 2004.

9-4 城镇居民家庭基本情况

年份 Year	调查户数(户) Number of Households Surveyed (household)	平均每户家庭人口(人) Average Number of people Per Household (person)	平均每户就业人口(人) Number of Employees Per Household (person)	每一就业者负担人数(人) Average Persons Supported by a Labor (person)
1963	240	5.30	1.63	3.25
1964	299	5.36	1.61	3.33
1965	370	5.22	1.60	3.26
1980	571	4.20	2.32	1.81
1985	1658	3.84	2.15	1.79
1987	1900	3.73	2.12	1.76
1988	1950	3.61	2.07	1.74
1989	1990	3.52	2.05	1.72
1990	1990	3.47	2.04	1.70
1991	1990	3.45	2.04	1.69
1992	1940	3.36	2.02	1.66
1993	1890	3.29	1.98	1.66
1994	1330	3.23	1.95	1.66
1995	1330	3.22	1.92	1.68
1996	1390	3.24	1.95	1.66
1997	1790	3.23	1.89	1.71
1998	1640	3.19	1.90	1.68
1999	1540	3.15	1.86	1.69
2000	1540	3.14	1.81	1.73
2001	1540	3.10	1.77	1.75
2002	1600	3.07	1.64	1.87
2003	1600	3.06	1.68	1.82
2004	1700	3.03	1.65	1.83
2005	1800	2.98	1.52	1.96
2006	1800	2.96	1.55	1.91
2007	1850	2.95	1.59	1.86
2008	1900	2.96	1.50	1.97
2009	1900	2.94	1.48	1.99
2010	1900	2.93	1.46	2.01
2011	1900	2.90	1.47	1.97
2012	1900	2.89	1.48	1.95
2013	1718	2.77	1.53	1.81
2014	3060	2.85	1.59	1.79
2015	3073	2.85	1.53	1.86
2016	3053	2.86	1.52	1.88

注：①2002年方法制度重新修订,部分指标有所变化：原“平均每人居住面积”改为“平均每人建筑总面积”;原“平均每人实际收入”改为“平均每人总收入”;原“平均每人实际支出”改为“平均每人总支出”。
②2014年起使用城乡一体化住户收支与生活状况调查数据,与之前的分城镇和农村住户调查的范围、方法、指标口径有所不同(此后相关表同)。
③2014年起为城镇常住居民人均可支配收入,与2014年以前不同。

BASIC CONDITIONS OF URBAN HOUSEHOLDS

平均每户就业面 (%) Percentage of Employed Persons Per Household (%)	平均每人 Per Capita		平均每人 Per Capita			平均每人建筑面积(平方米) Average Living Floor Space Per Cappita (sq.m)
	总收入 (元) Actual Income (yuan)	*可支配收入 (元) Disposable Income (yuan)	总支出 (元) Actual Expenditures (yuan)	消费性支出 Living Expenditures	*食品 Food	
30.75	238.1	238.1	237.2	218.4	133.9	
30.04	232.9	232.9	228.3	211.7	122.7	
30.65	224.3	224.3	218.8	204.4	118.0	3.3
55.24	413.7	413.7	394.2	369.3	210.6	5.1
55.99	713.3	704.2	693.1	644.2	324.5	7.9
56.84	960.6	951.8	919.1	836.1	443.2	8.4
57.34	1136.4	1128.1	1153.1	1058.8	538.9	8.9
58.24	1271.6	1262.6	1250.0	1130.7	607.0	9.1
58.79	1437.1	1427.2	1349.4	1220.3	652.4	9.8
59.13	1603.7	1592.9	1538.2	1380.2	717.4	9.6
60.12	1886.4	1874.2	1799.9	1577.7	799.0	9.9
60.18	2453.5	2438.7	2358.1	2097.6	941.5	10.5
60.37	3360.0	3346.0	3588.6	2733.1	1307.1	11.1
59.63	4031.9	4016.7	3977.3	3433.8	1680.6	11.9
60.19	4367.0	4350.2	4290.6	3713.5	1731.4	11.8
58.51	4693.8	4673.2	4549.7	3855.6	1773.6	12.8
59.56	4849.4	4826.4	4903.1	4074.4	1787.7	12.7
59.04	5234.5	5212.8	5333.8	4340.6	1783.4	13.2
57.64	5542.6	5524.5	5643.6	4644.5	1779.4	13.9
57.10	5888.7	5856.0	5774.8	4804.8	1799.4	15.2
53.42	7142.2	6789.0	7159.7	5608.9	2087.8	26.2
54.90	7745.8	7322.0	7551.1	5963.3	2279.6	26.3
54.46	8522.1	8022.8	8076.1	6398.5	2516.2	27.3
51.01	9395.1	8786.0	8582.8	6737.0	2625.4	29.9
52.36	10533.3	9803.0	9839.7	7397.0	2868.4	31.0
53.90	12421.8	11485.0	11476.7	8701.0	3456.0	32.3
50.68	14174.3	13153.0	12471.0	9478.0	3996.0	32.0
50.34	15698.0	14367.0	13868.0	10294.0	4160.5	32.8
49.83	17572.8	16058.4	15612.3	11451.0	4429.3	33.2
50.69	20193.3	18373.9	18123.4	13163.8	5363.7	35.5
51.21	22903.9	20839.6	20107.1	14496.0	5837.9	35.8
55.23	25180.5	22906.4	20419.5	15749.5	6259.2	38.8
55.73	27538.9	24852.3	23175.1	16681.4	3688.3	41.9
53.69	30057.4	27051.5	24798.4	18192.3	3897.6	43.2
53.23	32239.8	29385.8	27376.3	20040.0	4262.6	44.5

Note: ①" Per Capita Living Space (sq.m)" in the above table was changed into "Per Capita Living Floor Space(sq.m)";"Per Capita Actual Income(yuan)"into; "Per Capita Actual Expenditures(yuan)" into "Per Capita Total Expenditures(yuan)';owing to the changes of items in the reversion of 2002 mearurement system.

② The integrated household income and expenditure survey has been used since 2014, including both urban and rural households. The coverage ,methodology and definitions used in the survey are different from those used for the separate urban and rural household survey prior to 2014(…).

③ The concept is Per Capita Disposable Income of Rural Permanent Residents since 2014 ,different from that before 2014.

9-5 城镇居民家庭收支情况(2016)

单位: 元

项 目	Item	总 计 Total
调查户数(户)	Households Surveyed	3052.67
比 重(%)	Ratio	100.00
平均每户家庭人口(人)	Average Number of Residents Per Household	2.86
平均每户离退休人口(人)	Average Number of Retirees Per Household	0.43
平均每一就业者负担人数(人)	Average Persons supported by a Urban Labor	1.88
平均每户就业面(%)	Average Employment Rate Per Household	53.23
平均每人总收入	Per Capita Total Income	32239.85
#可支配收入	Disposable Income	29385.80
平均每人借贷收入	Income of Loans Per Capita	977.71
#提取储蓄存款	Savings Withdrawn	714.52
平均每人借贷支出	Expenditures of Loans Per Capita	699.14
#存入储蓄款	Money Saved	105.50
平均每人总支出	Total Expenditure Per Capita	27376.26
#消费性支出	Consumption Expenditure	20040.03
一、食品烟酒	Food Cigarettes and Wine	6294.26
食品	Food	4262.59
谷物	Grain	882.87
薯类	Patato	35.84
豆类	Bean	73.00
食用油	Edible Oil	179.08
蔬菜和食用菌	Vegetable and Edible Fungi	664.88
肉类	Meat	893.13
禽类	Poultry	178.15
水产品	Aquatic Products	316.19
蛋类	Egg	107.16
奶类	Milk	200.11
干鲜瓜果类	Fruits and Processed Products	370.97
糖果糕点类	Sweet	124.58
其他食品	Others	236.63
烟酒	Cigarettes and Wine	669.66
饮料	Drink	95.23
饮食服务	Food Service	1266.78
二、衣 着	Clothing	1557.43
衣类	Clothing	1250.26
鞋类	Shoes	307.17
三、居 住	Residence	4176.70
租赁房房租	Rent	168.83
住房维修及管理	Management	508.15
水电燃料及其他	Water and Power	783.28
自有住房折算租金	Converted Rent of Zts Own	2716.44
四、生活用品及服务	Household Facilities Articles and Services	1163.77
家具及室内装饰品	Furniture	154.96
家用器具	Appliances	294.89
家用纺织品	Drygoods	93.85
家庭日用杂品	Commodity	367.76
个人用品	Personal Helongings	203.88
家庭服务	Households Service	48.43
五、交通通信	Transport and Communication	2391.87
交通	Transport	1657.08
通信	Communication	734.79
六、教育文化娱乐	Education Culture and Recreation	2228.38
教 育	Education	1331.10
文化娱乐用品	Cultural Recreation Articals	241.91
文化娱乐服务	Cultural Recreation Services	655.36
七、医疗保健	Medicine and Medical Service	1792.04
医疗器具及药品	medical apparatus and instruments	495.16
医疗服务	Medical Service	1296.88
八、其他用品和服务	Miscellaneous Goods and Services	435.59
其他用品	Goods	213.34
其他服务	Services	222.25

注：2014年起城镇居民消费居住支出中自有住房折算租金指现住房为自有住房的住户为自身消费提供住房服务的折算价值，属于实物消费，不包括在现金消费支出中。

PER CAPITA INCOME AND EXPENDITURE OF URBAN HOUSEHOLDS(2016)

(yuan)

低收入户 Low Income Households	中低收入户 Lower Middle Income Households	中等收入户 Middle Income Households	中高收入户 Upper Middle Income Households	高收入户 High Income Households
613.33	615.58	611.75	611.17	600.83
20.09	20.17	20.04	20.02	19.68
3.37	3.19	2.80	2.66	2.26
0.19	0.32	0.46	0.66	0.52
2.02	1.86	1.82	1.92	1.75
49.53	53.71	54.93	52.21	57.25
14611.07	22513.31	30326.37	39494.35	66043.53
11449.27	20534.69	28148.19	37037.73	61156.98
885.60	655.75	1438.07	807.30	1186.06
544.27	572.33	1130.32	413.31	1002.31
355.57	302.03	580.05	946.90	1619.14
71.41	34.22	118.53	114.49	227.84
17706.85	19329.28	25654.27	30969.47	50908.75
12206.66	14323.92	18835.84	23867.55	36702.10
4115.75	5094.16	6243.74	7717.04	9626.00
3047.37	3611.70	4246.53	5135.70	5988.17
620.82	667.34	627.51	871.37	1902.10
28.34	37.15	36.22	42.56	37.03
61.28	68.30	78.07	88.03	73.33
155.55	167.67	183.33	207.48	191.83
515.07	604.88	719.96	800.71	746.51
648.18	787.63	977.72	1104.97	1055.42
127.44	156.76	183.47	238.34	207.16
208.34	257.20	343.48	436.87	385.21
83.12	98.52	116.25	131.76	115.36
135.94	165.18	230.78	249.17	249.53
225.54	297.45	380.41	502.15	526.34
77.17	100.21	125.62	162.10	184.38
160.57	203.41	243.71	300.20	313.97
421.16	563.17	663.01	776.79	1073.50
68.80	69.98	90.98	123.09	142.41
578.43	849.31	1243.22	1681.45	2421.92
811.63	1109.43	1435.88	1851.65	3102.45
632.73	884.23	1133.84	1469.97	2570.18
178.90	225.20	302.03	381.67	532.27
2715.51	2945.33	3860.14	5027.18	7465.33
143.03	144.24	153.29	251.61	164.15
458.62	301.45	301.62	576.42	1041.54
541.49	626.26	758.55	862.54	1300.93
1572.38	1873.37	2646.68	3336.61	4958.70
614.83	853.70	1019.89	1426.06	2288.09
65.15	99.38	103.19	207.34	369.40
163.97	220.77	251.83	363.06	567.55
39.91	74.23	77.17	133.48	176.46
214.83	287.56	358.42	434.68	641.70
114.13	138.65	188.96	231.28	414.98
16.83	33.11	40.32	56.22	117.99
1316.82	1250.48	2214.89	2706.83	5426.28
900.14	697.68	1508.96	1780.41	4150.40
416.68	552.81	705.93	926.42	1275.87
1520.76	1644.69	2057.64	2500.41	3988.13
1215.56	1146.69	1260.21	1309.88	1870.00
137.12	187.10	231.42	295.95	424.95
168.08	310.89	566.01	894.58	1693.19
876.70	1167.15	1558.54	2185.91	3857.11
291.66	319.04	450.07	664.12	901.90
585.05	848.11	1108.48	1521.78	2955.21
234.65	258.98	445.12	452.47	948.72
145.37	147.11	190.92	221.23	424.99
89.29	111.87	254.20	231.24	523.73

Note : Home ownership conversion in urban household residence consumption expenditure in 2014,refers to a resident who lives on a self-owned house now, provides housing service the conversion value for their own consumption. It belongs to material consumption, not included in cash consumption expenditure

9-6 城镇居民家庭平均每百户年末耐用品拥有量(2016)

品　名		Item		总平均 Total Average	低收入户 Low Income Households
摩托车	(辆)	Motorcycles	unit	30.50	45.62
助力车	(辆)	Auxiliary Drving Bikes	unit	27.35	34.94
家用汽车	(辆)	Cars for Household Use	unit	23.63	16.22
洗衣机	(台)	Washing Machins	unit	94.17	89.17
电冰箱	(台)	Refrigerators	unit	98.10	96.80
彩色电视机	(台)	Color TV Sets	unit	117.66	118.88
家用电脑	(台)	Computers	unit	74.43	56.60
组合音响	(套)	Hi-Fi Stereo Systems	unit	4.97	3.12
摄像机	(台)	TV Cameras	unit	4.23	1.60
照相机	(架)	Cameras	unit	18.80	8.86
中高档乐器	(件)	Medium and High-Grade Musical Instruments	unit	3.74	1.81
微波炉	(台)	Microwave Stove	unit	50.25	31.93
空调器	(台)	Air Conditioners	unit	139.62	105.89
热水器	(台)	Showers	unit	92.68	88.34
消毒碗柜	(台)	Disinfection cabinet	unit	8.40	3.92
洗碗机	(台)	Dishwasher	unit	1.22	0.44
健身器材	(件)	Health Care Instruments	unit	3.32	2.31
固定电话	(部)	Fixed telephone	set	28.70	24.24
移动电话	(部)	Mobile Phones	set	233.48	247.91

NUMBER OF DURABLE CONSUMER GOODS OWNED PER 100 URBAN HOUSEHOLDS AT THE YEAR-END BY INCOME LEVEL(2016)

中低收入户 Lower Middle Income Households	中等收入户 Middle Income Households	中高收入户 Upper Middle Income Households	高收入户 High Income Households
42.25	25.72	22.08	16.84
30.73	29.00	26.62	15.50
17.32	19.83	25.15	39.62
95.15	95.94	96.32	94.26
98.94	98.13	100.56	96.05
114.54	116.31	119.28	119.31
65.75	73.14	79.46	97.14
3.09	4.49	4.25	9.91
2.06	3.85	4.77	8.89
9.78	17.84	24.02	33.48
2.30	3.14	5.18	6.25
39.67	51.02	62.01	66.61
120.34	134.02	153.81	183.94
88.78	96.35	96.33	93.57
4.62	7.14	10.75	15.54
0.70	1.61	2.09	1.27
1.10	3.01	4.25	5.93
25.52	26.07	32.94	34.75
246.81	233.38	230.10	209.26

9-7 城镇居民家庭房屋居住分布情况
URABN HOUSEHOLDS HOUSING CONDITIONS

分组	Group	各组户数占总户数比重(%) Percentage of Household in Each Group of the Total Households				
		2012	2013	2014	2015	2016
总　　计	Total	1900	1718	3060	3073	3053
一、房屋产权	Building Property Right					
租赁公房	Leased Pubilc Houses	5.5	3.6	5.3	4.6	3.4
租赁私房	Leased Private Houses	1.9	7.5	7.7	6.4	5.4
原有私房	Original Private Houses	14.1	24.4	28.9	28.9	30.7
房改私房	Private Houses	44.1	28.3	24.5	23.5	22.3
商品房	Commercial Houses	32.4	32.8	26.1	28.9	29.6
借用房	Borrowed		1.4	1.1	0.9	1.0
其他	Others	1.0	1.9	6.3	6.8	7.6
二、住宅样式	Housing Pattens					
单栋住宅	Sole-Unit Houses	10.5	23.1	35.7	34.3	36.0
四居室	Four-Room Houses	4.9	3.8	3.2	3.7	3.7
三居室	Three-Room Houses	28.7	25.3	25.5	26.5	24.7
二居室	Two-Room Houses	43.6	35.2	27.0	26.7	27.9
一居室	One-Room Houses	4.2	5.8	6.3	6.4	5.6
普通楼房	Ordinary Houses	6.4	2.1	-	-	-
平房及其他	Bungalow and Others	1.7	4.6	2.2	2.5	2.1
三、用水情况	Waters					
独用自来水	Private Tap Water	99.8	97.8	94.7	95.0	95.8
公用自来水	Public Tap Water	0.2		-	-	-
井、河水	Water from Rivers and Wells		1.5	3.9	4.1	3.7
其他	Others		0.7	1.4	0.9	0.6
四、卫生设备	Sanitary Faciities					
无卫生设备	Have not	0.7	3.5	3.0	2.6	1.6
独立卫生设备	Independent Health Facilities	98.3	93.8	89.2	90.7	94.1
公用卫生设备	Public Health Facilities	1.0	2.6	7.8	6.7	4.3
五、取暖设备	Warming Facilities					
无取暖设备	Have not	22.5	29.5	33.8	37.3	37.5
空调设备	Air Conditioner	66.7		-	-	-
暖　气	Heater	5.2		-	-	-
其　他	Others	5.6	70.4	66.2	62.7	62.5
六、燃料使用情况	Fuel Material Usage Conditions					
煤	Coal	5.1	2.3	2.1	2.2	0.9
罐装液化石油气	LPG cylinders	43.0	47.5	30.6	30.5	46.5
管道液化石油气	LPG Pipeline	1.6	2.6	1.3	1.6	2.0
管道煤气	Piped Coal Gas	4.0	6.9	2.3	1.6	1.1
管道天然气	Gas pipeline	45.5	31.1	18.6	22.4	38.1
其　他	Others	0.8	9.2	45.1	41.8	11.4
七、通信设备使用情况	Telecommunication Facilities Usage Conditions					
1.每百户固定电话	Per 100 fixed telephone	59.3	39.2	41.7	33.91	28.70
2.每百户移动电话	Mobile Phones Per 100 Households	204.4	207.6	212.3	223.13	233.48

注：2014年起住宅样式为四居室的数据包含四居室及以上单元房的占比。
Note: The data refers to four bedroom and above for four bedroom units Since 2014.

9-8 农民家庭基本情况
BASIC CONDITIONS OF RURAL HOUSEHOLDS

年 份	调查户数 Number of Households Surveyed	常住人口(人) Permanent Residents (person)	平均每户常住人口(人) Average Permanent Residents Per Households (person)	平均每户整半劳动力(人) Average Full-Time and Part-Time Labors Per Household (person)	平均每个劳动力负担人口(人) Average Person Supported by Each Labor (person)
1982	948	5364	5.66	2.73	2.08
1983	1470	8267	5.62	2.99	1.88
1984	1510	8317	5.51	3.02	1.83
1985	3300	16473	5.07	2.98	1.71
1986	3300	16432	4.98	2.96	1.68
1987	3300	16195	4.91	2.94	1.67
1988	3300	15966	4.84	2.93	1.65
1989	3300	15567	4.72	2.86	1.65
1990	3300	15411	4.67	2.84	1.65
1991	3300	15094	4.57	2.66	1.72
1992	3300	14900	4.52	2.63	1.71
1993	3300	14651	4.44	2.65	1.67
1994	3300	14466	4.38	2.72	1.61
1995	3300	14447	4.38	2.77	1.58
1996	3300	14053	4.26	2.75	1.55
1997	3200	13453	4.20	2.64	1.60
1998	3200	13239	4.14	2.62	1.58
1999	3200	13082	4.09	2.63	1.55
2000	3300	13557	4.11	2.76	1.49
2001	3300	13490	4.09	2.75	1.49
2002	3300	13420	4.07	2.78	1.46
2003	3300	13385	4.06	2.86	1.42
2004	3300	13356	4.05	2.92	1.39
2005	3300	13228	4.01	2.99	1.34
2006	3300	13259	4.02	3.03	1.34
2007	3300	13186	4.00	3.06	1.30
2008	3300	13163	3.99	3.08	1.29
2009	3300	13151	3.99	3.12	1.28
2010	3300	13123	3.98	3.14	1.27
2011	3300	13120	3.98	3.12	1.27
2012	3300	13140	3.98	3.12	1.28
2013	2096	7921	3.78	2.88	1.31
2014	2522	7233	2.87	2.03	1.41
2015	2540	7309	2.88	2.04	1.41
2016	2549	7360	2.89	2.05	1.41

注: ①2014年起使用城乡一体化住户收支与生活状况调查数据,与之前的分城镇和农村住户调查的范围、方法、指标口径有所不同(此后相关表同)。
②2014年起农民人均纯收入改为农村常住居民人均可支配收入。

Note: ①The integrated household income and expenditure survey has been used since 2014 , including both urban and rural households. The coverage , methodology and definitions used in the survey are different from those used for the separate urban and rural household survey prior to 2014.(Related tables the same ever since).
②Per Capita Income of Rural Households has been changed into Per Capita Disposable Income of Rural Permanent Residents since 2014.

9-8 续表 1 continued

年 份 year	平均每户经营耕地面积(亩) Space of Cultivation land Per Household (mu)	平均每户年末拥有生产性固定资产原值(元) Value of Production Fixed Assets Per Household (yuan)	平均每户年内新建购房屋面积(平方米) Floor Space of Rooms Newly Built Per Household (sq.m)	平均每人年末使用房屋面积(平方米) Lving Space Per Capita (sq.m)
1982	0.57	159.20	5.36	16.45
1983	8.95	389.97	5.65	18.04
1984	8.66	530.20	6.70	19.03
1985	7.60	557.86	8.24	21.18
1986	7.48	610.47	8.45	22.63
1987	7.31	672.87	7.79	23.50
1988	7.04	759.61	4.90	24.15
1989	6.95	819.53	5.50	25.10
1990	6.79	861.91	6.20	25.73
1991	6.58	1068.45	4.56	27.33
1992	6.47	1146.94	4.07	27.94
1993	6.36	1281.66	3.75	25.80
1994	6.69	1542.58	3.91	25.22
1995	6.73	1775.57	4.66	25.92
1996	6.82	2291.60	4.25	26.58
1997	6.56	2688.67	4.98	27.99
1998	6.08	2604.21	4.74	28.38
1999	6.08	2543.61	4.19	29.87
2000	5.93	2482.02	3.48	30.11
2001	5.94	2773.52	2.98	31.19
2002	6.01	2953.37	4.65	31.55
2003	6.03	2989.82	4.01	32.44
2004	6.15	3046.47	2.82	33.68
2005	6.15	4121.20	3.88	36.05
2006	6.12	4297.19	4.22	36.77
2007	6.41	4996.00	3.36	37.96
2008	6.36	5434.99	5.90	39.04
2009	6.51	6368.83	4.40	40.11
2010	6.73	7078.46	5.05	40.99
2011	6.44	9636.11	7.88	44.24
2012	6.80	10813.13	5.46	44.98
2013	7.08	13839.73	6.06	41.84
2014	6.97	12048.41	5.81	54.78
2015	7.90	12226.49	4.08	55.61
2016	8.24	12709.63	2.51	57.67

9-8 续表 2 continued

年份	平均每户年末使用房屋价值(元) Value of Per Households Living Space (yuan)	平均每人总收入(元) Total Income Per Capita (yuan)	平均每人纯收入(元) Net Income Per Capita (yuan)	平均每人生活消费支出(元) Living Expenditures Per Capita (yuan)
1982	1261.51	311.51	286.07	226.96
1983	1688.93	405.14	299.24	252.47
1984	1786.54	525.86	392.29	305.03
1985	2068.78	569.74	421.24	334.63
1986	2319.44	605.67	445.13	373.53
1987	2514.22	638.64	460.66	408.69
1988	2751.40	710.47	497.84	450.62
1989	3095.15	820.70	571.84	540.13
1990	3545.50	957.01	670.80	607.58
1991	4661.58	936.57	626.92	615.40
1992	4885.77	1015.62	677.82	611.84
1993	5004.02	1135.77	783.18	722.09
1994	5887.81	1690.49	1170.06	1012.95
1995	6729.46	2184.20	1511.22	1245.10
1996	10050.26	2642.45	1863.62	1630.41
1997	11432.61	2913.16	2102.20	1660.13
1998	12966.45	2917.66	2172.24	1699.43
1999	13654.80	2871.62	2217.08	1572.90
2000	13717.28	3008.13	2268.50	1555.61
2001	16007.50	3124.10	2352.16	1649.18
2002	16581.94	3239.81	2444.06	1745.63
2003	19010.48	3378.80	2566.76	1801.63
2004	20254.50	3826.27	2890.01	2088.98
2005	24815.99	4221.81	3099.20	2430.19
2006	27772.00	4580.79	3419.35	2732.46
2007	31696.83	5365.78	3997.48	3090.00
2008	36250.27	6266.27	4656.38	3652.57
2009	41493.01	6663.13	5035.26	3725.40
2010	47606.56	7699.27	5832.27	4090.78
2011	61870.37	9387.20	6897.92	5010.74
2012	77338.15	10525.66	7851.71	5726.73
2013	101314.51	11896.06	8866.95	6279.52
2014	110492.00	14836.14	10849.06	8680.93
2015	125534.00	15819.16	11843.89	9803.15
2016	145244.08	16807.81	12724.97	10938.30

9-9 农民家庭年人均纯收入(可支配收入)及构成
PER CAPITA DISPOSABLE INCOME OF RURAL HOUSEHOLDS PER CAPITA AND COMPOSITION

单位：元 (yuan)

指标	Item	2005	2007	2008	2009	2010	2011	2012	2013	2014	2015	2016
全年总收入	Total Revenue	4221.81	5365.78	6266.27	6663.13	7699.27	9387.20	10525.66	11896.06	14836.14	15819.16	16807.81
全年纯收入	Annual Net Income	3099.20	3997.48	4656.38	5035.26	5832.27	6897.92	7851.71	8866.95	10849.06	11843.89	12724.97
工资性收入	Money Wage	941.64	1454.50	1742.33	1900.54	2186.11	2703.05	3189.84	3648.20	3298.61	3682.91	4023.04
家庭经营纯收入	House Business Revenue	2049.04	2379.82	2690.83	2828.53	3234.94	3731.34	4123.49	4616.55	5009.34	5281.41	5534.01
转移性收入	Transfer Income	91.71	125.46	182.40	247.81	304.30	379.08	472.51	518.07	2415.66	2718.79	3009.32
财产性收入	Property Income	16.81	37.70	40.82	58.37	106.92	84.45	65.87	84.13	125.44	160.78	158.60
比重(纯收入=100)	Ratio (net income = 100)											
工资性收入	Money Wage	30.38	36.39	37.42	37.74	37.48	39.19	40.63	41.14	30.40	31.10	31.62
家庭经营纯收入	House Business Revenue	66.12	59.53	57.79	56.17	55.47	54.09	52.52	52.06	46.17	44.59	43.49
转移性收入	Transfer Income	2.96	3.14	3.92	4.92	5.22	5.50	6.02	5.84	22.27	22.96	23.65
财产性收入	Property Income	0.54	0.94	0.88	1.16	1.83	1.22	0.84	0.95	1.16	1.35	1.25

注：2014年起为农村常住居民人均可支配收入、工资性收入、家庭经营净收入、财产净收入、转移净收入。
Note: It has been Per Capita Disposable Income of Rural Permanent Residents, Money Wage, House Business Revenue. Property Income, Transfer Income since 2014.

9-10 农民家庭年人均纯收入(可支配收入)分组
RURAL HOUSEHOLDS GROUPED BY PER CAPITA DISPOSABLE INCOME

单位：户 (household)

指标	Item	2005	2006	2007	2008	2009	2010	2011	2012	2013	2014	2015	2016
调查户总计	Total Households Surveyed	3300	3300	3300	3300	3300	3300	3300	3300	2096	2522	2540	2549
2000元以下	Below 2000 yuan	888	710	508	414	411	257	233	155	48	70	69	70
2000-3000元	2000-3000 yuan	840	787	659	519	478	365	295	197	83	57	51	35
3000-4000元	3000-4000 yuan	702	684	660	559	492	419	313	289	127	118	85	71
4000-5000元	4000-5000 yuan	413	479	510	510	460	469	373	286	170	139	147	117
5000元以上	5000 yuan and Over	457	640	969	1298	1459	1790	2086	2373	1668			
5000-10000元	5000-10000 yuan										814	796	689
10000-15000元	10000-15000 yuan										661	612	621
15000-20000元	15000-20000 yuan										353	349	386
20000元以上	20000 yuan and Over										311	431	561

注：2014年起为农村常住居民人均可支配收入分组。
Note: It has been Rural Permanent Grouped by Per Capita Disposable Income since 2014.

9-11 农民家庭年人均经营总收入
ANNUAL TOTAL INCME OF RURAL HOUSEHOLDS PER CAPITA

单位：元 (yuan)

指标	Item	2009	2010	2011	2012	2013	2014	2015	2016
家庭经营总收入	Total Income of Family Business	4435.68	5077.04	6134.62	6718.36	7022.00	8699.22	8928.74	9242.06
农业收入	Farming	2638.00	3115.06	3682.89	4056.77	4049.41	4663.10	4927.80	4875.69
林业收入	Forestry	59.33	65.63	79.26	88.49	140.80	272.35	292.41	345.81
牧业收入	Animal Husbandry	863.14	869.13	1013.07	1044.46	1077.50	1610.39	1235.80	1199.91
渔业收入	Fishery	311.80	329.55	389.88	423.50	403.93	476.41	696.02	654.65
工业收入	Industry	58.65	69.15	135.22	144.59	60.66	204.82	160.40	167.05
建筑业收入	Construction	133.29	154.25	167.18	177.49	307.83	188.27	110.67	261.24
交通运输邮电业收入	Transportation, Post Services	127.96	155.76	277.54	322.49	328.76	353.50	461.56	472.43
批零贸易餐饮业收入	Wholesales, Retail Sales and Catering	164.99	220.55	273.17	317.95	401.46	572.30	646.44	886.04
社会服务和文教卫生业收入	Social Services and Public Health Services	63.47	78.53	91.43	113.54	177.96	211.73	189.00	141.72
农林牧渔服务业收入	Agriculture and forestry services						133.44	171.08	189.94
其他家庭经营收入	Other Family Revenue	14.14	18.79	23.55	26.87	10.54	12.93	37.56	47.59

9-12 农民家庭年人均生产支出
ANNUAL PRODUCTION EXPENDITURES OF RURAL HOUSEHOLDS PER CAPITA

单位：元 (yuan)

指 标	Item	2009	2010	2011	2012	2013	2014	2015	2016
一、家庭经营费用支出	Expenditures of Family Business	1489.40	1713.15	2199.08	2402.73	2408.72	3413.49	3366.25	3412.31
农业生产支出	Agricultural Expenditures	746.68	866.74	1029.67	1076.28	1049.49	1329.35	1566.04	1535.20
林业生产支出	Forestry Expenditures	6.69	7.74	16.65	16.33	19.52	27.68	23.91	126.05
牧业生产支出	Animal Husbandary Expenditures	463.78	470.43	593.09	693.65	753.88	1279.08	923.32	765.09
渔业生产支出	Fishery Expenditures	104.37	125.68	216.01	230.50	174.04	217.63	366.77	276.83
工业生产支出	Industrial Expenditures	16.37	18.89	54.66	84.17	28.31	78.83	57.14	81.29
建筑业支出	Construction Expenditures	45.15	54.95	61.78	54.28	120.30	158.47	43.86	143.14
交通运输邮电业支出	Expenditures of Transportation and Post Services	38.14	60.29	107.32	120.00	81.99	74.77	136.61	114.81
批零贸易餐饮业支出	Expenditures of Wholesales, Retail Sales and Catering	51.96	88.76	90.88	100.13	82.03	166.42	175.88	276.11
社会服务和文教卫生业支出	Expenditures of Social Services and Public Health Services	13.73	14.89	19.82	20.52	69.33	39.98	18.10	25.19
农林牧渔服务业支出	Agriculture and forestry services						36.77	44.08	60.89
其他家庭经营支出	Other Family Expenditures	2.53	4.78	9.22	6.85	2.19	4.51	10.54	7.70
二、购置住房、生产性固定资产支出	Purchase of Housing, the Productive Expenditure of Fixed Assets	148.69	142.67	231.28	240.00	315.23	876.97	1244.33	862.13
三、税费支出	Expenditures of Taxation	11.21	10.28	9.28	11.09				

9-13 农民家庭年人均生活消费支出
LIVING EXPENDITURES OF RURAL HOUSEHOLDS PER CAPITA

单位: 元 (yuan)

指标	Item	2009	2010	2011	2012	2013	2014	2015	2016
全年总支出	Total Annual Expenditures	5537.59	6131.23	7971.52	8923.73	9477.33	16775.27	18257.83	19372.81
生活消费支出	Living Expenditures	3725.40	4090.78	5010.74	5726.73	6279.52	8680.93	9803.15	10938.30
一、食品消费	Food Consumption	1668.35	1763.05	1954.62	2154.01	2308.45	2724.10	2952.69	3295.30
主 食	Grain	320.19	329.34	334.56	350.86	334.10	440.21	446.36	466.19
副 食	Non-Staple Food	695.66	744.85	859.31	969.20	1037.53	1401.57	1539.65	1734.74
其他食品	Others	392.37	413.46	480.38	542.32	514.98	691.15	744.25	828.79
在外饮食	Travelling Catering Service	249.14	264.06	273.91	282.94	393.63	191.17	222.44	265.57
二、衣着消费	Clothing Consumption	195.45	217.61	272.12	316.41	347.67	495.73	549.14	568.71
三、居住消费	Residence Consumption	702.62	816.42	1086.86	1206.16	1415.73	1944.56	2150.27	2407.90
住 房	Housing	572.69	655.39	918.61	973.60	1013.20	1523.05	1693.72	1931.67
电 费	Electricity Fees	70.08	80.50	85.04	112.57	138.37	209.40	230.15	248.22
燃 料	Fuel	39.16	50.14	55.28	91.16	197.33	115.15	116.80	107.37
四、家庭设备用品及服务	Familty facilities and Services	229.32	262.26	359.57	397.86	425.00	574.31	599.92	669.01
耐用消费品	Durable Consumer Goods	133.42	158.37	230.49	238.55	249.85	298.95	298.90	328.12
日用杂品	Daily Necessities	88.20	94.33	116.88	142.41	164.10	260.06	286.12	320.73
五、交通通讯消费	Transportation and Telecommunication Fees	307.22	331.35	414.36	496.10	605.95	816.43	1218.42	1381.37
交通工具	Transportation	108.82	124.59	186.09	235.85	324.51	378.07	743.70	835.55
通讯工具	Telecommunication	23.71	34.86	33.04	39.84	45.85	76.43	89.87	94.07
交通、邮电服务费	Transport, Postal Services	174.70	171.90	195.23	220.41	235.48	361.94	384.85	451.76
六、教育文化娱乐	Culture, Education and Receation	281.68	288.12	341.87	394.63	407.42	1010.19	1118.15	1156.60
文教娱乐用品	Cultural, Educational and Receational Articles	61.71	62.30	94.96	107.87	104.20	122.61	156.33	145.88
学杂费	School Fees	146.81	102.61	139.02	136.21	159.18	98.51	90.58	93.95
技术培训费	Technical Training	5.44	7.19	10.43	12.85	28.88	20.89	36.57	51.56
一揽子教育服务费	Education Service Charge						661.05	712.83	693.66
文体休闲娱乐费	Sports Recreation Fee	9.92	13.81	17.44	23.05	35.58	62.47	78.67	76.99
七、医疗保健消费	Medicine and Medical Services Fees	236.31	295.24	438.20	591.87	624.40	907.33	985.09	1213.47
医疗保健用品	Health Care Supplies	71.18	71.61	102.19	117.28	127.71	200.10	225.14	269.73
医疗保健服务费	Health Care Service Fees	165.13	223.63	336.01	474.59	496.69	707.22	759.94	943.74
八、其他商品和服务	Other Commdities and Services	104.29	116.73	143.14	169.68	144.90	208.28	229.48	245.94

9-14 农民家庭年人均现金收支
ANNUAL CASH REVENUE AND EXPENDITURE OF RURAL HOUSEHOLDS PER CAPITA

单位：元 (yuan)

指 标	Item	2009	2010	2011	2012	2013	2014	2015	2016
期内现金收入合计	Total Cash Income at Year-End	5718.37	6664.44	8232.92	9337.04	10819.88	13243.58	13958.40	15145.85
一、工资性现金收入	Cash Income By Wages	1898.93	2185.60	2696.32	3186.99	3858.97	3282.57	3663.96	4000.55
二、家庭经营现金收入	Cash Income By Family Business	3509.20	4063.37	5011.97	5546.68	5959.60	7328.03	7336.22	7921.93
农业	Farm Products	1924.84	2306.34	2807.96	3096.78	3179.27	3614.71	3658.73	3873.47
林业	Forestry Products	55.54	60.38	80.14	88.34	142.91	163.40	172.04	241.80
牧业	Animal husbandary Products	658.16	675.22	773.47	837.81	891.19	1404.35	1039.15	995.89
渔业	Fishery Products	307.25	323.77	380.89	418.62	395.83	468.59	689.58	644.76
工业	Industry Products	58.65	69.15	135.22	144.59	60.66	204.82	160.40	167.05
建筑业	Building Industry	133.29	154.25	167.18	177.49	307.83	188.27	110.67	261.24
交通运输邮电业	Transportation and Post Service	127.96	155.76	277.54	322.49	328.76	353.50	461.56	472.43
批零贸易餐饮业	Retail Sales and Catering	164.99	220.55	273.17	317.95	401.46	572.30	646.44	886.04
社会服务和文教卫生业	Social services and educational sector	63.47	78.53	91.43	113.54	177.96	211.73	189.00	141.72
农林牧渔服务业	Agriculture and forestry services						133.44	171.08	189.94
其他家庭经营收入	Cash Income of Other	14.14	19.42	23.55	26.87	10.54	12.93	37.56	47.59
三、转移性现金收入	Transfer Cash Income	264.72	328.92	460.73	544.46	902.05	2497.66	2791.31	3053.31
四、财产性现金收入	Property Cash Income	45.52	86.55	63.91	58.91	99.26	135.33	166.91	170.07
期内现金支出合计	Total Cash Expenditures at Year-End	4723.52	5294.37	7194.75	8149.22	8563.81	14688.88	15923.32	16677.01
一、家庭经营费用现金支出	Cash Expenditures By Family Business	1368.00	1562.32	2051.67	2285.75	2243.66	3249.87	3222.08	3290.04
购买化肥	Fertilizers Purchases	313.95	320.80	377.07	374.44	396.06	456.72	515.12	482.81
购买农药	Purchases of Farm Chemical	87.72	94.03	125.52	129.82	112.80	140.48	142.26	154.19
购买农用薄膜	Purchase of Agricultural Film	3.40	5.07	6.80	6.31	4.80	7.94	8.01	8.65
二、购买住房、生产性固定资产支出	Purchase of Housing, the Productive Expenditure	148.38	142.17	231.28	240.00	315.23	876.97	1244.33	862.13
三、税费现金支出	Cash Expenditures of Taxations	11.20	10.28	9.28	10.85				
四、生活消费现金支出	Cash Expenditures of Living Consumption	3033.37	3406.12	4382.95	5070.68	5531.07	6738.17	7612.82	8364.76
五、转移性现金支出	Transfer Cash Expenditures	153.91	162.25	511.12	530.85	471.72	287.31	321.74	363.36
六、财产性现金支出	Property Cash Expenditures	8.33	10.74	8.45	11.10	2.13	8.67	6.12	11.47

9-15 农民家庭年人均出售主要农副产品情况
ANNUAL SELLING OF FARM AND SIDELINE PRODUCTS OF RURL HOUSEHOLDS PER CAPITA

单位：千克

品　名	Item	2005	2007	2008	2009	2010	2011	2012	2013	2014	2015	2016
粮食	Grain	383.48	386.98	390.60	422.65	447.78	451.98	489.22	591.56	770.96	888.88	982.69
小麦	Wheat	54.25	94.39	76.73	62.01	75.44	86.70	91.93	79.55	111.05	129.72	151.98
稻谷	Paddy	302.70	268.94	292.78	320.27	331.71	302.69	329.15	432.85	528.86	588.64	656.03
棉花	Cotton	55.95	81.48	70.09	76.43	55.03	88.30	93.94	72.29	48.98	30.33	19.31
油料	Oil Producer	77.73	61.27	65.14	77.04	72.15	60.91	58.57	73.99	77.34	52.15	45.97
糖料	Sugar	5.47	9.16	4.31	4.48	6.43	0.16	0.17	2.16	2.08	2.21	3.43
烟草	Tobacco	2.34	1.55	2.11	2.92	2.77	2.97	3.82	7.89	7.07	14.35	13.67
蔬菜	Vegetable	135.09	138.89	136.45	133.11	139.41	137.62	143.53	99.54	134.68	163.39	125.98
瓜类	Melon	14.21	16.20	14.80	19.07	19.69	17.40	17.60	40.74	33.63	10.12	15.49
水果	Fruits	69.54	82.72	90.38	99.70	78.09	66.13	109.87	62.86	111.30	97.70	93.46
茶叶	Tea	1.24	1.56	1.56	1.29	1.95	4.17	8.08	5.02	5.01	7.55	8.39
猪肉	Pork	29.70	26.03	26.38	28.70	30.92	22.91	25.68	28.51	58.86	41.76	32.19
家禽	Poultry	4.47	4.44	7.16	7.29	8.38	2.28	2.80	1.65	8.63	4.26	3.61
蛋类	Eggs	11.98	8.99	8.25	10.94	11.19	10.33	13.01	16.54	29.12	14.59	13.58
水产品	Aquatic Products	28.59	35.66	37.26	42.12	38.70	43.09	43.25	39.61	40.65	68.30	62.48

9-16 农民家庭主要生活用品购买量
ANNUAL PURCHASES OF ARTICLES FOR BAILY USE OF RURAL HOUSEHOLDS PER CAPITA

品 名	Item		2007	2008	2009	2010	2011	2012	2013	2014	2015	2016
粮 食	(千克/人) Grain	(Kg/person)	25.72	26.56	27.45	29.46	42.35	44.45	38.34	44.06	47.43	49.61
植物油	(千克/人) Edible Vegetable Oil	(Kg/person)	3.21	3.55	3.35	3.61	5.20	5.70	5.11	7.41	8.07	7.88
动物油	(千克/人) Edible Animal Oil	(Kg/person)	0.50	0.47	0.38	0.33	0.43	0.39	0.27	0.47	0.49	0.42
蔬菜	(千克/人) Vegetables	(Kg/person)	16.44	17.85	16.21	17.73	19.40	18.27	16.51	25.95	27.28	31.31
猪肉	(千克/人) Pork	(Kg/person)	6.27	6.22	7.04	7.43	8.38	8.71	8.76	13.13	14.32	13.80
牛羊肉	(千克/人) Beef and Mutton	(Kg/person)	0.49	0.41	0.41	0.51	0.56	0.47	0.54	0.85	1.04	1.14
家禽	(千克/人) Poultry	(Kg/person)	1.08	1.21	1.16	1.17	1.26	1.24	0.97	2.40	2.46	2.95
鲜蛋	(千克/人) Fresh Eggs	(Kg/person)	0.97	1.33	1.55	1.30	1.85	2.20		2.83	4.32	4.16
鲜活鱼类	(千克/人) Fresh Fish	(Kg/person)	7.69	7.29	6.97	6.99	7.11	7.06		9.58	10.13	10.31
卷烟	(盒/人) Tobacco	(pack/person)	29.06	28.88	27.51	27.50	31.12	31.42	26.93	41.00	40.03	40.62
酒	(千克/人) Wine	(Kg/person)	12.30	11.70	11.35	10.72	11.37	11.06	10.06	14.24	12.76	11.78
水 果	(千克/人) Fruits	(Kg/person)	6.87	6.80	6.72	6.22	6.87	8.27		17.63	19.69	23.07
服 装	(件/人) Clothing	(piece/person)	1.82	1.99	2.94	1.95	2.46	2.52				
鞋 类	(双/人) Footwear	(Two/person)	1.35	1.43	1.28	1.36	1.39	1.80		2.10	2.37	2.35
水 泥	(千克/人) Cement	(Kg/person)	85.93	134.97	137.25	150.72	236.88	149.81				
钢 材	(千克/人) Steel	(Kg/person)	5.84	10.45	10.11	10.21	13.85	9.72				
生活用煤	(千克/人) Coal	(Kg/person)	49.44	32.82	20.22	19.70	14.77	13.18		14.84	15.18	18.06
电视机	(台/百户) TV Sets	(set/100 households)	5.79	4.95	3.97	3.70	6.67	6.48	5.76	5.31	7.17	6.39
洗衣机	(台/百户) Washing Machine	(set/100 households)	1.92	2.73	2.67	3.21	6.09	5.09	4.44	4.93	4.35	4.48
电风扇	(台/百户) Electric Fans	(set/100 households)	8.85	9.73	11.45	10.52	10.79	13.67				
电冰箱	(台/百户) Refrigerators	(set/100 households)	4.18	5.64	7.06	7.00	8.30	7.12	6.16	6.03	6.61	6.62
自行车(含电动)	(辆/百户) Bycicle	(set/100 households)	5.40	6.80	7.04	4.67	7.18	7.30	6.54	6.99	6.27	5.63
摩托车	(辆/百户) Motocycle	(set/100 households)	5.28	4.73	4.26	3.88	6.09	5.30	3.91	3.65	3.51	3.18
热水器	(台/百户) Shower	(set/100 households)	2.06	3.11	3.79	4.36	6.18	5.70	3.58	2.75	3.20	3.19
电话机	(部/百户) Telephone Sets	(set/100 households)	4.52	4.33	4.37	3.36	3.41	2.76	1.86	1.03	1.37	0.83
手 机	(部/百户) Mobile Phones	(set/100 households)	12.97	13.82	14.42	18.92	25.39	28.00	33.40	39.75	39.44	34.97

9-17 农民家庭年人均主要食品消费量
RURAL HOUSEHOLD ANNUAL CONSUMPTION ON MAJOR FOOD PER CAPITA

单位：千克 (Kg)

品　名	Item	2007	2008	2009	2010	2011	2012	2013	2014	2015	2016
一、粮食	Grain	208.29	193.60	192.22	178.37	162.86	151.06	125.59	153.08	152.05	137.15
小麦	Wheat	21.80	22.02	19.87	17.60	17.41	15.55	10.17	16.74	17.90	14.74
稻谷	Paddy	168.61	155.37	155.18	146.13	135.87	126.67	104.27	121.21	118.83	107.22
豆类	Bean	3.82	3.30	3.27	3.22	2.53	1.97	3.85	7.25	7.86	8.72
二、蔬菜及菜制品	Fresh Vegetables and	143.57	132.58	137.04	137.51	131.68	119.33	88.16	118.03	123.06	123.22
鲜菜	Fresh Vegetables	140.57	130.05	134.69	136.22	130.67	118.25	86.56	116.30	121.40	121.10
三、油脂类	Oil and Fats	3.77	4.11	3.85	5.49	8.17	10.39	11.05	29.71	16.04	15.52
植物油	Edible Vegetable Oil	3.23	3.58	3.39	5.13	7.71	9.93	10.61	29.02	15.24	14.89
动物油	Edible Animal Oil	0.53	0.53	0.47	0.36	0.46	0.47	0.43	0.70	0.79	0.62
四、肉禽及其制品	Meat and Processed Products	22.70	22.21	22.99	22.79	22.90	22.80	22.91	29.82	31.20	29.15
猪肉	Pork	17.83	17.51	18.14	17.98	17.40	17.63	18.11	23.12	24.12	21.43
牛羊肉	Beef and Mutton	0.52	0.50	0.48	0.57	0.65	0.53	0.63	0.93	1.14	1.26
家禽	Poultry	3.30	3.23	3.22	2.91	3.23	2.94	2.87	4.19	4.27	4.60
五、蛋类及蛋制品	Eggs and Processed Products	4.17	4.69	4.93	4.47	5.03	5.02	4.68	6.65	8.31	8.08
六、奶及奶制品	Milk and Dariy Products	0.50	0.81	1.11	1.22	1.55	1.67	2.11	3.53	3.58	4.12
七、水产品	Aquatic Products	9.38	8.71	8.34	8.33	8.38	8.54	7.93	11.10	11.75	12.15
鱼类	Fish	9.03	8.40	7.97	7.93	8.03	8.09	7.58	10.55	10.97	11.20
八、干鲜瓜果	Fresh and Dry	18.66	16.01	16.84	15.70	16.38	16.83	13.33	20.74	22.42	26.28
九、酒类	Liquor and Drinks	12.35	11.76	11.41	10.77	11.40	11.12	10.08	14.25	12.78	11.85
白酒	Wine Spirit	3.87	3.85	3.94	3.70	3.69	3.52	3.65	5.82	5.51	5.22
啤酒	Beer	8.42	7.84	7.40	7.01	7.67	7.53	6.41	8.41	7.24	6.58

9-18 农民家庭每百户主要耐用消费品拥有量
POSSESSTION OF URABLE CONSUMER GOODS PER 100 RURAL HOUSEHOLDS

品名		Item		2007	2008	2009	2010	2011	2012	2013	2014	2015	2016
彩电	(台)	Color TV Set	(unit)	98.82	102.24	105.42	109.18	114.36	116.24	114.35	116.50	118.46	120.09
照相机	(架)	Camera	(unit)	1.82	2.06	2.58	2.64	3.55	3.64	5.24	4.89	3.84	2.97
洗衣机	(台)	Washing Machine	(unit)	34.68	37.12	41.70	47.97	57.09	62.42	53.79	57.94	65.02	73.13
电冰箱	(台)	Refrigerator	(unit)	26.18	30.52	41.36	51.48	73.73	80.18	75.82	79.53	84.75	93.01
摩托车	(辆)	Motocycle	(unit)	51.45	55.52	59.76	64.12	72.33	74.76	68.84	76.52	77.87	78.47
摄像机	(台)	Videorecorder	(unit)	1.06	0.91	0.52	0.70	1.42	1.52	0.62	0.50	0.44	0.37
抽油烟机	(台)	Ventilator	(unit)	5.03	6.10	7.70	10.03	13.70	15.82	10.94	13.59	14.89	14.86
空调机	(台)	Air Conditioner	(unit)	7.61	9.91	12.45	18.36	28.58	33.15	33.05	37.79	43.49	56.47
热水器	(台)	Shower	(unit)	12.21	16.03	22.73	32.00	48.24	55.91	52.16	58.01	61.71	68.63
电话机	(部)	Telephone Set	(set)	58.36	59.33	55.61	55.70	41.94	40.06	31.44	37.15	27.43	20.71
移动电话	(部)	Moblile Phone	(set)	104.67	117.88	134.21	152.27	204.82	215.06	211.52	223.46	232.18	236.26
家用计算机	(台)	PC	(unit)	2.00	3.00	5.15	7.39	15.58	19.73	22.14	25.72	26.23	27.04

9-19 市、州农民年人均纯收入(可支配收入)
ANAUAL NET INCOME OF RURAL HOUCEHOLD PER CAPITA IN CITIES AND PREFERCTURES

单位：元 (yuan)

地 区	Item	农村居民人均纯收入								农村常住居民人均可支配收入		
		2007	2008	2009	2010	2011	2012	2013	2013	2014	2015	2016
全 省	**Province**	**3997**	**4656**	**5035**	**5832**	**6898**	**7852**	**8867**	**9692**	**10849**	**11844**	**12725**
武汉市	Wuhan	5371	6349	7161	8295	9814	11190	12713	14390	16160	17722	19152
黄石市	Huangshi	3742	4374	4811	5524	6487	7477	8492	9781	10957	12004	12925
十堰市	Shiyan	2490	2841	3110	3499	4044	4566	5226	6212	7046	7779	8514
宜昌市	Yichang	4022	4686	5186	5980	7055	8046	9121	10458	11837	12990	14057
襄阳市	Xiangyang	4114	4880	5440	6365	7549	8684	9785	11176	12534	13650	14762
鄂州市	Ezhou	4393	5096	5718	6645	7909	9072	10210	11309	12692	13812	14813
荆门市	Jingmen	4652	5332	5956	6951	8248	9387	10615	12082	13481	14716	15811
孝感市	Xiaogan	3915	4636	5131	5943	7029	7988	9023	10360	11597	12655	13554
荆州市	Jingzhou	4140	4889	5464	6453	7664	8710	9909	11280	12625	13728	14707
黄冈市	Huanggang	3295	3744	4130	4634	5438	6142	6966	8385	9388	10252	11076
咸宁市	Xianning	3737	4411	4873	5606	6588	7505	8480	9709	10891	11940	12812
随州市	Suizhou	4177	4967	5457	6279	7427	8419	9490	10702	11984	13022	14077
恩施自治州	Enshi	2143	2519	2810	3255	3939	4571	5235	6364	7194	7969	8728
仙桃市	Xiantao	4695	5248	5856	6807	8006	9076	10365	11809	13193	14422	15462
天门市	Tianmen	4207	4761	5326	6207	7407	8507	9608	10809	12086	13178	14107
潜江市	Qianjiang	4378	4929	5531	6486	7684	8785	10017	11448	12862	14076	15113
神农架林区	Shennongjia	2850	3330	3707	4083	4640	5110	5677	6305	6920	7578	8342

注：2013年前分城镇和农村开展住户调查，指标为农民人均纯收入。2014年起使用城乡一体化住户收支与生活状况调查数据，指标改为农村常住居民人均可支配收入。

Note: Urban and rural household surveys are separate prior to 2013, the concept is Per Capita Net Income of Rural Households, The data from an integrated household income and expenditure survey has been used since 2014 , the concept was changed into Per Capita Disposable Income of Rural Permanent Residents.

主要统计指标解释

一、城镇住户调查(到2012年)

城镇家庭人口 指居住在一起,经济上合在一起共同生活的家庭成员。凡计算为家庭人口的成员其全部收支都包括在本家庭中。

城镇就业面 指就业人口占家庭人口的百分比。

城镇就业者负担人数 指家庭人口与就业人口之比。

城镇家庭总收入 指家庭成员得到的工资性收入、经营净收入、财产性收入、转移性收入之和,不包括出售财物收入和借贷收入。

城镇居民家庭可支配收入 指家庭成员得到可用于最终消费支出和其它非义务性支出以及储蓄的总和,即居民家庭可以用来自由支配的收入。它是家庭总收入扣除交纳的个人所得税、个人交纳的社会保障支出以及记账补贴后的收入。计算公式为:

城镇居民家庭可支配收入=家庭总收入-交纳所得税-个人交纳的社会保障支出-记帐补贴

城镇家庭总支出 指家庭除借贷支出以外的全部实际支出。包括现金消费支出、财产性支出、转移性支出、社会保障支出、购房与建房支出。

城镇家庭现金消费支出 指家庭用于日常生活的全部现金支出,包括食品、衣着、家庭设备及用品、交通通信、文教娱乐、医疗保健、其他等八大类支出。

城镇家庭服务性消费支出 指家庭用于支付社会提供的各种文化和生活方面的非商品性服务费用。

城镇家庭收入分组方法 是将所有调查户依户人均可支配收入由低到高排队,按10%,10%,20%,20%,20%,10%,10%的比例依次分成:最低收入户、较低收入户、中等偏下收入户、中等收入户、中等偏上收入户、高收入户、最高收入户等七组。总体中最低5%的户为困难户。

恩格尔系数 指食品支出在现金消费支出中所占的比例。计算公式为:

$$\text{恩格尔系数}=\frac{\text{食品支出}}{\text{现金消费支出}}\times 100\%$$

二、农村住户调查(到2012年)

农村住户 指农村常住户。农村常住户指长期(一年以上)居住在乡镇(不包括城关镇)行政管理区域内的住户,以及长期居住在城关镇所辖行政村范围内的农村住户。户口不在本地而在本地居住一年及以上的住户也包括在本地农村常住户范围内;有本地户口,但举家外出谋生一年以上的住户,无论是否保留承包耕地都不包括在本地农村住户范围内。

常住人口 指全年经常在家或在家居住6个月以上,而且经济和生活与本户连成一体的人口。外出从业人员在外居住时间虽然在6个月以上,但收入主要带回家中,经济与本户连为一体,仍视为家庭常住人口;在家居住,生活和本户连成一体的国家职工、退休人员也为家庭常住人口。但是现役军人、中专及以上(走读生除外)的在校学生、以及常年在外(不包括探亲、看病等)且已有稳定的职业与居住场所的外出从业人员,不算家庭常住人口。家庭常住人口主要作为计算农村住户平均每人收入、消费和积累水平及分析家庭人口状况的依据。

整、半劳动力 整劳动力指男子18周岁到50周岁,女子18周岁到45周岁;半劳动力指男子16周岁到17周岁,51周岁到60周岁;女子16周岁到17周岁,46周岁到55周岁,同时具有劳动能力的人。虽然在劳动年龄之内,但已丧失劳动能力的人,不应算为劳动力;超过劳动年龄,但能经常参加劳动,计入半劳动力数内。常住人口中的职工,若这些职工为劳动力,就包括在本户的整半劳动力中。

总收入 指调查期内农村住户和住户成员从各种来源渠道得到的收入总和。按收入的性质划分为工资性收入、家庭经营收入、财产性收入和转移性收入。

工资性收入 指农村住户成员受雇于单位或个人,靠出卖劳动而获得的收入。

家庭经营收入 指农村住户以家庭为生产经营单位进行生产筹划和管理而获得的收入。农村住户家庭经营活动按行业划分为农业、林业、牧业、渔业、工业、建筑业、交通运输业邮电业、批发和零售贸易餐饮业、社会服务业、文教卫生业和其他家庭经营。

财产性收入 指金融资产或有形非生产性资产的所有者向其他机构单位提供资金或将有形非生产性资产供其支配,作为回报而从中获得的收入。

转移性收入 指农村住户和住户成员无须付出任何对应物而获得的货物、服务、资金或资产所有权等,不包括无偿提供的用于固定资本形成的资金。一般情况下,是指农村住户在二次分配中的所有收入。

现金收入 指农村住户和住户成员在调查期内得到以现金形态表现的收入。按来源分成工资性收入、家庭经营现金收入、财产性收入、转移性收入。

农村居民家庭纯收入 指农村住户当年从各个来源得到的总收入相应地扣除所发生的费用后的收入总和。计算方法:

农村居民家庭纯收入=总收入-家庭经营费用支出-税费支出-生产性固定资产折旧-赠送农村内部亲支

纯收入主要用于再生产投入和当年生活消费支出,也可用于储蓄和各种非义务性支出。“农民人均纯收入”按人口平均的纯收入水平,反映的是一个地区农村居民的平均收入水平。

总支出 指农村住户用于生产、生活和再分配的全部支出。包括家庭经营费用支出、购置生产性固定资产支出、税费支出、消费支出、财产性支出和转移性支出。

三、一体化住户调查

从2012年四季度起,国家统计局对分别进行的城乡住户调查实施了一体化改革,统一了城乡居民收入指标名称、分类和统计标准,建立了城乡统一的一体化住户调查《住户收支与生活状况调查》,并据此获得全国居民有关数据。

居民可支配收入 居民可支配收入指居民可用于最终消费支出和储蓄的总和,即居民可用于自由支配的收入。既包括现金收入、也包括实物收入。按照收入的来源,可支配收入包含四项,分别为:工资性收入、经营性净收入、转移性净收入和财产性净收入。

居民消费支出 居民消费支出是指居民用于满足家庭日常生活消费需要的全部支出,既包括现金消费支出,也包括实物消费支出。消费支出可划分为食品烟酒、衣着、居住、生活用品及服务、交通和通信、教育文化和娱乐、医疗保健以及其他用品及服务八大类。

Explanatory Notes on Main Statistical Indicators

Ⅰ.Urban Households(to the year of 2012)

Population of Urban Households refer to members of the household living and sharing economically together. All income and expenditure of the population of the household are included in the income and expenditure of the household.

Proportion of Urban Employment referto the proportion of employed population to the population of urban households.

Number of Dependents per Urban Employee refers to the ratio between number of persons in urban households and the number of dependents.

Total Income of Urban Households refers to the sum of wage and salary, net business income, income from properties, and income from transfers of members of the households, excluding income from selling of properties and income from borrowings.

Disposable Income of Urban Households refers to the actual income at the disposal of members of the households which can be used for final consumption, other non-compulsory expenditure and savings. This equals to total income minus income tax, personal contribution to social security and sample household subsidy for keeping diaries. Following formula is used:

Disposable income = total household income – income tax – personal contribution to social security – sample household subsidy for keeping diaries

Total Expenditure of Urban Households refer to all expenditure of the households except expenditure on leading. It includes expenditure on consumption, on purchasing or building houses, on transfers, on properties and on social security.

Consumption Expenditure of Urban Households refers to total expenditure of the sample households for consumption in daily life, including expenditure on eight categories such as food, clothing, household appliances and services, health care and medical services, transport and communications, recreation, education and cultural services, housing, miscellaneous goods and services.

Expenditure of Urban Households on Consumption of Services refers to expenditure of households on services of various kinds provided by the society.

Urban Households by Income Group All households in the sample are grouped, by per capita disposable income of the household, into groups of lowest income, low income, lower middle income, middle income, upper middle income, high income and highest income, each group consisting of 10%, 10%, 20%, 20%, 20%, 10% and 10% of all households respectively. The lowest 5% of households are also referred to as poor households.

Engel Coefficient refers to the percentage of expenditure on food in the total consumption expenditure, using the following formula:

Engel Coefficient = (expenditure on food / total living consumption expenditure) x 100%

Ⅱ. Rural Households(to the year of 2012)

Rural Households refer to resident households in rural areas. Resident households in rural areas are the households residing for more than one year in the areas under the jurisdiction of administration of township governments (excluding county towns), and in the areas under the jurisdiction of administration of villages in county towns. Migrated households residing in the current addresses for over one year with their household registration in other places are included in the resident households of their current addresses. For households with their household registration in one place but all members of the households moving away for living in another place for over one year, they will not be included in the rural households of the area where they are registered, irrespective of whether they still keep their contracted land.

Resident Population refers to population staying at home permanently or for over 6 months during a year and sharing life economically with the household. Members of the household staying away from the household for over 6 months but keeping a close economic relation with the household by sending the majority of income to the household are regarded as resident population of the household. Government staff and workers or retirees living as close members of the household are also considered as resident population. However, servicemen, students of secondary technical schools or schools of higher education and persons with stable jobs and residence outside the household (excluding those visiting relatives or seeking medical service) are not included as resident population of the household. Resident population is used in calculating income, consumption, accumulation on per capita basis of rural households and in analyzing composition of rural households.

Full/Semi Labor Force Full labor force refers to persons capable of work, aged 18–50 for males and 18–45 for females. Semi labor force refers to persons capable of work, aged 16–17 and 51–60 for males and 16–17 and 46–55 for females. Persons at their working ages but not capable of work are not to be included as labor force. Persons not at working ages but participating regularly in work are included in semi labor force. For staff and workers as resident population of the household, they are included as full or semi labor force of the household if they are in the labor force.

Total Income refers to the sum of income earned from various sources by the rural households and their members during the reference period, and is classified as income from wages and salaries, income from household operations, income from properties and income from transfers.

Income from Wages and Salaries refers to income from labor earned by the members of rural households employed by other units or individuals.

Income from Household Operations refers to income by the rural households as units of production and operations. Operations by rural households are classified by economic activities as agriculture, forestry, animal husbandry, fishery, manufacturing, construction, transportation, post and telecommunications, wholesale, retail and catering, social service, culture, education, health, and other household operations.

Income from Properties refers to the income received as returns by owners of financial assets or tangible non–productive assets by providing capitals or tangible non–productive assets to other institutional units.

Income from Transfers refers to the receipt by rural households and their members of goods, services, capitals or rights of assets without giving or repaying accordingly, excluding capitals provided to them for the formation of fixed assets. In general, it refers to all income received by rural households through redistribution.

Cash Income refers to income received by rural households and their members in the form of cash during the reference period. It is classified, by source of income, into income from wages and salaries, cash income from household operations, income from properties and income from transfers.

Net Income refers to the total income of rural households from all sources minus all corresponding expenses. The formula for calculation is as follows:

Net income = total income – taxes and fees paid – household operation expenses – taxes and fees depreciation of fixed assets for production – subsidy for participating in household survey – gifts to non–rural relatives

Net income is mainly used as input for reproduction and as consumption expenditure of the year, and also used for savings and non–compulsory expenses of various forms. "Per capital net income of farmers" is the level of net income averaged by population which reflects the average income level of rural households in a given area.

Total Expenditure refers to total expenses of rural households on production, consumption and redistribution, including expenditure on household operations, on purchase of productive fixed assets, depreciation of productive fixed assets, taxes and fees, expenses on household consumption, expenses on properties and expenses on transfers.

Ⅲ. Integrated Household Survey

In the fourth quarter of 2012, the NBS launched its reform on the household survey programin order to produceaggregates with the same concepts and definitions for urban and rural population. This new survey program is an integrated one whereas there had existed two separate household surveys for the urban and rural households. The reform took a number of measures, including the integration of concepts, classifications and standards, which provided a basis for producing data covering all households. The new survey includes the following indicators:

Disposable Income of Households has a national coverage comparable between urban and rural households, and refers to the kind ofincome that households call have at them disposal. It includes income both in cash and in kind from four categories: income from wages and salaries, cash income from household operations, income from properties and income from transfers.

Consumption Expenditure of Households has anational coverage comparable between urban and rural households, and refers to the all the expenditures of households for consumption in daily life. It includes expenditure in cash and in kind on eight categories: food; clothing; housing; household appliances and services; transport and communications; education, cultural and recreational activities; and medical care. The expenditure on housing also includes rents, water, electricity, fuels and imputed rents Of owner—occupied dwellings.

10 城市概况

City Overview

10-1 主要城市土地面积、人口情况(2016)
LAND AREA AND PULATION OF MAJOR MUNICIPALITIES (2016)

城市	Municipalities	土地面积(平方公里) Land Area (sq.km)	常住人口(万人) Resident Population (10 000 persons)	当年出生人口(人) Births (persons)	当年死亡人口(人) Deaths (persons)	人口密度(人/平方公里) Population Desity (person/sq.km)
武汉	Wuhan Municipality	8494	1076.62	95436	45259	1267.51
黄石	Huangshi Municipality	4586	246.55	38570	16062	537.61
十堰	Shiyan Municipality	23680	340.90	44284	21782	143.96
宜昌	Yichang Municipality	21084	413.00	31299	24768	195.88
襄阳	Xiangyang Municipality	19724	563.90	66403	28590	285.90
鄂州	Ezhou Municipality	1596	106.85	14620	4912	669.49
荆门	Jingmen Municipality	12404	290.13	26712	11795	233.90
孝感	Xiaogan Municipality	8910	490.43	61657	24535	550.43
荆州	Jingzhou Municipality	14067	569.79	72054	25670	405.05
黄冈	Huanggang Municipality	17457	632.10	95426	33421	362.09
咸宁	Xianning Municipality	10049	252.60	47774	11036	251.37
随州	Suizhou Municipality	9636	220.18	29963	11016	228.50

10-2 主要城市就业情况(2016)
EMPLOYMENT OF MAJOR MUNICIPALITIES (2016)

单位：人 (persons)

城市	Municipalities	从业人员期末人数(城镇) Employment (year-end)	从业人员按三次产业分(城镇) Employment Grouped by Type of Industry			城镇私营和个体人数 Employment in Private Enterprises and Self-employed Individuals of Urban Areas
			第一产业 Primary Industry	第二产业 Secondary Industry	第三产业 Tertiary Industry	
武汉	Wuhan Municipality	2132591	3466	1053081	1076044	
黄石	Huangshi Municipality	307412	1091	182949	123372	360800
十堰	Shiyan Municipality	663163	7230	317207	338726	663100
宜昌	Yichang Municipality	942579	3855	521313	417411	938543
襄阳	Xiangyang Municipality	1009946	17452	522026	470468	368813
鄂州	Ezhou Municipality	220938	225	146975	73738	110925
荆门	Jingmen Municipality	394843	6922	211561	176360	379610
孝感	Xiaogan Municipality	825944	8372	460796	356776	722916
荆州	Jingzhou Municipality	424122	14145	181267	228710	1135300
黄冈	Huanggang Municipality	675332	22617	394556	258159	189295
咸宁	Xianning Municipality	229737	481	89553	139703	389728
随州	Suizhou Municipality	148402	612	70865	76925	318761

10-3 主要城市地区生产总值(2016)
GROSS DOMESTIC PRODUCTS OF MAJOR MUNICIPALITIES (2016)

城市	Municipalities	地区生产总值 (亿元) Gross Domestic Product (100 million yuan)	(当年价格) 第一产业 Primary Industry	第二产业 Secondary Industry	第三产业 Tertiary Industry	人均地区生产总值 (元) Per Capita GDP(yuan)
武汉	Wuhan Municipality	11912.61	390.62	5227.05	6294.94	111469
黄石	Huangshi Municipality	1305.55	114.07	721.47	470.01	53033
十堰	Shiyan Municipality	1429.15	173.40	681.59	574.16	42083
宜昌	Yichang Municipality	3709.36	398.89	2122.74	1187.73	89978
襄阳	Xiangyang Municipality	3694.51	430.90	2046.77	1216.84	65663
鄂州	Ezhou Municipality	797.82	97.21	434.58	266.03	74983
荆门	Jingmen Municipality	1521.00	213.15	789.51	518.34	52470
孝感	Xiaogan Municipality	1576.69	281.52	756.40	538.77	32236
荆州	Jingzhou Municipality	1726.75	382.72	736.39	607.64	30284
黄冈	Huanggang Municipality	1726.17	395.30	654.05	676.82	27373
咸宁	Xianning Municipality	1107.93	184.34	527.81	395.78	44027
随州	Suizhou Municipality	852.18	140.54	398.44	313.20	38801

10-4 主要城市固定资产投资(2016)
INVESTMENT IN FIXED ASSETS OF MAJOR MUNICIPALITIES (2016)

单位: 亿元 (100 million yuan)

城市	Municipalities	固定资产投资 Investment in Fixed Assets	房地产开发投资 Investment in Real Estate	#住宅 #Residential Buildings	新增固定资产 Newly Increased Fixed Assets	商品房屋销售面积(万平方米) Construction Floor Space of Commercial House Sold (10 000 sq.km)	#住宅 #Residential Buildings
武汉	Wuhan Municipality	7039.79	2517.44	1726.79	2404.13	3255.66	2931.06
黄石	Huangshi Municipality	1350.83	132.37	82.71	728.64	232.55	209.91
十堰	Shiyan Municipality	1323.81	87.28	60.57	842.94	219.56	209.98
宜昌	Yichang Municipality	3191.15	244.18	187.29	1841.07	586.92	550.02
襄阳	Xiangyang Municipality	3188.64	340.76	245.18	1558.18	625.22	554.23
鄂州	Ezhou Municipality	853.26	22.88	18.63	405.73	80.40	74.31
荆门	Jingmen Municipality	1531.46	100.39	71.72	858.69	305.96	286.85
孝感	Xiaogan Municipality	1899.43	160.02	116.09	1285.09	302.77	281.11
荆州	Jingzhou Municipality	2001.67	151.53	110.07	1088.79	243.40	227.67
黄冈	Huanggang Municipality	2041.65	265.73	198.99	1266.77	487.67	459.88
咸宁	Xianning Municipality	1438.29	56.99	40.54	839.62	307.02	284.06
随州	Suizhou Municipality	974.27	24.05	20.07	743.80	121.85	111.87

10-5 主要城市规上工业基本情况(2016)
BASIC STATISTICS ON INDUSTRY OF MAJOR MUNICIPALITIES (2016)

单位: 亿元 (100 million yuan)

城市	Municipalities	工业企业单位数(个) Number of Industrial Enterprises (unit)	主营业务收入 Major Business Income	利润总额 Total Profits
武汉	Wuhan Municipality	2529	12356.79	696.00
黄石	Huangshi Municipality	762	2416.19	76.82
十堰	Shiyan Municipality	911	1858.55	212.53
宜昌	Yichang Municipality	1487	5942.09	418.83
襄阳	Xiangyang Municipality	1884	5879.48	387.57
鄂州	Ezhou Municipality	525	1361.12	40.52
荆门	Jingmen Municipality	1155	3145.42	150.56
孝感	Xiaogan Municipality	1297	2677.17	126.79
荆州	Jingzhou Municipality	1271	2286.46	112.93
黄冈	Huanggang Municipality	1460	1677.17	80.62
咸宁	Xianning Municipality	845	1571.61	142.51
随州	Suizhou Municipality	677	1303.43	123.64

10-6 主要城市规上工业总产值(2016)
GROSS OUTPUT VALUE OF INDUSTRY OF MAJOR MUNICIPALITIES (2016)

单位:亿元 (100 million yuan)

城市	Municipalities	工业总产值(当年价) Total Value of Industry	内资企业 Inner Funded Enterprises	#国有企业	外商港澳台投资企业
武汉	Wuhan Municipality	13240.92	8860.32	1881.33	3430.52
黄石	Huangshi Municipality	2099.07	1733.95	7.00	186.34
十堰	Shiyan Municipality	1989.86	1517.67	24.93	467.05
宜昌	Yichang Municipality	6378.77	5778.15	14.27	97.97
襄阳	Xiangyang Municipality	6456.98	5968.31	67.20	420.44
鄂州	Ezhou Municipality	1424.30	1305.47	45.38	40.92
荆门	Jingmen Municipality	3319.48	3107.93	1.91	124.51
孝感	Xiaogan Municipality	2865.15	2589.93	5.72	83.55
荆州	Jingzhou Municipality	2474.76	2301.08	5.83	87.52
黄冈	Huanggang Municipality	1929.87	1805.74	7.88	47.46
咸宁	Xianning Municipality	1815.91	1672.08	4.37	58.54
随州	Suizhou Municipality	1346.22	1332.49	3.41	14.97

10-7 主要城市财政收支(2016)
GOVERNMENT REVENUE AND EXPENDITURES OF MAJOR MUNICIPALITIES (2016)

单位:亿元 (100 million yuan)

城市	Municipalities	公共财政收入 The public finance income	#各项税收 #Taxes	公共财政支出 The public finance expenditures	#社会保障和就业支出 #Subsides Expenditures for Social Security	#城乡社区事务支出 #Expenditures for City Maintenance
武汉	Wuhan Municipality	1322.10	1091.90	1523.09	235.62	244.80
黄石	Huangshi Municipality	105.47	67.42	222.53	39.72	17.10
十堰	Shiyan Municipality	100.27	67.30	322.54	48.64	17.17
宜昌	Yichang Municipality	300.04	176.71	538.63	59.05	74.76
襄阳	Xiangyang Municipality	320.70	188.67	639.74	73.75	110.30
鄂州	Ezhou Municipality	52.91	32.43	100.19	14.05	16.74
荆门	Jingmen Municipality	91.73	62.35	246.76	40.66	18.86
孝感	Xiaogan Municipality	129.23	81.06	355.12	55.48	23.72
荆州	Jingzhou Municipality	115.45	76.28	386.82	66.62	17.51
黄冈	Huanggang Municipality	119.52	74.59	452.54	76.05	11.48
咸宁	Xianning Municipality	83.34	50.01	216.20	29.70	7.98
随州	Suizhou Municipality	45.55	29.26	146.72	23.17	10.83

10-8 主要城市金融机构存贷款余额(2016)
DEPOSITS AND LOANS BALANCE OF BANKING INSTITUTIONS OF MAJOR MUNICIPALITIES (2016)

单位:亿元 (100 million yuan)

城市	Municipalities	年末金融机构人民币各项存款余额 Deposit Balance	#居民储蓄存款 #Savings Deposits from Residents	年末金融机构人民币各项贷款余额 Loans Balance
武汉	Wuhan Municipality	22196	6464.88	20755
黄石	Huangshi Municipality	1542	811.60	1013
十堰	Shiyan Municipality	2035	1142.51	1137
宜昌	Yichang Municipality	3130	1682.32	2353
襄阳	Xiangyang Municipality	3062	1961.96	1803
鄂州	Ezhou Municipality	582	335.03	391
荆门	Jingmen Municipality	1667	1097.94	873
孝感	Xiaogan Municipality	2079	1389.53	1023
荆州	Jingzhou Municipality	2553	1761.60	1186
黄冈	Huanggang Municipality	2681	1841.07	1161
咸宁	Xianning Municipality	1207	684.54	721
随州	Suizhou Municipality	1102	772.01	527

10-9 主要城市贸易、外经情况(2016)
DOMESTIC TRADE AND FOREIGN ECONOMY OF MAJOR MUNICIPALITIES (2016)

城市	Municipalities	社会消费品零售总额(亿元) Total Retail Sales of consumer Goods (100 million yuan)	进出口总额(亿美元) Total Import and Export (USD 100 million)	进口 Imports	出口 Exports	当年实际使用外资金额(亿美元) ActualForeign Direct Investment (USD 100 million)
武汉	Wuhan Municipality	5610.59	237.81	100.58	137.23	68.33
黄石	Huangshi Municipality	649.59	24.29	10.38	13.91	1.46
十堰	Shiyan Municipality	724.96	5.19	0.13	5.06	2.78
宜昌	Yichang Municipality	1240.33	26.74	3.42	23.31	3.91
襄阳	Xiangyang Municipality	1325.26	19.36	2.70	16.66	8.24
鄂州	Ezhou Municipality	298.45	4.86	2.52	2.34	2.71
荆门	Jingmen Municipality	614.23	10.62	2.00	8.62	3.76
孝感	Xiaogan Municipality	883.66	11.23	1.96	9.27	3.73
荆州	Jingzhou Municipality	1056.13	11.26	1.43	9.83	1.44
黄冈	Huanggang Municipality	973.94	7.06	1.05	6.02	1.29
咸宁	Xianning Municipality	442.54	4.29	1.38	2.92	0.70
随州	Suizhou Municipality	446.10	14.01	3.31	10.70	1.29

10-10 主要城市邮电、电力情况(2016)
POST SERVICE AND POWER IN MAJOR MUNICIPALITIES(2016)

城市	Municipalities	邮电业务收入(全市)(亿元) Revenue from Posts and Telecommunication Services(100 million yuan)	固定电话用户(万户) Telephones (10 000 Subscribers)	移动电话用户(万户) Mobile Telephones (10 000 Subscribers)	国际互联网用户(万户) Internet Service (10 000 Subscribers)	全年用电量(亿千瓦小时) Power Consumption (100 million kWh)	#城乡居民生活用电 #Urban and Rural Residents Power Consumption
武汉	Wuhan Municipality	221.67	221.73	1518.86	488.80	491.32	91.25
黄石	Huangshi Municipality	27.57	36.30	205.10	45.16	113.06	13.90
十堰	Shiyan Municipality	22.11	37.88	289.52	66.29	84.99	15.38
宜昌	Yichang Municipality	33.53	52.98	387.80	127.62	212.42	21.40
襄阳	Xiangyang Municipality	37.31	61.42	479.25	111.11	131.58	25.60
鄂州	Ezhou Municipality	9.16	15.78	94.71	23.56	67.15	6.08
荆门	Jingmen Municipality	21.01	29.78	216.55	47.60	88.84	12.68
孝感	Xiaogan Municipality	29.94	46.61	319.52	66.46	113.38	22.16
荆州	Jingzhou Municipality	37.82	59.89	396.30	131.37	109.32	27.86
黄冈	Huanggang unicipality	35.24	72.19	388.50	90.61	99.57	26.43
咸宁	Xianning Municipality	19.58	39.90	228.35	54.95	64.39	13.78
随州	Suizhou Municipality	13.83	21.13	168.84	38.79	34.83	9.65

10-11 主要城市居民收支情况(2016)
INCOME AND EXPENDITURE OF MAJOR URBAN HOUSEHOLDS (2016)

单位:元 (yuan)

城 市	Municipalities	城镇常住居民人均可支配收入 Per Capita Disposable Income of Urban Residents	城镇常住居民人均消费性支出 Per Capita Living Expenditure of Urban Residents	人均住房建筑面积(平方米) Per Capita Utility Floor Space of Residential Buildings (sq.m)
武汉	Wuhan Municipality	39737	26535	32.5
黄石	Huangshi Municipality	29906	18979	34.3
十堰	Shiyan Municipality	26030	15544	37.6
宜昌	Yichang Municipality	29735	18728	52.7
襄阳	Xiangyang Municipality	28794	17024	53.5
鄂州	Ezhou Municipality	26986	17103	56.3
荆门	Jingmen Municipality	28920	19539	29.6
孝感	Xiaogan Municipality	27939	18744	41.0
荆州	Jingzhou Municipality	27666	17152	49.8
黄冈	Huanggang Municipality	24796	17890	38.5
咸宁	Xianning Municipality	25839	17201	51.9
随州	Suizhou Municipality	24799	15926	45.0

10-12 主要城市居民消费支出、价格(2016)
LIVING EXPENDITURES AND PRICE OF MAJOR URBAN HOUSEHOLDS (2016)

单位:元 (yuan)

城 市	Municipalities	城镇常住居民人均消费性支出 Per Capita Living Expenditures for Consumption of Urban Residents				居民消费价格指数(上年=100) Consumer Price Index (preceding year=100)
		#医疗保健 #Medicine and Medicine and Medical Service	#交通和通讯 #Transport and Telecom-munication	#娱乐、教育、文化服务 #Recreation,Education and Cultural Services	#居住 #Residence	
武汉	Wuhan Municipality	1554	2944	2464	7415	102.4
黄石	Huangshi Municipality	1481	2378	2358	2959	102.1
十堰	Shiyan Municipality	1149	2018	1822	2534	101.9
宜昌	Yichang Municipality	1738	2242	2012	4169	102.3
襄阳	Xiangyang Municipality	1211	1902	1727	3448	102.2
鄂州	Ezhou Municipality	1546	1417	1746	2736	101.9
荆门	Jingmen Municipality	1932	1848	2452	3313	102.0
孝感	Xiaogan Municipality	1200	1708	2101	1927	102.2
荆州	Jingzhou Municipality	1308	1887	1932	3201	101.8
黄冈	Huanggang Municipality	1258	1590	2071	1928	101.4
咸宁	Xianning Municipality	1628	1735	2284	3681	101.7
随州	Suizhou Municipality	1146	1396	1869	2853	101.9

10–13 主要城市文教、科技、卫生情况(2016)
CULTURE, EDUCATION, SCIENCE AND TECHNOLOGY AND PUBLIC HEALTH OF MAJOR MUNICIPALITIES (2016)

城 市	Municipalities	普通高等学校在校学生数(万人) Number of Students Enrolled in Institutions of Higher Education (10 000 persons)	从事科技活动人员数(人) Number of Scientific and technical Personel (person)	公共图书馆图书总藏量(万册) Total Volume of Collection of Public Libraries (10 000 volumes)	医院、卫生院数(个) Number of Health Care Institutions (unit)	医院、卫生院床位数(万张) Number of Beds In Health Care Intitutions (10 000 units)	执业(助理)医师(万人) Practioner Doctors (Assitant) (10 000 persons)
武汉	Wuhan Municipality	94.88		1549.06	386	7.89	3.47
黄石	Huangshi Municipality	4.22	12838	139.70	71	1.54	0.53
十堰	Shiyan Municipality	5.25	14389	126.94	182	2.57	0.93
宜昌	Yichang Municipality	5.81	24068	618.97	177	2.49	1.05
襄阳	Xiangyang Municipality	5.02		203.32	221	3.21	1.32
鄂州	Ezhou Municipality	1.74	4109	42.00	489	0.58	0.22
荆门	Jingmen Municipality	1.27	13007	108.53	111	1.57	0.73
孝感	Xiaogan Municipality	4.37	18974	106.30	159	1.89	0.85
荆州	Jingzhou Municipality	9.18	10204	124.16	182	2.68	1.27
黄冈	Huanggang Municipality	4.05	9224	242.32	286	3.40	1.29
咸宁	Xianning Municipality	4.10	20120	94.84	95	1.37	0.67
随州	Suizhou Municipality	0.61	5248	32.93	106	1.04	0.42

主要统计指标解释

供水综合生产能力 指按供水设施取水、净化、送水、出厂输水干管等环节设计能力计算的综合生产能力。包括在原设计能力的基础上,经挖、革、改增加的生产能力。计算时,以四个环节中最薄弱的环节为主确定能力。

年末供水管道长度 指从送水泵至用户水表之间所有管道的长度。不包括新安装尚未使用的管道。

全年供水总量 指报告期供水企业(单位)供出的全部水量。包括有效供水量和漏损水量。

生活用水量 包括公共服务用水和居民家庭用水。公共服务用水指为城市社会公共生活服务的用水。包括行政事业单位、部队营区和公共设施服务、社会服务业、批发零售贸易业、旅馆饮食业以及其他公共服务业等单位的用水。居民家庭用水指城市范围内所有居民家庭的日常生活用水。包括城市居民、农民家庭、公共供水站用水。

用水普及率 指城市用水人口数与城市人口总数的比率。计算公式:

$$用水普及率=\frac{城市用水人口数}{城市人口总数}\times 100\%$$

供气管道长度 指报告期末从气源厂压缩机的出口或门站出口至各类用户引入管之间的全部已经通气投入使用的管道长度。不包括煤气生产厂、输配站、液化气储存站、灌瓶站、储配站、气化站、混气站、供应站等厂(站)内的管道。

全年供气总量 指全年燃气企业(单位)向用户供应的燃气数量。包括销售量和损失量。

用气普及率 指报告期末使用燃气的城市人口数与城市人口总数的比率。计算公式为:

$$用气普及率=\frac{城市用气人口数}{城市人口总数}\times 100\%$$

城市供热能力 指供热企业(单位)向城市热用户输送热能的设计能力。

城市供热总量 指在报告期供热企业(单位)向城市热用户输送全部蒸汽和热水的总热量。

城市供热管道长度 指从各类热源到热用户建筑物接入口之间的全部蒸汽和热水的管道长度。不包括各类热源厂内部的管道长度。

年末道路长度 指年末道路长度和与道路相通的广场、桥梁、隧道的长度,按车行道中心线计算。在统计时只统计路面宽度在3.5米(含3.5米)以上的各种铺装道路,包括开放型工业区和住宅区道路在内。

城市桥梁 指为跨越天然或人工障碍物而修建的构筑物。包括跨河桥、立交桥、人行天桥以及人行地下通道等。包括永久性桥和半永久性桥。

城市排水管道长度 指所有排水总管、干管、支管、检查井及连接井进出口等长度之和。

城市污水日处理能力 指污水处理厂(或处理装置)每昼夜处理污水量的设计能力。

年末运营车数 指年末公交企业(单位)用于运营业务的全部车辆数。以企业(单位)固定资产台帐中已投入运营的车辆数为准。

城市园林绿地面积 指报告期末用作园林和绿化的各种绿地面积。包括公共绿地、居住区绿地、单位附属绿地、防护绿地、生产绿地、道路绿地和风景林地面积。不包括:

1.屋顶绿化、垂直绿化、阳台绿化和室内绿化。

2.以物质生产为主的林地、耕地、牧草地、果园和竹园等。

3.城市总体规划中不列入绿地的水域。

公共绿地 指向公众开放的市级、区级、居住区级各类公园、街旁游园,包括其范围内的水域。其中居住区级公园应不小于

1万平方米，街旁游园的宽度不小于8米，面积不小于400平方米。

Explanatory Notes on Main Statistical Indicators

Production Capacity of Water Supply refers to the designed comprehensive production capacity of water facilities, covering the 4 links of water collection, purification, conveyance, and outflow through trunk pipelines. Increase capacity through transformation and innovation projects are included as well. The capacity is determined mainly on the weakest of the above-mentioned 4 links.

Length of Water Supply Pipelines at the Year-end refers to the total length of all the pipelines between the water pumps and the user抯 water meters, excluding pipelines newly installed but not used yet.

Annual Volume of Water Supply refers to the total volume of water supplied by water-works (units) during the reference period, including both the effective water supply and loss during the water supply.

Consumption of Water for Residential Use refers to the water consumption of households for daily life and the water consumption of public service facilities. The latter refers to water consumption for urban public services, including the consumption of government agencies and public institutions, military barracks, public facilities, wholesale and retail outlets, restaurants, hotels, and other units providing public services. Household water consumption refers to consumption of water for daily life of all households in the boundary of cities, including households of urban residents and farmers, and public water supply stations.

Percentage of Urban Population with Access to Tap Water refers to the ratio of the urban population with access to tap water to the total urban population. The formula is:

Percentage of population with access to tap water= (Urban population with access to tap water) / (Urban population) × 100%

Length of Gas Pipelines refers to the total length of pipelines in use between the outlet of the compressor of gas-work or outlet of gas stations and the leading pipe of users, excluding pipelines within gasworks, delivery stations, LPG storage stations, refilling stations, gas-mixing stations and supply stations.

Volume of Gas Supply refers to the total volume of gas provided to users by gas-producing enterprises (units) in a year, including the volume sold and the volume lost.

Percentage of Urban Population with Access to Gas refers to the ratio of the urban population with access to gas to the total urban population at the end of the reference period. The formula is:

Percentage of population with access to gas = (Urban population with access to gas / Urban population) x 100%

Heating Capacity in Urban Area refers to the designed capacity of heating enterprises (units) in supplying heating energy to urban users during the reference period.

Quantity of Heat Supplied in Urban Area refers to the total quantity of heat from steam and hot water supplied to urban users by heating enterprises (units) during the reference period.

Length of Heating Pipelines refers to the total length of steam or hot water pipelines for sources of heat to the leading pipelines of the buildings of the users, excluding internal pipelines in heat generating enterprises.

Length of Paved Roads at the Year-end refers to the length of roads with paved surface including squares bridges and tunnels connected with roads by the end of the year. Length of the roads is measured by the central lines for vehicles for paved roads with a width of 3.5 meters and over, including roads in open-ended factory compounds and residential quarters.

Urban Bridges refer to bridges built to cross over natural or man-made barriers, including bridges over rivers, overpasses for traffic and for pedestrian, underpasses for pedestrian, etc. Both permanent and semi-permanent bridges are included.

Length of Urban Sewage Pipes refers to the total length of general drainage, trunks. branch and inspection wells, connection wells, inlets and outlets, etc.

Daily Disposal Capacity of Urban Sewage refers to the designed 24 hour capacity of sewage disposal by the sewage treatment works or facilities.

Number of Vehicles under Operation at the Year-end refers to the total number of vehicles under operation by public transport enterprises (units) at the end of the year, based on the records of operational vehicles by the enterprises (units).

Area of Urban Gardens and Green Areas refers to the total area occupied for green projects at the end of the reference period, including public green land, green land in residential quarters, green land attached to institutions, protection green land, production green land, roadside green land and forest in scenic spots. It does not include the following:

(1) Greenery and plants on roofs, balconies, indoors and vertical green areas;

(2) Forest, cultivated land, grassland, orchards and bamboo grooves that are for production purpose; and

(3) Water areas that are not included in urban master plan as green land.

Public Green Area refers to green areas open to the public such as municipal, community and neighborhood parks and roadside parks, including waters within parks. Neighborhood parks should occupy an area larger than 10,000 square meters, and the width of road-side parks should occupy an area larger than 400 square meters, with a width of more that 8 meters.

11 资源和环境

Resources and Environment

11-1 “三废”排放和处理综合利用情况
"THREE WASTES" DISCHARGE AND TREATMENT UTILIZATION SITUATION

分　类	Item	2012	2013	2014	2015	2015	2016
一、废水排放总量(万吨)	Total Volume of Waste Water Discharged (10 000 ton)	290200	294054	301703	313785	313785	274787
工业废水排放总量	Total Volume of Industrial Waste Water Discharged	91609	84993	81657	80817	80817	49090
二、废气排放总量(亿标立方米)	Total Volume of Waste Gas Discharged (100 million cu.m)	19512	19986	21702	23643	23643	29519
三、废气中污染物排放量(万吨)	Pollutants Discharged in Waste Gas (10 000 ton)						
二氧化硫	Sulfur Dioxide	62.24	59.94	58.38	55.14	55.14	28.56
#工业二氧化硫	#Industrial Sulfur Dioxide	54.86	52.40	50.62	47.07	47.07	18.55
烟粉尘	Soot and Dust	34.97	35.95	50.40	44.69	44.69	27.58
四、工业固体废物产生量(万吨)	Volume of Industrial Solid Wastes Producced (10 000 ton)	7611	8181	8006	7750	7750	7109
已处置的	Teated	1561	1646	1701	2078	2078	1494
已综合利用的	Utilized In a Comprehensive Way	5737	6196	6139	5253	5253	4332
已贮存的	Stored	377	412	221	488	488	1505
工业固体废物排放量	Volume of Industrial Solid Wastes Emission	1.06	0.80	0.46	0.50	0.50	0.22
五、锅炉总数　(台)	Total Number of Boiler　(unit)	2451	2413	2617	3107	3107	2694
锅炉蒸吨数　(蒸吨)	Steam Tons of Boiler　(steam ton)	72444	75469	87176	83972	83972	81870
六、工业炉窑　(座)	Number of Industrial Kiln Stove　(unit)	2475	2298	2262	2157	2157	1589

11-2 工业污染治理情况

项目	Item	1990	1995	2000
一、汇总工业企业单位数 (个)	Total Number of Industrial Enterprises (unit)	991	613	583
二、污染治理项目本年投资来源合计 (万元)	Total Resource of Investment in Pollutant Treatment Projects (10 000 yuan)	18051	27433	85238
国家预算内资金	State Budgetary Funds	5568	3540	962
环境保护补助资金	Environmental Protection Subsidy Funds	2531	5430	1282
其　他	Others	1372	7966	61881
三、污染治理项目本年完成投资合计 (万元)	Total Investment in Pollutant Treatment Projects (10 000 yuan)			85238
治理废水	Waste Water	5637	12042	45653
治理废气	Waste Gas	9891	9164	26668
治理固体废物	Solid Waste	1371	5293	6072
治理噪声	Noise Abatement	534	583	644
其　他	Others	618	351	6201
四、本年施工项目数 (个)	Projects Carried Out in This Year (unit)	1545	939	851
治理废水	Waste Water	450	305	384
治理废气	Waste Gas	758	367	361
治理固体废物	Solid Waste	119	121	27
治理噪声	Noise Abatement	139	109	31
其　他	Others	79	37	48
五、本年竣工项目 (个)	Projects Completed in This Year (unit)	1312	832	692
治理废水	Waste Water	353	256	316
治理废气	Waste Gas	662	339	286
治理固体废物	Solid Waste	99	96	22
治理噪声	Noise Abatement	126	106	26
其　他	Others	72	35	42

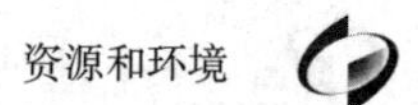

STATISTICS ON TREATMENT OF INDUSTRIAL POLLUTION

2005	2007	2008	2009	2010	2011	2012	2013	2014	2015	2016
336	342	307	225	159	232	171	147	152	161	305
148097	169405	161453	281332	277416	153812	154496	251745	262884	157944	169061
7591	4434	4244	5602	3892	7216	4128	3667	1890	1035	631
7385	5543	3713	4092	1894	1290	676	210	2177	992	631
133121	159428	153497	271638	271631	145306	149693	247868	258817	155917	167800
148097	169405	161453	281332	277416	153812	154496	251745	262884	157944	169061
48068	78246	82635	54002	35627	84573	35868	15873	18409	26067	39707
40008	74455	60834	213918	197293	47920	80510	216673	230712	120301	98518
11408	2004	3960	5970	9580	10505	3565	1720	2762	1375	8475
440	1411	1041	675	867	1081	1114	52	104	275	367
48173	13288	12983	6768	34050	9734	33439	17427	10896	9927	21994
473	504	406	318	226	364	136	113	127	199	302
191	224	178	126	98	158	43	28	38	63	99
176	188	139	132	74	122	56	59	78	96	151
15	21	23	11	13	17	7	3	2	7	21
20	21	15	11	12	18	8	1	4	5	4
71	50	51	38	29	49	22	22	5	28	27
428	442	345	273	195	331	117	148	134	146	238
174	197	152	108	84	143	42	42	37	41	80
160	168	115	111	64	112	49	83	88	73	116
11	18	19	10	10	16	7	3	1	4	17
18	20	14	9	10	18	6		3	5	4
65	39	45	35	27	42	13	20	5	23	21

11-3 排污费征收、使用和污染赔(罚)款情况
STATISTICS ON COLLECTION, REPARATIONS AND FINES ON POLLUTION DSICHARGES

项 目	Item	1990	1995	2000	2009	2010	2011	2012	2013	2014	2015	2016
交纳排污费单位 (个)	Number of Enterprises Charged (unit)	4072	9409	32581	15584	12017	10581	10895	7269	7566	8763	8817
本年征收排污费数 (万元)	Amount of Pollutant Fees (10 000 yuan)	7823	13870	20092	38176	40300	44975	50587	60161	65626	62645	65655

11-4 工业企业废水处理设施情况
STATISTICS ON INDUSTRIAL WASTE WATER TREATMENT FACILITES

项 目	Item	2000	2005	2010	2011	2012	2013	2014	2015	2016
汇总企业单位数 (个)	Total Number of Enterprises (unit)	2172	2313	2643	3911	3699	3590	3911	4555	4198
治理设施数量 (套)	Number of Treatment Facilities	2120	2163	2093	5296	2110	2084	2238	2562	1942
处理能力 (万吨/日)	Treatment Capacity(10 000 ton/day)		912	1037	1322	1023	1029	1043	1052	566
运行费用 (万元)	Operation Fees (10 000 yuan)	46651	77931	137920	344256	176058	168277	232869	224053	195593

主要统计指标解释

工业废水排放量 指经过企业厂区所有排放口排到企业外部的工业废水量。包括生产废水、外排的直接冷却水、超标排放的矿井地下水和与工业废水混排的厂区生活污水，不包括外排的间接冷却水(清污不分流的间接冷却水应计算在内)。

工业废气排放量 指报告期内企业厂区内燃料燃烧和生产工艺过程中产生的各种排入大气的含有污染物的气体的总量，以标准状态(273K，101325Pa)计算。

工业固体废物产生量 指报告期内企业在生产过程中产生的固体状、半固体状和高浓度液体状废弃物的总量，包括危险废物、冶炼废渣、粉煤灰、炉渣、煤矸石、尾矿、放射性废物和其他废物等；不包括矿山开采的剥离废石和掘进废石(煤矸石和呈酸性或碱性的废石除外)。酸性或碱性废石指采掘的废石其流经水、雨淋水的pH值小于4或pH值大于10.5者。

工业固体废物综合利用量 指报告期内企业通过回收、加工、循环、交换等方式，从固体废物中提取或者使其转化为可以利用的资源、能源和其他原材料的固体废物量(包括当年利用往年的工业固体废物贮存量)，如用作农业肥料、生产建筑材料、筑路等。综合利用量由原产生固体废物的单位统计。

Explanatory Notes on Main Statistical Indicators

Waste Water Discharged by Industry refers to the volume of waste water discharged by industrial enterprises through all their outlets, including waste water from production process, directly cooled water, groundwater from mining wells which does not meet discharge standards and sewage from households mixed with waste water produced by industrial activities, but excluding indirectly cooled water discharged (It should be included if the discharge is not separated with waste water).

Industrial Waste Air Emission refers to discharge into atmosphere of waste air containing pollutants generated from fuel burning and production process in enterprises within a given period of time.

Industrial Solid Wastes Produced refers to total volume of solid, semi-solid and high concentration liquid residues produced by industrial enterprises from production process in a given period of time, including hazardous wastes, slag, coal ash, gangue, tailings, radioactive residues and other wastes, but excluding stones stripped or dug out in mining (gangue and acid or alkaline stones not included). A stone is acid or alkaline depending on the pH value of the water below 4 or above 10.5 when the stone is in, or soaked by, the water.

Industrial Solid Wastes Utilized refers to volume of solid wastes from which useful materials can be extracted or which can be converted into usable resources, energy or other materials by means of reclamation, processing, recycling and exchange (including utilizing in the year the stocks of industrial solid wastes of the previous year). Examples of such utilizations include fertilizers, building materials and road materials. The information shall be collected by the producing units of the wastes.

12 农业

Agriculture

12-1 农村基层组织和农业基本情况
BASIC CONDITIONS OF RURAL GRASSROOTS UNITS AND AGRICULTURE

指 标	Item	2000	2005	2010	2013	2014	2015	2016
农村组织情况 (个)	**Rural Units (unit)**							
乡个数	Township	476	217	201	175	170	168	168
镇个数	Town Governments	853	737	742	757	761	761	759
村委会个数	Village Committees	32400	26678	26018	25452	25606	25343	25063
村民小组个数	Villager Group	259250	212587	209598	210108	208966	208546	208050
乡村户数、人口	**Rural Households,Population**							
乡村户数 (万户)	Rural Households (10 000 units)	983.94	1015.72	1062.14	1088.01	1094.98	1091.08	1089.71
乡村人口 (万人)	Rural Population (10 000 persons)	3947.26	3991.47	4031.73	4092.19	4110.29	4093.90	4076.46
乡村从业人员 (万人)	**Rural Employment (10 000 persons)**	**1781.70**	**1931.15**	**2154.44**	**2280.14**	**2308.72**	**2300.88**	**2290.90**
按性别分	Grouped by Sex							
男	Male	937.67	1026.48	1154.45	1217.97	1238.01	1237.43	1231.65
女	Female	844.03	904.67	999.99	1062.17	1070.71	1063.45	1059.25
按行业分	Grouped by Sector							
农林牧渔业	Farming, Forestry, Animal husbandary and Fishery	1159.13	1101.29	900.14	869.79	865.21	869.32	863.64
国营农林牧渔场从业人员	Employees in State-run Agriculture, forestry,animal husbandry, fishery Farm	54.94	55.73	54.31	47.38	51.69	51.23	57.90
农业从业人员	Agriculture Employees	34.08	35.27	31.56	27.93	28.96	28.65	31.67
非农业从业人员	Non-agriculture Employees	20.86	20.46	22.37	19.45	22.73	22.58	26.23
年末实有耕地面积 (千公顷)	**Cultivated Areas (Year-End) (1 000 hectares)**	**3282.96**	**3161.17**	**3323.92**	**3409.91**	**3420.51**	**3436.24**	**3444.31**
农业机械总动力(万千瓦)	Total Agricultural Machinery Power (10 000 kW)	1414.00	2057.37	2796.99	4081.05	4292.90	4465.51	4187.75
化肥施用量 (万吨)	Consumption of Chemical Fertilizers (10 000 tons)	247.08	285.83	350.77	351.93	348.27	333.87	327.96
农村用电量 (亿千瓦小时)	Electricity Consumed in Rural Areas (100 million kWh)	60.86	70.09	109.78	130.14	142.23	149.10	152.86
农作物总播种面积(千公顷)	Total Sown Area (1 000 hectares)	7584.07	7391.30	7997.57	8106.19	8112.26	7952.36	7843.51
#粮食	Grain Crops	4156.20	4068.15	4068.37	4258.40	4370.34	4466.03	4436.87
主要农产品产量(万吨)	**Volume of Major Agricultural Products (10 000 tons)**							
粮食	Grain Crops	2218.49	2177.38	2315.80	2501.30	2584.16	2703.28	2554.11
棉花	Cotton Crops	30.43	37.50	47.18	45.97	35.95	29.83	18.85
油料	Oil-Bearing Crops	269.98	293.90	311.80	333.17	341.73	339.60	329.75
肉类产量	Output of Meat	271.19	342.63	379.42	430.08	440.44	431.93	424.18
水产品产量	Output of Aquatic Products	234.34	318.21	353.09	410.37	433.30	455.80	470.84

注：主要农产品产量2006、2007年数据按农业普查数据进行衔接、调整。
Note:Statistics of output of major farm products of 2006,2007 is adusted according to Second Agriculture Survey.

12-2 耕地面积
AREAS UNDER CULTIVATION

单位:千公顷 (1 000 hectares)

年 份 Year	年末实有耕地面积 Cultivated Areas (Year-End)	水 田 Paddy Fields	旱 地 Dry Fields	年内减少 Dereased in Cultivated Areas in This Year	#国家基建占地 Capital Construction	人均占有耕地(公顷) Per Capita Cultivated Area (sq.m) 按乡村人口计算 By Rural Population	按农林牧渔业劳动力计算 By Farming, Forestry, Animal husbandry and Fishery Laborers
1949	2742.58	1765.11	1977.47			0.12	0.29
1952	4015.90	1876.62	2139.28			0.16	0.39
1957	4172.31	1945.05	2227.26			0.16	0.37
1962	4271.33	1847.19	2424.56			0.15	0.39
1965	4239.93	1966.38	2273.55			0.14	0.37
1970	3964.01	1982.20	1981.81			0.11	0.31
1975	3823.00	1996.10	1826.77	54.10		0.10	0.28
1978	3768.07	1959.63	1808.43	30.77	7.75	0.10	0.28
1979	3754.51	1940.27	1814.24	29.13	5.50	0.10	0.27
1980	3738.51	1929.50	1809.01	35.82	4.69	0.10	0.27
1985	3584.61	1864.15	1720.46	71.70	8.56	0.09	0.27
1986	3545.00	1847.63	1697.37	49.30	7.30	0.09	0.27
1987	3517.99	1845.17	1672.82	36.16	7.13	0.09	0.26
1988	3498.47	1838.37	1660.10	25.98	4.55	0.09	0.25
1989	3486.57	1858.25	1628.33	17.47	1.83	0.09	0.25
1990	3476.77	1871.77	1605.00	15.60	2.73	0.08	0.24
1991	3458.46	1869.19	1589.27	24.11	4.03	0.08	0.24
1992	3421.57	1845.31	1576.26	41.67	4.95	0.08	0.24
1993	3392.74	1815.75	1576.99	32.84	6.11	0.08	0.24
1994	3375.60	1805.42	1570.18	21.21	3.77	0.08	0.24
1995	3358.01	1780.40	1577.61	21.36	4.23	0.08	0.25
1996	3349.25	1800.00	1549.25	13.80	2.85	0.08	0.26
1997	3342.45	1796.07	1546.38	12.24	2.43	0.08	0.26
1998	3327.16	1788.95	1538.21	19.95	3.83	0.08	0.27
1999	3310.40	1786.34	1524.06	23.08	5.13	0.08	0.27
2000	3282.96	1757.63	1525.33	34.15	5.18	0.08	0.28
2001	3242.85	1742.69	1500.16	46.26	7.76	0.08	0.27
2002	3094.03	1708.58	1385.45	110.10	12.04	0.08	0.27
2003	3033.45	1665.49	1367.96	181.18	7.51	0.08	0.27
2004	3091.75	1789.10	1302.65	39.81	5.36	0.08	0.28
2005	3131.17	1856.17	1305.00	40.70	4.93	0.08	0.28
2006	3201.66	1881.74	1319.92	20.65	5.49	0.08	0.29
2007	3226.62	1890.04	1336.58	21.08	5.67	0.08	0.31
2008	3289.33	1914.07	1375.26	10.68	4.29	0.08	0.33
2009	3308.35	1928.67	1379.68	15.06	5.61	0.08	0.34
2010	3323.92	1932.05	1391.87	14.90	9.44	0.08	0.37
2011	3361.86	1954.61	1407.25	14.09	5.15	0.08	0.38
2012	3390.06	1963.13	1426.93	14.82	6.93	0.08	0.39
2013	3409.91	1976.12	1433.79	16.33	6.75	0.08	0.39
2014	3420.51	1986.01	1434.50	12.69	4.69	0.08	0.40
2015	3436.24	2010.40	1425.84	13.76	4.62	0.08	0.40
2016	3444.31	2026.67	1417.64	24.57	6.72	0.08	0.39

注：1996年及以后为农业普查接轨数(下同)。

Notes:Since 1996,the relative targers were in line with the data of agricultural gereral survey (the same as the following tables).

12-3 农林牧渔业总产值
GROSS OUTPUT VALUE OF FARMING, FORESTRY, ANIMAL HUSBANDRY AND FISHERY

单位:亿元　　当年价格　　(At current price, 100 million yuan)

年 份 Year	农林牧渔业总产值 Gross Output Value of FFAF	农业 Farming	林业 Foresty	畜牧业 Animal Husbandry	渔业 Fishery	农林牧渔服务业 Service Industry for Farming, Forestry, Animal husbandry and Fishery
1949	10.72	7.22	0.69	0.97	0.10	
1952	16.59	12.08	0.79	1.48	0.18	
1957	28.59	20.55	1.46	3.81	0.46	
1962	33.66	26.52	1.71	3.61	0.46	
1965	47.48	37.44	1.98	6.02	0.51	
1970	51.27	40.62	2.07	6.41	0.92	
1975	74.68					
1978	84.46					
1979	109.85					
1980	94.95	64.70	7.28	17.29	1.46	
1985	192.32	129.61	8.15	39.08	8.18	
1986	219.10	146.79	8.75	43.86	10.77	
1987	249.68	160.13	9.97	54.86	14.19	
1988	297.51	175.12	10.98	80.80	18.83	
1989	335.04	198.56	11.75	91.47	20.66	
1990	402.23	252.92	14.15	98.04	23.88	
1991	405.04	247.01	16.81	102.19	25.06	
1992	435.42	265.53	17.36	110.37	27.59	
1993	501.17	301.99	22.39	134.02	42.77	
1994	786.84	481.82	26.47	219.53	59.01	
1995	988.53	612.12	28.33	268.09	79.98	
1996	1140.76	670.27	33.62	337.02	99.86	
1997	1243.68	711.91	37.33	381.40	113.04	
1998	1222.58	688.06	41.29	371.37	121.86	
1999	1126.10	645.98	40.86	311.43	127.83	
2000	1125.64	615.74	40.24	338.77	130.89	
2001	1172.82	658.26	27.11	352.63	134.82	
2002	1203.30	671.20	28.33	354.84	148.93	
2003	1342.09	733.36	34.78	383.71	170.43	
2004	1695.44	921.59	31.78	514.52	205.68	21.87
2005	1775.58	932.15	37.30	545.40	236.49	24.24
2006	1842.20	995.46	40.50	487.09	221.42	97.73
2008	2940.47	1395.76	49.69	1008.65	372.98	113.39
2009	2985.19	1511.49	57.67	881.78	413.14	121.11
2010	3501.99	1921.67	65.37	925.04	458.58	131.33
2011	4252.90	2299.30	86.10	1205.80	508.80	152.90
2012	4732.10	2488.10	100.10	1334.00	626.20	183.70
2013	5161.00	2678.10	122.00	1395.40	748.40	216.70
2014	5452.80	2761.70	157.00	1427.60	844.20	262.30
2015	5728.56	2780.37	180.60	1503.34	922.77	341.48
2016	6278.35	2921.27	203.43	1715.18	1030.01	408.46

12-4 农、林、牧、渔业总产值指数
INDICES OF GROSS OUTPUT VALUE OF FARMING, FORESTRY, ANIMAL HUSBANDRY AND FISHERY

单位:%　　上年=100　　(preceding year=100)

年份 Year	合计 Total	农业 Farming	林业 Forestry	畜牧业 Animal Husbandry	渔业 Fishery	农林牧渔服务业 Service Industry for Farming, Forestry, Animal husbandry and Fishery
1978	104.00	103.10	104.90	107.60	94.20	
1980	88.80	83.70	102.80	108.10	111.30	
1985	106.30	101.70	103.00	127.80	133.30	
1986	103.40	100.60	98.50	107.30	129.80	
1987	102.70	101.20	104.50	101.00	120.10	
1988	97.20	93.90	90.60	105.40	105.60	
1989	105.00	104.50	101.60	105.20	108.30	
1990	107.10	108.40	106.00	104.90	106.70	
1991	100.70	97.66	118.80	104.23	104.94	
1992	107.50	107.50	103.27	108.00	110.10	
1993	115.10	113.73	128.97	121.43	155.02	
1994	157.00	159.55	118.27	163.80	137.93	
1995	125.63	127.04	106.99	122.12	135.54	
1996	115.40	109.50	118.67	125.71	124.87	
1997	109.02	106.21	111.04	113.17	113.20	
1998	98.30	96.65	110.61	97.37	107.80	
1999	92.11	93.88	98.95	83.86	104.90	
2000	99.96	95.32	98.48	108.78	102.39	
2001	104.19	106.91	67.37	104.09	103.00	
2002	102.60	101.97	104.50	100.63	110.47	
2003	111.53	109.26	122.77	108.14	114.44	
2004	126.33	125.67	91.37	134.09	120.68	
2005	104.73	101.15	117.37	106.00	114.98	110.84
2006	105.37	109.29	108.58	96.04	109.87	116.05
2007	124.68	115.73	103.36	140.88	140.38	108.33
2008	128.02	121.15	118.17	146.99	119.99	107.10
2009	101.52	108.29	116.10	87.42	110.77	106.81
2010	109.95	121.28	113.35	94.12	106.86	100.16
2011	121.40	119.70	137.70	130.40	110.90	116.40
2012	111.30	108.20	116.30	110.60	123.10	120.10
2013	109.06	107.64	121.88	104.60	119.51	117.96
2014	105.70	103.10	128.70	102.30	112.80	121.00
2015	105.70	104.70	129.40	100.30	105.70	130.90
2016	104.91	105.00	112.82	99.12	107.92	118.68

注: 2009年畜牧业数据变动原因为与农普数衔接。
Note: 2009 data changes due to livestock and agricultural census data convergence.

12-5 农、林、牧、渔业总产值指数
INDICES OF GROSS OUTPUT VALUE OF FARMING, FORESTRY, ANIMAL HUSBANDRY AND FISHERY

单位:% 1978年=100 (year 1978 =100)

年份 Year	合计 Total	农业 Farming	林业 Forestry	牧业 Animal Husbandry	渔业 Fishery
1980	97.3	91.4	104.7	127.9	121.5
1985	157.7	142.4	114.0	206.2	338.6
1987	167.5	145.0	117.3	282.7	527.8
1988	162.9	136.1	106.3	285.5	557.3
1989	171.0	142.3	108.0	301.0	603.6
1990	183.1	154.2	114.5	315.7	644.0
1991	181.7	147.7	125.9	334.0	631.8
1992	194.4	158.7	120.1	360.7	689.3
1993	207.4	168.0	129.5	410.9	936.1
1994	227.8	175.0	152.0	461.7	1203.0
1995	259.9	195.3	156.0	535.1	1530.2
1996	277.6	198.0	168.5	611.1	1732.0
1997	304.0	213.4	179.3	671.6	2007.4
1998	307.3	209.1	204.6	682.3	2164.0
1999	309.5	220.2	196.7	627.9	2270.0
2000	318.1	226.3	194.2	650.4	2324.5
2001	327.6	238.7	141.6	669.6	2382.4
2002	334.2	233.1	145.9	700.2	2677.3
2003	351.8	237.2	167.2	730.8	2824.4
2004	374.7	257.9	153.9	760.8	2979.6
2005	392.4	260.9	180.6	806.4	3425.9
2006	171.8	137.9	58.7	502.2	2214.2
2007	214.3	159.6	60.7	707.4	3108.3
2008	274.3	193.3	72.0	1039.8	3729.8
2009	278.5	209.3	83.6	909.1	4131.4
2010	326.7	266.2	94.7	953.6	4585.8
2011	396.7	318.5	124.8	1243.1	5088.0
2012	441.4	344.6	145.1	1375.3	6262.0
2013	481.4	370.9	176.8	1438.6	7484.0
2014	508.6	382.5	227.6	1471.8	8442.0
2015	534.4	400.5	294.5	1476.2	8923.2
2016	560.6	420.5	332.3	1463.2	9629.9

12-6 农、林、牧、渔业增加值(2016)
VALUE ADDED OF FARMING, FORESTRY, ANIMAL HUSBANDRY AND FISHERY(2016)

单位:亿元 (100 million yuan)

项 目	Item	合计 Total	农业 Farming	林业 Forestry	牧业 Animal Husbandry	渔业 Fishery	农林牧渔服务业 Service Industry for Farming, Forestry,Animal husbandry and Fishery
一、总产值(现价)	Gross Output Value(current price)	6278.35	2921.27	203.43	1715.18	1030.01	408.46
二、中间消耗	Intermedium-Consumption	2497.56	979.03	101.10	709.87	420.56	286.99
三、增加值	Value-Added	3780.79	1942.24	102.33	1005.32	609.44	121.47

12-7 农作物播种面积

单位:千公顷

年 份 Year	总播种面积 Total Sown Areas	粮食作物 Grain Crops	小麦 Wheat	稻谷 Rice	薯类 Tubers	玉米 Corn	大豆 Soybean	经济作物 Economic Crops
1978	7931.05	5544.78	1122.28	2894.63	427.23	403.14	173.43	971.53
1980	7477.06	5352.04	1292.29	2708.22	387.46	406.91	138.94	977.58
1985	7331.71	5108.25	1331.42	2538.57	354.01	374.17	134.64	1280.89
1990	7361.14	5200.01	1352.10	2636.47	391.90	386.11	164.65	1343.23
1991	7423.92	5194.50	1347.53	2622.79	402.38	395.19	150.61	1414.37
1992	7183.83	4955.35	1287.91	2537.49	392.59	376.18	140.23	1405.87
1993	7125.47	4812.05	1271.23	2377.82	384.33	365.96	181.69	1381.64
1994	7181.43	4797.95	1225.60	2373.26	203.39	373.02	201.52	1456.00
1995	7431.71	4776.65	1179.93	2408.66	397.65	393.77	188.01	1683.56
1996	7579.01	4880.28	1230.14	2448.58	419.53	405.07	174.71	1676.71
1997	7739.21	4944.66	1276.52	2467.51	415.74	400.30	182.51	1689.03
1998	7695.98	4737.15	1212.08	2244.74	431.02	442.84	201.32	1703.80
1999	7788.66	4673.11	1074.43	2284.98	448.72	460.82	207.01	1739.07
2000	7584.07	4156.20	845.10	1995.29	467.61	424.10	224.75	1984.76
2001	7488.99	4015.73	735.85	1953.77	237.75	401.11	218.01	1972.36
2002	7281.61	3816.08	679.02	1888.75	430.61	384.04	217.82	1981.04
2003	7153.24	3572.74	603.43	1808.75	208.56	349.81	196.47	2083.26
2004	7225.13	3817.89	605.08	2084.02	403.79	357.49	186.05	2079.51
2005	7391.30	4068.05	730.61	2162.39	397.75	428.79	179.79	1974.56
2006	7100.59	3902.27	1016.93	1975.07	218.67	431.93	118.40	1825.40
2007	7130.01	3981.43	1096.25	1978.82	219.19	436.34	114.75	1787.79
2008	7272.33	3906.69	1000.57	1978.94	216.09	470.37	206.79	1973.85
2009	7527.50	4012.53	993.36	2045.08	237.93	507.28	195.76	2018.78
2010	7997.57	4068.37	1000.11	2038.17	274.29	531.38	104.76	2116.92
2011	8009.57	4122.07	1013.61	2036.17	303.64	549.66	152.97	2127.49
2012	8105.69	4180.05	1065.50	2017.88	299.65	593.34	95.31	2204.36
2013	8106.19	4258.40	1094.80	2101.15	303.27	573.47	86.67	2159.12
2014	8112.26	4370.34	1074.33	2143.95	308.81	642.38	98.90	2102.34
2015	7952.36	4466.03	1093.43	2188.46	317.61	687.85	147.78	2172.36
2016	7843.51	4436.87	1108.27	2130.97	321.17	661.70	134.83	2054.52

注:2006、2007年度为农业普查衔接数据。本表经济作物不含蔬菜和瓜果。

TOTAL SOWN AREAS OF FARM CROPS

(1 000 hectares)

棉花 Cotton	油菜籽 Rape-Seed	花生 Peanuts	芝麻 Sesame	黄红麻 Jute and Ambary	甘蔗 Sugar-cane	甜菜 Beet-Roots	烤烟 Flue-Cured Tobacco	其他作物 Others
593.19	165.27	34.14	102.71	8.39	2.31	0.13	24.75	1414.73
591.67	175.75	40.76	113.51	12.17	1.49	0.12	9.69	1147.44
464.97	361.42	65.94	173.31	94.17	7.85	0.08	37.67	942.56
455.92	744.31	63.75	126.85	27.33	8.07	0.01	46.35	817.90
461.55	610.10	61.59	128.17	20.42	8.47	0.02	56.83	815.05
507.19	534.41	64.73	126.32	18.15	10.64	0.02	72.76	822.61
486.06	522.14	79.70	127.24	22.41	15.00	0.03	64.32	931.78
497.58	615.87	86.97	114.77	11.70	15.73		38.69	927.48
502.03	838.82	91.91	110.04	10.83	15.97	0.03	41.16	953.50
474.38	855.26	90.82	107.72	8.59	16.59		51.92	1022.02
480.56	829.80	95.20	107.35	10.10	18.00		70.99	1105.52
431.58	887.01	121.48	113.62	7.94	19.97		48.47	1255.03
310.70	1003.64	143.87	127.14	4.30	23.34		48.32	1376.48
318.07	1158.94	193.42	143.82	3.14	22.17		48.10	1443.11
346.65	1118.06	210.06	129.93	2.65	18.88		40.43	1500.90
286.37	1155.25	206.04	138.88	5.13	19.18		42.90	1484.49
355.02	1174.63	201.11	124.00	2.97	17.24		39.45	1497.24
408.30	1186.10	173.03	111.20	1.36	10.01		39.94	1327.73
360.95	1178.65	171.71	102.52	0.98	9.95		43.68	1348.69
496.40	1001.20	140.10	97.24	0.69	3.70		32.13	1372.92
514.22	927.10	137.80	94.67	0.59	3.60		32.70	1360.79
542.96	1089.61	142.26	92.18	0.50	6.62		46.78	1391.79
460.08	1165.88	183.73	99.64	0.35	10.35		55.87	1496.19
480.05	1159.88	189.26	92.46	0.11	8.05		40.76	1812.28
488.66	1141.38	192.17	89.16	0.10	7.80		47.65	1760.01
472.87	1167.33	239.80	88.19	0.09	7.75	0.03	52.06	1721.28
415.59	1226.30	200.35	84.37	0.08	7.50	0.02	49.64	1688.67
344.81	1248.70	198.52	89.88	0.05	7.56	0.02	39.17	1639.58
264.74	1232.13	199.12	86.35	0.06	8.46	0.02	42.84	1313.97
202.51	1150.43	206.07	85.60	0.09	8.90	0.02	44.62	1352.12

Note:Statistics of 2006 and 2007 are linkage data of Second Agricluture Survey.

12-8 主要农作物播种面积和产量(2016)
TOTAL SOWN AREAS AND OUTPUT OF FARM CROPS(2016)

指 标	Item	播种面积(千公顷) Sown Areas (1 000 hectares)	总产量(万吨) Total Output(10000 ton)
农作物总播种面积	**Total Sown Areas of Farm Crops**	**7843.51**	
粮食作物总计	**Total Grain**	**4436.87**	**2554.11**
夏粮	Summer Grain	1400.60	508.67
小麦	Wheat	1108.27	428.22
大麦	Barley	28.47	9.33
蚕豌豆	Broad and Dea Bean	65.12	14.73
秋粮	Autumn Grain	3036.27	2045.44
稻谷	Rice	2130.97	1693.52
#中稻	#Semilate Rice	1308.21	1193.76
双季晚稻	Late Double- crop Rice	410.68	283.63
秋薯	Tubers	96.33	32.42
玉米	Corn	661.7	296.76
高粱	Sorghum	2.87	1.1
大豆	Soybeans	134.83	20.90
绿豆	#Green Beans	5	1.14
经济作物(全口径)	**Economic Crops**	**3406.64**	
棉花	Cotton	202.51	18.85
油料	Oil-Bearing Crops	1452.91	329.75
#花生	#Peanuts	206.07	71.73
油菜籽	Rapeseed	1150.43	241.63
芝麻	Sesame	85.6	14.42
麻类	Hemp Crops	8.07	2.07
#黄麻	#Jute	0.09	0.01
苎麻	Ramie	7.97	2.05
糖类	Sugar Crops	8.98	37.51
#甘蔗	#Sugarcane	8.9	37.34
烟叶	Tobacco Crops	49.02	8.99
药材	Crude Drugs	174.92	0.38
蔬菜及食用菌面积	#Vegetable	1248.03	4001.70
瓜果类	Melon and Fruits	104.09	360.68
其他农作物	Others	158.11	
#花卉种植面积	Flower Gardening	47.54	

12-9 主要农产品产量
OUTPUT OF MAJOR FARM CROPS

单位:万吨 (10 000 ton)

年份 Year	粮食 Grain	夏粮 Summer Grain	秋粮 Autumn Grain	棉花 Cotton	油料 Oil Bearing Crops	#花生 Peanuts	#油菜籽 Rapeseed
1949	578.13	101.85	476.28	5.74	13.37	3.17	4.12
1952	747.54	148.81	598.73	12.17	22.34	4.56	7.09
1957	986.08	180.87	805.21	21.02	25.26	11.23	4.86
1962	960.41	246.34	714.07	14.22	18.30	3.81	4.29
1965	1241.34	255.01	986.33	38.29	22.32	5.15	6.76
1970	1268.67	187.06	1081.62	29.64	14.93	4.82	3.94
1975	1561.51	230.10	1331.41	40.61	21.44	5.12	10.65
1978	1725.60	315.04	1410.56	36.67	23.71	4.90	10.72
1980	1536.43	341.32	1195.11	31.63	20.58	5.85	11.59
1985	2216.13	429.58	1786.56	49.22	72.98	13.52	41.14
1990	2475.03	474.96	2000.07	51.73	95.75	12.79	70.90
1991	2244.10	476.20	1767.90	49.11	106.29	11.44	83.75
1992	2426.60	450.90	2022.83	60.99	99.74	15.72	70.86
1993	2325.70	471.87	1853.85	42.50	111.74	20.68	78.35
1994	2422.10	472.70	1949.40	45.00	137.77	24.81	98.07
1995	2463.84	447.20	2016.64	58.60	189.44	27.28	146.24
1996	2484.40	465.24	2019.16	43.01	181.82	30.77	134.88
1997	2634.40	542.60	2091.80	58.09	195.47	31.24	147.53
1998	2475.79	501.69	1974.10	32.50	216.69	42.87	154.76
1999	2451.88	392.71	2059.17	28.15	228.27	48.15	159.97
2000	2218.49	322.39	1896.10	30.43	269.98	53.46	192.40
2001	2138.49	319.14	1819.35	37.35	279.45	63.99	194.79
2002	2047.00	232.27	1841.73	32.26	245.29	72.25	151.40
2003	1921.02	255.65	1665.37	32.50	272.72	68.37	187.10
2004	2100.12	271.24	1828.96	39.54	314.38	63.19	235.12
2005	2177.38	302.49	1874.89	37.50	293.90	60.19	219.15
2006	2099.10	369.08	1730.02	55.20	254.45	48.40	191.83
2007	2185.44	406.44	1779.00	55.73	254.75	48.60	193.30
2008	2227.23	386.24	1840.99	51.30	283.56	49.41	214.89
2009	2309.10	398.45	1910.65	48.05	314.05	62.62	236.51
2010	2315.80	420.60	1895.18	47.18	311.80	64.45	232.57
2011	2388.53	425.83	1962.70	52.58	304.72	68.74	220.39
2012	2441.81	447.44	1994.37	53.15	319.66	74.34	230.03
2013	2501.30	501.00	2000.30	45.97	333.17	68.11	250.47
2014	2584.16	505.60	2078.56	35.95	341.73	69.06	257.16
2015	2703.28	504.45	2198.83	29.83	339.60	67.91	255.19
2016	2554.11	508.67	2045.44	18.85	329.75	71.73	241.63

注：2006、2007年为农业普查衔接数据。
Note:Statistics 2006 and 2007 are linkage data of Second Agriculture Survey.

12-10 人均占有主要农产品产量
PER CAPITA OUTPUT OF MAJOR FARM PRODUCTS

单位:千克/人 (kg/person)

年 份 Year	粮 食 Grain	棉 花 Cotton	油 料 Oil Bearing Crops	猪、牛、羊肉 Output of Pork, Beef and Mutton	水产品 Output of Aquatic Products
1952	275	4.5	8.2		2.9
1957	327	7.0	8.4		4.0
1962	302	4.4	5.8		2.3
1965	359	11.1	6.4		3.3
1970	319	7.5	3.8		2.8
1975	357	9.3	4.9		2.6
1978	379	8.1	5.2		2.4
1980	330	6.8	4.4	11.9	2.9
1985	452	10.0	14.9	20.7	7.6
1990	467	9.8	18.1	27.7	13.4
1991	415	8.9	19.6	29.0	12.9
1992	443	11.1	18.2	31.9	14.9
1993	416	7.6	20.0	35.3	18.1
1994	431	8.0	24.5	41.8	23.0
1995	429	10.2	33.0	48.6	26.3
1996	428	7.4	31.4	40.4	30.1
1997	450	9.9	33.4	44.4	34.6
1998	419	5.5	36.7	44.2	37.0
1999	413	5.0	38.4	44.8	38.6
2000	372	5.1	45.3	45.5	39.3
2001	358	6.3	46.8	48.3	40.5
2002	342	5.4	41.0	49.4	45.4
2003	316	6.5	45.5	51.4	47.8
2004	349	6.6	52.3	54.1	50.2
2005	361	6.2	48.7	56.8	52.8
2006	365	7.4	46.2	42.0	46.7
2007	360	9.2	42.0	42.5	49.1
2008	390	9.0	49.7	49.8	54.9
2009	404	8.4	54.9	53.5	59.1
2010	405	8.2	54.5	54.6	61.7
2011	416	9.2	53.1	55.2	62.1
2012	423	9.2	55.4	59.7	67.4
2013	431	7.9	57.5	61.9	70.8
2014	445	6.2	58.8	63.7	74.6
2015	462	5.1	58.0	77.1	77.9
2016	434	3.2	56.0	60.2	80

注:按全省常住人口计算的人均占有量。
Notes:The data is caculated by resident population.

12-11 蚕、茶、果生产情况
STATISTICS ON SILKWORM COCOONS, TEA AND FRUITS

指 标	Item	1995	2000	2005	2010	2013	2014	2015	2016
蚕茧产量 (万吨)	Silkworm Cocoons (10 000 tons)	2.24	1.22	1.07	0.71	0.77	0.64	0.67	0.63
茶叶产量 (万吨)	Tea (10 000 tons)	3.90	6.37	8.50	16.57	22.20	25.03	26.88	29.61
红茶	Red Tea	0.12		0.65	1.54	2.38	2.75	3.09	3.12
绿茶	Green Tea	3.05	5.15	6.72	13.71	17.04	18.65	19.45	21.21
其他茶	Others			0.18	0.33	0.44	0.39	0.31	0.61
园林水果产量 (万吨)	Garden fruit production (10 000 tons)	114.70	215.68	260.79	437.13	569.42	614.25	615.84	649.72
#苹果	#Apples	3.21	3.02	1.24	0.97	1.02	0.99	1.31	1.28
柑桔	Citrus	58.14	94.62	146.26	301.04	400.39	437.12	426.66	457.39
梨	Pears	26.02		46.80	48.05	56.31	54.63	50.92	47.42
葡萄	Grapes			4.97	13.12	23.68	27.15	27.07	29.09
桃子	Peaches	14.59	30.87	46.88	60.75	72.49	77.81	93.16	97.36
猕猴桃	Kiwi fruit			0.85	1.06	2.10	2.32	2.65	2.99
红枣	Dates			2.02	2.91	3.39	3.62	4.00	3.63
柿子	Persimmons			4.77	5.05	6.61	6.78	6.64	6.52
茶园面积 (千公顷)	Area of Tea Plantations (1 000 hectares)	113.39	121.02	138.43	214.61	291.77	303.80	324.11	339.41
#当年采摘面积	#Pick Area	7.42		101.62	155.92	205.39	218.90	231.27	243.32
果园 (千公顷)	Area of Orchards (1 000 hectares)	199.80	233.93	265.05	376.77	403.55	423.26	413.41	423.43
#苹果园	#Apples	13.66	8.98	3.30	0.17	1.63	1.33	1.23	1.29
柑桔园	Citrus	98.39	99.13	143.15	229.19	239.66	245.58	239.97	242.26
梨园	Pears	35.42	33.49	35.90	36.60	39.35	41.75	38.81	36.73
葡萄园	Grapes			4.77	5.57	10.01	12.65	11.90	13.87

12-12 林业生产情况
STATISTICS ON FORESTRY

单位:公顷 (hectare)

指标名称	Item	2014	2015	2016
造林面积	Build Forestry Areas	243799	246911	223534
用材林	Material Forests	85622	95377	79401
经济林	Economic Forests	51338	49235	49951
防护林	Windbreak Forests	105254	99746	91624
薪炭林	Firewood Forests	13	327	1693
特种用途林	Forests for Soecial Puppse	1572	2226	865
更新造林	Updateing Areas	3589	3918	4460
四旁(零星)植树	Planting	13786	14449	13309
育苗面积	Raise Seedlings Areas	39658	50269	47173
主要林产品产量(吨)	Output of Forestry Products (ton)			
生漆	Lacquer	6298	4092	3568
油桐籽	Tung-Oil Seeds	24895	24081	22066
乌桕籽	Tea-oil Seeds	18503	14136	11607
油茶籽	Tallow Seeds	127419	141857	142498
五倍子	Gallnut	3241	2937	2830
棕片	palm pieces	3714	2183	2444
松脂	Turpentine	44994	46174	43237
竹笋干	Bamboo Shoots	12299	18237	22880
核桃	Walnut	94241	94357	98075
板栗	Chestnut	414049	412402	415107
花椒	Pepper	3475	3693	1907
八角	Star anise	23	29	42
香菇	Mushroom(吨)	105849	125828	115128
黑木耳	Jew's-ear (吨)	25624	26715	22731
木材采伐量(万立方米)	Output of Timber Cut(10 000 cu.m)	333	398.5	335.8
竹材采伐量(万根)	Output of Bamboo Cut (10 000 cu.m)	3414	3123.7	3827.7

12-13 畜牧业生产情况
STATISTICS ON LIVESTOCK

指 标	Item	2000	2005	2010	2013	2014	2015	2016
牲畜年末存栏头数（万头）	(10 000 heads)							
大牲畜	Large Animals	431.50	384.32	327.54	345.29	353.19	362.23	355.95
牛	Cattles and Buffalloes	428.38	382.14	326.00	344.07	352.25	361.33	355.19
马	Horses	1.83	1.58	0.92	0.61	0.59	0.54	0.46
驴	Donkeys	0.98	0.44	0.46	0.41	0.26	0.29	0.24
骡	Mules	0.30	0.16	0.16	0.18	0.07	0.58	0.06
猪	Hogs	2132.79	2289.05	2476.10	2566.07	2550.67	2497.14	2432.16
羊 (万只)	Sheep (10 000 heads)	224.80	337.66	401.70	462.91	469.89	465.70	470.86
山羊	Goats	223.55	336.97	401.23	462.75	469.73	465.60	470.86
绵羊	Sheep	1.25	0.69	0.47	0.15	0.16	0.20	0.00
畜产品产量	**Livestock Products**							
猪牛羊出栏头数（万头）	Hogs, Sheep and Goats (10 000heads)	3023.96	3841.82	4459.80	5011.74	5169.09	5073.70	4939.39
当年肉猪出栏头数	Hogs	2714.44	3345.18	3827.40	4356.43	4475.11	4363.23	4223.61
当年出售和自宰的肉用牛	Ox by Sold and Killed	104.26	115.49	123.10	140.28	152.11	159.87	160.35
当年出售和自宰的肉用羊(万只)	Sheep by Slod and Killed (10 000heads)	205.26	381.15	509.30	515.03	541.87	550.60	555.43
肉类产量 (万吨)	Output of Meat (10 000 tons)	271.19	342.63	379.42	430.08	440.44	431.93	424.18
猪肉	Pork	215.84	271.23	287.00	330.60	339.60	331.50	322.17
牛肉	Beef	13.80	16.91	17.70	20.17	21.87	23.00	23.17
羊肉	Mutton	3.04	6.00	8.10	8.22	8.61	8.80	8.89
禽肉	Poultry	38.51	48.49	65.80	70.11	69.20	68.60	69.95
其他禽产品产量 (吨)	Others (tons)							
牛奶产量	Milk Cow	56400	122223	140000	154048	161000	168500	168600.00
绵羊毛产量	Sheep's Wool	34.57	4.00		3.56	4.00	7.00	8.00
山羊毛产量	Goats' Wool	52.17	16.00	13.73	73.82	74.00	104.00	105.00
蜂蜜	Cashmere	9187	7890	10182	23288.8	26504	27430.00	24203.00
禽蛋 (万吨)	Poultry Eggs (10 000 tons)	102.56	121.25	132.60	145.05	155.06	165.29	167.77

12-14 水产品产量
OUTPUT OF AQUATIC PRODUCTS

指 标	Item	2000	2005	2010	2013	2014	2015	2016
水产品产量 (万吨)	**Output of Aquatic Products (10 000 tons)**	**234.34**	**318.03**	**353.00**	**410.37**	**433.30**	**455.80**	**470.84**
鱼类产量	Fish	219.88	277.82	308.42	349.18	359.68	377.88	387.28
虾蟹产量	Shrimp, Prawn and Crab	7.51	7.71	35.93	51.00	56.83	69.66	74.87
贝类产量	Shell Fish	5.38	1.13	4.32	5.47	4.08	3.68	3.54
其它类产量	Others	1.58		3.66	4.72	5.62	4.66	5.15
养殖产量	Artificially Cultivated	194.84	274.45	321.56	371.06	399.64	436.79	451.82
捕捞产量	Captured	39.50	43.58	31.44	39.32	33.66	19.10	19.02
养殖按水面分类产量(万吨)	Grouped by waters (10 000 tons)	193.92	274.45	321.56	371.06	399.64	436.79	451.82
湖 泊	Lakes	20.84	28.44	33.03	32.96	33.77	32.70	31.68
水 库	Reservoir	8.15	12.52	19.96	19.56	20.66	19.94	18.91
塘 堰	Pools	33.05	38.87	26.61	32.60	35.07	33.35	32.42
精 养 池	Fine Cultivated Pools	122.96	177.54	224.86	283.98	297.99	322.29	337.14
河 沟	Rivers	2.90	6.03	2.03	1.78	1.71	1.50	1.42
其 它	Others	6.02	8.03	1.33	1.32	1.31	1.36	1.3
鱼苗产量 (亿尾)	Young Fry (100 million tons)	444.01	521.39	750.00	901.00	1050	1159	1207
鱼种产量 (万吨)	Advanced Fry (10 000 tons)	38.79	54.04	82.03	100.26	110.37	116.01	126.04
投放鱼种量 (万吨)	Volume of Advanced Fry (10 000 tons)	40.16	57.08	80.74	97.54	104.38	110.35	120.05
水产养殖面积 (千公顷)	**Aquatic Raised Areas (1 000 hectares)**							
湖 泊	Lakes	196.46	175.34	196.17	207.66	190.07	187.32	179.04
水 库	Reservoir	166.07	102.18	110.77	150.53	106.64	103.77	98.61
塘 堰	Pools	134.79	119.20	87.44	97.36	99.66	97.66	95.39
精 养 池	Fine Cultivated Pools	156.33	220.37	252.96	275.15	284.75	292.94	318.99
河 沟	Rivers	20.86	21.89	5.71	22.91	22.40	4.52	4.4
其 它	Others	32.92	34.56	3.67	28.91	21.68	2.46	2.47

注：数据来源于省水产局。

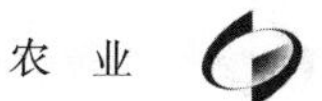

12-15 农业现代化情况

STATISTICS ON AGRICULTURAL MODERNIZATION

单位：千公顷

指 标	Item	2000	2005	2010	2013	2014	2015	2016
农业机械化情况	**Statistics on Agricultural Machinery**							
机耕面积	Areas Ploughed by Tractors	1969.55	2015.93	4517.14	5459.02	5847.00	6036.19	5938.37
机播面积	Seeded Areas by Tractors	255.69	233.66	815.61	1821.53	2091.28	2335.23	2493.92
机械植保面积	Plant Protection Area by Tractors	2426.95	2848.66	4074.38	4611.68	4792.82	4850.88	4776.82
机械收获面积	Harvest Area by Tractors	643.65	1407.62	2780.52	3746.95	4179.37	4233.67	4196.42
农村电气化情况	**Electrification of Rural Area**							
农村用电量 (亿千瓦小时)	Electricity Consumed in Rural Area (100 million kWh)	60.86	70.09	109.78	130.14	142.23	149.10	152.86
农用物资使用情况	**Used Agricultural Product Material**							
化肥施用量(折纯量) (万吨)	Consumption of Chemical Fertilizers (10 000 tons)	247.08	285.83	350.77	351.93	348.27	333.87	327.96
每亩耕地施用化肥(折纯量)(千克)	Per Mu Consumption of Chemical Fertilizers (kg)	50.17	60.28	70.35	68.81	67.88	64.77	63.48
农用塑料薄膜使用量 (万吨)	Used Plastic Film (10 000 tons)		5.46	6.38	6.63	6.92	7.13	6.73
农用柴油使用量 (万吨)	Used Diesel Oil (10 000 tons)	107.81	41.31	58.29	65.73	67.33	65.61	65.85
农药使用量 (万吨)	Used Agricultural Chemical Insecticides (10 000 tons)	11.54	11.02	14.00	12.72	12.61	12.07	11.74
农田水利情况	**Irrigation and Water Conservancy**							
有效灌溉面积	Effective Irrigation Area	2072.53	2064.59	2187.17	2291.17	2325.84	2359.60	2368.75
#机电排灌面积	#Electrical Well		1236.11	1320.53	1357.19	1416.82	1436.61	1453.30
占有效灌溉面积的比重(%)	Rate in Effective Irrigation Area (%)		59.9	60.4	59.2	60.9	60.9	61.4

12-16 主要农业机械和农产品加工机械拥有量

年 份 Year	农业机械总动力 (万千瓦) Total Power of Agricultural Machinery(1000 kW)	农用大中型拖拉机 (万台) Large and Medium Agricultural Tractors(10 000 units)	农用小型及手扶拖拉机(万台) Mini and Walking Agricultural Tractors (10 000 units)	农用排灌动力机械 (万千瓦) Machinery for Machinery for Agricultural Drainage and Irrigation (1000 kW)	农用水泵 (万台) Agricultual Water Pump(10 000 units)
1978	616.07	2.80	7.75		21.22
1980	772.53	3.60	10.90		23.70
1985	910.94	5.72	14.62	55.22	21.06
1990	1099.62	8.60	17.70	99.28	24.30
1991	1120.92	8.60	18.30	362.88	24.10
1992	1120.90	8.45	17.92	368.46	23.98
1993	1108.99	7.89	16.99	360.75	23.95
1994	1136.13	7.38	15.72	368.55	24.37
1995	1174.34	7.12	15.47	384.48	26.56
1996	1222.20	7.03	16.47	401.49	27.62
1997	1276.04	7.11	18.50	408.09	28.76
1998	1325.90	7.13	20.60	410.77	29.59
1999	1363.70	7.03	22.67	419.83	32.57
2000	1414.00	6.82	23.63	434.49	35.47
2001	1469.24	6.58	24.88	450.40	40.46
2002	1557.40	6.64	26.68	461.86	43.89
2003	1661.70	6.59	28.23	469.45	45.63
2004	1768.60	6.83	32.09	484.71	50.82
2005	2057.37	7.66	48.39	518.49	55.92
2006	2263.15	8.50	55.69	531.33	71.42
2007	2551.08	9.30	74.12	541.33	82.70
2008	2796.99	10.42	85.23	559.21	87.73
2009	3057.24	11.85	90.84	594.17	87.70
2010	3371.00	12.71	99.10	663.92	85.40
2011	3571.23	13.08	106.48	673.50	89.48
2012	3842.16	13.84	111.56	668.19	103.30
2013	4081.05	14.94	114.12	714.05	105.63
2014	4292.90	15.85	112.98	732.89	110.60
2015	4468.12	16.84	113.81	749.75	110.13
2016	4187.75	18.18	114.67	763.79	110.97

NUMBER OF AGRICULTURAL MACHINERY AND ACHINERY FOR PROCESSING FARM PRODUCTS OWNED AT YEAR-END

联合收割机 (台) Combine Hearvesters (unit)	机动脱粒机 (万台) Motorized Huller (10 000 units)	机动喷雾(粉)器 (万部) Motorized Duster (10 000 units)	大中型拖拉机配套农具 (万部) Large and Medium Tractors Towing Farm Machinery (10 000 units)	小型拖拉机配套农具 (万部) Mini Tractors Towing Farm Machinery (10 000 units)
425	15.00	0.78	4.66	4.92
602	17.40	1.00	4.99	7.20
479	15.22	0.60	2.39	4.95
2335	12.60	3.70	2.70	10.14
455	12.50	4.60	3.00	11.87
390	12.35	4.70	3.86	12.30
345	11.97	4.77	3.05	11.64
346	11.39	5.29	2.91	12.38
312	11.25	6.44	2.85	15.48
553	12.33	6.74	3.05	23.02
1521	11.11	7.36	3.63	29.46
2338	11.56	8.27	4.33	37.75
2559	11.56	8.00	4.80	42.84
2704	12.25	8.70	4.81	37.48
3363	12.79	9.07	5.22	41.12
5722	12.81	9.72	5.97	46.44
6708	12.62	10.26	6.21	49.03
10585	12.88	11.86	7.45	59.31
16085	14.33	15.98	9.36	96.69
22407	12.54	25.44	11.18	111.02
29803	13.14	30.58	12.96	149.08
34983	12.99	35.41	15.49	169.69
41904	15.37	38.40	20.37	178.55
50509	18.09	43.56	21.49	204.66
58398	23.33	48.73	24.01	211.97
66860	24.28	55.07	25.74	214.51
73808	26.43	60.41	28.00	215.42
81410	32.03	72.26	31.80	223.01
88704	35.21	73.02	37.13	222.44
95747	37.82	74.20	39.54	223.41

12-17 市、州乡村从业人员
RURAL EMPLOYMENT IN CITIES AND PREFECTURES

单位：万人

市、州	Municipalities and Prefecrures	2015	农林牧渔业从业人员 Employment in Farming, Forestry, Animal Husbandry and Fishery	2016	农林牧渔业从业人员 Employment in Farming, Forestry, Animal Husbandry and Fishery
全　省	**Province**	**2300.88**	**869.32**	**2290.90**	**863.64**
武汉市	Wuhan	136.42	44.52	136.14	45.86
黄石市	Huangshi	97.49	27.20	92.02	24.96
十堰市	Shiyan	138.73	53.21	143.25	53.60
荆州市	Jingzhou	242.89	99.79	243.43	99.13
宜昌市	Yichang	164.99	68.31	165.80	67.67
襄阳市	Xiangyang	220.84	77.13	217.47	76.11
鄂州市	Ezhou	39.97	18.57	40.20	17.50
荆门市	Jingmen	109.66	36.06	109.81	35.75
孝感市	Xiaogan	245.35	78.40	244.49	77.85
黄冈市	Huanggang	331.35	132.49	333.01	134.14
咸宁市	Xianning	113.19	44.10	113.85	44.32
随州市	Suizhou	106.87	38.58	106.69	38.98
恩施自治州	Enshi	183.44	87.46	181.40	88.12
仙桃市	Xiantao	67.28	29.35	68.37	28.73
天门市	Tianmen	60.58	17.33	59.07	16.88
潜江市	Qianjiang	39.32	15.32	33.16	12.54
神农架林区	Shennongjia	2.51	1.50	2.74	1.50

12-18 市、州耕地面积
CULTIVATED AREA OF CITIES AND PREFECTURES

市、州	Municipalities and Prefecrures	2000 年末耕地面积(千公顷) Cultivated Area at Year-end(1 000 hectares)	2000 人平耕地(亩) Cultivated Area Per Capita(Mu)	2010 年末耕地面积(千公顷) Cultivated Area at Year-end(1000 hectares)	2010 人平耕地(亩) Cultivated Area Per Capita(Mu)	2015 年末耕地面积(千公顷) Cultivated Area at Year-end(1000 hectares)	2015 人平耕地(亩) Cultivated Area Per Capita(Mu)	2016 年末耕地面积(千公顷) Cultivated Area at Year-end(1000 hectares)	2016 人平耕地(亩) Cultivated Area Per Capita(Mu)
全 省	**Province**	**3282.96**	**0.83**	**3323.92**	**0.87**	**3436.24**	**0.88**	**3444.31**	**0.88**
武汉市	Wuhan	217.84	0.40	204.79	0.31	196.46	0.28	190.09	0.26
黄石市	Huangshi	79.32	0.48	89.80	0.55	89.41	0.55	90.41	0.55
十堰市	Shiyan	181.54	0.79	169.91	0.76	174.92	0.78	177.85	0.78
宜昌市	Yichang	257.71	0.94	230.14	0.85	269.39	0.98	270.85	0.98
襄阳市	Xiangyang	412.96	1.09	436.91	1.19	453.87	1.21	462.17	1.23
鄂州市	Ezhou	40.28	0.59	41.05	0.59	46.27	0.66	40.85	0.57
荆门市	Jingmen	256.53	1.29	255.69	1.33	268.66	1.39	268.56	1.39
孝感市	Xiaogan	247.10	0.74	261.27	0.81	267.91	0.82	268.51	0.82
荆州市	Jingzhou	432.58	1.03	464.80	1.22	470.17	1.24	470.34	1.24
黄冈市	Huanggang	312.36	0.65	337.52	0.82	351.00	0.84	352.45	0.84
咸宁市	Xianning	145.94	0.81	155.85	0.95	167.37	1.00	169.96	1.01
随州市	Suizhou	136.58	0.85	144.94	1.00	143.39	0.98	144.14	0.98
恩施州	Enshi	280.59	1.11	255.89	1.17	260.37	1.17	261.05	1.17
仙桃市	Xiantao	98.68	1.01	90.59	1.16	90.33	1.17	90.33	1.18
潜江市	Qianjiang	66.99	1.01	70.22	1.11	72.19	1.13	72.64	1.13
天门市	Tianmen	107.62	1.00	108.36	1.15	109.93	1.28	109.81	1.28
神农架	Shennongjia	8.35	1.54	6.19	1.22	4.60	0.90	4.30	0.84

12-19 市、州农、林、牧、渔业总产值及指数

GROSS OUTPUT VALUE AND ITS INDICES OF FARMING, FORESTRY, ANIMAL HUSBANDRY AND FISHERY OF CITIES AND PREFECTURES

市、州	Municipalities and Prefecrures	绝对数(亿元) Absolute Number (100 milion yuan)					指数(%) Indices (%)				
		2000	2010	2014	2015	2016	2000	2010	2014	2015	2016
全　省	**Province**	**1125.64**	**3501.99**	**5452.80**	**5728.56**	**6278.35**	**102.8**	**110.0**	**105.7**	**105.7**	**104.9**
武汉市	Wuhan	126.94	281.09	559.44	620.28	669.65	105.3	111.6	105.5	104.9	103.6
黄石市	Huangshi	27.63	83.91	147.01	158.75	165.04	104.2	115.3	109.9	105.3	102.5
十堰市	Shiyan	44.65	133.19	273.11	286.78	317.13	111.1	119.0	109.2	105.2	105.2
荆州市	Jingzhou	147.69	423.79	616.16	631.45	692.78	91.0	110.1	106.5	105.2	104.0
宜昌市	Yichang	97.19	294.05	581.45	617.68	687.02	102.6	117.4	104.6	105.4	104.0
襄阳市	Xiangyang	158.15	409.04	704.46	725.55	775.91	93.5	111.8	103.8	105.2	104.8
鄂州市	Ezhou	13.92	92.82	143.13	149.83	169.85	106.7	115.8	103.3	105.6	104.3
荆门市	Jingmen	100.13	253.14	351.67	365.84	378.30	103.0	109.2	104.1	105.4	104.1
孝感市	Xiaogan	111.63	306.61	470.53	476.88	522.38	90.7	117.7	104.0	105.2	105.5
黄冈市	Huanggang	127.48	374.79	559.63	593.01	623.55	102.4	115.0	105.2	105.6	104.7
咸宁市	Xianning	52.87	168.52	280.29	301.15	310.21	104.5	120.2	105.9	105.4	103.8
随州市	Suizhou	58.06	150.29	225.93	244.36	257.67	141.5	113.9	104.2	105.3	103.2
恩施州	Enshi	76.78	174.25	237.01	247.39	262.71	102.3	114.3	104.3	105.3	104.5
仙桃市	Xiaotao	39.01	94.41	142.59	147.49	149.13	102.2	113.2	104.6	105.4	104.3
天门市	Tianmen	33.15	80.94	113.73	129.98	130.66	100.4	111.6	104.7	105.1	103.3
潜江市	Qianjiang	30.58	85.55	114.24	119.24	124.73	101.9	122.2	104.5	105.2	104.0
神农架	Shennongjia	0.99	2.59	3.77	4.07	4.20	87.1	112.6	106.1	104.6	102.0

注：本表产值按当年价格计算，指数按不变价格计算；全省合计数为调整数，故市、州相加不等于合计数。
Notes:The data of in this table is caculated at current prices of output valul,and the data of indices is calulaled at constort prices therefore,the total of provice is an adiusted number,and that of municipalities and prefecture if added are not egual to the total number.

12-20 市、州农、林、牧、渔业产值(现价)(2016)
GROSS OUTPUT VALUE OF FARMING, FORESTRY, ANIMAL HUSBANDRY AND FISHERY OF CITIES AND PREFECTURES (AT CURRENT PRICES)(2016)

单位：亿元 (100 million yuan)

市、州	Municipalities and Prefecrures	合计 Total	农业 Farming	林业 Forestry	牧业 Animal Husbandry	渔业 Fishery	农林牧渔服务业 Service Industry for Farming, Forestry, Animal Husbandry and Fishery
全省	**Province**	**6278.35**	**2921.27**	**203.43**	**1715.18**	**1030.01**	**408.46**
武汉市	Wuhan	669.65	392.27	8.14	139.30	101.80	28.13
黄石市	Huangshi	165.04	66.04	5.48	41.18	49.04	3.30
十堰市	Shiyan	317.13	181.30	15.00	100.49	18.30	2.04
荆州市	Jingzhou	692.78	260.14	8.38	153.02	237.95	33.29
宜昌市	Yichang	687.02	356.47	6.54	258.77	45.99	19.24
襄阳市	Xiangyang	775.91	351.56	8.27	344.11	32.72	39.25
鄂州市	Ezhou	169.85	38.53	2.88	46.08	81.83	0.54
荆门市	Jingmen	378.30	157.03	6.42	128.50	75.65	10.70
孝感市	Xiaogan	522.38	203.87	11.50	196.28	100.54	10.19
黄冈市	Huanggang	623.55	293.39	10.71	229.03	76.37	14.04
咸宁市	Xianning	310.21	158.70	14.72	73.68	60.69	2.42
随州市	Suizhou	257.67	134.65	5.65	96.57	12.16	8.64
恩施州	Enshi	262.71	147.20	10.39	101.93	1.09	2.10
仙桃市	Xiaotao	149.13	48.73	1.42	30.65	65.55	2.78
天门市	Tianmen	130.66	58.36	0.66	32.50	30.29	8.84
潜江市	Qianjiang	124.73	45.28	2.74	37.41	36.67	2.64
神农架	Shennongjia	4.20	2.63	0.51	0.98	0.03	0.05

12-21 市、州农、林、牧、渔业中间消耗(2016)
INTERMEDIATE-CONSUMPTION OF OF FARMING, FORESTRY, ANIMAL HUSBANDRY AND FISHERY OF CITIES AND PREFECTURES(2016)

单位：亿元 (100 million yuan)

市、州	Municipalities and Prefecrures	合计 Total	农业 Farming	林业 Forestry	牧业 Animal Husbandry	渔业 Fishery	农林牧渔服务业 Service Industry for Farming, Forestry, Animal Husbandry and Fishery
全省	**Province**	**2497.56**	**979.03**	**101.10**	**709.87**	**420.56**	**286.99**
武汉市	Wuhan	259.93	143.14	3.75	65.81	38.20	9.04
黄石市	Huangshi	48.41	17.65	1.26	15.70	13.02	0.79
十堰市	Shiyan	143.86	78.67	7.85	49.14	7.21	0.98
荆州市	Jingzhou	292.59	97.38	2.12	69.18	108.09	15.81
宜昌市	Yichang	277.19	139.49	2.69	107.79	18.80	8.42
襄阳市	Xiangyang	322.51	140.39	2.66	148.59	14.17	16.71
鄂州市	Ezhou	72.37	24.67	2.26	14.07	31.11	0.26
荆门市	Jingmen	158.48	56.90	2.10	62.50	32.91	4.08
孝感市	Xiaogan	235.69	84.70	5.01	90.95	50.02	5.01
黄冈市	Huanggang	218.22	102.70	5.77	85.23	20.50	4.02
咸宁市	Xianning	124.26	63.91	5.39	32.35	21.89	0.72
随州市	Suizhou	110.96	62.92	2.05	39.62	3.90	2.47
恩施州	Enshi	108.89	61.19	4.73	41.86	0.31	0.80
仙桃市	Xiaotao	60.12	15.72	1.12	11.28	31.00	1.00
天门市	Tianmen	49.24	26.43	0.27	10.54	9.82	2.18
潜江市	Qianjiang	51.18	15.17	0.85	25.53	8.33	1.30
神农架	Shennongjia	1.99	1.24	0.18	0.53	0.02	0.02

注：全省中间消耗为省级核算数，故市、州相加不等于合计数。

Note: The statistics of Intermedium Consumption is checked by Provincial Statistical Burea,thus the total of municipalities and prefecture do not equal to the total of the whole province.

12-22 市、州农、林、牧、渔业增加值(2016)
VALUE ADDED OF FARMING, FORESTRY, ANIMAL HUSBANDRY AND FISHERY OF CITIES AND PREFECTURES(2016)

单位：亿元 (100 million yuan)

市、州	Municipalities and Prefecrures	合计 Total	农业 Farming	林业 Forestry	牧业 Animal Husbandry	渔业 Fishery	农林牧渔服务业 Service Industry for Farming, Forestry, Animal Husbandry and Fishery
全省	**Province**	**3780.79**	**1942.24**	**102.33**	**1005.32**	**609.44**	**121.47**
武汉市	Wuhan	409.71	249.14	4.38	73.49	63.60	19.09
黄石市	Huangshi	116.63	48.39	4.23	25.48	36.02	2.51
十堰市	Shiyan	173.27	102.63	7.15	51.35	11.09	1.06
荆州市	Jingzhou	400.19	162.75	6.26	83.84	129.86	17.48
宜昌市	Yichang	409.83	216.98	3.85	150.98	27.19	10.82
襄阳市	Xiangyang	453.40	211.17	5.61	195.52	18.55	22.54
鄂州市	Ezhou	97.48	13.87	0.61	32.00	50.72	0.28
荆门市	Jingmen	219.81	100.12	4.32	66.00	42.74	6.62
孝感市	Xiaogan	286.69	119.17	6.49	105.33	50.52	5.18
黄冈市	Huanggang	405.32	190.69	4.94	143.80	55.87	10.02
咸宁市	Xianning	185.95	94.80	9.33	41.32	38.80	1.70
随州市	Suizhou	146.71	71.73	3.59	56.95	8.27	6.17
恩施州	Enshi	153.82	86.01	5.66	60.07	0.78	1.30
仙桃市	Xiaotao	89.02	33.01	0.30	19.37	34.55	1.78
天门市	Tianmen	81.41	31.93	0.39	21.95	20.48	6.67
潜江市	Qianjiang	73.55	30.11	1.89	11.88	28.35	1.34
神农架	Shennongjia	2.21	1.39	0.33	0.46	0.01	0.03

注：全省数为省级核算数，故分市州汇总不等于全省。

Note: The statistics of the whole province is checked by Provincial Statistical Burea, thus the total of municipalities and prefecture do not equal to the total of the whole province.

12-23 市、州主要农作物产量(2016)

单位：万吨

市、州	Municipalities and Prefecrures	粮食 Grain	稻谷 Rice	小麦 Wheat	玉米 Corn	薯类 Tubers	大豆 Soybean	棉花 Cotton
全省	**Province**	**2554.11**	**1693.52**	**428.22**	**296.76**	**96.70**	**20.90**	**18.85**
武汉市	Wuhan	110.01	87.94	5.94	8.88	3.56	1.97	0.76
黄石市	Huangshi	57.26	42.98	3.81	4.10	4.47	0.85	0.26
十堰市	Shiyan	105.64	22.88	24.17	31.17	20.77	4.07	0.01
荆州市	Jingzhou	371.51	301.65	40.33	14.35	4.32	7.07	5.03
宜昌市	Yichang	152.93	62.40	15.14	46.23	24.74	2.05	1.07
襄阳市	Xiangyang	500.14	178.48	214.47	83.71	19.33	1.56	1.82
鄂州市	Ezhou	31.12	25.63	1.16	0.28	2.48	0.63	0.41
荆门市	Jingmen	250.73	168.51	49.13	21.22	7.23	3.59	1.13
孝感市	Xiaogan	206.33	157.87	32.23	4.40	7.54	2.21	1.50
黄冈市	Huanggang	290.82	231.08	18.01	8.48	28.21	2.52	2.99
咸宁市	Xianning	96.45	76.55	2.60	7.88	6.61	1.43	0.24
随州市	Suizhou	157.40	95.37	43.78	6.29	8.99	0.76	0.85
恩施州	Enshi	149.77	32.97	1.40	61.63	47.45	3.83	0.00
仙桃市	Xiaotao	72.45	52.91	8.15	7.48	0.71	2.20	0.80
天门市	Tianmen	63.35	38.90	13.88	2.41	2.74	4.71	1.53
潜江市	Qianjiang	47.09	31.09	9.96	3.08	0.84	1.91	0.45
神农架	Shennongjia	2.00	0.05	0.10	0.78	0.94	0.06	

OUTPUT OF MAJOR FARM CROPS OF CITIES AND PREFECTURES(2016)

(10 000tons)

油料 Oil Bearing Crops	花生 Peanuts	油菜籽 Rapeseed	芝麻 Sesame	麻类 Hemp Crops	苎麻 Ramie	糖类 Sugar Crops	甘蔗 Crane	烟叶 Tobacoo Crops	烤烟 Tobacco
329.75	**71.73**	**241.63**	**14.42**	**2.07**	**2.05**	**37.51**	**37.34**	**8.99**	**7.89**
18.14	4.60	11.85	1.68	0.01	0.01	4.61	4.61		
9.78	1.08	7.33	1.36	0.85	0.85	0.16	0.16		
13.91	4.43	7.71	1.60			1.78	1.78	1.59	1.55
54.67	0.75	52.50	1.42	0.01		7.97	7.97		
23.99	3.60	19.77	0.53			0.30	0.30	0.74	0.53
26.10	14.52	10.35	1.11			0.72	0.72	0.82	0.82
6.06	0.33	5.08	0.50	0.03	0.03	3.50	3.50		
38.85	8.80	28.82	1.09			2.96	2.96	0.00	
23.57	7.75	14.99	0.82	0.01	0.01	2.57	2.57		
54.43	15.29	37.27	1.57	0.55	0.55	3.47	3.34		
10.80	1.72	8.44	0.64	0.61	0.61	5.84	5.84		
7.23	3.57	2.75	0.79			0.46	0.46		
10.70	2.15	7.75	0.07	0.00	0.00	0.01	0.01	5.82	4.98
12.86	0.23	11.95	0.55			2.61	2.58		
11.63	2.45	8.74	0.44			0.30	0.30		
7.02	0.45	6.32	0.24			0.24	0.24		
0.04	0.01	0.02	0.00					0.02	0.02

12-24 市、州大牲畜、羊、猪年末存栏、出栏、肉产量(2016)

市、州	Municipalities and Prefecrures	牛存栏(万只) Cattles and Bufflaoes	羊存栏 (万只) Sheep in Stock (10 000 heads)	山羊 Goats	年末生猪存栏 (万头) Hogs in Stock at Year-end(10 000 heads)
全省	**Province**	**355.19**	**470.86**	**470.86**	**2432.16**
武汉市	Wuhan	11.96	3.95	3.92	164.32
黄石市	Huangshi	4.44	4.29	4.29	68.03
十堰市	Shiyan	40.90	108.01	107.58	128.33
荆州市	Jingzhou	8.54	15.67	15.67	302.64
宜昌市	Yichang	17.75	134.22	134.22	404.09
襄阳市	Xiangyang	103.86	139.30	137.98	478.34
鄂州市	Ezhou	2.59	9.33	9.33	72.06
荆门市	Jingmen	25.56	49.85	49.74	260.50
孝感市	Xiaogan	46.86	22.67	22.60	232.43
黄冈市	Huanggang	108.19	105.74	103.63	449.52
咸宁市	Xianning	15.57	18.29	17.70	193.93
随州市	Suizhou	28.06	52.72	52.72	147.46
恩施州	Enshi	43.82	93.72	93.72	407.27
仙桃市	Xiaotao	0.31	0.27	0.19	50.32
天门市	Tianmen	7.32	1.86	1.86	68.91
潜江市	Qianjiang	2.67	1.71	1.71	52.45
神农架	Shennongjia	0.63	3.66	3.66	3.93

注：全省数为以省为总体的抽样调查数。

STATISTICS ON LIVE ANIMALS, SHEEP, HOGS IN STOCK AND OUT OF STOCK AT YEAR-END AND OUTPUT OF MEAT OF CITIES AND PREFECTURES(2016)

年内出栏肉猪 (万头) Hogs out of Stock at Year-end(10 000 heads)	年内出栏羊 (万只) Sheep out of Stock at Year-end(10 000 heads)	出笼禽 (万只) Poultry out of Stock at Year-end(10 000 heads)	猪肉产量 (万吨) Output of pork Meat (10 000 tons)	牛肉产量 beef	羊肉 muttom	禽蛋产量 (万吨) Output of Eggs (10 000 tons)
4223.61	**555.43**	**52195.94**	**322.17**	**23.17**	**8.89**	**167.77**
288.46	4.79	4047.01	22.58	0.81	0.12	18.92
113.50	5.14	2090.13	8.46	0.29	0.11	3.85
192.50	112.48	2536.00	14.44	2.02	1.69	5.14
467.00	18.65	6248.00	35.74	0.83	0.28	16.45
584.30	155.54	3060.00	48.61	1.47	3.25	6.02
596.20	165.56	6817.00	48.51	10.76	3.92	24.06
114.20	1.06	1245.00	8.87	0.34	0.02	4.75
392.50	62.34	4259.00	30.58	2.95	1.49	14.33
380.30	26.50	8856.00	28.62	2.42	0.58	32.46
473.20	81.01	4747.00	37.55	7.70	1.91	48.75
271.10	21.00	2956.00	20.33	0.44	0.52	2.95
230.50	57.91	6235.00	17.96	2.09	0.99	7.12
467.60	91.00	1300.00	38.36	2.45	1.79	2.85
97.77	0.54	631.00	7.33	0.21	0.01	4.16
95.93	1.08	985.00	8.59	0.46	0.03	4.70
101.10	2.30	1430.00	8.48	0.42	0.03	4.00
4.30	1.85	25.60	0.44	0.02	0.04	0.03

12-25 市、州主要土特产品产量(2016)
OUTPUT OF LOCAL SPECIALITY OF CITIES AND PREFECTURES(2016)

市、州	Municipalities and Prefecrures	茶叶 (万吨) Tea (10 000 tons)	蚕茧 (吨) Silkworm Coccons (ton)	桑蚕茧 Mulbeery Silkworm Coccons	园林水果 (万吨) Fruits (10 000 tons)	桃子 Peaches	柑橘 Citrus	苹果 Apples	黑木耳 (吨) Jew's Ear (ton)
全省	**Province**	**29.61**	**6336**	**6197**	**649.72**	**97.36**	**457.39**	**1.28**	**22731**
武汉市	Wuhan	0.35			12.25	3.27	4.97		300
黄石市	Huangshi	0.05	43	43	5.18	0.24	4.10		
十堰市	Shiyan	1.61	844	844	33.17	0.91	29.76	0.05	2414
荆州市	Jingzhou	0.03	5	5	51.59	0.83	34.60		22
宜昌市	Yichang	7.01	1285	1285	330.57	3.04	323.15	0.04	1300
襄阳市	Xiangyang	1.42	948	948	76.07	58.85	5.28	0.36	3588
鄂州市	Ezhou	0.01			4.64	0.34	3.35		
荆门市	Jingmen	0.03			38.22	3.57	14.92	0.03	1009
孝感市	Xiaogan	1.06			18.50	9.11	2.68	0.06	620
黄冈市	Huanggang	3.66	2937	2937	12.99	3.63	6.26	0.09	599
咸宁市	Xianning	4.57	17		7.30	0.96	3.64	0.08	258
随州市	Suizhou	0.28	122		16.43	10.10	0.80	0.16	12597
恩施州	Enshi	9.53	135	135	32.76	0.76	22.06	0.40	12
仙桃市	Xiaotao				2.93	0.37	1.13		
天门市	Tianmen				2.36	0.30	0.46		
潜江市	Qianjiang				4.74	1.06	0.23		12
神农架	Shennongjia	0.01			0.02	0.01			

12-26 市、州人平粮、棉、油、肉、水产品生产水平(2016)
PER CAPITA PRODUCTION LEVEL OF GRAIN,COTTON,OIL,MEAT AND AQUATIC PRODUCTS OF CITIES AND PREFECTURES(2016)

单位:千克 (kg)

市、州	Municipalities and Prefecrures	粮食 Grain	棉花 Cotton	油料 Oil Bearing Crops	猪肉 Pork	水产品 Aquatic Products	禽蛋 Eggs
按常住人口平均	Average of Total Population						
全省	Province	434.00	3.20	56.03	54.74	80.01	28.51
武汉市	Wuhan	102.19	0.71	16.85	20.97	47.30	17.58
黄石市	Huangshi	232.24	1.06	39.66	34.31	93.41	15.60
十堰市	Shiyan	309.88	0.03	40.79	42.36	23.23	15.09
荆州市	Yichang	652.01	8.83	95.94	62.72	239.89	28.87
宜昌市	Xiangyang	370.30	2.59	58.09	117.70	49.05	14.58
襄阳市	Ezhou	886.93	3.23	46.28	86.03	38.29	42.67
鄂州市	Jingmen	291.25	3.84	56.67	83.01	429.10	44.47
荆门市	Xiaogan	864.21	3.88	133.89	105.40	184.55	49.38
孝感市	Jingzhou	420.72	3.05	48.05	58.36	94.50	66.18
黄冈市	Huanggang	460.09	4.72	86.10	59.41	83.71	77.13
咸宁市	Xianning	381.83	0.97	42.77	80.48	105.07	11.66
随州市	Suizhou	714.87	3.84	32.82	81.57	43.91	32.36
恩施州	Enshi	447.61	0.00	31.98	114.64	2.22	8.50
仙桃市	Xiaotao	631.08	6.97	112.01	63.85	294.43	36.19
天门市	Qianjiang	492.38	11.90	90.41	66.77	102.83	36.54
潜江市	Tianmen	489.50	4.71	73.00	88.15	132.02	41.53
神农架	Shennongjia	260.08		5.28	57.22	3.64	3.73
按乡村人口平均	Average of Country Population						
全省	Province	626.55	4.62	80.89	79.03	115.50	41.16
武汉市	Wuhan	448.58	3.11	73.95	92.07	207.63	77.16
黄石市	Huangshi	336.74	1.54	57.51	49.75	135.44	22.62
十堰市	Shiyan	425.94	0.04	56.07	58.22	31.93	20.74
荆州市	Yichang	839.67	11.38	123.56	80.78	308.93	37.18
宜昌市	Xiangyang	555.88	3.88	87.20	176.69	73.62	21.89
襄阳市	Ezhou	1361.52	4.95	71.05	132.06	58.77	65.51
鄂州市	Jingmen	383.91	5.06	74.70	109.43	565.62	58.62
荆门市	Xiaogan	1299.81	5.83	201.38	158.53	277.58	74.26
孝感市	Jingzhou	499.96	3.62	57.10	69.35	112.29	78.65
黄冈市	Huanggang	486.04	4.99	90.96	62.76	88.43	81.48
咸宁市	Xianning	439.81	1.12	49.26	92.70	121.02	13.43
随州市	Suizhou	796.40	4.28	36.56	90.87	48.92	36.05
恩施州	Enshi	471.18	0.00	33.67	120.68	2.34	8.95
仙桃市	Xiaotao	619.00	6.84	109.87	62.63	288.80	35.50
天门市	Qianjiang	499.21	12.06	91.67	67.69	104.25	37.05
潜江市	Tianmen	784.44	7.54	116.99	141.26	211.57	66.55
神农架	Shennongjia	447.43		9.08	98.43	6.26	6.42

12-27 市、州农业机械、用电、化肥、水利情况(2016)
AGRICULTURAL MACHINERY, ELECTRICITY CONSUMPTION, CHEMICAL FERTILIZERS AND IRRAGATION IN CITIES AND PREFECTURES(2016)

市、州	Municipalities and Prefecrures	农业机械总动力(万千瓦特) Total Power of Agricultural Machinery (10 000kW)	当年实际机耕面积(千公顷) Actual Sown Areas (1 000 hectares)	农村用电量(万千瓦小时) Rural Electricity Consumption (1 000kW/h)	化肥施用量(折纯量)(万吨) Consumption of Chemical Fertilizers (pure) (10 000tons)	有效灌溉面积(千公顷) Effective Irrigation Area (1 000 hectares)
全省	**Province**	**4187.75**	**5938.37**	**1528617.00**	**327.96**	**2368.75**
武汉市	Wuhan	225.36	302.86	150159.00	12.54	150.99
黄石市	Huangshi	111.33	162.44	108617.30	5.20	57.64
十堰市	Shiyan	184.64	289.55	60833.02	13.47	38.10
荆州市	Jingzhou	607.84	851.62	165101.00	33.53	423.07
宜昌市	Yichang	286.06	403.53	113676.00	36.05	126.35
襄阳市	Xiangyang	605.60	829.85	107395.40	58.42	277.73
鄂州市	Ezhou	59.16	76.36	62935.00	8.45	26.62
荆门市	Jingmen	465.51	483.82	110684.50	29.90	216.21
孝感市	Xiaogan	249.98	429.14	140645.00	20.03	242.50
黄冈市	Huanggang	340.13	742.19	248639.60	33.60	258.10
咸宁市	Xianning	174.27	273.98	52139.69	11.81	94.76
随州市	Suizhou	206.12	268.66	49936.00	17.19	126.50
恩施州	Enshi	228.45	294.20	50888.78	27.70	73.30
仙桃市	Xiaotao	136.74	188.50	58296.00	5.92	85.09
天门市	Tianmen	159.35	203.19	34419.36	7.21	109.81
潜江市	Qianjiang	139.24	133.77	14252.00	6.48	60.86
神农架	Shennongjia	7.98	4.71	0.14	0.46	1.12

主要统计指标解释

农林牧渔业总产值 指以货币表现的农、林、牧、渔业全部产品和对农林牧渔业生产活动进行的各种支持性服务活动的价值总量，它反映一定时期内农林牧渔业生产总规模和总成果。1957年以前的农林牧渔业总产值中包括了厩肥和农民自给性手工业(如农民自制衣服、鞋、袜，自己从事粮食初步加工等)。1958年及以后，林业中增加了村及村以下竹木采伐产值；牧业中取消了厩肥产值；副业中取消了农民自给性手工业产值，增加了村及村以下办的工业产值；渔业中增加了海洋捕捞水产品产值。1980年及以后，在副业中增加了农民家庭兼营工业商品部分的产值。从1984年起村及村以下工业产值划归工业。从1993年起取消副业，将野生动物的捕猎划入牧业，野生植物采集和农民家庭兼营商品性工业划归农业。从2003年起，执行新的国民经济行业分类标准，农林牧渔业总产值中包括了农林牧渔服务业产值。林业中增加了森林采运业产值。农业中取消了家庭兼营商品性工业产值，将野生林产品的采集划归林业。第一次农业普查以后，由于畜牧业产品年报数据与普查数据之间存在一定的差距，国家统计局农调总队对畜牧业年报数据与普查数据进行衔接，对畜牧业产值进行相应调整。

农林牧渔业总产值的计算方法通常是按农、林、牧、渔业产品及其副产品的产量分别乘以各自单位产品价格求得；少数生产周期较长，当年没有产品或产品产量不易统计的，则采用间接方法匡算其产值；然后将四业产品产值相加即为农林牧渔业总产值。

粮食产量 指全社会的产量。包括国有经济经营的、集体统一经营的和农民家庭经营的粮食产量，还包括工矿企业办的农场和其他生产单位的产量。粮食除包括稻谷、小麦、玉米、高粱、谷子及其他杂粮外，还包括薯类和豆类。其产量计算方法，豆类按去豆荚后的干豆计算；薯类(包括甘薯和马铃薯，不包括芋头和木薯)1963年以前按每4公斤鲜薯折1公斤粮食计算，从1964年开始改为按5公斤鲜薯折1公斤粮食计算。城市郊区作为蔬菜的薯类(如马铃薯等)按鲜品计算，并且不作粮食统计。其他粮食一律按脱粒后的原粮计算。1989年以前全国粮食产量数据主要靠全面报表取得，1989年开始使用抽样调查数据。

棉花产量 指全社会的产量。包括春播棉和夏播棉。产量按皮棉计算。不包括木棉。

油料产量 指全部油料作物的生产量。包括花生、油菜籽、芝麻、向日葵籽、胡麻籽（亚麻籽）和其他油料。不包括大豆、木本油料和野生油料。花生以带壳干花生计算。

水产品产量 指人工养殖的水产品和天然生长的水产品的捕捞量。包括海水的鱼类、虾蟹类、贝类和藻类以及内陆水域的鱼类、虾蟹类和贝类，不包括淡水生植物。水产品产量是通过各级水产和统计部门逐级上报取得数据。1995年及以前，贝类中牡蛎按鲜肉计算；蚶、蛤、蛏按 5 斤鲜品折 1 斤计算。1996年以后则统一按鲜品计算。

猪、牛、羊肉产量指当年出栏并已屠宰、除去头蹄下水后带骨肉(即胴体重)的重量。包括全社会范围内的产量。1996年前为各级逐级上报数据。1996年第一次农业普查以后，由于畜牧业产品年报数据与普查数据之间存在一定的差距，国家统计局农调总队对畜牧业年报数据与普查数据进行衔接。1999年以后，国家统计局开展了猪、牛、羊、禽等主要畜禽品种的抽样调查，并用抽样数据作为国家定案数据使用。未开展抽样调查的品种，仍使用各级统计部门逐级上报数据。

期初(末)畜禽存栏头(只)数 指报告期初(末)农村各种合作经济组织和国营农场、农民个人、机关、团体、学校、工矿企业、部队等单位以及城镇居民饲养的大牲畜、猪、羊、家禽等畜禽的存栏数。数据上报方式及数据调整情况同猪、牛、羊肉产量。

常用耕地 是指耕地总资源中专门种植农作物并经常进行耕种、能够正常收获的土地。包括当年实际耕种的熟地；弃耕、休闲不满三年，随时可以复耕的地；开荒利用三年以上的土地。在统计口径上包括南方小于1米、北方小于2米宽的沟、渠、路和田埂。不包括临时种植农作物的坡度在25度以上的陡坡地；在河套、湖畔、库区临时开发的成片或零星土地；也不包括已列为国家和省（区、市）退耕计划但临时耕种的土地。常用耕地是国家需要重点保护的耕地，是反映我国农业综合生产能力的一个重要指标。

农作物播种面积 指实际播种或移植有农作物的面积。凡是实际种植有农作物的面积，不论种植在耕地上还是种植在非耕地上,均包括在农作物播种面积中。在播种季节基本结束后,因遭灾而重新改种和补种的农作物面积,也包括在内。它是反映我国耕地面积利用情况的一个重要指标。目前,农作物播种面积主要包括粮食、棉花、油料、糖料、麻类、烟叶、蔬菜和瓜类、药材和其他农作物九大类。

有效灌溉面积 指具有一定的水源,地块比较平整,灌溉工程或设备已经配套,在一般年景下,当年能够进行正常灌溉的耕地面积。在一般情况下,有效灌溉面积应等于灌溉工程或设备已经配备,能够进行正常灌溉的水田和水浇地面积之和。它是反映我国耕地抗旱能力的一个重要指标。

农用化肥施用量 指本年内实际用于农业生产的化肥数量,包括氮肥、磷肥、钾肥和复合肥。化肥施用量要求按折纯量计算数量。折纯量是指把氮肥、磷肥、钾肥分别按含氮、含五氧化二磷、含氧化钾的百分之百成份进行折算后的数量。复合肥按其所含主要成分折算。公式为:

折纯量=实物量×某种化肥有效成份含量的百分比

农业机械总动力 指主要用于农、林、牧、渔业的各种动力机械的动力总和。包括耕作机械、排灌机械、收获机械、农用运输机械、植物保护机械、牧业机械、林业机械、渔业机械和其他农业机械〔内燃机按引擎马力折成瓦(特)计算、电动机按功率折成瓦(特)计算〕。不包括专门用于乡、镇、村、组办工业、基本建设、非农业运输、科学试验和教学等非农业生产方面用的动力机械与作业机械。这个指标的统计数据主要来源于农机部门。

乡村从业人员 指乡村人口中劳动年龄在16周岁以上实际参加生产经营活动并取得实物或货币收入的人员,包括劳动年龄内经常参加劳动的人员,也包括超过劳动年龄但经常参加劳动的人员,但不包括户口在家的在外学生、现役军人和丧失劳动能力的人,也不包括待业人员和家务劳动者。从业人员按从事主业时间最长(时间相同按收入)分为农林牧渔业从业人员、工业从业人员、建筑业从业人员、交通运输业、仓储及邮电通信业从业人员、批零贸易业、餐饮业从业人员、其他非农行业从业人员。

Explanatory Notes on Main Statistical Indicators

Gross Output Value of Farming, Forestry, Animal Husbandry and Fishery refers to the total value of products of farming, forestry, animal husbandry and fishery, and total value of services rendered to support farming, forestry, animal husbandry and fishery activities. It reflects the total scale and results of agricultural production during a given period. Prior to 1957, Chinas gross agricultural output value included barnyard manure and handicraft products for self-consumption (clothes, shoes, stockings, and initial grain processing undertaken by peasants). Since 1958, cutting and felling of bamboo and trees by villages and other cooperative organizations under villages have been included in forestry; value of barnyard manure has been excluded from animal husbandry; self consumed handicrafts has been excluded from sideline occupations, while the output value of industries run by villages and cooperative organizations under village had been included in sideline occupations and the output value of fish catches by motor fishing boats has been added to fishery. Since 1980, the value of handicraft products made for sale by individuals in households had been added to sideline occupations. Since 1984, industries run by villages and under villages have been included in the sector of industry. Since 1993, the subdivision of sideline occupations has been canceled, and the hunting of wild animals has been classified into animal husbandry, and the gathering of wild plants and commodity industry run by rural household have been included in farming. A new industrial classification of economic activities was introduced in 2003. Under the new classification, value of services to farming, forestry, animal husbandry and fishery is included in the gross output value of agriculture, value of wood felling and transport is included in forestry, value of industrial output by rural households is not included in agriculture, and the collection of wild forest products is taken from agriculture and included in the forestry. The first agriculture census of China revealed some discrepancy between the production of animal products from the annual reports and that from the census. Efforts were made by the Rural Socio-economic Survey Organization of NBS to adjust the output value of animal husbandry to make the figures from the annual reports consistent with the census data.

Gross output value of agriculture is obtained by first multiplying the output of each product or by product by its price, resulting in the output value of each single item. For a small number of products, annual output of which is not available or difficult to get due to the long production (growing) process involved, the output value is estimated through an indirect approach. The sum of output value of all products of farming, forestry, animal husbandry and fishery is then equal to the gross output value of agriculture.

Grain Output refers to the total output in the whole country including grains produced by state farms, collective units, rural households, as well as by farms affiliated to industrial and mining enterprises and other production units. Grain includes rice, wheat, corn, sorghum, millet and other miscellaneous grains as well as tubers and bean. Output of beans refers to dry beans without pods. The output of tubers (sweet potatoes and potatoes, not including taros and cassava) was converted into that of grain at the ratio 4:1, i.e. 4 kilograms of fresh tubers was equivalent to 1 kilogram of grain up to 1963. Since 1964 the ratio for conversion has been 5:1. Tubers supplied as vegetables (such as potatoes) in cities and suburbs are calculated as fresh vegetables and their output is not included in the output of grain. Output of all other grains refers to husked grain. Data on grain production before 1989 were obtained through Comprehensive Statistical Reporting System. Since 1989, data from sample surveys are used.

Cotton Output refers to the cotton production in the whole country including cotton sown in spring and in autumn. Output is measured as the weight of ginned cotton. Ceiba is not included.

Output of Oil–bearing Crops refers to the total production of oil–bearing crops of various kinds, including peanuts, (dry, in shell) rapeseeds, sesame, sunflower seeds, flax seeds, and other oil–bearing crops. Soybeans, oil–bearing woody plants, and wild oil–bearing crops are not included.

Output of Aquatic Products refers to catches of both artificially cultured and naturally grown aquatic products, including fish, shrimps, crabs and shellfish in sea and inland water as well as seaweed. Freshwater plants are not included. Data on output of aquatic products are reported by aquatic product and statistical agencies level by level. Before 1995, among the shellfish, the oyster was counted as fresh meat; 5 kilograms of ark shell, clams and frogs are equivalent to 1 kilogram of fresh aquatic products; they are all counted as fresh aquatic products since 1996.

Output of Pork, Beef, and Mutton refers to the meat of slaughtered hogs, cattle, sheep and goats with head, feet, and offal taken away. Data refers to the production of the whole country. The first agriculture census of China in 1996 revealed some discrepancy between the production of animal products from the annual reports and that from the census. Efforts were made by the Rural Socio–economic Survey Organization of NBS to adjust the output value of animal husbandry to make the figures from the annual reports consistent with the census data. Since 1999, NBS conducted sample survey for the major animal husbandry products, such as hogs, cattle, sheep and goats and fowls, and the data from sample surveys are used as national finalized data. Those products, which are not covered by the sample survey, are still reported by statistical agencies level by level.

Number of Livestock or Poultry in Stock at Beginning (or End) refers to the total number of large animals, pigs, sheep, fowls, etc. raised by rural cooperative organizations, state farms, rural individuals, government agencies, schools, industrial and mining enterprises, army, and urban residents at the beginning (or end) of the reference period. Data reporting system and data adjustment are the same as that in the output of pork, beef and mutton.

Regularly Cultivated Land refers to farmland among the total land resources, which is exclusively used for farming and is under regular cultivation with harvest in normal years. Included are currently cultivated land, land that has been abandoned or put in idle for less than 3 years and could be re–used for cultivation at any time, and new–claimed land that has been put into cultivation for more than 3 years. According to statistical coverage, it includes the gouges, dykes, roads and ridges of field with 1 meter wide in Southern areas and 2 meters wide in Northern areas. Excluded under this category are steep slope land over 25 degrees under temporary cultivation, land (large or small plots) that is claimed along river bends, lake sides or banks of reservoirs, as well as land that has been designated under the "Green for Grain" programme of the state and provincial governments but is still temporarily under cultivation. The regularly cultivated land is the key protection land of the nation, an important indicator reflecting the comprehensive productivity of agriculture of China.

Sown Area of Crops refers to area of land sown or transplanted with crops regardless of being in cultivated area or non–cultivated area. Area of land re–sown due to natural disasters is also included. This is an important indicator that can reflect the utilization condition of the cultivated land in China. At present, the sown area of crops mainly include the following 9 categories of crops: grain, cotton, oil–bearing crops, sugar crops, fiber crops, Tobacco, Vegetables and melons, medicinal materials and other farm crops.

Irrigated Area refers to areas that are effectively irrigated, i.e. level land, which has water source and complete sets of irrigation facilities to lift and move adequate water for irrigation purpose under normal conditions. Under normal conditions, irrigated area is the sum of watered fields and irrigated fields where irrigation systems or equipment have been installed for regular irrigation purpose. This important indicator reflects drought resistance capacity of the cultivated land in China.

Consumption of Chemical Fertilizers in Agriculture refers to the quantity of chemical fertilizers applied in agriculture in the year, including nitrogenous fertilizer, phosphate fertilizer, potash fertilizer, and compound fertilizer. The consumption of chemical fertilizers is required in calculation to convert the gross weight into weight containing 100% effective component (e.g. 100% nitrogen content in nitrogenous fertilizer, 100% phosphorous pent oxide contents in phosphate fertilizer, 100% potassium oxide contents in potash fertilizer). Compound fertilizer is converted with its major component. The formula is :

Volume of effective component= physical quantity x effective component of certain chemical fertilizer (%)

Total Power of Farm Machinery refers to total mechanical power of machinery used in farming, forestry, animal husbandry, and fishery, including ploughing, irrigation and drainage, harvesting, transport, plant protection, stock breeding, forestry and fishery. The power of internal combustion engines is required to convert horsepower into watts and the power of electric motors is required to be converted into watts. Machinery employed for non–agricultural purposes, such as the machines used in township run and village–run industry, construction, non–agricultural transport, scientific experiments and teaching, is excluded. Data are mainly from agricultural machinery agencies.

Rural Employed Persons refer to rural labor forces aged over 16 years old who are engaged in real production and management activities and receive payment in kind or wages, including those covered within the age frame and regularly participating in production activities, and those who are out of the range of age frame and also participating in production activities regularly. Excluding students studying in other places with their permanent residence registered in local areas, servicemen and persons incapable of working; also excluding those who are waiting for jobs and those engaged in household work. Persons employed are classified as persons engaged in agriculture, forestry, animal husbandry or fishery activities; persons engaged in industrial activities; persons engaged in construction activities; persons engaged in transport, storage and telecommunications activities; persons engaged in whole sales and retail sales trade and catering activities; and persons engaged in other non–agriculture activities, depending upon the longest period of employment in major activities (or using income indicator when period of employment is the same).

13 工　业

Industry

工 业
INDUSTRY
2016

规模以上工业企业	Industrial Enterprises Above Designated Size		
工业总产值(现价)	Total Output Value (at current price)	48766.71	(亿元)
#轻工业	Light Industry	18027.68	(亿元)
重工业	Heavy Industry	30739.04	(亿元)
#大型企业	Large Scale Enterprises	16612.82	(亿元)
中型企业	Medium Scale Enterprises	11342.35	(亿元)
资产总计	Total Assets	37942.33	(亿元)
负债合计	Total Liability	20355.90	(亿元)
主营业务收入	Income from Major Business	45850.64	(亿元)
利税总额	Total Revenue	4754.74	(亿元)
从业人员年平均人数	Annually Average number of Employment	339.51	(万人)

规模以上工业总产值构成(%)
Composition of Industry above desginated size

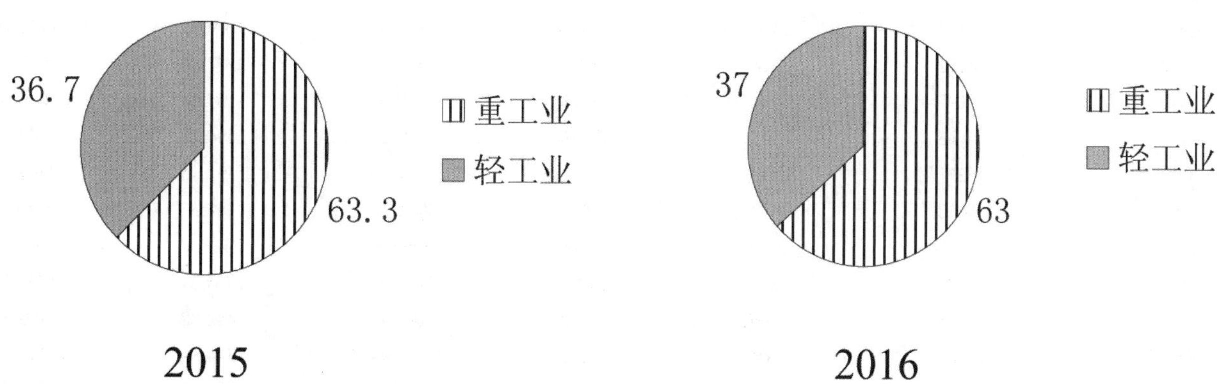

规模以上工业增加值(上年=100)

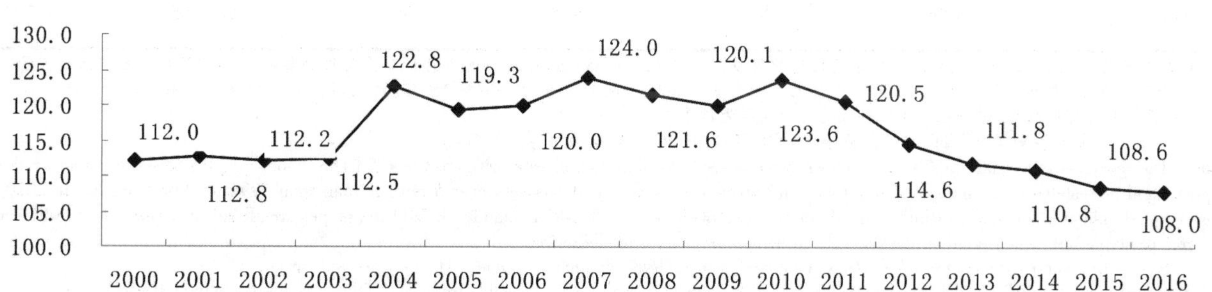

13-1 工业发展基本情况
THE BASIC SITUATION OF INDUSTRIAL DEVELOPMENT

年份 Year	工业企业单位数(个) Number of Industrial Enterprises (unit)	轻工业 Light industry	重工业 Heavy industry	工业总产值(当年价)(亿元) Total Output Value (currentprice) (100 million yuan)	轻工业 Light industry	重工业 Heavy industry
1979	16073	10100	5973	220.82	93.45	107.37
1985	25011	15309	9702	467.22	216.47	250.75
1986	27697	16890	10807	538.28	256.06	282.22
1987	26294	15528	10766	659.19	315.49	343.70
1988	26016	15279	10737	834.84	405.13	429.71
1989	25999	15035	10964	976.93	463.35	513.58
1990	25913	14885	11028	1008.20	476.76	531.44
1991	25204	14317	10887	1136.02	531.26	604.76
1992	23985	13428	10557	1373.66	605.11	768.55
1993	22600	11958	10642	1992.31	770.20	1222.11
1994	23275	12096	11179	3024.72	1360.78	1663.94
1995	27815	14827	12988	3697.91	1870.12	1827.79
1996	25986	13618	12368	4836.33	2470.90	2365.43
1997	24498	12723	11775	5977.00	3158.47	2818.53
1998	7399	3581	3818	6731.31	3534.67	3196.64
1999	6874	3308	3566	2831.70	1109.92	1721.78
2000	6282	3026	3256	3064.43	1177.24	1887.18
2001	6197	2981	3216	3239.51	1194.90	2044.61
2002	6183	2947	3236	3589.26	1184.78	2404.48
2003	6271	2789	3482	3631.29	1192.46	2438.82
2004	6232	2632	3600	4960.25	1180.07	3780.17
2005	6813	2953	3860	6066.96	1503.00	4563.95
2006	7546	3272	4274	7454.07	1898.34	5555.73
2007	8996	3808	5188	9601.52	2492.88	7108.64
2008	12067	4806	7261	13454.94	3344.80	10110.14
2009	14027	5515	8512	15567.02	4234.52	11332.50
2010	16106	6326	9780	21623.12	5935.78	15687.33
2011	10633	4347	6286	28072.73	8370.27	19702.45
2012	12441	5012	7429	33450.66	10941.70	22508.95
2013	14650	5855	8795	39208.98	13405.24	25803.74
2014	15957	6453	9504	43393.87	15378.14	28015.73
2015	16413	6646	9767	45809.57	16810.65	28998.91
2016	16296	6680	9616	48766.71	18027.68	30739.04

注：1.本表规模以上工业1997年及以前统计范围为乡及乡以上工业。1998-2006年为全部国有工业及年销售收入500万元以上非国有工业企业;2007年-2010年为主营业务收入500万元以上工业企业。2011年起为主营业务收入2000万元及以上的工业法人企业。(下表同)

2."国有及国有控股经济"一栏,1998年以前统计范围为国有工业。

3.2011年行业小类码按照《国民经济行业分类》(GB/T4754-2011)填写。(下表同)

Note: 1.The scopes of industrial statistics are all township and above town industrial enterprises before 1998.The scopes are all state-owned industrial enterprises and non-state-owned industrial enterprise with revenue from principal business over 5 million yuan from 1998 to 2006.For 2007 to 2010,the scopes are all industrial enterprices with revenue from principal business over 5 million yuan.From 2011,the scopes are all industrial enterprises with revenue from principal business over 20 millon yuan.The same applies to the talbe following.

2."State-owned and state-controlled economy"a column,prior to 1998 statistics the range of state-owned industries.

3.Accordring to GB/T4754-2011,the small classes code of industries are filled in the table from 2011.The same applies to the talbe following.

13-1 续表 continued

单位: 亿元 (100 million yuan)

年份 Year	主营业务收入(亿元) Main business income (100 million yuan)	利润总额(亿元) Total profit (100 million yuan)	利税总额(亿元) Total profits and taxes (100 million yuan)	职工人数(万人) Number of employees (1000 persons)
1979	163.52	20.70	34.19	161.98
1985	381.43	43.64	80.82	306.83
1986	438.95	40.22	82.14	333.63
1987	526.95	48.54	96.16	343.43
1988	654.72	58.85	117.28	356.43
1989	706.99	50.99	112.12	360.88
1990	705.97	26.73	88.40	358.65
1991	800.01	31.79	103.46	367.41
1992	1041.66	43.19	127.15	357.74
1993	1500.71	67.00	167.92	357.97
1994	1690.94	74.06	190.29	381.45
1995	2066.38	52.26	181.57	379.84
1996	2305.57	43.93	181.41	369.80
1997	2681.36	57.71	221.53	362.50
1998	2433.92	44.71	195.96	274.43
1999	2602.26	68.82	232.24	250.07
2000	2870.36	106.47	29.36	230.36
2001	3043.82	134.49	335.36	212.48
2002	3378.31	175.60	404.23	205.82
2003	3993.99	194.40	444.96	198.60
2004	4832.43	270.98	559.28	176.70
2005	5962.54	371.84	727.48	188.30
2006	7314.81	454.00	897.19	190.85
2007	9390.43	647.85	1229.16	200.35
2008	13081.90	909.03	1761.47	235.90
2009	15331.62	1092.47	1987.88	272.39
2010	21151.56	1668.55	2950.08	294.97
2011	27072.02	1864.46	3093.57	279.59
2012	32325.95	2046.28	3528.80	311.13
2013	38183.39	2475.07	4451.87	346.29
2014	41401.49	2402.63	4465.72	359.45
2015	43179.21	2456.00	4599.15	352.64
2016	45850.64	2713.46	4754.74	339.51

13-2 规模以上工业企业单位数和产销总值 (2016)

单位: 亿元

项 目	Item	企业单位数(个) Number of Enterprises (unit)
总　　计	**Total**	**16296**
一、按登记注册类型分组:	**Grouped by Type of Registration**	
内资企业	Inner Funded Enterprises	15479
国有企业	State Owned Enterprises	124
中央企业	Central Enterprises	42
地方企业	Local Enterprises	82
集体企业	Collective-owned Enterprise	82
股份合作企业	Share Holding Cooperative Enterprises	15
联营企业	Joint Owned Enterprise	3
国有联营企业	State Joint Ownership	
集体联营企业	Collective Joint Ownership	1
国有与集体联营企业	Joint State- Collective Ownership	1
其他联营企业	Other Joint Owned Enterprise	1
有限责任公司	Responsibility Co. Ltd	5637
国有独资公司	State Solely Funded Co.	126
其他有限责任公司	Others	5511
股份有限公司	Share Holding Co.Ltd.	719
私营企业	Private - owned enterprises	8857
私营独资企业	Solely Private - owned enterprises	226
私营合伙企业	Private Joint Venture	36
私营有限责任公司	Private Responsibility Co. Ltd	8110
私营股份有限公司	Private Share Holding Co.Ltd.	485
其他企业	Others	42
港、澳、台商投资企业	Hongkong, Macao and Taiwan Funded Enterprises	367
合资经营企业(港或澳、台资)	Joint Venture with Hongkong, Macao and Taiwan	154
合作经营企业(港或澳、台资)	Cooperate with Hongkong, Macao and Taiwan Funded	4
港澳台商独资经营企业	Enterprises Solely Funded by Hongkong, Macao and Taiwan Businessmen	191
港澳台商投资股份有限公司	Share Holding Co.Ltd. With Hongkong, Macao and Taiwan Investment	11
外商投资企业	Foreign Funded Enterprises	450
中外合资经营企业	Sino - Foreign Joint Funded Enterprises	245
中外合作经营企业	Sino - Foreign Cooperative Funded Enterprises	8
外资企业	Foreign Solely Funded Enterprises	181
外商投资股份有限公司	Foreign Funded Share Holding Co.Ltd.	14
二、在总计中:亏损企业	**Of the Total: enterprises running under deficit**	**1274**
在总计中:国有控股企业	Of the Total: State-Owned Share Holding Enterprises	772
在总计中:农村工业	Of the Total: Rural Industry	95
在总计中:轻工业	Of the Total: Light Industry	6680
重工业	Heavy Industry	9616
在总计中:大型企业	Of the Total: Large Scale Enterprises	358
中型企业	Medium Scale Enterprises	1817
小型企业	Small Enterprises	14121

THE NUMBER OF UNITS OF INDUSTRIAL ENTERPRISES ABOVE

工业总产值（当年价格）Total Output Value (current price)	工业销售产值(当年价格) Output Value of Industrial Products Sales (current price)	出口交货值 Delivery Value for Export
48766.71	**47295.43**	**1905.07**
41543.92	40209.23	1469.26
2501.36	2486.67	118.59
2387.41	2379.32	118.56
113.95	107.35	0.04
113.99	110.26	
16.59	15.51	
4.70	4.70	
2.99	2.93	
0.36	0.41	
1.36	1.36	
16398.04	15895.07	556.68
1745.81	1746.46	34.20
14652.24	14148.61	522.48
5174.15	4974.27	246.84
17264.84	16655.35	544.91
365.43	356.82	4.28
58.85	58.32	0.01
15544.86	15005.76	514.62
1295.70	1234.45	26.01
70.24	67.39	2.24
2068.01	2011.56	252.95
1077.15	1057.02	96.01
10.00	9.60	
903.72	865.68	156.41
32.24	33.39	0.52
5154.79	5074.64	182.86
4010.87	3944.52	60.41
58.43	57.57	1.67
871.23	853.76	113.33
213.11	217.90	7.01
2316.43	**2141.78**	**76.28**
11310.53	11136.77	334.68
195.15	190.04	
18027.68	17367.23	747.82
30739.04	29928.19	1157.25
16612.82	16357.11	819.26
11342.35	10918.90	610.99
20811.54	20019.42	474.82

13-2 续表 continued

单位: 亿元

项 目	Item	企业单位数 (个) Number of Enterprises(unit)
按行业分	**Grouped by sector**	
采矿业	**Mining and Qarrying**	**578**
煤炭开采和洗选业	Coal Mining and Processing	67
石油和天然气开采业	Petroleum and Natural Gas Extraction	1
黑色金属矿采选业	Ferrous Metals Mining and Processing	84
有色金属矿采选业	Non-ferrous Metals Mining and Processing	31
非金属矿采选业	Non-metal Minerals Mining and Processing	386
开采辅助活动	Mining Auxiliary Activities	4
其他采矿业	Other Minerals Mining and Processing	5
制造业	**Manufacturing**	**15371**
农副食品加工业	Food Processing	1785
食品制造业	Food Production	432
酒、饮料和精制茶制造业	Wine,Beverage and Refined Tea Production	492
烟草制品业	Tobacco Processing	7
纺织业	Textile Industry	966
纺织服装、服饰业	Textile,Garments, and Fashion Industry	566
皮革、毛皮、羽毛及其制品和制鞋业	Leather, Furs,Down and Related Products	172
木材加工和木、竹、藤、棕、草制品业	Timber Processing, Wood, Bamboo, Cane, Palm and Sraw Products	276
家具制造业	Furniture Manufacturing	162
造纸和纸制品业	Papermaking and Paper Products	272
印刷和记录媒介复制业	Printing and Record Processing	231
文教、工美、体育和娱乐用品制造业	Stationery, Education and Sports Goods	150
石油加工、炼焦和核燃料加工业	Petroleum Processing, Coking Products and Nuclear Fuel Processing	42
化学原料和化学制品制造业	Raw Chemical Material and Chemical Products	1090
医药制造业	Medical and pharmaceutical Products	410
化学纤维制造业	Chemical Fibers	20
橡胶和塑料制品业	Rubber and plastic products	654
非金属矿物制品业	Nonmetal Material Products	2023
黑色金属冶炼和压延加工业	Smelting and Pressing of Ferrous Metals	300
有色金属冶炼和压延加工业	Smelting and Pressing of Nonferrous Metals	144
金属制品业	Metal Products	797
通用设备制造业	Ordinary Machinery Manufacturing	717
专用设备制造业	Special Purpose Equipment Manufacturing	700
汽车制造业	Motor manufacturing	1457
铁路、船舶、航空航天和其他运输设备制造业	Railway,Watercraft,Aviation and other Transporlation Equipment manufacturing	160
电气机械和器材制造业	Electric Machinery and Equipment	681
计算机、通信和其他电子设备制造业	Telecommunication Computer,Equipment and Other Electronic Equipment Manufacturing	356
仪器仪表制造业	Instruments and Meters, Manufacturing	138
其他制造业	Other Manufacturing	78
废弃资源综合利用业	Waste Comprehensive Vtilization of Resources Industry	69
金属制品、机械和设备修理业	Metal products,Machinery and Equipment Repairing	24
电力、燃气及水的生产和供应业	**Electric Power, Gas and Water Production and Supply**	**347**
电力、热力生产和供应业	Electric Power, Steam and Hot Water Production and Supply	188
燃气生产和供应业	Gas Production and Supply	67
水的生产和供应业	Tap Water Production and Supply	92

(100 million Yuan)

工业总产值 (当年价格) Total Output Value(current price)	工业销售产值 (当年价格) Output Value of Industrial Products Sales(current price)	出口交货值 Delivery Value for Export
1119.18	**1088.68**	**0.78**
62.75	60.55	
31.43	31.46	0.76
277.83	277.14	
48.98	48.18	
636.05	611.45	
59.63	57.41	0.02
2.50	2.49	
45809.57	**44392.28**	**1904.30**
5259.62	5097.57	101.85
1342.62	1289.00	54.39
1960.53	1894.47	8.43
583.61	615.45	0.76
2445.95	2373.36	158.37
1054.02	1023.73	135.27
249.42	242.46	62.08
499.94	479.73	6.34
225.02	215.94	3.53
588.46	566.77	2.06
409.89	388.26	0.10
238.39	224.32	22.05
804.65	788.04	
4404.70	4246.99	146.96
1264.52	1202.71	116.85
74.48	73.58	3.94
1305.76	1272.43	4.41
3500.98	3371.79	26.88
1807.43	1787.44	73.34
948.97	937.51	12.49
1612.87	1556.08	22.09
1453.41	1386.33	70.44
1239.42	1184.92	30.46
6760.07	6675.43	60.77
787.74	752.67	64.84
2078.86	1934.82	94.50
2333.59	2261.27	608.50
205.02	193.08	4.43
150.54	146.80	4.47
160.40	153.89	3.72
58.68	55.42	
1837.96	**1814.47**	
1618.42	1606.25	
146.76	142.38	
72.79	65.84	

13-3 规模以上工业企业主要经济指标 (2016)

单位: 亿元

项 目	Item	企业单位数(个) Number of Enterprises (unit)
总 计	**Total**	**16296**
一、按登记注册类型分组:	**Grouped by Type of Registration**	
内资企业	Inner Funded Enterprises	15479
国有企业	State Owned Enterprises	124
中央企业	Central Enterprises	42
地方企业	Local Enterprises	82
集体企业	Collective-owned Enterprise	82
股份合作企业	Share Holding Cooperative Enterprises	15
联营企业	Joint Owned Enterprise	3
国有联营企业	State Joint Ownership	
集体联营企业	Collective Joint Ownership	1
国有与集体联营企业	Joint State- Collective Ownership	1
其他联营企业	Other Joint Owned Enterprise	1
有限责任公司	Responsibility Co. Ltd	5637
国有独资公司	State Solely Funded Co.	126
其他有限责任公司	Others	5511
股份有限公司	Share Holding Co.Ltd.	719
私营企业	Private - owned enterprises	8857
私营独资企业	Solely Private - owned enterprises	226
私营合伙企业	Private Joint Venture	36
私营有限责任公司	Private Responsibility Co. Ltd	8110
私营股份有限公司	Private Share Holding Co.Ltd.	485
其他企业	Others	42
港、澳、台商投资企业	Hongkong, Macao and Taiwan Funded Enterprises	367
合资经营企业(港或澳、台资)	Joint Venture with Hongkong, Macao and Taiwan	154
合作经营企业(港或澳、台资)	Cooperate with Hongkong, Macao and Taiwan Funded	4
港澳台商独资经营企业	Enterprises Solely Funded by Hongkong, Macao and Taiwan Businessmen	191
港澳台商投资股份有限公司	Share Holding Co.Ltd. With Hongkong, Macao and Taiwan Investment	11
外商投资企业	Foreign Funded Enterprises	450
中外合资经营企业	Sino - Foreign Joint Funded Enterprises	245
中外合作经营企业	Sino - Foreign Cooperative Funded Enterprises	8
外资企业	Foreign Solely Funded Enterprises	181
外商投资股份有限公司	Foreign Funded Share Holding Co.Ltd.	14
二、在总计中:亏损企业	**Of the Total: enterprises running under deficit**	**1274**
在总计中:国有控股企业	Of the Total: State-Owned Share Holding Enterprises	772
在总计中:农村工业	Of the Total: Rural Industry	95
在总计中:轻工业	Of the Total: Light Industry	6680
重工业	Heavy Industry	9616
在总计中:大型企业	Of the Total: Large Scale Enterprises	358
中型企业	Medium Scale Enterprises	1817
小型企业	Small Enterprises	14121

MAJOR ECONOMIC INDICATORS OF INDUSTRIAL

(100 million Yuan)

资产总计 Total Assets	流动资产合计 Circulating Funds	应收帐款净额 Net Value of Account Received	固定资产合计 Total Fixed Assets
37942.33	**17265.72**	**4373.47**	**13642.50**
32006.91	14181.89	3552.27	11594.85
4436.00	1490.52	205.31	1929.78
4243.15	1373.35	191.70	1878.90
192.86	117.18	13.62	50.88
48.00	23.31	8.17	15.36
9.91	7.65	2.61	1.61
3.52	1.78	0.69	1.70
2.65	1.18	0.37	1.47
0.71	0.56	0.31	0.12
0.15	0.04	0.01	0.11
12458.14	6300.65	1767.53	4334.39
2107.83	1011.96	180.02	836.87
10350.31	5288.69	1587.51	3497.52
7934.74	3048.95	687.64	2697.21
7094.11	3300.82	878.40	2604.35
80.91	34.37	8.68	33.73
14.73	6.34	1.15	5.70
6458.96	3009.70	809.10	2369.87
539.51	250.41	59.48	195.05
22.49	8.21	1.92	10.45
1699.13	830.43	219.68	620.66
888.65	470.93	112.90	301.72
11.59	4.80	1.08	2.04
665.94	275.44	95.13	293.36
62.53	19.05	8.15	15.63
4236.30	2253.41	601.52	1426.98
3156.59	1717.36	404.24	1005.53
30.03	10.41	0.97	18.49
718.36	424.11	177.82	228.30
330.02	100.99	18.15	174.05
3620.50	**1681.76**	**399.44**	**1339.58**
17098.93	6757.01	1295.28	6791.59
84.53	42.22	12.52	25.63
9289.23	4705.71	990.29	2989.51
28653.10	12560.01	3383.18	10652.98
19497.27	8395.61	1771.07	7120.83
7369.11	3646.16	1041.38	2663.00
11075.96	5223.96	1561.02	3858.66

13-3 续表 1 continued

单位: 亿元

项 目	Item	企业单位数(个) Number of Enterprises(unit)
按行业分	**Grouped by sector**	
采矿业	**Mining and Qarrying**	**578**
煤炭开采和洗选业	Coal Mining and Processing	67
石油和天然气开采业	Petroleum and Natural Gas Extraction	1
黑色金属矿采选业	Ferrous Metals Mining and Processing	84
有色金属矿采选业	Non-ferrous Metals Mining and Processing	31
非金属矿采选业	Non-metal Minerals Mining and Processing	386
开采辅助活动	Mining Auxiliary Activities	4
其他采矿业	Other Minerals Mining and Processing	5
制造业	**Manufacturing**	**15371**
农副食品加工业	Food Processing	1785
食品制造业	Food Production	432
酒、饮料和精制茶制造业	Wine,Beverage and Refined Tea Production	492
烟草制品业	Tobacco Processing	7
纺织业	Textile Industry	966
纺织服装、服饰业	Textile,Garments, and Fashion Industry	566
皮革、毛皮、羽毛及其制品和制鞋业	Leather, Furs,Down and Related Products	172
木材加工和木、竹、藤、棕、草制品业	Timber Processing, Wood, Bamboo, Cane, Palm and Sraw Products	276
家具制造业	Furniture Manufacturing	162
造纸和纸制品业	Papermaking and Paper Products	272
印刷和记录媒介复制业	Printing and Record Processing	231
文教、工美、体育和娱乐用品制造业	Stationery, Education and Sports Goods	150
石油加工、炼焦和核燃料加工业	Petroleum Processing, Coking Products and Nuclear Fuel Processing	42
化学原料和化学制品制造业	Raw Chemical Material and Chemical Products	1090
医药制造业	Medical and pharmaceutical Products	410
化学纤维制造业	Chemical Fibers	20
橡胶和塑料制品业	Rubber and Plastic Products	654
非金属矿物制品业	Nonmetal Material Products	2023
黑色金属冶炼和压延加工业	Smelting and Pressing of Ferrous Metals	300
有色金属冶炼和压延加工业	Smelting and Pressing of Nonferrous Metals	144
金属制品业	Metal Products	797
通用设备制造业	Ordinary Machinery Manufacturing	717
专用设备制造业	Special Purpose Equipment Manufacturing	700
汽车制造业	Motor manufacturing	1457
铁路、船舶、航空航天和其他运输设备制造业	Railway,Watercraft,Aviation and other Transporlation Equipment manufacturing	160
电气机械和器材制造业	Electric Machinery and Equipment	681
计算机、通信和其他电子设备制造业	Telecommunication Computer,Equipment and Other Electronic Equipment Manufacturing	356
仪器仪表制造业	Instruments and Meters, Manufacturing	138
其他制造业	Other Manufacturing	78
废弃资源综合利用业	Waste Comprehensive Vtilization of Resources Industry	69
金属制品、机械和设备修理业	Metal products,Machinery and Equipment Repairing	24
电力、燃气及水的生产和供应业	**Electric Power, Gas and Water Production and Supply**	**347**
电力、热力生产和供应业	Electric Power, Steam and Hot Water Production and Supply	188
燃气生产和供应业	Gas Production and Supply	67
水的生产和供应业	Tap Water Production and Supply	92

(100 million Yuan)

资产总计 Total Assets	流动资产合计 Circulating Funds	应收帐款净额 Net Value of Account Received	固定资产合计 Total Fixed Assets
812.88	**326.14**	**98.52**	**325.26**
37.61	13.47	1.43	13.93
104.91	11.23	0.82	79.64
139.07	61.18	20.28	54.56
54.21	18.73	3.54	23.61
376.31	170.88	36.01	108.17
94.34	47.62	34.73	42.78
6.42	3.02	1.71	2.57
32103.75	**16433.20**	**4184.08**	**9886.50**
1819.30	829.30	158.95	701.24
577.60	262.34	70.37	196.63
1179.18	730.92	71.59	297.84
443.30	342.07	27.43	98.54
919.97	401.89	84.55	388.31
404.16	212.08	44.29	123.96
98.18	50.00	14.88	34.96
243.85	96.58	17.78	97.51
136.60	55.63	10.88	61.68
377.63	186.50	47.50	137.61
226.43	127.85	44.36	70.48
225.30	142.24	13.41	28.99
290.99	129.10	27.49	151.98
3037.93	1153.21	181.80	1376.71
1235.78	527.95	129.50	336.90
62.81	23.98	4.98	16.24
656.00	331.26	87.29	204.03
2063.72	800.50	231.89	873.65
2496.78	849.89	111.26	1054.34
574.15	297.01	36.34	170.75
1004.17	572.15	156.07	305.12
1482.04	801.06	257.05	427.46
1021.88	629.36	185.92	263.98
6390.78	3603.01	950.03	1316.64
867.75	517.85	123.33	229.01
1452.51	873.40	361.57	426.71
2390.98	1637.75	659.91	372.12
175.68	102.92	36.74	50.98
96.07	56.24	9.71	29.73
121.13	68.50	20.41	36.20
31.12	20.66	6.81	6.17
5025.70	**506.39**	**90.87**	**3430.74**
4461.95	305.75	71.33	3207.10
215.09	69.74	7.40	109.87
348.66	130.91	12.14	113.76

13-3 续表 2 continued

单位: 亿元

项 目	Item	资产总计 Total Assets 固定资产原价 Original Price of Fixed Assets
总 计	Total	25426.04
一、按登记注册类型分组:	Grouped by Type of Registration	
内资企业	Inner Funded Enterprises	22019.83
国有企业	State Owned Enterprises	3857.08
中央企业	Central Enterprises	3776.69
地方企业	Local Enterprises	80.39
集体企业	Collective-owned Enterprise	29.64
股份合作企业	Share Holding Cooperative Enterprises	2.65
联营企业	Joint Owned Enterprise	3.39
国有联营企业	State Joint Ownership	
集体联营企业	Collective Joint Ownership	2.83
国有与集体联营企业	Joint State- Collective Ownership	0.40
其他联营企业	Other Joint Owned Enterprise	0.15
有限责任公司	Responsibility Co. Ltd	7005.61
国有独资公司	State Solely Funded Co.	1207.45
其他有限责任公司	Others	5798.16
股份有限公司	Share Holding Co.Ltd.	4440.01
私营企业	Private - owned enterprises	6666.38
私营独资企业	Solely Private - owned enterprises	68.34
私营合伙企业	Private Joint Venture	9.80
私营有限责任公司	Private Responsibility Co. Ltd	6233.50
私营股份有限公司	Private Share Holding Co.Ltd.	354.73
其他企业	Others	15.06
港、澳、台商投资企业	Hongkong, Macao and Taiwan Funded Enterprises	1057.90
合资经营企业(港或澳、台资)	Joint Venture with Hongkong, Macao and Taiwan	558.63
合作经营企业(港或澳、台资)	Cooperate with Hongkong, Macao and Taiwan Funded	5.58
港澳台商独资经营企业	Enterprises Solely Funded by Hongkong, Macao and Taiwan Business-men	458.90
港澳台商投资股份有限公司	Share Holding Co.Ltd. With Hongkong, Macao and Taiwan Investment	22.12
外商投资企业	Foreign Funded Enterprises	2348.31
中外合资经营企业	Sino - Foreign Joint Funded Enterprises	1630.03
中外合作经营企业	Sino - Foreign Cooperative Funded Enterprises	40.23
外资企业	Foreign Solely Funded Enterprises	383.71
外商投资股份有限公司	Foreign Funded Share Holding Co.Ltd.	293.82
二、在总计中:亏损企业	Of the Total: enterprises running under deficit	2249.28
在总计中:国有控股企业	Of the Total: State-Owned Share Holding Enterprises	11578.68
在总计中:农村工业	Of the Total: Rural Industry	93.30
在总计中:轻工业	Of the Total: Light Industry	7024.91
重工业	Heavy Industry	18401.13
在总计中:大型企业	Of the Total: Large Scale Enterprises	12861.92
中型企业	Medium Scale Enterprises	5548.93
小型企业	Small Enterprises	7015.19

(100 million Yuan)

累计折旧 Accumulated Depreciation	负债合计 Total Liability	流动负债合计 Total Circulating Liability	应付账款 Account Payable
12696.87	**20355.90**	**15643.54**	**4649.73**
11179.73	16831.23	12704.25	3465.46
1944.98	2837.98	2299.80	571.53
1907.73	2704.86	2238.76	565.24
37.25	133.12	61.04	6.29
16.46	27.81	20.16	6.89
1.40	6.56	4.68	1.07
1.69	1.16	1.16	0.65
1.37	0.72	0.72	0.38
0.28	0.42	0.42	0.26
0.04	0.03	0.03	0.01
2930.71	7356.53	5667.81	1700.43
463.73	1288.72	1033.34	311.82
2466.99	6067.81	4634.47	1388.61
1989.15	3454.52	2425.35	555.51
4290.62	3138.43	2278.41	627.44
35.62	25.04	17.01	4.07
4.54	6.10	2.19	0.60
4069.31	2866.20	2076.35	582.99
181.15	241.09	182.86	39.78
4.73	8.23	6.89	1.94
482.94	883.81	714.61	241.11
270.13	505.25	418.16	119.70
3.64	4.65	1.24	0.53
196.91	303.59	232.28	108.19
7.43	18.23	17.00	3.18
1034.20	2640.87	2224.67	943.16
723.72	2017.44	1768.80	748.44
23.94	17.00	14.14	1.80
166.27	393.38	315.28	147.42
120.10	212.63	126.06	45.38
1011.00	**2710.31**	**2023.78**	**605.89**
5047.57	9767.82	7647.31	2191.88
69.32	42.69	24.13	4.25
4401.60	4333.38	3186.40	815.01
8295.27	16022.52	12457.14	3834.72
6070.64	10997.79	8642.30	2517.32
3175.73	3929.21	3078.02	1028.64
3450.50	5428.89	3923.21	1103.76

13-3 续表 3 continued

单位: 亿元

项 目	Item	资产总计 Total Assets 固定资产原价 Original Price of Fixed Assets
按行业分	**Grouped by sector**	
采矿业	**Mining and Qarrying**	**707.71**
煤炭开采和洗选业	Coal Mining and Processing	18.21
石油和天然气开采业	Petroleum and Natural Gas Extraction	308.23
黑色金属矿采选业	Ferrous Metals Mining and Processing	96.91
有色金属矿采选业	Non-ferrous Metals Mining and Processing	31.62
非金属矿采选业	Non-metal Minerals Mining and Processing	178.33
开采辅助活动	Mining Auxiliary Activities	68.68
其他采矿业	Other Minerals Mining and Processing	5.73
制造业	**Manufacturing**	**19175.93**
农副食品加工业	Food Processing	2313.79
食品制造业	Food Production	762.58
酒、饮料和精制茶制造业	Wine,Beverage and Refined Tea Production	537.78
烟草制品业	Tobacco Processing	100.16
纺织业	Textile Industry	861.71
纺织服装、服饰业	Textile,Garments, and Fashion Industry	256.54
皮革、毛皮、羽毛及其制品和制鞋业	Leather, Furs,Down and Related Products	89.20
木材加工和木、竹、藤、棕、草制品业	Timber Processing, Wood, Bamboo, Cane, Palm and Sraw Products	173.93
家具制造业	Furniture Manufacturing	74.03
造纸和纸制品业	Papermaking and Paper Products	339.97
印刷和记录媒介复制业	Printing and Record Processing	149.06
文教、工美、体育和娱乐用品制造业	Stationery, Education and Sports Goods	115.61
石油加工、炼焦和核燃料加工业	Petroleum Processing, Coking Products and Nuclear Fuel Processing	239.54
化学原料和化学制品制造业	Raw Chemical Material and Chemical Products	2526.23
医药制造业	Medical and pharmaceutical Products	505.52
化学纤维制造业	Chemical Fibers	35.81
橡胶和塑料制品业	Rubber and Plastic Products	456.32
非金属矿物制品业	Nonmetal Material Products	1464.14
黑色金属冶炼和压延加工业	Smelting and Pressing of Ferrous Metals	2197.99
有色金属冶炼和压延加工业	Smelting and Pressing of Nonferrous Metals	275.58
金属制品业	Metal Products	529.08
通用设备制造业	Ordinary Machinery Manufacturing	644.72
专用设备制造业	Special Purpose Equipment Manufacturing	556.80
汽车制造业	Motor manufacturing	2159.07
铁路、船舶、航空航天和其他运输设备制造业	Railway,Watercraft,Aviation and other Transporlation Equipment manufacturing	286.93
电气机械和器材制造业	Electric Machinery and Equipment	688.43
计算机、通信和其他电子设备制造业	Telecommunication Computer,Equipment and Other Electronic Equipment Manufacturing	614.45
仪器仪表制造业	Instruments and Meters, Manufacturing	82.19
其他制造业	Other Manufacturing	68.22
废弃资源综合利用业	Waste Comprehensive Vtilization of Resources Industry	49.62
金属制品、机械和设备修理业	Metal products,Machinery and Equipment Repairing	20.91
电力、燃气及水的生产和供应业	**Electric Power, Gas and Water Production and Supply**	**5542.40**
电力、热力生产和供应业	Electric Power, Steam and Hot Water Production and Supply	5223.57
燃气生产和供应业	Gas Production and Supply	131.09
水的生产和供应业	Tap Water Production and Supply	187.74

(100 million Yuan)

累计折旧 Accumulated Depreciation	负债合计 Total Liability	流动负债合计 Total Circulating Liability	应付账款 Account Payable
405.47	**434.76**	**322.50**	**85.38**
4.88	16.25	10.31	0.65
228.59	47.73	35.85	13.52
46.66	78.79	59.42	11.84
13.22	28.16	21.51	5.51
81.24	189.00	121.90	29.69
27.55	70.69	70.39	23.61
3.33	4.12	3.11	0.56
10103.14	**17311.93**	**13725.67**	**4277.10**
1734.37	719.05	529.86	110.06
576.56	258.15	216.56	54.15
278.40	691.04	484.05	105.21
64.39	137.44	135.82	58.48
506.61	413.39	308.73	61.46
141.50	182.69	140.05	32.48
56.56	47.48	28.27	8.82
88.90	110.05	76.06	12.83
34.54	53.51	37.79	8.21
211.61	194.05	155.98	35.65
83.76	101.35	78.76	25.77
88.40	148.82	72.20	9.93
112.60	170.74	144.64	35.32
1210.31	1746.08	1201.01	265.32
184.77	546.54	395.66	76.99
20.72	25.87	16.94	6.35
267.83	289.95	211.32	56.38
642.03	900.29	648.41	197.92
1154.62	1630.31	1352.42	286.56
109.55	361.52	261.96	38.86
240.83	561.74	464.76	146.32
288.24	895.97	608.54	125.16
308.44	576.12	497.77	162.08
947.67	3438.15	3011.54	1334.22
107.05	625.66	533.80	193.08
279.54	811.31	680.22	276.23
258.31	1439.40	1252.46	502.70
31.92	89.36	72.92	24.55
42.19	57.14	44.36	8.40
16.00	71.01	52.39	12.08
14.89	17.75	10.41	5.53
2188.26	**2609.21**	**1595.37**	**287.24**
2077.22	2271.51	1398.20	242.96
29.22	136.84	114.59	31.01
81.81	200.85	82.58	13.27

13-3 续表 4 continued

单位: 亿元

项 目	Item	非流动负债合计 Total Non-current Liabilities	所有者权益合计 Total Rights of Owners
总　计	**Total**	**3436.06**	**17502.70**
一、按登记注册类型分组:	**Grouped by Type of Registration**		
内资企业	Inner Funded Enterprises	2995.02	15093.33
国有企业	State Owned Enterprises	526.37	1597.88
中央企业	Central Enterprises	465.84	1538.05
地方企业	Local Enterprises	60.53	59.82
集体企业	Collective-owned Enterprise	5.03	19.21
股份合作企业	Share Holding Cooperative Enterprises	0.13	3.08
联营企业	Joint Owned Enterprise		2.35
国有联营企业	State Joint Ownership		
集体联营企业	Collective Joint Ownership		1.94
国有与集体联营企业	Joint State- Collective Ownership		0.29
其他联营企业	Other Joint Owned Enterprise		0.12
有限责任公司	Responsibility Co. Ltd	1198.93	5082.16
国有独资公司	State Solely Funded Co.	241.33	819.10
其他有限责任公司	Others	957.60	4263.06
股份有限公司	Share Holding Co.Ltd.	901.18	4452.48
私营企业	Private - owned enterprises	362.78	3922.01
私营独资企业	Solely Private - owned enterprises	2.82	55.26
私营合伙企业	Private Joint Venture	1.89	8.63
私营有限责任公司	Private Responsibility Co. Ltd	327.52	3561.78
私营股份有限公司	Private Share Holding Co.Ltd.	30.55	296.34
其他企业	Others	0.61	14.18
港、澳、台商投资企业	Hongkong, Macao and Taiwan Funded Enterprises	149.31	814.84
合资经营企业(港或澳、台资)	Joint Venture with Hongkong, Macao and Taiwan	78.83	383.40
合作经营企业(港或澳、台资)	Cooperate with Hongkong, Macao and Taiwan Funded	2.83	6.94
港澳台商独资经营企业	Enterprises Solely Funded by Hongkong, Macao and Taiwan Businessmen	60.80	361.87
港澳台商投资股份有限公司	Share Holding Co.Ltd. With Hongkong, Macao and Taiwan Investment	0.72	44.30
外商投资企业	Foreign Funded Enterprises	291.73	1594.53
中外合资经营企业	Sino - Foreign Joint Funded Enterprises	173.05	1138.25
中外合作经营企业	Sino - Foreign Cooperative Funded Enterprises	2.86	13.04
外资企业	Foreign Solely Funded Enterprises	29.68	324.98
外商投资股份有限公司	Foreign Funded Share Holding Co.Ltd.	86.10	117.39
二、在总计中:亏损企业	**Of the Total: enterprises running under deficit**	**519.87**	**908.00**
在总计中:国有控股企业	Of the Total: State-Owned Share Holding Enterprises	1923.21	7324.67
在总计中:农村工业	Of the Total: Rural Industry	3.07	41.24
在总计中:轻工业	Of the Total: Light Industry	689.62	4914.21
重工业	Heavy Industry	2746.44	12588.49
在总计中:大型企业	Of the Total: Large Scale Enterprises	2022.31	8499.47
中型企业	Medium Scale Enterprises	637.43	3439.66
小型企业	Small Enterprises	776.32	5563.57

(100 million Yuan)

实收资本 Assets Recevied	国家资本 National Assets	所有者权益合计 Total Rights of Owners			
		集体资本 Collective Assets	法人资本 Corperative Assets	个人资本 Individual Assets	港澳台资本 Assets from Hongkong, Maco and Taiwan Funded Enterprises
9120.27	**2557.19**	**140.17**	**2788.56**	**2937.50**	**150.20**
7887.51	2330.32	129.87	2493.94	2905.96	6.60
753.04	736.84	1.93	13.00	1.27	
736.59	726.80	0.48	9.00	0.32	
16.46	10.05	1.46	4.00	0.95	
8.91	0.20	3.54	2.83	2.34	
1.69		0.53	1.08	0.08	
0.21		0.08	0.05	0.07	
0.02				0.02	
0.14		0.08	0.05		
0.05				0.05	
3896.03	1093.36	83.50	1087.26	1614.57	4.07
310.84	260.41	3.02	46.75	0.66	
3585.19	832.95	80.48	1040.51	1613.91	4.07
1454.95	493.29	17.54	590.26	347.07	1.12
1768.47	6.23	22.74	798.87	937.35	1.41
22.38		0.07	5.68	16.63	
3.50			1.56	1.94	
1619.69	6.23	20.19	749.29	840.69	1.41
122.90		2.48	42.34	78.08	
4.20	0.40		0.60	3.21	
378.07	17.82	4.26	109.25	14.25	121.03
171.06	14.68	4.26	68.74	7.94	42.44
5.35			3.75	0.20	0.15
179.36	3.14		28.83	4.14	74.18
13.01			7.24	1.95	0.04
854.69	209.05	6.05	185.37	17.28	22.56
649.52	205.49	5.81	150.96	16.08	11.54
11.12		0.22	5.53	0.11	
163.86	0.82		15.56	0.79	11.00
29.71	2.75	0.02	13.34	0.30	0.02
1306.66	**662.71**	**21.12**	**342.50**	**180.98**	**22.21**
3034.15	2078.90	29.48	570.91	164.18	2.67
13.82	0.68	2.45	3.17	7.39	0.12
1866.71	142.01	33.61	737.26	753.81	76.57
7253.57	2415.18	106.56	2051.30	2183.69	73.63
2933.46	1657.05	13.61	579.64	346.20	59.43
1560.66	274.13	44.98	683.34	370.64	40.76
4626.15	626.01	81.58	1525.58	2220.66	50.01

13-3 续表 5 continued

单位: 亿元

项 目	Item	非流动负债合计 Total Non-current Liabilities	所有者权益合计 Total Rights of Owners
按行业分	**Grouped by sector**		
采矿业	**Mining and Qarrying**	**58.83**	**375.07**
煤炭开采和洗选业	Coal Mining and Processing	1.02	19.16
石油和天然气开采业	Petroleum and Natural Gas Extraction	11.87	57.18
黑色金属矿采选业	Ferrous Metals Mining and Processing	11.55	59.42
有色金属矿采选业	Non-ferrous Metals Mining and Processing	4.14	26.04
非金属矿采选业	Non-metal Minerals Mining and Processing	29.54	187.31
开采辅助活动	Mining Auxiliary Activities	0.23	23.65
其他采矿业	Other Minerals Mining and Processing	0.47	2.30
制造业	**Manufacturing**	**2434.02**	**14711.14**
农副食品加工业	Food Processing	79.77	1095.45
食品制造业	Food Production	21.90	318.19
酒、饮料和精制茶制造业	Wine,Beverage and Refined Tea Production	72.57	487.64
烟草制品业	Tobacco Processing	1.62	305.86
纺织业	Textile Industry	66.92	498.51
纺织服装、服饰业	Textile,Garments, and Fashion Industry	20.04	219.28
皮革、毛皮、羽毛及其制品和制鞋业	Leather, Furs,Down and Related Products	7.22	50.42
木材加工和木、竹、藤、棕、草制品业	Timber Processing, Wood, Bamboo, Cane, Palm and Sraw Products	17.76	132.06
家具制造业	Furniture Manufacturing	9.92	82.69
造纸和纸制品业	Papermaking and Paper Products	24.83	179.79
印刷和记录媒介复制业	Printing and Record Processing	9.31	124.80
文教、工美、体育和娱乐用品制造业	Stationery, Education and Sports Goods	68.84	76.45
石油加工、炼焦和核燃料加工业	Petroleum Processing, Coking Products and Nuclear Fuel Processing	25.74	120.24
化学原料和化学制品制造业	Raw Chemical Material and Chemical Products	352.37	1285.25
医药制造业	Medical and pharmaceutical Products	131.84	688.11
化学纤维制造业	Chemical Fibers	2.13	20.87
橡胶和塑料制品业	Rubber and plastic products	36.34	364.45
非金属矿物制品业	Nonmetal Material Products	161.39	1156.18
黑色金属冶炼和压延加工业	Smelting and Pressing of Ferrous Metals	256.66	864.47
有色金属冶炼和压延加工业	Smelting and Pressing of Nonferrous Metals	93.21	212.63
金属制品业	Metal Products	57.78	437.11
通用设备制造业	Ordinary Machinery Manufacturing	252.47	580.06
专用设备制造业	Special Purpose Equipment Manufacturing	35.05	444.47
汽车制造业	Motor manufacturing	256.37	2945.24
铁路、船舶、航空航天和其他运输设备制造业	Railway,Watercraft,Aviation and other Transporlation Equipment manufacturing	79.12	242.05
电气机械和器材制造业	Electric Machinery and Equipment	101.07	639.76
计算机、通信和其他电子设备制造业	Telecommunication Computer,Equipment and Other Electronic Equipment Manufacturing	165.63	950.80
仪器仪表制造业	Instruments and Meters, Manufacturing	14.34	86.32
其他制造业	Other Manufacturing	6.69	38.62
废弃资源综合利用业	Waste Comprehensive Vtilization of Resources Industry	2.67	50.00
金属制品、机械和设备修理业	Metal products,Machinery and Equipment Repairing	2.47	13.37
电力、燃气及水的生产和供应业	**Electric Power, Gas and Water Production and Supply**	**943.21**	**2416.49**
电力、热力生产和供应业	Electric Power, Steam and Hot Water Production and Supply	826.58	2190.44
燃气生产和供应业	Gas Production and Supply	14.00	78.25
水的生产和供应业	Tap Water Production and Supply	102.63	147.80

(100 million Yuan)

实收资本 Assets Recevied	国家资本 National Assets	所有者权益合计 Total Rights of Owners			
		集体资本 Collective Assets	法人资本 Corperative Assets	个人资本 Individual Assets	港澳台资本 Assets from Hongkong, Maco and Taiwan Funded Enterprises
154.26	**46.68**	**6.62**	**38.79**	**62.13**	**0.02**
9.52	1.37	1.19	2.88	4.09	
37.54	23.09	1.75	5.94	6.76	
8.56	4.21	0.01	1.66	2.69	
80.70	0.89	3.36	28.16	48.24	0.02
14.96	14.85			0.11	
2.99	2.27	0.32	0.15	0.25	
8014.79	**1863.01**	**120.88**	**2595.78**	**2777.90**	**138.42**
385.39	10.96	10.47	138.13	199.02	8.05
133.90	8.26	0.83	49.58	56.54	4.51
182.44	8.04	1.73	39.50	87.91	15.09
45.26	26.08	1.05	18.13		
202.29	5.23	3.01	78.78	103.67	3.66
110.00	2.75	0.52	50.44	50.17	4.45
26.73		0.05	6.78	9.90	5.81
47.68	3.59	1.14	13.80	28.91	0.01
29.86		0.02	9.83	19.70	0.16
89.08	1.14	0.81	36.45	32.95	2.16
45.70	6.97	0.65	17.70	18.16	1.93
38.67	1.36	0.18	12.56	12.21	10.27
79.47	56.83	0.30	8.80	3.63	
913.89	497.76	12.60	191.75	173.40	6.11
190.30	19.57	7.31	88.78	56.63	12.05
12.82	0.11		1.93	2.51	
166.30	2.67	1.83	63.97	93.86	1.72
601.63	22.42	12.16	339.85	190.24	3.91
498.58	328.80	0.54	88.91	41.82	2.09
146.49	85.08	0.64	11.46	49.31	
221.45	37.84	4.79	89.67	78.80	5.27
238.74	51.42	5.33	90.76	77.56	4.06
223.61	28.53	3.68	126.58	54.72	1.38
1036.14	446.80	19.91	216.86	130.56	5.02
169.14	105.36	1.67	44.60	16.07	0.65
1640.92	38.56	19.08	426.74	1103.26	14.87
447.84	52.30	8.19	288.88	59.26	23.70
39.03	3.15	0.99	21.25	12.73	0.56
14.38	5.88	0.05	3.80	4.64	
28.55	4.53	0.49	14.72	7.87	0.95
8.53	1.01	0.85	4.78	1.89	
951.22	**647.50**	**12.67**	**153.99**	**97.47**	**11.76**
864.47	620.91	6.59	125.80	87.74	6.36
37.86	5.16	4.07	18.23	2.64	3.09
48.89	21.43	2.01	9.97	7.10	2.31

13-3 续表 6 continued

单位: 亿元

项 目	Item	所有者权益合计 Total owner 外商资本 Total Rights of the Owners Foreign Assets
总 计	Total	546.30
一、按登记注册类型分组:	Grouped by Type of Registration	
内资企业	Inner Funded Enterprises	20.47
国有企业	State Owned Enterprises	
中央企业	Central Enterprises	
地方企业	Local Enterprises	
集体企业	Collective-owned Enterprise	
股份合作企业	Share Holding Cooperative Enterprises	
联营企业	Joint Owned Enterprise	
国有联营企业	State Joint Ownership	
集体联营企业	Collective Joint Ownership	
国有与集体联营企业	Joint State- Collective Ownership	
其他联营企业	Other Joint Owned Enterprise	
有限责任公司	Responsibility Co. Ltd	13.27
国有独资公司	State Solely Funded Co.	
其他有限责任公司	Others	13.27
股份有限公司	Share Holding Co.Ltd.	5.67
私营企业	Private - owned enterprises	1.53
私营独资企业	Solely Private - owned enterprises	
私营合伙企业	Private Joint Venture	
私营有限责任公司	Private Responsibility Co. Ltd	1.53
私营股份有限公司	Private Share Holding Co.Ltd.	
其他企业	Others	
港、澳、台商投资企业	Hongkong, Macao and Taiwan Funded Enterprises	111.46
合资经营企业(港或澳、台资)	Joint Venture with Hongkong, Macao and Taiwan	33.00
合作经营企业(港或澳、台资)	Cooperate with Hongkong, Macao and Taiwan Funded	1.25
港澳台商独资经营企业	Enterprises Solely Funded by Hongkong, Macao and Taiwan Businessmen	69.06
港澳台商投资股份有限公司	Share Holding Co.Ltd. With Hongkong, Macao and Taiwan Investment	3.78
外商投资企业	Foreign Funded Enterprises	414.38
中外合资经营企业	Sino - Foreign Joint Funded Enterprises	259.64
中外合作经营企业	Sino - Foreign Cooperative Funded Enterprises	5.27
外资企业	Foreign Solely Funded Enterprises	135.69
外商投资股份有限公司	Foreign Funded Share Holding Co.Ltd.	13.29
二、在总计中:亏损企业	Of the Total: enterprises running under deficit	77.14
在总计中:国有控股企业	Of the Total: State-Owned Share Holding Enterprises	188.01
在总计中:农村工业	Of the Total: Rural Industry	
在总计中:轻工业	Of the Total: Light Industry	123.11
重工业	Heavy Industry	423.20
在总计中:大型企业	Of the Total: Large Scale Enterprises	277.53
中型企业	Medium Scale Enterprises	146.82
小型企业	Small Enterprises	121.96

(100 million Yuan)

营业收入 Proceeds Of Business	主营业务收入 Revenue of Major Business	营业成本 Operating Costs	主营业务成本 Cost of Major Business	营业税金及附加 Tax of Major Business	主营业务税金及附加 Tax of Major Business	其他业务收入 Revenue of Other Business	其他业务利润 Profit from Other Business	销售费用 Selling Expenses
46448.49	**45850.64**	**39459.85**	**38963.66**	**897.60**	**891.80**	**597.85**	**80.54**	**1346.46**
39657.01	39302.92	33823.84	33527.62	776.60	771.26	354.08	36.33	1118.48
2537.53	2525.36	2300.57	2278.76	9.59	9.16	12.17	1.67	37.38
2425.09	2415.49	2204.73	2184.44	9.09	8.73	9.60	0.98	33.53
112.44	109.86	95.84	94.32	0.50	0.43	2.57	0.69	3.85
110.61	110.41	96.33	96.21	1.40	1.40	0.20	0.01	3.08
12.54	12.41	10.58	10.56	0.08	0.08	0.13		0.57
4.93	4.93	3.81	3.81	0.09	0.09			0.16
3.16	3.16	2.45	2.45	0.04	0.04			0.04
0.41	0.41	0.40	0.40					
1.36	1.36	0.95	0.95	0.04	0.04			0.13
16198.50	15970.17	13687.05	13498.73	533.90	531.93	228.33	20.84	426.25
1942.77	1853.82	1270.80	1186.50	428.71	428.55	88.94	5.77	28.53
14255.73	14116.35	12416.25	12312.23	105.19	103.38	139.38	15.08	397.72
4808.06	4745.16	3851.97	3816.45	106.46	105.65	62.90	10.81	214.24
15919.77	15869.45	13816.46	13766.10	124.64	122.52	50.33	2.99	435.64
350.11	349.95	301.38	300.85	3.30	3.24	0.16		10.31
60.78	60.78	51.68	51.68	0.68	0.67			2.18
14392.70	14347.50	12510.53	12466.54	111.93	110.48	45.20	2.93	388.24
1116.19	1111.21	952.86	947.03	8.74	8.13	4.98	0.07	34.91
65.06	65.05	57.09	56.99	0.44	0.44	0.02	0.01	1.16
1980.28	1890.77	1658.66	1575.53	7.88	7.77	89.51	5.91	77.21
1031.12	985.25	854.56	811.67	4.26	4.21	45.87	3.70	39.35
9.54	9.52	8.40	8.39	0.04	0.04	0.02		0.49
858.32	816.13	738.28	698.93	3.06	3.00	42.19	1.72	31.38
35.44	34.12	29.56	28.74	0.19	0.19	1.32	0.49	0.80
4811.20	4656.95	3977.35	3860.51	113.12	112.77	154.25	38.30	150.78
3695.79	3556.10	3055.51	2949.24	104.47	104.35	139.70	35.96	106.73
57.59	57.25	51.48	51.46	0.37	0.37	0.34		0.59
841.51	829.16	699.11	690.80	6.16	6.07	12.35	2.05	28.91
215.42	213.54	170.80	168.55	2.11	1.96	1.87	0.29	14.52
2110.99	**2042.41**	**1977.10**	**1917.85**	**20.87**	**20.55**	**68.58**	**7.11**	**97.78**
11773.95	11458.88	9638.76	9381.31	625.66	624.02	315.07	60.62	284.96
168.19	168.19	149.09	149.09	1.63	1.62			4.28
16748.90	16627.42	13872.08	13773.85	480.49	478.12	121.47	7.92	618.51
29699.59	29223.22	25587.77	25189.81	417.11	413.68	476.37	72.62	727.96
16829.72	16431.11	13994.07	13675.54	686.33	685.05	398.61	57.85	482.69
10388.84	10272.27	8865.05	8762.01	71.13	69.18	116.56	14.94	303.88
19229.93	19147.26	16600.73	16526.11	140.13	137.57	82.67	7.75	559.89

13-3 续表 7 continued

单位:亿元

项 目	Item	所有者权益合计 Total owner 外商资本 Total Rights of the Owners Foreign Assets
按行业分	**Grouped by sector**	
采矿业	**Mining and Qarrying**	**0.02**
煤炭开采和洗选业	Coal Mining and Processing	
石油和天然气开采业	Petroleum and Natural Gas Extraction	
黑色金属矿采选业	Ferrous Metals Mining and Processing	
有色金属矿采选业	Non-ferrous Metals Mining and Processing	
非金属矿采选业	Non-metal Minerals Mining and Processing	0.02
开采辅助活动	Mining Auxiliary Activities	
其他采矿业	Other Minerals Mining and Processing	
制造业	**Manufacturing**	**518.46**
农副食品加工业	Food Processing	18.77
食品制造业	Food Production	13.83
酒、饮料和精制茶制造业	Wine,Beverage and Refined Tea Production	30.17
烟草制品业	Tobacco Processing	
纺织业	Textile Industry	7.93
纺织服装、服饰业	Textile,Garments, and Fashion Industry	1.67
皮革、毛皮、羽毛及其制品和制鞋业	Leather, Furs,Down and Related Products	4.20
木材加工和木、竹、藤、棕、草制品业	Timber Processing, Wood, Bamboo, Cane, Palm and Sraw Products	0.24
家具制造业	Furniture Manufacturing	0.16
造纸和纸制品业	Papermaking and Paper Products	15.57
印刷和记录媒介复制业	Printing and Record Processing	0.30
文教、工美、体育和娱乐用品制造业	Stationery, Education and Sports Goods	2.08
石油加工、炼焦和核燃料加工业	Petroleum Processing, Coking Products and Nuclear Fuel Processing	9.91
化学原料和化学制品制造业	Raw Chemical Material and Chemical Products	32.27
医药制造业	Medical and pharmaceutical Products	5.97
化学纤维制造业	Chemical Fibers	8.26
橡胶和塑料制品业	Rubber and plastic products	2.24
非金属矿物制品业	Nonmetal Material Products	33.04
黑色金属冶炼和压延加工业	Smelting and Pressing of Ferrous Metals	36.42
有色金属冶炼和压延加工业	Smelting and Pressing of Nonferrous Metals	
金属制品业	Metal Products	5.08
通用设备制造业	Ordinary Machinery Manufacturing	9.61
专用设备制造业	Special Purpose Equipment Manufacturing	8.71
汽车制造业	Motor manufacturing	216.99
铁路、船舶、航空航天和其他运输设备制造业	Railway,Watercraft,Aviation and other Transporlation Equipment manufacturing	0.78
电气机械和器材制造业	Electric Machinery and Equipment	38.40
计算机、通信和其他电子设备制造业	Telecommunication Computer,Equipment and Other Electronic Equipment Manufacturing	15.50
仪器仪表制造业	Instruments and Meters, Manufacturing	0.36
其他制造业	Other Manufacturing	
废弃资源综合利用业	Waste Comprehensive Vtilization of Resources Industry	
金属制品、机械和设备修理业	Metal products,Machinery and Equipment Repairing	
电力、燃气及水的生产和供应业	**Electric Power, Gas and Water Production and Supply**	**27.82**
电力、热力生产和供应业	Electric Power, Steam and Hot Water Production and Supply	17.07
燃气生产和供应业	Gas Production and Supply	4.67
水的生产和供应业	Tap Water Production and Supply	6.08

(100 million Yuan)

营业收入 Proceeds Of Business	主营业务收入 Revenue of Major Business	营业成本 Operating Costs	主营业务成本 Cost of Major Business	营业税金及附加 Tax of Major Business	主营业务税金及附加 Tax of Major Business	其他业务收入 Revenue of Other Business	其他业务利润 Profit from Other Business	销售费用 Selling Expenses
1016.93	**1001.50**	**865.74**	**849.25**	**17.67**	**17.51**	**15.43**	**0.31**	**32.95**
59.86	59.85	49.94	49.94	0.97	0.96	0.01		1.25
43.18	31.42	52.46	41.80	1.57	1.55	11.76		0.67
268.34	267.97	235.77	235.65	2.74	2.67	0.37	0.13	10.20
43.69	43.56	31.76	31.64	0.62	0.62	0.13		0.55
536.12	533.50	433.72	430.17	10.90	10.86	2.62	0.18	20.05
62.56	62.02	59.64	59.25	0.84	0.83	0.54		0.03
3.18	3.18	2.44	0.80	0.03	0.01			0.19
43587.44	**43032.83**	**37103.44**	**36641.70**	**863.96**	**858.73**	**554.61**	**72.66**	**1299.49**
4877.35	4865.69	4331.55	4319.48	20.68	20.44	11.66	0.65	109.23
1263.00	1251.21	1064.42	1056.16	7.21	7.17	11.78	0.61	58.88
1766.60	1744.17	1410.33	1402.61	28.11	27.73	22.43	0.56	122.17
632.27	609.93	152.40	130.37	361.01	361.01	22.34	0.27	9.40
2305.84	2300.71	1997.71	1992.77	18.85	17.91	5.12	0.26	59.41
965.66	964.06	844.02	841.35	7.14	7.08	1.60	0.47	26.35
230.95	230.11	207.69	206.85	1.07	1.01	0.84		4.30
443.23	441.43	383.10	381.41	5.16	5.00	1.80		11.45
199.19	198.41		169.54	1.18	1.17	0.77		6.79
536.83	534.78	470.80	469.53	3.07	3.03	2.06	0.33	17.14
367.62	366.60	300.97	299.18	2.98	2.98	1.02	0.35	11.72
213.02	212.25	180.62	179.82	1.63	1.63	0.77	0.05	5.94
894.51	870.16	713.79	689.55	141.93	141.93	24.35	2.94	3.79
4125.10	4085.00	3628.18	3595.93	24.67	24.37	40.10	3.00	115.34
1199.54	1196.91	896.87	894.94	7.20	6.97	2.63	0.63	104.95
74.61	74.41	66.59	66.59	0.35	0.35	0.20	0.16	1.44
1212.74	1206.64	1040.66	1036.43	8.45	8.44	6.11	0.41	32.91
3244.12	3236.63	2717.45	2712.34	32.19	31.90	7.50	1.12	114.20
1902.72	1806.41	1730.12	1636.22	7.59	7.50	96.31	2.57	28.21
1386.73	1382.22	1315.17	1311.74	2.22	2.22	4.51	0.79	8.00
1499.44	1471.79	1299.90	1274.15	9.75	9.67	27.65	0.36	49.32
1274.71	1269.58	1080.64	1075.92	7.63	7.23	5.13	0.51	39.39
1121.87	1114.69	965.77	959.74	6.59	6.43	7.18	0.48	34.84
6412.48	6237.58	5371.26	5244.32	127.31	126.45	174.90	45.71	182.45
656.65	648.92	588.09	570.09	4.04	3.72	7.73	0.58	9.49
1911.73	1865.58	1636.32	1603.40	15.09	14.76	46.15	4.97	54.91
2327.42	2310.99	2074.00	2060.02	6.87	6.72	16.44	4.35	63.16
188.46	187.01	150.72	149.99	1.17	1.10	1.45	0.10	8.11
146.10	145.21	121.85	121.43	1.82	1.82	0.89	0.17	3.97
160.97	158.08	152.50	150.25	0.75	0.75	2.89	0.05	1.64
45.97	45.65	39.63	39.60	0.25	0.25	0.32	0.20	0.62
1844.11	**1816.31**	**1490.67**	**1472.71**	**15.96**	**15.57**	**27.80**	**7.57**	**14.02**
1614.58	1595.15	1305.10	1292.31	14.43	14.12	19.43	5.42	3.41
152.86	149.13	123.41	121.08	0.95	0.91	3.73	0.76	5.59
76.67	72.03	62.16	59.33	0.58	0.54	4.64	1.39	5.02

13-3 续表 8 continued

单位: 亿元

项 目	Item	管理费用 Management Expense
总　计	**Total**	**1933.94**
一、按登记注册类型分组:	**Grouped by Type of Registration**	
内资企业	Inner Funded Enterprises	1621.72
国有企业	State Owned Enterprises	107.55
中央企业	Central Enterprises	99.37
地方企业	Local Enterprises	8.18
集体企业	Collective-owned Enterprise	5.26
股份合作企业	Share Holding Cooperative Enterprises	0.58
联营企业	Joint Owned Enterprise	0.29
国有联营企业	State Joint Ownership	
集体联营企业	Collective Joint Ownership	0.12
国有与集体联营企业	Joint State- Collective Ownership	0.03
其他联营企业	Other Joint Owned Enterprise	0.14
有限责任公司	Responsibility Co. Ltd	642.61
国有独资公司	State Solely Funded Co.	79.29
其他有限责任公司	Others	563.32
股份有限公司	Share Holding Co.Ltd.	285.30
私营企业	Private - owned enterprises	578.54
私营独资企业	Solely Private - owned enterprises	9.62
私营合伙企业	Private Joint Venture	2.89
私营有限责任公司	Private Responsibility Co. Ltd	522.03
私营股份有限公司	Private Share Holding Co.Ltd.	44.00
其他企业	Others	1.59
港、澳、台商投资企业	Hongkong, Macao and Taiwan Funded Enterprises	99.10
合资经营企业(港或澳、台资)	Joint Venture with Hongkong, Macao and Taiwan	65.17
合作经营企业(港或澳、台资)	Cooperate with Hongkong, Macao and Taiwan Funded	0.51
港澳台商独资经营企业	Enterprises Solely Funded by Hongkong, Macao and Taiwan Businessmen	31.28
港澳台商投资股份有限公司	Share Holding Co.Ltd. With Hongkong,	1.31
外商投资企业	Foreign Funded Enterprises	213.12
中外合资经营企业	Sino - Foreign Joint Funded Enterprises	155.56
中外合作经营企业	Sino - Foreign Cooperative Funded Enterprises	0.39
外资企业	Foreign Solely Funded Enterprises	44.72
外商投资股份有限公司	Foreign Funded Share Holding Co.Ltd.	12.22
二、在总计中:亏损企业	**Of the Total: enterprises running under deficit**	**149.61**
在总计中:国有控股企业	Of the Total: State-Owned Share Holding Enterprises	561.75
在总计中:农村工业	Of the Total: Rural Industry	6.20
在总计中:轻工业	Of the Total: Light Industry	686.41
重工业	Heavy Industry	1247.53
在总计中:大型企业	Of the Total: Large Scale Enterprises	701.53
中型企业	Medium Scale Enterprises	477.43
小型企业	Small Enterprises	754.98

(100 million Yuan)

税金 Tax	财务费用 Financial Expense	利息收入 Interest Income	利息支出 Interest Expense
96.35	**467.38**	**32.27**	**405.64**
86.20	431.81	33.47	364.38
5.76	51.66	7.45	56.45
5.41	50.76	7.42	55.76
0.34	0.91	0.03	0.69
0.16	0.51		0.41
	0.08		0.03
	0.12		0.01
	0.04		
	0.01		0.01
	0.07		
25.25	155.69	12.76	143.67
2.59	21.11	3.97	23.60
22.66	134.57	8.80	120.08
20.54	69.30	10.28	66.84
34.38	154.09	2.93	96.67
0.63	4.02	0.04	1.86
0.02	0.90	0.01	0.38
31.58	139.11	2.52	86.58
2.15	10.06	0.36	7.85
0.11	0.35	0.04	0.31
4.05	14.60	0.29	14.99
1.96	5.86	-0.56	8.39
0.03	0.23		0.22
1.85	7.62	0.10	5.50
0.15	0.63	0.01	0.47
6.10	20.96	-1.48	26.27
2.67	7.97	-1.84	15.95
0.02	0.38	0.03	0.40
2.63	5.50	0.12	3.24
0.78	7.11	0.21	6.69
5.17	**46.79**	**1.59**	**40.29**
16.24	146.54	22.50	172.67
0.30	1.71	0.46	1.24
50.82	141.47	6.55	108.47
45.53	325.91	25.73	297.17
35.85	174.94	23.22	194.53
21.39	97.74	4.47	86.23
39.11	194.70	4.59	124.88

13-3 续表 9 continued

单位: 亿元

项 目	Item	管理费用 Management Expense
按行业分	**Grouped by sector**	
采矿业	**Mining and Qarrying**	**53.62**
煤炭开采和洗选业	Coal Mining and Processing	3.53
石油和天然气开采业	Petroleum and Natural Gas Extraction	8.28
黑色金属矿采选业	Ferrous Metals Mining and Processing	10.05
有色金属矿采选业	Non-ferrous Metals Mining and Processing	4.32
非金属矿采选业	Non-metal Minerals Mining and Processing	22.56
开采辅助活动	Mining Auxiliary Activities	4.59
其他采矿业	Other Minerals Mining and Processing	0.28
制造业	**Manufacturing**	**1840.54**
农副食品加工业	Food Processing	143.98
食品制造业	Food Production	54.01
酒、饮料和精制茶制造业	Wine,Beverage and Refined Tea Production	77.70
烟草制品业	Tobacco Processing	19.70
纺织业	Textile Industry	85.28
纺织服装、服饰业	Textile,Garments, and Fashion Industry	34.56
皮革、毛皮、羽毛及其制品和制鞋业	Leather, Furs,Down and Related Products	8.01
木材加工和木、竹、藤、棕、草制品业	Timber Processing, Wood, Bamboo, Cane, Palm and Sraw Products	13.00
家具制造业	Furniture Manufacturing	6.92
造纸和纸制品业	Papermaking and Paper Products	17.45
印刷和记录媒介复制业	Printing and Record Processing	27.72
文教、工美、体育和娱乐用品制造业	Stationery, Education and Sports Goods	9.66
石油加工、炼焦和核燃料加工业	Petroleum Processing, Coking Products and Nuclear Fuel Processing	14.96
化学原料和化学制品制造业	Raw Chemical Material and Chemical Products	151.26
医药制造业	Medical and pharmaceutical Products	87.45
化学纤维制造业	Chemical Fibers	2.50
橡胶和塑料制品业	Rubber and plastic products	43.37
非金属矿物制品业	Nonmetal Material Products	132.27
黑色金属冶炼和压延加工业	Smelting and Pressing of Ferrous Metals	70.43
有色金属冶炼和压延加工业	Smelting and Pressing of Nonferrous Metals	30.18
金属制品业	Metal Products	65.09
通用设备制造业	Ordinary Machinery Manufacturing	69.40
专用设备制造业	Special Purpose Equipment Manufacturing	58.69
汽车制造业	Motor manufacturing	327.39
铁路、船舶、航空航天和其他运输设备制造业	Railway,Watercraft,Aviation and other Transporlation Equipment manufacturing	34.62
电气机械和器材制造业	Electric Machinery and Equipment	102.36
计算机、通信和其他电子设备制造业	Telecommunication Computer,Equipment and Other Electronic Equipment Manufacturing	125.53
仪器仪表制造业	Instruments and Meters, Manufacturing	14.14
其他制造业	Other Manufacturing	6.14
废弃资源综合利用业	Waste Comprehensive Vtilization of Resources Industry	4.00
金属制品、机械和设备修理业	Metal products,Machinery and Equipment Repairing	2.75
电力、燃气及水的生产和供应业	**Electric Power, Gas and Water Production and Supply**	**39.78**
电力、热力生产和供应业	Electric Power, Steam and Hot Water Production and Supply	26.87
燃气生产和供应业	Gas Production and Supply	5.21
水的生产和供应业	Tap Water Production and Supply	7.70

(100 million Yuan)

税金 Tax	财务费用 Financial Expense	利息收入 Interest Income	利息支出 Interest Expense
1.76	**13.05**	**0.80**	**9.46**
0.03	0.26		0.22
-0.13	1.34	0.02	1.33
0.57	2.66	0.14	1.91
0.14	0.40	0.02	0.35
1.12	7.88	0.54	4.96
0.03	0.45	0.09	0.67
	0.06		0.02
91.03	**384.54**	**30.62**	**333.10**
10.15	37.81	1.08	28.31
4.80	7.89	0.71	6.93
12.39	14.13	1.14	12.14
1.17	-0.79	0.32	
5.45	28.65	0.22	17.95
2.28	8.60	0.31	6.50
0.62	1.76		0.94
0.92	4.84	0.08	3.21
0.24	1.76	0.01	1.26
0.88	5.32	1.19	5.12
1.37	2.62	-0.11	1.96
0.53	2.40	0.02	1.15
0.23	2.45	2.85	5.20
6.88	50.70	0.90	44.10
6.67	13.14	1.40	13.31
0.08	0.93	0.03	0.62
2.04	12.73	0.21	10.25
6.62	40.19	1.43	27.43
5.97	45.47	4.86	44.35
0.76	8.24	5.05	10.27
2.25	15.13	1.04	11.50
2.25	21.28	1.10	10.26
1.96	11.72	0.40	8.55
7.47	14.64	7.11	27.27
0.52	8.47	1.48	9.86
3.28	13.89	0.23	10.45
2.12	5.76	-2.62	11.04
0.60	1.72	0.05	1.47
0.32	0.91	0.06	0.31
0.18	1.37	0.01	0.71
0.03	0.82	0.09	0.69
3.55	**69.78**	**0.86**	**63.08**
2.80	65.83	0.75	60.36
0.21	1.57	0.01	1.45
0.54	2.39	0.10	1.27

13-3 续表 10 continued

单位: 亿元

项 目	Item	营业利润 Operating Profit
总 计	**Total**	**2517.81**
一、按登记注册类型分组:	**Grouped by Type of Registration**	
内资企业	Inner Funded Enterprises	2054.04
国有企业	State Owned Enterprises	51.01
中央企业	Central Enterprises	47.00
地方企业	Local Enterprises	4.00
集体企业	Collective-owned Enterprise	3.98
股份合作企业	Share Holding Cooperative Enterprises	0.64
联营企业	Joint Owned Enterprise	0.46
国有联营企业	State Joint Ownership	
集体联营企业	Collective Joint Ownership	0.47
国有与集体联营企业	Joint State- Collective Ownership	-0.04
其他联营企业	Other Joint Owned Enterprise	0.03
有限责任公司	Responsibility Co. Ltd	738.59
国有独资公司	State Solely Funded Co.	118.04
其他有限责任公司	Others	620.55
股份有限公司	Share Holding Co.Ltd.	447.94
私营企业	Private - owned enterprises	807.61
私营独资企业	Solely Private - owned enterprises	21.44
私营合伙企业	Private Joint Venture	2.44
私营有限责任公司	Private Responsibility Co. Ltd	719.24
私营股份有限公司	Private Share Holding Co.Ltd.	64.49
其他企业	Others	3.81
港、澳、台商投资企业	Hongkong, Macao and Taiwan Funded Enterprises	121.23
合资经营企业(港或澳、台资)	Joint Venture with Hongkong, Macao and Taiwan	59.38
合作经营企业(港或澳、台资)	Cooperate with Hongkong, Macao and Taiwan Funded	0.01
港澳台商独资经营企业	Enterprises Solely Funded by Hongkong, Macao and Taiwan Businessmen	45.80
港澳台商投资股份有限公司	Share Holding Co.Ltd. With Hongkong, Macao and Taiwan Investment	2.85
外商投资企业	Foreign Funded Enterprises	342.54
中外合资经营企业	Sino - Foreign Joint Funded Enterprises	269.67
中外合作经营企业	Sino - Foreign Cooperative Funded Enterprises	4.37
外资企业	Foreign Solely Funded Enterprises	58.10
外商投资股份有限公司	Foreign Funded Share Holding Co.Ltd.	10.21
二、在总计中:亏损企业	**Of the Total: enterprises running under deficit**	**-196.22**
在总计中:国有控股企业	Of the Total: State-Owned Share Holding Enterprises	683.75
在总计中:农村工业	Of the Total: Rural Industry	5.20
在总计中:轻工业	Of the Total: Light Industry	960.64
重工业	Heavy Industry	1557.17
在总计中:大型企业	Of the Total: Large Scale Enterprises	984.06
中型企业	Medium Scale Enterprises	571.95
小型企业	Small Enterprises	961.80

(100 million Yuan)

政府补贴 subsidy	营业外收入 Non-operating Income	营业外支出 Non-operating Expense	利润总额 Total Profit	应交所得税 Income Tax	亏损企业亏损总额 Total Loss of Enterprises Running under Deficit
106.51	**254.45**	**58.41**	**2713.46**	**329.74**	**183.93**
73.17	206.65	47.99	2212.32	237.18	151.05
6.80	34.89	6.12	79.78	11.17	10.24
6.75	34.37	5.92	75.46	10.60	9.15
0.05	0.52	0.21	4.32	0.56	1.09
0.08	0.15	0.07	4.05	0.34	0.65
	0.01	0.04	0.61		0.03
0.04	0.04	0.01	0.49		
		0.01	0.46		
0.04	0.04		0.01		
			0.03		
34.07	110.57	21.99	826.79	117.33	67.11
3.56	11.35	2.63	126.76	34.96	10.46
30.51	99.22	19.37	700.03	82.37	56.65
25.38	44.77	7.52	485.18	63.21	56.46
6.77	16.20	12.23	811.58	44.90	16.56
	0.01	0.19	21.27	0.55	0.12
		0.11	2.34	0.07	
5.94	13.25	9.26	723.23	41.44	14.83
0.83	2.93	2.67	64.75	2.84	1.61
0.03	0.03		3.85	0.23	
4.62	11.41	3.34	129.30	20.73	7.00
1.86	7.26	1.73	64.92	9.52	2.51
	0.02		0.02	-0.07	0.14
0.75	2.04	1.20	46.64	7.82	4.22
1.31	1.33	0.01	4.17	0.52	
28.72	36.39	7.08	371.84	71.83	25.88
26.19	31.78	4.08	297.37	57.28	18.86
0.01	0.02	0.07	4.32	1.08	
1.05	2.83	1.54	59.40	10.92	7.00
1.47	1.74	1.39	10.55	2.52	0.02
11.59	**20.29**	**8.01**	**-183.93**	**0.18**	**183.93**
69.56	130.35	20.98	793.12	154.20	114.21
0.01	0.05	0.09	5.15	0.50	0.49
15.20	40.19	21.03	979.42	110.37	33.66
91.32	214.25	37.38	1734.04	219.37	150.28
65.19	163.87	27.50	1120.44	179.37	86.55
23.09	52.47	11.66	612.75	78.25	46.49
18.24	38.11	19.25	980.28	72.12	50.90

13-3 续表 11 continued

单位: 亿元

项 目	Item	营业利润 Operating Profit
按行业分	**Grouped by sector**	
采矿业	**Mining and Qarrying**	**28.45**
煤炭开采和洗选业	Coal Mining and Processing	3.90
石油和天然气开采业	Petroleum and Natural Gas Extraction	-24.30
黑色金属矿采选业	Ferrous Metals Mining and Processing	6.87
有色金属矿采选业	Non-ferrous Metals Mining and Processing	6.03
非金属矿采选业	Non-metal Minerals Mining and Processing	39.75
开采辅助活动	Mining Auxiliary Activities	-4.00
其他采矿业	Other Minerals Mining and Processing	0.19
制造业	**Manufacturing**	**2266.55**
农副食品加工业	Food Processing	232.10
食品制造业	Food Production	72.36
酒、饮料和精制茶制造业	Wine,Beverage and Refined Tea Production	117.04
烟草制品业	Tobacco Processing	91.52
纺织业	Textile Industry	116.13
纺织服装、服饰业	Textile,Garments, and Fashion Industry	45.18
皮革、毛皮、羽毛及其制品和制鞋业	Leather, Furs,Down and Related Products	8.30
木材加工和木、竹、藤、棕、草制品业	Timber Processing, Wood, Bamboo, Cane, Palm and Sraw Products	24.33
家具制造业	Furniture Manufacturing	12.24
造纸和纸制品业	Papermaking and Paper Products	23.17
印刷和记录媒介复制业	Printing and Record Processing	21.53
文教、工美、体育和娱乐用品制造业	Stationery, Education and Sports Goods	12.49
石油加工、炼焦和核燃料加工业	Petroleum Processing, Coking Products and Nuclear Fuel Processing	20.25
化学原料和化学制品制造业	Raw Chemical Material and Chemical Products	165.08
医药制造业	Medical and pharmaceutical Products	97.83
化学纤维制造业	Chemical Fibers	3.02
橡胶和塑料制品业	Rubber and plastic products	72.87
非金属矿物制品业	Nonmetal Material Products	209.03
黑色金属冶炼和压延加工业	Smelting and Pressing of Ferrous Metals	18.23
有色金属冶炼和压延加工业	Smelting and Pressing of Nonferrous Metals	10.03
金属制品业	Metal Products	59.30
通用设备制造业	Ordinary Machinery Manufacturing	58.49
专用设备制造业	Special Purpose Equipment Manufacturing	42.53
汽车制造业	Motor manufacturing	555.23
铁路、船舶、航空航天和其他运输设备制造业	Railway,Watercraft,Aviation and other Transporlation Equipment manufacturing	15.20
电气机械和器材制造业	Electric Machinery and Equipment	89.63
计算机、通信和其他电子设备制造业	Telecommunication Computer,Equipment and Other Electronic Equipment Manufacturing	47.27
仪器仪表制造业	Instruments and Meters, Manufacturing	12.64
其他制造业	Other Manufacturing	11.25
废弃资源综合利用业	Waste Comprehensive Vtilization of Resources Industry	0.12
金属制品、机械和设备修理业	Metal products,Machinery and Equipment Repairing	2.14
电力、燃气及水的生产和供应业	**Electric Power, Gas and Water Production and Supply**	**222.82**
电力、热力生产和供应业	Electric Power, Steam and Hot Water Production and Supply	205.88
燃气生产和供应业	Gas Production and Supply	16.67
水的生产和供应业	Tap Water Production and Supply	0.27

(100 million Yuan)

补贴收入 Income from subsidy	营业外收入 Non-operating Income	营业外支出 Non-operating Expense	利润总额 Total Profit	应交所得税 Income Tax	亏损企业亏损总额 Total Loss of Enterprises Running
1.08	**1.59**	**2.87**	**27.17**	**4.41**	**32.89**
	0.04	0.02	3.92	0.24	0.18
0.22	0.27	1.77	-25.81	-0.56	25.81
0.14	0.17	0.46	6.58	1.30	1.70
	0.04	0.25	5.82	1.00	0.08
0.38	0.61	0.29	40.06	1.97	1.43
0.33	0.39	0.05	-3.65	0.44	3.68
	0.07	0.02	0.25	0.03	
87.80	**226.06**	**50.51**	**2441.71**	**270.34**	**137.84**
3.15	6.27	5.30	233.07	13.01	3.80
0.88	2.17	0.64	73.88	8.23	1.55
1.76	6.03	6.70	116.37	19.27	3.97
0.23	0.42	1.18	90.76	25.05	0.05
0.68	6.15	0.67	121.23	8.93	3.40
0.31	0.81	0.82	45.17	3.53	1.44
0.05	0.35	0.25	8.40	0.51	0.10
0.78	1.30	0.16	25.47	1.23	0.30
0.04	0.07	0.03	12.28	0.74	0.24
1.36	2.35	0.33	25.18	3.43	2.14
0.64	1.03	0.40	22.16	3.15	1.25
0.33	0.53	0.24	12.77	1.19	0.40
0.24	0.78	1.15	19.89	4.90	0.74
7.54	16.18	5.86	175.40	23.48	21.49
2.25	5.04	2.26	100.61	9.56	2.97
0.04	0.13	0.04	3.11	0.35	0.03
1.34	2.18	0.82	74.22	6.29	1.04
5.70	8.93	4.74	213.23	15.76	4.21
0.48	22.76	3.67	37.33	7.74	6.53
0.61	1.82	0.52	11.33	1.67	1.04
0.83	8.18	1.67	65.82	5.74	5.73
2.35	7.78	1.39	64.89	4.88	2.77
1.90	3.87	0.62	45.79	5.20	12.05
32.25	42.76	5.97	592.01	71.94	28.49
2.53	3.64	0.25	18.59	2.50	9.14
4.14	8.91	2.22	96.33	11.45	15.98
12.25	60.07	2.26	105.07	8.27	4.73
1.54	2.08	0.17	14.55	1.32	1.00
0.21	0.53	0.06	11.72	0.60	0.02
1.35	2.81	0.10	2.82	0.23	0.98
0.02	0.15	0.02	2.27	0.21	0.25
17.64	**26.80**	**5.04**	**244.58**	**54.99**	**13.20**
17.08	24.03	3.93	225.98	50.95	9.20
0.05	0.80	0.86	16.61	3.54	0.45
0.51	1.98	0.25	2.00	0.50	3.55

13-3 续表 12 continued

单位: 亿元 (100 million Yuan)

项 目	Item	利税总额 Total Profit	本年应付职工薪酬 Wages Welfarism payable This Year
总 计	**Total**	**4754.74**	**2313.13**
一、按登记注册类型分组:	**Grouped by Type of Registration**		
内资企业	Inner Funded Enterprises	3923.45	1941.81
国有企业	State Owned Enterprises	159.96	299.80
中央企业	Central Enterprises	153.59	284.78
地方企业	Local Enterprises	6.38	15.02
集体企业	Collective-owned Enterprise	8.36	5.96
股份合作企业	Share Holding Cooperative Enterprises	0.90	0.65
联营企业	Joint Owned Enterprise	0.73	0.29
国有联营企业	State Joint Ownership		
集体联营企业	Collective Joint Ownership	0.63	0.08
国有与集体联营企业	Joint State- Collective Ownership	0.04	0.12
其他联营企业	Other Joint Owned Enterprise	0.07	0.09
有限责任公司	Responsibility Co. Ltd	1769.42	768.52
国有独资公司	State Solely Funded Co.	676.70	90.35
其他有限责任公司	Others	1092.72	678.17
股份有限公司	Share Holding Co.Ltd.	755.38	297.83
私营企业	Private - owned enterprises	1223.05	566.53
私营独资企业	Solely Private - owned enterprises	29.46	12.60
私营合伙企业	Private Joint Venture	3.99	2.17
私营有限责任公司	Private Responsibility Co. Ltd	1092.96	510.64
私营股份有限公司	Private Share Holding Co.Ltd.	96.64	41.11
其他企业	Others	5.65	2.23
港、澳、台商投资企业	Hongkong, Macao and Taiwan Funded Enterprises	188.96	99.10
合资经营企业(港或澳、台资)	Joint Venture with Hongkong, Macao and Taiwan	96.63	57.95
合作经营企业(港或澳、台资)	Cooperate with Hongkong, Macao and Taiwan Funded	0.28	0.52
港澳台商独资经营企业	Enterprises Solely Funded by Hongkong, Macao and Taiwan Businessmen	70.36	37.41
港澳台商投资股份有限公司	Share Holding Co.Ltd. With Hongkong, Macao and Taiwan Investment	5.09	2.13
外商投资企业	Foreign Funded Enterprises	642.34	272.21
中外合资经营企业	Sino - Foreign Joint Funded Enterprises	524.63	200.56
中外合作经营企业	Sino - Foreign Cooperative Funded Enterprises	8.08	1.35
外资企业	Foreign Solely Funded Enterprises	85.61	49.27
外商投资股份有限公司	Foreign Funded Share Holding Co.Ltd.	23.79	20.93
二、在总计中:亏损企业	**Of the Total: enterprises running under deficit**	**-123.06**	**198.24**
在总计中:国有控股企业	Of the Total: State-Owned Share Holding Enterprises	1868.09	824.73
在总计中:农村工业	Of the Total: Rural Industry	9.27	6.55
在总计中:轻工业	Of the Total: Light Industry	1872.41	748.52
重工业	Heavy Industry	2882.33	1564.61
在总计中:大型企业	Of the Total: Large Scale Enterprises	2339.27	1098.51
中型企业	Medium Scale Enterprises	940.96	576.81
小型企业	Small Enterprises	1474.51	637.80

13-3 续表 13 continued

单位: 亿元

项 目	Item	利税总额 Total Profit	本年应付职工薪酬 Wages Welfarism Payable this year
按行业分	**Grouped by sector**		
采矿业	**Mining and Qarrying**	**87.18**	**59.50**
煤炭开采和洗选业	Coal Mining and Processing	7.33	6.33
石油和天然气开采业	Petroleum and Natural Gas Extraction	-12.51	13.53
黑色金属矿采选业	Ferrous Metals Mining and Processing	16.71	8.38
有色金属矿采选业	Non-ferrous Metals Mining and Processing	8.78	3.67
非金属矿采选业	Non-metal Minerals Mining and Processing	65.86	18.33
开采辅助活动	Mining Auxiliary Activities	0.44	8.86
其他采矿业	Other Minerals Mining and Processing	0.57	0.42
制造业	**Manufacturing**	**4299.24**	**2088.12**
农副食品加工业	Food Processing	311.01	128.52
食品制造业	Food Production	112.62	51.38
酒、饮料和精制茶制造业	Wine,Beverage and Refined Tea Production	184.64	72.18
烟草制品业	Tobacco Processing	535.43	21.10
纺织业	Textile Industry	191.12	128.80
纺织服装、服饰业	Textile,Garments, and Fashion Industry	69.06	81.41
皮革、毛皮、羽毛及其制品和制鞋业	Leather, Furs,Down and Related Products	13.51	13.09
木材加工和木、竹、藤、棕、草制品业	Timber Processing, Wood, Bamboo, Cane, Palm and Sraw Products	39.06	17.98
家具制造业	Furniture Manufacturing	16.97	14.36
造纸和纸制品业	Papermaking and Paper Products	39.39	27.78
印刷和记录媒介复制业	Printing and Record Processing	35.63	22.56
文教、工美、体育和娱乐用品制造业	Stationery, Education and Sports Goods	18.09	10.27
石油加工、炼焦和核燃料加工业	Petroleum Processing, Coking Products and Nuclear Fuel Processing	192.18	35.14
化学原料和化学制品制造业	Raw Chemical Material and Chemical Products	279.07	123.57
医药制造业	Medical and pharmaceutical Products	157.47	67.16
化学纤维制造业	Chemical Fibers	4.72	3.42
橡胶和塑料制品业	Rubber and plastic products	112.68	49.77
非金属矿物制品业	Nonmetal Material Products	326.17	135.77
黑色金属冶炼和压延加工业	Smelting and Pressing of Ferrous Metals	96.00	153.52
有色金属冶炼和压延加工业	Smelting and Pressing of Nonferrous Metals	23.04	42.40
金属制品业	Metal Products	102.51	60.59
通用设备制造业	Ordinary Machinery Manufacturing	99.37	67.11
专用设备制造业	Special Purpose Equipment Manufacturing	75.38	68.92
汽车制造业	Motor manufacturing	892.92	369.64
铁路、船舶、航空航天和其他运输设备制造业	Railway,Watercraft,Aviation and other Transporlation Equipment manufacturing	34.44	50.67
电气机械和器材制造业	Electric Machinery and Equipment	147.86	91.53
计算机、通信和其他电子设备制造业	Telecommunication Computer,Equipment and Other Electronic Equipment Manufacturing	144.05	145.62
仪器仪表制造业	Instruments and Meters, Manufacturing	20.34	16.40
其他制造业	Other Manufacturing	16.58	8.20
废弃资源综合利用业	Waste Comprehensive Vtilization of Resources Industry	4.91	4.71
金属制品、机械和设备修理业	Metal products,Machinery and Equipment Repairing	3.02	4.56
电力、燃气及水的生产和供应业	**Electric Power, Gas and Water Production and Supply**	**368.32**	**165.51**
电力、热力生产和供应业	Electric Power, Steam and Hot Water Production and Supply	342.34	147.23
燃气生产和供应业	Gas Production and Supply	21.50	7.26
水的生产和供应业	Tap Water Production and Supply	4.48	11.02

13-3 续表 14 continued

单位: 亿元 (100 million Yuan)

项 目	Item	应交税金及附加 Tax and Extra Charges	本年应交增值税 Value Added Payable of the Current Year	全部从业人员年平均人数(万人) Average Number of Empolyment of the Current Year (10000 persons)
总 计	**Total**	**2467.37**	**1143.68**	**339.51**
一、按登记注册类型分组:	**Grouped by Type of Registration**			
内资企业	Inner Funded Enterprises	2034.50	934.52	296.15
国有企业	State Owned Enterprises	97.11	70.59	23.98
中央企业	Central Enterprises	94.15	69.04	21.87
地方企业	Local Enterprises	2.97	1.56	2.11
集体企业	Collective-owned Enterprise	4.80	2.90	1.43
股份合作企业	Share Holding Cooperative Enterprises	0.29	0.20	0.14
联营企业	Joint Owned Enterprise	0.25	0.16	0.07
国有联营企业	State Joint Ownership			
集体联营企业	Collective Joint Ownership	0.18	0.13	0.03
国有与集体联营企业	Joint State- Collective Ownership	0.03	0.03	0.03
其他联营企业	Other Joint Owned Enterprise	0.04		0.01
有限责任公司	Responsibility Co. Ltd	1085.20	408.73	117.50
国有独资公司	State Solely Funded Co.	587.48	121.23	9.71
其他有限责任公司	Others	497.72	287.50	107.80
股份有限公司	Share Holding Co.Ltd.	353.95	163.74	37.55
私营企业	Private - owned enterprises	490.75	286.83	114.89
私营独资企业	Solely Private - owned enterprises	9.38	4.90	2.47
私营合伙企业	Private Joint Venture	1.73	0.97	0.31
私营有限责任公司	Private Responsibility Co. Ltd	442.76	257.80	103.60
私营股份有限公司	Private Share Holding Co.Ltd.	36.89	23.16	8.52
其他企业	Others	2.15	1.36	0.57
港、澳、台商投资企业	Hongkong, Macao and Taiwan Funded Enterprises	84.45	51.78	16.80
合资经营企业(港或澳、台资)	Joint Venture with Hongkong, Macao and Taiwan	43.20	27.45	8.51
合作经营企业(港或澳、台资)	Cooperate with Hongkong, Macao and Taiwan Funded	0.21	0.22	0.09
港澳台商独资经营企业	Enterprises Solely Funded by Hongkong, Macao and Taiwan Businessmen	33.39	20.66	7.76
港澳台商投资股份有限公司	Share Holding Co.Ltd. With Hongkong, Macao and Taiwan Investment	1.58	0.73	0.31
外商投资企业	Foreign Funded Enterprises	348.42	157.38	26.56
中外合资经营企业	Sino - Foreign Joint Funded Enterprises	287.21	122.80	16.69
中外合作经营企业	Sino - Foreign Cooperative Funded Enterprises	4.86	3.39	0.17
外资企业	Foreign Solely Funded Enterprises	39.76	20.06	7.69
外商投资股份有限公司	Foreign Funded Share Holding Co.Ltd.	16.54	11.13	1.99
二、在总计中:亏损企业	**Of the Total: enterprises running under deficit**	**66.22**	**40.00**	**31.91**
在总计中:国有控股企业	Of the Total: State-Owned Share Holding Enterprises	1245.41	449.31	76.98
在总计中:农村工业	Of the Total: Rural Industry	4.92	2.49	1.43
在总计中:轻工业	Of the Total: Light Industry	1054.18	412.50	134.37
重工业	Heavy Industry	1413.19	731.18	205.14
在总计中:大型企业	Of the Total: Large Scale Enterprises	1434.06	532.51	114.17
中型企业	Medium Scale Enterprises	427.85	257.08	92.17
小型企业	Small Enterprises	605.46	354.10	133.16

13-3 续表 15 continued

单位: 亿元 (100 million Yuan)

项 目	Item	应交税金及附加 Tax and Extra Charges	本年应交增值税 Value Added Payable of the Current Year	全部从业人员年平均人数(万人) Average Number of Empolyment of the Current Year (10000 persons)
按行业分	**Grouped by sector**			
采矿业	**Mining and Qarrying**	**66.18**	**42.34**	**11.50**
煤炭开采和洗选业	Coal Mining and Processing	3.68	2.44	1.34
石油和天然气开采业	Petroleum and Natural Gas Extraction	12.61	11.73	1.50
黑色金属矿采选业	Ferrous Metals Mining and Processing	12.00	7.39	2.15
有色金属矿采选业	Non-ferrous Metals Mining and Processing	4.10	2.34	0.62
非金属矿采选业	Non-metal Minerals Mining and Processing	28.89	14.90	4.37
开采辅助活动	Mining Auxiliary Activities	4.56	3.25	1.42
其他采矿业	Other Minerals Mining and Processing	0.35	0.29	0.11
制造业	**Manufacturing**	**2218.90**	**993.56**	**313.00**
农副食品加工业	Food Processing	101.09	57.25	22.37
食品制造业	Food Production	51.77	31.53	10.09
酒、饮料和精制茶制造业	Wine,Beverage and Refined Tea Production	99.92	40.15	10.94
烟草制品业	Tobacco Processing	470.90	83.67	0.83
纺织业	Textile Industry	84.28	51.05	25.37
纺织服装、服饰业	Textile,Garments, and Fashion Industry	29.70	16.75	16.55
皮革、毛皮、羽毛及其制品和制鞋业	Leather, Furs,Down and Related Products	6.24	4.04	3.79
木材加工和木、竹、藤、棕、草制品业	Timber Processing, Wood, Bamboo, Cane, Palm and Sraw Products	15.72	8.42	3.95
家具制造业	Furniture Manufacturing	5.66	3.51	2.05
造纸和纸制品业	Papermaking and Paper Products	18.52	11.14	4.34
印刷和记录媒介复制业	Printing and Record Processing	18.00	10.49	3.41
文教、工美、体育和娱乐用品制造业	Stationery, Education and Sports Goods	7.04	3.69	2.53
石油加工、炼焦和核燃料加工业	Petroleum Processing, Coking Products and Nuclear Fuel Processing	177.43	30.36	1.05
化学原料和化学制品制造业	Raw Chemical Material and Chemical Products	134.03	79.00	21.37
医药制造业	Medical and pharmaceutical Products	73.09	49.66	11.37
化学纤维制造业	Chemical Fibers	2.04	1.27	0.58
橡胶和塑料制品业	Rubber and plastic products	46.78	30.01	10.44
非金属矿物制品业	Nonmetal Material Products	135.32	80.76	25.53
黑色金属冶炼和压延加工业	Smelting and Pressing of Ferrous Metals	72.38	51.08	12.10
有色金属冶炼和压延加工业	Smelting and Pressing of Nonferrous Metals	14.13	9.48	4.40
金属制品业	Metal Products	44.68	26.95	11.40
通用设备制造业	Ordinary Machinery Manufacturing	41.62	26.86	11.63
专用设备制造业	Special Purpose Equipment Manufacturing	36.76	23.00	10.76
汽车制造业	Motor manufacturing	380.31	173.60	41.47
铁路、船舶、航空航天和其他运输设备制造业	Railway,Watercraft,Aviation and other Transporlation Equipment manufacturing	18.87	11.81	7.09
电气机械和器材制造业	Electric Machinery and Equipment	66.26	36.44	15.36
计算机、通信和其他电子设备制造业	Telecommunication Computer,Equipment and Other Electronic Equipment Manufacturing	49.37	32.11	16.36
仪器仪表制造业	Instruments and Meters, Manufacturing	7.70	4.62	2.56
其他制造业	Other Manufacturing	5.78	3.04	1.51
废弃资源综合利用业	Waste Comprehensive Vtilization of Resources Industry	2.50	1.34	0.93
金属制品、机械和设备修理业	Metal products,Machinery and Equipment Repairing	0.98	0.49	0.87
电力、燃气及水的生产和供应业	**Electric Power, Gas and Water Production and Supply**	**182.28**	**107.78**	**15.01**
电力、热力生产和供应业	Electric Power, Steam and Hot Water Production and Supply	170.12	101.93	11.84
燃气生产和供应业	Gas Production and Supply	8.64	3.94	0.97
水的生产和供应业	Tap Water Production and Supply	3.53	1.91	2.19

13-4 国有控股工业企业单位数和主要经济指标 (2016)

单位: 亿元

项 目	Item	企业单位数(个) Number of Enterprises(unit)	工业总产值(当年价格) Total Output Value (current price)
总 计	**Total**	**772**	**11310.53**
在总计中:	Of the Total		
亏损企业	Enterprises running under Deficit	161	744.16
在总计中:	Of the Total:		
中央企业	Central Enterprises	42	2387.41
地方企业	Local Enterprises	82	113.95
在总计中:	Of the Total:		
轻工业	Light Industry	218	1348.68
重工业	Heavy Industry	554	9961.86
在总计中:	Of the Total:		
大型企业	Large Scale Enterprises	117	9080.34
中型企业	Medium Scale Enterprises	213	1354.43
小型企业	Small Enterprises	442	875.76
按行业分	Grouped by sector		
采矿业	**Mining and Qarrying**	**21**	**150.14**
煤炭开采和洗选业	Coal Mining and Processing	2	1.64
石油和天然气开采业	Petroleum and Natural Gas Extraction	1	31.43
黑色金属矿采选业	Ferrous Metals Mining and Processing	4	40.21
有色金属矿采选业	Non-ferrous Metals Mining and Processing	2	9.08
非金属矿采选业	Non-metal Minerals Mining and Processing	9	8.51
开采辅助活动	Mining Auxiliary Activities	3	59.26
其他采矿业	Other Minerals Mining and Processing		
制造业	**Manufacturing**	**598**	**9614.18**
农副食品加工业	Food Processing	46	185.72
食品制造业	Food Production	12	43.64
酒、饮料和精制茶制造业	Wine,Beverage and Refined Tea Production	12	26.86
烟草制品业	Tobacco Processing	6	583.13
纺织业	Textile Industry	18	70.40
纺织服装、服饰业	Textile,Garments, and Fashion Industry	7	20.08
皮革、毛皮、羽毛及其制品和制鞋业	Leather, Furs,Down and Related Products	1	3.38
木材加工和木、竹、藤、棕、草制品业	Timber Processing, Wood, Bamboo, Cane, Palm and Sraw Products	6	17.83
家具制造业	Furniture Manufacturing		
造纸和纸制品业	Papermaking and Paper Products	3	11.80
印刷和记录媒介复制业	Printing and Record Processing	16	37.50
文教、工美、体育和娱乐用品制造业	Stationery, Education and Sports Goods	5	11.42
石油加工、炼焦和核燃料加工业	Petroleum Processing, Coking Products and Nuclear Fuel Processing	8	507.09
化学原料和化学制品制造业	Raw Chemical Material and Chemical Products	51	1111.01
医药制造业	Medical and pharmaceutical Products	20	97.24
化学纤维制造业	Chemical Fibers		
橡胶和塑料制品业	Rubber and plastic products	7	33.92
非金属矿物制品业	Nonmetal Material Products	54	141.74
黑色金属冶炼和压延加工业	Smelting and Pressing of Ferrous Metals	18	866.60
有色金属冶炼和压延加工业	Smelting and Pressing of Nonferrous Metals	4	396.35
金属制品业	Metal Products	33	195.14
通用设备制造业	Ordinary Machinery Manufacturing	35	142.60
专用设备制造业	Special Purpose Equipment Manufacturing	30	177.59
汽车制造业	Motor manufacturing	86	3248.64
铁路、船舶、航空航天和其他运输设备制造业	Railway,Watercraft,Aviation and other Transporlation Equipment manufacturing	32	532.53
电气机械和器材制造业	Electric Machinery and Equipment	33	320.36
计算机、通信和其他电子设备制造业	Telecommunication Computer,Equipment and Other Electronic Equipment Manufacturing	31	742.26
仪器仪表制造业	Instruments and Meters, Manufacturing	13	37.42
其他制造业	Other Manufacturing	6	41.05
废弃资源综合利用业	Waste Comprehensive Vtilization of Resources Industry	2	4.67
金属制品、机械和设备修理业	Metal products,Machinery and Equipment Repairing	3	6.19
电力、燃气及水的生产和供应业	**Electric Power, Gas and Water Production and Supply**	**153**	**1546.22**
电力、热力生产和供应业	Electric Power, Steam and Hot Water Production and Supply	91	1438.80
燃气生产和供应业	Gas Production and Supply	11	62.39
水的生产和供应业	Tap Water Production and Supply	51	45.03

THE NUMBER OF STATE-OWNED SHARE HOLDING INDUSTRIAL ENTERPRISES AND THEIR TOTAL OUTPUT OF PRODUCTION AND SALES (2016)

(100 million yuan)

工业销售产值(当年价格) Output Value of Industrial Products Sales (current price)	出口交货值 Delivery Value for Export	资产总计 Total Assets	流动资产合计 Circulating Funds	固定资产合计 Total Fined Assets	固定资产原价 Original Value of Fixed Assets	主营业务收入 Revenue of Major Business	全部从业人员年平均人数(万人) Average Number of Empolyment of the Curreat Year (10 000 Bersons)
11136.77	**334.68**	**17098.93**	**6757.01**	**6791.59**	**11578.68**	**11458.88**	**76.98**
711.52	36.06	1785.98	724.69	769.04	1442.59	715.10	13.36
2379.32	118.56	4243.15	1373.35	1878.90	3776.69	2415.49	21.87
107.35	0.04	192.86	117.18	50.88	80.39	109.86	2.11
1360.40	24.09	1374.71	799.50	370.48	540.76	1347.59	9.63
9776.37	310.59	15724.22	5957.50	6421.11	11037.92	10111.29	67.35
9011.30	294.63	13790.42	5343.44	5404.68	9533.30	9331.22	58.27
1296.73	35.80	2062.24	966.07	737.12	1135.04	1297.46	13.12
828.75	4.26	1246.27	447.50	649.79	910.35	830.20	5.60
149.55	**0.78**	**289.69**	**90.44**	**157.26**	**442.35**	**152.07**	**3.78**
1.57		3.14	2.13	0.87	1.58	0.79	0.10
31.46	0.76	104.91	11.23	79.64	308.23	31.42	1.50
42.30		47.30	16.32	18.03	44.05	39.17	0.41
9.09		19.02	4.51	11.70	14.57	9.15	0.22
8.08		21.20	8.78	4.27	5.29	9.87	0.14
57.03	0.02	94.12	47.46	42.74	68.62	61.68	1.41
9457.23	**333.91**	**12389.89**	**6321.97**	**3510.76**	**6012.15**	**9761.29**	**60.05**
188.49		45.83	26.65	14.70	24.59	191.62	0.52
43.28	6.20	84.81	36.31	15.47	37.04	57.98	0.80
26.86		35.39	16.75	8.38	12.92	21.44	0.48
615.01	0.51	440.92	341.58	97.14	98.34	609.38	0.82
65.53	1.69	46.99	31.97	10.81	29.66	70.75	0.83
18.10	4.25	26.08	15.10	3.68	9.50	13.59	0.69
3.04		0.07	0.03	0.01	0.02	3.35	0.01
18.17		12.96	5.94	4.85	7.28	18.51	0.20
11.80		30.93	18.35	10.15	15.78	11.79	0.08
35.92		44.26	28.86	9.02	13.58	30.55	0.37
8.85	0.81	10.69	5.05	4.90	7.33	8.84	0.10
492.85		191.51	74.89	114.34	185.76	511.58	0.66
1082.18	70.24	1458.50	471.60	761.23	1187.55	1137.59	5.24
93.26	5.19	124.41	55.35	39.40	55.66	103.23	1.02
32.58	1.46	32.57	18.20	11.44	17.53	26.07	0.45
132.11	1.30	190.06	55.89	100.38	129.19	133.46	1.22
865.31	21.19	1990.09	639.21	805.59	1770.98	937.11	6.85
391.96	9.40	332.35	176.94	98.41	158.29	871.15	1.67
192.88	7.22	307.58	207.17	64.61	101.19	191.26	1.88
134.56	8.82	298.55	188.79	66.65	106.02	140.03	2.32
156.71	5.32	227.94	158.54	42.72	74.20	127.34	2.01
3223.33	25.05	4029.37	2217.09	702.80	1240.48	2989.04	16.61
511.39	62.81	752.41	452.97	191.34	215.75	423.10	4.95
321.73	6.53	375.86	224.56	119.64	165.33	332.52	2.55
703.60	94.61	1188.51	796.84	168.08	285.84	715.44	6.48
37.02	1.11	54.10	25.95	23.38	35.72	33.40	0.52
40.27	0.19	47.93	26.69	17.76	22.27	40.37	0.56
4.25		6.68	2.73	3.38	3.58	4.63	0.05
6.19		2.52	1.98	0.49	0.78	6.19	0.11
1530.00		**4419.36**	**344.60**	**3123.57**	**5124.19**	**1545.52**	**13.15**
1431.29		4024.35	203.63	2963.08	4895.95	1431.11	10.97
59.38		105.40	24.36	65.86	80.34	67.87	0.41
39.33		289.61	116.61	94.63	147.90	46.54	1.76

13-5 集体工业企业单位数和主要经济指标 (2016)

单位: 亿元

项 目	Item	企业单位数(个) Number of Enterprises (unit)	工业总产值(当年价格) Total Output Value (current price)
总 计	**Total**	**82**	**113.99**
在总计中:	Of the Total:		
亏损企业	Enterprises running under Deficit	13	7.56
在总计中:	Of the Total:		
农村工业	Rural Industry	12	15.28
在总计中:	Of the Total:		
轻工业	Light Industry	17	23.46
重工业	Heavy Industry	65	90.52
在总计中:	Of the Total:		
大型企业	Large Scale Enterprises		
中型企业	Medium Scale Enterprises	9	27.16
小型企业	Small Enterprises	73	86.83
按行业分	Grouped by sector		
采矿业	**Mining and Qarrying**	**17**	**38.99**
煤炭开采和洗选业	Coal Mining and Processing	1	3.05
石油和天然气开采业	Petroleum and Natural Gas Extraction		
黑色金属矿采选业	Ferrous Metals Mining and Processing	4	13.55
有色金属矿采选业	Non-ferrous Metals Mining and Processing		
非金属矿采选业	Non-metal Minerals Mining and Processing	12	22.38
开采辅助活动	Mining Auxiliary Activities		
其他采矿业	Other Minerals Mining and Processing		
制造业	**Manufacturing**	**61**	**71.99**
农副食品加工业	Food Processing		
食品制造业	Food Production	1	3.61
酒、饮料和精制茶制造业	Wine,Beverage and Refined Tea Production	2	1.4
烟草制品业	Tobacco Processing		
纺织业	Textile Industry	1	3.86
纺织服装、服饰业	Textile,Garments, and Fashion Industry	3	1.3
皮革、毛皮、羽毛及其制品和制鞋业	Leather, Furs,Down and Related Products		
木材加工和木、竹、藤、棕、草制品业	Timber Processing, Wood, Bamboo, Cane, Palm and Sraw Products		
家具制造业	Furniture Manufacturing		
造纸和纸制品业	Papermaking and Paper Products	1	0.46
印刷和记录媒介复制业	Printing and Record Processing	2	2.68
文教、工美、体育和娱乐用品制造业	Stationery, Education and Sports Goods		
石油加工、炼焦和核燃料加工业	Petroleum Processing, Coking Products and Nuclear Fuel Processing		
化学原料和化学制品制造业	Raw Chemical Material and Chemical Products	4	8.32
医药制造业	Medical and pharmaceutical Products	2	2.6
化学纤维制造业	Chemical Fibers		
橡胶和塑料制品业	Rubber and plastic products	5	6.23
非金属矿物制品业	Nonmetal Material Products	11	19.38
黑色金属冶炼和压延加工业	Smelting and Pressing of Ferrous Metals	4	5.5
有色金属冶炼和压延加工业	Smelting and Pressing of Nonferrous Metals	4	2.47
金属制品业	Metal Products	3	1.2
通用设备制造业	Ordinary Machinery Manufacturing	1	0.36
专用设备制造业	Special Purpose Equipment Manufacturing		
汽车制造业	Motor manufacturing	8	7.83
铁路、船舶、航空航天和其他运输设备制造业	Railway,Watercraft,Aviation and other Transporlation Equipment manufacturing	3	2.38
电气机械和器材制造业	Electric Machinery and Equipment		
计算机、通信和其他电子设备制造业	Telecommunication Computer,Equipment and Other Electronic Equipment Manufacturing		
仪器仪表制造业	Instruments and Meters, Manufacturing	1	0.27
其他制造业	Other Manufacturing		
废弃资源综合利用业	Waste Comprehensive Vtilization of Resources Industry	3	1.61
金属制品、机械和设备修理业	Metal products,Machinery and Equipment Repairing	2	0.53
电力、燃气及水的生产和供应业	**Electric Power, Gas and Water Production and Supply**	**4**	**3.01**
电力、热力生产和供应业	Electric Power, Steam and Hot Water Production and Supply		
燃气生产和供应业	Gas Production and Supply		
水的生产和供应业	Tap Water Production and Supply	4	3.01

THE NUMBER OF COLLECTIVE-OWNED INDUSTRIAL ENTERPRISES(2016)

(100 million yuan)

工业销售产值(当年价格) Output Value of Industrial Products Sales (current price)	出口交货值 Delivery Value for Export	资产总计 Total Assets	流动资产合计 Circulating Funds	固定资产合计 Total Fined Assets	固定资产原价 Original Value of Fixed Assets	主营业务收入 Revenue of Major Business	全部从业人员年平均人数(万人) Average Number of Empolyment of the Curreat Year (10 000 Bersons)
110.26		**48.00**	**23.31**	**15.36**	**29.64**	**110.41**	**1.43**
7.34		9.99	6.30	1.94	2.79	9.56	0.38
15.12		5.63	1.67	3.33	3.54	13.86	0.17
21.78		6.37	2.19	1.81	2.30	21.97	0.18
88.49		41.63	21.11	13.55	27.35	88.44	1.26
26.90		13.25	5.84	5.60	13.70	27.37	0.55
83.36		34.75	17.47	9.76	15.95	83.04	0.89
38.19		**16.13**	**7.09**	**7.65**	**12.7**	**37.68**	**0.41**
2.92		1.12	0.3	0.62	0.72	3.06	0.07
13.3		4.77	3.16	1.33	4.88	13.3	0.08
21.97		10.24	3.63	5.71	7.1	21.32	0.26
69.32		**29.85**	**16.03**	**7.25**	**16.43**	**70.09**	**1.00**
3.37		0.42	0.31	0.11	0.24	3.37	0.02
0.35		0.34	0.1	0.08	0.09	1.38	0.03
3.86		0.62	0.08			3.59	
1.28		0.59	0.37	0.08	0.15	1.29	0.04
0.46		0.08	0.07	0.02	0.05	0.46	0.01
2.68		0.49	0.25	0.1	0.15	2.68	0.02
8		1.56	0.98	0.58	0.8	7.64	0.06
2.58		1.23	0.53	0.7	0.74	2.58	0.02
6.1		1.86	1.12	0.49	0.79	5.88	0.06
19.19		3.73	2.21	1.25	1.65	19.11	0.16
5.35		4.04	1.28	1.41	8.27	5.29	0.08
2.44		1.74	1.37	0.17	0.54	2.49	0.05
1.04		1.68	1.18	0.19	0.37	1.15	0.02
0.36		0.18	0.12	0.06	0.02	0.31	0.01
7.62		3.87	1.91	0.41	0.76	5.95	0.1
2.29		1.43	1.18	0.15	0.27	2.29	0.08
0.27		0.23	0.23		0.02	0.26	0.02
1.56		3.79	2	1.35	1.3	3.89	0.16
0.52		1.94	0.73	0.11	0.2	0.49	0.07
2.75		**2.02**	**0.19**	**0.45**	**0.52**	**2.64**	**0.03**
2.75		2.02	0.19	0.45	0.52	2.64	0.03

13-6 外商投资和港澳台商投资工业企业单位数和主要经济指标(2016)

单位:亿元

项 目	Item	企业单位数(个) Number of Enterprises (unit)
总计	**Total**	**817**
在总计中:	Of the Total:	
亏损企业	Enterprises running under Deficit	134
在总计中:	Of the Total:	
港、澳、台商投资企业	Hongkong, Macao and Taiwan Funded Enterprises	367
合资经营企业(港或澳、台资)	Joint Venture with Hongkong, Macao and Taiwan	154
合作经营企业(港或澳、台资)	Cooperate with Hongkong, Macao and Taiwan Funded	4
港澳台商独资经营企业	Enterprises Solely Funded by Hongkong, Macao and Taiwan Businessmen	191
港澳台商投资股份有限公司	Share Holding Co.Ltd.With Hongkong,Macao and Taiwan Businessmen	11
其他港澳台投资	Othes	7
外商投资企业	Foreign Funded Enterprises	450
中外合资经营企业	Sino – Foreign Joint Funded Enterprises	245
中外合作经营企业	Sino – Foreign Cooperative Funded Enterprises	8
外资企业	Foreign Solely Funded Enterprises	181
外商投资股份有限公司	Foreign Funded Share Holding Co.Ltd.	14
其他外商投资	Othes	2
在总计中:	Of the Total:	
国有控股企业	State–Owned Share Holding Enterprises	46
在总计中:	Of the Total:	
农村工业	Rural Industry	1
在总计中:	Of the Total:	
轻工业	Light Industry	348
重工业	Heavy Industry	469
在总计中:	Of the Total:	
大型企业	Large Scale Enterprises	74
中型企业	Medium Scale Enterprises	226
小型企业	Small Enterprises	517
按行业分	Grouped by sector	
采矿业	**Mining and Qarrying**	**5**
煤炭开采和洗选业	Coal Mining and Processing	
石油和天然气开采业	Petroleum and Natural Gas Extraction	
黑色金属矿采选业	Ferrous Metals Mining and Processing	1
有色金属矿采选业	Non–ferrous Metals Mining and Processing	1
非金属矿采选业	Non–metal Minerals Mining and Processing	3
开采辅助活动	Mining Auxiliary Activities	
其他采矿业	Other Minerals Mining and Processing	
制造业	**Manufacturing**	**765**
农副食品加工业	Food Processing	41
食品制造业	Food Production	34
酒、饮料和精制茶制造业	Wine,Beverage and Refined Tea Production	27
烟草制品业	Tobacco Processing	
纺织业	Textile Industry	50
纺织服装、服饰业	Textile,Garments, and Fashion Industry	41
皮革、毛皮、羽毛及其制品和制鞋业	Leather, Furs,Down and Related Products	15
木材加工和木、竹、藤、棕、草制品业	Timber Processing, Wood, Bamboo, Cane, Palm and Sraw Products	3
家具制造业	Furniture Manufacturing	4
造纸和纸制品业	Papermaking and Paper Products	24
印刷和记录媒介复制业	Printing and Record Processing	8
文教、工美、体育和娱乐用品制造业	Stationery, Education and Sports Goods	12
石油加工、炼焦和核燃料加工业	Petroleum Processing, Coking Products and Nuclear Fuel Processing	1
化学原料和化学制品制造业	Raw Chemical Material and Chemical Products	46
医药制造业	Medical and pharmaceutical Products	37
化学纤维制造业	Chemical Fibers	3
橡胶和塑料制品业	Rubber and plastic products	17
非金属矿物制品业	Nonmetal Material Products	40
黑色金属冶炼和压延加工业	Smelting and Pressing of Ferrous Metals	9
有色金属冶炼和压延加工业	Smelting and Pressing of Nonferrous Metals	2
金属制品业	Metal Products	30
通用设备制造业	Ordinary Machinery Manufacturing	31
专用设备制造业	Special Purpose Equipment Manufacturing	20
汽车制造业	Motor manufacturing	172
铁路、船舶、航空航天和其他运输设备制造业	Railway,Watercraft,Aviation and other Transporlation Equipment manufacturing	6
电气机械和器材制造业	Electric Machinery and Equipment	49
计算机、通信和其他电子设备制造业	Telecommunication Computer,Equipment and Other Electronic Equipment Manufacturing	33
仪器仪表制造业	Instruments and Meters, Manufacturing	5
其他制造业	Other Manufacturing	1
废弃资源综合利用业	Waste Comprehensive Vtilization of Resources Industry	3
金属制品、机械和设备修理业	Metal products,Machinery and Equipment Repairing	1
电力、燃气及水的生产和供应业	**Electric Power, Gas and Water Production and Supply**	**47**
电力、热力生产和供应业	Electric Power, Steam and Hot Water Production and Supply	19
燃气生产和供应业	Gas Production and Supply	23
水的生产和供应业	Tap Water Production and Supply	5

THE NUMBER OF FOREIGN FUNDED AND HONGKONG MACO AND TAIWAN FUNDED INDUSTRIAL ENTERPRISES AND THEIR TOTAL OUTPUT OF PRODUCTION AND SALES (2016)

(100 million yuan)

工业总产值(当年价格) Total Output Value (current price)	工业销售产值(当年价格) Output Value of Industrial Products Sales (current price)	出口交货值 Delivery Value for Export	资产总计 Total Assets	流动资产合计 Circulating Funds	固定资产合计 Total Fined Assets	固定资产原价 Original Value of Fixed Assets	主营业务收入 Revenue of Major Business	全部从业人员年平均人数(万人) Average Number of Empolyment of the curreat Year (10 000 Bersons)
7222.80	**7086.20**	**435.81**	**5935.42**	**3083.83**	**2047.64**	**3406.21**	**6547.72**	**43.36**
333.79	306.91	15.06	512.59	238.09	197.03	268.20	309.89	3.76
2068.01	2011.56	252.95	1699.13	830.43	620.66	1057.90	1890.77	16.80
1077.15	1057.02	96.01	888.65	470.93	301.72	558.63	985.25	8.51
10.00	9.60		11.59	4.80	2.04	5.58	9.52	0.09
903.72	865.68	156.41	665.94	275.44	293.36	458.90	816.13	7.76
32.24	33.39	0.52	62.53	19.05	15.63	22.12	34.12	0.31
44.90	45.88		70.42	60.20	7.92	12.67	45.75	0.13
5154.79	5074.64	182.86	4236.30	2253.41	1426.98	2348.31	4656.95	26.56
4010.87	3944.52	60.41	3156.59	1717.36	1005.53	1630.03	3556.10	16.69
58.43	57.57	1.67	30.03	10.41	18.49	40.23	57.25	0.17
871.23	853.76	113.33	718.36	424.11	228.30	383.71	829.16	7.69
213.11	217.90	7.01	330.02	100.99	174.05	293.82	213.54	1.99
1.15	0.90	0.44	1.30	0.53	0.62	0.53	0.90	0.02
2525.74	2523.22	15.10	2228.95	1238.87	706.36	1156.35	2246.14	9.12
0.34	0.34		0.54	0.51	0.03	0.17	0.33	
1903.44	1812.92	138.28	1149.22	610.47	381.54	727.12	1645.87	16.23
5319.36	5273.28	297.53	4786.20	2473.37	1666.11	2679.09	4901.85	27.13
4339.13	4313.28	264.72	3560.64	1876.48	1193.10	1990.23	3940.13	24.72
1842.03	1770.31	99.81	1455.80	774.68	500.59	838.44	1633.82	12.23
1041.63	1002.60	71.28	918.98	432.67	353.96	577.54	973.78	6.42
31.32	**30.45**		**8.83**	**3.71**	**2.48**	**12.77**	**25.79**	**0.11**
17.83	17.05		0.92	0.85	0.05	0.05	17.07	0.02
7.26	7.26		6.33	2.37	1.53	1.8	3.67	0.05
6.22	6.15		1.58	0.49	0.9	10.91	5.04	0.04
6995.41	**6862.3**	**435.81**	**5499.19**	**2978.60**	**1785.18**	**3042.54**	**6323.30**	**42.28**
353.24	319.94	13.35	140.73	85	43.11	77.13	287.75	1.16
207.65	200.07	6.11	99.03	39.62	43.41	120.68	194	1.53
309.79	294.68	0.05	209.79	119.07	65.14	127.05	257.08	1.75
201.55	194.61	25.42	76.27	32.95	35.82	68.51	191.46	2.43
101.71	100.13	23.63	56.36	34.83	8.27	15	90.61	1.96
33.46	33.05	11.04	19.9	7.53	10.62	14.17	28.25	1.64
6.04	5.95		3.35	0.63	1.3	1.5	3.38	0.12
10.22	9.07	1.29	4.74	2.8	0.97	1.8	8.47	0.13
126.68	117.93	1.82	149.67	79.91	53.11	111.87	112.15	0.76
10.67	10.72		13.91	9.62	3.77	7.63	10.9	0.17
41.49	37.3	1.58	35.67	21.33	4.94	15.54	37.56	0.46
24.61	22.56		31.63	16.91	12.7	19.1	8.94	0.06
363.65	349.9	38.22	306.94	68.58	183.33	265.41	357.43	1.42
247.25	242.66	32.56	204.91	99.66	64.35	91.06	224.27	2.29
15.13	14.82	2.44	11.99	4.04	6.66	12.09	13.44	0.09
28.56	28.25	0.13	28.24	16.88	6.71	12.08	26.69	0.2
231.33	236.73	6.2	397.92	116.81	211.58	362.43	227.21	2.21
128.91	130.41	21.02	176.75	54.89	112.57	182.64	140.76	0.79
63.81	62.86		7.49	2.73	2.2	3.25	63.08	0.09
130.47	122.67	1.69	75.31	30.64	38.92	67.39	120.03	0.57
72.16	69.17	12.11	82.3	55.04	20.93	28.25	66.89	0.8
62.11	61.01	17.56	60.4	33.36	14.1	19.72	63.33	0.97
3364.08	3357.37	23.38	2658.96	1631.46	674.63	1137.97	3023.78	14.47
9.38	8.78	3.39	10.5	8.48	1.44	2.86	8.53	0.12
430.79	424.5	52.03	303.53	175.14	106.25	193.65	397.11	2.77
399.91	386.88	139.56	321.57	223.05	55.29	80.02	340.01	2.93
8.73	8.4	1.21	5.08	2.66	2.33	3.06	8.29	0.37
0.38	0.24	0.02	0.13	0.12	0.01	0.06	0.24	0.01
11.44	11.4		5.55	4.48	0.58	0.44	11.4	0.02
0.24	0.24		0.55	0.36	0.15	0.16	0.25	0.01
196.07	**193.44**		**427.4**	**101.52**	**259.98**	**350.9**	**198.63**	**0.98**
120.65	119.78		290.95	59.16	193.76	269.48	115.57	0.25
70.93	69.88		106.57	35.88	56.98	69.08	79.06	0.55
4.5	3.78		29.88	6.48	9.24	12.34	4.01	0.18

13-7 私营工业企业单位数和主要经济指标 (2016)

单位:亿元

项 目	Item	企业单位数(个) Number of Enterprises (unit)	工业总产值(当年价格) Total Output Value (current price)
总计	**Total**	**8857**	**17264.84**
在总计中:	Of the Total:		
亏损企业	Enterprises running under Deficit	429	407.14
在总计中:	Of the Total:		
轻工业	Light Industry	3890	8226.28
重工业	Heavy Industry	4967	9038.56
在总计中:	Of the Total:		
大型企业	Large Scale Enterprises	63	1584.64
中型企业	Medium Scale Enterprises	691	4093.88
小型企业	Small Enterprises	8103	11586.32
按行业分	Grouped by Sector		
采矿业	**Mining and Qarrying**	**342**	**477.19**
煤炭开采和洗选业	Coal Mining and Processing	43	33.55
石油和天然气开采业	Petroleum and Natural Gas Extraction		
黑色金属矿采选业	Ferrous Metals Mining and Processing	40	76.75
有色金属矿采选业	Non-ferrous Metals Mining and Processing	18	24.85
非金属矿采选业	Non-metal Minerals Mining and Processing	238	340.27
开采辅助活动	Mining Auxiliary Activities		
其他采矿业	Other Minerals Mining and Processing	3	1.77
制造业	**Manufacturing**	**8444**	**16706.99**
农副食品加工业	Food Processing	1191	3141.66
食品制造业	Food Production	212	604.38
酒、饮料和精制茶制造业	Wine,Beverage and Refined Tea Production	281	439.64
烟草制品业	Tobacco Processing		
纺织业	Textile Industry	594	1404.65
纺织服装、服饰业	Textile,Garments, and Fashion Industry	342	568.15
皮革、毛皮、羽毛及其制品和制鞋业	Leather, Furs,Down and Related Products	131	157.53
木材加工和木、竹、藤、棕、草制品业	Timber Processing, Wood, Bamboo, Cane, Palm and Sraw Products	166	279.71
家具制造业	Furniture Manufacturing	92	125.42
造纸和纸制品业	Papermaking and Paper Products	144	251.27
印刷和记录媒介复制业	Printing and Record Processing	104	160.21
文教、工美、体育和娱乐用品制造业	Stationery, Education and Sports Goods	87	97.02
石油加工、炼焦和核燃料加工业	Petroleum Processing, Coking Products and Nuclear Fuel Processing	19	27.69
化学原料和化学制品制造业	Raw Chemical Material and Chemical Products	600	1665.89
医药制造业	Medical and pharmaceutical Products	169	317.36
化学纤维制造业	Chemical Fibers	12	51.63
橡胶和塑料制品业	Rubber and plastic products	382	713.05
非金属矿物制品业	Nonmetal Material Products	1285	2055.87
黑色金属冶炼和压延加工业	Smelting and Pressing of Ferrous Metals	135	357.3
有色金属冶炼和压延加工业	Smelting and Pressing of Nonferrous Metals	78	232.21
金属制品业	Metal Products	422	680.63
通用设备制造业	Ordinary Machinery Manufacturing	348	608.71
专用设备制造业	Special Purpose Equipment Manufacturing	341	532.99
汽车制造业	Motor manufacturing	680	941.63
铁路、船舶、航空航天和其他运输设备制造业	Railway,Watercraft,Aviation and other Transporlation Equipment manufacturing	62	165.3
电气机械和器材制造业	Electric Machinery and Equipment	274	409.8
计算机、通信和其他电子设备制造业	Telecommunication Computer,Equipment and Other Electronic Equipment Manufacturing	152	465.86
仪器仪表制造业	Instruments and Meters, Manufacturing	51	70.01
其他制造业	Other Manufacturing	49	78.31
废弃资源综合利用业	Waste Comprehensive Vtilization of Resources Industry	35	97.44
金属制品、机械和设备修理业	Metal products,Machinery and Equipment Repairing	6	5.65
电力、燃气及水的生产和供应业	**Electric Power, Gas and Water Production and Supply**	**71**	**80.66**
电力、热力生产和供应业	Electric Power, Steam and Hot Water Production and Supply	40	44.68
燃气生产和供应业	Gas Production and Supply	15	22.89
水的生产和供应业	Tap Water Production and Supply	16	13.09

THE NUMBER OF PRIVATE-OWNED INDUSTRIAL ENTERPRISES AND THEIR MAJOR ECONOMIC INDICATORS (2016)

(100 million yuan)

工业销售产值(当年价格) Output Value of Industrial Products Sales(current price)	出口交货值 Delivery Value for Export	资产总计 Total Assets	流动资产合计 Circulating Funds	固定资产合计 Total Fined Assets	固定资产原价 Original Value of Fixed Assets	主营业务收入 Revenue of Major Business	全部从业人员年平均人数(万人) Average Number of Empolyment of the Curreat Year (10 000 Bersons)
16655.35	**544.91**	**7094.11**	**3300.82**	**2604.35**	**6666.38**	**15869.45**	**114.89**
376.68	9.92	445.09	214.54	144.32	209.41	326.23	5.04
7948.45	318.05	2939.83	1312.18	1114.15	3699.28	7628.29	57.34
8706.90	226.86	4154.28	1988.65	1490.21	2967.10	8241.16	57.56
1546.70	63.06	690.74	353.93	276.63	821.77	1466.04	10.31
3952.17	301.14	1593.70	771.26	632.66	2185.86	3728.96	31.93
11156.49	180.71	4809.67	2175.64	1695.06	3658.75	10674.45	72.65
459.86		**232.30**	**89.28**	**86.59**	**141.17**	**425.92**	**3.62**
31.41		20.26	6.38	8.02	9.87	32.03	0.72
74.93		41.76	14.14	20.58	24.5	71.45	0.48
24.29		17.78	7.25	6.54	9.38	23.11	0.21
327.47		151.49	61.19	51.05	97.14	298.52	2.18
1.77		1.06	0.32	0.4	0.29	0.82	0.03
16117.89	**544.91**	**6745.28**	**3178.08**	**2461.49**	**6447.37**	**15373.19**	**110.72**
3049.49	54.36	1000.03	468.78	355.69	1591.04	2948.4	12.91
576.21	5.01	195.89	85.63	66.35	479.94	540.23	3.73
419.06	5.08	190.34	85.4	69.21	109.25	405.03	3.07
1366.96	88.25	454.63	176.27	217.57	564.4	1311.99	13.56
556.05	54.14	198.92	90.12	72.31	174.25	522.52	8.26
152.88	48.76	54.07	27.95	16.98	65.25	151.68	1.29
267.14	5.09	101.46	41.13	37.95	79.85	245.43	1.89
121.53	1.64	80.01	27.02	44.86	52.08	107.51	1.05
242.98	0.02	102.49	44.55	36.25	80.11	231.98	1.73
155.35	0.01	72.75	31.46	30.41	73.35	147.04	1.4
94.11	8.4	45.15	22.64	11.74	66.7	87.15	1.28
27.5		11.76	5.09	5.78	5.93	24.59	0.11
1608.64	9.86	687.63	281.82	289.14	724.91	1458.79	7.13
301.68	27.91	163.56	79.23	54.44	98.3	288.27	2.22
50.88	0.31	18.59	9.93	5.42	12.22	49.68	0.28
695.34	0.51	304.38	139.24	109.46	290.71	655.22	4.69
1968.82	6.45	872.42	362.04	350.12	595.72	1892.4	14.04
347.24	0.01	123.26	59.65	49.62	114.32	336.09	1.87
228.69	1.01	80.71	38.61	33.16	49.84	224.25	1.23
655.02	3.13	267.66	144.3	87.44	179.51	640.09	4.71
582.18	4.78	255.03	131.88	87.78	227.95	562.46	4.11
517.9	5.83	340.24	194.15	110.88	251.63	487	3.66
899.24	5.9	532.74	274.85	168.09	240.69	810.81	7.6
154	0.04	55.68	25.23	21.31	40.94	147.1	1.2
387.24	6.06	224.21	119.82	73.15	157.36	373.8	3.09
450.98	197.31	207.86	147.35	29.65	45.02	496.24	2.72
64.79	0.8	35.08	23.13	7.91	16.8	62.37	0.75
76.27	4.24	18.4	8.54	7.11	40.06	75.33	0.69
94.16		48.3	30.98	11.37	18.7	85.02	0.32
5.55		2.03	1.29	0.33	0.58	4.71	0.13
77.60		**116.48**	**33.46**	**56.28**	**77.83**	**70.33**	**0.55**
42.38		94.97	25.38	46.11	61.4	36.74	0.3
22.84		12.96	4.69	5.83	9.01	21.83	0.1
12.37		8.55	3.39	4.34	7.42	11.76	0.15

13-8 大中型工业企业单位数和产销总值(2016)

单位:亿元

项 目	Item	企业单位数(个) Number of Enterprises (unit)
总 计	**Total**	**2175**
一、按登记注册类型分组:	Grouped by Type of Registration	
内资企业	Inner Funded Enterprises	1875
国有企业	State Owned Enterprises	56
中央企业	Central Enterprises	33
地方企业	Local Enterprises	23
集体企业	Collective-owned Enterprise	9
股份合作企业	Share Holding Cooperative Enterprises	
联营企业	Joint Owned Enterprise	
国有联营企业	State Joint Ownership	
集体联营企业	Collective Joint Ownership	
国有与集体联营企业	Joint State- Collective Ownership	
其他联营企业	Other Joint Owned Enterprise	
有限责任公司	Responsibility Co. Ltd	842
国有独资公司	State Solely Funded Co.	49
其他有限责任公司	Others	793
股份有限公司	Share Holding Co.Ltd.	213
私营企业	Private - owned enterprises	754
私营独资企业	Solely Private - owned enterprises	9
私营合作企业	Private Joint Venture	
私营有限责任公司	Private Responsibility Co. Ltd	670
私营股份有限公司	Private Share Holding Co.Ltd.	75
其他企业	Others	1
港、澳、台商投资企业	Hongkong, Macao and Taiwan Funded Enterprises	137
合资经营企业(港或澳、台资)	Joint Venture with Hongkong, Macao and Taiwan	63
合作经营企业(港或澳、台资)	Cooperate with Hongkong, Macao and Taiwan Funded	1
港澳台商独资经营企业	Enterprises Solely Funded by Hongkong, Macao and Taiwan Businessmen	66
港澳台商投资股份有限公司	Share Holding Co.Ltd. With Hongkong, Macao and Taiwan Investment	5
其他港澳台投资	Others	2
外商投资企业	Foreign Funded Enterprises	163
中外合资经营企业	Sino - Foreign Joint Funded Enterprises	91
中外合作经营企业	Sino - Foreign Cooperative Funded Enterprises	2
外资企业	Foreign Solely Funded Enterprises	61
外商投资股份有限公司	Foreign Funded Share Holding Co.Ltd.	9
其他外商投资	Others	
二、在总计中:亏损企业	**Of the Total: enterprises running under deficit**	**208**
在总计中:国有控股企业	Of the Total: State-Owned Share Holding Enterprises	330
在总计中:农村工业	Of the Total: Rural Industry	10
在总计中:轻工业	Of the Total: Light Industry	1047
重工业	Heavy Industry	1128
在总计中:大型企业	Of the Total: Large Scale Enterprises	358
中型企业	Medium Scale Enterprises	1817
按行业分	Grouped by Sector	
采矿业	**Mining and Qarrying**	**54**

NUMBER OF LARGE AND MEDIUM SCALE INDUSTRIAL ENTERPRISES AND THEIR TOTAL VALUE OF PRODUCTION AND SALES (2016)

(100 million yuan)

工业总产值(当年价格) Total Output Value (current price)	工业销售产值(当年价格) Output Value of Industrial Products Sales (current price)	出口交货值 Delivery Value for Export
27955.18	**27276.01**	**1430.25**
21774.01	21192.41	1065.72
2431.23	2419.37	118.59
2376.88	2368.82	118.56
54.35	50.55	0.04
27.16	26.90	
9320.57	9075.88	354.52
1580.85	1596.77	34.10
7739.72	7479.11	320.42
4315.26	4170.11	228.42
5678.52	5498.87	364.20
28.69	28.50	4.28
5015.54	4859.65	353.00
634.29	610.71	6.93
1.28	1.29	
1636.27	1594.53	235.77
852.46	839.54	83.12
3.71	3.85	
723.62	691.68	152.13
17.61	20.14	0.52
38.88	39.32	
4544.89	4489.07	128.76
3673.76	3625.44	37.90
42.61	41.91	
632.43	620.53	85.10
196.09	201.19	5.76
1365.03	**1235.32**	**52.17**
10434.77	10308.02	330.43
101.41	99.47	
9451.87	9105.33	519.94
18503.31	18170.68	910.31
16612.82	16357.11	819.26
11342.35	10918.9	610.99
353.4	**347.12**	**0.78**

13-8 续表1 continued

单位: 亿元

项 目	Item	企业单位数(个) Number of Enterprises(unit)
煤炭开采和洗选业	Coal Mining and Processing	10
石油和天然气开采业	Petroleum and Natural Gas Extraction	1
黑色金属矿采选业	Ferrous Metals Mining and Processing	13
有色金属矿采选业	Non-ferrous Metals Mining and Processing	4
非金属矿采选业	Non-metal Minerals Mining and Processing	22
开采辅助活动	Mining Auxiliary Activities	3
其他采矿业	Other Minerals Mining and Processing	1
制造业	**Manufacturing**	**2066**
农副食品加工业	Food Processing	145
食品制造业	Food Production	87
酒、饮料和精制茶制造业	Wine,Beverage and Refined Tea Production	61
烟草制品业	Tobacco Processing	3
纺织业	Textile Industry	251
纺织服装、服饰业	Textile,Garments, and Fashion Industry	155
皮革、毛皮、羽毛及其制品和制鞋业	Leather, Furs,Down and Related Products	15
木材加工和木、竹、藤、棕、草制品业	Timber Processing, Wood, Bamboo, Cane, Palm and Sraw Products	24
家具制造业	Furniture Manufacturing	12
造纸和纸制品业	Papermaking and Paper Products	36
印刷和记录媒介复制业	Printing and Record Processing	29
文教、工美、体育和娱乐用品制造业	Stationery, Education and Sports Goods	20
石油加工、炼焦和核燃料加工业	Petroleum Processing, Coking Products and Nuclear Fuel Processing	5
化学原料和化学制品制造业	Raw Chemical Material and Chemical Products	136
医药制造业	Medical and pharmaceutical Products	73
化学纤维制造业	Chemical Fibers	4
橡胶和塑料制品业	Rubber and plastic products	73
非金属矿物制品业	Nonmetal Material Products	148
黑色金属冶炼和压延加工业	Smelting and Pressing of Ferrous Metals	46
有色金属冶炼和压延加工业	Smelting and Pressing of Nonferrous Metals	28
金属制品业	Metal Products	70
通用设备制造业	Ordinary Machinery Manufacturing	76
专用设备制造业	Special Purpose Equipment Manufacturing	66
汽车制造业	Motor manufacturing	242
铁路、船舶、航空航天和其他运输设备制造业	Railway, Watercraft, Aviation and other Transporlation Equipment manufacturing	37
电气机械和器材制造业	Electric Machinery and Equipment	103
计算机、通信和其他电子设备制造业	Telecommunication Computer,Equipment and Other Electronic Equipment Manufacturing	80
仪器仪表制造业	Instruments and Meters, Manufacturing	14
其他制造业	Other Manufacturing	13
废弃资源综合利用业	Waste Comprehensive Vtilization of Resources Industry	8
金属制品、机械和设备修理业	Metal products,Machinery and Equipment Repairing	6
电力、燃气及水的生产和供应业	**Electric Power, Gas and Water Production and Supply**	**55**
电力、热力生产和供应业	Electric Power, Steam and Hot Water Production and Supply	30
燃气生产和供应业	Gas Production and Supply	7
水的生产和供应业	Tap Water Production and Supply	18

(100 million yuan)

工业总产值(当年价格) Total Output Value	工业销售产值(当年价格) Output Value of Industrial Products Sales (current price)	出口交货值 Delivery Value for Export
22.60	22.50	
31.43	31.46	0.76
108.85	109.39	
19.74	19.75	
111.14	106.61	
59.26	57.03	0.02
0.38	0.38	
26129.80	**25468.97**	**1429.48**
2081.71	2003.46	59.77
767.50	735.31	41.66
1413.50	1375.38	0.17
578.55	610.41	0.51
1379.78	1343.94	130.18
590.46	571.99	116.99
56.66	55.94	10.64
140.47	135.98	
68.21	66.58	
293.14	281.86	1.04
166.22	151.58	0.07
92.76	86.93	14.75
735.88	733.88	
2650.06	2557.70	129.38
673.34	641.28	90.72
24.44	23.98	1.45
562.63	553.11	2.41
962.71	936.71	12.10
1437.69	1432.13	72.96
685.37	678.98	11.40
606.23	584.31	15.38
566.45	544.69	65.75
550.02	526.63	21.05
5192.38	5156.19	42.89
613.75	598.82	62.23
1257.43	1160.88	73.24
1762.86	1711.10	445.98
70.10	68.76	2.35
81.16	79.38	0.64
31.98	27.81	3.72
36.34	33.29	
1471.97	**1459.92**	
1388.39	1379.89	
54.57	55.09	
29.01	24.94	

13-8 续表2 continued

单位: 亿元

项 目	Item	资产总计 Total Assets
总 计	**Total**	**26866.37**
一、按登记注册类型分组:	Grouped by Type of Registration	
内资企业	Inner Funded Enterprises	21849.93
国有企业	State Owned Enterprises	4335.32
中央企业	Central Enterprises	4227.86
地方企业	Local Enterprises	107.46
集体企业	Collective-owned Enterprise	13.25
股份合作企业	Share Holding Cooperative Enterprises	
联营企业	Joint Owned Enterprise	
国有联营企业	State Joint Ownership	
集体联营企业	Collective Joint Ownership	
国有与集体联营企业	Joint State- Collective Ownership	
、其他联营企业	Other Joint Owned Enterprise	
有限责任公司	Responsibility Co. Ltd	8084.51
国有独资公司	State Solely Funded Co.	1868.17
其他有限责任公司	Others	6216.34
股份有限公司	Share Holding Co.Ltd.	7132.07
私营企业	Private - owned enterprises	2284.45
私营独资企业	Solely Private - owned enterprises	6.27
私营合作企业	Private Joint Venture	
私营有限责任公司	Private Responsibility Co. Ltd	2023.24
私营股份有限公司	Private Share Holding Co.Ltd.	254.94
其他企业	Others	0.34
港、澳、台商投资企业	Hongkong, Macao and Taiwan Funded Enterprises	1368.67
合资经营企业(港或澳、台资)	Joint Venture with Hongkong, Macao and Taiwan	772.90
合作经营企业(港或澳、台资)	Cooperate with Hongkong, Macao and Taiwan Funded	9.71
港澳台商独资经营企业	Enterprises Solely Funded by Hongkong, Macao and Taiwan Businessmen	466.29
港澳台商投资股份有限公司	Share Holding Co.Ltd. With Hongkong, Macao and Taiwan Investment	55.94
其他港澳台投资	Others	63.83
外商投资企业	Foreign Funded Enterprises	3647.77
中外合资经营企业	Sino - Foreign Joint Funded Enterprises	2842.90
中外合作经营企业	Sino - Foreign Cooperative Funded Enterprises	5.32
外资企业	Foreign Solely Funded Enterprises	477.64
外商投资股份有限公司	Foreign Funded Share Holding Co.Ltd.	321.91
其他外商投资	Others	
二、在总计中:亏损企业	**Of the Total: enterprises running under deficit**	**2216.68**
在总计中:国有控股企业	Of the Total: State-Owned Share Holding Enterprises	15852.66
在总计中:农村工业	Of the Total: Rural Industry	35.63
在总计中:轻工业	Of the Total: Light Industry	5530.86
重工业	Heavy Industry	21335.51
在总计中:大型企业	Of the Total: Large Scale Enterprises	19497.27
中型企业	Medium Scale Enterprises	7369.11
按行业分	Grouped by Sector	
采矿业	**Mining and Qarrying**	**373.72**

(100 million yuan)

			主营业务收入	全部从业人员年平均人数(万人)
流动资产合计 Circulating Funds	固定资产合计 Total Fined Assets	固定资产原价 Original Value of Fixed Assets	Revenue of Major Business	Average Number of Empolyment of the Curreat Year (10 000 Bersons)
12041.77	**9783.84**	**18410.85**	**26703.38**	**206.35**
9390.61	8090.15	15582.18	21129.44	169.40
1431.34	1901.12	3805.69	2453.66	23.08
1369.69	1868.48	3756.40	2402.67	21.72
61.65	32.65	49.28	50.99	1.36
5.84	5.60	13.70	27.37	0.55
4226.16	2756.34	4590.03	9460.30	71.75
914.57	730.91	1049.94	1701.54	8.71
3311.59	2025.44	3540.09	7758.76	63.04
2601.80	2517.74	4164.92	3991.82	31.74
1125.18	909.29	3007.63	5195.00	42.24
2.68	3.49	5.99	28.50	0.46
1009.93	801.42	2823.49	4658.80	37.39
112.57	104.38	178.15	507.70	4.39
0.29	0.06	0.21	1.29	0.04
695.06	481.51	839.96	1504.23	14.13
413.53	262.59	473.62	793.01	7.39
4.12	1.28	4.49	3.85	0.05
204.84	199.84	334.42	646.34	6.37
15.99	12.70	18.34	21.71	0.24
56.59	5.10	9.09	39.31	0.08
1956.10	1212.17	1988.71	4069.71	22.81
1575.77	878.86	1414.23	3242.19	14.68
2.98	2.34	7.20	41.58	0.10
280.90	160.05	277.01	588.11	6.10
96.45	170.92	290.26	197.83	1.94
1024.22	**843.89**	**1607.15**	**1228.15**	**20.96**
6309.51	6141.80	10668.33	10628.68	71.39
19.66	9.20	66.59	82.23	0.67
2926.78	1715.13	4411.06	8739.78	78.28
9114.99	8068.70	13999.79	17963.61	128.07
8395.61	7120.83	12861.92	16431.11	114.17
3646.16	2663.00	5548.93	10272.27	92.17
138.32	**182.63**	**491.26**	**312.01**	**6.37**

13-8 续表3 continued

单位: 亿元

项 目	Item	资产总计 Total Assets
煤炭开采和洗选业	Coal Mining and Processing	10.20
石油和天然气开采业	Petroleum and Natural Gas Extraction	104.91
黑色金属矿采选业	Ferrous Metals Mining and Processing	71.14
有色金属矿采选业	Non-ferrous Metals Mining and Processing	25.71
非金属矿采选业	Non-metal Minerals Mining and Processing	62.96
开采辅助活动	Mining Auxiliary Activities	94.12
其他采矿业	Other Minerals Mining and Processing	4.67
制造业	**Manufacturing**	**22584.48**
农副食品加工业	Food Processing	711.26
食品制造业	Food Production	348.17
酒、饮料和精制茶制造业	Wine,Beverage and Refined Tea Production	897.91
烟草制品业	Tobacco Processing	433.36
纺织业	Textile Industry	547.88
纺织服装、服饰业	Textile,Garments, and Fashion Industry	269.42
皮革、毛皮、羽毛及其制品和制鞋业	Leather, Furs,Down and Related Products	29.97
木材加工和木、竹、藤、棕、草制品业	Timber Processing, Wood, Bamboo, Cane, Palm and Sraw Products	89.61
家具制造业	Furniture Manufacturing	60.00
造纸和纸制品业	Papermaking and Paper Products	186.96
印刷和记录媒介复制业	Printing and Record Processing	98.95
文教、工美、体育和娱乐用品制造业	Stationery, Education and Sports Goods	60.62
石油加工、炼焦和核燃料加工业	Petroleum Processing, Coking Products and Nuclear Fuel Processing	253.92
化学原料和化学制品制造业	Raw Chemical Material and Chemical Products	2211.25
医药制造业	Medical and pharmaceutical Products	911.00
化学纤维制造业	Chemical Fibers	20.21
橡胶和塑料制品业	Rubber and plastic products	317.32
非金属矿物制品业	Nonmetal Material Products	863.97
黑色金属冶炼和压延加工业	Smelting and Pressing of Ferrous Metals	2329.11
有色金属冶炼和压延加工业	Smelting and Pressing of Nonferrous Metals	480.67
金属制品业	Metal Products	516.73
通用设备制造业	Ordinary Machinery Manufacturing	1010.99
专用设备制造业	Special Purpose Equipment Manufacturing	572.59
汽车制造业	Motor manufacturing	5418.45
铁路、船舶、航空航天和其他运输设备制造业	Railway,Watercraft,Aviation and other Transporlation Equipment manufacturing	757.59
电气机械和器材制造业	Electric Machinery and Equipment	923.95
计算机、通信和其他电子设备制造业	Telecommunication Computer,Equipment and Other Electronic Equipment Manufacturing	2056.88
仪器仪表制造业	Instruments and Meters, Manufacturing	84.75
其他制造业	Other Manufacturing	53.89
废弃资源综合利用业	Waste Comprehensive Vtilization of Resources Industry	46.94
金属制品、机械和设备修理业	Metal products,Machinery and Equipment Repairing	20.17
电力、燃气及水的生产和供应业	**Electric Power, Gas and Water Production and Supply**	**3908.17**
电力、热力生产和供应业	Electric Power, Steam and Hot Water Production and Supply	3612.47
燃气生产和供应业	Gas Production and Supply	78.12
水的生产和供应业	Tap Water Production and Supply	217.58

(100 million yuan)

流动资产合计 Circulating Funds	固定资产合计 Total Fined Assets	固定资产原价 Original Value of Fixed Assets	主营业务收入 Revenue of Major Business	全部从业人员年平均人数(万人) Average Number of Empolyment of the Curreat Year (10 000 Bersons)
5.03	3.54	5.68	21.88	0.67
11.23	79.64	308.23	31.42	1.50
32.22	24.73	56.57	105.86	1.30
7.11	13.37	16.56	16.22	0.30
33.10	16.60	30.38	72.80	1.12
47.46	42.74	68.62	61.68	1.41
2.18	2.01	5.21	2.16	0.06
11627.46	**6871.76**	**13337.52**	**24922.94**	**187.42**
310.15	320.56	1453.42	1916.18	8.77
151.50	121.21	634.61	698.97	6.45
619.97	182.05	360.18	1261.25	7.21
335.32	96.46	94.98	605.48	0.78
246.31	228.16	501.92	1323.26	16.56
148.12	76.74	163.88	536.16	10.83
14.01	13.71	21.94	50.97	2.23
31.84	41.73	85.16	124.07	1.57
21.85	33.99	22.70	54.83	0.74
99.90	68.41	214.16	264.51	2.09
63.51	27.76	56.43	144.22	1.44
33.42	11.58	45.11	84.49	1.13
112.63	135.67	218.30	802.57	0.78
802.30	1083.84	1744.17	2507.73	13.24
367.79	226.93	341.24	679.44	7.65
8.93	7.97	23.97	23.24	0.39
175.02	88.24	198.09	502.64	5.14
274.79	417.87	701.08	883.61	9.31
753.57	1005.21	2094.32	1461.82	9.92
251.97	136.60	218.02	1125.80	3.27
309.56	152.19	254.79	545.66	5.00
548.54	291.41	367.23	451.29	5.73
364.18	153.46	343.29	473.10	5.37
3045.51	1059.85	1814.61	4795.54	29.92
447.30	199.41	230.19	506.20	5.78
549.15	297.32	454.88	1111.78	9.80
1434.00	315.11	532.90	1778.09	13.17
39.65	34.84	52.74	63.92	1.27
28.89	21.49	51.77	79.28	0.88
24.99	17.20	22.73	43.25	0.41
12.79	4.81	18.70	23.62	0.59
275.98	**2729.45**	**4582.07**	**1468.43**	**12.56**
178.34	2614.01	4416.74	1373.28	10.68
24.74	42.56	52.16	62.60	0.50
72.90	72.88	113.17	32.56	1.38

13-9 规模以上工业企业生产能力(2016)

OUTPUT OF MAJOR PRODUCTS OF INDUSTRY ABOVE DESIGNATED SIZE (2016)

产品名称		Item		年初生产能力 Capacity at the Beginning of the Year	年末生产能力 Capacity at the End of the Year
原煤	吨	Coal	ton	23751357	25233475
天然原油	吨	Crude Petroleum Oil	ton	680670	573880
卷烟	万支	Cigarettes	10000 pieces	19159875	18079875
棉纺锭/纺纱量	锭/吨	Knitting Spindle/Capacity	spindle/ton	9901769	9789314
气流纺锭/纺纱量	头/吨	Air Spindle/Capacity	spindle/ton	560211	585501
棉布织机/布	台/万米	Cotton Loom/Cloth	piece/10000 meters	440444	521500
原油加工能力/原油加工量	吨/吨	Crude Oil Processing pacity	ton/ton	14000000	14500000
焦炭	吨	Coke	ton	9960000	9416000
烧碱(折100%)	吨	Caustic Soda (100%)	ton	1268000	1183000
碳化钙(电石,折300升/千克)	吨	Calcium Carbide (300 L/kg)	ton	555000	583500
农用氮、磷、钾化学肥料总计(折纯)	吨	Chemical Fertilizers	ton	18230287	17331793
初级形态塑料	吨	Primary Plastic	ton	2534927	2640878
化学纤维	吨	Chemical Fiber	ton	221714	279814
硅酸盐水泥熟料	吨	Portland Cement Clinker	ton	65458156	67800036
水泥	吨	Cement	ton	141050826	147219766
平板玻璃	重量箱	Plain Glass	weight case	96997130	97447330
生铁	吨	Pig Ion	ton	27894670	24488025
粗钢	吨	Crude Steel	ton	39832500	36554500
钢材	吨	Rolled Steel	ton	43273793	43394094
铁合金	吨	Ferroalloy	ton	439016	422025
原铝(电解铝)	吨	Electrolyzed Aluminum	ton	148000	148000
金属切削机床	台	Metal-cutting Machine Tools	piece	6389	6377
汽车	辆	Automobile	unit	2665050	2868780
其中:基本型乘用车(轿车)	辆	Cars	unit	1972220	2232800
家用电冰箱	台	Home Refrigerators	piece	4815000	5017000
房间空气调节器	台	Air Conditioners	piece	16600000	16800000
微型计算机设备	台	computers	piece	36206868	36206868
移动通信手持机(手机)	台	Mobile Phones	piece	165002130	145001521
发电设备容量总计/发电量	万千瓦/万千瓦小时	Generating Capacity	10000 kwh	6071	6256
其中:火电设备容量/发电量		Thermal Power	10000 kwh	2401	2517
水电设备容量/发电量		Hydropower	10000 kwh	3456	3461
风电设备容量/发电量		Wind Power	10000 kwh	173	218

13-10 规模以上工业主要产品产量(2016)
SCALE INDUSTRIAL OUTPUT OF MAIN ProduCTS (2016)

名 称		name		产品产量
原煤	吨	Original Coal	ton	5474220.0
1.无烟煤	吨	1.Anthracite	ton	3744487.0
2.烟煤	吨	2.Bituminous Coal	ton	1729733.0
其中:一般烟煤	吨	General Bituminous Coal	ton	1729733.0
洗煤	吨	Washed Coal	ton	583323.0
其中:洗精煤	吨	Cleaned Coal	ton	583323.0
天然原油	吨	Natural Oil	ton	580939.0
天然气	万立方米	Natural Gas	10000 cu.m	13051.0
铁矿石原矿	吨	Iron Ore	ton	29049956.8
铁矿石成品矿	吨	Finished Iron Ore	ton	1135856.2
其中:铁精矿	吨	Iron ore concentrate	ton	672937.0
铜金属含量	吨	Copper	ton	68221.5
锌金属含量	吨	Zinc	ton	
锡金属含量	吨	Tin	ton	111.1
锑金属含量	吨	Antimony	ton	83.0
稀有稀土金属矿	吨	Rare earth metal ore	ton	2263.8
其中:钨精矿折合量(折三氧化钨65%)	吨	Tungsten Concentrate Equivalent Amount (65% of Tungsten Trioxide)	ton	1109.7
其中:钼精矿折合量(折纯钼45%)	吨	Molybdenum Concentrate Equivalent Amount (45% of Pure Mo)	ton	1000.1
石灰石	吨	limestone	ton	27023108.8
建筑用天然石料	立方米	Natural stone for construction	cu.m	451691.0
高岭土(瓷土)	吨	Kaolin(China clay)	ton	455364.1
硫铁矿石(折含硫35%)	吨	Pyrite Stone (35% of Sulfur)	ton	80176.0
磷矿石(折含五氧化二磷30%)	吨	Phosphate Rock (30% of Phosphorus Pentoxide)	ton	51803379.1
原盐	吨	Crude Salt	ton	4060882.0
小麦粉	吨	Wheat Flour	ton	6567905.8
大米	吨	Rice	ton	29217840.1
饲料	吨	Feed	ton	20004050.8
其中:配合饲料	吨	Compound Feed	ton	11746614.7
混合饲料	吨	Mixed feed	ton	3328298.4
精制食用植物油	吨	Refined Edible Vegetable oil	ton	7735400.5
鲜、冷藏肉	吨	Fresh and Chilled Meat	ton	1758193.7
冻肉	吨	Frozen meat	ton	7438.1
熟肉制品	吨	Cooked meat products	ton	8271.6
冷冻水产品	吨	Frozen Seafood	ton	552420.9
冷冻蔬菜	吨	Frozen vegetables	ton	104351.2
膨化食品	吨	Puffed food	ton	58629.8
焙烤松脆食品	吨	Baked crisp food	ton	19429.0
糖果	吨	Candy	ton	273420.7

13-10 续表1 continued

名 称		name		产品产量
速冻食品	吨	Quick-Frozen Food	ton	66777.3
其中:速冻米面食品	吨	Frozen Rice\Flour Food	ton	66182.3
方便面	吨	Instant Noodles	ton	191409.1
乳制品	吨	Dairy Products	ton	1139864.9
液体乳	吨	Liquid Dairies	ton	1125423.8
固体及半固体乳制品	吨	Dairy\Solid or Semi-Solid Food	ton	14441.1
其中:乳粉	吨	Milk Powder	ton	5201.7
罐头	吨	Can	ton	1751126.1
味精(谷氨酸钠)	吨	Monosodium glutamate	ton	10309.0
酱油	吨	Soy Sauce	ton	155815.0
营养、保健食品	吨	Nutraceuticals	ton	45580.0
冷冻饮品	吨	Frozen Drinks	ton	299652.7
食品添加剂	吨	Food Additives	ton	347424.1
饲料添加剂	吨	Feed Additices	ton	13720.9
发酵酒精(折96度,商品量)	千升	Fermentation of Alcohol	kl	22436.0
饮料酒	千升	Alcoholic Beverage	kl	3173975.6
其中:白酒(折65度,商品量)	千升	Liquor (of 65 degrees, the amount of goods)	kl	903237.1
啤酒	千升	Beer	kl	1805187.9
黄酒	千升	Yellow wiue	kl	8057.3
葡萄酒	千升	Wine	kl	866.9
果酒及配制酒	千升	Fruit and concoction wiue	kl	128844.2
软饮料	吨	Soft Drinks	ton	10052663.4
其中:碳酸型饮料(汽水)	吨	Carbonated Beverages (soft drinks)	ton	853926.0
包装饮用水	吨	Packaging of Drinking Water	ton	3619458.9
果汁和蔬菜汁类饮料	吨	Fruit Juice and Vegetable Juice	ton	1173363.0
蛋白饮料	吨	Protein drinks	ton	469522.5
精制茶	吨	Refined Tea	ton	480575.2
卷烟	万支	Cigarette	10000 pieces	1220958.0
纱	吨	Yarn	ton	3215451.9
1、棉纱	吨	Cotton Yarn	ton	1809638.7
2、棉混纺纱	吨	Cotton Blended Yarn	ton	525165.3
3、化学纤维纱	吨	Chemical Fiber Yarn	ton	880648.0
布	万米	Fabric	10000 meters	784907.4
其中:色织布(含牛仔布)	万米	Dyed Fabric (including jean)	10000 meters	531.2
其中:1.棉布	万米	1.Cotton	10000 meters	636322.5
2.棉混纺布	万米	2.Cotton Blended Cloth	10000 meters	122148.0
化学纤维短纤布	万米	Chemical staple fiber cloth	10000 meters	26436.9
印染布	万米	Dyed Cloth	10000 meters	44995.5
毛机织物(呢绒)	万米	Wool woven fabric	10000 meters	3099.1
亚麻布(含亚麻≥55%)	万米	Linen Fabric (containing linen≥ 55%)	10000 meters	362.2

13–10 续表2 continued

名 称		name		产品产量
苎麻布(含苎麻≥55%)	万米	Ramie fabric (containing linen ≥ 55%)	10000 meters	1697.0
蚕丝	吨	Silk	ton	1077.2
化纤长丝机织物	万米	Woren fabrics of synthetic filament yarn	10000 meters	5580.0
蚕丝被	万条	Silk Quilt	10000 pieces	158.6
无纺布(无纺织物)	吨	Non–woven Fabric	ton	408226.7
帘子布	吨	Cord fabric	ton	3420.0
服装	万件	Clothing	10000 pieces	110354.6
1.梭织服装	万件	Tated Garments	10000 pieces	85685.8
其中:羽绒服	万件	Down Jacket	10000 pieces	342.8
西服套装	万件	Western–style	10000 pieces	1561.4
衬衫	万件	Shirt	10000 pieces	1322.7
运动类服装	万件	Sparswear	10000 pieces	990.0
2.针织服装	万件	Knitted Garments	10000 pieces	24668.8
轻革	平方米	Light Leather	sq.m	1201051.0
手提包(袋)、背包	万个	Handbag/Bachpack	10000 pieces	269.0
天然毛皮服装	万件	Leather Clothes	piece	48.1
鞋	万双	Footwear	10000 pairs	4403.5
其中:纺织面鞋	万双	Textile Footwear	10000 pairs	545.4
皮革鞋靴	万双	Leather Footwear	10000 pairs	2357.9
胶鞋	万双	Rubber Footweau	10000 pairs	107.5
人造板	立方米	Artificial Board	cu.m	9784523.0
其中:胶合板	立方米	Plywood	cu.m	3502355.9
纤维板	立方米	FibreBoard	cu.m	3953434.8
刨花板	立方米	Shaving Board	cu.m	200386.0
细木工板	立方米	Joinery Boowd	cu.m	38211.0
人造板表面装饰板	平方米	Artificial Board for Surface Decoration	sq.m	92975954.0
实木木地板	平方米	Solid Wood Flooving	sq.m	692090.9
复合木地板	平方米	Composite Wood Flooring	sq.m	48704448.8
竹地板	平方米	Bamboo Flooring	sq.m	867938.0
家具	件	Furniture	piece	6692567.0
其中:木质家具	件	Wood Furniture	piece	2734008.0
金属家具	件	Metal Furniture	piece	418243.0
软体家具	件	Upholstered Furniture	piece	372653.0
纸浆(原生浆及废纸浆)	吨	Pulp (original pulp and waste paper pulp)	ton	134430.0
机制纸及纸板(外购原纸加工除外)	吨	Machine Made Paper and PaperBoard (excludingprocessing outsourcing base paper)	ton	2511330.9
其中:未涂布印刷书写用纸	吨	Uncoating Writing Paper	ton	600729.5
其中:新闻纸	吨	Newsprint	ton	13117.0
卫生用纸原纸	吨	Toilet Paper	ton	121814.2
包装用纸及纸板	吨	Wrapping Paper and cardboard	ton	55645.4

13-10 续表3 continued

名 称		name		产品产量
其中:箱纸板	吨	Case Board	ton	16702.4
纸制品	吨	Paper Products	ton	3596227.0
其中:瓦楞纸箱	吨	Corrugated	ton	2146565.3
卫生用纸制品	吨	Toilte Paper	ton	4846.0
单色印刷品	令	Monochrome Print	ream	6450476.4
多色印刷品	对开色令	Multi-color Print	folio color ream	20744307.0
原油加工量	吨	Crude Oil Processing Capacity	ton	12334284.0
汽油	吨	Gasoline	ton	3241348.6
煤油	吨	Kerosene	ton	982521.6
柴油	吨	Diesel Fuel	ton	4265778.5
润滑油	吨	Lubricating Oil	ton	65976.0
燃料油	吨	Fuel Oil	ton	18941.6
石脑油	吨	Naphtha	ton	
液化石油气	吨	LPG	ton	607843.01
石油焦	吨	Petroleum Coke	ton	976061.3
石油沥青	吨	Petroleum Pitch	ton	59049.9
焦炭	吨	Coke	ton	8917209.0
硫酸(折100%)	吨	Sulfuric Acid (100% discount)	ton	7427103.7
盐酸(氯化氢,含量31%)	吨	Hydrochloric Acid (hydrogen chloride, 31%)	ton	606179.0
浓硝酸(折100%)	吨	Concentrated Nitric Acid (100% discount)	ton	5553.0
磷酸(含量85%)	吨	Ortho-phosphoric acid (85%)	ton	12021.1
烧碱(折100%)	吨	Caustic Soda (100% discount)	ton	1089425.0
其中:离子膜法烧碱(折100%)	吨	Ionic Membrane Method(100% discount)	ton	899700.0
纯碱(碳酸钠)	吨	Soda Ash (sodium carbonate)	ton	1647798.4
碳化钙(电石,折300升/千克)	吨	Calcium acetylide (of 300 litre per kilgogram)	ton	400381.7
乙烯	吨	ethylene	ton	728928.7
丙烯	吨	propylene	ton	377757.8
纯苯	吨	purified petroleum benzine	ton	458389.0
精甲醇	吨	Refined Methanol	ton	459452.0
合成氨(无水氨)	吨	Anhydrous Amonia	ton	4687275.0
农用氮、磷、钾化学肥料总计(折纯)	吨	Agricultural Nitrogen, Phosphorus and Potassium Fertilizer	ton	11560535.2
1、氮肥(折含N100%)	吨	1.N (of N 100%)	ton	5354419.9
其中:尿素(折含N100%)	吨	Urea (of N 100%)	ton	1367437.0
2、磷肥(折五氧化二磷100%)	吨	2.P (of 100% phosphorus pentoxide)	ton	6206115.3
磷酸一铵(实物量)	吨	MAP (physical quantity)	ton	9509472.1
磷酸二铵(实物量)	吨	DAP (physical quantity)	ton	4886031.9
化学农药原药(折有效成分100%)	吨	Chemical Pesticide Active Compound	ton	278105.3
其中:杀虫剂(杀螨剂)原药	吨	Pesticide Active Compound	ton	69046.0

13-10 续表4 continued

名 称		name		产品产量
除草剂原药	吨	Herbicide Active Compound	ton	180666.0
涂料	吨	Paint	ton	407348.6
初级形态塑料	吨	Primary Form Plastic	ton	2247433.1
其中:低密度聚乙烯树脂(LDPE)	吨	LDPE Resin	ton	7367.4
高密度聚乙烯树脂(HDPE)	吨	HDPE Rsein	ton	245564.6
线型低密度聚乙烯树脂(LLDPE)	吨	LLDPE Resin	ton	265614.4
聚丙烯树脂	吨	Polypropylene Resin	ton	641198.4
聚氯乙烯树脂	吨	PVC Resin	ton	637079.0
聚苯乙烯树脂	吨	Polystyrene Resin	ton	32064.0
ABS树脂	吨	ABS Resin	ton	24388.0
硅橡胶	吨	Silicon Rwbber	ton	116248.0
合成橡胶	吨	Synthetic Rubber	ton	26902.0
合成纤维单体	吨	Synthetic Fiber Monomer	ton	323264.1
合成纤维聚合物	吨	Synthetic Fiber Polymer	ton	20226.0
化学试剂	吨	Chemical Reagent	ton	711752.3
表面活性剂	吨	Swface Active Agent	ton	14519.2
活性炭	吨	Acticarbon	ton	17318.0
多晶硅	千克	Polycrystalline Silion	kg	7074174.9
合成洗涤剂	吨	Synthetic Detergent	ton	215135.0
液体洗涤剂	吨	Lignid Detergent	ton	2250.0
化学药品原药	吨	Original Drug Chemicals	ton	284196.0
中成药	吨	Chinese Patent Medicine	ton	460575.0
兽用药品	吨	Veterinary Medicine	ton	5114.8
化学纤维用浆粕	吨	Chemical Fiber Pulp	ton	8990.0
化学纤维	吨	Chemical Fiber	ton	274932.4
人造纤维(纤维素纤维)	吨	Artificid Fiber	ton	94927.0
其中:粘胶短纤维	吨	Fibranne	ton	85816.0
粘胶纤维长丝	吨	Viscose Filament	ton	9111.0
合成纤维	吨	Synthetic Fiber	ton	180005.4
涤纶纤维	吨	Polyester Fiber	ton	101147.3
丙纶纤维	吨	Polypropylene Fiber	ton	73974.0
橡胶轮胎外胎	条	Rubber Cover Tyre	piece	10541289.0
其中:乘用车橡胶轮胎外胎	条	Passenger car Rubber Cover Tyre	piece	6985686.0
载货汽车橡胶轮胎外胎	条	Truck Rubber Cover Tyre	piece	3555603.0
其中:子午线轮胎外胎	条	Radial Tire	piece	7678269.0
塑料制品	吨	Plastic Products	ton	5946798.5
其中:塑料薄膜	吨	Plastic Film	ton	228125.9
其中:农用薄膜	吨	Agricultural Film	ton	69882.1
泡沫塑料	吨	Foam	ton	279409.0
塑料人造革、合成革	吨	Plastic Leather and Synthetic Leather	ton	54134.4

13-10 续表5 continued

名 称		name		产品产量
日用塑料制品	吨	Household Plastic Products	ton	664873.1
硅酸盐水泥熟料	吨	Cement Clinker	ton	50714574.0
其中:窑外分解窑水泥熟料	吨	Cement Kiln Clinker	ton	40924108.3
水泥	吨	Cement	ton	115866591.3
其中:强度等级42.5水泥(含R型)	吨	Strength Grade 42.5 Cement (including R-type)	ton	16668943.5
强度等级52.5水泥(含R型)	吨	Strength Grade 52.5 Cement (including R-type)	ton	94792.0
石灰	吨	Lime	ton	3194773.8
商品混凝土	立方米	Concrete	cu.m	68863021.8
水泥混凝土排水管	千米	Concrete Drainage Pipe	km	9204.1
水泥混凝土压力管	千米	Concrete Pressure Pipe	km	6142.2
水泥混凝土电杆	根	Cement Concrete Pole	piece	889171.0
预应力混凝土桩	米	Prestressed Concrete Pile	meter	88837326.5
石膏板	万平方米	Gypsum Board	10000 sq.m	77574.3
砖	万块	Brick	10000 pieces	7576143.7
瓦	万片	Tile	10000 pieces	347930.3
瓷质砖	平方米	Porcelain Tile	sq.m	275678644.8
陶质砖	平方米	Ceramic Tile	sq.m	141042240.3
天然大理石建筑板材	平方米	Natural Marble Building Boards	sq.m	33946735.3
天然花岗石建筑板材	平方米	Natural Granite Building Boards	sq.m	46958454.0
沥青和改性沥青防水卷材	平方米	Asphalt and Modified Bitumen Sheet	sq.m	61137739.6
隔热、隔音人造矿物材料及其制品	吨	Thermal and Sound Insulated Manufactured mineral and Pwdwts	ton	34017.2
平板玻璃	重量箱	Plate Glass	weight case	86966562.4
钢化玻璃	平方米	Tempered Glass	sq.m	14152805.0
夹层玻璃	平方米	Laminated Glass	sq.m	1755740.8
中空玻璃	平方米	Insulating Glass	sq.m	10426103.5
日用玻璃制品	吨	Daily Glass Products	ton	781949.0
玻璃包装容器	吨	Glass Containers	ton	1930446.8
玻璃保温容器	个	Glass Thermal Cowtainers	piece	24800000.0
玻璃纤维纱	吨	Glass Fiber Yarn	ton	18388.7
纤维增强塑料制品	吨	Fiber Reinforced Plastic Products	ton	9164.8
卫生陶瓷制品	件	Sanitary Ceramic Products	piece	20975292.0
耐火材料制品	吨	Refractory Products	ton	2055476.4
石墨及炭素制品	吨	Graphite and Carbon Products	ton	292534.0
生铁	吨	Pig Iron	ton	23233046.6
粗钢	吨	Crude Steel	ton	29484760.3
铸铁件	吨	Iron Casting	ton	2856955.7
铸钢件	吨	Steel Casting	ton	987489.6
钢材	吨	Steel	ton	35637878.8
1.铁道用钢材	吨	1. Railway Steel	ton	449432.0
重轨	吨	Heavy Rail	ton	448985.0

13-10 续表6 continued

名 称		name		产品产量
2.大型型钢	吨	2. Large-scale Steel	ton	53971.0
3.中小型型钢	吨	3. Small and Medium Scale Steel	ton	1335131.0
4.棒材	吨	4. Bar	ton	2471265.0
5.钢筋	吨	5. Steel Bar	ton	6495910.1
6.线材(盘条)	吨	6. Wire (coil)	ton	4258597.4
7.特厚板	吨	7. Special Plate	ton	324269.0
8.厚钢板	吨	8. Thick Steel Plate	ton	607177.0
9.中板	吨	9. Middle Plate	ton	1065898.2
10.热轧薄板	吨	10. Hot-rolled Sheet	ton	39075.0
11.冷轧薄板	吨	11. Cold-rolled Sheet	ton	1679611.6
12.中厚宽钢带	吨	12. Thick Wide Strip	ton	4318557.0
13.热轧薄宽钢带	吨	13. Hot-rolled Thin Wide Strip	ton	2324830.3
14.冷轧薄宽钢带	吨	14. Cold-rolled Wide Strip	ton	2656521.4
15.热轧窄钢带	吨	15. Hot-rolled Narrow Strip	ton	256388.0
16.冷轧窄钢带	吨	16. Cold-rolled Narrow Strip	ton	49275.0
17.镀层板(带)	吨	17. Coated Plate	ton	3640422.7
18.涂层板(带)	吨	18. Coated Plate	ton	515364.3
19.电工钢板(带)	吨	19. Electrical Shect	ton	1546741.1
20.无缝钢管	吨	Seamless steel tube	ton	1232502.0
21.焊接钢管	吨	Welded Steel	ton	37610.2
22.其他钢材	吨	Other steel	ton	279329.5
用外购钢材再加工生产钢材	吨	Process steel by outsourcing steel	ton	37.3
用外购国产钢材再加工生产钢材	吨	Process steed by outsourcing olomestic	ton	37.3
铁合金	吨	Ferroalloy	ton	302191.4
其中：电炉硅铁(折合含硅75%)	吨	Electnic Ferrosilicon (of Silicon 75%)	ton	19774.7
锰硅合金(折合含锰硅量合计82%)	吨	Manganese Silicon alloy (of/Manganese Sililong 82%)	ton	80615.0
十种有色金属	吨	10 Kinds of Nonferrous Metals	ton	874714.0
精炼铜(电解铜)	吨	Refined Copper (electrolytic copper)	ton	435830.3
铅	吨	Lead	ton	360831.0
镍	吨	Nickel	ton	1628.0
锑品	吨	Antimory	ton	8881.0
原铝(电解铝)	吨	Electrolytic Aluminum	ton	67543.7
黄金	千克	Gold	kg	23965.1
白银(银锭)	千克	Silver (silver bullion)	kg	1126068.7
铜合金	吨	Copper Alloy	ton	53879.0
铝合金	吨	Aluminum Alloy	ton	110332.0
铜材	吨	Copper	ton	328790.6
铝材	吨	Aluminum	ton	1169319.7
钢结构	吨	Steel structure	ton	491172.3

13-10 续表7 continued

名 称		name		产品产量
金属门窗及类似制品	吨	Metal doors and windows and similar proatucts	ton	88415.7
金属切削工具	万件	Metal Cutting Tools	10000 pieces	39508.9
金属压力容器	吨	Metal pressure vessel	ton	1641.0
钢丝	吨	Wire	ton	100164.0
钢丝绳	吨	Wire Rope	ton	26178.0
钢绞线	吨	Strand	ton	229809.1
不锈钢日用制品	吨	Stainless steel daily products	ton	24771.6
锻件	吨	Forge Piece	ton	701680.1
粉末冶金零件	吨	Powder Metallurgy	ton	90909.9
工业锅炉	蒸发量吨	Industrial Boiler	ton	2809.6
发动机	千瓦	Engine	kw	137734204.0
其中:汽车用发动机	千瓦	Automotive Engine	kw	135247016.0
电站用汽轮机	千瓦	Power Plant Steam Turbine	kw	701400.0
电站水轮机	千瓦	Turbine	kw	18200.0
金属切削机床	台	Metal Cutting Machine	piece	4945.0
其中:数控金属切削机床	台	CNC Metal Cutting Machine	piece	530.0
金属成形机床	台	Metal Forming Machine	piece	33843.0
其中: 数控金属成形机床(数控锻压设备)	台	CNC Metal Forming Machine	piece	132.0
铸造机械	台	Foundry Machine	piece	64264.0
电焊机	台	Electric Welding Machine	piece	515.0
机床数控装置	套	Machine Digital Control Device	piece	1813.0
起重机	吨	Crane	piece	26253.7
电动车辆(电动叉车)	台	Electric Vehicles (electric forklift)	piece	42641.0
内燃叉车	台	Internal Combustion Forklift	piece	156.0
输送机械(输送机和提升机)	吨	Transportation Machinery (conveyors and elevators)	ton	189249.0
电梯、自动扶梯及升降机	台	Elevatows,Escalatovs and Lifters	piece	1034.0
电梯	台	Elevators	piece	1034.0
泵	台	Pump	piece	470202.0
其中:真空泵	台	Vacuum Pump	piece	3964.0
真空应用设备	台	Vacuum Application Equipmeut	piece	12.0
气体压缩机	台	Gas Compressor	piece	30709781.0
制冷设备用压缩机	台	Refrigeration Equipment with Compressor	piece	30704140.0
非制冷设备用压缩机	台	Non Refrigeration Equipnent with Compressor	piecen	5641.0
阀门	吨	Valve	ton	81647.9
液压元件	件	Hydraulic Components	piece	901529.0
气动元件	件	Pneumatic components	piece	2176715.0
滚动轴承	万套	Roller	10000 pieces	7300.9
齿轮	吨	Gear	ton	430578.7
风机	台	Fans	piece	37129.0
其中:鼓风机	台	Blower	piece	5998.0

13-10 续表8 continued

名 称		name		产品产量
工商用制冷、空调设备	万台(套)	Industnial and commereial refrigeration equipment and air conalitioner	10000 pieces	283.6
其中:工商用空调设备	万台(套)	Industrial and Commercial Air Conditioner	10000 pieces	282.9
其中:车用空调设备	万台(套)	Vehicular Air Conditionev	10000 pieces	282.9
电动手提式工具	台	Electric Hand Tools	piece	168449.0
衡器(秤)	台	Weighing Apparatws	piece	1023.0
包装专用设备	台	Special Equipment Package	piece	13734.0
影像投影仪	台	Image Projector	piece	4732.0
金属密封件	万件	Metal Sealing Element	10000 pieces	2373.6
金属紧固件	吨	Metal Fastenings	ton	61728.6
弹簧	吨	Spring	ton	50154.0
减速机	台	Reducer	piece	336824.0
矿山专用设备	吨	Mining Special Equipment	ton	95286.9
石油钻井设备	台(套)	petroleum Drilling Equipment	piece	347.0
建筑工程用机械	台	Construction Machiney	piece	476.0
其中:挖掘、铲土运输机械	台	Digging and Scraper Transport Machinery	piece	476.0
水泥专用设备	吨	Cement Special Equipment	ton	15800.0
混凝土机械	台	Concrete Machinery	piece	730.0
金属冶炼设备	吨	Metal Smelting Equipment	ton	987.6
金属轧制设备	吨	Metal Rolling Equipment	ton	7273.4
炼油、化工生产专用设备	吨	Oil Refining and Chemical Production Special Equipment	ton	571327.6
塑料加工专用设备	台	Plastics Processing Special Equipment	piece	234.0
模具	套	Mold	piece	697538.0
食品制造机械	台	Food Manfacturing Machiney	piece	114611.0
农产品加工专用设备	台	Equipmeut for Agvicultural Prodwtion manufactuming	piece	99339.0
农产品初加工机械	台	Equipment for Agricultural Products Pretreating	piece	1138106.0
饲料生产专用设备	台	Equipment for Feed Production	piece	10856.0
电子工业专用设备	台	Equipment for Ealectronic prodults	piece	72489.0
小型拖拉机	台	Small Tractor	piece	57684.0
机械化农业及园艺机具	台	Mechanized Agnculture and Horticultural Machiney	piece	884575.0
其中:土壤耕整机械	台	Soil Tiuage Machiney	piece	48370.0
种植施肥机械	台	Planting and Fevtilizing Machiney	piece	1065.0
收获机械	台	Harvesting Machinery	piece	5197.0
其中:谷物收获机械	台	Cereal Harvesting Machinery	piece	5197.0
收获后处理机械	台	Post-harvesting Processing Machinery	piece	58651.0
其中:棉花加工机械	台	Cotton Processing Machinery	piece	871.0
医疗仪器设备及器械	台	Equipmewl and Apparatus for Medical Treatweut	piece	59418.0
环境污染防治专用设备	台(套)	Equipment for Environmental Pollution Control	piece	89628.0
大气污染防治设备	台(套)	Air Pollution Control Equipment	piece	83980.0
水质污染防治设备	台(套)	Water Pollution Control Equipment	piece	4616.0
固体废弃物处理设备	台(套)	Solid Waste Handling Equipment	piece	777.0

13-10 续表9 continued

名 称		name		产品产量
放射性污染防治和处理设备	台(套)	Equipweut for Prevention and Treatment of Radioactive Pollution	piece	255.0
工业机器人	套	Industrial Robot	piece	6116.0
汽车	辆	Car	piece	2436913.0
其中:基本型乘用车(轿车)	辆	Passenger Vehicles	piece	1065549.0
1升<排量≤1.6升	辆	(1) 1.0 Liter < Displacement ≤ 1.6 Liter	piece	877633.0
1.6升<排量≤2.0升	辆	(2) 1.6 Liter < Displacement ≤ 2.0 Liter	piece	182753.0
2.0升<排量≤2.5升	辆	(3) 2.0 Liter < Displacement ≤ 2.5 Liter	piece	5162.0
2.5升<排量≤3.0升	辆	(4) 2.5 Liter < Displacement ≤ 3.0 Liter	piece	1.0
多功能乘用车(MPV)	辆	MPV	piece	129692.0
运动型多用途乘用车(SUV)	辆	SUV	piece	827402.0
客车	辆	Bus	piece	97484.0
(1)大型客车(车长>10米)	辆	(1) Large Passenger Bus (car length>10 m)	piece	172.0
(2)中型客车(7米<车长≤10米)	辆	(2) Medium Passenger Bus(7 m<car length≤10 m)	piece	4509.0
(3)轻型客车(车长≤7米)	辆	(3) light buses (car length≤ 7 m)	piece	92803.0
载货汽车	辆	Lorry	piece	313794.0
其中:新能源汽车	辆	New Euevgy Car	piece	24033.0
改装汽车	辆	Modified Cars	piece	271638.0
低速载货汽车	辆	Low Speed Truck	piece	6632.0
铁路货车	辆	Railway Wagon	piece	4550.0
城市轨道车辆	辆	Urban rail vehicle	piece	14.0
民用钢质船舶	载重吨	Civil Steel Ships	ton	1506612.9
钢质机动货船	载重吨	Steel Mobile Freightev	ton	1472812.9
其中:散货船	载重吨	Bulk Cowgo Ship	ton	917544.9
钢质机动非货船	载重吨	Steed Mobile Non Fveightev	ton	16050.0
钢质非机动船	载重吨	Steel non motorized vessel	ton	17750.0
电动自行车	辆	Electric Bicycle	piece	924986.0
发电机组(发电设备)	千瓦	Generating Units (power equipment)	kw	679600.0
其中:水轮发电机组	千瓦	Generator Group	kw	7600.0
汽轮发电机组	千瓦	Turbonator	kw	672000.0
电动机	千瓦	Motors	kw	1553672.0
交流电动机	千瓦	AC Motors	kw	1178703.0
变压器	千伏安	Transformer	kva	31315285.0
互感器	台	Mutual Inductor	kva	255895.0
高压开关板	面	High-voltage Switch Board	piece	234295.0
低压开关板	面	Low-voltage Switch Board	piece	261119.0
高压开关设备(11万伏以上)	台	High Voltage Switchgear (11 KV and above)	piece	27905.0
安全、自动化监控设备	台(套)	Equipment for safety and automation mouitoring	pieces	18331
通信及电子网络用电缆	对千米	Communication and Electronic Networks Cables	km	1778742.0
电力电缆	千米	Power Cable	km	673181.0
光纤	千米	Optical fibre	km	14761488.0
光缆	芯千米	Optical Cable	km	74185660.6
绝缘制品	吨	Insulation Products	ton	89922.4
锂离子电池	只(自然只)	Li-ion Battery	piece	206068104.0
铅酸蓄电池	千伏安时	Lead-acid Battery	kvah	26571469.5
碱性蓄电池	只(自然只)	Alkaline Battery	piece	8884666.0
原电池及原电池组(非扣式)	万只	Primary Cells and Primary Batteries	10000 pieces	9443.0
太阳能电池(光伏电池)	千瓦	Solar Battery	kw	1276734.2

13-10 续表10 continued

名 称		name		产品产量
家用电冰箱(家用冷冻冷藏箱)	台	Household Refrigerator	piece	3920630.0
家用冷柜(家用冷冻箱)	台	Household Refrigerator (household freezers)	piece	1394553.0
房间空气调节器	台	Room Air Conditioners	piece	12063787.0
家用吸排油烟机	台	Home Ventilator	piece	7889.0
家用电热水器	台	Water Heater	piece	2205968.0
家用燃气灶具	台	Kitchen Range	piece	1443183.0
太阳能热水器	平方米	Solar Water Heater	sq.m	406492.0
电光源	万只	Light Sources	10000 pieces	192156.8
其中:白炽灯泡	万只	Incandescent Bulb	10000 pieces	43529.0
荧光灯	万只	Fluorescent Lamp	10000 pieces	11167.4
灯具及照明装置	万套(台、个)	Lamps and Lighting Fittings	10000pieces	1981.8
电子计算机整机	台	Computers	piece	8402677.0
微型计算机设备	台	Micro-computer Equipment	piece	8402677.0
平板电脑	台	Tablet computer	piece	7997738.0
显示器	台	Monitor	piece	21851183.0
移动通信基站设备	信道	Equipment for Mobile Communication Base Station		185982.0
移动通信手持机(手机)	台	Mobile Handset (cell phone)	piece	62206750.0
其中:智能手机	台	Smartphoue	piece	49037918.0
彩色电视机	台	Colow Television	piece	89286.0
液晶(LCD)电视机	台	LCD Television	piece	89286.0
电视接收机顶盒	台	Television Set-top BO	piece	294773.0
半导体分立器件	万只	Semiconductor Discrete Devices	10000 pieces	1235198.5
集成电路圆片	万片	IC Wafer	10000 pieces	23.5
光电子器件	万只(片、套)	Optoelectronic Devices	10000 pieces	991073.4
其中:发光二极管(LED)	万只	Light-emitting Diode (LED)	10000 pieces	369517.0
液晶显示屏	片	LCD Screen	piece	4504400.0
液晶显示模组	套	LCD module	piece	1432700.0
电子元件	万只	Electronic Component	10000 pieces	1353891.8
其中:电声器件	万只	Electroacoustic Device	10000 pieces	194.8
印制电路板	平方米	Printed Board	sq.m	2674540.0
工业自动调节仪表与控制系统	万台(套)	Automatic Adjustment and Control System of Industrial Instrumentation	10000 piece	12.8
电工仪器仪表	台	Electric Instrument	piece	1822.0
工业仪表	万台(个)	Industrial Instrumeut	10000 pieces	45.7
分析仪器及装置	台(套)	Analytical Instrument	piece	961.0
试验机	台	Testing Machinery	piece	565.0
环境监测专用仪器仪表	台	Instrumeut for Environmeutal monitoring	piece	31786.0
汽车仪器仪表	台	Car Instrument	piece	7149397.0
光学仪器	万台(个)	Optical Instrument	10000 piece	3465.9
发电量	万千瓦小时	Power Generation	10000 kwh	224231363.31
其中:火力发电量	万千瓦小时	Thermal Capacity	10000 kwh	10119875.15
水力发电量	万千瓦小时	Hydroelectricity	10000 kwh	13792968.70
风力发电量	万千瓦小时	Wind Power Capacity	10000 kwh	276847.93
煤气生产量	万立方米	Coal Gas	10000 cu.m	2870078.00
自来水生产量	万立方米	Water Production	10000 cu.m	246174.7

13-11 规模以上工业企业主要经济效益指标(2016)

项 目	Item	企业亏损面(%) Enterprises deficit (%)
总　计	**Total**	**7.8**
一、按登记注册类型分组:	**Grouped by Type of Registration**	
内资企业	Inner Funded Enterprises	7.4
国有企业	State Owned Enterprises	22.6
中央企业	Central Enterprises	23.8
地方企业	Local Enterprises	22.0
集体企业	Collective-owned Enterprise	15.9
股份合作企业	Share Holding Cooperative Enterprises	13.3
联营企业	Joint Owned Enterprise	
国有联营企业	State Joint Ownership	
集体联营企业	Collective Joint Ownership	
国有与集体联营企业	Joint State- Collective Ownership	
其他联营企业	Other Joint Owned Enterprise	
有限责任公司	Responsibility Co. Ltd	10.4
国有独资公司	State Solely Funded Co.	23.0
其他有限责任公司	Others	10.1
股份有限公司	Share Holding Co.Ltd.	11.7
私营企业	Private - owned enterprises	4.8
私营独资企业	Solely Private - owned enterprises	1.8
私营合作企业	Private Joint Venture	
私营有限责任公司	Private Responsibility Co. Ltd	4.8
私营股份有限公司	Private Share Holding Co.Ltd.	6.8
其他企业	Others	
港、澳、台商投资企业	Hongkong, Macao and Taiwan Funded Enterprises	16.6
合资经营企业(港或澳、台资)	Joint Venture with Hongkong, Macao and Taiwan	16.9
合作经营企业(港或澳、台资)	Cooperate with Hongkong, Macao and Taiwan Funded	25.0
港澳台商独资经营企业	Enterprises Solely Funded by Hongkong, Macao and Taiwan Businessmen	17.3
港澳台商投资股份有限公司	Share Holding Co.Ltd. With Hongkong, Macao and Taiwan Investment	
外商投资企业	Foreign Funded Enterprises	16.2
中外合资经营企业	Sino - Foreign Joint Funded Enterprises	14.3
中外合作经营企业	Sino - Foreign Cooperative Funded Enterprises	12.5
外资企业	Foreign Solely Funded Enterprises	19.9
外商投资股份有限公司	Foreign Funded Share Holding Co.Ltd.	7.1
二、在总计中:亏损企业	**Of the Total: enterprises running under deficit**	**100.0**
在总计中:国有控股企业	Of the Total: State-Owned Share Holding Enterprises	20.9
在总计中:农村工业	Of the Total: Rural Industry	5.3
在总计中:轻工业	Of the Total: Light Industry	6.3
重工业	Heavy Industry	8.9
在总计中:大型企业	Of the Total: Large Scale Enterprises	9.2
中型企业	Medium Scale Enterprises	9.6
小型企业	Small Enterprises	7.5

MAJOR ECONOMIC INDICATORS OF INDUSTRIAL ENTERPRISES ABOVE DESIGNATED SIZE (2016)

总资产贡献率(%) Contributing Ratie of Tatal Assets(%)	资产负债率(%) Assets Liability Ratio(%)	流动资产周转率(次/年) Current Asset Tuinover (Times/year)	成本费用利润率(%) Ratio of Riofits to Industrial Cost(%)	产品销售率(%) Propovtion of Produts Sold(%)
13.52	**53.65**	**2.69**	**6.28**	**96.98**
13.29	52.59	2.80	5.98	96.79
4.71	63.98	1.70	3.19	99.41
4.76	63.75	1.77	3.16	99.66
3.65	69.03	0.96	3.97	94.21
18.25	57.95	4.75	3.85	96.73
9.34	66.22	1.64	5.19	93.49
21.11	33.07	2.77	11.19	99.92
23.84	26.98	2.67	17.26	98.00
5.91	58.83	0.73	1.19	115.65
45.24	18.12	36.54	2.21	100.00
15.25	59.05	2.57	5.54	96.93
33.04	61.14	1.92	9.06	100.04
11.63	58.62	2.70	5.18	96.56
10.23	43.54	1.58	10.97	96.14
18.56	44.24	4.82	5.42	96.47
38.65	30.95	10.19	6.54	97.64
29.60	41.42	9.59	4.05	99.10
18.22	44.38	4.78	5.33	96.53
19.30	44.69	4.46	6.21	95.27
26.31	36.57	7.92	6.39	95.94
11.99	52.02	2.38	6.99	97.27
11.88	56.86	2.19	6.73	98.13
4.28	40.09	1.99	0.23	95.95
11.38	45.59	3.12	5.77	95.79
8.87	29.16	1.86	12.91	103.57
15.82	62.34	2.14	8.52	98.45
17.18	63.91	2.15	8.94	98.35
28.13	56.60	5.53	8.18	98.52
12.35	54.76	1.98	7.63	97.99
9.17	64.43	2.13	5.16	102.25
−2.33	**74.86**	**1.26**	**−8.10**	**92.46**
11.80	57.13	1.74	7.46	98.46
11.90	50.51	3.98	3.20	97.38
21.25	46.65	3.56	6.39	96.34
11.01	55.92	2.36	6.22	97.36
12.88	56.41	2.00	7.30	98.46
13.88	53.32	2.85	6.29	96.27
14.40	49.02	3.68	5.41	96.19

13-11 续表 continued

项 目	Item	企业亏损面(%) Enterprises Deficit (%)
按行业分	Grouped by Sector	
采矿业	**Mining and Qarrying**	**8.8**
煤炭开采和洗选业	Coal Mining and Processing	9.0
石油和天然气开采业	Petroleum and Natural Gas Extraction	100.0
黑色金属矿采选业	Ferrous Metals Mining and Processing	14.3
有色金属矿采选业	Non-ferrous Metals Mining and Processing	9.7
非金属矿采选业	Non-metal Minerals Mining and Processing	6.7
开采辅助活动	Mining Auxiliary Activities	75.0
其他采矿业	Other Minerals Mining and Processing	
制造业	**Manufacturing**	**7.6**
农副食品加工业	Food Processing	4.2
食品制造业	Food Production	5.8
酒、饮料和精制茶制造业	Wine,Beverage and Refined Tea Production	5.7
烟草制品业	Tobacco Processing	14.3
纺织业	Textile Industry	6.5
纺织服装、服饰业	Textile,Garments, and Fashion Industry	5.5
皮革、毛皮、羽毛及其制品和制鞋业	Leather, Furs,Down and Related Products	3.5
木材加工和木、竹、藤、棕、草制品业	Timber Processing, Wood, Bamboo, Cane, Palm and Sraw Products	4.0
家具制造业	Furniture Manufacturing	4.3
造纸和纸制品业	Papermaking and Paper Products	10.7
印刷和记录媒介复制业	Printing and Record Processing	11.7
文教、工美、体育和娱乐用品制造业	Stationery, Education and Sports Goods	4.7
石油加工、炼焦和核燃料加工业	Petroleum Processing, Coking Products and Nuclear Fuel Processing	16.7
化学原料和化学制品制造业	Raw Chemical Material and Chemical Products	9.3
医药制造业	Medical and pharmaceutical Products	11.5
化学纤维制造业	Chemical Fibers	5.0
橡胶和塑料制品业	Rubber and plastic products	4.3
非金属矿物制品业	Nonmetal Material Products	5.6
黑色金属冶炼和压延加工业	Smelting and Pressing of Ferrous Metals	11.0
有色金属冶炼和压延加工业	Smelting and Pressing of Nonferrous Metals	13.9
金属制品业	Metal Products	7.5
通用设备制造业	Ordinary Machinery Manufacturing	7.8
专用设备制造业	Special Purpose Equipment Manufacturing	8.6
汽车制造业	Motor manufacturing	11.4
铁路、船舶、航空航天和其他运输设备制造业	Railway,Watercraft,Aviation and other Transporlation Equipment manufacturing	11.3
电气机械和器材制造业	Electric Machinery and Equipment	9.8
计算机、通信和其他电子设备制造业	Telecommunication Computer,Equipment and Other Electronic Equipment Manufacturing Other Electronic Equipment Manufacturing	12.1
仪器仪表制造业	Instruments and Meters, Manufacturing	9.4
其他制造业	Other Manufacturing	2.6
废弃资源综合利用业	Waste Comprehensive Vtilization of Resources Industry	23.2
金属制品、机械和设备修理业	Metal products,Machinery and Equipment Repairing	25.0
电力、燃气及水的生产和供应业	**Electric Power, Gas and Water Production and Supply**	**15.9**
电力、热力生产和供应业	Electric Power, Steam and Hot Water Production and Supply	16.5
燃气生产和供应业	Gas Production and Supply	3.0
水的生产和供应业	Tap Water Production and Supply	23.9

总资产贡献率(%) Contributing Ratie of Tatal Assets(%)	资产负债率(%) Assets Liability Ratio(%)	流动资产周转率(次/年) Current Asset Tuinover (Times/year)	成本费用利润率(%) Ratio of Riofits to Industrial Cost(%)	产品销售率(%) Propovtion of Produts Sold(%)
11.79	**53.48**	**3.12**	**2.81**	**97.27**
20.06	43.21	4.44	7.13	96.49
-10.67	45.49	3.85	-41.12	100.09
13.29	56.65	4.39	2.54	99.75
16.82	51.96	2.33	15.70	98.37
18.68	50.22	3.14	8.27	96.13
1.08	74.93	1.31	-5.64	96.27
9.17	64.23	1.05	8.37	99.66
14.33	**53.92**	**2.65**	**6.01**	**96.91**
18.59	39.52	5.88	5.04	96.92
20.57	44.69	4.81	6.23	96.01
16.59	58.60	2.42	7.16	96.63
120.71	31.00	1.85	50.22	105.45
22.70	44.94	5.74	5.58	97.03
18.62	45.20	4.55	4.94	97.13
14.71	48.36	4.62	3.79	97.21
17.30	45.13	4.59	6.18	95.96
13.33	39.17	3.58	6.61	95.96
11.47	51.39	2.88	4.93	96.31
16.65	44.76	2.88	6.46	94.72
8.53	66.06	1.50	6.43	94.10
66.86	58.68	6.93	2.71	97.94
10.61	57.48	3.58	4.45	96.42
13.71	44.23	2.27	9.13	95.11
8.45	41.19	3.11	4.35	98.79
18.71	44.20	3.66	6.57	97.45
17.07	43.62	4.05	7.10	96.31
5.43	65.30	2.24	1.99	98.89
4.92	62.97	4.67	0.83	98.79
11.25	55.94	2.62	4.60	96.48
7.32	60.46	1.59	5.36	95.38
8.17	56.38	1.78	4.28	95.60
14.29	53.80	1.78	10.04	98.75
4.93	72.10	1.27	2.90	95.55
10.88	55.86	2.19	5.33	93.07
6.60	60.20	1.42	4.63	96.90
12.39	50.87	1.83	8.33	94.18
17.52	59.47	2.60	8.82	97.52
4.63	58.63	2.35	1.77	95.94
11.62	57.04	2.22	5.18	94.43
8.57	**51.92**	**3.64**	**15.15**	**98.72**
9.01	50.91	5.28	16.13	99.25
10.67	63.62	2.19	12.23	97.02
1.62	57.61	0.59	2.58	90.46

13-12 规模以上工业企业产销总值及主要经济指标(分地区) (2016)

单位: 亿元

地区	Region	企业单位数(个) Number of Enterprises(unit)	亏损企业 Enterprises Running under Deficit
全省	**Province**	**16296**	**1274**
武汉	Wuhan	2529	340
黄石	Huangshi	762	91
十堰	Shiyan	911	117
宜昌	Yichang	1487	94
襄阳	Xiangyang	1884	94
鄂州	Ezhou	525	41
荆门	Jingmen	1155	69
孝感	Xiaogan	1297	90
荆州	Jingzhou	1271	79
黄冈	Huanggang	1460	105
咸宁	Xianning	845	56
随州	Suizhou	677	30
恩施	Enshi	520	18
仙桃	Xiantao	400	26
潜江	Qianjiang	263	14
天门	Tianmen	298	4
神农架	Shennongjia	12	6

13-12 续表 1 continued

单位: 亿元

地区	Region	资产总计 Total Assets	流动资产合计 Circulating Funds	应收帐款净额 Net Account Received
全省	**Province**	**37942.33**	**17265.72**	**4373.47**
武汉	Wuhan	13733.09	7098.78	2070.25
黄石	Huangshi	1955.97	989.02	163.32
十堰	Shiyan	3141.46	1549.03	311.42
宜昌	Yichang	5370.95	1551.94	301.02
襄阳	Xiangyang	3375.24	1688.92	501.43
鄂州	Ezhou	698.43	265.98	64.77
荆门	Jingmen	1620.65	599.30	109.27
孝感	Xiaogan	1519.21	647.52	165.70
荆州	Jingzhou	1597.22	762.71	208.61
黄冈	Huanggang	1128.45	482.16	126.98
咸宁	Xianning	934.85	373.78	79.71
随州	Suizhou	710.03	302.57	81.55
恩施	Enshi	484.36	163.11	32.94
仙桃	Xiantao	527.51	241.24	64.85
潜江	Qianjiang	575.45	282.04	52.44
天门	Tianmen	524.28	246.79	36.60
神农架	Shennongjia	45.17	20.83	2.62

TOTAL VALUE OF PRODUCTION AND SALES AND MAJOR ECONOMIC INDICATORS OF INDUSTRIAL ENTERPRISES ABOVE DESIGNATED SIZE (BY REGIONS) (2016)

(100 million yuan)

工业总产值(当年价格) Total Output Value(current price)	工业销售产值(当年价格) Output Value of Industrial Products(current price)	出口交货值 Delivery Value for Export
48766.71	**47295.43**	**1905.07**
13240.92	12828.32	823.37
2099.07	2049.56	74.13
1989.86	1925.46	24.99
6378.77	6168.15	206.83
6456.98	6271.76	124.97
1424.30	1388.02	21.42
3319.48	3242.02	58.20
2865.15	2774.69	66.22
2474.76	2403.78	65.14
1929.87	1808.27	29.21
1815.91	1736.25	52.71
1346.22	1343.10	67.00
404.97	392.34	4.98
979.81	959.49	157.09
1117.02	1100.73	73.39
916.27	898.17	55.42
7.35	5.31	

(100 million yuan)

固定资产合计 Total Value of Fixed Assets	固定资产原价 Original Price of Fixed Assets	累计折旧 Accumulated
13642.50	**25426.04**	**12696.87**
4329.79	7403.18	3322.10
718.48	1093.45	417.44
526.87	796.50	318.89
2511.22	3943.11	1456.32
1156.52	1659.73	586.01
295.22	484.92	194.35
667.54	1416.23	806.98
681.01	2794.73	2175.75
660.47	2619.01	2130.70
456.42	601.49	176.60
382.39	457.79	146.54
280.44	322.64	74.14
257.84	358.51	115.23
225.67	381.18	162.05
221.22	514.61	302.56
252.94	553.27	302.16
18.45	25.66	9.04

13-12 续表 2 continued

单位: 亿元

地区	Region	负债合计 Total Liability	流动负债合计 Total Circulating Liability	应付账款 Account	非流动负债合计 Tatal Non-current Liability	所有者权益合计 Total Rights of Owners
全省	**Province**	**20355.90**	**15643.54**	**4649.73**	**3436.06**	**17502.70**
武汉	Wuhan	8569.32	7137.32	2484.13	1261.84	5147.09
黄石	Huangshi	1154.53	751.63	196.72	252.19	800.73
十堰	Shiyan	1383.12	1175.14	376.90	156.90	1752.68
宜昌	Yichang	2747.48	1896.46	308.91	773.14	2608.44
襄阳	Xiangyang	1721.41	1219.45	395.05	214.03	1632.01
鄂州	Ezhou	402.86	329.70	84.89	48.42	289.46
荆门	Jingmen	660.74	476.81	99.71	101.80	959.90
孝感	Xiaogan	741.34	408.41	99.32	131.73	777.23
荆州	Jingzhou	719.99	597.00	162.66	77.15	877.23
黄冈	Huanggang	551.34	414.05	108.06	69.14	576.61
咸宁	Xianning	389.45	285.71	89.84	61.66	538.28
随州	Suizhou	301.70	209.57	48.73	57.64	407.10
恩施	Enshi	261.19	185.67	27.12	68.82	222.68
仙桃	Xiantao	220.69	164.73	56.06	38.20	305.88
潜江	Qianjiang	247.06	201.34	61.12	32.65	321.58
天门	Tianmen	246.25	164.69	48.35	79.15	278.03
神农架	Shennongjia	37.42	25.85	2.15	11.57	7.75

13-12 续表 3 continued

单位: 亿元

地区	Region	所有者权益合计 Total Rights of the Owners	主营业务收入	主营业务成本
		外商资本 Foreign Assets	Revenue of Major Business	Cost of Major Business
全省	**Province**	**546.30**	**45850.64**	**38963.66**
武汉	Wuhan	298.23	12356.79	10221.69
黄石	Huangshi	64.89	2416.19	2173.79
十堰	Shiyan	45.62	1858.55	1601.10
宜昌	Yichang	30.77	5942.09	5014.45
襄阳	Xiangyang	36.46	5879.48	4987.36
鄂州	Ezhou	0.43	1361.12	1181.82
荆门	Jingmen	10.62	3145.42	2710.28
孝感	Xiaogan	20.81	2677.17	2303.28
荆州	Jingzhou	14.43	2286.46	2021.74
黄冈	Huanggang	8.95	1677.17	1481.12
咸宁	Xianning	4.81	1571.61	1310.98
随州	Suizhou	3.80	1303.43	1065.52
恩施	Enshi	0.24	381.20	305.44
仙桃	Xiantao	5.51	951.65	775.17
潜江	Qianjiang	0.55	1138.04	1055.65
天门	Tianmen	0.17	898.23	750.44
神农架	Shennongjia		6.04	3.84

(100 million Yuan)

实收资本 Assets Recevied	国家资本 National Assets	所有者权益合计 Total Rights of Owners			
		集体资本 Collective Assets	法人资本 Corperative Assets	个人资本 Individual Assets	港澳台资本 Assets from Hongkong, Maco and Taiwan
9120.27	**2557.19**	**140.17**	**2788.56**	**2937.50**	**150.20**
3469.38	979.65	49.45	816.41	1258.13	67.50
334.80	113.86	7.29	83.07	59.41	6.28
540.75	286.71	12.48	95.62	99.13	1.19
699.38	212.49	14.70	188.29	243.31	9.82
1110.60	227.46	14.10	642.25	186.41	3.92
238.48	109.90	1.70	94.23	30.70	1.53
345.96	81.29	5.65	99.72	144.67	4.02
427.17	43.54	2.55	101.58	251.98	6.36
718.25	418.31	12.00	88.57	182.16	2.78
291.14	25.94	5.27	106.42	130.35	14.21
191.30	3.83	3.72	88.60	84.04	6.30
220.85	15.81	4.01	61.99	128.36	6.88
115.63	26.03	3.50	30.35	55.23	0.28
113.24	4.58	1.28	46.26	38.46	17.15
175.43	5.62	2.07	155.11	11.49	0.60
122.45	1.63		89.16	30.11	1.37
5.44	0.53	0.42	0.94	3.56	

(100 million Yuan)

主营业务税金及附加 Tax of Major Business	其他业务收入 Revenue of Other Business	其他业务利润 Profit from Other Business	销售费用 Selling Expenses	管理费用 Management Expense	
					税金 Tax
891.80	**597.85**	**80.54**	**1346.46**	**1933.94**	**96.35**
559.39	228.17	49.32	373.45	577.45	19.21
15.80	104.75	4.49	52.95	71.48	2.95
21.77	72.40	8.22	69.88	123.73	2.06
43.25	35.34	6.01	198.34	224.11	13.26
42.27	25.03	3.28	133.31	308.29	9.24
7.92	34.56	3.07	54.61	66.57	2.12
80.17	10.37	0.98	81.99	97.47	3.91
36.19	8.35	0.82	87.19	98.98	5.70
12.66	24.06	1.54	55.83	80.38	18.82
11.52	9.61	0.93	38.70	50.33	3.16
12.28	9.59	0.23	44.36	45.11	1.65
8.69	4.72	0.69	41.92	46.70	2.28
3.43	1.93	0.43	15.23	18.06	0.61
5.16	2.06	0.25	51.52	54.48	7.60
27.28	26.69	0.25	14.39	27.65	0.55
3.66	0.20	0.02	30.70	42.57	3.21
0.35	0.01	0.01	2.09	0.59	0.02

13-12 续表 4 continued

单位: 亿元

地区	Region	财务费用 Financial Expense	利息支出 Interest Expense	营业利润 Operating Profit	政府补贴 Subsidy
全省	**Province**	**467.38**	**405.64**	**2517.81**	**106.51**
武汉	Wuhan	108.23	111.28	566.05	51.04
黄石	Huangshi	23.40	23.35	75.28	3.97
十堰	Shiyan	4.23	12.43	202.83	5.51
宜昌	Yichang	88.57	83.95	398.44	21.40
襄阳	Xiangyang	48.57	37.82	374.87	9.08
鄂州	Ezhou	13.99	10.96	40.87	0.18
荆门	Jingmen	26.95	21.46	149.74	1.89
孝感	Xiaogan	34.38	16.51	120.67	3.03
荆州	Jingzhou	21.65	15.49	107.41	3.78
黄冈	Huanggang	18.41	12.20	77.35	1.17
咸宁	Xianning	15.58	8.77	141.09	1.77
随州	Suizhou	17.42	11.72	122.33	0.45
恩施	Enshi	10.17	8.90	27.47	1.06
仙桃	Xiantao	8.67	7.65	57.18	0.95
潜江	Qianjiang	8.89	6.58	3.96	1.16
天门	Tianmen	17.34	16.18	53.36	0.07
神农架	Shennongjia	0.93	0.39	-1.09	0.02

13-12 续表 5 continued

单位: 亿元

地区	Region	应交税金及附加 Tax alafor Business	本年应付工资薪酬 Wases Welfarism Payable This Year
全省	**Province**	**2467.37**	**2313.13**
武汉	Wuhan	1106.77	807.09
黄石	Huangshi	80.87	100.49
十堰	Shiyan	81.26	150.16
宜昌	Yichang	288.92	235.56
襄阳	Xiangyang	208.95	195.15
鄂州	Ezhou	62.23	36.61
荆门	Jingmen	151.06	77.61
孝感	Xiaogan	103.08	111.41
荆州	Jingzhou	82.19	89.85
黄冈	Huanggang	46.10	76.35
咸宁	Xianning	55.66	54.94
随州	Suizhou	45.92	44.09
恩施	Enshi	17.94	19.31
仙桃	Xiantao	53.41	68.14
潜江	Qianjiang	47.43	184.17
天门	Tianmen	34.62	61.21
神农架	Shennongjia	0.94	1.01

(100 million Yuan)

营业外收入 Non-operating Income	营业外支出 Non-operating Expense	利润总额 Total Profit	应交所得税 Income Tax	亏损企业亏损总额 Total Loss of Enterprises Running under Deficit	利税总额 Total Profit
254.45	**58.41**	**2713.46**	**329.74**	**183.93**	**4754.74**
145.50	15.55	696.00	128.55	82.81	1655.00
9.97	8.44	76.82	15.82	7.38	138.92
12.05	2.35	212.53	9.17	6.91	282.56
29.71	9.32	418.83	64.10	14.55	630.40
20.30	7.22	387.57	38.44	9.35	548.84
1.52	1.87	40.52	8.60	1.51	92.04
4.74	3.92	150.56	6.58	6.31	291.12
7.65	1.52	126.79	8.14	8.04	216.04
7.26	1.73	112.93	11.08	3.93	165.22
4.27	1.00	80.62	5.00	3.24	118.57
2.83	1.41	142.51	12.03	1.88	184.50
2.78	1.47	123.64	2.49	1.71	164.78
2.83	0.36	29.94	2.74	0.63	44.53
1.47	0.16	58.50	7.28	2.64	97.02
1.41	1.92	3.44	1.32	30.93	49.01
0.12	0.08	53.40	8.32	0.09	76.48
0.05	0.09	-1.14	0.08	2.04	-0.30

(100 million Yuan)

本年应交增值税 Value Added Payable of the Current Year	全部从业人员年平均人数(万人) Average Number of Empolyment of the Current Year (10000 persons)
1143.68	**339.51**
397.84	82.87
46.20	18.16
47.72	18.98
167.98	34.82
118.07	36.12
43.51	8.17
60.28	16.92
52.77	23.29
39.48	19.52
25.89	19.29
29.00	12.11
32.35	10.07
11.13	4.50
33.32	12.49
18.24	9.36
19.43	12.70
0.48	0.14

13-13 分市州规模以上工业企业主要经济效益指标(2016)

单位：%

地 区	Item	企业亏损面 Loss Making Rate of Enterprises	总资产贡献率 Contributing Rate of Total Assets
全省	**Province**	**7.8**	**13.52**
武汉市	Wuhan	13.4	12.85
黄石市	Huangshi	11.9	7.97
十堰市	Shiyan	12.8	8.96
宜昌市	Yichang	6.3	13.25
襄阳市	Xiangyang	5.0	17.30
鄂州市	Ezhou	7.8	14.61
荆门市	Jingmen	6.0	19.27
孝感市	Xiaogan	6.9	15.29
荆州市	Jingzhou	6.2	11.24
黄冈市	Huanggang	7.2	11.53
咸宁市	Xianning	6.6	20.52
随州市	Suizhou	4.4	24.78
恩施市	Enshi	3.5	11.02
仙桃市	Xiantao	6.5	19.83
潜江市	Qianjiang	5.3	9.62
天门市	Tianmen	1.3	17.67
神农架林区	Shennongjia	50.0	0.20

MAJOR INDICATORS OF ECONOMIC BENEFITS OF ABOVE DESIGNATEDSIZE INDUSTRIAL ENTERPRISES BY REGION(2016)

资产负债率 Assets Liability Ratio	流动资产周转率(次/年) Current Asset Turnover(Times/Year)	成本费用利润率 Ratio of Profits to Industrial Cost	产品销售率 Proportion of Products Sold
53.65	**2.69**	**6.28**	**96.98**
62.40	1.77	6.07	96.88
59.03	2.55	3.18	97.64
44.03	1.25	11.42	96.76
51.15	3.85	7.55	96.70
51.00	3.50	7.05	97.13
57.68	5.25	3.00	97.45
40.77	5.27	5.15	97.67
48.80	4.15	5.01	96.84
45.08	3.03	5.15	97.13
48.86	3.50	5.05	93.70
41.66	4.23	9.97	95.61
42.49	4.32	10.50	99.77
53.92	2.35	8.55	96.88
41.84	3.95	6.56	97.93
42.93	4.13	0.30	98.54
46.97	3.64	6.35	98.02
82.85	0.29	-15.26	72.15

主要统计指标解释

工业 指从事自然资源的开采，对采掘品和农产品进行加工和再加工的物质生产部门。具体包括：(1)对自然资源的开采，如采矿、晒盐等(但不包括禽兽捕猎和水产捕捞)；(2)对农副产品的加工、再加工，如粮油加工、食品加工、缫丝、纺织、制革等；(3)对采掘品的加工、再加工，如炼铁、炼钢、化工生产、石油加工、机器制造、木材加工等，以及电力、自来水、煤气的生产和供应等；(4)对工业品的修理、翻新，如机器设备的修理、交通运输工具(如汽车)的修理等。

工业统计调查单位为独立核算法人工业企业。

独立核算法人工业企业指从事工业生产经营活动的单位。独立核算法人工业企业应同时具备以下条件：①依法成立，有自己的名称、组织机构和场所，能够承担民事责任；②独立拥有和使用资产，承担负债，有权与其他单位签订合同；③独立核算盈亏，并能够编制资产负债表。

本年鉴中涉及的企业登记注册类型：

国有及国有控股企业 指国有企业加上国有控股企业。国有企业(即原全民所有制工业或国营工业)指企业全部资产归国家所有，并按《中华人民共和国企业法人登记管理条例》规定登记注册的非公司制的经济组织。包括国有企业、国有独资公司和国有联营企业。1957年以前的公私合营和私营工业，后均改造为国营工业，1992年改为国有工业，这部分工业的资料不单独分列时，均包括在国有企业内。国有控股企业是对混合所有制经济的企业进行的“国有控股”分类。它是指这些企业的全部资产中国有资产(股份)相对其他所有者中的任何一个所有者占资(股)最多的企业。该分组反映了国有经济控股情况。

集体企业 指企业资产归集体所有，并按《中华人民共和国企业法人登记管理条例》规定登记注册的经济组织。是社会主义公有制经济的组成部分。包括城乡所有使用集体投资举办的企业，以及部分个人通过集资自愿放弃所有权并依法经工商行政管理机关认定为集体所有制的企业。

股份合作企业 指以合作制为基础，由企业职工共同出资入股，吸收一定比例的社会资产投资组建，实行自主经营，自负盈亏，共同劳动，民主管理，按劳分配与按股分红相结合的一种集体经济组织。

联营企业 指两个及两个以上相同或不同所有制性质的企业法人或事业单位法人，按自愿、平等、互利的原则，共同投资组成的经济组织。联营企业包括：

国有联营企业指国有企业与国有企业间的联营；

集体联营企业指集体企业与集体企业间的联营；

国有与集体联营企业指国有企业与集体企业间的联营。

有限责任公司 指根据《中华人民共和国公司登记管理条例》规定登记注册，由两个以上，五十个以下的股东共同出资，每个股东以其所认缴的出资额对公司承担有限责任，公司以其全部资产对其债务承担责任的经济组织。

有限责任公司包括国有独资公司以及其他有限责任公司。

股份有限公司 指根据《中华人民共和国企业法人登记管理条例》规定登记注册，其全部注册资本由等额股份构成并通过发行股票筹集资本，股东以其认购的股份对公司承担有限责任，公司以其全部资产对其债务承担责任的经济组织。

私营企业 指由自然人投资设立或由自然人控股，以雇佣劳动为基础的营利性经济组织。包括按照《公司法》、《合伙企业法》、《私营企业暂行条例》规定登记注册的私营有限责任公司、私营股份有限公司、私营合伙企业和私营独资企业。

港、澳、台商投资企业 指企业注册登记类型中的港、澳、台资合资、合作、独资经营企业和股份有限公司之和。

外商投资企业 指企业注册登记类型中的中外合资、合作经营企业、外资企业和外商投资股份有限公司之和。

“三资”企业系指港、澳、台商投资企业和外资企业的简称。

轻工业 指主要提供生活消费品和制作手工工具的工业。按其所使用的原料不同，可分为两大类：(1)以农产品为原料的轻工业，是指直接或间接以农产品为基本原料的轻工业。主要包括食品制造、饮料制造、烟草加工、纺织、缝纫、皮革和毛皮制作、造纸以及印刷等工业；(2)以非农产品为原料的轻工业，是指以工业品为原料的轻工业。主要包括文教体育用品、化学药品制造、合成纤维制造、日用化学制品、日用玻璃制品、日用金属制品、手工工具制造、医疗器械制造、文化和办公用机械制造等工业。

重工业 指为国民经济各部门提供物质技术基础的主要生产资料的工业。按其生产性质和产品用途，可以分为下列三类：(1)采掘(伐)工业，是指对自然资源的开采，包括石油开采、煤炭开采、金属矿开采、非金属矿开采等工业；(2)原材料工业，指向国民经济各部门提供基本材料、动力和燃料的工业。包括金属冶炼及加工、炼焦及焦炭、化学、化工原料、水泥、人造板以及电力、石油和煤炭加工等工业；(3)加工工业，是指对工业原材料进行再加工制造的工业。包括装备国民经济各部门的机械设备制造工业、金属结构、水泥制品等工业，以及为农业提供的生产资料如化肥、农药等工业。

根据上述划分原则，修理业中以重工业产品为修理作业对象的划为重工业，反之划为轻工业。

工业总产值

(1)定义：

工业总产值是以货币形式表现的，工业企业在一定时期内生产的工业最终产品或提供工业性劳务活动的总价值量。它反映一定时间内工业生产的总规模和总水平。

(2)计算原则：

工业生产的原则，即凡是企业在报告期生产的经检验合格的产品，不管是否在报告期销售，均包括在内。

最终产品的原则，即凡是计入工业总产值的产品，必须是本企业生产的经检验合格的，不需要再进行任何加工的最终产品。如果企业有中间产品(半成品)对外销售，则对外销售的中间产品应视为企业的最终产品。

工厂法原则，即工业总产值是以工业企业作为基本计算(核算)单位，即按企业的最终产品计算工业总产值。按这种方法计算的工业总产值，不允许同一产品价值在企业内部重复计算，不能把企业内部各个车间(分厂)生产的成果相加，但允许企业间的重复计算。

(3)内容及计算方法：

1995年全国工业普查对工业总产值(原规定)的内容及计算原则和方法做了某些修订，修订后的工业总产值(新规定)包括三项内容：即本期生产成品价值、对外加工费收入、在制品半成品期末期初差额价值三部分。

本期生产成品价值：指企业本期生产，并在报告期内不再进行加工，经检验、包装入库的全部工业成品(半成品)价值合计，包括企业生产的自制设备及提供给本企业在建工程、其他非工业部门和福利部门等单位使用的成品价值。本期生产成品价值为按自备原材料生产的产品的数量乘以本期不含增值税(销项税额)的产品实际销售平均单价计算；会计核算中按成本价格转帐的自制设备和自产自用的成品，按成本价格计算生产成品价值。生产成品价值中不包括用定货者来料加工的成品(半成品)价值。

对外加工费收入：指企业在报告期内完成的对外承接的工业品加工(包括用定货者来料加工产品)的加工费收入和对外工业修理作业所取得的加工费收入。对外加工费收入按不含增值税(销项税额)的价格计算，可根据会计"产品销售收入"科目的有关资料取得。

对于本企业对内非工业部门提供的加工修理、设备安装的劳务收入，如果企业会计核算基础较好，能取得这部分资料，而且这部分价值所占比重较大，应包括在对外加工费收入中。

自制半成品在制品期末期初差额价值：指企业报告期在制品期末减期初的差额价值，本指标一般可以从会计核算资料中取得。如果会计产品成本核算中不计算半成品、在制品的成本，则总产值中也不包括这部分价值，反之则包括。

(4)工业总产值统计范围变化和计算方法修订情况：

1984年以前工业总产值不包括村办工业，村办工业总产值划归农业。1984年以后工业总产值包括村办工业。

1995年工业普查对工业总产值计算方法做了修订，即从1995年始按新修订(新规定)方法计算工业总产值。新规定与原规定的区别如下：

全价与加工费的计算原则不同：新规定为凡自备原材料，不论其生产繁简程度如何，一律按全价计算工业总产值；凡来料加工，允许按加工费计算工业总产值。原规定则视生产加工的繁简程度不同，规定哪些行业按全价，哪些行业按加工费计算工业总产值。

自制半成品、在产品期末期初差额价值的计算原则不同：新规定要求，凡会计产品成本核算时计算了成本的差额价值，总产值中就应包括，否则可不包括；原规定则按生产周期六个月的界限区分，凡生产周期六个月以上的企业，总产值计算中应包括这部分差额价值，否则可不包括。

计算价格不同：新规定按不含增值税(销项税额)的价格计算；原规定则按含增值税(销项税额)的价格计算。

工业增加值 指工业企业在报告期内以货币表现的工业生产活动的最终成果。

工业增加值有两种计算方法：一是生产法，即工业总产出减去工业中间投入加上应交增值税；二是收入法，即从收入的角度出发，根据生产要素在生产过程中应得到的收入份额计算，具体构成项目有固定资产折旧、劳动者报酬、生产税净额、营业盈余，这种方法也称要素分配法。本年鉴中的工业增加值是以生产法计算的。

生产法工业增加值的计算方法为：

工业增加值=工业总产出-工业中间投入+应交增值税

(1)工业总产出：指工业企业在一定时期内工业生产活动的总成果。工业总产出包括：成品生产价值，对外加工费收入，自制半成品、在产品期末期初差额价值。1995年后用新规定计算的工业总产值代替。

(2)工业中间投入：指工业企业在工业生产活动中消耗的外购物质产品和对外支付的服务费用。服务费用包括支付给物质生产部门(工业、农业、批发零售贸易业、建筑业、运输邮电业)的服务费用和支付给非物质生产部门(如保险、金融、文化教育、科学研究、医疗卫生、行政管理等)的服务费用。工业中间投入的确定须遵循以下原则：必须从外部购入的，并已计入工业总产出的产品和服务价值；必须是本期投入生产，并一次性消耗掉(包括本期摊销的低值易耗品等)的产品和服务价值。

工业中间投入包括直接材料费用、制造费用中的工业中间投入、管理费用中的工业中间投入、销售费用中的工业中间投入和利息支出五部分。

资产总计 指企业拥有或控制的能以货币计量的经济资源，包括各种财产、债权和其他权利。资产按流动性分为流动资产、长期投资、固定资产、无形资产、递延资产和其他资产。该指标根据企业会计“资产负债表”中“资产总计”项目的期末数增列。

流动资产 指企业可以在一年内或者超过一年的一个生产周期内变现或者耗用的资产，包括现金及各种存款、短期投资，应收及预付款项、存货等。

流动资产平均余额 指企业在报告期内全部流动资产的平均余额。

固定资产原价 指企业在建造、购置、安装、改建、扩建、技术改造某项固定资产时所支出的全部货币总额。它一般包括买价、包装费、运杂费和安装费等。

固定资产净值年平均余额 指固定资产净值在报告期内余额的平均数。计算公式为：

$$\text{固定资产净值年平均余额}=\frac{\text{1至12月各月月初、月末固定资产净值之和}}{24}$$

该指标根据“资产负债表”中“固定资产原价”、“累计折旧”指标的期初、期末数计算填列。

固定资产净值指固定资产原价减去历年已提折旧额后的净额。计算公式为：

固定资产净值=固定资产原价-累计折旧

负债合计 指企业所承担的能以货币计量，将以资产或劳务偿付的债务，偿还形式包括货币、资产或提供劳务。负债一般按偿还期长短分为流动负债和长期负债。根据会计“资产负债表”中“负债合计”的年末数填列。

所有者权益 指企业投资人对企业净资产的所有权。企业净资产等于企业全部资产减去全部负债后的余额，包括企业投资人对企业的最初投入的实际到位的资产及资本公积金、盈余公积金和未分配利润。所有者权益合计数小于零，表示企业资不抵债。

主营业务收入 指会计“利润表”中对应指标的本年累计数。未执行2001年《企业会计制度》的企业，用“产品销售收入”的本期累计数代替。

主营业务成本 指会计“利润表”中对应指标的本年累计数。未执行2001年《企业会计制度》的企业，用“产品销售成本”的本期累计数代替。

主营业务税金及附加 指会计"利润表"中对应指标的本年累计数。未执行2001年《企业会计制度》的企业，用"产品销售税金及附加"的本期累计数代替。

利润总额 指企业生产经营活动的最终成果，是企业在一定时期内实现的盈亏相抵后的利润总额(亏损以"–"号表示)，它等于营业利润加上补贴收入加上投资收益加上营业外净收入再加上以前年度损益调整。

本年应交增值税 指企业在报告期内应交纳的增值税额。它等于本年销项税额加上出口退税加上进项税额转出数减去本年进项税额。小规模纳税企业直接按全年计税销售额乘以征收率计算取得。

从业人员平均人数 是指报告期内每天拥有的从业人员人数。其计算公式为：

$$季平均人数=\frac{季内各月平均人数之和}{3}$$

$$月平均人数=\frac{报告月内每天实有人数之和}{报告月日历日数}$$

$$年平均人数=\frac{年内各月平均人数之和}{12}$$

总资产贡献率 反映企业全部资产的获利能力，是企业经营业绩和管理水平的集中体现，是评价和考核企业盈利能力的核心指标。计算公式为：

$$总资产贡献率(\%)=\frac{利润总额+税金总额+利息支出}{平均资金总额}\times 100\%$$

公式中：税金总额为产品销售税金及附加与应交增值税之和；平均资产总额为期初期末资产之和的算术平均值。

资产负债率 该指标既反映企业经营风险的大小，也反映企业利用债权人提供的资金从事经营活动的能力。计算公式为：

$$资产负债率(\%)=\frac{负债总额}{资产总额}\times 100\%$$

资产与负债均为报告期期末数。

流动资产周转次数 指一定时期内流动资产完成的周转次数，反映投入工业企业流动资金的周转速度。计算公式为：

$$流动资产周转资转次数=\frac{产品销售收入}{全部流动资产平均余额}$$

公式中：全部流动资产平均余额为期初和期末的流动资产之和的算术平均值。

成本费用利润率 反映企业投入的生产成本及费用的经济效益，同时也反映企业降低成本所取得的经济效益。计算公式为：

$$成本费用利润率(\%)=\frac{利润总额}{成本费用总额}\times 100\%$$

公式中：成本费用总额为产品销售成本、销售费用、管理费用、财务费用之和。

全员劳动生产率 该指标反映企业的生产效率和劳动投入的经济效益。计算公式为：

$$全员劳动生产率(元/人)=\frac{工业增加值}{全部从业人员平均人数}$$

产品销售率 该指标反映工业产品已实现销售的程度，是分析工业产销衔接情况，研究工业产品满足社会需求的指标。计算公式为：

$$产品销售率(\%)=\frac{工业销售产值}{工业总产值（现价）}\times 100\%$$

Explanatory Notes on Main Statistical Indicators

Industry refers to the material production sector which is engaged in extraction of natural resources and processing and reprocessing of minerals and agricultural products, including (1) extraction of natural resources, such as mining, salt production (but not including hunting and fishing); (2) processing and reprocessing of farm and sideline produces, such as rice husking, flour milling, wine making, oil pressing, silk reeling, spinning and weaving, and leather making; (3) manufacture of industrial products, such as steel making, iron smelting, chemicals manufacturing, petroleum processing, machine building, timber processing; water and gas production and electricity generation and supply; (4)repairing of industrial products such as the repairing of machinery and means of transport (including cars).

Units of industrial statistics survey corporate industrial enterprises with independent accounting system.

Corporate industrial enterprises with independent accounting system refer to enterprises engaging in industrial production activities, which meet the following requirements: (1)They are established legally, having their own names, organizations, location, able to take civil liability; (2)They possess and use their assets independently, assume liabilities, and are entitled to sign contracts with other units; (3)They are financially independent and compile their own balance sheets.

Enterprises covered in the industrial statistics in the Yearbook include following categories by their registration:

State–owned and State–holding Enterprises refer to state–owned enterprises plus state–holding enterprises. State–owned enterprises (originally known as state–run enterprises with ownership by the whole society) are non–corporate economic entities registered in accordance with the Regulation of the People's Republic of China on the Management of Registration of Legal Enterprises, where all assets are owned by the state. Included in this category are state–owned enterprises, state–funded corporations and state–owned joint–operation enterprises. Joint state–private industries and private industries, which existed before 1957, were transformed into state–run industries since 1957, and into state–owned industries after 1992. Statistics on those enterprises are included in the state–owned industries instead of grouping them separately. State–holding enterprises is a sub–classification of enterprises with mixed ownership, referring to enterprises where the percentage of state assets (or shares by the state) is larger than any other single share holder of the same enterprise. This sub–classification illustrates the control of the state over a particular industry.

Collective–owned Enterprises refer to economic entities registered in accordance with the Regulation of the People's Republic of China on the Management of Registration of Legal Enterprises, where assets are owned by collectively. Collective enterprises constitute an integral part of the socialist economy with public ownership. They include urban and rural enterprises invested by collectives, and some enterprises registered in industrial and commercial administration agency as collective units where funds are pulled together by individuals who voluntarily give up their right of ownership.

Share–holding Cooperative Enterprises refer to economic units set up on cooperative basis, with funding partly from members of the enterprise and partly from outside investment, where the operation and management is decided by the members who also participate in the production, and the distribution of income is based both on work (labour input) and on shares (capital input).

Joint–operation enterprises refer to economic units that are established by joint investment by two or more corporate enterprises or institutions of the same or different types of ownership on voluntary, equal and mutual–beneficial basis. They include:

a) state–owned joint–operation enterprises (joint operation between state–owned enterprises);

b) collective joint–operation enterprises (joint operation between collective enterprises; and

c) state–collective joint–operation enterprises (joint operation between state and collective enterprises).

Limited Liability Corporations refer to economic units registered in accordance with the Regulation of the People's Republic of China on the Management of Registration of Corporations, with capitals from 2 to 49 investors, each investor bears limited liability to the corporation depending on his/her holding of shares, and the corporation bears liability to its debt to the maximum of its total assets.

Share–holding Corporations Ltd. refer to economic units registered in accordance with the Regulation of the People's Republic of China on the Management of Registration of Corporate Enterprises, with total registered capitals divided into equal shares and raised through issuing stocks. Each investor bears limited liability to the corporation depending on the holding of shares, and the corporation bears liability to its debt to the maximum of its total assets.

Private Enterprises refer to economic units invested or controlled (by holding the majority of the shares) by natural persons who hire labours for profit–making activities. Included in this category are private limited liability corporations, private share–holding corporations Ltd., private partnership enterprises and private sole investment enterprises registered in accordance with the Corporation Law, Partnership Enterprise Law and Tentative Regulation on Private Enterprises.

Enterprises with Funds from Hong Kong, Macao and Taiwan refers to all industrial enterprises registered as the joint–venture, cooperative, sole (exclusive) investment industrial enterprises and limited liability corporations with funds from Hong Kong, Macao and Taiwan.

Foreign Funded Enterprises refers to all industrial enterprises registered as the joint–venture, cooperative, sole (exclusive) investment industrial enterprises and limited liability corporations with foreign funds.

Enterprise with Hong Kong, Macao, Taiwan and foreign fund refer to all the enterpries with funds from Hong Kong Macao and Taiwan and foreign funded enterprises.

Light Industry refers to the industry that produces consumer goods and hand tools. It consists of two categories, depending on the materials used:

(1) Industries using farm products as raw materials. These are branches of light industry which directly or indirectly use farm products as basic raw materials, including the manufacture of food and beverages, tobacco processing, textile, clothing, fur and leather manufacturing, paper making, printing, etc.

(2) Industries using non farm products as raw materials. These are branches of light industry which use manufactured goods as raw materials, including the manufacture of cultural, educational articles and sports goods, chemicals, synthetic fiber, chemical products for daily use, glass products for daily use, metal products for daily use, hand tools, medical apparatus and instruments, and the manufacture of cultural and clerical machinery.

Heavy Industry refers to the industry which produces capital goods, and provides various sectors of the national economy with necessary material and technical basis. It consists of the following three branches according to the purpose of production or the use of products:

(1) Mining, quarrying and logging industry refers to the industry that extracts natural resources, including extraction of petroleum, coal, metal and non–metal ores.

(2) Raw materials industry refers to the industry that provides various sectors of the national economy with raw materials, fuels and power. It includes smelting and processing of metals, coking and coke chemistry, chemical materials and building materials such as cement, plywood, and power, petroleum refining and coal dressing.

(3) Manufacturing industry refers to the industry that processes raw materials. It includes machine–building industry which equips sectors of the national economy, industries of metal structure and cement products, industries producing means of agricultural production, such as chemical fertilizers and pesticides.

According to the above principle of classification, the repairing trades, which are engaged primarily in repairing products of heavy industry are classified into heavy industry while these engaged in repairing products of light industry are classified into light industry.

Gross Industrial Output Value

(1) Definition: Gross industrial output value is the total volume of final industrial products produced and industrial services provided during a given period. It reflects the total achievements and overall scale of industrial production during a given period.

(2) Principles for calculation:

Statistics on industrial production follow the principle that all products produced by the enterprises and accepted during the reference period are to be included no matter whether they are sold or not during the reference period.

Determination of final products follow the principle that all products that are included in the calculation of grow industrial output value are the final products of the enterprise which have been accepted through quality check and require no further processing. If an enterprise has intermediate (semi–finished) products to sell, these intermediate products are considered as the final products of the enterprise.

Gross industrial output value is calculated following the principle of factory approach, i.e. industrial enterprise is used as the basic accounting unit in calculating the gross industrial output value. By this approach, value of the same product is not to be double counted, and the output value of different workshops (branch factories) should not be added. However, this approach does not exclude the possibility of double counting between enterprises.

(3) Content and calculation method: The old definition of gross industrial output value was modified during the national industrial census in 1995. The revised (new) definition of gross industrial output value consists of 3 components: value of the finished products during the reference period, income from external processing, and value of change in semi–finished products at the end and at the beginning of the reference period.

Value of the finished products during the reference period: refers to the value of all finished (semi–finished) industrial products that are produced during the reference period without the need for further processing, checked for acceptance, packed and put into the warehouse of the enterprise, including the value of own–produced equipment and the value of products provided to the projects under construction of the enterprise, and to other non–industrial or welfare units. Value of finished products during the reference period is calculated by the quantity of products produced using own materials multiplied by the average unit prices at which products are sold (excluding value–added tax). Own–produced equipment and products produced for own use are value at cost prices as in the case of enterprise accounting. Value of finished products does not include the value of finished products (semi–finished products) that are produced using the materials from the clients who make the orders.

Income from external processing: refers to income from contracted external processing of industrial products (including processing of industrial products using materials from the clients), and the income from industrial repairing work provided to other units. Income from external processing is calculated using information from the item "products sales income" in the enterprise accounting at the prices excluding value–added tax.

For income from services such as processing, repairing and installation of equipment provided to non–industrial units within the enterprise, if the accounting work of the enterprise is good enough to separate it from other records, and the share of such services is significant, it should also be included in the income from external processing.

Value of change in semi–finished products at the end and at the beginning of the reference period: refers to the value of change in semi–finished products at the end and at the beginning of the reference period, which generally can be obtained from accounting records of enterprises. If the enterprise accounting excludes the cost of semi–finished products, then it should not be included in the gross industrial output value, and vice versa.

(4) Changes in the coverage and method of calculation of gross industrial output value

Prior to 1984, the value of rural industry run by villages was classified into agriculture instead of industry. Since 1984, it has been in–

cluded in the gross industrial output value. Method of calculation for the gross industrial output value was modified in the industrial census in 1995. The difference in the new method as compared with the old one is outlined below:

Principle in using full value vs. processing fee: The new method stipulates that all products produced using own materials are to be calculated with full value in reporting the gross industrial output value irrespective of sophistication of production, and for external processing, it allows calculation using processing fee. In the old method, however, the use of full value or processing fee was determined by the degree of sophistication of production in different branches of industries.

Principle in determining the value of change in semi–finished products: The new method requires that value of the change in semi–finished products should be included in the gross industrial output value if it is included in the accounting record of the enterprise, otherwise it should not be included. By the old method, it is determined by the type of enterprises in terms of production cycle. If the production cycle is over 6 months, the value of change in semi–finished products is included in the gross industrial output value, otherwise it is excluded.

Difference in prices: The new method uses prices excluding value–added tax in the calculation of gross industrial output value, while the old method used prices including value–added tax.

Value–added of Industry refers to the final results of industrial production of industrial enterprises in money terms during the reference period.

Industrial value–added can be calculated by two approaches: the production approach, i.e. gross industrial output value minus intermediate input plus value–added tax, and the income approach, i.e. income for various factors used in the course of production, including depreciation of fixed assets, remuneration of labourers, net of production tax, and operating surplus. Value–added of industry in the Yearbook is calculated by production approach as following:

Value–added of industry = gross industrial output industrial intermediate input + value–added tax

(1) Gross industrial output: refers to the total achievements of industrial production during a given period. Gross industrial output includes value of finished products, income from external processing, and value of change in semi–finished products at the end and at the beginning of the reference period. Since 1995, it was substituted by the gross industrial output value by new method.

(2) Industrial intermediate input: refers to purchased goods and paid services consumed during the industrial production of enterprises. Fees paid for services include fees paid for the services provided by material production sectors (industry, agriculture, wholesale and retail trade, construction, transport, post and telecommunications) and by non–material production sectors (insurance, banking, culture, education, scientific research, health and medical care, public administration, etc.). The determination of industrial intermediate input follows the principle that the goods and services must be purchased from outside and included in the gross industrial output, and that the goods and services are inputted into production and consumed (include low–value consumables) during the reference period.

Industrial intermediate input includes 5 components, namely direct consumption of materials, industrial intermediate input in manufacturing cost, industrial intermediate input in management cost, industrial intermediate input in marketing cost and expenditure on interest.

Total Assets refer to all economic resources, in monetary terms, that is owned or controlled by enterprises, including properties, creditors equity and other economic rights of all forms. Classified by the degree of equitability, total assets include circulating assets, long–term investment, fixed assets, intangible assets and deferred assets, and other assets. Data on this indicator can be obtained by the year–end figures of total assets in the Assets and Liability Table of accounting records of enterprises.

Working Capitals refer to capitals that an enterprise can cash or use during one year or one production cycle that may exceeds one year, including cash and savings deposits of various forms, short–term investment, money receivable and prepaid money, inventories, etc.

Annual Average Value of Working Capitals refers to the average value of all working capitals of the enterprise during the reference period.

Original Value of Fixed Assets refers to the total value, in monetary terms, that an enterprise spent on fixed assets, through construction, purchase, installation, transformation, expansion or technical upgrading. Generally, it covers cost of purchase, packing, transportation and installation, etc.

Annual Average of Net Value of Fixed Assets refer to average of the net value of fixed assets during the reference period, calculated with the following formula:

Annual Average of Net Value of Fixed Assets = sum of net value of fixed assets at the beginning and at the end of each month from January to December / 24.

Information on this indicator can be obtained from the beginning and ending figures of the original value of fixed assets and cumulative depreciation from the Assets and Liability Table of enterprises.

Net value of fixed assets refers to the original value of fixed assets minus depreciation over the years, i.e.:

Net value of fixed assets = original value of fixed assets cumulative depreciation

Total Liabilities refer to payable liabilities of enterprises that have to repay in terms of money, assets or labour services. In terms of payment, it can be divided into liquid liabilities and long–term liabilities. Data on this item is obtained from the ending figures on total liabilities from theAssets and Liability Table from the enterprises.

Owner's Equity refers to the ownership of net assets of enterprise by its investors. The net assets equal the total assets minus total liabilities of the enterprise, including the actual assets invested into the enterprise by investors, accumulation of capitals and operating surplus and non–distributed profits. The enterprise's assets is less than its liabilities if the sum of owner's equity is smaller than zero.

Revenue from Principal Business refers to the annual accumulation of corresponding item in the "profit table" of the accountant. For enterprises that do not follow the 2001 Enterprise Accounting Standards, the year–end accumulation of revenue from the sales of products is used as a substitute.

Cost of Principal Business refers to the annual accumulation of corresponding item in the "profit table" of the accountant. For enterprises that do not follow the 2001 Enterprise Accounting Standards, the year–end accumulation of cost for the sales of products is used as a substitute.

Tax and Extra Charges from Principal Business refer to the annual accumulation of corresponding item in the "profit table" of the accountant. For enterprises that do not follow the 2001 Enterprise Accounting Standards, the year–end accumulation of tax and extra charges from the sales of products is used as a substitute.

Total Profits refer to the final achievements of production and operation of the enterprises, represented by the total profits after deducting losses (loss is expressed by the negative figure). It is the sum of profits from operation, income from subsidies, investment earnings, net income from activities other than operation, and adjustment of profits and losses of previous years.

Value–added Tax Payable refers to the amount of the value–added tax which should be paid by the enterprises during the reference period. It is the sum of tax on sales, export rebate, and transferred tax on purchases of the current year, minus the tax on purchases of the current year. Value–added tax payable of small–size enterprises is determined by the taxable sales of the year multiplied by the tax rate.

Average Annual Number of Employed Persons Employed persons refer to all those who are employed in enterprises and receive remunerations therefrom, including currently working employees, retirees who are re–employed, teachers of local–run schools, as well as foreigners, staff from Hong Kong, Macao and Taiwan, part–time employees and persons with second job who are employed by the enterprise, and employees of other units temporarily working in the enterprises, but excluding former employees who left the enterprise with their employment records still kept by the enterprises.

Average number of employed persons refers to the number of employees everyday during the reference period, calculated with the following formula:

Monthly average number = sum of actual employees everyday in reference month/number of calendar dates in reference month

Quarterly average number = sum of monthly average number in reference quarter/3

Annual average number = sum of monthly average number in reference year/12

Ratio of Profits, Taxes and Interests to Average Assets reflects the profit–making capability of all assets of the enterprise and is a key indicator manifesting the performance and management and evaluating the profit–making potential of the enterprise. It is calculated as follows:

Ratio of Profits, Taxes and Interests to Average Assets (%) = [(total profits + total taxes + interest payment) / average assets] × 100%

In the above formula, total taxes is the sum of tax and extra charges on the sales of products and value–added tax payable; and average assets is the arithmetic mean of the sum of beginning assets and ending assets.

Ratio of Debts to Assets reflect both the operation risk and the capability of the enterprise in making use of the capital from the creditors. It is calculated as follows:

Ratio of Debts to Assets (%) = (total debts / total assets) × 100%

Both assets and debts are figures at the end of the reference period.

Turnover of Working Capitals refers to the number of times of turnover of working capital in a given period of time, which reflects the speed of the turnover of working capital of industrial enterprises, and is calculated as follows:

Turnover of Working Capital=(sales revenue of products) / (average balance of total working capital)

In the above formula, average balance of total working capital refers to the arithmetic mean of the sum of working capital at the beginning and at the end of the reference period.

Ratio of Profits to Total Industrial Costs refers to the ratio of profits realized in a given period to the total costs in the same period, which reflects the economic efficiency of input cost and is calculated as follows:

Ratio of Profits to Total Industrial Cost (%)=(total profits/ total costs) × 100%

Total costs in the above formula is the sum of cost of products sold, marketing cost, management cost and financial cost.

Overall Labour Productivity is an indicator reflecting the production efficiency of an enterprise and the economic efficiency of its labour input, calculated by the formula:

Overall Labour Productivity (yuan/person) = industrial value–added / average of all persons engaged

Sales Ratio of Products is an indicator reflecting the actual sale of industrial products, analyzing the production–selling and supply–demand relations. It is calculated as:

Sales Ratio of Products (%) = value of industrial sales / gross industrial output value (current prices) * 100%

14 建筑业

Construction

建　筑　业

Construction

2016

建筑施工企业个数	Number of Construction Enterprises	3534	（个）
建筑施工企业职工平均人数	Average Number of Staff and Workers in Construction Enterprises	269.17	（万人）
建筑业总产值	Total Output Value of Construction Industry	11862.40	（亿元）
施工房屋面积	Construction Area	72759.57	（万平方米）
建筑业全员劳动生产率	Overall Labor Productivity of Construction Industry	44.07	（万元/人）

建筑业总产值(亿元)

Gross Output Value of Construction Enterprises (100 million yuan)

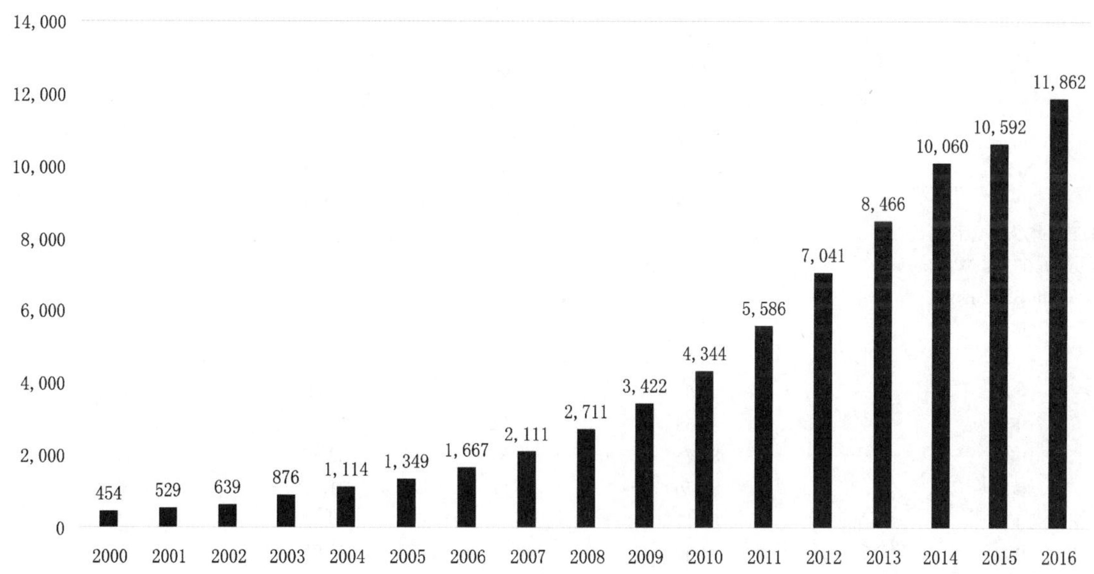

附：建筑业产值构成(%)

	2007	2008	2009	2010	2011	2012	2013	2014	2015	2016
国有经济	50.5	49.2	47.4	52.6	52.5	48.7	46.5	47.3	44.3	46.8
乡镇企业及其他经济	46.3	51.3	50.3	45.9	45.9	49.4	52.7	52.0	55	53.2

14-1 建筑企业概况
BASIC STATISTICS ON CONSTRUCTION ENTERPRISES

项 目 Item	总 计 Total	国有经济 State-Owned	地 方 Local - Owned	中 央 Central- Owned	其他经济 Others
企业单位个数(个) Number of Enterprises (unit)					
1995	912	323	277	46	50
1996	1696	403	250	53	95
1997	1761	429	378	51	125
1998	1838	433	379	54	199
1999	2120	491	432	59	332
2000	2070	488	440	48	409
2001	1661	393	350	43	459
2002	1625	363	327	36	782
2003	1808	558	488	70	906
2004	2357	433	378	55	2566
2005	2114	524	448	76	1322
2006	2238	320	279	41	1695
2007	2516	449	383	66	1876
2008	2975	440	374	66	2374
2009	2878	396	331	65	2330
2010	2845	388	334	54	2315
2011	2640	376	330	46	2134
2012	2952	390	335	55	2440
2013	3376	399	334	66	2879
2014	3217	386	324	62	2741
2015	3346	384	323	61	2875
2016	3534	389	325	64	3145
职工平均人数(万人) Average Staff and Workers (10000 persons)					
1995	57.28	38.05	18.86	19.19	2.61
1996	76.51	36.83	18.58	18.25	3.48
1997	76.09	36.36	18.60	17.76	3.77
1998	82.63	38.22	19.22	19.00	5.59
1999	85.72	39.57	22.57	17.00	9.46
2000	82.76	36.58	21.73	14.83	10.82
2001	83.11	36.16	19.99	16.44	17.65
2002	93.50	34.20	21.25	12.95	35.80
2003	108.82	50.20	30.72	19.48	41.64
2004	105.30	44.40	28.10	16.30	48.70
2005	110.09	41.70	22.85	18.85	56.79
2006	114.25	27.26	15.18	12.08	76.71
2007	136.14	39.73	19.52	20.21	86.97
2008	137.61	38.51	18.40	20.11	92.49
2009	146.02	41.68	18.76	22.92	97.12
2010	170.71	54.40	22.31	32.09	110.74
2011	141.88	42.61	15.06	27.55	94.49
2012	169.33	50.83	15.10	35.73	114.29
2013	174.18	40.50	14.83	25.67	130.64
2014	206.37	49.04	19.48	29.56	153.98
2015	232.85	55.21	19.07	36.14	174.45
2016	269.17	61.15	17.25	43.91	208.02

14-1 续表 1 continued

项 目 Item	总 计 Total	国有经济 State-Owned	地 方 Local - Owned	中 央 Central- Owned	其他经济 Others
建筑业总产值(亿元) Gross Output Value of Construction Enterprises (100 million yuan)					
1995	227.41	178.51	58.96	119.55	15.19
1996	284.43	187.00	60.83	126.17	18.29
1997	305.97	199.53	63.59	135.94	21.75
1998	343.65	223.80	73.98	149.82	26.70
1999	399.02	246.58	88.07	158.51	45.13
2000	454.35	266.03	106.76	159.27	64.86
2001	529.02	279.39	112.32	167.07	131.93
2002	639.11	301.93	143.90	158.03	238.29
2003	876.26	535.71	227.72	307.99	257.56
2004	1114.33	676.45	285.29	391.16	370.63
2005	1349.32	776.70	268.77	507.92	502.71
2006	1667.00	545.64	184.87	360.77	1048.92
2007	2110.80	1065.26	234.03	831.23	976.85
2008	2710.80	1333.87	241.63	1092.24	1319.41
2009	3421.89	1621.66	191.86	1429.80	1722.37
2010	4344.39	2287.08	414.78	1872.30	1996.10
2011	5586.45	2934.99	501.47	2433.52	2566.42
2012	7040.65	3428.40	627.89	2800.51	3478.70
2013	8465.50	3933.36	757.54	3175.82	4465.39
2014	10059.59	4755.30	921.65	3833.65	5232.75
2015	10591.71	4695.04	1072.67	3622.37	5825.87
2016	11862.40	5549.57	1071.13	4478.43	6312.83
施工房屋面积(万平方米) Floor Space of Buildings Under Construction (10000 sq.m)					
1995	3284.30	2122.80	1185.20	937.60	293.90
1996	4548.80	2224.60	1203.30	1021.30	315.80
1997	4604.20	2330.60	1226.90	1103.70	388.30
1998	5310.00	2488.80	1288.80	1200.00	573.70
1999	5797.00	2703.40	1578.40	1125.00	764.20
2000	6256.50	2889.10	1564.50	1324.60	919.20
2001	6662.59	2792.50	1480.20	1312.30	1817.10
2002	7215.88	2836.00	1452.00	1384.00	2637.90
2003	8933.44	3817.50	2102.60	1714.90	3541.10
2004	11772.31	5089.10	2522.60	2566.50	5334.30
2005	12091.16	4568.90	1993.30	2575.60	6257.50
2006	14478.24	3811.18	1016.18	2795.00	9545.40
2007	16679.70	5503.80	1666.40	3837.40	10139.80
2008	18376.50	5703.90	1060.40	4643.50	11920.60
2009	20499.30	5672.40	522.50	5149.90	14027.50
2010	25046.70	6752.80	968.80	5784.00	17660.30
2011	31023.80	9209.70	1549.00	7660.70	21031.70
2012	39112.20	10747.20	1661.70	9085.50	27459.10
2013	48937.96	14424.51	1734.33	12690.18	33914.19
2014	62227.88	22903.06	2137.75	20765.31	38763.33
2015	62195.32	21339.76	2258.52	19081.24	40349.12
2016	72759.57	32325.74	3165.63	29160.12	40433.82

14-1 续表 2 continued

项 目 Item	总 计 Total	国有经济 State-Owned	地 方 Local - Owned	中 央 Central- Owned	其他经济 Others
竣工房屋面积(万平方米) Floor Space of Buildings Completed (10000 sq.m)					
1995	1175.90	622.20	466.90	155.30	69.40
1996	1880.70	653.30	501.30	152.00	103.90
1997	1982.30	765.30	522.10	243.20	92.50
1998	2374.00	836.00	624.00	212.00	239.40
1999	2873.00	1023.10	776.10	247.00	365.60
2000	3150.10	1096.30	836.10	260.20	481.80
2001	3673.40	1237.00	828.30	408.70	1102.30
2002	4146.60	1261.80	889.30	372.50	1738.80
2003	4840.80	1578.80	1143.40	435.40	2268.30
2004	6647.10	2561.30	1563.20	998.10	3265.30
2005	6896.90	2125.60	923.70	1201.90	3979.80
2006	7376.20	1137.10	450.40	686.70	5560.30
2007	8425.00	1620.90	858.60	762.30	5895.30
2008	9256.10	1386.00	537.90	848.10	7394.00
2009	10280.70	1587.10	255.90	1331.20	8198.90
2010	12813.40	2185.70	364.50	1821.20	10174.90
2011	16468.10	2593.00	600.00	1993.00	13274.20
2012	20395.20	1938.00	649.80	1288.30	17751.90
2013	22773.70	2278.00	571.70	1706.30	20077.10
2014	24867.30	2393.00	1105.00	1288.00	22165.10
2015	26825.20	3717.00	908.50	2808.50	22719.00
2016	28599.93	4714.59	772.76	3941.82	23885.34
房屋建筑面积竣工率(%) Rate of Floor Space of Buildings Completed (%)					
1995	35.80	41.20	39.40	16.60	23.60
1996	41.30	29.40	41.70	14.90	32.90
1997	43.10	32.70	42.60	22.00	23.80
1998	44.70	33.60	48.40	17.70	41.70
1999	49.60	37.80	49.20	22.00	47.80
2000	50.30	37.90	53.40	19.60	52.40
2001	55.10	44.30	56.00	31.10	60.70
2002	57.50	44.50	61.20	26.90	65.90
2003	54.20	41.30	51.10	25.40	64.10
2004	56.50	50.30	62.00	38.90	61.20
2005	57.00	46.50	46.30	46.70	63.60
2006	50.90	29.80	44.30	24.60	58.30
2007	50.50	29.50	51.50	19.90	58.10
2008	50.40	24.30	50.70	18.30	62.00
2009	50.20	28.00	49.00	25.80	58.40
2010	51.20	32.40	37.60	31.50	57.60
2011	53.10	28.20	38.70	26.00	63.10
2012	52.10	18.00	39.10	14.20	64.60
2013	46.50	15.80	33.00	13.40	59.20
2014	40.00	10.40	51.70	6.20	57.20
2015	43.10	17.40	40.20	14.70	56.30
2016	39.31	14.58	24.41	13.52	59.07

注： 本表资料包括施工总承包和专业承包企业，不含劳务分包企业(下同)。
Note: In this table, the data including general contract and specilized contract enterprises under construction, excluding labor divided contract (the same as the following tables)

14-2 分市州建筑业企业生产情况(2016)
STATISTICS ON PRODUCTION OF CONSTRUCTION ENTERPRISES OF CITIES AND PREFECTURE(2016)

单位：亿元 (100 million yuan)

项目	Item	建筑业总产值 Total Output Value of Construction Industry	建筑工程产值 Output Value of Construction Projects	安装工程产值 Output Value of Installation Projects	其他产值 Output Value of Other Projects	竣工产值 Output Value of Projects Completed
湖北省	**Hubei**	**11862.40**	**10612.09**	**922.89**	**327.42**	**6341.37**
武汉市	Wuhan	6980.37	6193.06	578.55	208.76	3456.11
黄石市	Huangshi	329.57	311.23	13.82	4.51	246.32
十堰市	Shiyan	388.92	373.63	10.99	4.30	146.58
宜昌市	Yichang	901.36	841.52	48.80	11.03	314.31
襄阳市	Xiangyang	825.96	739.63	73.82	12.52	433.36
鄂州市	Ezhou	145.70	113.78	20.24	11.69	83.15
荆门市	Jingmen	144.62	126.65	10.24	7.73	97.42
孝感市	Xiaogan	425.31	361.60	53.70	10.01	345.58
荆州市	Jingzhou	233.34	212.61	14.49	6.24	177.82
黄冈市	Huanggang	874.93	797.86	52.94	24.13	635.62
咸宁市	Xianning	138.39	124.09	7.42	6.88	106.15
随州市	Suizhou	90.17	78.38	6.96	4.83	69.84
恩施州	Enshi	140.70	129.04	8.21	3.44	93.69
仙桃市	Xiantao	55.24	53.30	1.42	0.51	33.85
潜江市	Qianjiang	101.55	86.35	12.24	2.97	51.48
天门市	Tianmen	78.75	62.71	8.89	7.15	43.62
神农架	Shennongjia	7.51	6.64	0.16	0.71	6.46

14-3 按登记注册类型分的企业数及合同情况(2016)

单位：亿元

指标名称	Item	有工作量的建筑业企业个数(个) Number of Construction Enterprises with Work (unit)
总计	**Total**	**3366**
其中:国有及国有控股企业	State-owned and State-holding Enterprises	380
一、按登记注册类型分组	Grouped by Status of Registration	
内资企业	**Domestic Funded Enterprises**	**3350**
国有企业	State-owned Enterprises	162
集体企业	Collective-owned Enterprises	75
股份合作企业	Cooperative Enterprises	3
联营企业	Joint Ownership Enterprises	1
国有联营企业	State Joint Ownership Enterprises	
集体联营企业	Collective Joint Ownership Enterprises	1
国有与集体联营企业	Joint State-collective Enterprises	
其他联营企业	Other Joint Ownership Enterprises	
有限责任公司	Limited Liability Corporations	1504
国有独资公司	State Sole Funded Corporations	51
其他有限责任公司	Other Limited Liability Corporations	1453
股份有限公司	Share-holding Corporations Ltd.	143
私营企业	Private Enterprises	1462
私营独资企业	Private-funded Enterprises	9
私营合伙企业	Private Partnership Enterprises	
私营有限责任公司	Private Limited Liability Corporations	1382
私营股份有限公司	Private Share-holding Corporations Ltd.	71
其他企业	Other Enterprises	
港、澳、台商投资企业	**Enterprises with Funds from Hong Kong,Macao and Taiwan**	**14**
合资经营企业(港或澳、台资)	Joint-venture Enterprises	10
合作经营企业(港或澳、台资)	Cooperative Enterprises	
港、澳、台商独资经营企业	Enterprises with Sole Fund	3
港、澳、台商投资股份有限公司	Share-holding Corporations Ltd.	1
其他港澳台投资	Other Enterprises with Funds from Hong Kong,Macao and Taiwan	
外商投资企业	**Foreign Funded Enterprises**	**2**
中外合资经营企业	Joint-venture Enterprises	2
中外合作经营企业	Cooperative Enterprises	
外资企业	Enterprises with Sole Fund	
外商投资股份有限公司	Share-holding Corporations Ltd.	
其他外商投资	Other Foreign Funded Enterprises	

Basic Statistics on Number of Enterprises and Contracts by Status of Registration(2016)

(100 million yuan)

合同情况(亿元) Condition on Contracts (100 million yuan)		
签订的合同额 Total Value of Contracts	1.上年结转合同额 Value from Contracts Signed in Last Year	2.本年新签合同额 Value from New Contracts Signed in This Year
25130.15	**10284.50**	**14845.64**
15976.60	6986.21	8990.39
25069.55	**10268.88**	**14800.67**
560.19	204.04	356.15
69.53	11.52	58.01
4.24	1.16	3.08
0.56	0.02	0.54
0.56	0.02	0.54
20145.19	8540.45	11604.74
6417.45	2711.78	3705.68
13727.74	5828.67	7899.07
1007.40	440.73	566.66
3282.45	1070.97	2211.48
8.89	2.71	6.18
2957.23	949.34	2007.88
316.33	118.91	197.42
4.51	**0.92**	**3.59**
4.07	0.77	3.30
0.17	0.07	0.10
0.27	0.09	0.18
56.08	**14.69**	**41.39**
56.08	14.69	41.39

14-4 按登记注册类型分的建筑业总产值(2016)

单位：亿元

指标名称	Item	建筑业总产值 Total Output Value
总计	**Total**	**11862.40**
其中:国有及国有控股企业	State-owned and State-holding Enterprises	5573.24
一、按登记注册类型分组	Grouped by Status of Registration	
内资企业	**Domestic Funded Enterprises**	**11812.38**
国有企业	State-owned Enterprises	376.79
集体企业	Collective-owned Enterprises	72.40
股份合作企业	Cooperative Enterprises	4.98
联营企业	Joint Ownership Enterprises	0.54
国有联营企业	State Joint Ownership Enterprises	
集体联营企业	Collective Joint Ownership Enterprises	0.54
国有与集体联营企业	Joint State-collective Enterprises	
其他联营企业	Other Joint Ownership Enterprises	
有限责任公司	Limited Liability Corporations	8303.42
国有独资公司	State Sole Funded Corporations	1866.86
其他有限责任公司	Other Limited Liability Corporations	6436.56
股份有限公司	Share-holding Corporations Ltd.	640.12
私营企业	Private Enterprises	2409.95
私营独资企业	Private-funded Enterprises	12.53
私营合伙企业	Private Partnership Enterprises	1.53
私营有限责任公司	Private Limited Liability Corporations	2134.98
私营股份有限公司	Private Share-holding Corporations Ltd.	260.91
其他企业	Other Enterprises	4.19
港、澳、台商投资企业	**Enterprises with Funds from Hong Kong,Macao and Taiwan**	**9.88**
合资经营企业(港或澳、台资)	Joint-venture Enterprises	4.11
合作经营企业(港或澳、台资)	Cooperative Enterprises	
港、澳、台商独资经营企业	Enterprises with Sole Fund	5.61
港、澳、台商投资股份有限公司	Share-holding Corporations Ltd.	0.16
其他港澳台投资	Other Enterprises with Funds from Hong Kong,Macao and Taiwan	40.13
外商投资企业	**Foreign Funded Enterprises**	**40.13**
中外合资经营企业	Joint-venture Enterprises	
中外合作经营企业	Cooperative Enterprises	
外资企业	Enterprises with Sole Fund	
外商投资股份有限公司	Share-holding Corporations Ltd.	
其他外商投资	Other Foreign Funded Enterprises	

Total Output Vaule of Construction by Status of Registration(2016)

(100 million yuan)

其中:装饰装修产值 Output Value of Decoration	其中:在外省完成的产值 Output Value Completed in Other Provinces	建筑工程产值 Output Value of Construction	安装工程产值 Output Vaule of Installation	其他产值 Others
525.47	**4413.36**	**10612.25**	**922.65**	**327.50**
82.57	3448.46	5009.76	420.94	142.54
519.44	**4405.23**	**10565.38**	**920.17**	**326.83**
2.16	49.17	290.97	29.10	56.72
0.86	0.24	61.97	9.76	0.67
0.00	0.00	4.98	0.00	0.00
0.14	0.00	0.44	0.07	0.03
0.14	0.00	0.44	0.07	0.03
266.06	3926.73	7461.97	688.15	153.30
14.89	1393.58	1713.40	139.77	13.68
251.18	2533.15	5748.57	548.37	139.62
14.97	87.37	558.43	50.14	31.55
235.15	341.69	2182.45	142.96	84.54
0.08	0.00	12.36	0.11	0.07
0.68	0.00	1.53	0.00	0.00
231.60	336.87	1914.79	139.38	80.81
2.78	4.82	253.78	3.48	3.66
0.10	0.03	4.17	0.00	0.02
3.49	**1.21**	**6.74**	**2.48**	**0.66**
2.24	1.18	4.00	0.08	0.03
1.21	0.03	2.70	2.28	0.63
0.05	0.00	0.05	0.12	0.00
2.54	6.93	40.13	0.00	0.00
2.54	**6.93**	**40.13**		**0.00**

14-5 按隶属关系和资质等级分的建筑业总产值的构成(2016)

单位：亿元

指标名称	Item	建筑业总产值 Total Output Value
总计	**Total**	**11862.40**
一、按隶属关系分组	**Grouped by Jurisdiction of Management**	
中央	Centre	4463.62
省(自治区、直辖市)	Province (Autonomous Region、Municipality)	516.10
地区(州、盟、省辖市)	Region (State、League、Provincial Municipality)	1370.70
县(区、市、旗)	County (District、City、Banner)	1029.17
街道	Street	265.30
镇	Town	138.00
乡	Countryside	29.57
居委会	Residents' Committee	12.44
村委会	Village Committee	9.09
其他	Others	4028.42
二、按企业资质等级分组	**Grouped by Qualification Criteria**	
企业资质等级(施工总承包)	General Contracting	11153.63
特级	Special Grade	3558.61
一级	First Grade	4674.23
二级	Second Grade	2052.73
三级及以下	Third Grade and Below	868.06
企业资质等级(专业总承包)	Professional Contraction Construction	708.77
一级	First Grade	362.65
二级	Second Grade	161.85
三级及以下	Third Grade and Below	184.28

Composition of Total Output Value of Construction Enterprises by Jurisdiction of Management and Qualification Criteria (2016)

(100 million yuan)

其中:装饰装修产值 Output Value of Decoration	其中:在外省完成的产值 Output Value Completed in Other Provinces	建筑工程产值 Output Value of Construction	安装工程产值 Output Vaule of Installation	其他产值 Others
525.47	**4413.36**	**10612.25**	**922.65**	**327.50**
53.01	3251.79	4075.84	303.38	84.40
10.06	51.43	426.47	71.64	17.99
43.07	212.80	1182.37	125.39	62.93
32.82	166.09	930.06	76.16	22.94
25.64	77.60	228.98	33.46	2.86
0.75	17.06	130.86	5.79	1.35
0.14	0.00	29.42	0.13	0.03
0.86	0.00	10.61	0.88	0.95
0.01	0.00	8.86	0.16	0.06
359.12	636.59	3588.78	305.66	133.98
349.56	4250.33	10173.44	734.58	245.61
73.49	2608.09	3381.52	145.80	31.29
149.10	1485.81	4157.64	385.01	131.58
90.19	145.22	1863.38	141.32	48.03
36.78	11.21	770.89	62.45	34.71
175.92	163.03	438.81	188.07	81.88
131.14	78.44	207.76	89.34	65.54
36.66	29.85	100.49	51.06	10.30
8.11	54.75	130.56	47.67	6.05

14-6 按登记注册类型分的建筑业企业完成房屋建筑竣工面积(2016)

单位:万平方米

指标名称	Item	合计 Total
总计	**Total**	**28613.46**
其中:国有及国有控股企业	State-owned and State-holding Enterprises	4661.43
按登记注册类型分组	Grouped by Status of Registration	
内资企业	**Domestic Funded Enterprises**	**28499.26**
国有企业	State-owned Enterprises	191.61
集体企业	Collective-owned Enterprises	390.56
股份合作企业	Cooperative Enterprises	5.05
联营企业	Joint Ownership Enterprises	4.94
国有联营企业	State Joint Ownership Enterprises	
集体联营企业	Collective Joint Ownership Enterprises	4.94
国有与集体联营企业	Joint State-collective Enterprises	
其他联营企业	Other Joint Ownership Enterprises	
有限责任公司	Limited Liability Corporations	17516.99
国有独资公司	State Sole Funded Corporations	1936.26
其他有限责任公司	Other Limited Liability Corporations	15580.73
股份有限公司	Share-holding Corporations Ltd.	1711.02
私营企业	Private Enterprises	8636.50
私营独资企业	Private-funded Enterprises	100.98
私营合伙企业	Private Partnership Enterprises	6.07
私营有限责任公司	Private Limited Liability Corporations	7554.34
私营股份有限公司	Private Share-holding Corporations Ltd.	975.11
其他企业	Other Enterprises	42.59
港、澳、台商投资企业	**Enterprises with Funds from Hong Kong,Macao and Taiwan**	**52.81**
合资经营企业(港或澳、台资)	Joint-venture Enterprises	3.01
合作经营企业(港或澳、台资)	Cooperative Enterprises	
港、澳、台商独资经营企业	Enterprises with Sole Fund	49.80
港、澳、台商投资股份有限公司	Share-holding Corporations Ltd.	0.00
外商投资企业	**Foreign Funded Enterprises**	**61.39**
中外合资经营企业	Joint-venture Enterprises	61.39
中外合作经营企业	Cooperative Enterprises	
外资企业	Enterprises with Sole Fund	
外商投资股份有限公司	Share-holding Corporations Ltd.	
其他外商投资	Other Foreign Funded Enterprises	

Completed Floor Space of Buildings Constructed by Construction Enterprises by Status of Registration (2016)

(10 000sq.m)

住宅房屋 Residential Buildings	商业及服务用房屋 Houses for Business and Service	办公用房屋 Office Buildings	科研、教育、医疗用房屋 Houses for Scientific Research、Education and Medical Treatment	文化、体育、娱乐用房屋 Houses for Culture、Sports and Entertainment	厂房及建筑物 Workshop and Buildings	仓库 Storage	其他未列明的房屋建筑物* Others
20047.1254	**2240.58**	**1621.89**	**1168.40**	**287.00**	**2682.49**	**76.59**	**489.37**
2729.0432	724.79	431.74	205.43	97.58	428.38	3.39	41.08
20009.7635	**2218.15**	**1601.49**	**1167.20**	**286.85**	**2668.45**	**65.97**	**481.39**
105.0525	8.56	23.27	18.26	8.90	24.88	2.05	0.62
301.4712	38.03	7.22	14.45	0.16	25.35	0.02	3.86
4.3264	0.00	0.00	0.23	0.00	0.49	0.00	0.00
1.5056	0.57	0.82	1.14	0.00	0.76	0.00	0.15
1.5056	0.57	0.82	1.14	0.00	0.76	0.00	0.15
11909.3505	1593.97	920.56	866.62	227.25	1679.80	35.48	283.95
938.3729	353.93	238.26	104.10	31.97	267.94	1.34	0.34
10970.9776	1240.04	682.29	762.52	195.28	1411.86	34.14	283.61
962.1875	267.93	102.95	117.98	29.75	167.00	17.62	45.59
6685.9897	309.08	546.67	148.52	20.79	768.42	9.82	147.22
84.5758	0.46	2.20	0.00	0.00	2.54	0.00	11.20
0	0.00	6.06	0.00	0.01	0.00	0.00	0.00
5809.5122	291.53	430.03	143.91	20.58	719.12	8.89	130.77
791.9017	17.09	108.37	4.61	0.20	46.77	0.92	5.25
39.8801	0.00	0.00	0.00	0.00	1.74	0.96	0.00
9.7365	**8.93**	**8.12**	**1.20**	**0.15**	**14.04**	**10.63**	**0.00**
0	0.00	0.00	0.00	0.00	3.01	0.00	0.00
9.7365	8.93	8.12	1.20	0.15	11.04	10.63	0.00
0	0.00	0.00	0.00	0.00	0.00	0.00	0.00
27.6254	**13.51**	**12.28**	**0.00**	**0.00**	**0.00**	**0.00**	**7.98**
27.6254	13.51	12.28	0.00	0.00	0.00	0.00	7.98

14–7 按隶属关系和资质等级分的建筑业企业工程完成情况(2016)

单位：万平方米

指标名称	Item	房屋建筑施工面积 Floor Space of Buildings under Construcion
一、按隶属关系分组	**Grouped by Jurisdiction of Management**	
中央	Centre	2916.01165
省(自治区、直辖市)	Province (Autonomous Region、Municipality)	177.46448
地区(州、盟、省辖市)	Region (State、League、Provincial Municipality)	696.01952
县(区、市、旗)	County (District、City、Banner)	794.52465
街道	Street	150.79736
镇	Town	66.70675
乡	Countryside	13.41585
居委会	Residents´ Committee	5.6328
村委会	Village Committee	5.38863
其他	Others	2457.54
四、按企业资质等级分组	**Grouped by Qualification Criteria**	
企业资质等级(施工总承包)	Enterprises Qualification Criteria (General Contracting)	7205.71054
特级	Special Grade	2771.26236
一级	First Grade	2548.70099
二级	Second Grade	1357.74666
三级及以下	Third Grade and Below	528.00053
企业资质等级(专业总承包)	Enterprises Qualification Criteria (Professional Contraction Construction)	77.79449
一级	First Grade	27.04314
二级	Second Grade	26.26416
三级及以下	Third Grade and Below	24.49

Project Completion Situation on Construction Enterprises by Jurisdiction of Management and Qualification Criteria (2016)

(10 000 sq.m)

本年新开工面积 Floor Space of New Construction This Year	实行投标承包面积 Contracting Space of Bidding	房屋建筑竣工面积 Floor Space of Buildings Completed	住宅房屋 Residential Buildings	商业及服务用房屋 Houses for Business Use
688.76	1212.85	394.18	234.13	67.60
68.91	137.60	50.47	27.07	0.52
426.72	528.75	366.02	262.74	12.03
457.14	565.04	453.40	283.49	63.20
94.57	121.51	101.56	51.76	11.97
51.58	38.13	48.78	28.56	0.94
6.59	11.61	13.11	10.90	0.12
4.52	3.68	4.20	2.98	0.48
3.67	2.41	4.52	3.96	0.00
1467.77	1633.35	1425.09	1099.12	67.21
3225.02	4211.76	2811.93	1983.38	222.28
1025.33	1100.54	712.22	478.81	83.27
1120.25	2039.32	1022.49	698.19	83.82
755.06	767.34	747.65	574.42	38.55
324.38	304.57	329.57	231.96	16.64
45.20	43.17	49.41	21.33	1.78
14.11	17.15	15.88	2.89	0.00
15.62	12.02	16.17	6.62	0.72
15.48	14.01	17.36	11.83	1.06

14-8 分市州建筑业企业工程完成情况(2016)
STATISTICS ON PROJECTS COMPLETION OF CONSTRUCTION ENTERPRISES BY CITIES AND PREFECTURES (2016)

单位：万平方米 (10 000 sq.m)

项 目	Item	房屋建筑施工面积 Floor Space of Housing Construction	本年新开工面积 Beginning projects in This Year	实行投标承包面积 Actual Floor Space by Contracts and Bids	房屋建筑竣工面积 Floor Space of Housing Projects Completed	#住 宅 Residential Buildings	#办公用房 Office Buildings
湖北省	**Hubei**	**72759.57**	**32692.01**	**42544.24**	**28599.93**	**20042.13**	**1618.56**
武汉市	Wuhan	44516.58	16723.06	22939.89	13612.73	9402.96	805.71
黄石市	Huangshi	2082.07	1109.69	1416.27	1201.83	823.20	52.26
十堰市	Shiyan	1473.18	774.74	847.73	636.45	505.32	23.72
宜昌市	Yichang	3423.90	1707.06	2882.83	1278.91	985.08	49.27
襄阳市	Xiangyang	4177.42	2127.90	3078.81	1886.78	1342.73	83.46
鄂州市	Ezhou	791.75	442.06	406.73	427.65	295.03	6.31
荆门市	Jingmen	1086.74	646.98	923.69	447.83	303.88	33.68
孝感市	Xiaogan	3191.22	2226.38	1701.19	2244.99	1680.49	83.32
荆州市	Jingzhou	1482.92	810.33	881.48	762.28	491.60	31.48
黄冈市	Huanggang	6591.29	3937.74	4660.38	3831.47	2702.31	284.38
咸宁市	Xianning	768.70	529.27	487.95	566.98	472.31	27.17
随州市	Suizhou	846.83	384.06	640.07	433.79	341.25	25.16
恩施州	Enshi	784.16	468.84	455.66	455.19	208.08	80.23
仙桃市	Xiantao	313.64	220.13	221.14	200.67	156.54	9.63
潜江市	Qianjiang	699.12	282.63	643.80	313.95	120.81	9.68
天门市	Tianmen	490.66	277.22	332.50	276.77	200.13	12.61
神农架	Shennongjia	39.38	23.90	24.12	21.66	10.43	0.47

主要统计指标解释

建筑业统计单位 指从事房屋、构筑物建造和设备安装活动的法人企业。建筑业法人企业应具有建筑业资质并能够独立核算,同时其应具备以下条件:①依法成立,有自己的名称、组织机构和场所,能够承担民事责任;②独立拥有和使用资产,承担负债,有权与其他单位签订合同;③独立核算盈亏,能够编制资产负债表。

建筑业总产值 是以货币形式表现的建筑业企业在一定时期内生产的建筑业产品和提供的服务的总和。建筑业总产值包括:

(1)建筑工程产值:指列入建筑工程预算内的各种工程价值。

(2)安装工程产值:指设备安装工程价值,不包括被安装设备本身的价值。

(3)其他产值:建筑业总产值中除建筑工程、安装工程以外的产值。包括房屋构筑物修理产值、非标准设备制造产值、总包企业向分包企业收取的管理费以及不能明确划分的施工活动所完成的产值。

a.房屋构筑物修理产值:指房屋和构筑物修理所完成的产值,但不包括被修理房屋、构筑物本身价值和生产设备的修理产值。

b.非标准设备制造产值:指加工制造没有定型的非标准生产设备的加工费和原材料价值(如化工厂、炼油厂用的各种罐、槽,矿井生产统一使用的各种漏斗、三角槽、阀门等)以及附属加工厂为本企业承建工程制作的非标准设备的价值。

建筑业增加值 指建筑业企业在报告期内以货币形式表现的建筑业生产经营活动的最终成果。

从2004年第一次全国经济普查开始,建筑业现价增加值按生产法和分配法(收入法)两种方法计算,以收入法的计算结果为准,即从收入的角度出发,根据生产要素在生产过程中应得的收入份额计算。具体计算方法:经济普查年度建筑业增加值按照《经济普查年度GDP核算方案》计算,非经济普查年度建筑业增加值按照《非经济普查年度GDP核算方案》计算。

房屋建筑施工面积 指在报告期内施过工的全部房屋建筑面积,包括本期新开工的房屋面积、上期施工跨入本期继续施工的房屋面积、上期停缓建在本期恢复施工的房屋面积、本期竣工的房屋面积及本期施工后又停缓建的房屋面积。

房屋建筑竣工面积 指在报告期内房屋建筑按照设计要求全部完工,达到了使用条件,经验收鉴定合格,正式移交使用单位的房屋建筑面积。

Explanatory Notes on Main Statistical Indicators

Statistical Unit in Construction refers to corporate enterprise engaged in the construction of buildings and structures and in the installation of equipment. A corporate construction enterprise should have qualification certificates with independent accounting system, and should meet the following 3 requirements: a) being set up in line with relevant legal basis, having its full name, organization and location, and capable of taking civil liabilities; b) independently possessing and using its assets and assuming its liabilities, and entitled to sign contracts with other institutions; and c) making independent accounts of its profits and losses, and capable of compiling its own balance sheet.

Gross Output Value of Construction refers to total of construction products and services, expressed in money terms, produced or rendered by construction and installation enterprises during a given period of time. It includes:

(1) Output value of construction projects, that is the value of projects covered by the project budgets;

(2) Output value of installation projects, that is the value of the installation of equipment, (excluding the value of the equipment to be

installed);

(3) Output value of others, that is the output value of construction industry excluding that of construction projects and installation projects. It includes: output value of repair of buildings and structures; output value of non–standard equipment manufacturing; overhead expenses received by contracted enterprises to the sub–contracted enterprises and the completed output value of construction activities that have no clear definition.

a. Output value of repair of buildings and structures, that is the value created through the repairs of buildings or structures, but does not include the value of buildings or structures being repaired and the value of the repair of production equipment;

b. Output value of manufactured non–standard equipment, that is the value of non–standard production equipment including raw materials and manufacturing cost made for the construction project (i.e., chemical plant; kettles or tanks used by refineries; various fillers, triangle tanks, valves used by mines), and the output value of equipment manufactured by subsidiary workshops.

Value–added of Construction refers to the final result of the activities of production and management of construction industry in monetary terms in the reference period.

Starting from the 2004 economic census, value–added of construction is calculated by both production approach and income approach, with the income approach as the final approach, where the calculation is based on the share of production factor in the production process. Specifically, value–added of construction for census years is calculated in accordance with the Programme of Compilation of GDP and National Accounts for the Year of Economic Census, and value–added of construction for other years is calculated in accordance with the Programme of Compilation of GDP and National Accounts for the Non Economic Census Years.

Floor Space of Buildings Under Construction refers to floor space of buildings under construction during the reference period, including newly started buildings, buildings started earlier and continued during the reference period, and buildings suspended earlier but restarted during the reference period, buildings completed during the reference period, and buildings under construction and then suspended during the reference period.

Floor Space of Buildings Completed refers to the floor space of buildings that are completed in the reference period in accordance with the requirements of the design, up to the standard for putting them into use, and have been checked and accepted by concerned departments as qualified ones.

15 交通运输、邮电

Transportation, Post and Telecommunications Services

交通运输、邮电

Transportation,Post and Telecommunication Service 2016

全社会客运量	Passenger Capacity of The Whole Society	105813.14 (万人)
#公路	Public Road	88220.89 (万人)
全社会货运量	Volume of Freight Traffic	165124.84 (万吨)
#公路	Public Road	122654.50 (万吨)
邮电业务总量	Postal Service Portfolio	1400.01 (亿元)
#函件	Letters	6318.24 (万件)
年末固定电话用户	Local Telephone Subscriber End of Year	731.65 (万户)
年末移动电话用户	Mobile Phone Subscriber End of Year	4683.75 (万户)

全 社 会 客 货 运 量

Passenger Capactity of The Whole Society

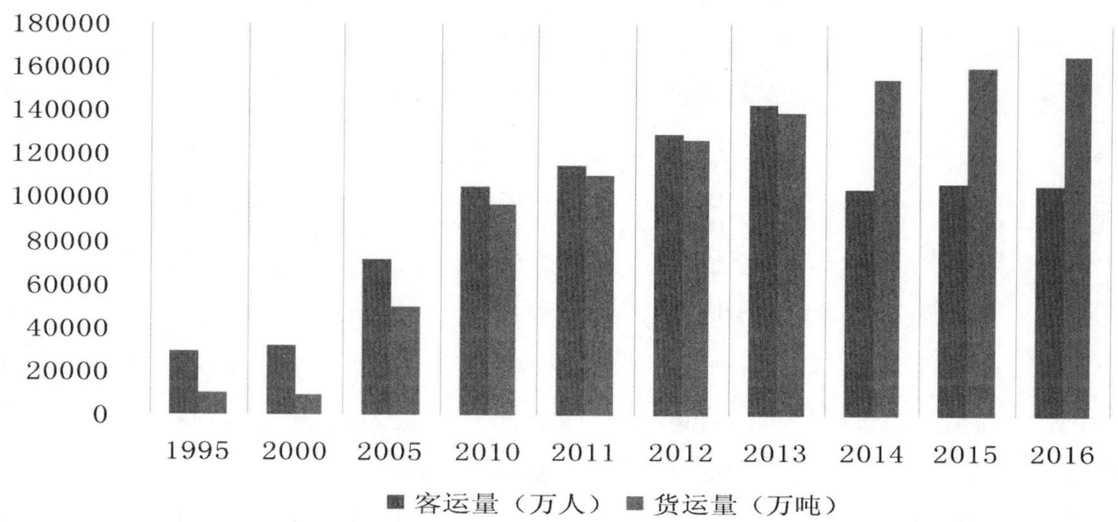

附:全社会客货运量

Passenger Capacity of The Whole Society

年份 Year	客运量(万人) Passenger Capacity (10 000 persons)	货运量(万吨) volume of freight traffic (10 000 tons)
1995	28508	10174
2000	31593	9345
2005	71892	49924
2010	105132	96938
2012	129511	126195
2013	143100	139740
2014	103672	154736
2015	104694	156357
2016	105813	165125

说明： 2014年因公路运输调整统计方法,与前期数据不可比(下同)。

Note:In 2014,the statistics method of transportation has been changed, the data can not be compared by the previous(the same below).

15-1 交通运输业基本情况

指　标	1995	2000	2005	2010
运输线路长度 (公里)				
铁路营业里程	1940	2025	2758	3032
公路通车里程	48728	57850	91131	206212
#等级公路里程	30910	48062	76075	187812
#高速公路		569	1649	3674
一级公路	641	611	1092	2210
二级公路	4967	7911	15225	16159
内河航道里程	8969	8309	8988	8988
客运量总计 (万人)	28508.20	31593.00	71892.00	105415.50
铁路	2300.00	3469.00	4615.00	7281.30
公路	24315.00	27184.00	66183.00	96873.00
水运	1745.00	679.00	601.00	375.80
民用航空	150.00	261.00	494.00	885.40
旅客周转量 (亿人公里)	285.29	398.32	803.90	1262.26
货物运输量总计 (万吨)	10173.62	9345.19	49923.52	97006.94
铁路	3986.00	3857.00	8491.00	10145.60
公路	2600.00	2228.00	33481.00	71020.00
水运	3585.00	3255.00	7944.00	15832.00
货物周转量 (亿吨公里)	776.44	831.64	1682.48	3370.37
民用车辆拥有量 (万辆)			393.90	761.11
#民用汽车拥有量	34.89	47.55	103.04	224.60
#载客汽车	14.96	24.69	53.40	151.51
载货汽车	18.61	21.72	30.96	53.29
#营运汽车			20.33	36.60
#私人汽车		41.72	59.66	165.39
民用运输船舶拥有量 (艘)		5905	5362	5502
机动船		4188	4158	4634
驳船		1717	1204	868
港口货物吞吐量 (万吨)		4113.46	13992.51	18782.67

注:2014年因公路运输统计方法调整,数据与前期不可比。

Note:From 2014, due to the statistics method of road transport has been adjusted, the data can not be compared with the previous period.

TRANSPORTATION

2012	2013	2014	2015	2016
3463	4794	4059	4062	4140
218151	226912	236932	252980	260179
203145	212893	224184	240936	249819
4006	4333	5096	6204	6204
2515	2789	3344	5231	5460
17233	17576	18033	21555	22005
8988	8988	9066	9066	9066
129510.90	143100.28	103671.80	104693.75	105813.14
9177.40	12101.80	14302.70	15083.90	15855.30
118369.00	129533.75	87804.00	87953.26	88220.89
443.50	528.00	533.80	574.46	572.22
933.50	936.73	1031.30	1082.13	1164.73
1576.97	1761.10	1458.24	1490.81	1521.05
126194.64	139740.26	154735.73	156356.93	165124.84
9177.40	9010.40	7681.30	6579.00	6744.20
97136.00	108824.21	116280.00	115800.30	122654.50
19070.00	24408.00	30765.00	33968.00	35715.80
4351.80	5036.80	5798.12	5908.40	6159.90
879.01	967.23	1042.36	959.35	902.95
305.07	363.68	439.39	504.36	593.33
277.76	282.29	345.84	424.70	515.17
62.69	68.62	72.73	70.16	69.71
40.37	42.04	42.95	55.25	51.92
238.64	292.00	300.61	433.90	524.16
4895	4938	4744	4357	4010
4531	4794	4500	4155	3857
364	232	244	202	153
23518.12	26219.00	28969.15	32949.52	35191.90

15-2 客 运 量
PASSENGER TRAFFIC

单位：万人 (10 000 persons)

年份 Year	总计 Total	铁路 Railway	公路 Highway	水运 Waterway	民用航空 Civil Aviation
1978	12009.20	2854.00	7429.00	1722.00	4.20
1980	16629.26	3217.00	11282.00	2123.00	7.26
1985	28178.22	3353.00	22378.00	2433.00	14.22
1990	32145.93	2107.00	27333.00	2693.00	12.93
1991	33982.62	2016.00	29279.00	2654.00	33.62
1992	34726.00	2077.00	29635.00	2894.00	120.00
1993	30152.00	2265.00	25116.00	2665.00	106.00
1994	29607.00	2358.00	24819.00	2210.00	120.00
1995	28508.20	2300.00	24315.00	1743.00	150.00
1996	29045.40	2248.00	25180.00	1449.00	168.00
1997	29503.08	2127.00	25684.00	1538.00	154.08
1998	28208.00	2218.00	24540.00	1306.00	144.00
1999	29360.14	2545.00	25596.00	1080.00	139.14
2000	63306.00	3469.00	58897.00	679.00	261.00
2001	62696.00	3632.00	58018.00	767.00	279.00
2002	63382.00	3813.00	58623.00	638.00	308.00
2003	62880.00	3602.00	58371.00	573.00	334.42
2004	68167.00	4072.00	63127.00	522.00	446.11
2005	71892.00	4615.00	66183.00	601.00	494.00
2006	75440.00	4850.00	69335.00	706.00	549.00
2007	84088.00	5125.00	77514.00	736.00	712.70
2008	89720.00	6027.00	82532.00	388.00	774.00
2009	96219.00	6440.00	88703.00	371.00	705.00
2010	105415.50	7281.30	96873.00	375.80	885.40
2011	114736.92	8503.80	104971.00	347.60	914.52
2012	129510.90	9764.90	118369.00	443.50	933.50
2013	143100.28	12101.80	129533.75	528.00	936.73
2014	103671.40	14302.70	87804.00	533.80	1031.30
2015	104693.73	15083.90	87953.26	574.46	1082.13
2016	105813.14	15855.30	88220.89	572.22	1164.73

注： 2014年因公路运输统计方法调整，数据与前期不可比。

Note:From 2014, due to the statistics method of road transport has been adjusted, the data can not be compared with the previous period .

15-3 旅客周转量
TURNOVER VOLUME OF PASSENGER TRAFFIC

单位：亿人公里 (100 million person-kms)

年份 Year	总计 Total	铁路 Railway	公路 Highway	水运 Waterway	民用航空 Civil Aviation
1978	69.38	30.72	24.85	13.54	0.17
1980	95.88	41.79	36.20	17.52	0.37
1985	185.25	84.00	81.33	19.40	0.52
1990	225.85	82.83	112.83	29.28	0.91
1991	257.68	98.09	126.70	30.19	2.70
1992	286.35	104.89	135.61	34.72	11.13
1993	281.28	113.60	123.64	33.50	10.54
1994	283.98	121.91	121.40	28.71	11.96
1995	285.29	129.47	117.76	22.71	15.35
1996	285.04	121.17	124.97	21.09	17.81
1997	282.53	118.62	123.39	24.14	16.38
1998	278.66	126.68	118.51	18.79	14.68
1999	300.38	146.54	124.46	14.09	15.29
2000	563.78	232.00	297.46	8.84	25.48
2001	574.24	248.00	293.35	5.87	27.02
2002	633.6.9	283.00	317.02	3.60	30.07
2003	617.68	271.00	309.00	4.00	33.68
2004	703.95	322.80	334.00	3.20	43.95
2005	803.90	389.40	358.00	4.20	52.30
2006	847.42	408.10	374.80	5.10	59.42
2007	947.71	440.80	423.80	5.30	77.81
2008	1077.68	474.01	522.57	2.30	78.80
2009	1096.31	466.70	562.34	2.49	64.78
2010	1262.26	528.90	631.39	2.92	99.05
2011	1444.66	639.15	700.06	2.49	102.97
2012	1576.00	663.60	804.07	2.94	106.36
2013	1761.10	756.40	892.25	3.14	109.31
2014	1458.24	854.40	483.89	2.85	120.10
2015	1490.81	869.30	489.29	3.32	128.90
2016	1521.05	895.80	487.33	3.35	134.57

15-4 货 运 量
FREIGHT TRAFFIC

单位：万吨 (10 000 tons)

年份 Year	总计 Total	铁路 Railway	公路 Highway	水运 Waterway	*内河 Inland Waterway	*海运 Seashipping
1978	10199	3513	3556	3130		
1980	8420	3211	2199	3110		
1985	11059	2659	3852	3463		
1990	10916	3901	2941	3784		
1991	11217	3957	2999	3996		
1992	11565	4018	2828	4364		
1993	11184	4029	2734	4248		
1994	10663	3964	2666	3641		
1995	10174	3986	2600	3585		
1996	9928	3779	2537	3268		
1997	9389	3882	2280	3119		
1998	10154	3999	2009	4040		
1999	10517	3964	2141	4313		
2000	40949	6558	27863	6270	6202	68
2001	41476	7094	29851	4275	4198	77
2002	42064	7400	28777	5630	5390	240
2003	44661	7825	30348	6195	5830	365
2004	47073	7872	31584	7259	6823	436
2005	50317	8491	33481	7944	7466	478
2006	52885	8990	35361	8242	7679	536
2007	58523	9728	39568	9027	7765	1262
2008	75778	10202	52759	12681	8182	4499
2009	82714	9839	59563	13305	8108	5197
2010	97007	10145	71020	15832	9916	6082
2011	110168	10059	82741	17358	10817	6536
2012	125392	9177	97136	19070	11836	7275
2013	139740	9010	108824	21897	13575	8042
2014	154736	7681	116280	30765	21152	8476
2015	156357	6579	115800	33968	27564	6226
2016	165125	6744	122655	35716	29898	5728

15-5 货物周转量
TURNOVER VOLUME OF FREIGHT TRAFFIC

单位：亿吨公里 (100 million ton-km)

年份 Year	总计 Total	铁路 Railway	公路 Highway	水运 Waterway	#内河 Inland Waterway	#沿海 Seashipping
1978	281.09	191.72	9.22	80.15		
1980	326.85	206.14	9.85	110.85		
1985	507.57	320.37	16.59	169.94		
1990	670.53	415.17	14.72	235.04		
1991	720.23	455.00	14.67	245.41		
1992	757.00	461.81	13.89	272.70		
1993	753.52	477.64	11.99	259.90		
1994	743.21	505.57	10.23	222.32		
1995	776.44	544.40	9.62	222.20		
1996	775.79	552.32	9.93	208.05		
1997	725.34	501.77	8.72	212.21		
1998	696.62	465.81	7.59	220.63		
1999	696.27	457.70	8.25	227.76		
2000	1156.57	618.37	227.16	305.29	295.07	10.22
2001	1097.60	634.90	218.97	237.31	226.15	11.16
2002	1212.82	680.00	211.49	313.60	271.30	42.29
2003	1313.13	703.80	224.00	377.00	315.38	61.61
2004	1485.76	781.83	235.60	461.08	395.75	65.33
2005	1689.86	987.60	251.00	443.20	391.05	105.00
2006	1730.93	1021.40	266.10	437.90	379.81	58.10
2007	1902.17	1138.20	302.09	458.00	361.93	95.83
2008	2699.97	1096.90	789.37	810.46	416.17	394.29
2009	2808.46	1032.40	930.10	845.18	402.82	442.36
2010	3370.37	1144.60	1079.13	1145.52	547.77	470.00
2011	4044.45	1226.80	1277.71	1538.83	625.26	609.61
2012	4693.61	1194.10	1565.45	1590.65	740.76	683.36
2013	4883.01	1195.70	1818.18	1868.08	946.02	756.69
2014	5798.12	1109.10	2340.56	2347.32	1347.07	891.82
2015	5908.40	995.70	2380.62	2530.91	1851.27	618.02
2016	6159.90	971.50	2506.85	2680.34	2040.82	600.69

15-6 全省民用车辆拥有量(2016)
NUMBER OF CIVIL MOTOR VEHICLES OWNED BY WHOLE PROVINCE(2016)

单位：辆 (unit)

指标	Item	总计 Total	营运 Working	非营运 Non-Working
合计	**Total**	**9029512**	**627072**	**8391819**
汽车	Civil Vehicles	5933346	519174	5403551
载客汽车	Passenger Vehicles	5151650	134145	5006884
#大型	Lage Scale	54692	38061	11521
中型	Medium Scale	31927	11833	14591
小型	Small Scale	5040637	84244	4956385
#轿车	Cars	3173912	77628	3096284
载货汽车	Trucks	697055	355987	341068
#重型	Heavy Scale	164891	151170	13721
中型	Medium Scale	63633	55318	8315
轻型	Light Scale	467862	149339	318523
#普通载货	Ordinary Trucks	324812	69264	255548
其他汽车	Other Vehicles	84641	29042	55599
#三轮汽车	Tricycle Motocars	6651	2065	4586
低速汽车	Low Speed Vehicles	39763	19157	20606
摩托车	Motorear	3053785	66721	2987064
#普通	Ordinary Motor	3025755	66706	2959049
轻便	Light Motor	28030	15	28015
挂车	Freight Trailers	42124	41049	1075
其他类型车	Other Motor Vehicles	257	128	129

注：本表“其他汽车”中，包括三轮和四轮农用运输车。
Note:Tricycles and four-wheel farming vehicles are inclued in “Other Vehicles”.

15-7 私人车辆拥有量
NUMBER OF PRIVATE – OWNED VEHICLES

单位：辆 (unit)

指 标	Item	2000	2005	2010	2013	2014	2015	2016
民用汽车	Civil Vehicles	475500	596601	1653948	2919992	3566489	4338967	5241602
载客汽车	Passenger Vehicles	245500	297095	1153728	2366962	3006050	3796713	4704592
#大型	#Lage Scale	29200	3312	2939	1011	951	770	650
轿车	Cars		177650	773727	1556798	1953696	2414210	2938643
载货汽车	Ordinary Trucks	211400	135352	327509	452886	478775	473513	478375
#重型	#Heavy Scale		8766	33281	51217	59171	59388	63829
其它汽车	Others		164154	172711	100144	81664	68741	58635
摩托车	Motors	1241000	2853113	4971619	4793599	4792901	4501871	3046392
载货挂车	Freight Trailers	4400	1714	6467	10255	10893	11405	12684

15-8 水路运输工具拥有量(2016)
NUMBER OF WATER TRANSPORT TOOLS(2016)

指 标	Item	机动船 Power Boat	客船 Passenger Ship	货船 Cargo Ship	拖船 Tugboat
数量 (艘)	Quantity (ship)	3857	627	3134	96
总载重量 (吨位)	Total Carrying Capacity (tonage)	7471437		7471437	
净载重量 (吨位)	Net Load (tonage)	7307685		7307685	
载客量 (客位)	Passenger Carrying Capacity (person)	45012	45012		
标准箱位	TEU	3718		3718	
功率 (千瓦)	Power (kw)	2165576	98196	2008944	58436

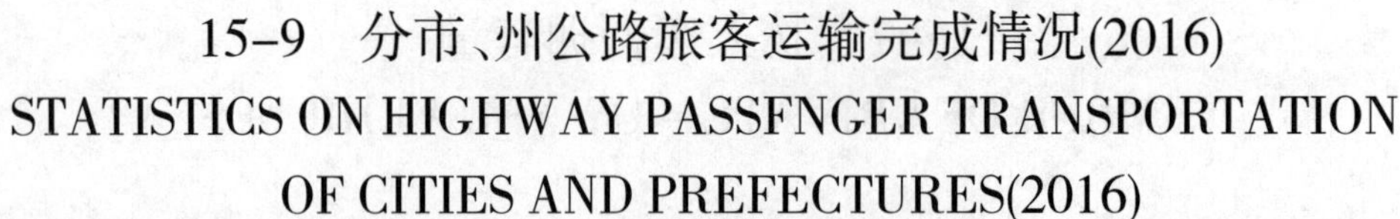

15-9 分市、州公路旅客运输完成情况(2016)
STATISTICS ON HIGHWAY PASSFNGER TRANSPORTATION OF CITIES AND PREFECTURES(2016)

地区	Region	旅客运输量(万人) Passenger Traffic (10,000 person)	旅客周转量 (万人公里) Turnover Volume of Passenger Traffic (100 million person-km)	货物运输量(万吨) Freight Traffic (10 000 ton)	货物周转量 (亿吨公里) Turnover Volume of Freight Traffic (100 million ton-km)
武汉市	Wuhan	11484	813818	28891	6366116
黄石市	Huangshi	3391	218062	5849	1166022
十堰市	Shiyan	3326	299803	5478	1191248
宜昌市	Yichang	10899	542514	8761	1432680
襄阳市	Xiangyang	10974	529836	25335	5248345
鄂州市	Ezhou	2029	125945	1519	346911
荆门市	Jingmen	2949	177974	3106	1036723
孝感市	Xiaogan	6941	305869	3287	614589
荆州市	Jingzhou	6404	346077	7306	1494794
黄冈市	Huanggang	10165	489963	7904	1645217
咸宁市	Xianning	5889	333042	8795	1026152
随州市	Suizhou	3316	175942	6632	1256341
恩施自治州	Enshi	3765	235270	3733	818105
仙桃市	Xiantao	2055	80661	1447	343995
潜江市	Qianjiang	1817	77336	2374	551300
天门市	Tianmen	2240	99670	1766	415571
神农架林区	Shennongjia	578	21487	500	116501

15-10 邮电业务基本情况
BASIC CONDITIONS OF THE POST AND TELECOMMUNICATION SERVICES

指　　标	Item	2005	2010	2014	2015	2016
邮电业务总量 (亿元)	**Total Volume of Post and Telecommunication Services (100 million yuan)**	**373.63**	**1028.09**	**720.35**	**962.66**	**1400.01**
邮政业务总量	Postal Services	23.40	55.71	98.66	137.41	192.10
电信业务总量	Telecommunication Services	350.20	972.38	621.69	825.25	1207.91
函件 (亿件)	Letters (100 million pcs)	1.30	1.00	0.67	0.68	0.63
包件 (万件)	Parcels (10 000 pcs)	320.00	210.10	141.70	105.80	71.94
快递业务量 (万件)	Special Express (10 000 pcs)	685.30	5476.60	72570.70	50847.30	77348.11
报刊期发数 (万份)	Newspaper and Magzines Circulation (10 000 pcs)	643.00	55102.50	72570.40	70907.10	67450.92
固定电话用户 (万户)	Fixed telephone subscribers (10 000 subscribers)	1236.00	1026.40	907.40	872.50	731.65
年末城市电话 (万户)	Urban Telephone Subscribers at Year-end (10 000 subscribers)	900.00	670.70	613.00	632.50	531.70
年末农村电话 (万户)	Rural Telephones (10 000 subscribers)	336.00	355.70	294.40	240.00	199.90
年末移动电话用户 (万户)	Mobile Telephone Subscribers at Year-end (10 000 subscribers)	1401.00	3454.70	4606.80	4650.60	4683.75
互联网宽带接入用户 (万户)	Internet Users (10 000 subscribers)	128.00	459.40	869.70	983.50	1131.88
邮路总长度(单程) (公里)	Length of Postal Routes and Rural Delivery (One Way) (km)		57483	161205	62159	74638
邮路线路总条数 (条)	Routes		411	718	653	726
农村投递线路条数 (条)	Highway Routes		4198	3567	3562	3539
农村投递线路长度(单程) (公里)	Railway Routes(One Way) (km)		194656	207494	205502	194241
邮电通信工具拥有量	Telecommunication Facilities					
移动电话交换机容量 (万户)	Mobile Telephone Swicthboard Capacity (10 000 units)		5862.70	8450.70	8748.70	8748.70
固定长途电话交换机容量 (万路端)	Capacity of Long Distance Telephone Switchborad (circuit)	46.60	49.00	17.30	17.00	7.40
长途光缆线路长度 (万公里)	Length of Long Distance Optical Cable (km)		2.70	3.03	3.14	3.23

注:邮电业务总量统计口径2011年发生变化,与以前各年份不可比。
Note:The statistic on total volume of post and telecommunication have been reconfigured from 2011.Datas of other year can not compare with the data of 2011.
2016年工信部调整了统计口径,2015年电信业务数据与2016年电信业务数据不可比。

15-11 邮电通信水平
LEVEL OF POST AND TELECOMMUNICATION SERVICES

指　　标	Item	2005	2010	2013	2014	2015	2016
每百人平均函件量 (件/百人)	Average Number of Letters Mailed Per 100 Persons (unit/100 person)	228.0	174.7	181.1	114.8	115.5	107.4
每百人平均订阅报刊量 (份/百人)	Average Number of Newspaper and Periodicals Subscribed Per 100 Persons (unit/100 person)	977.9	962.7	1254.9	1247.8	1211.8	1146.1
每百人平均包件 (件/百人)	Average Number of Parcels Per 100 Persons (unit/100 person)	5.6	3.4	2.9	2.4	1.8	1.2
电话普及率 (部/百人)	Rate of Popularization of Telephone (unit/100 person)	43.9	78.3	93.1	94.8	94.4	92.0
移动电话普及率 (部/百人)	Rate of Popularization of Mobile Phones (unit/100 person)	23.3	60.4	76.2	79.2	79.5	79.6

主要统计指标解释

铁路营业里程 又称营业长度(包括正式营业和临时营业里程),指办理客货运输业务的铁路正线总长度。凡是全线或部分建成双线及以上的线路,以第一线的实际长度计算;复线、站线、段管线、岔线和特殊用途线以及不计算运费的联络线都不计算营业里程。该指标可以反映铁路运输业基础设施的发展水平,也是计算客货周转量、运输密度和机车车辆运用效率等指标的基础资料。

公路里程指在一定时期内实际达到《公路工程[WTBZ]技术标准JTJ01-88》规定的等级公路,并经公路主管部门正式验收交付使用的公路里程数。包括大中城市的郊区公路以及通过小城镇街道部分的公路里程和桥梁、渡口的长度,不包括大中城市的街道、厂矿、林区生产用道和农业生产用道的里程。两条或多条公路共同经由同一路段,只计算一次,不得重复计算里程长度。该指标可以反映公路建设的发展规模,也是计算运输网密度等指标的基础资料。

内河航道里程 也称内河通航里程,指在一定时期内,能通航运输船舶及排筏的天然河流、湖泊水库、运河及通航渠道的长度。包括全年季节性通航累计三个月以上的航道,不包括仅供零散流放竹、木排的河道。该指标可以反映内河水运网的规模、水平和发展情况。

民用航空航线里程 指民航运输定期班机飞行的航线长度的总和。航线长度按机场之间的距离计算,通常有两种计算方法:一是将每条航线长度相加称为重复计算航线里程;一是将两线或两条以上航线经过同一区段里程,只计算一次航线长度称为不重复计算航线里程。一般常用的是后者,该指标可以确切反映民航运输网的规模,是表明民航事业为国民经济服务和方便人民生活程度的主要指标。

货(客)运量 指在一定时期内,各种运输工具实际运送的货物(旅客)数量。该指标是反映运输业为国民经济和人民生活服务的数量指标,也是制定和检查运输生产计划、研究运输发展规模和速度的重要指标。货运按吨计算,客运按人计算。货物不论运输距离长短、货物类别,均按实际重量统计。旅客不论行程远近或票价多少,均按一人一次客运量统计;半价票、小孩票也按一人统计。

货物(旅客)周转量 指在一定时期内,由各种运输工具运送的货物(旅客)数量与其相应运输距离的乘积之总和。该指标可以反映运输业生产的总成果,也是编制和检查运输生产计划,计算运输效率、劳动生产率以及核算运输单位成本的主要基础资料。计算货物周转量通常按发出站与到达站之间的最短距离,也就是计费距离计算。计算公式为:

货物(旅客)周转量=∑(货物(旅客)运输量×运输距离)

民用汽车拥有量 指报告期末,在公安交通管理部门按照《机动车注册登记工作规范》,已注册登记领有民用车辆牌照的全部汽车数量。汽车拥有量统计的主要分类:根据汽车结构分为载客汽车、载货汽车及其他汽车;根据汽车所有者不同分为个人(私人)汽车、单位汽车;根据汽车的使用性质分为营运汽车、非营运汽车;根据汽车大小规格不同载客汽车分为大型、中型、小型和微型,载货汽车分为重型、中型、轻型和微型。

邮电业务总量 指以价值量形式表现的邮电通信企业为社会提供各类邮电通信服务的总数量。邮电业务量按专业分类包括函件、包件、汇票、报刊发行、邮政快件、特快专递、邮政储蓄、集邮、公众电报、用户电报、传真、长途电话、出租电路、无线寻呼、移动电话、分组交换数据通信、出租代维等。计算方法为各类产品乘以相应的平均单价(不变价)之和,再加上出租电路和设备、代用户维护电话交换机和线路等的服务收入。该指标综合反映了一定时期邮电业务发展的总成果,是研究邮电业务量构成和发展趋势的重要指标。计算公式为:

邮电业务总量=∑(各类邮电业务量×不变单价)+出租代维及其他业务收入

邮政业务总量+电信业务总量

移动电话用户 指通过移动电话交换机进入移动电话网、占用移动电话号码的各类电话用户。包括签约用户和智能网预付费用户。一个移动电话号码统计为一户。

互联网上网人数 指平均每周使用互联网至少1小时的中国公民人数。

本地电话用户 指接入本地电信运营商固定电话网上的电话用户。包括:住宅用户、单位用户、公用电话用户等。按电话用户位置又分为市内电话用户和农村电话用户。1997年以前,"市内电话用户"是指接入县城及县以上城市的电话网上的电话用户;"农村电话用户"是指接入县邮电局农话台及县以下农村电话交换点,以县城为中心(除市话用户外)联通县、乡(镇)、行政村、村民小组的用户。从1997年起,电话用户数分组调整为以用户所在区域划分为"城市电话用户"和"乡村电话用户",与过去的按市内电话和农村电话划分方法不同。而电话用户总数、电话机总部数统计范围不变。

城市电话用户 指直辖市、省辖市、地级市、县级市的市区、市郊区及县城(包括县人民政府所在地的县城关区或行政建制相当于县人民政府所在地的镇)范围内接入局用交换机的电话用户数,包括分布在农村地区的独立工矿区、林区、驻军等电话用户数。

农村电话用户 指按行政区划属于城市范围以外的乡(镇)、村的电话用户数。

住宅电话用户 指安装在居民住宅或农民家里并按照住宅电话用户登记注册和收费的电话用户。包括私人付费、单位付费和按规定免费安装的住宅电话用户。

长途电话交换机容量 指用于接入长途电话网的电话交换机设备的额定容量,包括国际电话交换机容量。

局用交换机容量 指安装在电信运营企业内用于接续本地固定电话的电话交换机容量,包括现用和备用的人工或自动交换机的全部容量。不包括用户交换机容量。

移动电话交换机容量 指移动电话交换机根据一定话务模型和交换机处理能力计算出来的最大同时服务用户的数量。

Explanatory Notes on Main Statistical Indicators

Length of Railways in Operation refers to the total length of the trunk line under passenger and freight transportation (including both full operation and temporary operation). The calculation is based on the actual length of the first line even if this line has a full or partial double track or more tracks, excluding double tracks, station sidings, tracks under the charge of stations, branch lines, special-purpose lines and the non-payable connecting lines. The length of railways in operation is an important indicator to show the development of the infrastructure for the railway transport, and also the essential data to calculate volume of passenger freight transport, traffic density and utilization efficiency of the locomotives and carriages.

Length of Electrified Railways refers to the length of the section of railways in operation in which the power supply lines and other equipment are installed for the running of electrified locomotives. The proportion of the length of electrified railways to the total length of railways in operation is an important indicator to show the modernization of railways.

Automatic-blocking and Semi-automatic-blocking Length of Railways refer to length of railways installed with equipment to perform automatic or manual blocking of trains. Blocking is a spacing technique by which a section of the railway only allows one train to pass at a time in the aim of ensuring the traffic safety. the proportion of automatic/semi-automatic blocking length to the total length of railways in operation is an important indicator to show the modernization of railways.

Length of Highways refers to the length of highways which are built in conformity with the grades specified by the highway engineering standard formulated by the Ministry of Communications, and have been formally checked and accepted by the departments of highways and put into use. The length of highways includes that of the suburb highways at large and medium-sized cities, highways passing through streets at small cities and towns, and also the length of bridges and ferries. It does not include the length of streets in big and medium-sized cities and highways built for the production purpose at factories, mines, forest areas and agricultural areas. If two or more highways go the same section of the way, the length of the section is only calculated for once and no duplication is allowed. The length of highways is an important indicator to show the development of the highway construction and to provide essential information to calculate the transport network density.

Length of Navigable Inland Waterways itis an indicator reflecting the size and development of inland water network, it refers to the length of the natural rivers, lakes, reservoirs, canals, and ditches open to navigation during a given period, which enables the transport by ships and rafts. It includes the channels open to navigation for over an accumulative 3 months in a year, yet this does not include the river courses, which are only used to float odd logs and bamboo rafts. This indicator can reflect the scale, level and development situation of the inland waterway network.

Length of Civil Aviation Routes refers to the length of all routes for regular civil aviation flights. There are usually two ways to calculate the distance between airports connected by the route length: One is to put the length of all air routes together, called duplicated calculation of the length of the routes; the other is not to allow the duplication in calculation when two or more routes passing the same section of aviation routes. The latter is usually used, as it can precisely show the size of the civil aviation network and indicate the extent of civil aviation serving the national economy and the people.

Length of Oil (Gas) Pipelines used as an indicator to show the development, scale and level of the pipeline transportation, it refers to the actual transport distance of oil (or gas) products, and is in general calculated in the length of single pipeline. If the length of the double pipelines and alternate pipeline are included, it is called the extension length of the oil (gas) pipelines, which indicates the actual length of the pipelines built, excluding double pipelines.

Freight (Passenger) Traffic refers to the volume of freight (passenger) transported with various means. Freight transport is calculated in tons and passenger traffic is calculated in the number of persons. Despite the type of freight and traveling distance, the freight transport is calculated in the actual weight of the goods: and despite the traveling distance and ticket price, the passenger traffic is calculated by the principle that one person can be counted only once in one travel. The passengers who travel with a half price ticket or a child ticket is also calculated as one person. The freight (passenger) traffic provides a quantitative measure to show how the transport industry serves the national economy and people, and is also an important indicator for planning the transport industry and for studying the development scale and speed of the transport industry.

Freight (Passenger) Traffic Density refers to the freight (passenger) traffic volume carried by a particular means of transportation during a given period through one kilometer of a specific section of transportation route. The formula is as follows:

Freight (Passenger) traffic density=[freight ton–kilometers (passenger–kilometers)] / (length of route in operation)

Freight (passenger) traffic density reflects the degree of business of freight (passenger) traffic on transportation routes, and therefore provides important information for balancing transport capability, planning construction and upgrading of transport routes and studying the distribution of transport network.

Freight Ton–kilometers (Passenger–kilometers) refer to the sum of the products of the volume of transported cargo (passengers) multiplying by the transport distance. It is an important indicator to reflect the achievement of transportation industry. Normally, the shortest distance between the departure station and the destination station (i.e., the payable distance) is the basis to calculate the freight ton–kilometers. This is an important indicator to show the total results of the transport industry, to prepare and examine the transport plan and to measure the efficiency, the labour productivity and the unit cost of transport.

The formula is as follows:

Freight ton–kilometers (passenger–kilometers) = Σ {freight (passenger) traffic × distance of transportation}

Possession of Civil Motor Vehicles refer to the total numbers of vehicles that are registered and received vehicles license tags according to the Work Standard for Motor Vehicles Registration formulated by transport management office under department of public security at the end of reference period. They are divided into following categories according to the structure of motor vehicles: passenger vehicles, trucks and others; and private vehicles and vehicles for units use according to ownerships; working vehicles and non–working vehicles according to kind of usage; large passenger vehicles, medium passenger vehicles, small passenger vehicles and mini passenger vehicle, heavy trucks, light–heavy trucks, light trucks and mini trucks according to sizes of vehicles.

Business Volume of Post and Telecommunications refers to the total amount of post and telecommunication services, ex–

pressed in value terms, provided by the post and telecommunications departments for the society. Post and telecommunication services can be classified as letters, parcels, remittance, issue of newspapers and magazines, fast mail service, express mail service, savings deposits, stamps for collection, public and individual telegraph service, facsimiles, long-distance telephone service, leasing of telephone lines, urban paging service, mobile telephone service, data transfer and transmission, etc. The accounting approach is to multiply the service products of all types with their average unit price (constant price) to get sum of business value, plus income from other services such as leasing of telephone lines and equipment, maintenance of telephone switchboards and lines on behalf of customers. This indicator reflects the overall results of post and telecommunications service during a given period, and is important to study the composition of business service and the development of post and telecommunications service.

The formula is as follows:

Business volume of post and telecommunications= $\sum$ (Transaction of post and telecommunication service x constant price) + Income from leasing, maintenance and other services = business volume of postal service + business volume of telecommunications service

Subscribers of Wireless Paging Services Wireless paging service refers the service by which telephone users send audio, digital or character signals to persons carrying small-size pagers within the designated areas through wireless paging centers. The page carriers who have registered in paging centers are counted as paging subscribers.

Mobile Telephone Subscribers refer to the persons who own mobile telephone numbers and are connected with the mobile telephone communication network through the mobile telephone switchboards, including contracted subscribers and pre-paid subscribers for intelligent network. One mobile telephone is taken as a subscriber.

Internet Users refer to the number of Chinese citizens who use Internet at least for one hour each week.

Local Telephone Subscribers refer to subscribers that are connected to the local telecommunication service provider through fix line network, including household subscribers, institutional subscribers and public telephones. They are also classified as city subscribers and rural subscribers according to locations. Before 1997, city subscribers referred to those connected to city telephone networks in county towns and cities, while village subscribers referred to those connected to village telephone stations at and below counties. Since 1997, the classification of telephone subscribers was modified on the basis of physical location of the subscribers as urban telephone subscribers and rural telephone subscribers, which is different from the previous classification of categorizing local telephones and rural telephones, while the definition of total subscribers and total number of telephones remain unchanged.

Urban Telephone Subscribers refer to number of telephone subscribers, located at municipalities, cities under the jurisdiction of province, cities at prefecture level, downtown and suburb of city at county level town and county towns (including country towns where county government located, and towns of county level according to the administrative organizational system), that are connected to the public line telephone network, including rural mineral area, forest area, military area.

Rural Telephone Subscribers refer to telephone subscribers, located at counties (towns) and villages outside the range of cities according to administrative jurisdiction.

Household Telephone Subscribers refer to telephone sets installed in the dwelling units of urban or rural residents, and registered as residence subscribers for payment, including 3 types of payment for the service: private payment, public payment and free service.

Capacity of Long Distance Telephone Exchanges refers to the rated capacity of telephone exchanges to connect long distance telephone network, including capacity of international telephone exchanges.

Capacity of Office Telephone Exchanges refers to the capacity (measured in gate) of telephone exchanges installed in the offices of telecommunication service providers for communication between fixed telephones. It includes the capacity of both manual and automatic exchanges in use and for stand-by purpose, excluding the capacity of subscribers exchanges.

Capacity of Mobile Telephone Exchanges refers to the capacity of the maximum services provided to subscribers at one time basing on a certain model and transacting capacity of the mobile telephone exchanges.

16 国内贸易

Domestic Trade

国内贸易

Domestic Trade
2016

社会消费品零售总额	Total Retail Sales of Consumption Goods	15649.22	(亿元)
商品零售额	Retail Sales	14094.07	(亿元)
餐饮收入额	Amount of Food and beverage revenue	1555.15	(亿元)

社会消费品零售总额(亿元)
Total Value of Retail of Consumption Goods(100 million yuan)

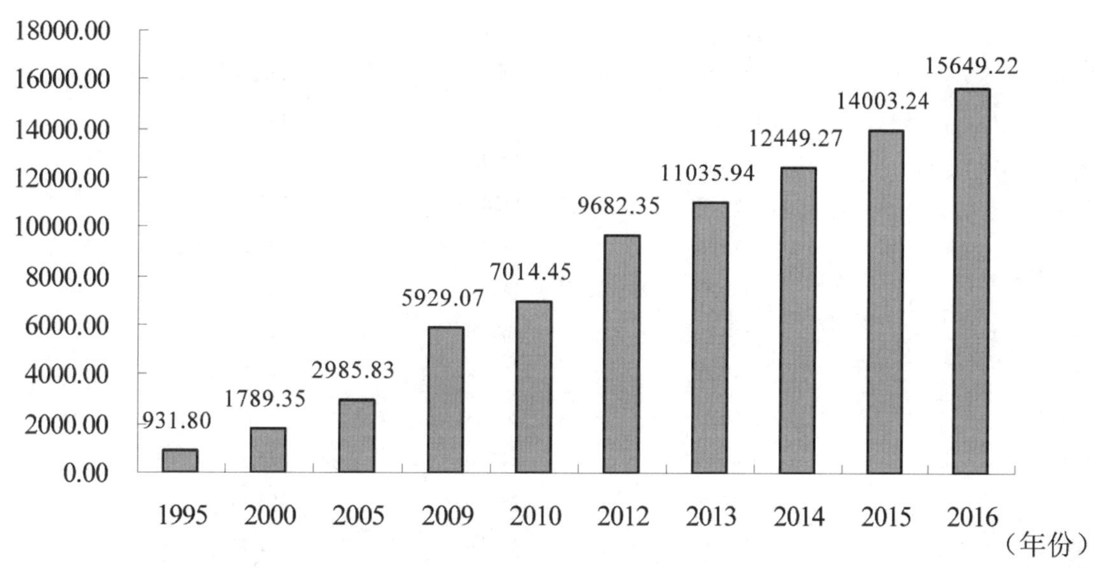

社会消费品零售总额(亿元)

Total Value of Retail Sales of Consumption Goods(100 million yuan)

年份 year	1995	2000	2005	2009	2010	2012	2013	2014	2015	2016
社会消费品零售总额 Total Value of Retail of Consumption Goods	931.80	1789.35	2985.83	5929.07	7014.45	9682.35	11035.94	12449.27	14003.24	15649.22

16-1 按地区分社会消费品零售总额
TOTAL RETAIL SALES OF CONSUMER GOODS BY REGION

单位:亿元 (100 million yuan)

年份 Year	零售额 Total Retail Sales of Consumer Goods	市 City	县 County	县以下 Below County Level
1978	59.84	19.24	16.56	24.04
1980	81.91	28.98	17.01	35.92
1985	181.17	75.26	31.64	74.17
1990	326.36	166.44	45.62	114.30
1991	362.26	190.65	50.04	121.57
1992	411.52	221.59	55.04	134.89
1993	521.35	293.82	68.88	158.65
1994	723.75	411.63	101.74	210.38
1995	931.80	539.79	127.76	264.25
1996	1145.73	688.40	130.28	327.05
1997	1345.34	802.37	146.61	396.36
1998	1481.38	896.08	156.07	429.23
1999	1617.14	1019.58	150.95	446.61
2000	1789.35	1128.47	177.65	483.23
2001	1975.16	1267.09	194.21	513.86
2002	2129.38	1429.83	200.69	498.86
2003	2358.69	1603.34	222.86	587.66
2004	2619.47	1819.80	246.21	277.44
2005	2985.83	2081.31	279.43	625.09
2006	3461.09	2430.05	325.66	705.38
2007	4115.78	2889.08	393.38	833.33
2008	5109.74	3587.49	491.44	1030.80
2009	5929.07	4128.16	586.81	1213.45
2010	7014.45	(城镇)5937.80	(城区)5030.80	(乡村)1076.10
2011	8363.34	(城镇)7003.70	(城区)5954.80	(乡村)1271.50
2012	9682.35	(城镇)8112.60	(城区)6873.80	(乡村)1449.90
2013	11035.94	(城镇)9163.80	(城区)7682.40	(乡村)1722.10
2014	12449.27	(城镇)10494.82	(城区)8396.70	(乡村)1954.45
2015	14003.24	(城镇)11775.38	(城区)9412.84	(乡村)2227.85
2016	15649.22	(城镇)13149.57	(城区)10505.68	(乡村)2499.65

注：1.1996年及以后社会消费品零售总额及各分组指标中不含售给城乡居民生活用住房的零售额。
2.2004、2008年为经普数据，2005-2007年为按国家统计局制定的修订方法修订数据，1993-2003年原则根据原各年环比发展速度和2004年经济普查数据调整。
3.2010年起采用国家新制定的城乡划分标准：城镇(其中:城区)、乡村

Notes:a)Since 1996, the residential house was exclued in the total retail sales of consumer goods and all the targets by groups.
b)The figures of 2004 and 2008 were from general economic Survey, that of the 2005-2007 were from statistics according to the reqirment of general economic survey; while the figures of 1993-2003 were from each year's indices (previous year =100) and readjusted according to the data of general economic survey.
c)Since 2010, a new towm and country division national standard is applied:town(including urban area), country.

16-2 分市、州社会消费品零售总额
TOTAL RETAIL SALES OF CONSUMER GOODS BY DISTRICT

单位:亿元　　　　(100 million yuan)

地区	Region	2008	2009	2010	2012	2013	2014	2015	2016
全省	**Province**	**5109.74**	**5929.07**	**7014.45**	**9682.35**	**11035.94**	**12449.27**	**14003.24**	**15649.22**
武汉	Wuhan	1895.89	2164.09	2570.40	3467.37	3916.60	4369.32	5102.24	5610.59
黄石	Huangshi	221.60	256.09	301.63	413.50	468.86	519.71	582.36	649.59
十堰	Shiyan	217.17	254.25	308.88	424.80	491.51	548.65	639.41	724.96
宜昌	Yichang	399.41	470.41	552.72	766.19	881.93	964.53	1089.47	1240.33
襄阳	Xiangyang	425.01	500.56	613.34	839.51	966.31	1030.57	1165.10	1325.26
鄂州	Ezhou	107.89	126.68	135.55	182.20	208.68	230.28	261.95	298.45
荆门	Jingmen	194.26	228.82	263.08	362.85	414.68	451.78	541.43	614.23
孝感	Xiaogan	278.18	326.90	388.77	535.50	608.68	689.33	797.14	883.66
荆州	Jingzhou	381.19	445.42	505.34	688.36	781.36	831.44	946.14	1056.13
黄冈	Huanggang	292.33	340.07	408.71	559.37	635.02	715.65	880.91	973.94
咸宁	Xianning	140.72	165.88	209.63	289.54	330.58	361.77	401.04	442.54
随州	Suizhou	156.67	182.05	215.21	293.51	333.86	354.37	399.57	446.10
恩施	Enshi	97.49	114.04	136.76	188.82	218.28	243.55	445.97	500.39
仙桃	Xiantao	108.87	127.87	146.79	200.81	229.00	233.58	266.17	297.19
潜江	Qianjiang	74.40	86.36	101.13	137.36	156.31	150.19	186.14	208.50
天门	Tianmen	115.42	135.21	151.57	206.91	237.50	231.05	258.90	289.21
神农架	Shennongjia	3.25	3.72	4.38	5.92	6.75	7.52	13.54	14.96

注：1.本表各市、州数据包含了"其他"部分的全口径数据；
　　2.2008年以前的全省的数据根据经济普查的结果进行了调整。

Notes:a)"Others " was included in the total retail sales of consumer goods in the form.
　　b)Before 2008,Total was adjusted accoding to the economic census data.

16-3 批发和零售业连锁经营情况
BASIC CONDITIONS OF WHOLESALES, RETAIL SALES, CATERING CHAIN STORES INDUSTRIES

指标名称	Item	合计 Total		直营店 Direct Sales Store		加盟店 League Store	
		2015	2016	2015	2016	2015	2016
一、门店总数 (个)	Number of Stores (unit)	7765	8665	6808	7140	957	1525
其中:批发业 (个)	Number of Stores (unit)	517	900	506	537	11	363
零售业 (个)	Number of Stores (unit)	7248	7765	6302	6603	946	1162
二、营业面积 (百平方米)	Floor Space of Business (100 sq.m)	71820	71162	70911	69788	908	1373
其中:批发业 (百平方米)	Floor Space of Business (100 sq.m)	2807	4052	2807	3368		684
零售业 (百平方米)	Floor Space of Business (100 sq.m)	69013	67110	68105	66421	908	689
三、从业人员 (人)	Person Engaged (person)	136590	130171	132061	125529	4529	4642
其中:批发业 (人)	Person Engaged (person)	10473	10007	10413	9165	60	842
零售业 (人)	Person Engaged (person)	126117	120164	121648	116364	4469	3800
四、商品购进总额 (亿元)	Total Value of Commodities Purchaesd (100 000 000 yuan)	1646.21	1665.07	1613.28	1655.82	32.93	9.25
#统一配送商品购进额	#Total Purchasing Value	1178.44	1168.78	1151.48	1165.66	26.96	3.12
#自有配送中心配送商品购进额	#Commodities Purchased From Dispatching Center	961.80	926.69	935.39	924.26	26.41	2.43
#非自有配送中心配送商品购进额	#Commodities Purchased From Nondispatching Center	54.80	74.64	54.68	74.38	0.12	0.27
五、商品销售额 (亿元)	Sales Amount (100 000 000 yuan)	1882.47	1863.80	1843.67	1850.24	38.80	13.55
#零售额	#Retail Sales	1584.18	1615.32	1554.24	1610.62	29.94	4.70

16-4 住宿和餐饮业连锁经营情况
BASIC CONDITIONS OF HOTELS AND CATERING SERVICES

指标名称	Item	合计 Total		直营店 Direct Sales Store		加盟店 League Store	
		2015	2016	2015	2016	2015	2016
一、门店总数 (个)	Number of Stores (unit)	828	947	826	946	2	1
二、营业面积 (百平方米)	Floor Space of Business (100 sq.m)	3650	5480	3640	5480	10	
三、从业人员 (人)	Person Engaged (person)	36999	45047	36899	45021	100	26
四、客房数 (间)	Number of Hotel Rooms (unit)	6590	6400	6528	6338	62	62
五、床位数 (个)	Number of Beds (unit)	8470	8096	8372	7998	98	98
六、餐位数 (位)	Restaurant Seating Capacity (unit)	135738	144908	135638	144908	100	
七、商品购进总额 (万元)	Total Value of Commodities Purchaesd (10 000 yuan)	108948	156571	108746	156569	202	2
#统一配送商品购进额	#Total Purchasing Value	90436	127845	90434	127843	2	2
#自有配送中心配送商品购进额	#Commodities Purchased From Dispatching Center	18933	42564	18930	42562	2	2
#非自有配送中心配送商品购进额	#Commodities Purchased From Nondispatching Center	39557	55182	39557	55182		
八、营业额 (万元)	Turnover (10 000 yuan)	570703	637213	570164	637000	539	214
#餐费收入	Meals Revenue	552447	619478	552147	619478	300	
#商品销售额	Merchandise Sales	556019	3228	555718	3226	302	2

16-5 限额以上批发零售业基本情况(2016)
BASIC CONDITIONS OF ENTERPRISES ABOVE DESIGNATED SIZE IN WHOLESALES AND RETAILSALES TRADE (2016)

(按登记注册类型分)

(Grouped by Registration Type)

登记注册类型	Type of Registration	法人企业数(个) Number of Corperations (unit)	年末从业人数(人) Person Engaged at Year-end (person)	零售营业面积(万平方米) Floor Space of Retail Business (10 000 sq.m)
总 计	**Total**	**8030**	**529596**	**2308.33**
一、批发业	**Wholesales**	**2949**	**192853**	**561.45**
按登记注册类型分组	Grouped by Registration Type			
内资	**Domestic Funded Enterprises**	**2903**	**175717**	**488.62**
国有	State-owned Enterprises	80	13580	21.09
集体	Collective-owned Enterprises	15	756	0.91
股份合作	Cooperative Enterprises	5	206	0.51
联营企业	Joint Ownership Enterprises			
国有联营	State Joint Ownership Enterprises			
集体联营	Collective Joint Ownership Enterprises			
国有与集体联营	Joint State-collective Enterprises			
其他联营	Other Joint Ownership Enterprises			
有限责任公司	Limited Liability Corporations	1195	69072	204.25
国有独资公司	State Sole Funded Corporations	35	8546	14.55
其他有限责任公司	Other Limited Liability Corporations	1160	60526	189.69
股份有限公司	Share-holding Corporations Ltd.	70	43298	60.44
私营企业	Private Enterprises	1445	43477	186.47
私营独资	Private-funded Enterprises	64	1149	7.89
私营合伙	Private Partnership Enterprises			
私营有限责任公司	Private Limited Liability Corporations	1356	41396	174.62
私营股份有限公司	Private Share-holding Corporations Ltd.	25	932	3.96
其他	Other Enterprises	93	5328	14.95
港澳台商投资企业	**Enterprises with Funds from Hongkong, Macao and Taiwan**	**23**	**4620**	**2.53**
合资经营	Joint-venture Enterprises	5	426	0.06
合作经营	Cooperative Enterprises	1	5	0.07
独资经营	Enterprises with Sole Investment	16	3323	2.39
独资股份有限公司	Sole Investment Co. Ltd. With Investment	1	866	
外商投资企业	**Foreign Funded Enterprises**	**23**	**12516**	**70.31**
中外合资经营	Sino-foreign Joint-venture Enterprises	10	2039	0.02
外资企业	Enterprises with Sole Foreign Investment	8	5592	0.29
外商投资股份有限公司	Share-holding Co. Ltd. with Foreign Investment	1	14	
其他外资企业	Other Enterprises with Sole Foreign Investment	4	4871	70.00

16-5 续表 continued

登记注册类型	Type of Registration	法人企业数(个) Number of Corperations (unit)	年末从业人数(人) Person Engaged at Year-end (person)	零售营业面积(万平方米) Floor Space of Retail Business (10 000 sq.m)
二、零售业	**Retail Trade**	**5081**	**336743**	**1746.88**
按登记注册类型分组	Grouped by Registration Type			
内资	**Domestic Funded Enterprises**	**5025**	**314704**	**1661.31**
国有	State-owned Enterprises	85	4343	15.43
集体	Collective-owned Enterprises	93	10526	54.98
股份合作	Cooperative Enterprises	7	292	2.63
联营企业	Joint Ownership Enterprises	3	141	0.22
国有联营	State Joint Ownership Enterprises			
集体联营	Collective Joint Ownership Enterprises			
国有与集体联营	Joint State-collective Enterprises	2	127	0.16
其他联营	Other Joint Ownership Enterprises	1	14	0.06
有限责任公司	Limited Liability Corporations	1858	135107	656.60
国有独资公司	State Sole Funded Corporations	19	3024	6.39
其他有限责任公司	Other Limited Liability Corporations	1839	132083	650.21
股份有限公司	Share-holding Corporations Ltd.	117	53312	481.00
私营企业	Private Enterprises	2783	107873	442.90
私营独资	Private-funded Enterprises	448	8174	48.48
私营合伙	Private Partnership Enterprises	21	668	2.04
私营有限责任公司	Private Limited Liability Corporations	2262	96106	377.88
私营股份有限公司	Private Share-holding Corporations Ltd.	52	2925	14.50
其他	Other Enterprises	79	3110	7.55
港澳台商投资企业	**Enterprises with Funds from Hongkong, Macao and Taiwan**	**34**	**9665**	**29.66**
合资经营	Joint-venture Enterprises	11	856	3.82
合作经营	Cooperative Enterprises			
独资经营	Enterprises with Sole Investment	23	8809	25.84
独资股份有限公司	Sole Investment Co. Ltd. With Investment			
外商投资企业	**Foreign Funded Enterprises**	**22**	**12374**	**55.91**
中外合资经营	Sino-foreign Joint-venture Enterprises	6	2022	7.18
外资企业	Enterprises with Sole Foreign Investment	14	10087	47.24
外商投资股份有限公司	Share-holding Co. Ltd. with Foreign Investment	1	205	1.30
其他外资企业	Other Enterprises with Sole Foreign Investment	1	60	0.20

16-6 限额以上批发零售业基本情况(2016)
BASIC CONDITIONS OF ENTERPRISES ABOVE DESIGNATED SIZE IN WHOLESALES AND RETAILSALES TRADE (2016)

(按国民经济行业分)

(Grouped by Sector)

项　目	Item	法人企业数(个) Number of Corperations (unit)	年末从业人数(人) Person Engaged at Year-end (person)	零售营业面积(万平方米) Floor Space of Retail Business (10 000 sq.m)
总　计	**Total**	**8030**	**529596**	**2308.33**
一、批发业	**Wholesales**	**2949**	**192853**	**561.45**
农、林、牧产品批发业	Wholesales of Agriculture, Forestry and Animal Husbandry Products	302	12288	86.06
食品、饮料及烟草制品批发业	Wholesales of Foods, Beverage and Tobacco	580	54404	127.15
米、面制品及食用油批发业	Wholesales of Rice, Noodles and Edible Oil	101	6428	13.42
烟草制品批发业	Wholesales of Tobacco	29	10846	0.82
纺织、服装及日用品批发业	Wholesales of Textile Products, Garments and Daily Used Articles	184	13416	79.35
服装批发业	Wholesales of Garments	54	5491	71.33
家用电器批发业	Wholesales of Home Appliances	38	2948	1.24
文化、体育用品及器材批发业	Wholesales of Cultural and Sports Goods and Equipments	48	6762	14.20
医药及医疗器材批发业	Wholesales of Medicnes and Medical Appliances	332	39065	42.75
矿产品、建材及化工产品批发业	Wholesales of Mineral Products, Building Materials and Chemical Products	948	50570	170.30
煤炭及制品批发业	Wholesales of Coal and Coal-made Products	109	2653	13.59
石油及制品批发业	Wholesales of Petroleum Products	109	27620	78.18
非金属矿及制品批发	Wholesales of Non-metal and Non-metal Mines	42	889	3.78
金属及金属矿批发业	Wholesales of Metal and Metal Mines	248	6051	15.98
建材批发业	Wholesales of Construction Materials	169	4086	26.52
化肥批发业	Wholesales of Chemical Fertilizers	105	5064	18.23
机械设备、五金交电及电子产品批发	Wholesales of Machinery Equipment, Hardware, Transport and Electronic Products	461	13878	22.35
汽车批发业	Wholesales of Cars	72	3498	6.49
计算机、软件及辅助设备批发业	Wholesales of Computers, Softwares and Assisted Equipments	27	857	0.23
贸易经纪与代理	Trade Agent	9	158	0.04
其他批发业	Other Wholesales	85	2312	19.26
二、零售业	**Retail Sales**	**5081**	**336743**	**1746.88**
综合零售业	Retail Sales of Department	915	149126	931.59
百货零售业	Department Stores	457	55489	565.96
超级市场零售业	Supermarkets	347	86376	342.06
食品、饮料及烟草制品专门零售业	Monopoly Retail of Foods, Beverage and Tobacco	566	25931	68.49
纺织、服装及日用品专门零售业	Monopoly Retail of Textile, Garments,and Daily Used Articles	305	20129	61.86
服装零售业	Retail Sales of Garments	172	12437	44.79
文化、体育用品及器材专门零售业	Monopoly Retail of Cultural, Sports Products and Equipments	223	9632	35.84
体育用品零售业	Retail Sales of Sports Products	10	216	2.36
图书报刊零售业	Retail Sales of Books, Newspapers and Periodicals	74	3957	9.66
医药及医疗器材专门零售业	Monopoly Retail of Medicine and Medical Appliances	297	22559	57.39
药品零售业	Retail Sales of Medicine	257	21436	55.92
汽车、摩托车、燃料及零配件专门	Monopoly Retail of Cars, and Motorcars Parts	1376	66300	313.17
汽车零售业	Retail Sales of Cars	1075	52641	253.99
机动车燃料零售业	Retail Sales of Motor Vehicles Fuels	131	10252	47.05
家用电器及电子产品专门零售业	Monopoly Retail of Home Appliances and Electronic Products	745	21791	134.89
家用视听设备零售业	Retail Sales of Home Audio-visual Equipment	180	4861	23.12
计算机、软件及辅助设备零售业	Retail Sales of Computers, Softwares and Assisted Equipments	173	3714	8.36
通讯设备零售业	Retail Sales of Communication Equipments	46	1473	4.04
五金、家具及室内装修材料专门零售业	Monopoly Retail of Hardware, Furnitures and Decorative Materials	398	9875	105.88
货摊、无店铺及其他零售业	Retail Sales of Stalls、Storeless and Others	256	11400	37.76
互联网零售	Retail Sales of Internet	114	7349	8.06

16-7 限额以上住宿和餐饮业基本情况(2016)
BASIC CONDITIONS OF ENTERPRISES ABOVE DESIGNATED SIZE IN HOTELS AND CATERING SERVICES (2016)

(按登记注册类型分)

(Grouped by Registeration Type)

项　目	Item	法人企业数(个) Number of Corperations (unit)	年末从业人数(人) Person Engaged at Year-end (person)	餐饮营业面积(万平方米) Floor Space of Catering Business (10 000 sq.m)
一、住宿业	**Hotel Trade**	**793**	**58923**	**176.09**
按登记注册类型分组	**Grouped by Registration Type**			
内资	**Domestic Funded Enterprises**	**769**	**54422**	**171.07**
国有	State-owned Enterprises	38	4009	11.19
集体	Collective-owned Enterprises	8	965	1.67
股份合作	Cooperative Enterprises	2	88	0.38
联营企业	Joint Ownership Enterprises			
国有联营	State Joint Ownership Enterprises			
集体联营	Collective Joint Ownership Enterprises			
国有与集体联营	Joint State-collective Enterprises			
其他联营	Other Joint Ownership Enterprises			
有限责任公司	Limited Liability Corporations	312	25354	73.37
国有独资公司	State Sole Funded Corporations	10	1618	3.24
其他有限责任公司	Other Limited Liability Corporations	302	23736	70.13
股份有限公司	Share-holding Corporations Ltd.	20	2712	5.57
私营企业	Private Enterprises	376	21019	78.52
私营独资	Private-funded Enterprises	34	999	4.78
私营合伙	Private Partnership Enterprises	10	414	2.40
私营有限责任公司	Private Limited Liability Corporations	321	18890	68.82
私营股份有限公司	Private Share-holding Corporations Ltd.	11	716	2.53
其他	Other Enterprises	13	275	0.37
港澳台商投资企业	Enterprises with Funds from Hongkong, Macao and Taiwan	19	3997	3.99
合资经营	Joint-venture Enterprises	4	811	0.63
合作经营	Cooperative Enterprises	1	336	0.24
独资经营	Enterprises with Sole Investment	11	2387	2.51
投资股份有限公司	Share-holding Co. Ltd. With Investment	3	463	0.61
外商投资企业	Foreign Funded Enterprises	5	504	1.04
中外合资经营	Sino-foreign Joint-venture Enterprises	1	217	0.20
中外合作经营	Sino-foreign Cooperative Enterprises			
外资企业	Enterprises with Sole Foreign Investment	3	255	0.54
外商投资股份有限公司	Share-holding Co. Ltd. with Foreign Investment	1	32	0.30
二、餐饮业	**Catering Trade**	**1630**	**94617**	**345.98**
按登记注册类型分组	**Grouped by Registration Type**			
内资	**Domestic Funded Enterprises**	**1606**	**80827**	**317.83**
国有	State-owned Enterprises	14	767	1.92
集体	Collective-owned Enterprises	4	118	1.24
股份合作	Cooperative Enterprises	1	120	0.20
联营企业	Joint Ownership Enterprises			
国有联营	State Joint Ownership Enterprises			
集体联营	Collective Joint Ownership Enterprises			
国有与集体联营	Joint State-collective Enterprises			
其他联营	Other Joint Ownership Enterprises			
有限责任公司	Limited Liability Corporations	507	36312	120.90
国有独资公司	State Sole Funded Corporations	6	1022	1.00
其他有限责任公司	Other Limited Liability Corporations	501	35290	119.90
股份有限公司	Share-holding Corporations Ltd.	13	894	3.39
私营企业	Private Enterprises	1004	41047	181.17
私营独资	Private-funded Enterprises	277	6506	33.70
私营合伙	Private Partnership Enterprises	11	392	2.34
私营有限责任公司	Private Limited Liability Corporations	696	32888	141.01
私营股份有限公司	Private Share-holding Corporations Ltd.	20	1261	4.13
其他	Other Enterprises	63	1569	9.01
港澳台商投资企业	**Enterprises with Funds from Hongkong, Macao and Taiwan**	**16**	**9967**	**21.76**
合资经营	Joint-venture Enterprises	6	385	0.94
合作经营	Cooperative Enterprises			
独资经营	Enterprises with Sole Investment	10	9582	20.82
投资股份有限公司	Share-holding Co. Ltd. With Investment			
外商投资企业	**Foreign Funded Enterprises**	**8**	**3823**	**6.39**
中外合资经营	Sino-foreign Joint-venture Enterprises	1	470	0.60
外资企业	Enterprises with Sole Foreign Investment	7	3353	5.79
外商投资股份有限公司	Share-holding Co. Ltd. with Foreign Investment			
其他外商投资企业	Other Enterprises with Sole Foreign Investment			

16-8 限额以上住宿和餐饮业基本情况(2016)
BASIC CONDITIONS OF ENTERPRISES ABOVE DESIGNATED SIZE IN HOTELS AND CATERING SERVICES (2016)

(按国民经济行业分)

(Grouped by Sector)

行　业	Item	法人企业数(个) Number of Corperations (unit)	年末从业人数(人) Person Engaged at Year-end (person)	餐饮营业面积(万平方米) Floor Space of Catering Business (10 000 sq.m)
总　计	**Total**	**2423**	**153540**	**522.07**
一、住宿业	**Hotel**	**793**	**58923**	**176.09**
按国民经济行业分组	Grouped by Sector			
旅游饭店	Tourist Hotel	410	41861	110.26
一般旅馆	Regular Hotel	363	15798	61.11
其他住宿服务	Other Accomodation Service	20	1264	4.73
二、餐饮业	**Catering**	**1630**	**94617**	**345.98**
按国民经济行业分组	Grouped by Sector			
正餐服务业	Dinner	1590	80612	317.51
快餐服务业	Fast Food	24	10929	24.09
饮料及冷饮服务业	Beverage and Cold Drink Services	8	1927	2.53
其他餐饮服务业	Others	8	1149	1.85

16-9 限额以上住宿和餐饮业经营情况(2016)
BUSINESS OF ENTERPRISES ABOVE DESIGNATED SIZE OF HOTELS AND CATERING SERVICES (2016)

(按国民经济行业分)

(Grouped by Sector)

行业	Item	营业额(亿元) Turnover (100 million yuan)	客房收入 Revnue from Guest Rooms	餐费收入 Revenue from Catering Bills	商品销售收入 Revenue from Commodity Sales	其他收入 Revenue from Others	年末住宿和餐饮企业拥有床位数(万个) Number of Beds owned by Hotels and Catering Enterprises at Year-end (10 000 units)	年末住宿和餐饮企业拥有餐位数(万位) Number of Seats owned by Hotels and Catering Enterprises at Year-end (10 000 units)
总计	**Total**	**371.31**	**83.04**	**264.75**	**13.34**	**10.17**	**34.88**	**107.18**
一、住宿业	**Hotel**	**118.21**	**60.53**	**45.35**	**5.05**	**7.28**	**23.68**	**32.06**
按国民经济行业分组	Grouped by Sector							
旅游饭店	Tourist Hotel	79.83	38.81	32.55	1.96	6.53	14.94	24.80
一般旅馆	Regular Hotel	34.01	20.10	11.86	1.46	0.59	8.36	6.65
其他住宿服务	Other Accomodation Service	4.37	1.63	0.94	1.63	0.16	0.38	0.60
二、餐饮业	**Catering**	**253.10**	**22.51**	**219.41**	**8.29**	**2.90**	**11.19**	**75.12**
按国民经济行业分组	Grouped by Sector							
正餐服务业	Dinner	200.33	22.38	166.91	8.15	2.89	11.13	67.88
快餐服务业	Fast Food	39.23	0.04	39.09	0.10		0.02	5.43
饮料及冷饮服务业	Beverage and Cold Drink Services	7.12		7.09	0.03		0.01	1.50
其他餐饮服务业	Others	6.42	0.09	6.32	0.01	0.01	0.03	0.32

16-10 限额以上住宿和餐饮业经营情况(2016)

(按登记注册类型分)

单位:亿元

项　目	Item	营业额 Turnover	客房收入 Revnue from Guest Rooms
总　计	**Total**	**371.31**	**83.04**
一、住宿业	**Hotels**	**118.21**	**60.53**
按登记注册类型分组	**Grouped by Registration Type**		
内资	Domestic Funded Enterprises	109.45	55.77
国有	State-Owned Enterprises	5.33	2.40
集体	Collective-owned Enterprises	1.73	0.81
股份合作	Cooperative Enterprises	0.10	0.05
联营企业	Joint Ownership Enterprises		
国有联营	State Joint Ownership Enterprises		
集体联营	Collective Joint Ownership Enterprises		
国有与集体联营	Joint State-collective Enterprises		
其他联营	Other Joint Ownership Enterprises		
有限责任公司	Limited Liability Corporations	48.76	26.44
国有独资公司	State Sole Funded Corporations	4.80	1.60
其他有限责任公司	Other Limited Liability Corporations	43.95	24.84
股份有限公司	Share-holding Corporations Ltd.	4.14	1.78
私营企业	Private Enterprises	48.68	23.63
私营独资	Private-funded Enterprises	6.61	3.54
私营合伙	Private Partnership Enterprises	0.95	0.34
私营有限责任公司	Private Limited Liability Corporations	40.18	19.15
私营股份有限公司	Private Share-holding Corporations Ltd.	0.94	0.59
其他	Other Enterprises	0.72	0.66
港澳台商投资企业	Enterprises with Funds from Hongkong, Macao and Taiwan	8.04	4.37
合资经营	Joint-venture Enterprises	1.99	1.01
合作经营	Cooperative Enterprises	0.79	0.45
独资经营	Enterprises with Sole Investment	4.24	2.25
投资股份有限公司	Share-holding Co. Ltd. With Investment	1.02	0.65
外商投资企业	Foreign Funded Enterprises	0.72	0.39
中外合资经营	Sino-Foreign Joint-venture Enterprises	0.29	0.15
外资企业	Enterprises with Sole Foreign Investment	0.37	0.20
外商投资股份有限公司	Share-holding Co. Ltd. with Foreign Investment	0.06	0.04
其他外商投资企业	Other Foreign Founded Enterprises		
二、餐饮业	**Catering Trade**	**253.10**	**22.51**
按登记注册类型分组	**Grouped by Registration Type**		
内资	**Domestic Funded Enterprises**	**205.09**	**22.22**
国有	State-Owned Enterprises	1.14	0.29
集体	Collective-owned Enterprises	0.87	0.03
股份合作	Cooperative Enterprises	0.21	0.05
联营企业	Joint Ownership Enterprises		
国有联营	State Joint Ownership Enterprises		
集体联营	Collective Joint Ownership Enterprises		
国有与集体联营	Joint State-collective Enterprises		
其他联营	Other Joint Ownership Enterprises		
有限责任公司	Limited Liability Corporations	79.94	9.59
国有独资公司	State Sole Funded Corporations	2.91	0.15
其他有限责任公司	Other Limited Liability Corporations	77.04	9.44
股份有限公司	Share-holding Corporations Ltd.	2.05	0.22
私营企业	Private Enterprises	114.41	11.69
私营独资	Private-funded Enterprises	29.65	2.17
私营合伙	Private Partnership Enterprises	0.56	0.13
私营有限责任公司	Private Limited Liability Corporations	81.21	9.15
私营股份有限公司	Private Share-holding Corporations Ltd.	2.99	0.24
其他	Other Enterprises	6.47	0.35
港澳台商投资企业	**Enterprises with Funds from Hongkong, Macao and Taiwan**	**37.94**	**0.13**
合资经营	Joint-venture Enterprises	0.57	0.04
合作经营	Cooperative Enterprises		
独资经营	Enterprises with Sole Investment	37.36	0.08
投资股份有限公司	Share-holding Co. Ltd. With Investment		
外商投资企业	**Foreign Funded Enterprises**	**10.07**	**0.16**
中外合资经营	Sino-Foreign Joint-venture Enterprises	0.64	
外资企业	Enterprises with Sole Foreign Investment	9.44	0.16
外商投资股份有限公司	Share-holding Co. Ltd. with Foreign Investment		
其他外商投资企业	Other Foreign Funded Enterprises		

BUSINESS OF ENTERPRISES ABOVE DESIGNATED SIZE OF HOTELS AND CATERING SERVICES (2016)

(Grouped by Registeration Type)

(100 million yuan)

餐费收入 Revenue from Catering Bills	商品销售收入 Revenue from Commodity Sales	其他收入 Revenue from Others	年末床位数 (万个) Number of Beds at Year-end (10 000 units)	年末餐位数 (万位) Number of Seats at Year-end (10 000 units)
264.75	**13.34**	**10.17**	**34.88**	**107.18**
45.35	**5.05**	**7.28**	**23.68**	**32.06**
41.97	5.01	6.71	22.91	31.10
2.45	0.12	0.36	0.87	1.88
0.73	0.06	0.13	0.13	0.42
0.04		0.01	0.02	0.03
16.36	1.67	4.28	11.59	17.78
1.58	0.23	1.39	0.40	0.59
14.77	1.44	2.90	11.18	17.19
1.81	0.13	0.42	0.50	1.10
20.56	3.01	1.48	9.69	9.77
2.69	0.35	0.03	0.43	0.56
0.55	0.06		0.13	0.24
16.98	2.60	1.45	8.94	8.53
0.34			0.20	0.44
0.02	0.02	0.02	0.11	0.12
3.11	0.03	0.53	0.65	0.73
0.85		0.13	0.15	0.17
0.32		0.01	0.05	0.07
1.59	0.03	0.36	0.36	0.41
0.34		0.03	0.09	0.09
0.27	0.01	0.04	0.12	0.23
0.12		0.02	0.03	0.08
0.15	0.01	0.01	0.07	0.13
		0.02	0.02	0.02
219.41	**8.29**	**2.90**	**11.19**	**75.12**
171.91	**8.26**	**2.70**	**11.07**	**67.94**
0.60	0.19	0.06	0.12	0.59
0.84			0.03	0.55
0.16			0.02	0.05
66.54	2.19	1.62	5.11	29.83
1.39	0.58	0.79	0.05	0.63
65.15	1.61	0.83	5.06	29.20
1.70	0.12	0.01	0.12	0.69
96.53	5.21	0.99	5.55	34.48
25.30	1.84	0.34	0.51	7.33
0.43			0.05	0.31
68.33	3.12	0.61	4.91	25.91
2.47	0.24	0.03	0.09	0.93
5.55	0.55	0.02	0.14	1.75
37.62	**0.02**	**0.16**	**0.07**	**5.56**
0.39	0.01	0.13	0.05	0.21
37.24	0.01	0.03	0.02	5.35
9.87		**0.04**	**0.05**	**1.62**
0.64				0.20
9.23		0.04	0.05	1.42

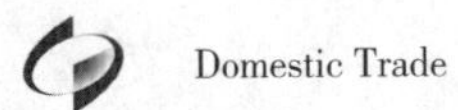

16-11 限额以上批发和零售业商品购、销、存总额(2016)
TOTAL PURCHASES, SALES AND STOCK OF ENTERPRISES ABOVE DESIGNATED SIZE OF WHOLESALE AND RETAIL TRADES(2016)

(按登记注册类型分)

(Grouped by Registeration Type)

单位:亿元 (100 million yuan)

项目	Item	购进总额 Total Purchasing Value	销售总额 Total Sales Value	批发 Whole-sales	零售 Retail Sales	年末库存总额 Total Value of Inventory at Year-end
总计	**Total**	**16566.12**	**18358.74**	**10618.74**	**7739.99**	**1281.56**
一、批发业	**Wholesales**	**9829.30**	**10881.62**	**9839.34**	**1042.28**	**636.94**
按登记注册类型分组	**Grouped by Registration Type**					
内资	Domestic Funded Enterprises	8666.12	9400.24	8447.04	953.20	594.07
国有	State-owned Enterprises	589.71	752.20	728.46	23.74	162.55
集体	Collective-owned Enterprises	13.26	14.50	13.35	1.16	0.76
股份合作	Cooperative Enterprises	2.47	2.70	2.07	0.63	0.13
联营企业	Joint Ownership Enterprises					
国有联营	State Joint Ownership Enterprises					
集体联营	Collective Joint Ownership Enterprises					
国有与集体联营	Joint State-collective Enterprises					
其他联营	Other Joint Ownership Enterprises					
有限责任公司	Limited Liability Corporations	4886.77	5169.30	4722.79	446.51	203.97
国有独资公司	State Sole Funded Corporations	1619.97	1689.68	1591.56	98.12	27.61
其他有限责任公司	Other Limited Liability Corporations	3266.80	3479.63	3131.24	348.39	176.36
股份有限公司	Share-holding Corporations Ltd.	1735.74	1886.86	1617.81	269.05	123.58
私营企业	Private Enterprises	1376.38	1502.44	1311.99	190.46	101.04
私营独资	Private-funded Enterprises	35.29	39.28	30.94	8.34	0.80
私营合伙	Private Partnership Enterprises					
私营有限责任公司	Private Limited Liability Corporations	1306.14	1422.30	1247.11	175.19	98.76
私营股份有限公司	Private Share-holding Corporations Ltd.	34.95	40.87	33.94	6.93	1.48
其他	Other Enterprises	61.78	72.23	50.57	21.66	2.04
港澳台商投资企业	**Enterprises with Funds from Hongkong, Macao and Taiwan**	**188.69**	**215.10**	**206.51**	**8.59**	**13.86**
合资经营	Joint-venture Enterprises	16.07	17.89	15.00	2.89	1.10
合作经营	Cooperative Enterprises	0.27	0.27	0.25	0.02	0.07
独资经营	Enterprises with Sole Investment	159.57	184.58	178.89	5.68	12.27
投资股份有限公司	Share-holding Co. Ltd. With Investment	12.78	12.36	12.36		0.42
外商投资企业	**Foreign Funded Enterprises**	**974.48**	**1266.28**	**1185.79**	**80.49**	**29.01**
中外合资经营	Sino-foreign Joint-venture Enterprises	677.45	914.36	914.36		24.73
外资企业	Enterprises with Sole Foreign Investment	223.21	258.49	258.10	0.39	3.93
外商投资股份有限公司	Share-holding Co. Ltd. with Foreign Investment	0.76	0.97	0.97		
其它外商投资企业	Other Foreign Funded Enterprises	73.06	92.47	12.38	80.10	0.35
二、零售业	**Retail Trade**	**6736.82**	**7477.12**	**779.40**	**6697.71**	**644.62**
按登记注册类型分组	**Grouped by Registration Type**					
内资	**Domestic Funded Enterprises**	**6475.96**	**7175.71**	**772.75**	**6402.96**	**627.01**
国有	State-owned Enterprises	91.66	100.78	6.86	93.92	4.46
集体	Collective-owned Enterprises	162.88	176.46	8.20	168.26	9.76
股份合作	Cooperative Enterprises	3.98	4.04	0.09	3.95	0.11
联营企业	Joint Ownership Enterprises	3.04	3.11		3.11	0.03
国有联营	State Joint Ownership Enterprises					
集体联营	Collective Joint Ownership Enterprises					
国有与集体联营	Joint State-collective Enterprises	2.77	2.84		2.84	0.03
其他联营	Other Joint Ownership Enterprises	0.27	0.27		0.27	
有限责任公司	Limited Liability Corporations	3638.85	3981.00	577.20	3403.80	348.65
国有独资公司	State Sole Funded Corporations	142.10	192.10	17.07	175.03	7.58
其他有限责任公司	Other Limited Liability Corporations	3496.76	3788.90	560.14	3228.76	341.07
股份有限公司	Share-holding Corporations Ltd.	1022.49	1158.67	68.04	1090.64	112.52
私营企业	Private Enterprises	1519.32	1714.59	110.05	1604.54	149.93
私营独资	Private-funded Enterprises	111.31	124.38	10.30	114.07	6.92
私营合伙	Private Partnership Enterprises	4.65	5.36	0.04	5.32	0.27
私营有限责任公司	Private Limited Liability Corporations	1346.77	1523.29	96.51	1426.77	137.90
私营股份有限公司	Private Share-holding Corporations Ltd.	56.59	61.56	3.19	58.38	4.83
其他	Other Enterprises	33.73	37.07	2.32	34.75	1.55
港澳台商投资企业	**Enterprises with Funds from Hongkong, Macao and Taiwan**	**149.43**	**172.17**	**4.46**	**167.71**	**9.18**
合资经营	Joint-venture Enterprises	7.76	9.16	3.99	5.18	0.70
合作经营	Cooperative Enterprises					
独资经营	Enterprises with Sole Investment	141.67	163.01	0.48	162.53	8.49
投资股份有限公司	Share-holding Co. Ltd. With Investment					
外商投资企业	**Foreign Funded Enterprises**	**111.43**	**129.23**	**2.19**	**127.05**	**8.42**
中外合资经营	Sino-foreign Joint-venture Enterprises	23.16	29.53	2.19	27.34	1.11
外资企业	Enterprises with Sole Foreign Investment	84.71	95.55		95.55	7.09
外商投资股份有限公司	Share-holding Co. Ltd. with Foreign Investment	1.04	1.37		1.37	0.01
其它外商投资企业	Other Foreign Funded Enterprises	2.53	2.79		2.79	0.21

16-12 限额以上批发和零售业商品购、销、存总额(2016)

TOTAL PURCHASES, SALES AND STOCK OF ENTERPRISES ABOVE DESIGNATED SIZE OF WHOLESALE AND RETAIL TRADES (2016)

(按国民经济行业分)

(Grouped by Sector)

单位:亿元 (100 million yuan)

行业	Item	购进总额 Total Purchasing Value	销售总额 Total Sales Value	批发 Whole-sales	零售 Retail Sales	年末库存总额 Total Value of Inventory at Year-end
总计	**Total**	**16566.12**	**18358.74**	**10618.74**	**7739.99**	**1281.56**
一、批发业	**Wholesales**	**9829.30**	**10881.62**	**9839.34**	**1042.28**	**636.94**
农、林、牧产品批发业	Wholesales of Agriculture, Forestry and Animal Husbandry Products	338.84	366.21	308.61	57.60	102.94
食品、饮料及烟草制品批发业	Wholesales of Foods, Beverage and Tobacco	1550.78	1847.27	1602.66	244.61	138.48
米、面制品及食用油批发业	Wholesales of Rice, Noodles and Edible Oil	179.61	189.13	159.24	29.89	10.14
烟草制品批发业	Wholesales of Tobacco	493.16	670.32	663.54	6.77	84.74
纺织、服装及日用品批发业	Wholesales of Textile Products, Garments and Daily Used Articles	336.75	395.67	292.16	103.51	26.69
服装批发业	Wholesales of Garments	141.85	174.74	88.57	86.17	4.91
家用电器批发业	Wholesales of Home Appliances	134.71	151.49	144.70	6.78	9.82
文化、体育用品及器材批发业	Wholesales of Cultural and Sports Goods and Equipments	192.81	235.01	215.14	19.87	18.45
医药及医疗器材批发业	Wholesales of Medicnes and Medical Appliances	1143.06	1260.24	1070.89	189.35	129.81
矿产品、建材及化工产品批发业	Wholesales of Mineral Products, Building Materials and Chemical Products	4793.93	5026.03	4671.89	354.13	156.90
煤炭及制品批发业	Wholesales of Coal and Coal-made Products	171.08	183.42	165.32	18.11	13.31
石油及制品批发业	Wholesales of Petroleum Products	2582.87	2761.82	2499.77	262.04	61.75
非金属及金属矿批发业	Wholesales of Non-metellic Mineral and Metal Industry	16.46	17.53	15.22	2.31	0.85
金属及金属矿批发业	Wholesales of Metal and Metal Mines	1424.26	1446.87	1426.90	19.97	58.34
建材批发业	Wholesales of Construction Materials	113.71	123.22	106.64	16.58	6.99
化肥批发业	Wholesales of Chemical Fertilizers	210.98	201.86	195.70	6.16	7.56
机械设备、五金交电及电子产品批发	Wholesales of Machinery Equipment, Hardware, Transport and Electronic Products	1385.91	1660.12	1594.27	65.86	57.80
汽车批发业	Wholesales of Cars	743.30	983.71	962.47	21.24	26.83
计算机、软件及辅助设备批发业	Wholesales of Computers, Softwares and Assisted Equipments	294.84	295.39	282.06	13.33	2.45
贸易经纪与代理	Trade Agent	39.59	37.39	37.26	0.13	3.20
其他批发业	Other Wholesales	47.64	53.68	46.47	7.21	2.68
二、零售业	**Retail Sales**	**6736.82**	**7477.12**	**779.40**	**6697.71**	**644.62**
综合零售业	Retail Sales of Department	1637.79	1874.85	67.33	1807.52	190.80
百货零售业	Department Stores	910.37	1041.86	42.08	999.78	115.28
超级市场零售业	Supermarkets	658.63	760.71	22.81	737.90	69.79
食品、饮料及烟草制品专门零售业	Monopoly Retail of Foods, Beverage and Tobacco	345.71	398.67	51.06	347.61	23.18
纺织、服装及日用品专门零售业	Monopoly Retail of Textile, Garments,and Daily Used Articles	201.13	235.89	38.79	197.09	23.08
服装零售业	Retail Sales of Garments	145.92	163.37	34.26	129.11	15.83
文化、体育用品及器材专门零售业	Monopoly Retail of Cultural, Sports Products and Equipments	91.58	107.31	6.41	100.89	13.60
体育用品零售业	Retail Sales of Sports Products	3.65	4.48		4.48	0.16
图书报刊零售业	Retail Sales of Books, Newspapers and Periodicals	31.23	32.83	3.17	29.65	5.99
医药及医疗器材专门零售业	Monopoly Retail of Medicine and Medical Appliances	521.99	610.11	41.08	569.04	46.12
药品零售业	Retail Sales of Medicine	505.05	585.77	37.29	548.48	44.83
汽车、摩托车、燃料及零配件专门零售	Monopoly Retail of Cars, and Motorcars Parts	2433.41	2659.92	182.32	2477.60	283.43
汽车零售业	Retail Sales of Cars	2057.34	2232.32	130.74	2101.58	273.55
机动车燃料零售业	Retail Sales of Motor Vehicles Fuels	316.51	365.51	45.49	320.01	5.13
家用电器及电子产品专门零售业	Monopoly Retail of Home Appliances and Electronic Products	1056.41	1068.43	373.66	694.77	50.02
家用视听设备零售业	Retail Sales of Home Audio-visual	84.52	91.70	5.86	85.83	7.15
计算机、软件及辅助设备零售业	Retail Sales of Computers, Softwares and Equipment Assisted Equipments	46.89	52.56	8.00	44.56	3.23
通讯设备零售业	Retail Sales of Communication Equipments	14.29	15.55	1.07	14.49	1.65
五金、家具及室内装修材料专门零售业	Monopoly Retail of Hardware, Furnitures and Decorative Materials	132.78	155.11	11.84	143.27	8.88
货摊、无店铺及其他零售业	Retail Sales of Stalls、Storeless and Others	316.00	366.83	6.92	359.91	5.50
互联网零售	Retail Sales of Internet	279.53	321.42	4.05	317.37	3.90

16-13 限额以上批发和零售业企业资产及负债(2016)

ASSETS AND LIABILITIES OF ENTERPRISES ABOVE DESIGNATED SIZE OF WHOLESALE AND RETAIL TRADES (2016)

单位:亿元 (100 million yuan)

项目	Item	流动资产合计 Total Circulating Funds	固定资产原价 Original Price of Fixed Assets	资产总计 Total Assets	负债合计 Total Liabilities	所有者权益合计 Total Creditor's Equity
总计	**Total**	**4823.60**	**1382.19**	**6819.18**	**4883.25**	**1935.93**
一、批发业	**Wholesales**	**3056.84**	**641.23**	**3959.19**	**2844.56**	**1114.63**
1. 按登记注册类型分组	Grouped by Registration Type					
内资	Domestic Funded Enterprises	2683.26	620.15	3550.95	2476.92	1074.03
国有	State-owned Enterprises	267.08	66.43	319.58	200.28	119.30
集体	Collective-owned Enterprises	8.67	1.52	10.23	9.29	0.94
股份合作	Cooperative Enterprises	0.48	0.12	0.58	0.39	0.19
联营企业	Joint Ownership Enterprises					
国有联营	State Joint Ownership Enterprises					
集体联营	Collective Joint Ownership Enterprises					
国有与集体联营	Joint State-collective Enterprises					
其他联营	Other Joint Ownership Enterprises					
有限责任公司	Limited Liability Corporations	1422.99	240.33	1799.65	1316.58	483.07
国有独资公司	State Sole Funded Corporations	123.44	92.66	213.33	153.02	60.30
其他有限责任公司	Other Limited Liability Corporations	1299.54	147.67	1586.32	1163.55	422.77
股份有限公司	Share-holding Corporations Ltd.	396.03	212.75	696.88	421.56	275.32
私营企业	Private Enterprises	576.16	90.18	698.07	514.95	183.12
私营独资	Private-funded Enterprises	2.78	2.46	5.63	1.94	3.69
私营合伙	Private Partnership Enterprises					
私营有限责任公司	Private Limited Liability Corporations	566.68	84.32	680.29	507.07	173.22
私营股份有限公司	Private Share-holding Corporations Ltd.	6.70	3.40	12.16	5.94	6.22
其他	Other Enterprises	11.85	8.84	25.96	13.87	12.09
港澳台商投资企业	**Enterprises with Funds from Hongkong, Macao and Taiwan**	**69.82**	**14.53**	**85.09**	**71.39**	**13.70**
合资经营	Joint-venture Enterprises	10.47	0.23	10.64	9.01	1.63
合作经营	Cooperative Enterprises	0.09	0.02	0.10	0.06	0.04
独资经营	Enterprises with Sole Investment	55.90	14.24	70.97	58.96	12.01
投资股份有限公司	Share-holding Co. Ltd. With Investment	3.36	0.04	3.37	3.36	0.02
外商投资企业	**Foreign Funded Enterprises**	**303.76**	**6.55**	**323.15**	**296.25**	**26.90**
中外合资经营	Sino-foreign Joint-venture Enterprises	172.04	3.35	185.65	151.85	33.80
外资企业	Enterprises with Sole Foreign Investment	99.54	2.01	103.47	111.94	-8.46
外商投资股份有限公司	Share-holding Co. Ltd. with Foreign Investment	0.59	0.01	0.59	0.02	0.58
其他外资企业	Other Enterprises with Sole Foreign Investment	31.59	1.18	33.44	32.45	0.99
2. 按国民经济行业分组	**Grouped by Sector**					
农、林、牧产品批发业	Wholesales of Agriculture, Forestry and Animal Husbandry Products	185.69	42.10	241.83	179.00	62.83
食品、饮料及烟草制品批发业	Wholesales of Foods, Beverage and Tobacco	644.36	152.66	836.76	486.46	350.31
米、面制品及食用油批发业	Wholesales of Rice, Noodles and Edible Oil	81.89	13.63	133.26	81.10	52.16
烟草制品批发业	Wholesales of Tobacco	171.96	57.01	214.27	105.41	108.86
纺织、服装及日用品批发业	Wholesales of Textile Products, Garments and Daily Used Articles	126.89	10.55	144.30	132.44	11.86
服装批发业	Wholesales of Garments	48.73	3.81	56.60	54.70	1.90
家用电器批发业	Wholesales of Home Appliances	53.76	3.23	58.35	54.62	3.73
文化、体育用品及器材批发业	Wholesales of Cultural and Sports Goods and Equipments	91.14	11.61	107.52	74.66	32.85
医药及医疗器材批发业	Wholesales of Medicnes and Medical Appliances	712.53	66.25	842.53	639.99	202.54
矿产品、建材及化工产品批发业	Wholesales of Mineral Products, Building Materials and Chemical Products	770.25	326.46	1207.28	836.17	371.11
煤炭及制品批发业	Wholesales of Coal and Coal-made Products	69.99	5.32	80.14	50.99	29.15
石油及制品批发业	Wholesales of Petroleum Products	158.16	271.67	469.64	277.74	191.90
非金属及金属矿批发业	Wholesales of Non-metellic Mineral and Metal Industry	6.54	3.65	11.85	7.63	4.22
金属及金属矿批发业	Wholesales of Metal and Metal Mines	399.36	18.91	456.88	367.31	89.57
建材批发业	Wholesales of Construction Materials	24.09	9.40	35.78	22.02	13.76
化肥批发业	Wholesales of Chemical Fertilizers	41.68	7.94	55.10	36.95	18.15
机械设备、五金交电及电子产品批发	Wholesales of Machinery Equipment, Hardware, Transport and Electronic Products	502.20	25.16	546.54	475.09	71.45
汽车批发业	Wholesales of Cars	206.47	5.81	226.48	188.38	38.1
计算机、软件及辅助设备批发业	Wholesales of Computers, Softwares and Assisted Equipments	139.77	0.40	141.17	126.80	14.37
贸易经纪与代理	Trade Agent	11.5	0.31	11.76	9.29	2.47
其他批发业	Other Wholesales	12.29	6.13	20.67	11.45	9.22

16-13 续表 continued

单位:亿元 (100 million yuan)

项目	Item	流动资产合计 Total Circulating Funds	固定资产原价 Original Price of Fixed Assets	资产总计 Total Assets	负债合计 Total Liabilities	所有者权益合计 Total Creditor's Equity
二、零售业	**Retail Trade**	**1766.76**	**740.96**	**2859.99**	**2038.69**	**821.29**
1. 按登记注册类型分组	**Grouped by Registration Type**					
内资	Domestic Funded Enterprises	1640.61	691.38	2676.02	1900.66	775.36
国有	State-owned Enterprises	11.33	6.16	18.94	7.67	11.27
集体	Collective-owned Enterprises	14.45	18.98	29.93	25.04	4.89
股份合作	Cooperative Enterprises	0.60	0.63	1.04	0.46	0.58
联营企业	Joint Ownership Enterprises	0.56	0.12	0.67	0.10	0.58
国有联营	State Joint Ownership Enterprises					
集体联营	Collective Joint Ownership Enterprises					
国有与集体联营	Joint State-collective Enterprises	0.53	0.12	0.64	0.09	0.55
其他联营	Other Joint Ownership Enterprises	0.03		0.03		0.03
有限责任公司	Limited Liability Corporations	945.24	300.23	1471.99	1073.06	398.93
国有独资公司	State Sole Funded Corporations	61.54	15.94	90.21	61.89	28.32
其他有限责任公司	Other Limited Liability Corporations	883.69	284.29	1381.77	1011.16	370.61
股份有限公司	Share-holding Corporations Ltd.	170.11	213.15	450.27	315.75	134.52
私营企业	Private Enterprises	493.21	142.50	689.86	474.79	215.07
私营独资	Private-funded Enterprises	15.46	22.46	37.79	10.62	27.17
私营合伙	Private Partnership Enterprises	1.12	1.35	2.51	1.04	1.47
私营有限责任公司	Private Limited Liability Corporations	434.77	113.84	599.18	424.36	174.83
私营股份有限公司	Private Share-holding Corporations Ltd.	41.85	4.86	50.38	38.77	11.61
其他	Other Enterprises	5.12	9.62	13.31	3.80	9.51
港澳台商投资企业	**Enterprises with Funds from Hongkong, Macao and Taiwan**	**73.36**	**15.36**	**88.17**	**68.12**	**20.05**
合资经营	Joint-venture Enterprises	2.90	2.32	5.13	3.85	1.28
合作经营	Cooperative Enterprises					
独资经营	Enterprises with Sole Investment	70.46	13.03	83.04	64.27	18.77
投资股份有限公司	Share-holding Co. Ltd. With Investment					
外商投资企业	**Foreign Funded Enterprises**	**52.79**	**34.22**	**95.80**	**69.91**	**25.89**
中外合资经营	Sino-foreign Joint-venture Enterprises	8.77	2.56	19.31	12.53	6.78
外资企业	Enterprises with Sole Foreign Investment	43.56	30.03	74.52	55.10	19.42
外商投资股份有限公司	Share-holding Co. Ltd. with Foreign Investment	0.18	0.85	0.95	1.14	-0.19
其他外资企业	Other Enterprises with Sole Foreign Investment	0.28	0.77	1.02	1.15	-0.13
2. 按国民经济行业分组	**Grouped by Sector**					
综合零售业	Retail Sales of Department	362.30	309.70	751.46	534.88	216.58
百货零售业	Department Stores	205.93	185.41	451.66	305.91	145.76
超级市场零售业	Supermarkets	147.42	116.89	284.33	219.25	65.08
食品、饮料及烟草制品专门零售业	Monopoly Retail of Foods, Beverage and Tobacco	89.54	33.25	130.31	55.72	74.59
纺织、服装及日用品专门零售业	Monopoly Retail of Textile, Garments,and Daily Used Articles	118.88	21.08	144.73	110.47	34.25
服装零售业	Retail Sales of Garments	98.37	16.20	118.81	97.16	21.65
文化、体育用品及器材专门零售业	Monopoly Retail of Cultural, Sports Products and Equipments	47.01	17.77	70.61	43.89	26.71
体育用品零售业	Retail Sales of Sports Products	0.39	0.21	0.74	1.69	-0.95
图书报刊零售业	Retail Sales of Books, Newspapers and Periodicals	24.68	9.62	34.09	14.19	19.90
医药及医疗器材专门零售业	Monopoly Retail of Medicine and Medical Appliances	215.76	23.78	265.18	201.05	64.14
药品零售业	Retail Sales of Medicine	205.77	22.83	254.02	194.07	59.94
汽车、摩托车、燃料及零配件专门零售业	Monopoly Retail of Cars, and Motorcars Parts	702.38	236.51	1128.15	866.31	261.84
汽车零售业	Retail Sales of Cars	674.91	166.61	1004.92	779.41	225.51
机动车燃料零售业	Retail Sales of Motor Vehicles Fuels	16.47	64.87	105.45	76.73	28.73
家用电器及电子产品专门零售业	Monopoly Retail of Home Appliances and Electronic Products	116.75	54.38	190.96	103.01	87.94
家用视听设备零售业	Retail Sales of Home Audio-visual Equipment	15.96	9.96	26.30	11.03	15.28
计算机、软件及辅助设备零售业	Retail Sales of Computers, Softwares and Assisted Equipments	11.90	7.22	22.88	14.42	8.45
通讯设备零售业	Retail Sales of Communication Equipments	3.48	1.99	5.26	3.47	1.78
五金、家具及室内装修材料专门零售业	Monopoly Retail of Hardware, Furnitures and Decorative Materials	59.92	19.78	94.58	68.75	25.83
货摊、无店铺及其他零售业	Retail Sales of Stalls、Storeless and Others	54.23	24.71	84.01	54.62	29.39
互联网零售	Retail Sales of Internet	33.27	11.08	48.27	33.61	14.67

16-14 限额以上批发和零售业企业主要财务指标(2016)
MAIN FINANCIAL INDICATORS OF ENTERPRISES ABOVE DESIGNATED SIZE OF WHOLESALE AND RETAIL TRADES (2016)

单位:亿元 (100 million yuan)

项目	Item	主营业务收入 Revenue of Major Business	主营业务成本 Cost of Major Business	其他业务利润 Profits of Other Business	利润总额 Total Profits
总计	**Total**	**15274.50**	**13671.60**	**84.03**	**394.49**
一、批发业	**Wholesales**	**9383.98**	**8500.10**	**43.51**	**250.40**
1. 按登记注册类型分组	**Grouped by Registration Type**				
内资	**Domestic Funded Enterprises**	**8176.26**	**7503.23**	**27.94**	**214.52**
国有	State-owned Enterprises	612.95	459.31	0.36	61.66
集体	Collective-owned Enterprises	12.82	12.41		0.06
股份合作	Cooperative Enterprises	2.47	2.05		0.17
联营企业	Joint Ownership Enterprises				
国有联营	State Joint Ownership Enterprises				
集体联营	Collective Joint Ownership Enterprises				
国有与集体联营	Joint State-collective Enterprises				
其他联营	Other Joint Ownership Enterprises				
有限责任公司	Limited Liability Corporations	4507.57	4242.46	3.14	77.10
国有独资公司	State Sole Funded Corporations	1454.22	1402.55	0.07	16.82
其他有限责任公司	Other Limited Liability Corporations	3053.35	2839.90	3.07	60.28
股份有限公司	Share-holding Corporations Ltd.	1583.58	1473.62	22.34	22.83
私营企业	Private Enterprises	1390.35	1257.53	2.10	48.51
私营独资	Private-funded Enterprises	36.82	29.26	0.04	3.28
私营合伙	Private Partnership Enterprises				
私营有限责任公司	Private Limited Liability Corporations	1317.89	1194.64	2.06	44.39
私营股份有限公司	Private Share-holding Corporations Ltd.	35.64	33.63		0.85
其他	Other Enterprises	66.52	55.85		4.18
港澳台商投资企业	**Enterprises with Funds from Hongkong, Macao and Taiwan**	**234.45**	**212.58**	**0.81**	**2.78**
合资经营	Joint-venture Enterprises	15.27	14.24	0.01	-0.04
合作经营	Cooperative Enterprises	0.27	0.21		0.01
独资经营	Enterprises with Sole Investment	208.34	188.69	0.80	2.80
投资股份有限公司	Share-holding Co. Ltd. With Investment	10.57	9.44		0.01
外商投资企业	**Foreign Funded Enterprises**	**973.27**	**784.29**	**14.76**	**33.10**
中外合资经营	Sino-foreign Joint-venture Enterprises	658.98	560.25	0.65	25.61
外资企业	Enterprises with Sole Foreign Investment	222.51	150.30	0.34	6.74
外商投资股份有限公司	Share-holding Co. Ltd. with Foreign Investment	0.83	0.65		0.09
其他外资企业	Other Enterprises with Sole Foreign Investment	90.96	73.10	13.77	0.67
2. 按国民经济行业分组	**Grouped by Sector**				
农、林、牧产品批发业	Wholesales of Agriculture, Forestry and Animal Husbandry Products	325.53	303.73	0.25	11.44
食品、饮料及烟草制品批发业	Wholesales of Foods, Beverage and Tobacco	1533.30	1157.85	2.03	118.15
米、面制品及食用油批发业	Wholesales of Rice, Noodles and Edible Oil	173.20	156.48	0.07	4.98
烟草制品批发业	Wholesales of Tobacco	531.17	372.15	0.34	61.38
纺织、服装及日用品批发业	Wholesales of Textile Products, Garments and Daily Used Articles	350.00	308.78	14.36	2.02
服装批发业	Wholesales of Garments	160.29	133.38	13.81	0.46
家用电器批发业	Wholesales of Home Appliances	125.44	119.10	0.05	0.24
文化、体育用品及器材批发业	Wholesales of Cultural and Sports Goods and Equipments	197.50	178.57	0.85	6.98
医药及医疗器材批发业	Wholesales of Medicnes and Medical Appliances	1092.76	1004.04	4.77	25.87
矿产品、建材及化工产品批发业	Wholesales of Mineral Products, Building Materials and Chemical Products	4461.54	4260.66	19.93	60.37
煤炭及制品批发业	Wholesales of Coal and Coal-made Products	172.94	153.79	0.03	10.24
石油及制品批发业	Wholesales of Petroleum Products	2338.91	2225.49	18.96	27.61
非金属及金属矿批发业	Wholesales of Non-metellic Mineral and Metal Industry	17.42	13.97		1.42
金属及金属矿批发业	Wholesales of Metal and Metal Mines	1313.17	1287.61	0.62	6.21
建材批发业	Wholesales of Construction Materials	109.31	96.58	0.07	5.40
化肥批发业	Wholesales of Chemical Fertilizers	190.48	180.37	0.03	4.38
机械设备、五金交电及电子产品批发	Wholesales of Machinery Equipment, Hardware, Transport and Electronic Products	1339.43	1209.51	1.20	23.49
汽车批发业	Wholesales of Cars	722.98	622.20	0.97	25.27
计算机、软件及辅助设备批发业	Wholesales of Computers, Softwares and Assisted Equipments	269.31	264.35		5.10
贸易经纪与代理	Trade Agent	32.22	31.93	0.01	0.09
其他批发业	Other Wholesales	51.71	45.05	0.11	1.98

16-14 续表 continued

单位:亿元 (100 million yuan)

项目	Item	主营业务收入 Revenue of Major Business	主营业务成本 Cost of Major Business	其他业务利润 Profits of Other Business	利润总额 Total Profits
二、零售业	**Retail Trade**	**5890.52**	**5171.50**	**40.52**	**144.09**
1. 按登记注册类型分组	**Grouped by Registration Type**				
内资	**Domestic Funded Enterprises**	**5631.48**	**4950.83**	**23.52**	**127.45**
国有	State-owned Enterprises	92.22	77.77	0.16	4.83
集体	Collective-owned Enterprises	149.05	135.06	0.20	2.20
股份合作	Cooperative Enterprises	3.84	3.39		0.20
联营企业	Joint Ownership Enterprises	2.56	2.39		0.07
国有联营	State Joint Ownership Enterprises				
集体联营	Collective Joint Ownership Enterprises				
国有与集体联营	Joint State-collective Enterprises	2.30	2.13		0.07
其他联营	Other Joint Ownership Enterprises	0.27	0.27		
有限责任公司	Limited Liability Corporations	3076.97	2756.48	9.78	52.45
国有独资公司	State Sole Funded Corporations	147.53	139.57	0.30	2.09
其他有限责任公司	Other Limited Liability Corporations	2929.44	2616.91	9.49	50.36
股份有限公司	Share-holding Corporations Ltd.	659.63	557.99	8.66	17.72
私营企业	Private Enterprises	1610.35	1387.74	4.69	47.09
私营独资	Private-funded Enterprises	120.72	95.38	0.07	11.04
私营合伙	Private Partnership Enterprises	6.06	4.78	0.01	0.75
私营有限责任公司	Private Limited Liability Corporations	1429.53	1238.72	4.53	33.76
私营股份有限公司	Private Share-holding Corporations Ltd.	54.03	48.87	0.09	1.54
其他	Other Enterprises	36.85	30.00	0.02	2.90
港澳台商投资企业	**Enterprises with Funds from Hongkong, Macao and Taiwan**	**151.73**	**135.28**	**15.67**	**12.18**
合资经营	Joint-venture Enterprises	8.19	6.76	0.22	0.31
合作经营	Cooperative Enterprises				
独资经营	Enterprises with Sole Investment	143.54	128.51	15.45	11.87
投资股份有限公司	Share-holding Co. Ltd. With Investment				
外商投资企业	**Foreign Funded Enterprises**	**107.31**	**85.40**	**1.33**	**4.46**
中外合资经营	Sino-foreign Joint-venture Enterprises	26.25	20.54	0.02	1.60
外资企业	Enterprises with Sole Foreign Investment	77.45	61.62	1.28	2.83
外商投资股份有限公司	Share-holding Co. Ltd. with Foreign Investment	1.25	1.03		0.03
其他外资企业	Other Enterprises with Sole Foreign Investment	2.36	2.20	0.03	
2. 按国民经济行业分组	**Grouped by Sector**				
综合零售业	Retail Sales of Department	1298.72	1086.53	31.45	46.44
百货零售业	Department Stores	676.38	571.90	25.77	36.94
超级市场零售业	Supermarkets	554.47	456.55	5.58	7.33
食品、饮料及烟草制品专门零售业	Monopoly Retail of Foods, Beverage and Tobacco	359.90	291.86	1.02	26.64
纺织、服装及日用品专门零售业	Monopoly Retail of Textile, Garments,and Daily Used Articles	218.75	183.97	0.24	-1.30
服装零售业	Retail Sales of Garments	153.77	133.58	0.16	1.86
文化、体育用品及器材专门零售业	Monopoly Retail of Cultural, Sports Products and Equipments	97.12	78.70	0.56	5.52
体育用品零售业	Retail Sales of Sports Products	4.24	3.63		0.27
图书报刊零售业	Retail Sales of Books, Newspapers and Periodicals	30.95	23.19	0.24	2.73
医药及医疗器材专门零售业	Monopoly Retail of Medicine and Medical Appliances	549.68	482.41	1.15	7.52
药品零售业	Retail Sales of Medicine	526.27	465.65	1.14	5.60
汽车、摩托车、燃料及零配件专门零售业	Monopoly Retail of Cars, and Motorcars Parts	2528.65	2329.82	3.29	29.50
汽车零售业	Retail Sales of Cars	2155.90	1993.81	3.01	19.92
机动车燃料零售业	Retail Sales of Motor Vehicles Fuels	314.66	288.68	0.24	6.15
家用电器及电子产品专门零售业	Monopoly Retail of Home Appliances and Electronic Products	367.61	307.68	1.68	18.08
家用视听设备零售业	Retail Sales of Home Audio-visual Equipments	83.49	68.09	0.11	4.55
计算机、软件及辅助设备零售业	Retail Sales of Computers, Softwares and Assisted Equipments	49.10	41.89	0.22	2.11
通讯设备零售业	Retail Sales of Communication Equipments	14.64	12.29	0.01	0.65
五金、家具及室内装修材料专门零售业	Monopoly Retail of Hardware, Furnitures and Decorative Materials	136.71	109.27	0.12	8.12
货摊、无店铺及其他零售业	Retail Sales of Stalls、Storeless and Others	333.37	301.25	1.01	3.58
互联网零售	Retail Sales of Internet	287.13	264.47	0.07	-0.40

16-15 限额以上餐饮业企业资产及负债(2016)
ASSETS AND LIABILITIES OF ENTERPRISES ABOVE DESIGNATED SIZE OF CATERING SERVICES (2016)

单位:亿元 (100 million yuan)

项　目	Item	流动资产合计 Total Circulating Funds	固定资产原价 Original Price of Fixed Assets	资产总计 Total Assets	负债合计 Total Liabilities	所有者权益合计 Total Creditor's Equity
总　计	**Total**	**80.94**	**131.34**	**239.45**	**161.21**	**78.25**
1. 按国民经济行业分组	**Grouped by Sector**					
正餐服务业	Dinner	76.59	120.81	220.67	149.21	71.45
快餐服务业	Fast Food	1.92	8.43	12.89	9.40	3.49
饮料及冷饮服务业	Beverage and Cold Drink Services	1.75	1.44	4.62	1.95	2.68
其他餐饮服务业	Others	0.69	0.65	1.27	0.65	0.63
2. 按登记注册类型分组	**Grouped by Registration Type**					
内资	**Domestic Funded Enterprises**	**75.05**	**116.23**	**214.85**	**141.62**	**73.23**
国有	State-Owned Enterprises	0.60	1.25	1.69	0.70	0.99
集体	Collective-owned Enterprises	0.16	0.37	0.50	0.20	0.30
股份合作	Cooperative Enterprises	0.02	0.08	0.09	0.01	0.09
联营企业	Joint Ownership Enterprises					
国有联营	State Joint Ownership Enterprises					
集体联营	Collective Joint Ownership Enterprises					
国有与集体联营	Joint State-collective Enterprises					
其他联营	Other Joint Ownership Enterprises					
有限责任公司	Limited Liability Corporations	42.96	50.25	111.45	93.70	17.75
国有独资公司	State Sole Funded Corporations	2.05	1.70	3.04	1.91	1.13
其他有限责任公司	Other Limited Liability Corporations	40.91	48.55	108.41	91.80	16.62
股份有限公司	Share-holding Corporations Ltd.	0.81	0.81	2.81	1.98	0.84
私营企业	Private Enterprises	29.62	61.16	94.96	44.28	50.68
私营独资	Private-funded Enterprises	3.95	8.49	11.50	3.69	7.81
私营合伙	Private Partnership Enterprises	0.15	0.70	0.81	0.22	0.60
私营有限责任公司	Private Limited Liability Corporations	24.27	50.17	78.49	37.97	40.51
私营股份有限公司	Private Share-holding Corporations Ltd.	1.24	1.80	4.16	2.40	1.76
其他	Other Enterprises	0.88	2.30	3.34	0.76	2.59
港澳台商投资企业	**Enterprises with Funds from Hongkong, Macao and Taiwan**	**3.67**	**9.76**	**16.07**	**11.83**	**4.23**
合资经营	Joint-venture Enterprises	1.00	2.14	2.85	3.51	-0.66
合作经营	Cooperative Enterprises					
独资经营	Enterprises with Sole Investment	2.68	7.62	13.22	8.32	4.90
投资股份有限公司	Share-holding Co. Ltd. With Investment					
外商投资企业	**Foreign Funded Enterprises**	**2.22**	**5.35**	**8.54**	**7.76**	**0.78**
中外合资经营	Sino-Foreign Joint-venture Enterprises	0.19	0.01	0.19	0.19	
外资企业	Enterprises with Sole Foreign Investment	2.04	5.34	8.35	7.57	0.78
外商投资股份有限公司	Share-holding Co. Ltd. with Foreign Investment					
其他外商投资企业	Other Enterprises with Sole Foreign Investment					

16-16 限额以上餐饮业企业主要财务指标(2016)
MAIN FINANCIAL INDICATORS OF ENTERPRISES ABOVE DESIGNATED SIZE OF CATERING SERVICES (2016)

单位:亿元 (100 million yuan)

项目	Item	主营业务收入 Revenue of Major Business	主营业务成本 Cost of Major Business	其他业务利润 Profits of Other Business	利润总额 Total Profits
总计	Total	242.08	137.99	1.02	16.84
1. 按国民经济行业分组	Grouped by Sector				
正餐服务业	Dinner	194.18	117.39	1.02	14.37
快餐服务业	Fast Food	38.76	17.96	-0.01	1.28
饮料及冷饮服务业	Beverage and Cold Drink Services	7.03	1.77		1.25
其他餐饮服务业	Others	2.12	0.87		-0.07
2. 按登记注册类型分组	Grouped by Registration Type				
内资	Domestic Funded Enterprises	194.39	117.50	0.90	14.56
国有	State-Owned Enterprises	1.07	0.63	0.02	0.02
集体	Collective-owned Enterprises	0.85	0.77		
股份合作	Cooperative Enterprises	0.21	0.10		0.06
联营企业	Joint Ownership Enterprises				
国有联营	State Joint Ownership Enterprises				
集体联营	Collective Joint Ownership Enterprises				
国有与集体联营	Joint State-collective Enterprises				
其他联营	Other Joint Ownership Enterprises				
有限责任公司	Limited Liability Corporations	72.55	40.45	0.35	2.10
国有独资公司	State Sole Funded Corporations	2.91	1.93		0.25
其他有限责任公司	Other Limited Liability Corporations	69.64	38.52	0.35	1.85
股份有限公司	Share-holding Corporations Ltd.	2.04	1.00	0.02	0.26
私营企业	Private Enterprises	111.37	70.13	0.51	11.17
私营独资	Private-funded Enterprises	28.98	19.95	0.05	4.11
私营合伙	Private Partnership Enterprises	0.56	0.35		0.06
私营有限责任公司	Private Limited Liability Corporations	79.10	48.10	0.46	6.85
私营股份有限公司	Private Share-holding Corporations Ltd.	2.72	1.73	0.01	0.16
其他	Other Enterprises	6.31	4.43		0.95
港澳台商投资企业	Enterprises with Funds from Hongkong, Macao and Taiwan	37.73	16.56	0.12	2.21
合资经营	Joint-venture Enterprises	0.53	0.18		-0.23
合作经营	Cooperative Enterprises				
独资经营	Enterprises with Sole Investment	37.21	16.38	0.12	2.44
投资股份有限公司	Sole Investment Co. Ltd. With Investment				
外商投资企业	Foreign Funded Enterprises	9.96	3.93	-0.01	0.07
中外合资经营	Sino-Foreign Joint-venture Enterprises	0.64	0.55		0.04
外资企业	Enterprises with Sole Foreign Investment	9.32	3.38	-0.01	0.03
外商投资股份有限公司	Share-holding Co. Ltd. with Foreign Investment				
其他外商投资企业	Other Enterprises with Sole Foreign Investment				

16-17 限额以上住宿业企业资产及负债(2016)
ASSETS AND LIABILITIES OF ENTERPRISES ABOVE DESIGNATED SIZE OF HOTELS SERVICES (2016)

单位:亿元 (100 million yuan)

项目	Item	流动资产合计 Total Circulating Funds	固定资产原价 Original Price of Fixed Assets	资产总计 Total Assets	负债合计 Total Liabilities	所有者权益合计 Total Creditor's Equity
总计	**Total**	**90.55**	**219.84**	**325.68**	**204.17**	**121.51**
1. 按国民经济行业分组	**Grouped by Sector**					
旅游饭店	Tourist Hotel	66	178	255.62	160.94	94.68
一般旅馆	Regular Hotel	20	36	58.79	35.14	23.65
其他住宿服务	Other Accomodation Service	5	6	11.27	8.09	3.18
2. 按登记注册类型分组	**Grouped by Registration Type**					
内资	**Domestic Funded Enterprises**	**84.75**	**199.24**	**305.06**	**188.62**	**116.44**
国有	State-Owned Enterprises	3.39	11.13	10.54	6.03	4.51
集体	Collective-owned Enterprises	1.70	7.79	6.41	1.72	4.69
股份合作	Cooperative Enterprises	0.07	0.72	0.76	0.73	0.03
联营企业	Joint Ownership Enterprises					
国有联营	State Joint Ownership Enterprises					
集体联营	Collective Joint Ownership Enterprises					
国有与集体联营	Joint State-collective Enterprises					
其他联营	Other Joint Ownership Enterprises					
有限责任公司	Limited Liability Corporations	46.82	107.04	179.49	108.65	70.84
国有独资公司	State Sole Funded Corporations	2.97	10.75	29.85	11.34	18.50
其他有限责任公司	Other Limited Liability Corporations	43.86	96.29	149.65	97.31	52.34
股份有限公司	Share-holding Corporations Ltd.	5.89	10.90	18.80	11.44	7.35
私营企业	Private Enterprises	26.68	61.27	88.66	59.96	28.71
私营独资	Private-funded Enterprises	1.66	2.18	3.92	2.11	1.81
私营合伙	Private Partnership Enterprises	0.18	0.61	0.68	0.24	0.43
私营有限责任公司	Private Limited Liability Corporations	23.94	57.88	81.90	56.18	25.73
私营股份有限公司	Private Share-holding Corporations Ltd.	0.90	0.60	2.16	1.42	0.74
其他	Other Enterprises	0.20	0.40	0.39	0.09	0.31
港澳台商投资企业	**Enterprises with Funds from Hongkong, Macao and Taiwan**	**4.49**	**18.13**	**17.37**	**12.92**	**4.44**
合资经营	Joint-venture Enterprises	1.09	11.33	7.35	4.57	2.79
合作经营	Cooperative Enterprises	0.45	0.34	0.61	0.23	0.38
独资经营	Enterprises with Sole Investment	2.32	5.98	8.42	7.31	1.10
投资股份有限公司	Share-holding Co. Ltd. With Investment	0.62	0.49	0.99	0.82	0.17
外商投资企业	**Foreign Funded Enterprises**	**1.31**	**2.46**	**3.25**	**2.63**	**0.62**
中外合资经营	Sino-foreign Joint-venture Enterprises	1.05	1.28	1.93	1.24	0.69
外资企业	Enterprises with Sole Foreign Investment	0.25	0.27	0.56	0.48	0.07
外商投资股份有限公司	Share-holding Co. Ltd. with Foreign Investment	0.02	0.91	0.76	0.91	-0.14
其他外商投资企业	Other Enterprises with Sole Foreign Investment					

16-18 限额以上住宿业企业主要财务指标(2016)
MAIN FINANCIAL INDICATORS OF ENTERPRISES ABOVE DESIGNATED SIZE OF HOTELS SERVICES (2016)

单位:亿元 (100 million yuan)

项　目	Item	主营业务收入 Revenue of Major Business	主营业务成本 Cost of Major Business	其他业务利润 Profits of Other Business	利润总额 Total Profits
总　计	**Total**	**115.28**	**56.32**	**0.91**	**-0.93**
1. 按国民经济行业分组	**Grouped by Sector**				
旅游饭店	Tourist Hotel	77.75	35.12	0.69	-2.71
一般旅馆	Regular Hotel	33.25	18.14	0.12	1.64
其他住宿服务	Other Accomodation Service	4.28	3.06	0.11	0.13
2. 按登记注册类型分组	**Grouped by Registration Type**				
内资	**Domestic Funded Enterprises**	**106.82**	**53.64**	**0.81**	**-0.57**
国有	State-Owned Enterprises	5.21	2.11	0.03	
集体	Collective-owned Enterprises	1.69	0.51	0.07	0.05
股份合作	Cooperative Enterprises	0.10	0.07		
联营企业	Joint Ownership Enterprises				
国有联营	State Joint Ownership Enterprises				
集体联营	Collective Joint Ownership Enterprises				
国有与集体联营	Joint State-collective Enterprises				
其他联营	Other Joint Ownership Enterprises				
有限责任公司	Limited Liability Corporations	47.13	21.57	0.40	-2.06
国有独资公司	State Sole Funded Corporations	4.68	3.16		-0.08
其他有限责任公司	Other Limited Liability Corporations	42.45	18.41	0.40	-1.98
股份有限公司	Share-holding Corporations Ltd.	3.92	1.24		0.25
私营企业	Private Enterprises	48.05	27.66	0.32	1.12
私营独资	Private-funded Enterprises	6.58	4.46	0.01	0.76
私营合伙	Private Partnership Enterprises	0.94	0.65	0.03	0.04
私营有限责任公司	Private Limited Liability Corporations	39.61	22.16	0.28	0.31
私营股份有限公司	Private Share-holding Corporations Ltd.	0.93	0.39		
其他	Other Enterprises	0.71	0.46		0.07
港澳台商投资企业	**Enterprises with Funds from Hongkong, Macao and Taiwan**	**7.80**	**2.40**	**0.10**	**-0.27**
合资经营	Joint-venture Enterprises	1.90	0.26	0.07	-0.12
合作经营	Cooperative Enterprises	0.75	0.34		-0.11
独资经营	Enterprises with Sole Investment	4.16	1.28		-0.10
独资股份有限公司	Sole Investment Co. Ltd. With Investment	0.99	0.53	0.03	0.05
外商投资企业	**Foreign Funded Enterprises**	**0.66**	**0.28**		**-0.09**
中外合资经营	Sino-Foreign Joint-venture Enterprises	0.29	0.05		-0.07
外资企业	Enterprises with Sole Foreign Investment	0.31	0.19		
外商投资股份有限公司	Share-holding Co. Ltd. with Foreign Investment	0.06	0.04		-0.02
其他外商投资企业	Other Enterprises with Sole Foreign Investment				

16-19 亿元以上商品交易市场基本情况(2016年)
BASIC STATISTICS ON COMMODITY EXCHANGE MARKETS OF TRANSACTION VALUE OVER 100 MILLION YUAN (2016)

单位:亿元 (100 million yuan)

市　　场	Market	市场数量(个) Number of Markets (unit)	摊位数(个) Number of Booths (unit)	营业面积(万平方米) Operating Area (10 000 sq.m)	成交额(亿元) Turnover (100 million yuan)
总　计	**Total**	151	86427	625.46	2210.42
综合市场	**Integrated Markets**	46	31809	195.07	632.54
生产资料综合市场	Production Comprehensive Market	3	6621	77.02	125.02
工业消费品综合市场	Industrial Consumable Comprehensive Markets	8	7717	47.13	104.88
农产品综合市场	Farm Produce Comprehensive Markets	19	8370	31.94	229.72
其他综合市场	Other Comprehensive Markets	16	9101	38.97	172.92
专业市场	**Special Markets**	105	54618	430.39	1577.88
生产资料市场	Production Markets	17	5511	57.23	270.93
农业生产用具市场	Agricultural Production Equipment Markets				
农用生产资料市场	Agricultural Production Markets				
煤炭市场	Coal and Charcoal Markets				
木材市场	Wood Markets				
建材市场	Building Material Markets	9	2830	29.35	78.51
化工材料及制品市场	Chemical Materials and Products Markets				
金属材料市场	Metal Materials Markets	7	2341	27.28	189.31
机械设备市场	Mechanical Equipments Markets	1	340	0.60	3.11
其他生产资料市场	Others				
农产品市场	Farm Produce Markets	20	12034	75.12	467.64
粮油市场	Grain and Oil Markets	1	235	2.40	1.24
肉禽蛋市场	Meat, Poultry and Eggs Markets				
水产品市场	Aquatic Products Markets	4	4497	28.35	272.30
蔬菜市场	Vegetables Markets	6	1459	10.77	34.05
干鲜果品市场	Dried and Fresh Melons and Fruits Markets	4	4256	24.58	143.57
棉麻土畜、烟叶市场	Cotton, Local & Livestock Products, and Tobacco Markets				
其他农产品市场	Others	5	1587	9.02	16.49
食品、饮料及烟酒市场	Food, Beverages, Tobacco and Liquor Markets	6	3210	17.12	53.57
食品饮料市场	Food and Beverages Markets	3	1031	14.55	17.87
茶叶市场	Tea Markets	2	1335	0.76	15.07
烟酒市场	Tobacco and Liquor Markets				
其他食品饮料及烟酒市场	Others	1	844	1.81	20.62
纺织、服装、鞋帽市场	Textiles, Clothing, Shoes and Hats Markets	22	20059	77.89	205.25
布料及纺织品市场	Cloth and Textiles Markets	2	235	1.10	3.15
服装市场	Clothing Markets	14	13402	65.39	173.89
鞋帽市场	Shoes and Hats Markets	2	720	5.00	4.11
其他纺织服装鞋帽市场	Others	4	5702	6.40	24.10
日用品及文化用品市场	Daily Use Articles and Cultural Goods Markets	6	1966	16.78	66.12

16-19 续表 continued

单位:亿元 (100 million yuan)

市　场	Market	市场数量(个) Number of Markets (unit)	摊位数(个) Number of Booths (unit)	营业面积(万平方米) Operating Area (10 000 sq.m)	成交额(亿元) Turnover (100 million yuan)
小商品市场	Merchandise Markets	1	326	0.40	2.65
箱包市场	Luggage Markets	1	360	4.70	3.00
玩具市场	Toys Markets				
文具市场	Stationary Markets				
图书、报刊杂志市场	Books, Newspapers and Magazines Markets	1	427	0.41	6.50
音像制品及电子出版物市场	Video Products and E-journal Markets				
体育用品市场	Sports Markets				
其他日用品及文化用品市场	Others	3	853	11.27	53.97
黄金、珠宝、玉器等首饰市场	Gold, Jewelry, Jade Markets				
电器、通讯器材、电子设备市场	Electrical Appliances, Communication Appliances and Electronical Appliances Markets	6	2121	10.94	29.09
家电市场	Household Appliances Markets	1	280	0.84	1.25
通讯器材市场	Communication Appliances Markets	3	961	5.10	22.01
照相、摄像器材市场	Cameras and Video Equipments Markets				
计算机及辅助设备市场	Computer and Auxiliary Equipments Markets	2	880	5.00	5.84
其他电器、通讯器材、电子设备市场	Others				
医药、医疗用品及器材市场	Medicine, Medical Materials and Medical Instruments Markets				
中药材市场	Chinese Medicine Markets				
其他医药、医疗用品及器材市场	Others				
家具、五金及装饰材料市场	Furniture, Hardware and Decoration Materials Markets	22	6962	124.22	177.35
家具市场	Furniture Markets	7	1130	20.32	13.15
装饰材料市场	Decoration Materials Markets	14	5283	100.21	159.25
灯具市场	Lamps Markets				
厨具、盥洗设备市场	Kitchen Utensils, Washing Equipments Markets				
五金材料市场	Hardware Materials Markets	1	549	3.68	4.95
其他装修市场	Others				
汽车、摩托车及零配件市场	Cars, Motorcycles and Spare Parts Markets	6	2755	51.09	307.94
汽车市场	Cars Markets	5	755	25.09	168.84
摩托车市场	Motorcycles Markets				
机动车零配件市场	Vehicle Spare Parts Markets	1	2000	26.00	139.10
花、鸟、鱼、虫市场	Flower, Bird, Fish and Insects Markets				
花卉市场	Flower Markets				
鸟市场	Bird Markets				
观赏鱼市场	Fish Markets				
其他花鸟鱼虫市场	Others				
旧货市场	Second Hand Markets				
古玩、古董、字画市场	Antiques,Calligraphy and Painting Markets				
邮票、硬币市场	Stamps and Coins Markets				
其他旧货市场	Others				
其他专业市场	Others				

主要统计指标解释

社会消费品零售总额 指批发和零售业、餐饮业、新闻出版业、邮政业和其他服务业等，售予城乡居民用于生活消费的商品和社会集团用于公共消费的商品之总量。社会消费品零售总额包括：

一、批发和零售业企业(单位)：

1.售予城乡居民的各种生活消费品；

2.售予入境旅游的外国人、华侨、港澳台同胞的各类商品；

3.售予行政事业单位、社会团体、军队和武警等机构的商品，以及以零售方式售予各类企业的商品。具体包括：用于非生产和社会交往的办公用品，如通讯设备、计算器具和设备、电讯网络设备、文印设备、音像视听器材和设备、纸张、本册、文具及装订文印材料、家具、日用电器、针纺织品、清洁卫生用品、文体用品、奖品、纪念品、礼品等；供内部人员乘坐的交通工具和燃料；用于办公设施修缮的各类配件、材料、工具等；用于取暖和防暑降温的设备、燃料、材料及食品等；专用于教学的用品和设备；非营利医疗机构的中、西药品、中药材和医疗设备器材；非专用的劳动保护用品；不对外营业的内部食堂用的餐具、炊具、设备、清洁卫生工具和食品、燃料等；军队、武警用于其人员生活的衣着品和个人用品；其他各类非生产性设备和用品。

二、餐饮业出售的主食、菜肴、烟酒饮料和其他商品。

三、新闻出版业、邮政业售予城乡居民、企事业单位、军队和武警等机构的书报杂志、音像制品、邮品等。

四、其他服务业出售的食品、烟酒饮料、服装鞋帽、日常生活用品、医药保健用品、艺术品、工艺美术品、玩具、殡葬用品以及其他消费品。

批发零售业商品购、销、存总额 指各种登记注册类型的批发、零售业企业(单位)以本企业(单位)为总体的，从国内、国外市场购进的商品总量，销售和出口的商品总量、库存商品总量等情况。该指标可以反映商品流转过程中商品的购进、销售、库存之间的比例关系和存在的问题。

商品购进总额 指从本企业(单位)以外的单位和个人购进(包括从境外直接进口)作为转卖或加工后转卖的商品总额。它反映批发零售贸易业从国内、国外市场上购进商品的总量。商品购进总额包括：(1)从工农业生产者购进的商品；(2)从出版社、报社的出版发行部门购进的图书、杂志和报纸；(3)从各种登记注册类型的批发零售贸易企业(单位)购进的商品；(4)从其他单位购进的商品，如从机关、团体、企业等单位购进的剩余物资，从餐饮业、服务业购进的商品，从海关、市场管理部门购进的缉私和没收的商品，从居民手中收购的废旧商品等；(5)从国(境)外直接进口的商品。不包括企业(单位)为自身经营用和未通过买卖行为而收入的商品以及销售退回、商品升溢等。

商品销售总额 指对本企业(单位)以外的单位和个人出售(包括对境外直接出口)的商品总额。它反映批发零售贸易业在国内市场上销售商品以及出口商品的总量。商品销售总额包括：(1)售给城乡居民和社会集团消费用的商品；(2)售给工业、农业、建筑业、运输邮电业、批发零售贸易业、餐饮业、服务业等作为生产、经营使用的商品；(3)售给批发零售贸易业作为转卖或加工后转卖的商品；(4)对国(境)外直接出口的商品。不包括出售本企业(单位)自用的废旧包装用品、未通过买卖行为付出的商品、经本单位介绍，由买卖双方直接结算，本单位只收取手续费的业务、购货退出的商品以及商品损耗和损失等。

批发零售业库存 指报告期末各种登记注册类型的批发零售贸易企业(单位)已取得所有权的商品。它反映批发零售贸易企业(单位)的商品库存情况和对市场商品供应的保证程度。期末库存包括：(1)存放在批发零售贸易业经营单位(如门市部、批发站、经营处)仓库、货场、货柜和货架中的商品；(2)挑选、整理、包装中的商品；(3)已记入购进而尚未运到本单位的商品，即发货单或银行承兑凭证已到而货未到的部分;(4)寄放他处的商品,如因购货方拒绝承付而暂时存放在购货方的商品和已办完加工成品收回手续而未提回的商品;(5)委托其他单位代销(未作销售或调出)尚未售出的商品;(6)代其他单位购进尚未交付的商品。不包括所有权不属于本单位的商品、拨付除批发零售贸易业以外的其他行业所属独立核算加工厂等加工生产尚未收回成品的商品、代国家物资储备部门保管的商品等。

库存总额采用的计算价格是:农副产品采购单位按购进价计算;批发单位按进货价计算;零售单位按核算价格计算,即按什么价格核算就按什么价格计算。

住宿餐饮业营业额 指住宿和餐饮业法人企业、产业活动单位在经营活动中因提供服务或销售商品等取得的收入,包括客房收入、餐费收入、商品销售收入和其他收入。客房收入指住宿和餐饮业法人企业、产业活动单位在经营活动中因提供住宿服务取得的客房收入。餐费收入指住宿和餐饮业法人企业、产业活动单位因为顾客提供就餐服务取得的收入,包括经烹饪、调制加工后出售的各种食品,如主食、炒菜、凉拌菜等的收入。商品销售收入指住宿和餐饮业法人企业、产业活动单位伴随服务而出售商品所取得的收入。其他收入指营业收入中除客房收入、餐费收入、商品销售收入以外的其他收入,包括娱乐、健身和商务服务等。

亿元商品交易市场成交额 指年成交额达到亿元以上,经工商部门批准、专门从事商品批发、零售业务活动的市场。其市场所有摊位成交总额称为商品交易市场成交额。

连锁企业(或称连锁店、连锁公司) 指在核心企业或总店的领导下,由分散的、经营同类商品或服务的企业或活动单位,采取共同方针,实行集中采购和分散销售的有机结合,通过规范化经营,实现规模效益的经济联合组织形式。一般连锁店应由若干个分店组成。其经营特征:(1)经营同类商品;(2)使用统一商号;(3)统一采购配送,采购与销售相分离(部分商品可根据物流合理和保质保鲜原则,由供应商直接送货到门店,其余均由总部统一配送)。

连锁门店包括下列三种形式:

直营连锁:也叫正规连锁。连锁门店均由总部独资或控股开设,在总部的直接领导下统一经营。总部采取纵深似的管理方式,直接下令掌管所有的零售门店,零售门店也必须完全接受总部指挥。他是大型垄断商业资本通过吞并、兼并或独资、控股等途径,发展壮大自身实力和规模的一种形式。

特许连锁:各连锁门店(被特许人)通过合同形式,取得使用总部(特许人)商标、商号、经营技术和销售总部开发的商品的特许权,各加盟连锁门店为独立法人,在总部指导下统一经营。

自由连锁:也称自愿连锁。连锁公司的门店均为独立法人,各自的资产所有权关系不变,在公司总部的指导下共同经营。各成员店使用共同的店名,与总部订阅有关购、销、宣传等方面的合同,并按合同开展经营活动。在合同规定的范围之外,各成员店可以自由活动。根据自愿原则,各成员店可自由加入连锁体系,也可自由退出。

特许连锁加上自由连锁等于加盟连锁。

Explanatory Notes on Main Statistical Indicators

Total Retail Sales of Consumer Goods refer to the sum of retail sales of commodities sold by wholesale, retail, catering, publishing, post and telecommunications and other service industries to urban and rural households for private consumption and to social institutions for public consumption. Retail sales of consumer goods include:

1) Sales by wholesale and retail units:

a) of consumer goods sold to urban and rural households

b) of commodities sold to foreigners, overseas Chinese and Chinese compatriots from Hong Kong, Macao and Taiwan visiting in China

c)of commodities sold to government agencies, institutions, social organizations, military and armed police units, and commodities sold to enterprises in the form of retail sales. More specifically, they include: office facilities and articles for non-production purposes such as communications equipment, computing equipment and instruments, TV and network equipment, printing and copying equipment, audio–visual equipment and instruments, paper, notebooks, stationeries, furniture, electric appliances, knitwear, sanitation and cleaning articles, cultural and sport articles, articles for prizes, souvenirs, etc.; transport vehicles and fuels for employees; materials, spare parts and tools for the maintenance of office facilities; equipment, fuels, materials and food for winter heating or summer cooling purposes; articles and equipment for teaching purpose; Chinese and western medicines and medical equipment and facilities purchased by non profit–making medical institutes; non–specialized work safety articles; cooking utensils, tableware, equipment, cleaning articles, food and fuels purchased by internal cafeterias; clothes and personal articles purchased by military or armed police units for their officials and soldiers; and other equipment and articles for non–production purposes.

2) Sales of stable food, cooked dishes, beverages, tobaccos and other articles by catering units.

3) Sales of books, newspapers, magazines, audio–visual products and post products by publishing, post and telecommunications departments to urban and rural households and to enterprises, institutions, military and armed police units.

4) Sales of food, beverages, tobaccos, clothing, hats, footwear, articles for daily use, medicines, medical and health articles, work of art, handicrafts, toys, funeral articles and other articles by other service industries.

Purchase, Sales and Stock of Commodities by Wholesale and Retail Trades refer to the total volume of commodities purchased, total volume of sales and exports, and the stock of commodities by wholesale and retail enterprises (establishments) of different status of registration from domestic and overseas markets. This indictor reflects the relationship among purchase, sales and stock of commodities in the circulation of goods and reveals the existing problems.

Total Purchases of Commodities refer to the total value of purchases of commodities by the enterprises (establishments) from other establishments or individuals (including direct import from abroad) for the purpose of re–selling, either with or without further processing of the commodities purchased. This indicator is used to show the total value of purchases of commodities by wholesale and retail establishments from domestic and overseas markets. The total purchases include: (1) agricultural and industrial products purchased from producers; (2) books, magazines and newspapers purchased from distribution departments of the publishers; (3) commodities purchased from wholesale and retail establishments of different status of registration; (4) commodities purchased from other units, such as surplus materials purchased from government agencies, enterprises or institutions, commodities purchased from catering and service establishments, confiscated goods purchased from customs authorities or market management agencies, second–hand goods and wastes purchased from residents; and (5) commodities directly imported from abroad. Excluded are commodities purchased by enterprises (establishments) for use in their own business operation, commodities obtained without buying or selling procedures, rejected commodities, etc.

Total Sales of Commodities refer to value of commodities sold by the establishments to other establishments and individuals (including direct export). This indicator is used to show the total value of sales of commodities at domestic markets and export. The total sales include: (1) commodities sold to urban and rural residents and social groups for their consumption; (2) commodities sold to establishments in industry, agriculture, construction, transportation, post and telecommunications, wholesale and retail trades, catering trade and public utility for their production and operation; (3) commodities sold to wholesale and retail establishments for re selling, with or without further processing; and (4)commodities for direct export to other countries. Excluded are selling of waste packaging materials used by the establishments (units) themselves, commodities transferred without buying or selling procedures, commission income from brokerage in transactions whose settlement is directly handled by buyers and sellers, rejected commodities in the purchase, loss in commodities, etc.

Commodity Stock of Wholesale and Retail Enterprises refers to total commodities possessed by wholesale and retail enterprises (units) of various types of registration status at the end of the reference period, which reflects the commodity stock level of various wholesale and retail enterprises and the potential for market supply. It includes: (1) commodities located in storage, garages, counters, and shelves of operating units (such as sale stores, wholesale centers, and operating offices) of wholesale and retail enterprises; (2) commodities in the process of selecting, sorting, and packing; (3) commodities not arrived but recorded as purchase in the account, i.e. commodities not arrived but payment receipts for the commodities from the sellers or the banks arrived; (4) commodities deposited in other places rather than places mentioned above, for instance: commodities in the hold of purchasers temporarily due to the refusal of payment and commodities not taken back after going through the formalities; (5) commodities entrusted to other units to sell but not sold yet; (6) commodities purchased for other units but not delivered yet. Commodities not included as stock are those not owned by the enterprises (units), those allocated to financially independent factories rather than wholesale and retail enterprises for processing but not taken back yet, and finally those put in stock by wholesale and retail enterprises on behalf of the state material reserves units.

For the calculation of the value of commodities stock, the value is calculated at purchasing prices in agricultural goods purchasing units and wholesale units, and at the accounting prices in retail units.

Business Revenue of Hotels and Catering Services refer to revenue received from providing services or selling commodities by corporate enterprises and establishments engaged in hotel and catering services, including income from hotel rooms, from catering services, from selling of commodities and from other services. Income from hotel rooms refers to income of corporate enterprises and establishments by providing lodging services. Income from catering services refers to income of corporate enterprises and establishments by providing catering services, including selling of cooked or prepared foods such as stable food, cooked dishes or cold dishes. Income from selling of commodities refers to income of corporate enterprises and establishments by selling commodities that accompany the services they provide. Income from other activities refers to income received other than income from hotel rooms, catering services or selling of commodities, such as income from providing recreation, fitness or business services.

Volume of Transaction at Large Commodity Markets (with transaction value over 100 million yuan) refers to markets approved by the industrial and commercial administration departments, which specialize in wholesale and retail of commodities with an annual transaction of over 100 million yuan. The sum of sales of all sellers in the markets makes up the transaction value of the markets.

Chain Enterprises (also called chain stores or chain corporations) refer to a form of joint economic entities under which scattered enterprises or establishments engaged in providing homogeneous commodities or services, with the central leadership of core enterprise or headquarters and guided by common policies, conduct centralized purchase and distributed selling of commodities, in order to gain better efficiency through standardized operation. Consisting of a number of branch stores, the chain stores have in general following features: 1) homogeneous commodities, 2) unique name of stores, 3) centralized purchase and delivery which is separated from distributed selling operation (most commodities are delivered from the headquarters except some items which, from logistics, quality or freshness considerations, might be delivered by the suppliers directly).

Chain stores have 3 categories:

a) Chain stores under direct management: These are formal chain stores invested or controlled by the headquarters. They operate under the direct and unified management from the headquarters. Adopting a direct management approach, the headquarters give orders and control all retail stores, which follow completely the directives from the headquarters. Large monopolized commercial companies develop and expand their business through purchasing, merging, direct investment and controlling of shares.

b) Chain stores through special permit: Through contracts, chain stores (or their owners) obtain licenses from the headquarters to use designated trade marks, names, operation know-how, and to sell the commodity developed by the headquarters. Under this arrangement, each store in the chain is an independent legal entity and operates under the guidance from the headquarters.

c) Chain stores through voluntary arrangement: Under this arrangement, all stores operate together under the guidance of the headquarters, while maintaining their status of independent legal entities with full ownership of their assets. They use the same store name, sign contracts with the headquarters concerning purchase, sale, publicity, etc. and operate under the contract. They are free to engage in other activities which are not bounded in the contract. They could join or leave the chain on voluntary basis.

Chain stores through special permit and those through voluntary arrangement make up chain stores through license arrangement.

17 科技和教育

Science, Technology and Education

17-1 科技活动基本情况
BASIC STATISTICS ON PERSONEL ENGAGED IN SCIENTIFIC AND TECHNICAL ACTIVITIES

项　目	Item	2010	2012	2013	2014	2015	2016
科技活动人员 (人)	Personels Engaged in Scientific and Technical Activities (person)	282604	339786	365502	388430	378828	393333
R&D人员 (人)	R & D Personels	142683	185703	205172	218094	220977	218322
R&D经费内部支出 (万元)	Inner Expenditures of R & D Funds (10 000 yuan)	2637885	3845239	4462690	5108973	5617415	6000422
基础研究	Basic Research	102494	203953	218994	186200	230593	258642
应用研究	Practical Research	472497	561485	679021	691267	705635	738875
实验发展	Experiment Development	2062893	3079800	3564675	4231507	4681187	5002905

17-2 科技活动项目、成果与机构情况
BASIC STATISTICS ON SCIENTIFIC AND TECHNICAL PROJECTS, ACHIEVEMENT AND INSTITUTIONS

项　目	Item	2012	2013	2014	2015	2016
发表科技论文 (篇)	Scientific Research Papers Published (piece)	89714	90209	93590	93190	92176
出版科技专著数 (种)	Scientific and Techincal Books Published (kind)	2672	2618	2900	2827	3014
科技项目(课题)数 (个)	Number of Scientific Projects (unit)	48669	53088	55777	56218	58613
科技项目经费支出 (万元)	Expenses for Scientific Projects (10 000 yuan)	3208902	3433884	3768678	4504527	4930193
科学研究与开发机构数 (个)	Number of Scientific Research Institutions and Development Organizations (unit)	1744	1946	2002	2245	2158
科研机构R&D人员数 (人)	R & D Staff (person)	67997	74696	68151	75338	69351
科研机构R&D内部支出(万元)	Inner Expenditures of R & D Funds (10 000 yuan)	1464692	1938710	1901466	2111784	2014238
科研机构年末仪器设备资产原价 (万元)	Original Price of Fixed Assets of Scientific Research Institutions and Organizations at Year-end (10 000 yuan)	2293613	2553205	2591182	2635298	2793709

17-3 政府部门所属科学研究与开发机构科技活动情况
BASIC STATISTICS ON STATE-OWNED RESAEARCH AND DEVELOPMENT INSTITUTIONS

项　目	Item	机构(个) Number of Institu-tions (unit)	科技活动人员(人) Persons Engaged (person)	大学本科及以上学历 Bachelor's Degrees and Above	#R&D人员 Research and Development Persons	收费收入(万元) Revenue (10 000 yuan)	#政府拨款 Government Appropriations
2014年总计	**Total of 2013**	256	9938	7159	7077	458906	281806
一、自然科学和技术领域	Natural Science and Technology	239	9038	6423	6650	433627	259948
县级政府部门属	Department of County	134	1151	234	175	14631	5443
市、州级政府部门属	Department of Cities and Prefecture	59	1617	938	717	36475	19505
省政府部门属	Department of Province	51	3800	3029	1917	171818	103203
国务院部门属	Department of State Council	12	3370	2958	4268	235982	172074
#中科院武汉分院属	#Chinese Academy of Science Wuhan Branch	6	1889	1690	3566	123589	97124
二、社会、人文科学领域	Sosiety and Humanity	7	325	274	208	10785	10601
2015年总计	**Total of 2014**	239	9298	6975	6869	528259	345156
一、自然科学和技术领域	Natural Science and Technology	223	8521	6334	6520	502541	322521
县级政府部门属	Department of County	121	988	208	95	16001	5436
市、州级政府部门属	Department of Cities and Prefecture	51	1465	870	602	37344	19126
省政府部门属	Department of Province	39	2824	2316	1420	166296	93879
国务院部门属	Department of State Council	12	3244	2940	4403	282899	204078
#中科院武汉分院属	#Chinese Academy of Science Wuhan Branch	6	1714	1559	3528	138456	111859
二、社会、人文科学领域	Sosiety and Humanity	7	312	255	182	11143	10794
2016年总计	**Total of 2015**	212	8630	6604	6878	554772	369793
一、自然科学和技术领域	Natural Science and Technology	195	7721	5838	6419	521150	340391
县级政府部门属	Department of County	105	827	191	88	15643	5922
市、州级政府部门属	Department of Cities and Prefecture	45	1299	832	552	40567	25706
省政府部门属	Department of Province	33	2367	1963	1305	165422	87741
国务院部门属	Department of State Council	12	3228	2852	4474	299517	221021
#中科院武汉分院属	#Chinese Academy of Science Wuhan Branch	6	1660	1532	3456	143244	123345
二、社会、人文科学领域	Sosiety and Humanity	8	349	275	256	14476	14284

17-3 续表 continued

项　目	Item	经费支出(万元) Expenditures (10 000 yuan)	#科技经费支出 Expenditure on Science & Technology	#R&D经费内部支出 Inner Expenditure of R & D	研究课题数(个) Number of Projects	课题经费投入(万元) Investment on Subject Study (10 000 Yuan)	参加课题组(人年) Number of Persons Engaged in Subjects Study (person/year)
2014年总计	**Total of 2013**	434547	326067	182264	3884	150800	7044
一、自然科学和技术领域	Natural Science and Technology	412198	308486	174852	3817	149140	6631
县级政府部门属	Department of County	14947	7729	398	37	567	190
市、州级政府部门属	Department of Cities and Prefecture	32101	25007	7001	259	7125	702
省政府部门属	Department of Province	152770	92057	38017	881	22993	2124
国务院部门属	Department of State Council	234729	201272	136847	2707	120113	4028
#中科院武汉分院属	#Chinese Academy of Science Wuhan Branch	122286	104885	101373	1642	73891	2833
二、社会、人文科学领域	Sosiety and Humanity	10496	7896	4708	20	413	140
2015年总计	**Total of 2014**	516130	394399	208946	4011	179430	6743
一、自然科学和技术领域	Natural Science and Technology	492199	375146	201072	3931	177450	6444
县级政府部门属	Department of County	15238	7978	468	37	647	120
市、州级政府部门属	Department of Cities and Prefecture	31269	23787	7202	222	4741	589
省政府部门属	Department of Province	153526	92416	35275	813	30200	1675
国务院部门属	Department of State Council	292165	250964	158126	2859	141862	4060
#中科院武汉分院属	#Chinese Academy of Science Wuhan Branch	146046	128094	121098	1790	86273	2796
二、社会、人文科学领域	Sosiety and Humanity	11582	9118	6045	17	527	75
2016年总计	**Total of 2015**	511288	393131	226536	4411	209941	6055
一、自然科学和技术领域	Natural Science and Technology	482874	372076	216617	4249	204030	5615
县级政府部门属	Department of County	16483	6198	393	30	610	97
市、州级政府部门属	Department of Cities and Prefecture	37568	24841	6714	220	5232	544
省政府部门属	Department of Province	141800	89492	31381	912	27974	1321
国务院部门属	Department of State Council	287022	251543	178129	3087	170212	3653
#中科院武汉分院属	#Chinese Academy of Science Wuhan Branch	133984	118371	113700	1930	87436	2228
二、社会、人文科学领域	Sosiety and Humanity	13195	9722	6880	74	4379	249

注：1.本表数据没有包括科技情报文献机构数据，但包括了县政府所属科技综合服务机构数。
2.科技部门的课题数包括生产性活动课题。

Notes:a)The data of intelligence literature is not included in this table.
b)The number of projects in science and technology department includes projects of production activities.

17-4 科学情报文献机构情况
STATISTICS ON SCIENTIFIC INTELLIGENCE LITERATURE ORGANIZATIONS

项 目	Item	2000	2005	2010	2012	2013	2014	2015	2016
机构 (个)	Institutions (unit)	14	12	11	11	11	10	9	9
职工总数 (人)	Total Number of Employees (person)	564	546	553	596	610	592	513	586
从事科技活动人员	Persons engaged in Scientific Activities	511	456	512	554	573	575	465	560
#大学本科及以上学历	#Bachelor's degrees and Above	337	306	347	422	455	462	386	491
经费收入总额 (万元)	Funds (10 000 yuan)	2629	6677	8706	11650	15472	14493	14573	19145
#政府拨款	#Government Appropriations	1679	5210	6009	8476	12131	12515	11840	15117
经费支出总额 (万元)	Expendtitures (10 000 yuan)	2340	6778	7955	10460	13584	11852	12348	15158
#劳务费	#Service Charge	970	1179	2668	4038	4105	4328	4210	6228

17-5 高等院校科技活动情况
BASIC STATISTICS ON SCIENTIFIC AND TECHNICAL ACTIVITIES OF INSTITUTIONS OF HIGHER EDUCATION

项 目	Item	2015			2016		
		合计 Total	自然科学和技术领域 Natural Science and Technology	社会、人文科学领域 Sosiety and Humanity	合计 Total	自然科学和技术领域 Natural Science and Technology	社会、人文科学领域 Sosiety and Humanity
科学研究与开发机构数 (个)	Institutions of Research and Development (unit)	594	405	189		478	217
科技活动人员数 (人)	Number of Personels in Scientific and Technical Activities (person)	77421	50173	27248		55984	28978
研究与发展经费内部支出 （万元）	Inner Expenditures of Research and Development (10 000 yuan)	545156	472507	72649		411606	69567
研究课题数 (个)	Number of Research Projects (unit)	42709	24050	18659		30469	19783
项目(课题)经费投入 (万元)	Funds Invested in Research Projects (10 000 yuan)	443381	388583	54799		646310	54788
项目(课题)参加人员折合全时当量 (人年)	Number of Persons Engaged in Projects (person-year)	15275	10711	4565		12912	4391

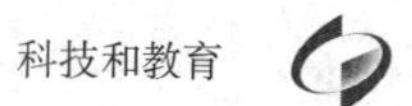

17-6 大中型工业企业科技活动情况
STATISTICS ON RESEARCH AND DEVELOPMENT ACTIVITIES OF LAREGE AND MEDIUM-SIZED INDUSTRIAL ENTERPRISES

单位:万元 (10 000 yuan)

项　目	Item	2010	2012	2013	2014	2015	2016
大中型企业个数 (个)	Large and Medium Enterprises (unit)	1421	2022	2274	2277	2204	2175
有R&D活动的企业数 (个)	Number of Enterprises with Scientific Activities (unit)	559	478	584	633	717	776
从事科技活动人员数 (人)	Number of Persons Engaged in Scientific Activities (person)	120581	155116	157520	170579	163587	167797
研究与发展人员数 (人)	Persons Engaged in Research and Development (person)	64329	93825	99563	107656	105848	105525
企业办研发机构数 (个)	Number of Research and Development Organizations Opened by Enterprises (unit)	457	454	478	432	534	479
R&D项目数 (个)	Number of R&D Projects (unit)	4602	5668	6095	6400	4954	5554
全部R&D项目经费支出 (万元)	Expenses for Development Projects (10 000 yuan)	1193793	1978154	1892653	2172256	2627715	2786500
研究与发展经费支出 (万元)	Expenditures for Research and Development (10 000 yuan)	1429050	2287148	2521324	2978369	3272348	3347523
新产品开发费支出 (万元)	Expenditures for Developing New Products (10 000 yuan)	1760964	2488079	2606672	2896732	2856350	3056850
技术改造经费支出 (万元)	Expenditures for Technical Innovation (10 000 yuan)	1326521	921059	883841	916673	835034	487186
技术引进经费支出 (万元)	Expenditures for Technology Introduction (10 000 yuan)	190418	153336	121278	128533	147979	141254
消化吸收经费支出 (万元)	Expenditures for Technology Utilization (10 000 yuan)	29408	42406	39464	38330	16046	15780
购买国内技术经费支出 (万元)	Expenditures for Purchasing Domestic Technology (10 000 yuan)	21561	38037	72594	53481	50314	23891

17-7 有研发活动的规模以上工业企业主要分组指标

指 标	Item	有R&D活动企业(个) Number of Enterprises with R & D Activities (unit)	
		2015	2016
总 计	**Total**	**2421**	**2979**
一、按登记注册类型分	**Grouped by Type of Registration**		
内资企业	Domestic-funded Enterprises	2245	2786
国有企业	State-owned Enterprises	34	31
集体企业	Collective-owned Enterprises	3	4
股份合作企业	Cooperative Enterprises	2	3
联营企业	Associated Enterprises		
有限责任公司	Limited Liability Companies	959	1138
股份有限公司	Share Holding Co., Ltd	244	297
私营企业	Private Enterprises	995	1310
其他企业	Others	8	3
港、澳、台商投资企业	Hongkong, Maco and Taiwan-invested Enterprises	71	80
合资经营企业(港或澳、台资)	Joint Ventures (Hongkong, Maco or Taiwan Invested Enterprises)	46	80
合作经营企业(港或澳、台资)	Cooperative Ventures(Hongkong, Maco or Taiwan Invested Enterprises)		45
港、澳、台商独资经营企业	Enterprises Solely Funded by hongkong, Maco and Taiwan Businessmen	23	33
港、澳、台商投资股份有限公司	Hongkong, Maco and Taiwan Funded Share Holding Co.Ltd.	2	2
其他港澳台投资企业	Other Hongkong, Maco and Taiwan Funded Share Holding Co., Ltd.		
外商投资企业	Foreign-invested Enterprises	105	113
中外合资经营企业	Sino-Foreign Joint Ventures	78	84
中外合作经营企业	Sino-Foreign Contractual Joint Ventures		
外资企业	Foreign Funded Enterprises	25	25
外商投资股份有限公司	Foreign Funded Share Holding Co., Ltd.	1	1
其他外商投资企业	Other Enterprises Invested by Foreign Businessmen	1	1
二、按行业分	**Grouped by Sector**		
煤炭开采和洗选业	Coal Mining and Processing		
石油和天然气开采业	Petroleum and Natural Gas Extraction	1	1
黑色金属矿采选业	Ferrous Metals Mining and Processing	8	4
有色金属矿采选业	Non-ferrous Metals Mining and Processing	1	2
非金属矿采选业	Non-metal Minerals Mining and Processing	18	21
开采辅助活动	Mining Auxiliary	1	1
其他采矿业	Other Mining	1	1
农副食品加工业	Primary Products and Food Processing Industry	176	224

MAJOR INDIENTORS OF INDUSTRIAL ABOVE DESIGNATED ENTERPRISES WITH RESEARCH AND DEVELOPMENT ACTIVITIES

有研发机构的企业(个) Number of Enterprises with R&D Activities (unit)		R&D人员合计(人) R & D Personels (person)		R&D经费支出(万元) Funding for R & D Expenditure (10 000 yuan)		新产品开发经费支出(万元) Funding for New Product Development Expenditures (10 000 yuan)		新产品销售收入(万元) Revenue of New Product Sales (10 000 yuan)	
2015	2016	2015	2016	2015	2016	2015	2016	2015	2016
1117	**1004**	**140381**	**149571**	**4072726**	**4459622**	**3644392**	**4076507**	**56769152**	**67132019**
1053	945	122395	133428	3402384	3808749	2981211	3420562	42560779	58159499
25	21	13742	10320	578624	386718	538530	467952	2911532	2990210
1	1	22	21	755	1099	1484	671	22932	3097
1		65	125	543	783	543	544	7900	4266
408	368	52169	58937	1400940	1705297	1203691	1477586	18584506	24589188
121	117	30775	31065	765757	831024	687647	766868	8815980	13917271
493	436	25357	32905	651899	881449	546398	705574	12156747	16625628
4	2	265	55	3865	2381	2919	1367	61182	29839
30	24	6144	5842	168996	199664	153932	3480648	3021361	3433294
25	18	4255	3403	126127	125945	114544	2597564	2352167	2587194
3	5	1722	2340	38236	71377	33572	856262	599932	815097
2	1	167	99	4633	2342	5817	26822	69262	31003
34	35	11842	10301	501346	451209	509249	10123355	11187013	9938693
20	24	8913	7677	415986	376346	456036	9088666	10399606	8910826
1	1		8		704		62968	150	52969
11	9	1683	1675	48517	42570	50827	792369	483345	813075
1	1	1222	917	36632	31302	2387	174925	300648	157398
1		24	24	211	286		4426	3264	4426
1	4	609	797	1774	2082	134	22610	21821	22461
1	1	92	62	4020	5072	1387	240211		240211
1		31	322	165	1053				1702
6	2	263	322	8846	1871	411	75479	48182	75494
	6	58	270	914	9173	432	66201		65096
		15	82	157	2000	96			
96		4880		127561	628	112248		4490255	5535063

17-7 续表 continued

指　标	Item	有R&D活动企业(个) Number of Enterprises with R & D Activities (unit)	
		2015	2016
食品制造业	Food Production	51	72
酒、饮料和精制茶制造业	Beverage Production	73	101
烟草制品业	Tabacco Processing	2	3
纺织业	Textile Industry	64	67
纺织服装、服饰业	Textile Wearing Apparel and Accessaries	9	17
皮革、毛皮、羽毛及其制品和制鞋业	Leather, Fur, Feather and Related Products		6
木材加工及木、竹、藤、棕、草制品业	Timber Processing and Wood, Bamboo, Rattan, Palm and Sraw Products	30	31
家具制造业	Furniture Manufacturing	8	9
造纸及纸制品业	Papermaking and Paper Products	15	30
印刷和记录媒介复制业	Printing and Record Processing	23	33
文教、工美、体育和娱乐用品制造业	Stationery, Education, Art, Sport and Entertainment Products	12	21
石油加工、炼焦及核燃料加工业	Petroleum Processing, Coking Products and Nuclear Fuel Processing	11	12
化学原料及化学制品制造业	Raw Chemical Material and Chemical Products	258	318
医药制造业	Medical and pharmaceutical Products	162	183
化学纤维制造业	Chemical Fibers	6	7
橡胶和塑料制品业	Rubber Products and Plastic Products	67	105
非金属矿物制品业	Nonmetal Material Products	143	207
黑色金属冶炼及压延加工业	Smelting and Processing of ferrous Metals	30	35
有色金属冶炼及压延加工业	Smelting and Processing of Nonferrous Metals	34	34
金属制品业	Metal Products	110	137
通用设备械制造业	Ordinaryly Machinery Manufacturing	197	197
专用设备制造业	Special Purpose Equipment Manufacturing	177	205
汽车制造业	Automobile Manufacturing	279	333
铁路、船舶、航空航天和其他运输设备制造业	Realway, Ship, Aircraft and Other Transport Equipment Manufacturing	41	47
电气机械及器材制造业	Electric Machinery and Equipment	200	249
通信设备、计算机及其他电子设备制造业	Telecommunication Equipment, Computer and Other Electronic Equipment Manufacturing	134	151
			64
仪器仪表及文化办公用机械制造业	Instruments, Meters, Cultural and Official Machinery	44	15
其他制造业	Other Manufacturing	13	11
废弃资源和废旧材料回收加工业	Waste Resources and Junk Material Recycled	5	6
金属制品、机械和设备修理业	Repairing of Metal and Mechanical Equipment	5	6
电力、热力的生产和供应业	Electric Power, Steam and Hot Water Production and Supply	10	11
煤气生产和供应业	Gas Production and Supply	2	2
水的生产和供应业	Tap Water Production and Supply		2

有研发机构的企业(个) Number of Enterprises with R & D Units (unit)		R&D人员合计(人) R & D Personels (person)		R&D经费支出(万元) Funding for R & D Expenditure (10 000 yuan)		新产品开发经费支出(万元) Funding for New Product Development Expenditures (10 000 yuan)		新产品销售收入(万元) Revenue of New Product Sales (10 000 yuan)	
2015	2016	2015	2016	2015	2016	2015	2016	2015	2016
31		1613		91012		68203		772453	1469547
39		2044		66964		67514		534672	919422
1		206		8265		8157		3428	52616
39		3846		63640		65454		980762	1213914
9		696		10077		14740		168437	319769
						62			48969
12		927		18096		16772		332304	476954
4		59		830		2286		30192	51560
8		517		12786		12412		147730	185127
7		966		16577		17251		215473	269319
6		310		4814		6043		117043	95084
4		335		32714		1672		300061	1772821
129		16134		499146		266100		7652936	9332073
90		10110		189298		173693		2959834	3033463
1		714		7260		7065		78483	187228
41		3270		65357		61456		1295079	1827522
61		5101		125921		77764		1513837	2050236
17		6167		373812		311726		2692026	3537280
16		2952		172691		56809		2911164	3276981
62		4650		86762		97357		1412768	1650295
80		7907		146689		128104		2628373	2815002
57		6481		130212		128896		1511909	1665237
119		19360		703213		798084		13303183	13933735
23		9687		137081		151609		1622180	1829648
73		11437		286513		291517		4652699	4771646
49		15109		588490		621370		3295873	3065770
19		1584		34613		45209		397371	392991
8		1020		21236		18700		280256	364056
3		114		2135		364		213484	311150
1		255		5707		3565		15849	19377
2		538		18406		9735		84725	128961
1		324		8973.0				84312.0	121451
									2791

17-8 全省高新技术产业发展情况(2016)
STATISTICS ON NEW AND HIGH TECHNIC INDUSTRY DEVELOPMENT IN THE WHOLE PROVINCE(2016)

单位:亿元 (100 million yuan)

项目	Item	全省 the Whole Province	增幅(%) Increase(%)
"四上"高新技术产业增加值	Four Up Added Value of High-tech Industry	5488.29	13.9
其中:高新服务业增加值	Added Value of High-tech Service	726.67	22.6
高新制造业增加值	Added Value of High-tech Manufacturing	4761.62	13.0
1.电子信息	1.Electronic Information	551.48	15.6
2.先进制造	2.Advanced Manufacturing	1853.92	11.4
3.新材料	3.New Material	1015.93	13.4
4.生物医药与医疗机械	4.Bio-medicine and Medical Instrument	433.66	13.6
高新制造业产值*	Output Value of High-tech Manufacturing	20250.39	11.5
高新制造业产品出口交货值*	Export Value of High-tech Manufacturing	1413.96	21.9
高新制造业产品销售收入*	Revenue of High-tech Manufacturing	18443.58	13.1
高新制造业利税总额*	Tax on High-tech Manufacturing	1559.58	14.4
"四下"高新技术产业增加值	Four Up Added Value of High-tech Industry	86.25	5.0

注:带"*"号的指标口径为规模以上工业企业。
Note:Data with "*" cover industrial enterprises above designated size(the same below).

17–9 市州高新技术产业发展情况(2016)

STATISTICS ON THE DEVELOPMENT OF HIGH AND NEW TECHNOLOGY INDUSTRIE OF CITIES AND PREFECTURE (2016)

单位:亿元

(100 million yuan)

地 区	Region	增加值 Value Added	增加值* Value Added	增速* Increase(%)
全省合计	**Total of the Province**	**5574.54**	**5488.29**	**13.9**
武 汉 市	Wuhan	2423.18	2348.69	12.4
黄 石 市	Huangshi	156.57	155.94	8.7
十 堰 市	Shiyan	187.14	181.06	17.3
宜 昌 市	Yichang	666.24	664.59	17.0
襄 阳 市	Xiangyang	924.50	922.90	14.3
鄂 州 市	Ezhou	130.14	130.09	12.3
荆 门 市	Jingmen	195.00	194.77	15.1
孝 感 市	Xiaogan	198.80	198.58	13.9
荆 州 市	Jingzhou	162.75	162.63	11.3
黄 冈 市	Huanggang	156.81	156.21	13.4
咸 宁 市	Xianning	98.58	98.35	9.9
随 州 市	Suizhou	94.58	94.56	14.7
恩 施 州	Enshi	10.30	10.17	11.6
仙 桃 市	Xiantao	66.22	66.17	13.4
潜 江 市	Qianjiang	57.93	57.93	61.9
天 门 市	Tianmen	45.74	45.66	17.8
神农架林区	Shennongjia	0.06		

注:带"*"号的指标口径为规模以上工业企业。
Note:Data with "*" cover industrial enterprises above designated size(the same below).

17-10 申报登记省、部级以上成果分类及经济效益
CLASSIFICATION AND ECONOMIC BENEFITS OF SCIENTIFIC ACHIEVEMENTS APPLIED AND REGISTERED ABOVE PROVINCIAL AND MINISTRIAL LEVEL

单位:项 (unit)

项　目	Item	2000	2005	2010	2012	2013	2014	2015	2016
成果总类	**Total Calsses of Achievement**	**571**	**717**	**750**	**1567**	**1621**	**1778**	**1933**	**2022**
一、按成果水平分类	Grouped by Level								
国际首创/领先	International Innovation/ Leading	19	28	52	101	81	100	130	166
国际先进	Internationl Advanced Technology	97	172	195	254	326	353	373	324
国内首创/领先	Domestic Innovation/ Leading	276	394	362	745	751	706	743	685
国内先进	Domestic Advanced Technology	84	72	69	176	177	270	413	299
其它	Others	18	3	39	14	31	299	216	500
二、按成果类型分类	Grouped by Type								
基础理论研究	Basic Theory Research	37	15	15	24	22	13	16	17
应用开发研究	Applicable Development	494	669	717	1507	1570	1728	1875	1974
其它	Others	40	33	18	36	29	37	42	31
三、按成果产业属性分类	Grouped by Sector Property								
工业类成果	Industrial Achievements	145	225	226	532	514	560	693	579
农业类成果	Agricultural Achievements	79	129	124	197	251	371	320	334
医学类成果	Medical Achievements	199	291	231	414	441	446	394	467
其他类成果	Others	148	74	169	424	415	401	526	642
四、按成果完成单位分类	Grouped by Units								
高等院校完成	Institutions of Higher Education	149	169	137	160	246	271	198	283
研究单位完成	Scientific Research Institutions	92	92	64	86	74	116	99	122
厂矿企业完成	Industrial and Mineral Enterprises	137	176	303	1136	911	966	1233	1206
其他单位完成	Others	193	280	246	185	390	425	403	411
五、经济效益　(亿元)	Economic Benefits　(100 million yuan)								
总收入	Total Income	78.33	199.50		1212.78	331.33	462.80	379.48	492.26
本年度节约资金	Capital Saved in This Year	6.33	28.28	36.85	401.37	56.38	551.61	23.19	77.65

17-11 科学技术协会组织与活动
ORGANIZATIONS AND ACTIVITIES OF SCIENTIFIC AND TECHNOLOGICAL ASSOCIATION

项 目	Item	2015	2016
一、机构与人员	**Organizations and Personels**		
1.省级学会 (个)	Provincal Institute (unit)	133	143
会员 (人)	Members (person)	153948	152621
高级(资深)会员 (人)	Senoir Members (person)	20349	18998
外国会员 (人)	Foreign Members (person)	5	6
2.市、州学会数 (个)	City and Prefecture Institute (unit)	673	544
3.省级科协 (个)	Provincal Scientific Assosiations (unit)	1	1
市、州科协 (个)	City and Prefecture Scientific Assosiations (unit)	13	13
县(区)科协 (个)	County (District) Scientific Assosiations (unit)	103	102
二、学术活动	**Academic Activities**		
省级学会及县以上科协	**Provincial Institutes and Scientific Assosiations above County level**		
国内学术会议 (次)	Domestic Academic Conference (time)	757	826
参加人数 (人次)	Number of Person Participated (person-time)	73001	82901
论文数 (篇)	Number of Scholary Paper (piece)	16866	13924
境内国际学术会议 (次)	Domestic International Academic Conference (time)	60	103
参加人数 (人次)	Number of Person Participated (person-time)	10792	13667
论文数 (篇)	Number of Scholary Paper (piece)	3925	2339
三、科普活动	**Science and Technology Popularization Activities**		
省级学会及县以上科协	**Provincial Institutes and Scientific Assosiations above County level**		
举办科普宣讲活动 (次)	Events of Science Popularization Lectures (time)	11471	12266
宣讲活动受众人数 (人次)	People Participated (person-time)	6945017	6138853
举办实用技术培训 (次)	Technical Training (time)	12058	8065
实用技术培训人数 (人次)	People Participated (person-time)	1887086	1430592
播放科技广播、影视节目 (分钟)	Scientific Radio and Video Programs (mimute)	439379	324990
参加活动科技人员 (人次)	People Participated (person-time)	154045	86366
四、青少年科技教育	**Education in Science and Technology for the Adolescents**		
省级学会及县以上科协	**Provincial Institutes and Scientific Assosiations above County level**		
举办青少年科技竞赛 (项)	Adolescent Technology Competition (unit)	473	460
参加人数 (人次)	Number of Person Participated (person-time)	1996254	1903876
获奖人数 (人次)	Number of Person Rewarded (person-time)	77884	53885
举办青少年科学营 (次)	Adolescent Technology Campus	268	83
参加人数 (人次)	Number of Person Participated (person-time)	20031	7216
举办青少年科技教育培训 (次)	Adolescent Technology Education Training	1101	88
培训人数 (人次)	Number of Person Participated (person-time)	614058	185142
五、科普基础设施建设	**Infrastructure Construction of Science Popularization**		
县以上科协	**Scientific Assosiations above County Level**		
科技场馆 (个)	Science and Technology Museum (unit)	68	65
建筑面积 (平方米)	Construction Area (square metre)	197956	221272
展厅面积 (平方米)	Exhibition Area (square metre)	81454	94888
全年参观人数 (人次)	Year-round Visitor (person-time)	2385092	3951424
科普活动站 (个)	Science Popularization Station (unit)	12003	11171
科普画廊建筑面积 (平方米)	Science Popularization Gallery Construction Area (square metre)	132060	128266
省级科普教育基地 (个)	Provincial Education Base of Science Popularization (unit)	145	153
农村科普示范基地 (个)	Rural Demonstration Base of Science Popularization (unit)	1547	1487
六、为科技工作者服务	**Serve for Scientists**		
省级学会及县以上科协	**Provincial Institutes and Scientific Assosiations above County level**		
反映科技工作者建议 (条)	Reported Suggestions of Scientists	1466	1122
其中:获上级领导批示的建议 (条)	Answered by Leaders	311	269
答复人大政协代表(委员)提案 (件)	Replied Proposal of NPC and CPPCC Representatives(Committees) (piece)	117	35
走访看望(慰问)科技工作者 (人次)	Visit Scientific Workers (person-time)	3757	
科学道德与学风建设宣讲活动 (场次)	Preach Ethics of Science	9	231
宣讲活动受众人数 (人次)	Number of Audience (person-time)	2262	41632
参加宣讲活动专家数 (人次)	Number of Specialists (person-time)	129	579
技术创新方法培训班 (场次)	Technology Innovation Training Class	114	149
继续教育培训班 (场次)	Continuing Education Class	118	204
培训结业人数 (人次)	Number of People Completed Courses (person-time)	28359	20762
宣传科技工作者人数 (人)	Propagating Scientific and Technology Workers (person)	6694	585
表彰奖励科技工作者 (人次)	Rewarded Scientific and Technology Workers (person-time)	3794	3880

17-12 专利受理量、批准量及分布状况
NUMBER OF PATENT APPLICATIONS EXAMINATION, APPROVAL AND DISTRITUTION

单位:项 (unit)

项目	Item	受理量 Number of Patent Applications Examined				批准量 Number of Patent Applications Approved			
		2005	2010	2015	2016	2005	2010	2015	2016
合计	**Total**	**11534**	**31311**	**74240**	**95157**	**3860**	**17362**	**38781**	**41822**
发明	Creations and Inventions	2038	7410	30204	43789	733	2025	7766	8517
实用新型	Utility Models	4835	12792	35676	42181	2238	10431	25298	27209
外观设计	Designs	4661	11109	8360	9187	889	4906	5717	6096
在合计中	**Of This Total**								
个人	Individual	7400	10844	18512	24182	2189	4990	8874	9136
大专院校	Universities and Colleges	1365	3265	11380	15487	574	1972	6468	7382
科研单位	Insitutions of Scientific Research	182	1112	1756	2453	101	532	799	922
工矿企业	Industrial and Mineral Enterprises	2305	15856	36702	48420	901	9744	22193	23864
机关团体	Government Agencies and Organizations	283	234	5889	4615	98	124	447	518

17-13 按市州分三种专利申请与授权状况(2016)
THREE KINDS OF PATENT APPICATION AND AUTHORIZATION BY MUNICIPALITIES AND PREFECTURES(2016)

单位:项 (item)

市、州	Municipalities and Prefecture	申请 当年累计 Patent Application Total of year	发明 Invention	实用新型 New type of practicial Utility	外观设计 Design	授权 当年累计 Authorization Total of year	发明 Invention	实用新型 New type of practicial Utility	外观设计 Design
全省合计	**Total of the Province**	**95157**	**43789**	**42181**	**9187**	**41822**	**8517**	**27209**	**6096**
武汉	Wuhan	44690	20611	20443	3636	22925	6512	13962	2451
黄石	Huangshi	3566	1575	3304	497	3667	522	2820	325
十堰	Shiyan	3521	1361	4777	420	2638	286	1995	357
荆州	Jingzhou	9874	4677	1477	514	1770	243	1122	405
宜昌	Yichang	8829	5028	1969	599	1912	189	1229	494
襄阳	Xiangfan	1553	765	1932	228	1436	111	1164	161
鄂州	Ezhou	2867	1227	1609	662	1403	156	863	384
荆门	Jingmen	4299	1731	1639	547	1311	116	972	223
孝感	Xiaogan	3406	1135	1359	281	1116	57	807	252
黄冈	Huanggang	3749	1563	1207	454	1156	97	854	205
咸宁	Xianning	2465	804	551	306	700	34	419	247
随州	Suizhou	1602	745	393	395	483	57	187	239
恩施州	Enshi	1258	497	619	111	421	47	304	70
仙桃	Xiantao	1445	715	426	335	231	19	160	52
潜江	Qianjiang	972	640	265	67	423	46	268	109
天门	Tianmen	1018	688	198	132	208	18	72	118
神农架林区	Shennongjia	43	27	13	3	22	7	11	4

17-14 各类技术合同签定及执行情况
SIGNING AND IMPEMENTATION OF VARIOUS TECHNICAL CONTRACTS

项　目	Item	合同数(项) Number of Contracts (unit)	合同金额(万元) Value of Contracts (10 000 yuan)
2010	2010	6641	909167
技术开发合同	Technology Development Contracts	2390	502290
技术转让合同	Technology Transfer Contracts	199	126505
技术咨询合同	Technology Consultation Contracts	1321	71932
技术服务合同	Technology Service Contracts	2731	208439
2011	2011	7799	1214103
技术开发合同	Technology Development Contracts	4101	661014
技术转让合同	Technology Transfer Contracts	327	99063
技术咨询合同	Technology Consultation Contracts	1358	88232
技术服务合同	Technology Service Contracts	2013	365793
2012	2012	12908	2345655
技术开发合同	Technology Development Contracts	7698	1000226
技术转让合同	Technology Transfer Contracts	447	482601
技术咨询合同	Technology Consultation Contracts	1391	87457
技术服务合同	Technology Service Contracts	3372	775371
2013	2013	14909	4187410
技术开发合同	Technology Development Contracts	9473	1614052
技术转让合同	Technology Transfer Contracts	574	342631
技术咨询合同	Technology Consultation Contracts	1082	238981
技术服务合同	Technology Service Contracts	3780	1991746
2014	2014	21696	6017367
技术开发合同	Technology Development Contracts	11695	1398146
技术转让合同	Technology Transfer Contracts	518	279765
技术咨询合同	Technology Consultation Contracts	1496	389802
技术服务合同	Technology Service Contracts	7987	3949654
2015	2015	22787	8300672
技术开发合同	Technology Development Contracts	11318	2155738
技术转让合同	Technology Transfer Contracts	547	390390
技术咨询合同	Technology Consultation Contracts	1408	316786
技术服务合同	Technology Service Contracts	9514	5437758
2016	2016	24248	9277311
技术开发合同	Technology Development Contracts	11637	2512842
技术转让合同	Technology Transfer Contracts	696	385274
技术咨询合同	Technology Consultation Contracts	1819	372867
技术服务合同	Technology Service Contracts	10096	6006327

17-15 全省技术买卖情况(2016)
PURCHASE AND SELLING OF TECHNOLOGY IN THE WHOLE PROVINCE (2016)

卖方类别 Type of the Seller / 买方类别 Type of the Buyer		合计 Total		机关法人 Organ Corporations		事业法人 Institutions Corporations		社团法人 Associations Corporations	
		合同数(项) Number of Contracts	成交额(万元) Contracted Value (10 000 yuan)	合同数(项) Number of Contracts	成交额(万元) Contracted Value (10 000 yuan)	合同数(项) Number of Contracts	成交额(万元) Contracted Value (10 000 yuan)	合同数(项) Number of Contracts	成交额(万元) Contracted Value (10 000 yuan)
总计	**Total**	**24248**	**9277311**	**282**	**152693**	**11483**	**1422586**	**278**	**106034**
机关法人	Departments	5679	2735455	240	148967	3201	584350	269	102989
事业法人	Institutions	4237	655528	24	3574	2679	209859		
社团法人	Social Groups	400	55740	1	16	349	28581		
企业法人	Corporations	13616	5629173	17	137	5121	438831	9	3045
自然人	Natural Person	53	1808			17	476		
其他组织	Other Organizations	263	199608			116	160490		

17-15 续表 continued

卖方类别 Type of the Seller / 买方类别 Type of the Buyer		企业法人 Corporations		自然人 Natural Person		其他组织 Other Organizations	
		合同数(项) Number of Contracts	成交额(万元) Contracted Value (10 000 yuan)	合同数(项) Number of Contracts	成交额(万元) Contracted Value (10 000 yuan)	合同数(项) Number of Contracts	成交额(万元) Contracted Value (10 000 yuan)
总计	**Total**	12127	7512880	10	1554	68	81563
机关法人	Departments	1941	1892859	1	50	27	6240
事业法人	Institutions	1533	442075			1	20
社团法人	Social Groups	50	27143				
企业法人	Corporations	8422	5110592	8	1487	39	75081
自然人	Natural Person	35	1316	1	17		
其他组织	Other Organizations	146	38895			1	222

17-16 地震观测及地方地震工作情况
STATISTICS ON EARTHQUAKE OBSERVATION AND LOCAL EFFORTS ON EARTHQUAKE WORKS

项 目	Item	2014	2015	2016
职工总数 (人)	Total Number of Staff and Workers (person)	445	407	388
专业技术人员 (人)	Professtional Technical Personel (person)	309	303	288
高级技术人员 (人)	Senior Technical Personel (person)	75	82	89
市州级地震局 (个)	Number of Earthquake Agency (unit)	17	17	17
重点县地震办公室 (个)	Number of Earthquake Offices in Key Counties (unit)	32	32	32
地方地震工作人员 (人)	Local Seismologist (person)	641	641	736
地震观测台(网)人员 (人)	Number of Staff in Earthquake Observation Station (person)	73	73	74
#观测技术人员 (人)	#Technical Personel (person)	53	53	68
地震台站 (个)	Earthquake Observation Station (unit)	52	47	47
国家台	National Station	5	5	5
省级台	Provincial Station	47	42	42
GPS测量 (千米/点)	GPS Measurement (km/point)	120000/180	210000/430	140000/280
流动重力测量 (千米/点)	Flow Gravity Measurement (km/point)	90000/482	70000/420	63000/381

17-17 气象部门基本情况
BASIC CONDITIONS OF METEOROLOGICAL DEPARTMENT

项 目	Item	2000	2005	2010	2013	2014	2015	2016
一、气象观测人员总数 (人)	Total Number of Staff in Meteorological Depaartment (person)	333	375	378	415	469	446	396
地面观测	Groud Observation	285	320	330	367	410	376	328
高空观测	Upper Air Observation	24	18	18	14	24	34	32
雷达观测	Radar Observation	24	20	30	34	35	36	36
特种观测	Special Observation							
二、气象台站总数 (个)	Total Number of Meteorological Obervatory (unit)	85	87	87	89	89	89	89
气象台	Meteorological Obervatory	13	14	14	14	14	14	14
气象站	Weather Station	70	71	71	73	73	73	73
独立农试站	Independent Agricultural Station	2	2	2	2	2	2	2
三、卫星云图接收站点数 (个)	Number of Stations Receiving Satellite Image (unit)	11	25	15	17	17	17	17
极轨卫星	Polar Orbiting Meteorological Satellite	2	23	5	4	4	4	4
同步卫星	Geostationary Satellite	9	7	10	13	13	13	13
接收卫星云图图片数	Number of Satellite Image Pictures Received							
使用云图单位数	Number of Pictures Used	144						
四、拥有雷达数 (部)	Number of Radar Owned (unit)	11	12	15	17	14	14	14
701测风	701 Wind Sensing	4	4					
3厘米	3 cm	2	2	1	1	1	1	1
5厘米	5 cm	2	1	1	1			
10厘米	10 cm	3	5	10	7	10	10	10
1波段	1 Wave Band			3	8	3	3	3

17-18 质量技术监督检查情况
STATISTICS ON SUPERVISION AND EXAMINATION OF QUALITY TECHNOLOGY

年份 Year	机构(个) Institutions (unit)	职工人数(人) Number of Staff and Workers (person)	#专业技术人员 #Professional Technic Personel	经费收入(万元) Revenue (10 000 yuan)	经费支出(万元) Expenditures (10 000 yuan)	固定资产(万元) Fixed Assets (10 000 yuan)	#仪器设备 #Equipment and Devices	计量器具检定台(万套件) Number of Measuring Equipment Tested (10 000 units)	#衡具 #Measuring Instrument	#强制检定 #Compulsory Test
1980	88	1211	327	308	306	1667	512	60		
1985	107	1668	356	640	515	3234	1402	146	36	
1990	105	3299	1409	3063	2610	7994	3760	136	68	118
1995	167	6275	2121	10095	10374	21213	6327	150	64	140
1996	102	2265	1252	3237	3177	6985	3261	136	61	108
1997	101	2337	1337	3491	3418	6751	3680	150	62	110
1998	106	2479	1439	4 079	4034	6314	3810	126	50	100
1999	105	2531	1446	4 515	4532	6732	3713	120	43	103
2000	104	2790	1478	4 568	4853	8829	5286	150	43	105
2001	91	1632	911	3005	2899	6537	3881	132	33	65
2002	360	9583	4059	36371	34024	39461	9806	165	40	138
2003	403	9137	3960	44450	41317	47323	12114	154	45	118
2004	376	9034	4703	50520	48383	53579	14549	128	23	114
2005	398	9046	3953	59089	56152	62607	19986	120	22	98
2006	398	9050	4094	67864	64078	72440	23840	119	22	110
2007	393	9065	4072	79698	75988	81822	26984	119	19	102
2008	392	9055	3732	93140	89653	94547	27832	109	16	96
2009	395	9077	3718	111477	110965	111627	35047	128	18	107
2010	388	9133	3815	116319	109915	129113	38963	125	17	119
2011	387	8828	3693	134901	135563	150114	44143	142	15	135
2012	385	8997	3645	153332	146310	159772	45440	175	16	155
2013	383	8981	3655	197287	180390	183786	57740	199	15	188
2014	379	8420	3160	191091	177558	234080	64785	202	20	156
2015	409	8297	2996	206214	202262	248957	80114	261	20	232
2016	409	8452	2816	227598	225075	275586	83466	265	17	183

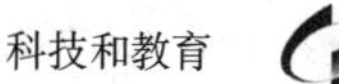

17-19 标准事业基本情况
BASIC STATISTICS ON STANDARD ENTERPRISES

项　目	Item	2000	2005	2010	2013	2014	2015	2016
质量监督机构 (个)	Quality Supervision Institution (unit)	86	99	99	99	99	99	99
固定人员 (人)	Fixed Personel (person)	1 007						
制定标准 (项)	Standard Established (unit)	29	36	81	69	77	92	108
修定标准 (项)	Standard Revised (unit)			4	4	21	11	3
废止标准 (项)	Standard Abolished (unit)							17
当年采用国际标准 (项)	International Standard Adopted (unit)	4	129	193	106			
受检产品质量监督 (种)	Number of Products under Quality Supervision (kind)	99					59	60
质量监督检测 (批次)	Quality Supervision Test (batch)	20093	26548	40288	40317	6429	4797	4621
标准文件馆藏 (万件)	Standard Document Collection (10 000 units)	25	22	30	121	160	140	145.37

17-20 档案事业基本情况
BASIC STATISTICS ON ARCHIVES

指　标		Item		2013	2014	2015	2016
各级各类档案馆数量	(个)	Number of Institutions	(unit)				
国家综合档案馆		National Comprehensive Archives		116	116	115	115
专门档案馆		National Special Archives		14	14	14	14
部门档案馆		Department Archives		7	7	14	14
各级各类档案馆馆藏		Number of Collections					
全宗	(个)	Fonds	(unit)	15403	15587	15882	16033
案卷	(万卷)	Archives	(10 000 volumes)	1659.54	1734.76	1820.69	1747.80
以件为保管单位档案	(万件)	Archives	(10 000 pieces)	678.24	632.00	712.21	971.90
照片	(万张)	Photos	(10 000 sheets)	141.00	161.00	156.72	140.00
馆藏资料	(万册)	Files	(10 000 volumes)	291.08	275.00	279.37	226.80
国家综合档案馆面积	(万平方米)	The Area of National Comprehensive Archives	(10 000 square meters)				
总建筑面积		Floor Space		20.66	21.98	23.15	25.3
库房面积		The Area of Storerooms		8.76	9.21	9.51	10.27
全省档案专业技术职称人员	(人)	Full-time Personnel	(person)				
研究馆员		Research Librarian		21	30	42	24
副研究馆员		Associate Research Librarian		247	250	395	161
馆员		Librarian		940	945	909	562
助理馆员		Associate Librarian		776	630	535	397
全省档案馆本年度利用档案		Utilized Archives					
利用档案人数	(万人次)	Use of Material	(10 000 person-times)	30.08	37.84	42.55	44.28
利用档案卷次	(万人次)	Number of Archives Used	(10 000 person-times)	74.16	92.00	85.73	99.42
举办展览	(个)	Display Organized	(unit)	604	550	560	564
接待参观	(万人次)	Visitors	(10 000 person-times)	41.15	42.38	42.50	60.00
全省本年编研档案资料		Materials Edited This Year					
公开出版种数	(种)	Number of Materials Open Published	(kind)	76	90	96	80
公开出版字数	(万字)	Number of Words Open Published	(10 000 words)	1929.56	1942.64	1906.21	2838.80
内部参考种数	(种)	Number of Materials for Inner Reference	(kind)	197	224	328	292
内部参考字数	(万字)	Number of Words for Inner reference	(10 000 words)	2062.96	2170.68	2778.51	3120.00

17-21 各级各类学校数
NUMBER OF SCHOOLS OF VARIOUS LEVELS

单位:所 (unit)

学校分类	Type of Shool	2008	2009	2010	2011	2012	2013	2014	2015	2016
普通高等学校	Regular Institutions of Higher Education	87	120	120	122	122	123	123	126	129
#地方院校	#Local Schools	79	112	112	114	114	115	115	118	121
中等职业学校	Secondary Vocation Schools	462	402	413	341	332	310	301	289	289
普通中学	Regular Middle School	3011	2897	2787	2707	2622	2576	2552	2545	2558
#初中	#Junior High Schools	2356	2275	2184	2122	2047	2013	2011	2013	2026
城区	Urban	431	383	362	507	507	509	535	548	582
镇区	Township	564	622	671	929	953	945	955	968	967
乡村	Rural	1361	1270	1151	686	587	559	521	497	477
高中	Senior High School	655	622	603	585	575	563	541	532	532
城区	Urban	295	267	243	313	318	318	314	311	321
镇区	Township	271	268	278	222	220	212	201	193	188
乡村	Rural	89	87	82	50	37	33	26	28	23
小学	Primary School	9302	8544	7749	7415	6614	5746	5513	5398	5383
城区	Urban	845	722	685	1015	1007	997	1061	1062	1124
镇区	Township	715	847	937	1636	1629	1536	1556	1543	1545
乡村	Rural	7742	6975	6127	4764	3978	3213	2896	2793	2714
特殊教育学校	Special Education School	76	76	76	76	77	80	83	83	84
幼儿园	Kindergarten	2880	2995	4395	4670	5321	6011	6491	6814	7500
技工学校	School of Technology	208		206				131	132	124

17-22 各级各类学校在校学生数
ENROLLMENT IN SCHOOLS OF VARIOUS LEVELS

单位:人 (person)

学校分类	Type of Shool	2005	2010	2011	2012	2013	2014	2015	2016
普通高等学校	Regular Institutions of Higher Education	1012665	1296920	1340298	1386086	1421434	1419699	1408738	1399948
#地方院校	#Local Schools	824960	1098570	1129010	1183416	1217155	1216228	1207217	1200494
中等职业学校	Secondary Vocation Schools	606014	903834	720915	500540	411194	372601	364893	375637
普通中学	Regular Middle School	4466879	3418299	3208399	2652208	2471869	2294899	2241286	2259904
#初中	#Junior High Schools	3172392	2180937	2040702	1577701	1483710	1375940	1365319	1414864
城区	Urban	494739	413930	561141	543902	529708	538778	547028	589002
镇区	Township	750903	848967	994830	743679	689455	627833	625858	646844
乡村	Rural	1926750	918040	484731	290120	264547	209329	192433	179018
高中	Senior High School	1294487	1237362	1167697	1074507	988159	918959	875967	845040
城区	Urban	541404	427334	596728	580248	555182	529827	512284	509424
镇区	Township	553411	633319	465734	435656	386923	357324	332446	311557
乡村	Rural	199672	176709	105235	58603	46054	31808	31237	24059
小学	Primary School	4291881	3655512	3773446	3267498	3282579	3211598	3358095	3461337
城区	Urban	787812	713491	1005861	1027061	1050497	1120918	1202479	1307462
镇区	Township	593090	974019	1273914	1160375	1187536	1209864	1281967	1321295
乡村	Rural	2910979	1968002	1493671	1080062	1044546	880816	873649	832580
特殊教育学校	Special Education School	9444	15349	12893	10557	10576	11080	11057	11831
幼儿园	Kindergarten	594481	1118360	1324714	1355395	1473371	1538200	1625793	1699519
技工学校	School of Technology	136000	229000				93400	89400	79156

17-23 各级各类学校招生数
NEW ENROLLMENT IN SCHOOLS OF VARIOUS LEVELS

单位：人 (person)

学校分类	Type of Shool	2005	2010	2011	2012	2013	2014	2015	2016
普通高等学校	Regular Institutions of Higher Education	315560	387612	413600	406957	403860	400307	391157	397623
#地方院校	#Local Schools	269042	337621	358933	356113	352544	350391	342310	349234
中等职业学校	Secondary Vocation Schools	273789	283610	212318	143530	130995	126656	132594	132075
普通中学	Regular Middle School	1469777	1053418	981191	838372	804312	749560	740206	782004
#初中	#Junior High Schools	1011186	657947	619213	510866	487841	454284	461592	504948
城区	Urban	162324	132571	179751	181591	177436	178772	182684	209080
镇区	Township	241579	251823	295975	237380	225227	206959	213860	232105
乡村	Rural	607283	273553	143487	91895	85178	68553	65048	63763
高中	Senior High School	458591	395471	361978	327506	316471	295276	278614	277056
城区	Urban	187976	138260	184335	178360	179553	168688	161996	166665
镇区	Township	197496	199177	144925	131519	123402	116662	106275	102144
乡村	Rural	73119	58034	32718	17627	13516	9926	10343	8247
小学	Primary School	567411	680166	692317	634766	607979	597543	625609	623202
城区	Urban	113284	126070	179176	186695	188925	203429	217723	233312
镇区	Township	81622	176073	228466	220893	211576	217982	232628	231143
乡村	Rural	372505	378023	284675	227178	207478	176132	175258	158747
特殊教育学校	Special Education School	1038	2047	1622	1483	1788	2113	2047	2413
幼儿园	Kindergarten	396082	761044	807017	785848	825253	656652	613990	575076
技工学校	School of Technology	73000	57000				38000	34700	34694

17-24 各级各类学校毕业生数
NUMBER OF GRADUATES FROM SCHOOLS OF VARIOUS LEVELS

单位:人 (person)

学校分类	Type of Shool	2000	2005	2010	2012	2013	2014	2015	2016
普通高等学校	Regular Institutions of Higher Education	51932	187920	331303	353014	361572	390921	388621	393627
#地方院校	#Local Schools	26461	144529	285599	305545	313748	342171	339709	344834
中等职业学校	Secondary Vocation Schools	125593	129436	335776	272883	200196	147158	125735	111352
普通中学	Regular Middle School	883828	1438503	1288944	988034	924920	826599	778302	753920
#初中	#Junior High Schools	718015	1055083	854395	575799	533709	477114	461384	448251
城区	Urban	198402	169257	149922	183511	176905	175225	179771	186265
镇区	Township	61909	239870	326945	277376	257033	224495	213005	203963
乡村	Rural	457704	645956	377528	114912	99771	77394	68608	58023
高中	Senior High School	165813	383420	434549	412235	391211	349485	316918	305669
城区	Urban	98353	161281	147307	216107	216067	197220	183878	185881
镇区	Township	41382	164517	228146	173191	157143	138866	121045	111441
乡村	Rural	26078	57622	59096	22937	18001	13399	11995	8347
小学	Primary School	1160203	1020710	611620	513818	489395	451925	466221	499292
城区	Urban	281706	149766	120208	162653	162408	162339	170042	190560
镇区	Township	84207	134340	160359	177913	180709	167271	180809	194145
乡村	Rural	794290	736604	331053	173252	146278	122315	115370	114587
特殊教育学校	Special Education School	1310	1498	2261	1292	1227	1218	1112	1246
幼儿园	Kindergarten					572085	585677	617733	640751
技工学校	School of Technology	24848	45000				34900	30000	27034

17-25 各级各类学校教职工数
NUMBER OF FACULTIES AT SCHOOLS OF VARIOUS LEVELS

单位:人 (person)

学校分类	Type of Shool	2000	2005	2010	2012	2013	2014	2015	2016
普通高等学校	Regular Institutions of Higher Education	72265	107459	123491	127921	128185	128878	129118	131014
#地方院校	#Local Schools	35120	73079	89205	94170	94777	95718	96039	96571
中等职业学校	Secondary Vocation Schools	28816	36658	40985	33442	30845	29809	27532	27672
普通中学	Regular Middle School	237500	273146	263055	259884	254716	250873	246443	244193
城区	Urban	97054	75581	68468	104952	105801	108068	108438	113631
镇区	Township	28889	78027	107371	115008	110983	109553	106896	103052
乡村	Rural	111557	119538	87216	39924	37932	33252	31109	27510
小学	Primary Schools	299994	232888	211247	193609	198262	199033	197577	196452
城市	Urban	84877	47727	42100	54139	55015	58137	60500	64156
县镇	Township	23515	33532	51059	67003	69933	71558	71355	72377
农村	Rural	191602	151629	118088	72467	73314	69338	65722	59919
特殊教育学校	Special Education School	1676	1679	1744	1826	1921	1997	1955	2028
幼儿园	Kindergarten	40484	33094	66202	92024	110376	122017	134279	152252
技工学校	School of Technology	13070	9934				9196	9383	8597

17-26 各级各类学校专任教师数
NUMBER OF FULL-TIME TEACHERS AT SCHOOLS OF VARIOUS LEVELS

单位:人 (person)

学校分类	Type of Shool	2000	2005	2010	2012	2013	2014	2015	2016
普通高等学校	Regular Institutions of Higher Education	30363	59009	74685	80665	81784	82821	83444	83517
#地方院校	#Local Schools	15995	43240	57264	62913	64032	64908	65440	65068
中等职业学校	Secondary Vocation Schools	15549	24036	28476	23796	22555	21905	20550	20657
普通中学	Regular Middle School	198486	233517	227962	212305	205306	201758	198342	195685
#初中	#Junior High Schools	154543	169084	156836	141409	135580	133632	131325	129157
城区	Urban	49752	31803	30409	44766	44122	45998	46819	49710
镇区	Township	13138	39851	59014	69143	65457	64544	63263	61032
乡村	Rural	91653	97430	67413	27500	26001	23090	21243	18415
高中	Senior High School	43943	64433	71126	70896	69726	68126	67017	66528
城区	Urban	27663	28330	26883	39579	40383	39873	39755	40852
镇区	Township	10336	27235	35091	27221	26097	25762	24716	23609
乡村	Rural	5944	8868	9152	4096	3246	2491	2546	2067
小学	Primary School	274979	215693	196078	191699	196556	199172	200158	202014
城区	Urban	75377	42127	37873	55297	56547	60085	62736	67632
镇区	Township	21459	30351	47480	65828	68204	71378	72318	74021
乡村	Rural	178143	143215	110725	70574	71805	67709	65104	60361
特殊教育学校	Special Education School	1231	1317	1477	1560	1647	1712	1682	1741
幼儿园	Kindergarten	29889	20018	38494	49153	57736	63006	68761	78005
技工学校	School of Technology	6182	7064				8069	7794	7639

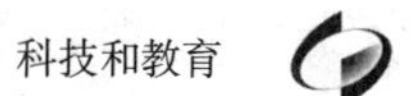

17-27 各级各类学校专任教师学历分类

STATISTICS ON ACADEMIC DEGREE OF FULL-TIME TEACHERS AT SCHOOLS OF VARIOUS LEVELS

单位:人 (person)

学历分类	Type of School	2012	2013	2014	2015	2016
一、中等职业学校	Secondary Vocational School	23796	22555	21905	20550	20657
高等学校本科毕业及以上	Graduated from Universities and Above	19604	19172	19026	18105	18344
高等学校专科毕业	Graduated from Colleges	3861	3148	2696	2308	2145
高中阶段及以下	Degree Below Senior High School	331	235	183	137	168
二、普通中学	Regular Secondary Schools	212305	205306	201758	198342	195685
高等学校本科毕业及以上	Graduated from Universities and Above	156745	156715	158575	158861	159582
高等学校专科毕业	Graduated from Colleges	52938	47284	41857	38500	35415
中专、高中毕业的	Graduated from Secondary and High Schools	2521	1257	1266	981	688
三、小学	Primary School	191699	196556	199172	200158	202014
中师、高中毕业及以上的	Graduated from Teacher Schools and Degrees Above	191282	196300	199012	199969	201896
四、幼儿园(不包括园长)	Kindergarten (President is Excluded)	49153	57736	63006	68761	78005
中师、高中毕业及以上的	Graduate from Teacher Schools and Degrees Above	47040	55669	61096	66395	75600

17-28 高等学校分类别情况

单位:所、人

学校分类	Type of School	2000 学校数 Number of Colleges and Universities	2000 在校生数 Students Enrollment in Schools	2000 招生数 New Enroll-ment	2000 毕业生数 Graduates	2005 学校数 Number of Colleges and Universities	2005 在校生数 Students Enrollment in Schools	2005 招生数 New Enroll-ment	2005 毕业生数 Graduates
总 计	Total	54	346568	1E+05	51932	85	989754	306775	184706
综合大学	Comprehensive Universities	6	79303	28489	13871	10	196454	48591	48617
理工院校	Colleges and Universities of Science	11	124501	47724	18603	49	545277	181361	92857
农业院校	Colleges and Universities of Agriculture	2	13111	4311	1775	1	15715	3999	2763
林业院校	Colleges and Universities of Forestry	4	10770	4095	1068	1	1678	1062	121
医药院校	Colleges and Universities of Medicine	7	39694	17186	5950	3	26534	7686	5238
师范院校	Colleges and Universities of Teacher-Training	4	26218	9923	4466	5	52581	15687	12960
语文院校									
财经院校	Colleges and Universities of Finance	1	2482	974	448	6	93524	30319	12771
政法院校	Colleges and Universities of Politics and Law	1	2787	915	515	3	12389	3416	2369
体育院校	Colleges and Universities of Physical Education	2	2255	749	318	1	8837	2735	1154
艺术院校	Colleges and Universities of Art	2	12719	4298	2584	4	8834	4378	814
民族院校	Colleges and Universities of Minority Groups	14	32728	21002	2334	2	27931	7539	5042

CLASSIFICATION OF HIGHER EDUCATION INSTITUTIONS

(unit, person)

2010				2015				2016			
学校数 Number of Colleges and Universities	在校生数 Students Enrollment in Schools	招生数 New Enroll-ment	毕业生数 Graduates	学校数 Number of Colleges and Universities	在校生数 Students Enrollment in Schools	招生数 New Enroll-ment	毕业生数 Graduates	学校数 Number of Colleges and Universities	在校生数 Students Enrollment in Schools	招生数 New Enroll-ment	毕业生数 Graduates
120	1290243	386984	327208	126	1408738	391157	388621	129	1399948	397623	393627
8	166008	44736	39434	8	175368	41640	45686	8	170123	41992	45299
74	773095	238873	202148	79	848861	243049	239337	82	842829	247310	244748
1	18239	4600	3892	1	18796	4607	4241	1	18755	4611	4391
1	5721	2051	1461	1	10132	3031	2651	1	9293	2819	3543
4	38173	10979	10031	4	40827	10258	10428	4	40488	10395	10650
7	78905	24018	18007	8	91256	27337	24750	8	96080	30821	25763
				1	8057	2145	3004	1	8820	2706	1885
12	123204	37315	30366	11	124607	34449	36217	11	123227	33324	33883
4	11698	2877	4157	4	14224	4790	3289	4	14373	4269	3956
2	14826	4298	2855	3	16234	4240	4128	3	16456	4391	4045
5	26179	8000	6898	4	18388	5602	4663	4	18828	5387	4764
2	34195	9237	7959	2	41988	10009	10227	2	40676	9598	10700

17-29 大学、中专专任教师职称情况
STATISTICS ON RANKS AND TITLES OF FULL-TIME TEACHERS AT SCHOOLS OF VARIOUS LEVELS

单位:人 (person)

职称	Ranks and Titles	2000	2005	2010	2011	2012	2013	2014	2015	2016
普通高等学校专任教师数	**Number of Full-Time Teachers of Regular Higher Education Institutions**	**30363**	**59009**	**74685**	**78952**	**80665**	**81784**	**82821**	**83444**	**83517**
正高级	Senoir	3253	6434	8674	9378	9998	10217	10622	10901	10955
副高级	Associate Senoir	9448	17843	22047	23013	24373	24959	25927	26572	27072
中　级	Junior	9847	19169	26077	29013	30244	31147	31273	30983	31186
初　级	Primary	5741	10311	13656	13475	11883	11242	10544	9981	9379
无职称	No Title	2074	5252	4231	4073	4167	4219	4455	5007	4925
中等职业学校专任教师数	**Number of Full-Time Teachers of Specialized Schools**	15549	24036	28476	26208	23796	22555	21905	20550	20657
正高级	Senoir								97	96
副高级	Associate Senoir	3523	5152	6441	5958	5644	5495	5507	5262	5170
中　级	Junior	7229	11467	12935	11960	10760	10187	10040	9258	9263
初　级	Primary	4399	5889	7229	6856	6082	5762	5289	4961	4988
无职称	No Title	398	1528	1871	1434	1310	1111	1069	972	1140

17-30 各级各类学校校舍建筑面积情况(2016)
STATISTICS ON FLOOR SPACE OF SCHOOL HOUSES UNDER CONSTRUCTION IN SCHOOLS OF VARIOUS LEVELS(2016)

单位:万平方米 (10 000 sq.m)

项 目	Item	学校占地面积	校舍建筑面积	其中:教学及辅助用房
普通中学	Regular Middle School	10067.91	4240.73	1427.65
城区	Urban	3927.51	1855.38	706.89
镇区	Township	4715.39	1873.58	562.56
乡村	Rural	1425.01	511.78	158.20
其中:初中	#Junior High Schools	6325.74	2437.00	845.97
城区	Urban	1680.60	758.91	324.27
镇区	Township	3359.85	1241.90	384.19
乡村	Rural	1285.29	436.19	137.51
其中:高中	Senior High School	3742.17	1803.73	581.68
城区	Urban	2246.91	1096.47	382.62
镇区	Township	1355.54	631.67	178.37
乡村	Rural	139.72	75.59	20.69
小学	Primary School	9284.93	2886.61	1423.31
城区	Urban	1758.60	772.42	430.49
镇区	Township	3121.90	1030.90	500.25
乡村	Rural	4404.43	1083.29	492.57
特殊学校	Special Education School	71.94	35.59	16.08
城区	Urban	41.28	22.04	9.68
镇区	Township	24.37	11.27	5.34
乡村	Rural	6.29	2.28	1.06

17-31 初中毕业生升入高中和小学毕业生升入初中的升学率

STATISTICS ON PROPORTION OF MIDDLE-SCHOOL STUDENTS ENTERING HIGH SCHOOL AND PROPORTION OF PRIMARY-SCHOOL STUDENTS ENTERING MIDDLE SCHOOL

年份 Year	初中毕业生升入高中升学率 Proportion of Middle-School Students Entering High-School			小学毕业生升学率 Proportion of Primary-School Students Entering Middle-School		
	初中毕业生数(万人) Number of Middle-School Graduates (10 000 persons)	高中招生数(万人) Number of High-School Graduates (10 000 persons)	升学率(%) Proportion of Students Entering Schools of Higher Level(%)	小学毕业生数(万人) Number of Primary School Graduates (10 000 persons)	初中招生数(万人) Number of Middle-School Graduates (10 000 persons)	升学率(%) Proportion of Students Entering Schools of Higher Level(%)
1965	7.60	3.75	49.4	29.60	24.95	84.3
1975	49.25	31.26	63.5	116.05	110.11	94.9
1978	98.80	43.33	43.9	132.37	119.46	90.3
1980	52.23	25.04	47.7	107.64	88.93	82.6
1985	49.92	19.13	38.3	104.89	69.21	66.0
1990	51.71	16.78	32.5	89.96	66.63	74.1
1995	57.85	19.88	34.4	90.76	80.53	88.7
1996	59.33	19.86	33.5	90.19	83.59	92.7
1997	64.70	21.29	32.9	95.35	89.30	93.7
1998	69.23	24.53	35.4	103.75	96.10	92.6
1999	69.60	27.20	39.1	111.24	101.40	91.2
2000	71.80	31.43	43.8	116.02	109.06	94.0
2001	76.34	35.31	46.3	121.00	113.49	93.8
2002	82.93	42.45	51.2	122.17	120.07	98.3
2003	91.61	39.61	43.2	118.70	117.83	99.3
2004	99.32	42.97	43.3	109.93	109.69	99.8
2005	105.51	45.86	43.5	102.07	101.85	99.8
2006	106.18	45.55	42.9	94.66	97.07	102.6
2007	99.77	43.98	44.1	83.29	87.27	104.8
2008	96.10	43.91	45.7	71.51	77.75	108.7
2009	92.38	42.38	45.9	64.68	69.63	107.7
2010	85.44	39.55	46.3	61.16	65.79	107.6
2011	77.14	36.20	46.9	58.34	61.92	106.1
2012	57.58	32.75	56.9	51.38	51.09	99.4
2013	53.37	31.65	59.3	48.94	48.78	99.7
2014	47.71	29.53	61.9	45.19	45.43	100.5
2015	46.14	27.86	60.39	46.62	46.16	99.01
2016	44.83	27.71	61.81	49.93	50.49	101.13

17-32 小学学龄儿童入学率
STATISTICS ON PROPORTION OF CHILDREN AT SCHOOLING AGE ENTERING PRIMARY SCHOOLS

年份 Year	学龄儿童数(万人) Number of Children at Schooling Age (10 000 person)	已入学学龄儿童数(万人) Number of Children Entering School (10 000 persons)	入学率(%) Proportion of Students Entering Schools of Higher Level (%)
1975	629.50	611.00	97.1
1978	616.86	597.73	96.9
1980	594.80	576.86	97.0
1985	496.69	489.38	98.5
1990	485.00	480.32	99.0
1991	556.39	549.35	98.7
1992	571.44	563.44	98.6
1993	574.54	566.84	98.7
1994	599.47	593.88	99.1
1995	637.12	632.34	99.2
1996	661.72	658.38	99.5
1997	681.52	678.95	99.6
1998	685.87	682.53	99.5
1999	669.16	665.88	99.5
2000	641.60	638.57	99.5
2001	585.99	583.29	99.5
2002	538.02	535.98	99.6
2003	490.29	488.68	99.7
2004	440.03	438.66	99.7
2005	397.52	396.11	99.7
2006	363.99	362.14	99.5
2007	345.49	344.77	99.8
2008	340.59	340.08	99.9
2009	343.63	342.74	99.7
2010	350.95	350.82	99.96
2011	362.77	362.74	99.96
2012	317.15	317.06	99.97
2013	320.48	320.41	99.98
2014	315.77	315.72	99.99
2015	330.72	330.69	99.99
2016	340.52	340.51	100.00

17-33 各级各类学校服务的人口及每万人口中在校学生数

STATISTICS ON THE NUMBER OF POPULATION SERVED BY SCHOOLS OF VARIOUS LEVELS AND THE NUMBER OF STUDENTS AT SCHOOL PER 10000 PERSONS

项　目	Item	2000	2005	2010	2011	2012	2013	2014	2015	2016
每一学校服务的人口数 (万人)	**Number of Population Served by Each School (10 000 persons)**									
普通高等学校	Regular Institutions of Higher Education	111.63	70.95	47.70	47.20	47.37	47.15	47.28	46.44	45.62
成人高等学校	Adults Higher Education	188.37	354.76	408.86	411.29	412.79	414.21	415.43	417.96	420.36
普通中等专业学校	Specialized Secondary School	29.69	13.80	13.86	16.89	17.41	18.71	19.32	20.25	20.36
普通高中	RegualrHigh-School								11.00	11.06
普通初中	Regualr Middle-School								2.91	2.90
小学	Primary School	0.26	0.48	0.74	0.78	0.87	1.01	1.05	1.08	1.09
幼儿园	Kindergarten	1.61	2.58	1.30	1.23	1.09	0.96	0.90	0.86	0.78
每万人口中的学生数 (人)	**Number of Students at School per 10 000 Persons (person)**									
普通高等学校	Regular Institutions of Higher Education	57.49	167.91	226.58	232.77	239.85	245.12	244.10	240.75	258.96
成人高等学校	Adults Higher Education	35.94	37.05	45.79	46.19	47.59	48.77	47.31	40.78	34.64
普通中等专业学校	Specialized Secondary School	46.22	100.48	157.90	125.20	86.61	70.91	64.06	62.36	63.83
普通高中	RegualrHigh-School								149.70	143.59
普通初中	Regualr Middle-School								233.33	240.42
小学	Primary School	1107.77	711.64	638.63	655.34	565.41	566.06	552.20	573.89	588.16
幼儿园	Kindergarten	120.56	98.57	195.38	230.06	234.54	254.07	264.48	277.84	288.79

17-34 各级各类学校每个专任教师负担的学生数
STATISTICS ON STUDENT-TEACHER RATIO BY LEVELS OF SCHOOL

单位:人 (person)

项　　目	Item	2000	2005	2008	2009	2010	2011	2012	2013	2014	2015	2016
普通高等学校	Regular Institutions of Higher Education	11.41	15.86	15.29	15.7	17.37	16.98	17.18	17.35	17.14	15.73	15.63
中等职业学校	Secondary Vocation School	17.92	25.21	33.8	35.74	31.74	27.51	21.03	18.23	17.01	17.76	18.18
普通中学	Regular High School	17.68	19.13	16.82	15.77	15.00	14.22	12.49	12.04	11.37	11.30	11.55
#初中	#Junior Middle Schools	18.19	18.76	15.96	14.71	13.91	13.23	11.16	10.94	10.30	10.40	10.95
高中	Senior High School	15.89	20.09	18.83	18.18	17.40	16.37	15.16	14.17	13.49	13.07	12.70
小学	Primary School	24.28	19.90	17.92	12.09	18.64	20.46	17.04	16.7	16.12	16.78	17.13
幼儿园	Kindergarten	24.31	29.70	29.95	18.13	29.05	30.71	27.58	25.52	24.41	23.64	21.79

17-35 各级学校女学生和女教师数
NUMBER OF FEMALE STUDENTS AND FEMALE TEACHERS AT SCHOOL OF VARIOUS LEVELS

单位:万人 (10 000 persons)

项　目	Item	2000	2005	2010	2011	2012	2013	2014	2015	2016
一、女学生数	Number of Female Students	506.17	473.27	426.07	416.40	360.95	350.98	337.8	341.05	346.19
普通高等学校	Regular Institutions of Higher Education	11.93	44.11	62.25	65.13	67.70	69.12	69.04	68.46	68.15
中等专业学校	Specialized Secondary School	14.33	29.14	44.22	34.96	24.58	19.84	17.90	16.96	17.1
普通中学	Regualr High School	155.66	203.98	154.98	145.44	119.94	112.14	104.22	102.39	103.44
小学	Primary School	317.45	194.85	164.62	170.87	148.73	149.88	146.64	153.24	157.5
二、女学生占学生总数 %	Percentage of Female Students in School	46.2	45.5	46.2	46.1	46.2	46.3	46.3	46.2	46.2
普通高等学校	Regular Institutions of Higher Education	34.4	43.6	48.0	48.6	48.8	48.6	48.6	48.5	48.6
中等专业学校	Specialized Secondary School	51.4	48.1	48.9	48.5	49.1	48.3	48.0	46.5	45.5
普通中学	Regualr High School	44.4	45.7	45.3	45.3	45.2	45.4	45.4	45.7	45.8
小学	Primary School	47.5	45.4	45.0	45.3	45.5	45.7	45.7	45.6	45.5
三、女教师数	Number of Female Teachers	20.33	21.58	22.43	22.61	22.4	22.81	23.43	22.87	24.25
普通高等学校	Regular Institutions of Higher Education	1.02	2.34	3.16	3.42	3.51	3.59	3.65	3.72	3.77
中等专业学校	Specialized Secondary School	0.60	0.94	1.17	1.07	0.99	0.94	0.92	0.83	0.63
普通中学	Regualr High School	6.26	7.94	8.4	8.43	8.22	8.15	8.21	8.26	8.35
小学	Primary School	12.07	10.32	9.7	9.69	9.68	10.13	10.65	10.06	11.5
四、女教师占教师总数 %	Percentage of Female Teachers in School	38.3	40.4	42.5	43.0	44.0	45.1	46.3	47.1	48.9
普通高等学校	Regular Institutions of Higher Education	33.6	39.7	42.3	43.3	43.5	43.9	44.1	44.6	45.1
中等专业学校	Specialized Secondary School	38.5	39.1	41.0	40.8	41.5	41.5	41.8	42.3	43.1
普通中学	Regualr High School	31.5	34.0	36.9	37.4	38.7	39.7	40.7	41.7	42.7
小学	Primary School	43.9	47.9	49.5	49.7	50.5	51.5	53.5	54.5	57.0

17-36 各级各类成人学校在校学生数
NUMBER OF ADULT STUDENTS ENROLLED AT SCHOOLS OF VARIOUS LEVELS

单位:万人 (10 000 persons)

各类学校	Item	2000	2005	2010	2011	2012	2013	2014	2015	2016
成人高等学校	Adult Higher Education	21.66	22.34	26.21	26.60	27.5	28.28	27.51	23.86	20.39
广播电视大学	Radio and TV Universities	2.78	2.52	0.54	0.61	0.45	0.43	0.33	0.35	0.2
职工大学	Schools of Higher Education for Staff	1.36	0.22	0.04	0.01	0.01	0.004			
管理干部学院	Colleges for Management and Caders	0.90	0.60	0.35	0.20	0.06	0.04	0.02	0.004	0.02
教育学院	Pedagogical College	0.94	0.89	0.37	0.26	0.24	0.24	0.23	0.18	0.17
普通高等学校办函授部、夜大学	Correspondence and Evening College Run by Regualr High Education	15.16	18.11	24.91	25.52	26.74	27.57	26.93	23.33	20
成人中等学校	Secondary Schools for Adults	139.75	35.90	81.77	49.27	43.85	45.06	39.46	28.16	34.71
中学	Middle School	0.61	2.42	3.69	2.64	4.57	4.24	3.67	3.36	3.37
技术培训学校	Technical Training Schools	131.86	33.48	78.08	46.63	39.28	40.82	35.79	24.8	31.35

注:成人高等学校学生数是本、专科学生数。

Note:The number of students in Adults Higher Education refers to the number of students in vocational schools.

17-37 研究生基本情况
BASIC CONDTIONS ABOUT POST-GRADUATES

单位:人 (person)

项目	Item	2012	2013	2014	2015	2016
高等学校在校研究生数	Number of Post-graduates at School in Institutions of Higher Education	108528	112707	114260	117085	119676
攻读博士学位研究生	Post-graduate Studying for Doctor's Degree	20927	22367	21509	22049	23088
攻读硕士学位研究生	Post-graduate Studying for Master's Degree	87601	90340	92751	95036	96588
招收研究生数	New Students Enrollment	37371	39027	38867	39785	40014
攻读博士学位研究生	Post-graduate Studying for Doctor's Degree	4766	5070	4891	4940	5023
攻读硕士学位研究生	Post-graduate Studying for Master's Degree	32605	33957	33976	34845	34991
毕业研究生数	Number of Graduates	32201	34585	31992	34116	34838
攻读博士学位研究生	Post-graduate Studying for Doctor's Degree	3692	3948	4038	3520	3669
攻读硕士学位研究生	Post-graduate Studying for Master's Degree	28509	30637	27954	30596	31169
科研单位在学研究生数	Number of Post-graduates Studying in Research Institutions	2328	2362	2399	2812	2443
攻读博士学位研究生	Post-graduate Studying for Doctor's Degree	760	819	845	883	925
攻读硕士学位研究生	Post-graduate Studying for Master's Degree	1568	1543	1554	1929	1518
招收研究生数	New Students Enrollment	777	779	790	778	791
攻读博士学位研究生	Post-graduate Studying for Doctor's Degree	220	229	246	237	251
攻读硕士学位研究生	Post-graduate Studying for Master's Degree	557	550	544	541	540
毕业研究生数	Number of Graduates	646	650	624	615	634
攻读博士学位研究生	Post-graduate Studying for Doctor's Degree	174	160	208	196	205
攻读硕士学位研究生	Post-graduate Studying for Master's Degree	472	490	416	419	429

主要统计指标解释

科技活动 指在自然科学、农业科学、医药科学、工程与技术科学、人文与社会科学领域(简称科学技术领域)中,与科技知识的产生、发展、传播和应用密切相关的有组织的活动。可分为研究与试验发展(R&D)、研究与试验发展成果应用及相关的科技服务三类活动。该定义是联合国教科文组织考虑成员国特别是发展中国家开展科技统计工作的需要,而对科技活动所作的统计界定。

科技活动人员 指直接从事科技活动、以及专门从事科技活动管理和为科技活动提供直接服务,累计的实际工作时间占全年制度工作时间10%及以上的人员。(1)直接从事科技活动的人员包括:在独立核算的科学研究与技术开发机构、高等学校、各类企业及其他事业单位内设的研究室、实验室、技术开发中心及中试车间(基地)等机构中从事科技活动的研究人员、工程技术人员、技术工人及其它人员;虽不在上述机构工作,但编入科技活动项目(课题)组的人员;科技信息与文献机构中的专业技术人员;从事论文设计的研究生等。(2)专门从事科技活动管理和为科技活动提供直接服务的人员,包括:独立核算的科学研究与技术开发机构、科技信息与文献机构、高等学校、各类企业及其他事业单位主管科技工作的负责人,专门从事科技活动的计划、行政、人事、财务、物资供应、设备维护、图书资料管理等工作的各类人员,但不包括保卫、医疗保健人员、司机、食堂人员、茶炉工、水暖工、清洁工等为科技活动提供间接服务的人员。该指标用来反映投入科技活动人力的规模。

科学家与工程师 指科技活动人员中具有高、中级技术职称(职务)的人员和不具有高、中级技术职称(职务)的大学本科及以上学历人员。该指标用来反映投入科技活动人力的素质。

研究与试验发展(R&D) 指在科学技术领域,为增加知识总量,以及运用这些知识去创造新的应用进行的系统的创造性的活动,包括基础研究、应用研究、试验发展三类活动。国际上通常采用R&D活动的规模和强度指标反映一国的科技实力和核心竞争力。

专业技术人员 指从事专业技术工作和专业技术管理工作的人员,即企事业单位中已经聘任专业技术职务从事专业技术工作和专业技术管理工作的人员,以及未聘任专业技术职务,现在专业技术岗位上工作的人员。包括工程技术人员,农业技术人员,科学研究人员,卫生技术人员,教学人员,经济人员,会计人员,统计人员,翻译人员,图书资料、档案、文博人员,新闻出版人员,律师、公证人员,广播电视播音人员,工艺美术人员,体育人员,艺术人员及企业政治思想工作人员,共十七个专业技术职务类别。用来反映科技人力资源情况。

科技活动经费筹集 指从各种渠道筹集到的计划用于科技活动的经费,包括政府资金、企业资金、事业单位资金、金融机构贷款、国外资金和其他资金等。反映各社会经济主体对促进科技进步所做的努力。

新产品 指采用新技术原理、新设计构思研制、生产的全新产品,或在结构、材质、工艺等某一方面比原有产品有明显改进,从而显著提高了产品性能或扩大了使用功能的产品。既包括政府有关部门认定并在有效期内的新产品,也包括企业自行研制开发,未经政府有关部门认定,从投产之日起一年之内的新产品。用来反映科技产出及对经济增长的直接贡献。

专利 是专利权的简称,是对发明人的发明创造经审查合格后,由专利局依据专利法授予发明人和设计人对该项发明创造享有的专有权。包括发明、实用新型和外观设计。反映拥有自主知识产权的科技和设计成果情况。

发明 指对产品、方法或者其改进所提出的新的技术方案。是国际通行的反映拥有自主知识产权技术的核心指标。

普通高等学校 指按照国家规定的设置标准和审批程序批准举办的,通过全国普通高等学校统一招生考试,招收高中毕业生为主要培养对象,实施高等教育的全日制大学、独立设置的学院和高等专科学校、高等职业学校和其他机构。

大学、独立设置的学院主要实施本科层次以上教育,高等专科学校、高等职业学校实施专科层次教育,其他机构是承担国家普通招生计划任务不计校数的机构。包括普通高等学校分校和批准筹建的普通高等学校等。

成人高等学校 指按照国家规定的设置标准和审批程序批准举办的,通过全国成人高等学校统一招生考试,招收具有高中毕业或同等学历的在职从业人员为主要培养对象，利用函授、业余、脱产等多种形式对其实施高等学历教育的学校。包括职工高等学校、农民高等学校、管理干部学院、教育学院、独立函授学院、广播电视大学、其他机构等。其他机构是承担国家成人招生计划任务不计校数的机构。

小学学龄儿童净入学率 指调查范围内已入小学学习的学龄儿童占校内外学龄儿童总数(包括弱智儿童，不包括盲聋哑儿童)的比重。计算公式为：

$$\text{小学学龄儿童净入学率}=\frac{\text{已入学的小学学龄儿童数}}{\text{校内外小学学龄儿童总数}}\times 1000‰$$

Explanatory Notes on Main Statistical Indicators

Scientific and Technological Activities (S&T Activities) refer to organized activities which are closely related with the creation, development, dissemination and application of the scientific and technical knowledge in the fields of natural sciences, agricultural science, medical science, engineering and technological science, humanities and social sciences (referred to as scientific and technological fields). S&T activities can be classified in to 3 categories: research and development (R&D) activities, application of R&D results, and related S&T services. This statistical definition is made by UNICHIEF for scientific and technological activities to meet the need of carrying out statistical work in this field for its member countries in particular those developing countries.

Personnel Engaged in S&T Activities efer to personnel directly engaged in S&T activities, in the management of S&T activities, and in providing direct service to S&T activities, who spend over 10% of the total working hours in a year in S&T activities. (1) Personnel directly engaged in S&T activities include researchers, engineers, technicians and other related personnel engaged in S&T activities in independent-accounting R&D institutions, institutions of higher learning, and in research institutes, laboratories, technology development centers and central experiment workshops under enterprises and institutions. Also included are people working in S&T research project teams, professional and technical personnel working in S&T information archiving institutes, and graduate students working on the design of their thesis. (2) Personnel engaged in the management of S&T activities and in providing direct service to S&T activities include senior management people responsible for S&T activities in independent-accounting R&D institutions, S&T information archiving institutes, institutions of higher learning, and in enterprises and institutions where S&T activities are undertaken. Also included are people responsible for the planning, administration, personnel management, financial management, logistics supply, equipment maintenance, information and library management that are related with S&T activities. People providing indirect services are excluded, such as security, medical service, drivers, plumbers, cleaners and those providing catering and related service. This indicator reflects the size of personnel engaged in S&T activities.

Scientists and Enginee rsrefer to persons engaged in S&T activities who have obtained titles of senior and middle level professional positions, and those without such position but have completed university or higher education. This indicator reflects the quality of personnel engaged in S&T activities.

Research and Development (R&D) refers to systematic and creative activities in the field of science and technology aiming at increasing the knowledge and using the knowledge for new application. R&D includes 3 categories of activities: basic research, applied research and experiments and development. The scale and intensity of R&D are widely used internationally to reflect the strength of S&T and the core competitiveness of a country in the world.

Professional and Technical Personnel refer to persons engaged in professional and technical work or in the management of professional and technical activities, i.e., people with professional or technical positions who are engaged in professional and technical work or in the management of professional and technical activities, and people without professional or technical positions but are working on professional or technical posts. They include professionals and technicians working in 17 categories of technical occupations including engineering, agriculture, scientific researches, medical service, teaching, economic research and application, accounting, statistics, translation, libraries, archives, cultural and museum service, journalism and publication, lawyers, notarization service, radio and television broadcasting, handicraft and fine arts, sports, performing art, and political workers in enterprises. This indicator reflects the condition of human resources in S&T.

Funding for S&T Activities refers to funds obtained from various sources for S&T activities, including government funds, self-raised funds by enterprises, self-raised funds by institutions, loans from financial institutions, foreign funds and other funds. This indicator reflects the efforts made by various social economic entities in promoting the development of S&T.

New Products refer to new products produced with new technology and new design, or products that represent noticeable improvement in terms of structure, material, or production process so as to improve significantly the character or function of the older versions. They include new products certified by relevant government agencies within the period of certification, as well as new products designed and produced by enterprises within a year without certification by government agencies. This indictor reflects the direct contribution of S&T output to economic growth.

Patentis an abbreviation for the patent right andrefers to the exclusive right of ownership by the inventors or designers for the creation or inventions, given from the patent offices after due process of assessment and approval in accordance with the Patent Law. Patents are granted for inventions, utility models and designs. This indicator reflects the achievements of S&T and design with independent intellectual property.

Inventions refer to the new technical proposals to the products or methods or their modifications. This is universal core indicator reflecting the technologies with independent intellectual property.

Regular Institutions of Higher Learning refer to educational establishments set up according to the government evaluation and approval procedures, enrolling graduates from senior secondary schools and providing higher education courses and training for senior professionals. They include full-time universities, colleges, high professional schools, high professional vocational schools and others.

Universities and colleges are mainly providing undergraduate courses; those high professional schools and high professional vocational schools are mainly providing professional trainings; and others refer to educational establishments, which are responsible for enrolling students but not covered in the total number of schools, including: branch schools of universities and colleges, and universities and colleges that have been proved and prepared to construct.

Institutions of Higher Learning for Adults refer to educational establishments, set up in line with relevant rules approved by the government, enrolling staff and workers with senior secondary school or equivalent education, and providing higher education courses in many forms of correspondence, spare time, or full time for adults. Professionals thus trained receive a qualification equivalent to graduates studying regular courses at regular universities, colleges and professional colleges. Institutions of higher learning for adults include schools of high education for staff and workers, schools of high education for peasants, colleges for management cadres, pedagogical colleges, independent correspondence colleges, Radio and TV universities and other educational establishments. Other educational establishments are responsible for enrolling adult students but not covered in the number of schools.

Enrollment Rate of Primary School Age Children refers to the proportion of school age children enrolled at schools to the total number of school age children both in and outside schools (including retarded children, but excluding blind, deaf and mute children). The formula is:

Enrollment Rate of Primary School-age Children = (Total Primary School-age Children at Schools)/(TotalPrimary School age Children Both at and OutsideSchools) x 100%

18 卫生和社会服务

Public Health and Social Services

18-1 卫生机构数
NUMBER OF HEALTH CARE INSTITUTIONS

单位：个 (unit)

年份 Year	总计 Total	医院 Hospitals	综合医院 General Hospitals	中医医院 Hosptials Specialized in Traditional Chinese Medicine	专科医院 Specialized Hosptials	基层医疗卫生机构 Basic Medical Institutions	社区卫生服务中心(站) Community Health Service Centers	街道卫生院 Urban Health Centers	乡镇卫生院 Township Health Centers
2006	10052	575	401	82	82		664	55	1140
2007	11093	580	393	83	93		1089	53	1160
2008	10305	593	389	86	106		1115	48	1155
2009	32790	614	409	86	105		1142	48	1134
2010	34269	602	394	87	107		1294	44	1149
2011	35625	608	393	91	111	34509	1278	34	1161
2012	35240	650	414	95	126	34063	1220	34	1165
2013	35631	711	444	98	153	34042	1231	36	1152
2014	36077	771	483	102	169	34503	1175	36	1150
2015	36173	869	532	109	208	34569	1189	29	1140
2016	36261	928	550	115	237	34706	1236	31	1136

注：卫生事业机构数从2009年起包含村卫生室数量。
Note: The statistics of health care units, hospital beds and health care professionals started to include the village clinics since 2012.

18-1 续表 continued

单位：个 (unit)

年 份 Year	村卫生室 Village Clinices	门诊部(所) Outpatient Department	专业公共卫生机构 Specialized Public Health Institutions	疾病预防控制中心 Center for Disease Control and Prevention	专科疾病防治院(所/站) Specialized Disease Prevention & Treatment Institution	妇幼保健院(所/站) Women and Children Care Agencies	卫生监督所(中心) Health Inspection Institution (center)
2006		7116		114	116	95	72
2007		7677		113	118	100	83
2008		6871		110	109	99	93
2009	22405	6936		112	87	99	97
2010	24112	6729		115	84	100	98
2011	25204	6832	425	112	83	100	98
2012	24976	6668	438	111	83	100	109
2013	24941	6682	779	113	75	101	102
2014	24919	7223	696	112	76	100	103
2015	24796	7415	577	113	76	103	107
2016	24788	7515	559	115	74	104	109

18-2 卫生机构人员数
NUMBER OF PERSONS ENGAGED IN HEALTH CARE INSTITUTIONS

单位：万人 (10 000 persom)

年份 Year	总计 Total	卫生技术人员 Medical Technical Personel	执业(助理)医师 Licensed (Assistant) Doctors	执业医师 Licensed Doctors	注册护士 Pegistertered Nurses	药师(士) Pharmacist	乡村医生和卫生员 Village Doctors and Assistants	每千人口医生数(人) Number of Doctors per 1000 Population (person)
1970	10.30	8.33	4.15		1.83			1.03
1975	15.05	11.85	4.91		2.05			1.11
1980	19.94	15.59	6.32		3.09			1.35
1985	23.58	18.48	7.27		3.77			1.47
1990	26.75	20.92	8.68		5.66			1.62
1991	27.51	21.55	8.79		5.97			1.62
1992	28.24	22.15	9.02		6.25			1.64
1993	28.91	22.46	9.16		6.49			1.64
1994	29.31	22.84	9.38		6.64			1.66
1995	29.55	23.20	9.58		6.83			1.68
1996	29.65	23.47	9.72		7.00			1.67
1997	30.38	23.90	9.96		7.21			1.70
1998	30.31	23.96	10.11		7.29			1.71
1999	30.40	24.05	10.31		7.41			1.74
2000	30.14	23.88	10.30		7.53			1.74
2001	29.48	23.41	10.21		7.51			1.72
2002	25.30	20.59	8.63		6.35			1.43
2003	25.62	20.83	8.72		6.38			1.45
2004	26.06	21.38	8.99		6.62			1.49
2005	26.22	21.50	8.98		6.94			1.49
2006	26.53	21.80	9.01		7.06			1.49
2007	27.80	22.70	9.20	7.65	7.69			1.52
2008	28.48	23.38	9.20	7.7	8.06			1.51
2009	33.71	24.70	9.79	8.22	8.73		3.86	1.59
2010	34.95	25.58	9.95	8.37	9.38	1.77	4.15	1.62
2011	36.52	26.81	10.21	8.53	10.21	1.77	4.41	1.66
2012	38.64	28.87	10.91	9.01	11.57	1.74	4.30	1.89
2013	41.12	30.93	11.72	9.65	12.79	1.77	4.29	1.90
2014	43.82	33.55	12.61	10.39	14.40	1.78	4.22	2.17
2015	47.55	36.76	13.60	11.22	16.51	1.82	4.09	2.32
2016	49.54	38.54	14.24	11.74	17.52	1.85	4.04	2.42

注：卫生人员数从2009年起包含村卫生室卫生人员数量。
Note: The statistics of health care units, hospital beds and health care professionals started to include the village clinics since 2012.

18-3 卫生机构床位数
NUMBER OF BEDS IN HEALTH CARE INSTITUTIONS

单位：万张 (10 000 beds)

年份 Year	总计 Total	医院 Hospitals	基层医疗卫生机构 Basic Medical Institutions	乡镇卫生院 Township Health Centers	专业公共卫生机构 Specialized Public Health Institutions	每千人口卫生机构床位数(张) Beds of Medical InstitutionsPer 1000Population (bed)
1970	6.14	5.56				1.38
1975	9.90	9.02				2.05
1980	12.59	11.22				2.40
1985	14.70	11.52				2.34
1990	16.34	13.16				2.45
1991	16.52	13.43				2.47
1992	16.62	13.46				2.44
1993	16.30	13.48				2.41
1994	16.13	13.40				2.36
1995	15.78	13.08				2.29
1996	14.42	13.08				2.24
1997	15.30	13.08				2.24
1998	15.09	13.03				2.21
1999	14.90	12.91				2.07
2000	14.96	12.99				2.18
2001	14.62	12.91				2.18
2002	12.72	8.53				2.12
2003	13.59	9.39				2.26
2004	13.78	9.52				2.29
2005	13.96	9.67				2.31
2006	14.24	9.81				2.35
2007	15.06	10.36				2.48
2008	16.73	11.32				2.75
2009	18.72	12.66		4.33		2.82
2010	20.04	13.50		4.64		3.26
2011	22.40	15.20	6.23	5.05	0.96	3.63
2012	25.30	17.38	6.83	5.58	1.09	4.38
2013	28.82	20.05	7.47	6.18	1.32	4.97
2014	31.83	22.20	8.15	6.77	1.48	5.47
2015	34.38	24.66	8.39	6.90	1.57	5.87
2016	36.16	25.73	8.82	7.21	1.61	6.14

18-4 分等级医疗卫生机构情况(2016)
HEALTH CARE INSTITUTIONS BY LEVEL(2016)

单位:个 (Unit)

项目	Iem	合计 Total	三级 Thrid-level	二级 Second-level	一级 First-level	其他 Others
医院	Hospitals	928	121	302	252	253
其中:综合医院	General Hospitals	550	68	157	168	157
中医医院	Hosptials Specialized in Traditional Chinese Medicine	115	20	63	19	13
中西医结合医院	Hospitals of Traditional Chinese Medicine and Western Medicine	20	3	3	8	6
民族医院	Minortiy Hospitals	3		3		
专科医院	Specialized Hosptials	237	32	76	57	72
妇幼保健院	Women and Children Care Agencies	96	12	83		1
专科疾病防治院	Specialized Prevention & Treatment Centers	11		2	2	7

18-5 医院业务工作开展情况
BASIC STATISTICS ON HOSPITAL BUSINESS

项　目	Item	2000	2005	2010	2014	2015	2016
机构数 (个)	Number of Institutions (unit)	507	574	603	771	869	928
诊疗总人次数 (万人次)	Number of Clients (10 000 person-times)	4616.20	5452.11	7710.20	11399.93	12111.16	12668.59
#门、急诊人次数 (万人次)	#Number of Outpacients and Emergency (10 000 person-times)	4396.10	5107.19	7533.44	10976.72	11721.98	12384.24
出院人数 (万人)	Number of discharged Patients (10 000 persons)	158.93	219.45	423.28	735.70	780.05	836.90
死亡 (万人)	Dead (10 000 persons)	1.59	2.28	3.13	3.29	3.81	4.31
病死率 (%)	Rate of Death from Illness (%)	1.08	1.04	0.74	0.45	0.49	0.51
病床平均周转次数 (次)	Average times of Beds Usage (time)	18.66	23.99	32.50	35.40	33.98	34.26
病床平均工作日 (日)	Average Day of Beds Usage (day)	218.79	268.24	350.40	350.90	337.40	335.46
病床使用率 (%)	Utilization Rate of Beds (%)	59.94	73.49	96.01	96.14	92.44	91.91
出院者平均住院日 (日)	Average Days for Hospitalization Discharged (day)	11.12	10.71	10.50	9.70	9.83	9.65

18-6 农村村级卫生组织情况
STATISTICS ON HEALTH CARE INSTITUTIONS AT VILLAGE LEVEL

项 目	Item	2000	2005	2010	2014	2015	2016
行政村数 (个)	Number of Villages (unit)	32400	26678	26018	25448	25109	25064
村设置的医疗点数 (个)	Medical care Station Set by Villages (unit)	26879	21136	24057	24918	24795	24788
#村或集体办	#Set by Villages or Collective Set	14666	11207	15395	15551	15495	15497
联合办	Set with Village Doctors	4640	3777	2815	2445	2984	2983
医院设点	Set by Hospital	2403	2410	3348	4085	3559	3603
私人办	Set by Individual	4344	2907	1833	1998	1922	1860
其他	Others	826	835	666	839	835	845
乡村医生和卫生员人数 (人)	Number of Village Doctors and Medical Working Personel (person)	57511	34417	41473	42304	40897	40429
#乡村医生	#Village Doctors	44490	33375	40425	40502	38970	38506
卫生员	Medical Working Personel	1301	1042	1048	1802	1927	1923

主要统计指标解释

卫生机构 包括医疗机构、疾病预防控制中心(防疫站)、采供血机构、卫生监督及监测(检验)机构、医学科研和在职培训机构、健康教育所等。

医疗机构 包括医院、社区卫生服务中心(站)、疗养院、卫生院、门诊部、诊所(卫生所、医务室)、妇幼保健院(所、站)、专科疾病防治院(所、站)、急救中心(站)和临床检验中心。医疗机构分为非赢利性医疗机构和赢利性医疗机构。

医院 包括综合医院、中医医院、中西医结合医院、民族医院、各类专科医院和护理院。

卫生技术人员 指卫生机构中医生、护理人员 、药剂人员、检验人员等卫生技术人员。

医生 指在医疗、预防保健机构工作且取得《执业医师证书》的执业医师和执业助理医师。

Explanatory Notes on Main Statistical Indicators

Health Care Institutions include medical institutions, disease prevention and control centers (epidemic prevention stations), blood gathering and supplying institutions, health supervision and inspection (check up) institutions, medicinal scientific research and on-job training institutions, health education and so on.

Medical Organizations include hospitals, health service centers (stations) of communities, nursing homes, health centers, clinics, clinics (health stations and infirmaries), maternity and child care agencies (centers and stations), special disease prevention and curing agencies (centers and stations), first aid centers (stations) and clinical inspection centers. Medical organizations are grouped by two types: profit-making and non-profit-making medical organizations.

Hospitals include polyclinics, traditional Chinese medical hospitals, hospitals integrated with traditional Chinese therapeutics and western therapeutics, ethical hospitals, various specialties hospitals and nursing hospitals.

Medical Technical Personnel refers to doctors, assistant nurses, pharmacists, and laboratory technicians working in medical institutions.

Doctors refer to certified physicians and certified assistant physicians with certifications working in medical and health care and prevention agencies.

19 文化和体育

Culture and Sports

19-1 文化事业机构、人员数
NUMBER OF CULTURAL INSTITUTIONS AND PERSONEL

单位：个、人 (unit, person)

项 目	Item	2010	2011	2012	2013	2014	2015	2016
艺术业机构	Art Performing Institution		239	295	363	328	340	366
#剧团	#Troupes		172	226	307	273	282	308
#剧场	#Theater		65	66	53	52	58	58
文物事业机构	Historical Relics Institutions	166	175	214	291	300	302	310
#博物馆	#Museums	121	125	161	170	174	175	183
图书馆事业机构	Library Institutions	107	109	111	112	112	112	112
群众文化事业机构	Public Culture Institutions	1378	1378	1379	1382	1390	1399	1402
文化馆	Cultural Centers				120	121	122	123
文化站	Art Center				1262	1269	1277	1279
艺术业人员数	Number of People Engaged in Art Performing		5018	10976	10384	9774	10596	9969
#剧团人员	#Staff in Troupes		4580	9216	9005	8520	8999	8699
#剧场人员	#Staff in Theater		437	1750	1367	1241	1597	1270
文物事业人员数	Number of Historical Relics Staffs	3297	3596	4334	4713	4928	5025	5162
#博物馆人员	#Number of staff in Library	2298	2380	3078	3360	3380	3449	3556
图书馆事业人员数	Number of People Engaged in Library	2151	2149	2219	2226	2231	2212	2198
群众文化事业人员数	Number of People Engaged in Public Art	4943	5022	5044	4912	5045	4869	4945
文化馆人员	Number of People in Cultural Centers				2270	2294	2230	2220
文化站人员	Number of People in Art Centers				2642	2751	2639	2725
#乡镇文化站	#Township Cultural Stations	2175	2221	2256	2046	2234	2109	2159

19-2 公共图书馆发展情况
DEVELOPMENT STATISTICS ON PUBLIC LIBRARIES

项 目		Item		2005	2010	2012	2013	2014	2015	2016
机构数	(个)	Number of Library	(unit)	102	107	111	112	112	112	112
藏书数	(万册)	Total Collections	(10 000 volumes)	1923	2361	2521	2648	2822	3003	3318
书架单层总长度	(万米)	Total Length of Bookshelves	(10 000 m)	101	111	51	53	53	54	56
有效借书证数	(万个)	Valid Library card number	(10 000 units)	72	104	138	108	128	144	167
图书流通情况		Number of Circulation								
公共图书馆流通人次	(万人次)	The public library circulation	(10 000 person-times)	1145	1516	1516	1763	1868	1955	2082
册次	(万册数)	Volume-time	(10 000 volume-times)	927	1846	1386	1570	1755	1816	1882
为读者服务举办各种活动		Service for Readers								
次数	(次)	Times	(time)	1621	1790	2928	3098	3498	3615	4874
参加人数	(万人次)	Number of Readers Involved	(10 000 person-times)	176	105	128	178	173	163	233
当年新购图书	(万册)	New Books Purchaesd in 2012	(10 000 volume-times)	43	60	111	138	161	185	296
图书费	(万元)	Purchase Expenses	(10 000 yuan)	1296	1847	4210	5076	5713	7302	7948

19-3 公共图书馆藏书及分类情况
STATISTICS ON BOOKS AND TYPE OF BOOKS IN PUBLIC LIBRARIES

单位：万册 (10 000 volumes)

年份 Year	合 计 Total	#外 文 #Foreign	#古 籍 #Ancient	#图书 #New Books	其它藏量 Other Reserves
1996	1472	82	97		
1997	1533	81	97		
1998	1599	81	96		
1999	1643	81	96		
2000	1678	82	97		
2001	1709	83	98		
2002	1759	81	99		
2003	1819	83	98		
2004	1867		94		
2005	1923		97		
2006	1981		100		
2007	2037		96		
2008	2106		97		
2009	2181		96		
2010	2361		95		
2011	2410		98	1860	453
2012	2521		98	2008	415
2013	2648		99	2156	393
2014	2822		101	2295	426
2015	3003		101	2462	441
2016	3318		98	2752	468

注：其它藏量包括报刊、视听文献、缩微制品、电子图书和其它

Note: Other reserves include newspapers, audiovisual documents, microform, electronic books and other materials.Contains a total electronic books

19-4 图书、报纸、期刊出版情况
STATISTICS ON PUBLICATION OF BOOKS, NEWSPAPERS AND PERIODICALS

项 目	Item	2000	2005	2010	2013	2014	2015	2016
一、图书出版种数 (种)	Category of Library Books Published (kind)	4529	6535	10464	13900	16043	15543	15105
新出版 (种)	New Publications (kind)	2443	3739	6328	8445	9662	8932	7911
总印数 (千册)	Total Prints (1 000 volume)	288416	345510	275330	262740	271933	262997	270444
总印张 (千印张)	Total Number of Paper Printed (1 000 pages)	1552128	2495183	1997639	2088169	2288053	2250020	2236382
二、杂志出版种数 (种)	**Category of Magazines Published** (kind)	391	407	407	408	409	412	414
总印数 (千册)	Total Prints (1000 volume)	220280	196800	300770	309375	280895	251249	185441
总印张 (千印张)	Total Number of Paper Printed (1 000 pages)	746145	745526	1482345	1781708	1662398	1458924	1027425
三、报刊出版种数 (种)	Category of Newspapers and Periodicals Published (kind)	164	193	130	130	130	129	129
总印数 (千份)	Total Prints (1 000 copies)	1342282	1956980	1816720	1982020	1910667	1539203	1226957
总印张 (万印张)	Total Number of Paper Printed (10 000 pages)	339434	520833	889514	858508	826749	538040	348483

19-5 艺术活动、群众文化活动、图书馆及博物馆活动情况
STATISTICS ON ART ACTIVITIES, PUBLIC CULTURE ACTIVITIES, LIBRARY AND MUSEUM

项 目	Item	2000	2005	2010	2013	2014	2015	2016
艺术表演团体	Art Performance Troupes							
演出场次 (万场次)	Number of Performances (10 000shows)				3.73	3.9	3.85	3.85
国内演出观众人数 (万人次)	Number of Domestic Audience (10 000 person-times)				2880	3344	2902	3052
艺术表演场馆	Art Performance Places							
演(映)出场次 (万场次)	Number of Performances (10 000shows)				2.50	2.71	3.49	5.42
观众人次 (万人次)	Number of Audience (10 000 person-times)				256	262	288	329
群众文化活动	Public Culture Activities							
举办展览个数 (个)	Number of Expo Displayed (unit)	2785	2653	4276	4045	4467	4399	5542
举办训练班结业人数 (万人次)	Number of Training Activities (10 000 person-times)	9.90	13.00	10.80	87.8	95.1	97.6	124.0
图书馆活动	Library Activities							
书刊文献外借人次 (千人次)	Number of Circulation (1000 person-times)					10525	9918	10279
图书流通册次 (千册)	Number of Circulation (1000 volumes)	9485	9267	18462	15701	17554	18164	18821
博物馆活动	Museum Activities							
基本陈列展览 (个)	Displays Exhibition (unit) (unit)	210	218	686	796	857	964	988
参观人数 (千人次)	Visitors (1000 persons) (time)	1819	2194	19212	23576	25996	26239	26712

19-6 文化、文物事业经费支出及基本建设情况
BASIC CONDITIONS ABOUT EXPENDITURES ON CULTURE AND HISTORICAL RELICS AND ITS CONSTRUCTION

单位：万元 (10 000 yuan)

项　目	Item	2012	2013	2014	2015	2016
文化、文物事业经费支出总计	Total Expenditures on Culture and Historical Relics	286344	333675	357361	450545	571068
文化事业	Culture	218712	249298	270471	338057	416761
艺术表演团体	Art Performing Groups	43492	52952	54940	63525	74001
艺术表演场所	Art Performing Places	5245	9233	10163	9784	10828
图书馆	Library	34313	43633	45054	50295	49833
群众文化	Public Culture	36247	39667	43503	51708	68180
中等专业学校	Secondary Vocation School	3511	3276	2972	12412	22985
干部训练	Cadre Taining					
其他文化事业	Others	95833	100466	113768	150333	191165
文物事业	Historical Relics	67632	84377	86890	112488	154307
博物馆	Museum	38330	54176	56199	59126	101517
文物事业机构	Institutions of Historical Relics	19254	16912	12956	21621	24814
其它文物事业	Others	10048	13290	17735	31741	27976
文化、文物基本建设完成投资	Investment in Culture & Historical Relics Cause Construction	31446	83300	64377	35872	45187
文化事业	Culture Cause	21360	52887	39263	17955	25945
文物事业	Historical Relics Cause	10086	30413	25114	17917	19242

19-7 广播电视从业人员基本情况(2016)
BASIC STATISTICS ON PERSONEL ENGAGED IN BROADCASTING AND TELEVISION (2016)

单位：人 (person)

项目	Item	全省合计 Total of the Province	省级 Provincial Level	市州级 Municiple and Prefecture Level	县级 County Level
从业人员	Personel	39999	24590	6475	8934
其中：长期职工	#Long-term Staff and Workers	38236	23485	6320	8431
党员	Party Members(Communists)	15854	8429	2976	4449
按岗位分：	Classified by Job Division:				
管理人员	Management Personel	6852	3712	1230	1910
专业技术人员	Professional Technical Personel	21433	12569	4158	4706
编辑、记者	Editors and Reporters	6959	2558	2145	2256
播音员、主持人	Announcers and Hosts	1223	414	420	389
按学历分：	Classified by Academic Qualifications:				
研究生及以上	#Graduate and Above	1113	707	288	118
本科及大专	Undergraduate and Post-secondary	25995	15012	5296	5687
高中及以下	High School and Below	12891	8871	891	3129
按职称分：	Classified According to Occupation:				
正高	Senior	348	282	63	3
副高	Vice-senior	1384	852	464	68
中级	Medium	7162	3270	1884	2008
初级及以下	Primary and Below	20736	13738	3092	3906
按年龄分：	Classified by Age:				
35岁以下	35 and Below	13481	8878	2318	2285
36岁至50岁	36-50	20305	12386	3008	4911
50岁以上	50 and Above	6213	3326	1149	1738

19-8 广播电视传输覆盖与经济效益
STATISTICS ON BROADCASTING AND TV COVERAGE RATING AND ECONOMIC BENEFITS

项 目	Item	2010	2013	2014	2015	2016
广播覆盖率 (%)	Broadcasting Coverage Rate (%)	98.10	98.80	98.90	99.08	99.33
电视覆盖率 (%)	TV Coverage Rate (%)	98.11	98.81	98.89	98.98	99.15
有线电视用户 (万户)	Cable Television Users (10 000 household)	894.07	1045.31	1070.89	1067.80	1060.80
中短波发射转播台/机 (座/部)	Medium and Short-Wave Transmitting Stations (set)	26/76	28/86	28/86	28/88	28/89
中短波发射转播台功率 (千瓦)	Power of Medium and Short-Wave Transmitters (kw)	1256.00	1371	1371	1391	1401
调频电视发射转播台 (座/部)	FM and TelevisionTransmitting Stations (set)				481/484	478/486
调频发射机 (部)	FM Transmitters (set)	584	609	611	484	486
调频发射机功率 (千瓦)	Power of FM Transmitters (kw)	520.31	558.91	564.91	623.69	633.97
电视发射转播台 (座/部)	Television Transmitting Station (set)	991/1275	908/1191	885/1170	481/753	478/751
电视发射转播台功率 (千瓦)	Power of Television Transmitters (kw)	592.22	583.88	586.70	598.69	590.21
微波线路站数/长度 (座/公里)	Length of Micro-Wave Route Per Station (set/km)	121/ 2961.05	116/ 2906.05	116/ 2906.05	126/ 2875.05	122/ 2829.05
创收收入 (亿元)	Revenue (100 million yuan)	48.57	73.12	89.02	89.40	91.23
固定资产原值 (亿元)	Original Price of Fixed Assets(100 million yuan)	90.43	95.31	104.43	110.89	121.93

19-9 广播电视宣传、节目制作和电影活动
RADIO TELEVISION PROGRAMME PRODUCTION AND FILM PROMOTION ACTIVITIES

项　　目		Item		2005	2010	2014	2015	2016
广播电台	(座)	Broadcasting Station	(unit)	11	11	6	6	6
电视台	(座)	TV Station	(unit)	12	12	8	8	6
广播电视台	(座)	Radiated TV Station	(unit)	71	71	76	81	77
广播节目套数	(套)	Number of Radio Programs	(unit)	81	85	87	87	88
广播平均日播音时间	(小时)	Average Broadcasting Hour per Week	(h)	1040.40	1225.65	1296.97	1308.36	1318.63
广播节目年制作能力	(万小时)	Annual Capacity of Radio Program Production	(10 000 h)	20.59	23.54	24.29	24.63	26.71
电视节目套数	(套)	Number of TV Programs	(unit)	113	114	117	114	113
电视平均周播出时间	(万小时)	Average TV Hour per Week	(10 000 h)	1.05	1.26	1.32	1.31	1.31
电视节目年制作能力	(万小时)	Annual Capacity of TV program Production	(10 000 h)	7.93	9.48	10.92	10.77	10.99
电视剧制作	(部/集)	Production of TV Series	(episode)	11/ 208	11/314	20/854	19/835	17/613
城市电影活动		Movie of city						
放映场次数数	(万场)	Times Projected	(10 000 times)			162.47	231.71	334.99
观众人数	(千人次)	Number of the audience	(1000 person-times)			43905	66425	75536

19-10 分单位类型、分人员类型体育系统从业人员数(2016)
NUMBER OF STAFF AND WORKERS IN SPORTS COMMISSIONS(2016)

单位：人 (person)

项目	Item	合计 Total	公务员 Civilian	管理人员 Adminis-trator	专业技术人员 小计 Subtotal	其中：教练员 Coach	其中：科研人员 Scientific research personnel	其中：卫生技术人员 Health technical personnel	运动员 Athlete	工勤人员 Worker	其他 Others
合计	**Total**	**6358**	**1012**	**1189**	**2043**	**837**	**29**	**41**	**1113**	**549**	**452**
体育行政机关	Sports Administrative Authority	1228	1012	–	–	–	–	–	–	78	138
运动项目管理部门 (优秀运动队)	Sports Management Department	1128	–	148	225	206		9	713	42	
本科院校	Undergraduate School	1223	–	159	674	36		28	325	65	
体育运动学校	Sports School for athelets	491	–	79	376	147	5	2		36	
少年儿童体育学校	Sports School for Kids	684	–	181	391	304	2	1	72	29	11
体育中学	Middle School for Athelets	61	–	10	47	18	3			4	
训练基地	Training Base	155	–	58	47	32			3	37	10
体育场馆	Stadium	822	–	341	232	94		1		229	20
体育科研机构	Sports Science Reaserch Institution	50	–	10	40		19				
其他事业单位	Other Institution	497	–	191	11					25	270
其它	Others	19	–	12						4	3

19-11 等级裁判员、运动员情况
NUMBER OF ATHLETES AND REFEREES IN GRADES

单位：人 (person)

项 目	Item	2000	2005	2010	2011	2012	2013	2014	2015	2016
等级裁判员合计	Number of Referees in Grades	1195	787	1504	1870	1667	2335	1725	3021	1570
国际裁判	International Referees									7
国家级裁判	National Referees	29	25	24	23	15	27		4	21
一级裁判	First Grade	143	115	352	378	403	377	394	317	176
二级裁判	Second Grade	1023	647	1128	1469	1249	1931	1331	2700	1366
等级运动员合计	Number of Athletes in Grade	418	1149	1639	1570	1723	2109	2111	1556	1230
国际运动健将	International Master of Sports	6		1	5	8		4	4	
运动健将	Master of Sports	36	36	21	54	54	61	41	68	77
一级运动员	First Grade	10	247	180	227	328	214	359	316	385
二级运动员	Second Grade	366	866	1437	1284	1333	1834	1707	1168	768

19-12 体育竞赛成果情况
STATISTICS ON ACHIEVEMENT IN SPORTS COMPETITION

项 目	Item	2000	2005	2010	2012	2013	2014	2015	2016
世界比赛获奖牌数 (枚)	**Number of Medals Won in International Games (unit)**	**13**	**5**	**12**	**64**	**51**	**86**	**66**	**107**
金牌	Gold Medal	4	3	2	30	25	41	29	50
银牌	Silver Medal	6	2	3	21	9	23	32	32
铜牌	Bronze Medal	3		7	13	17	22	5	25
亚洲比赛获奖牌数 (枚)	**Number of Medals Won in Asia Games (unit)**	**5**	**7**	**13**	**24**	**11**	**26**	**35**	**44**
金牌	Gold Medal	4	5	8	15	5	17	17	23
银牌	Silver Medal		2	4	7	4	3	9	16
铜牌	Bronze Medal	1		1	2	2	6	9	5
全国比赛获前六名 (人)	**Top Six Places in National Games (person)**		**155**	**134**	**461**	**356**	**356**	**502**	**655**
第一名	First Place	35	24	21	82	57	48	75	116
第二名	Second Place	22	23	21	74	72	53	78	102
第三名	Third Place	21	27	17	76	82	69	85	131
第四名	Fourth Place	35	24	23	68	48	55	76	91
第五名	Fifth Place	29	31	30	86	65	87	109	126
第六名	Sixth Place	26	26	22	75	32	44	79	89

19-13 新建健身场地设施情况(2016)
SITUATION OF NEW-BUILT FITNESS FACILITIES(2016)

项目	Item		合计 Total	村级农民体育健身工程 Town-based Peasant Fitness Project	乡镇体育健身工程 County-based Fitness Project	全民健身路径工程 Citizen "Fitness Path" Project	全民健身活动中心 Citizen Fitness Center
数量 (个)	Number	(unit)	7797	2521	73	4892	6
器材件数 (件)	Number of Instrument	(piece)	31355	–	–	31269	
场地面积 (平方米)	Area	(sq. m)	2852254.76	1791067	135761	441722.76	16240
场地长度 (米)	Length	(m)	103600	–	–	–	
投资总额 (万元)	Total Invenstment	(10 000 Yuan)	53402	4427	1704	7224	2629

19-13 续表

项目	Item		户外健身场地设施 Outdoor Fitness Facilities					其他场地设施 Other Fitness Facilities
			体育公园 Fitness Park	全民健身广场 Citizen Fitness Square	户外体育营地 Outdoor Fitness Center	社区运动场地 Community-based Fitness Square	健身步道 Fitness Path	
数量 (个)	Number	(unit)	3	35	1	69	6	191
器材件数 (件)	Number of Instrument	(piece)	–	–	–	–	–	86
场地面积 (平方米)	Area	(sq. m)	55000	147500	45688	92086	–	127190
场地长度 (米)	Length	(m)	–	–	–	–	103600	–
投资总额 (万元)	Total Invenstment	(10 000 Yuan)	25084	2286	54	1723	4110	4160

19-14 分市州文化及相关产业“三上”法人单位数(2016)
NUMBER OF LEGAL PERSONS OF CULTURE AND RELAVANT INDUSTRY ABOVE DESIGNATED BY REGION(2016)

单位：个 (unit)

地 区	Region	“三上”法人单位数 Legal Persons	规上文化制造业 Cultual Manufacturing	限上文化批发和零售业 Wholesale and Rerail of Culture	规上文化服务业 Services of Culture
全 省	**Province**	**1814**	**569**	**452**	**793**
武汉市	Wuhan	505	73	90	342
黄石市	Huangshi	46	21	7	18
十堰市	Shiyan	43	14	14	15
宜昌市	Yichang	311	92	61	158
襄阳市	Xiangyang	360	100	111	149
鄂州市	Ezhou	31	11	8	12
荆门市	Jingmen	51	24	21	6
孝感市	Xiaogan	108	64	30	14
荆州市	Jingzhou	70	28	29	13
黄冈市	Huanggang	100	43	37	20
咸宁市	Xianning	63	36	9	18
随州市	Suizhou	32	20	8	4
恩施州	Enshi	54	15	24	15
仙桃市	Xiantao	18	15	2	1
潜江市	Qianjiang	7	6		1
天门市	Tianmen	10	7	1	2
神农架	Shennongjia	5			5

19-15 分市州规模以上文化制造业企业基本情况(2016)
BASIC CONDITIONS CULTURAL MANUFACTURING ENTERPRISES ABOVE DESIGNATED SIZE BY REGION(2016)

单位：万元 (10 000 yuan)

地 区	Region	企业单位数(个) Number of Enterprises (unit)	年末从业人员(人) Engaged Person at Year-end (person)	资产总计 Total Assets	营业收入 Business Revenue	营业税金及附加 Taxes and Extra Charges on Business	营业利润 Operating Profit	应交增值税 Value-added Tax Payable
全 省	**Province**	**569**	**100662**	**7900663.6**	**11859901**	**78617.3**	**571238.2**	**259724.8**
武汉市	Wuhan	73	14941	2914742	2134659.2	5709.5	121960.6	47536.6
黄石市	Huangshi	21	3901	126862.3	159010.2	1369	10313.2	1691.8
十堰市	Shiyan	14	1489	102546.4	76434.8	2479	4469.2	3528
宜昌市	Yichang	92	18970	1722807.4	2449497.9	10226.1	128517.4	63995.6
襄阳市	Xiangyang	100	20696	1110702.3	2689848.7	13924.7	92242.3	54022.2
鄂州市	Ezhou	11	974	42954.4	270326.7	2208.2	9589.8	13240.8
荆门市	Jingmen	24	2612	169371.1	361748.6	6502.7	26019.9	3853.7
孝感市	Xiaogan	64	9053	495928.4	1322724.1	23894	62089.1	29649.9
荆州市	Jingzhou	28	6301	325020.4	832970.5	1328.1	14673.5	9963.8
黄冈市	Huanggang	43	6649	294510.8	338927	1770.6	12081.6	8032.2
咸宁市	Xianning	36	4950	261413.2	453984.9	2741.7	31848.8	6084.9
随州市	Suizhou	20	3047	108248.5	220860.8	1089.8	15481.6	3326.8
恩施州	Enshi	15	1688	42228.8	77122.8	697.4	6909.2	1468.7
仙桃市	Xiantao	15	2892	107344	269264.5	2852.2	22577.1	10873.6
潜江市	Qianjiang	6	370	16211.9	93479.4	1398.9	6032	201.5
天门市	Tianmen	7	2129	59771.7	109041.1	425.4	6432.9	2254.7
神农架	Shennongjia							

19-16 分市州限额以上文化批发和零售企业基本情况(2016)
BASIC CONDITIONS OF ENTERPRISES OF WHOLESALE AND RETAIL OF CULTURE ABOVE DESIGNATED SIZE BY REGION(2016)

单位：万元 (10 000 yuan)

地区	Region	企业单位数(个) Number of Enterprises (unit)	年末从业人员(人) Engaged Person at Year-end (person)	资产总计 Total Assets	营业收入 Business Revenue	营业税金及附加 Taxes and Extra Charges on Business	营业利润 Operating Profit	应交增值税 Value-added Tax Payable
全省	**Province**	**452**	**21742**	**1932293.7**	**3215987.4**	**30273.8**	**202630.1**	**44486.8**
武汉市	Wuhan	90	10449	1093471.3	1446736.1	5717.6	51523.7	16373.9
黄石市	Huangshi	7	269	17944.8	21277.2	175.6	1624.6	154.5
十堰市	Shiyan	14	466	30810.4	40247.5	261.6	3579.2	47
宜昌市	Yichang	61	3078	265899	526131	3305.8	21895.4	8844.6
襄阳市	Xiangyang	111	2615	137789.5	572331.8	15558.9	61965.6	13083.8
鄂州市	Ezhou	8	350	9307.2	54186.1	33.1	840	144.3
荆门市	Jingmen	21	390	23961.8	32098.7	674.1	3845.4	806
孝感市	Xiaogan	30	1029	59474.7	191672.8	647.4	27063.4	1607.1
荆州市	Jingzhou	29	713	46152.3	77075.4	918.7	5873.6	600.3
黄冈市	Huanggang	37	1150	78800.5	101816.2	633.3	7241.9	1432.1
咸宁市	Xianning	9	170	14062.8	36774.2	285.5	5291.7	40.9
随州市	Suizhou	8	251	25228.6	28710.3	373.5	4373.5	351.5
恩施州	Enshi	24	656	82112.6	53730.2	374.1	4421.8	522.9
仙桃市	Xiantao	2	96	11341.3	10853	197.3	1313.4	175.9
潜江市	Qianjiang							
天门市	Tianmen	1	60	35936.9	22346.9	1117.3	1776.9	302
神农架	Shennongjia							

19-17 分市州规模以上文化服务业企业基本情况(2016)
BASIC CONDITIONS OF ENTERPRISES OF SERVICES OF CULTURE ABOVE DESIGNATED BY REGION(2016)

单位：万元

(10 000 yuan)

地 区	Region	企业单位数(个) Number of Enterprises (unit)	年末从业人员(人) Engaged Person at Year-end (person)	资产总计 Total Assets	营业收入 Business Revenue	营业税金及附加 Taxes and Extra Charges on Business	营业利润 Operating Profit	应交增值税 Value-added Tax Payable
全 省	**Province**	**793**	**131493**	**15925929**	**7485656.9**	**113885.4**	**604724.5**	**241297.5**
武汉市	Wuhan	342	102889	13580422	6690406.8	95168.7	517015.2	224414
黄石市	Huangshi	18	1176	35714.5	26261.7	651.1	-575.1	571.4
十堰市	Shiyan	15	1967	187670	46200.1	313.7	5090.3	961.8
宜昌市	Yichang	158	10194	632701.3	329923	7608.1	49623.7	7543.3
襄阳市	Xiangyang	149	6943	567461.4	185522.7	7112.5	24641.9	3454.3
鄂州市	Ezhou	12	849	44689.4	17064.8	43.5	2218.6	183.9
荆门市	Jingmen	6	594	19989.8	12303.6	64.6	934.3	387
孝感市	Xiaogan	14	885	65015.2	15416.8	444.5	3085.4	489.2
荆州市	Jingzhou	13	851	38755.8	18499.9	75.5	245.9	195.1
黄冈市	Huanggang	20	1390	177027.6	29844.5	462.6	396.5	1145
咸宁市	Xianning	18	1420	147371.5	45552	774.7	513.3	-88.5
随州市	Suizhou	4	142	1091.2	1917.9	28.6	-30.4	48.9
恩施州	Enshi	15	1440	257098.9	34310.9	821.5	-1843.3	992.4
仙桃市	Xiantao	1	27	90	49.1	2.1	2.3	
潜江市	Qianjiang	1	22	425.7	1364.4	5.1	31.8	2.5
天门市	Tianmen	2	163	33171	10871.3	53.6	2022.2	459.5
神农架	Shennongjia	5	541	137232.8	20147.4	255	1351.9	537.7

主要统计指标解释

文化事业机构 指从事专业文化工作和为专业文化工作服务的独立建制的单位。不包括这些单位另外举办独立核算的其他机构和各部门的业余文化组织。该指标主要反映文化事业机构发展规模水平。

艺术表演团体 指从事戏曲、音乐、舞蹈、杂技等专业艺术表演，有独立帐户的单位，不包括半工半艺、半农半艺和民间职业剧团。该指标主要反映全国专业艺术表演团体发展规模水平。

艺术表演观众人数(人次) 指售票、包场演出或民族地区免费演出的艺术表演观众人次数，不包括彩排审查和内部观摩演出的观看人次数。该指标主要反映全国观看专业艺术表演团体演出的效益规模。

等级运动员 是指经考核正式批准授予运动员称号的运动员，等级称号由高到低依次为国际级运动健将、运动健将、一级运动员、二级运动员、三级运动员。

广播节目综合人口覆盖率 指根据国家广电总局制定的《广播电视人口覆盖率统计技术标准和方法》进行统计调查的，在对象区能接收到由中央、省、地区或县通过无线、有线或卫星等技术方式传播的各级广播节目的人口数占全国总人口数的百分比。

电视节目综合人口覆盖率 指根据国家广电总局制定的《广播电视人口覆盖率统计技术标准和方法》进行统计调查的，在对象区能接收到由中央、省、地区或县通过无线、有线或卫星等技术方式传播的各级电视节目的人口数占全国总人口数的百分比。

Explanatory Notes on Main Statistical Indicators

Cultural Institutions refer to units, which have their own organizational system and independent accounting system and specialize in or serve cultural development. They exclude other establishments run by these cultural institutions and amateur cultural groups established by various departments. This indicator reflects the development of cultural units.

Art Troupe refers to the troupe which is engaged in drama, opera, music, dance, acrobatics or other art performance, opens independent accounts with banks and has self-supporting accounting system; excluding the troupes which are engaged partly in industrial or agricultural activities, partly in art performance and the professional troupes organized by the people. This indicator reflects the development of national professional art troupes.

Number of Audience at Art Performance refers to the number of attendants at commercial shows, completely booked shows or free shows given in minority national areas, and does not include the number of spectators at rehearsals for examination and internal shows for study.

Certified Grade Athletes refer to those who are awarded the title of athletes through assessment. The titles rank from high to low as: international level athletes, national level athletes, first grade athletes, second grade athletes and third grade athletes.

Radio Coverage of Population refers to the percentage of population, which can receive central, provincial, city, prefecture, and county radio programs relayed by wireless, cable, satellite and other technical means, in the surveying area, to national total population, according to Statistical Standard and Method on Television and Radio Coverage of Population established by the State Administration of Broadcasting, Film and Television.

Television Coverage of Population refers to the percentage of population, which can receive central, provincial, city, prefecture, and county television programs relayed by wireless, cable, satellite and other technical means, in the surveying area, to national total population, according to Statistical Standard and Method on Television and Radio Coverage of Population established by the State Administration of Broadcasting, Film and Television.

20 公共管理及其他

Public Management and Other

20-1 工会组织情况
BASIC STATISTICS ON LABOR UNION

年 份 Year	工会基层组织数(个) Number of Grassroot Labor Union Organizations (unit)	全省已建工会的基层单位职工与会员人数(万人) Number of Grassroot Staff and Workers and Members of Established Labor Union in the Province(10 000 persons)				工会专职工作人员人数(万人) Number of Full-time Workers in Labor Union (10 000 persons)
		职工人数 Number of Staff and Workers	#女职工 #Women Workers	会员人数 Number of Members	#女会员 #Women Members	
1975	18872	280.22	83.18	174.72	56.24	0.87
1980	22802	387.95	139.20	299.41	94.91	1.04
1985	25286	484.68	192.32	404.58	156.62	2.76
1990	33990	559.00	227.00	498.00	198.00	3.40
1995	28461	564.34	230.90	511.11	207.49	1.81
1996	28459	584.30	238.16	527.09	213.08	2.88
1997	20151	472.60	192.65	419.72	168.89	2.68
1998	17488	445.80	183.90	400.90	163.90	2.30
1999	18976	442.97	178.21	396.90	155.03	3.18
2000	45251	532.31	197.81	475.57	176.87	2.45
2001	111309	728.94	218.68	660.82	198.25	2.45
2004	50391	755.90	276.69	721.46	262.74	2.95
2005	54893	856.07	298.78	771.95	279.94	3.09
2006	61627	904.15	314.67	856.95	296.39	3.76
2007	69886	1004.92	358.44	972.30	345.64	3.94
2008	79048	1099.78	382.72	1073.22	377.43	4.48
2009	83436	1160.45	418.82	1127.68	411.12	4.75
2010	88647	1220.52	437.50	1184.88	429.00	5.80
2011	107995	1319.08	462.18	1267.28	453.11	6.10
2012	120561	1336.09	491.49	1292.06	481.87	6.44
2013	130513	1348.45	494.94	1312.16	487.57	6.36
2014	130326	1325.35	495.91	1285.13	487.36	6.67
2015	130118	1355.78	505.27	1301.52	490.43	6.61
2016	131582	1385.96	515.29	1338.23	503.98	6.62

注：因文革期间工会统计中断，表中1975年数据根据年平均增长值推算

Note:The data in 1975 were calculated by the average growth rate because Labor Union statistics had been suspended in the period of "The Great Cultural Revolution".

20-2 基层政权和村(居)委会情况
BASIC STATISTICS ON GRASSROOT REGIME AND VILLAGE COMMITTEES

单位:个 (unit)

年份 Year	镇 Township	乡 Villages	街道办事处 Regional Office	居委会个数 Number of Committees	村委会个数 Number of Village Committees
1986	859	3700	178	3257	32796
1987	836	1257	186	3394	32738
1988	828	1260	215	3483	32354
1989	840	1143	298	3545	32094
1990	849	1123	293	3573	32703
1991	849	1121	307	3709	32595
1992	852	1117	297	3830	32716
1993	857	1097	214	3921	32674
1994	864	1092	218	3998	32636
1995	865	1038	236	4110	32547
1996	823	567	252	4170	32486
1997	840	552	252	4287	32393
1998	847	543	253	4364	32293
1999	850	488	271	4425	32187
2000	860	466	283	3619	32001
2001	735	228	250	3468	31191
2002	738	224	272	3265	27667
2003	735	224	273	3351	27127
2004	738	224	274	3356	26470
2005	733	217	277	3465	29534
2006	737	210	277	3545	25828
2007	734	210	279	3653	25722
2008	735	207	285	3794	25551
2009	740	204	283	3882	25517
2010	741	199	290	3983	25763
2011	742	194	297	4051	25643
2012	746	188	298	4032	25575
2013	757	175	300	4208	25452
2014	761	170	302	4187	25448
2015	761	168	304	4294	25109
2016	759	168	307	4390	25064

20-3 社会福利事业、企业单位机构及人员数

BASIC STATISTICS ON NUMBER OF SOCIAL WELFARE ENTERPRISES AND PERSONS ENGAGED

单位：个 (unit)

项　目	Item	机构数 Number of Institutions					
		2010	2012	2013	2014	2015	2016
全省合计	**Total of the Province**	**6149**	**8251**	**12000**	**12453**	**16451**	**16979**
事业单位	Institution	5395	7545	11375	11919	15973	16581
其中：提供住宿服务	Adoptive Institutions	2520	2545	2213	2008	1658	1881
优抚休(疗)养院	Special Care Nursing Home	97	102	105	101	74	74
社会福利收养院	Welfare Homes	2423	2443	2108	1816	1492	1519
军休所							101
社会福利医院							2
儿童福利机构							24
未成年人救助保护中心	Protection Centre for Street Children	13	78	66	65	55	48
救助管理站	Home for Beggers and Vagrants	63	87	86	87	86	84
军供站	Military Supply Station	9	9	9	9	9	9
其他							20
其中：非收养性事业单位	Non-Adoptive Institutions	2875	5000	9162	9917	12931	14700
社区服务机构	Community Service Centre	2315	4330	8466	9216	12165	14152
低保服务机构							71
救灾储备单位	Relief Unit	42	44	47	48	45	37
福利彩票发行单位	Lottery Tickets Issuing Units	52	54	54	54	53	46
军队离退休干部管理机构	Managing Organizations on Veterans	106	106	108	107	108	4
烈士纪念建筑物管理单位	Managing Organizations on Martyrs Memorials	46	52	55	56	56	52
婚姻登记服务单位	Marriage Registration Service Center	97	93	99	97	95	95
殡葬事业单位	Funeral Units	132	147	172	178	175	159
#殡仪馆	#Funeral Home	83	84	88	85	84	78
其他							84
社会福利企业	Social Welfare Enterprises	754	706	625	534	478	398

注：从2016年起，社会福利机构统计口径发生变化。

20-3 续表 continued

单位：人 (person)

项 目	Item	机 构 数 Number of Institutions					
		2010	2012	2013	2014	2015	2016
全省合计	**Total of the Province**	**74891**	**84733**	**95296**	**99577**	**111933**	**102579**
事业单位	Institution	33401	44100	56987	64951	80785	75582
其中：提供住宿服务	Adoptive Institutions	18835	19754	19871	23511	26183	20997
优抚休(疗)养院	Special Care Nursing Home	2723	2776	3088	3790	3457	3599
社会福利收养院	Welfare Homes	16112	16978	16783	19721	14820	14220
军休所							797
社会福利医院							352
儿童福利机构							495
未成年人救助保护中心	Protection Centre for Street Children	183	547	541	335	289	270
救助管理站	Home for Beggers and Vagrants	553	805	871	886	863	860
军供站	Military Supply Station	247	247	236	229	218	204
其他							200
其中：非收养性事业单位	Non-Adoptive Institutions	14566	24346	37116	41440	54602	54585
社区服务机构	Community Service Centre	7919	16586	28863	33648	44384	47785
低保服务机构							646
救灾储备单位	Relief Unit	127	132	131	127	134	115
福利彩票发行单位	Lottery Tickets Issuing Units	430	488	536	380	439	439
军队离退休干部管理机构	Managing Organizations on Veterans	871	882	879	859	874	57
烈士纪念建筑物管理单位	Managing Organizations on Martyrs Memorials	597	670	695	690	682	635
婚姻登记服务单位	Marriage Registration Service Center	487	549	603	591	589	594
殡葬事业单位	Funeral Units	3152	3440	3761	3695	3631	3582
#殡仪馆	#Funeral Home	2552	2575	2592	2449	2499	2435
其他							732
社会福利企业	Social Welfare Enterprises	41490	40633	38309	34626	31148	26997

注：从2016年起，社会福利机构统计口径发生变化。

20-4 社会保险基本情况
BASIC CONDITIONS ABOUT SOCIAL INSURANCE

年 份 year	失业保险 Unemployment Insurance		城镇职工基本养老保险 Basic Endowment Insurance for Urban and Rural Employees		工伤保险年末参保人数（万人）Participants at Year-end (10 000 persons)	年末参加生育保险人数（万人）Number of People Participated in Maternity Insurance at Year-end (10 000 persons)
	年末参保人 数（万人）Participants at Year-end (10 000 persons)	全年发放失业保险金（亿元）Unemployed Relief Released (100 million yuan)	年末参保职工人数（万人）Participants at Year-end (10 000 persons)	年末参保离退休人数（万人）Retirees (10 000 persons)		
1996	392.9	0.4	353.2		177.6	137.8
1997	381.2	0.5	355.8		188.5	165.5
1998	378.2	0.5	413.1	107.4	190.0	168.8
1999	517.6	0.6	455.3	122.4	183.8	189.0
2000	459.6	1.6	465.6	130.4	185.0	191.3
2001	420.8	3.2	474.4	136.6	182.3	182.1
2002	416.1	5.4	532.7	154.5	183.2	182.7
2003	390.1	5.6	554.5	167.5	189.2	182.1
2004	391.3	4.0	586.1	194.7	187.2	179.9
2005	391.5	4.0	597.6	206.4	230.3	175.9
2006	395.5	3.7	630.2	220.5	275.5	194.5
2007	405.4	3.8	651.4	235.3	328.0	225.0
2008	422.6	3.6	671.7	252.4	350.7	315.4
2009	437.0	3.6	701.9	273.7	396.5	350.6
2010	464.5	3.9	749.1	301.3	444.5	388.7
2011	496.0	3.7	766.0	341.4	467.3	412.9
2012	501.4	3.8	801.4	367.3	505.8	444.7
2013	511.9	4.2	822.0	396.0	541.0	457.9
2014	520.9	5.1	847.0	419.3	576.7	480.6
2015	531.2	5.8	874.9	440.6	640.1	500.2
2016	542.5	7.7	897.1	457.9	651.1	511.9

20-5　参加基本养老保险人数
NUMBER OF PRESONS PARTICIPATED IN BASIC ENDOEMENT INSURANCE

年份 Year	合计 Total	职工 Number of Employees	企业(含其他) Enterprises (including others)	离退休人员 Number of Retirees	企业(含其他) Enterprises (including others)
1996	353.2	353.2	353.2		
1997	355.8	355.8	355.8		
1998	520.5	413.1	413.1	107.4	107.4
1999	577.7	455.3	455.3	122.4	122.4
2000	596.0	465.6	465.6	130.4	130.4
2001	611.0	474.4	474.4	136.6	136.6
2002	687.2	532.7	481.5	154.5	147.2
2003	722.0	554.5	501.1	167.5	158.6
2004	780.8	586.1	530.6	194.7	184.5
2005	804.0	597.6	539.8	206.4	195.1
2006	850.7	630.2	570.0	220.5	207.5
2007	886.7	651.4	602.6	235.3	223.0
2008	924.1	671.7	628.7	252.4	238.7
2009	975.6	701.9	660.5	273.7	259.2
2010	1050.4	749.1	690.9	301.3	258.3
2011	1107.4	766.0	725.5	341.4	325.6
2012	1168.7	801.4	757.8	367.3	351.2
2013	1217.9	822.0	779.1	396.0	379.7
2014	1266.2	847.0	802.5	419.3	402.1
2015	1315.5	874.9	830.7	440.6	422.9
2016	1355.0	897.1	853.8	457.9	439.5

20-6 城乡各种福利院基本情况
BASIC CONDITIONS OF WELFARE HOUSES IN URBAN AND RURAL AREAS

年份 Year	单位数(个) Number of Units (unit)	职工人数(人) Number of Staff and Workers (person)	床位数(张) Number of Beds (unit)	收养人数(人) Number of People Adopted (person)
1986	3955	12373	52912	46818
1987	3655	12360	57698	49356
1988	3300	11901	57356	47448
1989	3285	11759	57022	47075
1990	3252	11854	57878	48017
1991	3130	11966	57839	47684
1992	3114	12361	61878	50885
1993	3101	12955	61389	51638
1994	3066	13280	63451	52866
1995	2977	13607	64417	53662
1996	2907	13664	65853	54987
1997	2715	14163	69970	57471
1998	2650	14392	72284	59753
1999	2603	14552	76203	63326
2000	2459	14203	77871	63901
2001	2191	14173	78119	62590
2002	2145	14414	79522	65564
2003	2123	14856	117511	103320
2004	2359	16344	156461	144042
2005	2755	18132	189486	168800
2006	2770	17705	198458	179385
2007	2616	17157	206049	188308
2008	2553	18395	210342	180286
2009	2504	18190	216211	185933
2010	2596	19571	228375	189782
2011	2690	21159	233503	190917
2012	2710	21106	240985	193466
2013	2365	21283	241671	183140
2014	2265	21970	277345	183173
2015	1884	20451	241573	153705
2016	1881	20997	257488	154119

20-7 婚姻登记和离婚情况
STATISTICS ON MARRIAGE REGISTERATION AND DIVORCE

年份 Year	准予登记结婚(对) Marriage Registeration Granted (couple)	初婚(人) First Marriage (person)	再婚(人) Digamist(person)	离婚(对) Divorce (couple)	离婚率(‰) Rate of Divorce (‰)
1986	402315	785319	19311	6322	0.25
1987	417552	809808	25296	6660	0.26
1988	362654	698447	26861	7389	0.29
1989	413460	801171	25749	9203	0.35
1990	408688	790477	26899	9477	0.35
1991	424708	820092	29324	9584	0.35
1992	463279	897899	28659	10793	0.39
1993	425276	822044	28508	11937	0.43
1994	457324	884817	29831	12910	0.46
1995	482063	930832	33294	13340	0.46
1996	442532	851577	33487	14590	0.50
1997	426460	820615	32305	21260	0.72
1998	399900	763163	36637	24711	0.84
1999	376961	716175	37747	19519	0.66
2000	353781	673294	34268	21255	0.71
2001	335421	632188	38654	22077	0.74
2002	321517	605055	37979	24003	0.80
2003	329256	614244	44268	29375	0.98
2004	381472	710633	52311	46369	1.54
2005	394093	717495	70691	53394	1.77
2006	445672	822294	69050	57682	1.91
2007	485278	896768	73788	65876	2.17
2008	542251	1025496	59006	76003	2.49
2009	565400	1058851	71949	81133	2.84
2010	570810	1068715	72905	89549	3.11
2011	626912	1169771	84053	98874	3.18
2012	615861	1155365	76357	109862	3.81
2013	645767	1201344	90190	127604	4.40
2014	621946	1182271	61621	133723	4.60
2015	572954	1079852	66056	144684	4.90
2016	513823	971991	55655	160236	5.40

20-8 残疾人基本情况
BASIC STATISTICS ON THE DISABLED

单位：人 (10 000 persons)

项目		Item		2015	2016
康复		Rehabilitation			
视力残疾康复		Rehabilitation of Persons with Visual Disability			
白内障复明手术	(例)	Sight-restoring Surgeries for Cataract Patients	(cases)	26409	2256
低视力者配用助视器	(人)	Persons with Low-vision Fitted with Vision-aids	(persons)	5753	1020
盲人定向行走训练	(人)	Blind Persons Receiving Orientation Skill Training	(persons)	5762	1950
听力语言残疾康复		Rehabilitation of Persons with Hearing and Speech Disability			
新收训聋儿	(人)	Deaf Children Newly Trained in the year	(persons)	922	1423
培训聋儿家长	(人)	Parents Trained	(persons)	1155	695
肢体残疾康复		Rehabilitation of Persons with Physical Disability			
肢体残疾(脑瘫)儿童机构康复训练	(人)	Rehabilitation Training Institutions for Children with Mobility Impairment(Cerebral Palsy)	(persons)	2492	3014
肢体残疾人社区、家庭康复训练	(人)	Persons with Mobility Impairment Receiving Rehabilitation Training in Communities and Families	(persons)	9749	6919
智力残疾康复		Rehabilitation of Persons with Intellectual Disability			
智力残疾儿童康复训练	(人)	Children with Intellectual Disability Receiving Rehabilitation Training	(persons)	6687	2080
孤独症儿童机构训练	(人)	Children with Autism Trained in Institutions	(person)	819	864
残疾人辅助器具供应服务		Provision of Assistive Devices			
辅助器具供应	(件)	Assistive Devices Provided	(pieces)	32573	15232
残疾人假肢装配	(件)	Prosthesis Installed for the Disabled	(pieces)	1305	1389
残疾人矫形器装配	(例)	Orthotic Devices for the Disabled	(cases)	843	464
教育		Education			
未入学学龄残疾儿童少年	(人)	School-age Disabled Children Unable to Enter School	(persons)	3243	5635
特殊教育普通高中在校生	(人)	Students at Special Education Senior High Schools	(persons)	320	322
残疾人中等职业教育在校生	(人)	Students at Secondary Vocational Schools for PWDs	(persons)	145	145
高等院校录取残疾考生	(人)	Disabled Students Admitted to Higher Education Institutions	(persons)	351	358
社会保障	(人)	Social Security	(persons)		
残疾居民参加城乡社会养老保险		Urban Worker with Disabilities Covered by Social Pension Insurance Urban Worker with Disabilities Covered by Medical Insurance		1088793	1131985
城乡残疾人纳入最低生活保障托养残疾人		Disabled residents in Urban and Rural Social endowment Insurance		660135	521162
扶贫		Poverty Alleviation			
扶持农村贫困残疾人	(人次)	Impoverished PWDs Assited in Rural Areas	(persons-times)	133611	148795
农村残疾人实用技术培训	(人次)	Vocational Skills Training for PWDs	(persons-times)	29744	24533
农村贫困残疾人危房改造	(户)	Dilapidated House Renovation for Poor PWDs	(households)	290	280
受益残疾人	(人)	PWDs Benefited	(persons)	334	393
维权		Rights Protection			
贫困残疾人家庭无障碍改造	(户)	Barrier Free Home Renovation for Poor PWDs	(households)	1880	1900
残疾人机动轮骑车燃油补贴	(人)	Fuel Subsidy for Motor Wheelchairs of PWDs	(persons)	49043	50791
组织建设		Organization Development			
残疾人人口库持证残疾人	(万人)	PWDs with Disability Certificate in the PWD Database	(10 000 persons)	125.8	129.9

注：2016年起，残疾人事业统计口径发生变动，与上年不可比。

20-9 刑事案件发、破案情况
STATISTICS ON OCCURANCE AND CLEARING UP OF CRIMINAL CASES

指 标	Item	2000	2005	2010	2012	2013	2014	2015	2016
刑事案件发案总数 (件)	Number of Criminal Cases Occurred (case)	114866	147004	221735	335813	279638	265260	299522	275707
刑事案件破案总数 (件)	Number of Criminal Cases Cleared (case)	72796	71455	76401	139738	118092	90652	77355	69775
刑事案件破案率 (%)	Rate of Criminal Cases Cleared (%)	63.4	48.6	34.5	41.6	42.2	34.2	25.8	25.3

20-10 城市交通事故与火灾情况
BASIC STATISTICS ON TRAFFIC ACCIDENTS AND FIRE ACCIDENTS

指 标	Item	2000	2005	2010	2012	2013	2014	2015	2016
交通事故处理发生件数 (起)	Number of Traffic Accidents (case)	20148	9585	6465	6007	5798	5268	4627	19269
死亡人数 (人)	Deaths (person)	3792	2417	1967	1822	1801	1771	1694	6560
受伤人数 (人)	Injuries (person)	16492	10555	7684	6818	6353	5468	4638	18111
折合经济损失 (万元)	Losses Converted into Money (10 000 yuan)	7041	4958	3294	5391	4473	5071	5176	9801
火灾发生数 (起)	Number of Fire Accsidents (case)	6780	9356	9333	4951	2695	2322	2121	1964
死亡人数 (人)	Deaths (person)	54	56	17	11	22	2	3	4
受伤人数 (人)	Injuries (person)	106	47	7	10	72	10	3	12
折合经济损失 (万元)	Losses Converted into Money (10 000 yuan)	1754	1945	3565	4927	4791	5520	4142	4380

注:2016年起,交通事故统计口径发生变动,与上年不可比。

20-11 审查批捕、起诉情况
STATISTICS ON EXAMINATION, ARREST AND PROSECUTION

项 目		Item		2000	2005	2010	2012	2013	2014	2015	2016
受理批捕件数	(件)	Number of Cases	(case)	20378	19846	9120	28905	27194	28267	28860	28605
受理批捕人数	(人)	Number of People Arrested	(person)	31245	29427	13391	43040	37801	38379	38400	38587
批准逮捕	(人)	Number of Arrests Granted	(person)	25114	27063	12081	38468	31813	32398	32400	31332
不批捕人数	(人)	Number of Non-Arrest	(person)	4329	1522	1001	3725	5616	5305	5388	6588
受理审查起诉件数	(件)	Number of Cases Received	(case)	17660	21966	10028	46382	36882	39980	42337	43596
受理审查起诉人数	(人)	Number of Prosecution Accepted	(person)	25416	33410	15280	75876	52541	55410	57002	58036
起诉人数	(人)	Prosecutor	(person)	22396	26926	11600	47348	44947	45740	46609	48207
不起诉人数	(人)	Non-prosecutor	(person)	1019	982	329	1343	1806	2115	2235	2369

20-12 检察机关查办职务犯罪情况
STATISTICS ON CRIMES COMMITTED BY TAKING ADVANTAGE OF DUTY BY PROCURATORIAL ORGAN

项 目		Item		2000	2005	2010	2012	2013	2014	2015	2016
受理案件件数	(件)	Number of Cases Dealt	(case)	8343	3125	1074	1840	2168	2703	2947	2397
立案件数	(件)	Registered Cases	(case)	2034	1552	988	1651	1935	2438	2542	2059
立案人数	(人)	Registered Offenders	(person)	2312	1682	1228	2127	2374	2897	3021	2421
贪污贿赂件数	(件)	Number of Corruption and Bribe Cases	(case)	1821	1363	801	1290	1508	1864	1947	1563
渎职侵权件数	(件)	Number of Malversation Cases	(case)	213	189	187	361	427	574	595	496
查办大案件数	(件)	Large Cases	(case)	882	887	1039	1120	1429	1972	2127	1764
#5万元以上件数		#Money Involved Above 50000 yuan		850	839	936	911	1319	1580	1722	1433
查办要案人数	(人)	Number of Offender Involved in Large Cases	(person)	108	139	133	152	173	267	218	223
#厅局级人数		#Number of Offenders at Bureau Level		11	17	10	16	15	55	218	223
提起公诉人数	(人)	Number of People Prosecuted	(person)	1490	1265	1725	1871	2053	2145	1841	2028

20-13 律师、公证、调解工作基本情况
BASIC STATISTICS ON LAWYERS, NOTARIZATION AND MEDIATION

项 目		Item		2005	2010	2012	2013	2014	2015	2016
一、律师工作		**Lawyers**								
律师事务所	(个)	Number of Lawyer Office	(person)	387	466	512	549	595	665	717
专职律师		Number of Full-Time Lawyer		3722	5869	7300	7805	8502	9419	10314
兼职律师		Number of Part-Time Lawyer		165	252	306	334	351	363	376
担任法律顾问	(家)	Number of Units with Legal Advisors	(unit)	9565	12059	14046	14339	16973	34772	55269
民事案件诉讼代理	(件)	Agent of Civil Cases	(case)	27079	45403	61052	63917	64479	79913	81013
刑事诉讼辩护及代理	(件)	Defender and Agent of Criminal Cases	(case)	11341	17724	17095	19043	18155	19076	20457
非诉讼法律事务	(件)	Agent of Non-Litigious Legal Affairs	(case)	34674	37521	38011	24310	24928	26276	21731
解答法律咨询	(万人次)	Agent of Legal Advisory Services	(10 000 (person-times)	15.23	11.01	12.58	11.12	12.12	14	13.98
代写法律事务文件	(万件)	Agent of Legal Document Written on Behalf of Clients	(10 000 cases)	3.49	1.59	2.09	2.3	1.8	3.02	2.35
二、公证工作		**Notarization**								
公证机构	(个)	Number of Notary Offices	(unit)	118	116	117	117	117	117	117
#公证员		#Notaries		455	353	367	387	397	424	449
公证员助理		Assistant Notaries		62	167	372	244	236	254	256
办理公证文件	(万件)	Number of Domestic Notarized Document	(10 000 cases)	31.04	32.65	33.79	28.6	35.84	42.04	47
#涉外公证	(件)	#Foreign Notarized Documents	(case)	65498	79723	88877	91467	107445	113143	112384
三、人民调解工作		**People's Mediation**								
人民调解委员会	(万个)	Number of People's Mediation Committees	(10 000 units)	3.70	3.62	3.43	3.44	3.36	3.37	3.32
调解人员	(万人)	Number of Mediators	(10 000 persons)	17.20	20.43	15.81	15.87	14.51	14.73	14.28
调解纠纷总数	(万件)	Number of Disputes Mediated	(10 000 cases)	21.62	22.85	28.33	30.00	32.13	32.15	31.03
调解成功总数	(万件)	Number of Successful Mediation	(10 000 cases)	21.13	22.14	27.60	29.33	31.50	31.44	30.46

20-14 涉外公证文书分类情况
FOREIGN-RELATED NOTARIAL DOCUMENTS BY TYPE

单位：件 (case)

分类	Item	2005	2010	2011	2012	2013	2014	2015	2016
合 计	**Total**	**65498**	**79723**	**80818**	**88877**	**91467**	**107445**	**113143**	**112384**
出生	Births	7243	11567	12956	14791	10812	12074	15972	13923
学历	Academic Degree	10078	7181	6138	5367	6754	8555	10140	10844
经历	Personal Experience	806	863	875	1068	294	775	2222	1452
生存和居住	Survival and Residence	102	67	54	62	88	127	110	126
死亡	Death	109	103	82	106	137	146	173	194
收养子女	Children Adoption	539	692	591	470	269	271	321	237
亲属关系	Kinship	3962	6605	7811	8562	7247	9322	11665	10269
婚姻状况	Marital Status	3691	5774	5464	6670	3072	2795	2555	3120
继承权	Rights of Inheritance	28	94	81	35	122	788	100	113
遗嘱	Testament	18	82	75	38	48	19	21	23
职称	Title	141	172	239	131	15	7	67	34
身份	Identity	150	719	697	546	82	36	417	505
组织资格	Qualification of Organization	16	31	12	13	14	24	4	6
委托书	Trust Deed	293	643	948	1184	1916	3385	2313	2385
公司章程	Chapter of Company	24	39	31	38	15	5	6	8
副本与原本相符	Confirmation of Copy and Photo-offset Copies to Originals	7861	12982	11230	16069	19897	24379	26754	28389
证书(执照)	Operation Document	186	285	264	1035	2392	6672	13767	12766
声明书	Declaration	3972	1140	1526	1649	1255	1486	820	1632
合同(协议)	Contract(Agreement)	372	46	36	18	28	37	20	34
受、未受刑事处分	Criminal Record & Uncriminal Record	6126	10359	11279	12788	7770	10078	12704	13244
其他	Others	9916	11943	12339	9799	24622	20528	12992	13080

20-15 履行法律监督情况
SUPERVISION ON LAW ENFORCEMENT

单位：人、件 (person, case)

项　目	Item	2000	2005	2010	2012	2013	2014	2015	2016
监督公安机关立案件数	Number of Cases Registered by Public Security	247	554	1088	2218	3243	2429	1412	1107
监督追捕人数	Number of Criminals Hunted under Supervision	300	204	903	2166	3063	2253	1985	1830
监督追诉人数	Number of People Being Prosecuted	61	78	1130	2103	3746	2347	1484	1359
刑事抗诉件数	Number of Cases Against Crimnal Prosecutions	192	123	119	274	357	470	433	467
监督刑罚执行纠错人次	Person-times of Error Correction of Execution of Punishment	3546	51	499	1587	4635	4362	3700	3440
民事行政监督抗诉件数	Number of Counterappeal Civil Cases	894	514	432	435	303	218	155	114

20-16 调解民间纠纷分类
CIVIL DISPUTES MEDIATION BY TYPE

项　目	Item	调解纠纷(件) Number of Disputes Mediated (case)				各种纠纷所占比重(%) Proportion (%)			
		2013	2014	2015	2016	2013	2014	2015	2016
合计	**Total**	**102052**	**63013**	**71671**	**72599**	**100.0**	**100.0**	**100.0**	**100.0**
婚姻	Marriage	22568	21441	18596	18442	22.1	34.0	26.0	25.4
继承	Rights of Inheritance	613	505	658	702	0.6	0.8	0.9	1.0
房地产开发	Real Estate Development	1229	964	1158	1061	1.2	1.5	1.6	1.5
运输合同	Transportation Contracts	210	293	257	315	0.2	0.5	0.4	0.4
买卖合同	Selling and Purchasing Contracts	6096	6416	6083	6911	6.0	10.2	8.5	9.5
借款合同	Loans Contracts	14684	15128	12740	14862	14.4	24.0	17.8	20.5
劳动争议	Labor Disputes	3337	3484	2727	2956	3.3	5.5	3.8	4.1
人身权	Personal Rights	13297	12005	15487	14541	13.0	19.1	21.6	20.0
所有权	Right of Ownership	3067	1845	1378	1267	3.0	2.9	1.9	1.7
其他	Others	36951	932	12587	11542	36.2	1.5	17.6	15.9

20-17 人民法院审理一审案件情况
STATISTICS ON FIRST INSTANCE CASES IN PEOPLE'S COURT

单位：件 (case)

年份 Year	收案 Cases Received	刑事 Criminal Cases	民商事 Civil Cases	海事海商 Maritime	行政 Administration
1985	63079	12709	40660	26	
1990	227618	29086	166960		568
1995	257312	21391	174908	456	4359
1998	252403	17763	171025	606	6368
1999	238715	19598	151191	647	6247
2000	228804	19204	146838	618	6754
2001	251003	21741	222702	745	6560
2002	211464	19548	188163	525	3753
2003	193780	18943	171282	488	3555
2004	172889	18833	150682	592	3374
2005	155478	19672	132585	745	3221
2006	156885	19914	133584	606	3387
2007	161728	21719	137328	459	2681
2008	165099	22364	140072	746	2663
2009	173032	23481	147319	710	2232
2010	179631	22963	154299	781	2369
2011	280572	25074	249792	1458	5706
2012	395414	31489	354789	1501	9136
2013	422427	31621	387593	1914	3213
2014	344515	33931	306601	1951	3983
2015	316619	37034	272384	2022	7201
2016	326240	37309	281705	2212	7226

注：一审案件指人民法院按照诉讼级别管辖按第一审程序审理的案件。
Note: First instance cases refer to cases in the first instance process in People's Court.

20-18 人民法院刑事一审案件收结案情况
END OF FIRST INSTANCE CASES IN PEOPLE'S COURT OF CRIMINAL LAWSUITS

单位：件 (case)

项 目	Item	收案 Cases Received				结案 Cases Closed			
		2013	2014	2015	2016	2013	2014	2015	2016
合 计	**Total**	**31621**	**33931**	**37034**	**37309**	**31188**	**33183**	**35766**	**38326**
危害公共安全罪	Crimes Harming Public Security	5564	6520	8187	9633	5455	6381	8094	9760
破坏社会主义市场经济秩序罪	Crimes Harming Socialism Market Economy Order	1590	1415	1409	1449	1566	1358	1320	1438
侵害公民人生权利民主权利罪	Crimes against Rights in Human Life and Democratic Rights	6650	6844	6521	6429	6518	6784	6312	6600
侵犯财产罪	Property Violation	9086	9453	9936	9887	9134	9271	9677	10167
妨害社会管理秩序罪	Crimes Harming Social Management Order	7233	8105	9453	8528	7097	7929	9286	8658
危害国防利益罪	Crimes Harimg National Defense Interests	6	19	10	13	7	17	14	14
贪污贿赂罪	Corruption and Bribe	1242	1305	1319	1160	1188	1194	893	1478
渎职罪	Malversation	235	259	195	207	211	236	168	207
其他	Others	15	11	4	3	12	13	2	4
合计中含自诉案件	Self-Suing Cases	184	155	217	218	184	151	199	212

20-19 人民法院刑事案件中青少年犯罪情况

STATISTICS ON JUVENILE DELINQUENCY IN PEOPLE'S COURT OF CRIMINAL LAWSUITS

单位：人 (person)

年份 Year	刑事犯罪总数 Total Number of Criminal Cases	青少年犯罪（25岁以下） Juvenile Delinquency (Under the age of 25)	不满18岁 Juvenile Age under 18	18-25岁 Age 18-25	青少年罪犯刑事罪犯率% Percentage of Juvenile Delinquency in Criminal Cases %
1999	20534	6836	1302	5534	33.3
2000	20076	5922	1279	4643	29.5
2001	22911	6597	1774	4823	28.8
2002	20868	5669	1901	3768	27.2
2003	20908	6207	2328	3879	29.7
2004	20429	5838	2633	3205	28.6
2005	21669	6283	2939	3344	29.0
2006	22876	6933	2945	3988	30.3
2007	17368	7459	3131	4328	43.0
2008	26682	6810	3030	3780	25.5
2009	28507	7700	2930	4770	27.0
2010	27928	7058	2287	4771	25.3
2011	29280	7263	2229	5034	24.8
2012	35419	7327	2050	5277	20.7
2013	33871	5398	1365	4033	15.9
2014	34599	4721	1170	3551	13.6
2015	43918	6011	1084	4927	13.7
2016	40797	4731	668	4063	11.6

20-20 人民法院民事一审案件收结案情况(2016)
STATISTICS ON END OF FIRST INSTANCE CASES IN PEOPLE'S COURT OF CIVIL LAWSUITS (2016)

单位：件 (case)

项 目	Item	收案 Cases Received	结案 Cases Ended	调解 Mediated	判决 Judgement	驳回 Cases Rejected	撤诉 Cases Withdraw	其他 Others
合 计	**Total**	**281705**	**290398**	**72599**	**135409**	**7335**	**58954**	**16101**
婚姻家庭	Marriage	52766	54419	18442	22715	590	12296	376
继承	Rights of Inheritance	1430	1603	702	612	30	241	18
知识产权	Intelligence Property Rights	157	171	14	20		129	8
房地产开发	Real Estate Development	55123	6117	1061	3236	120	1667	33
运输合同	Transportation Contracts	904	946	315	420	15	161	35
买卖合同	Selling and Purchasing Contracts	24385	24255	6911	10660	439	5942	303
借款合同	Loans Contracts	60720	62736	14862	34355	1674	10969	876
劳动争议	Labor Disputes	12103	12838	2956	6928	544	2070	340
海事海商	Martial Commerce	2212	1933	504	1018	13	354	44
人身权	Personal Right	38399	40243	14541	20448	259	4780	215
特别程序	Special Procedure	16262	16583	95	2393	1233	674	12188
破产	Bankruptcy	89	92		1	4	7	80
所有权及与其相关合同	Rights of Ownership and Relevant Contracts	7031	7398	1267	3427	463	2117	124
其他	Others	10124	61064	10929	29176	1951	17547	1461

注：结案中含上年旧存。
Note: The statistics of ended cases include statistics of last year.

20-21 人民法院行政一审案件收结案情况(2016)
STATISTICS ON END OF FIRST INSTANCE CASES IN PEOPLE'S COURT OF ADMINISTRATION (2016)

单位：件 (case)

项 目	Item	收案 Cases Received	结案 Cases Ended	维持 Cases Maintained	撤消 Cases Cancled	驳回 Cases Rejected	撤诉 Cases Withdraw	单独赔偿 Sole Compensation	其他 Others
合 计	**Total**	**7226**	**7257**	**176**	**515**	**1510**	**1943**	**16**	**3097**
土 地	Land	604	641	8	56	95	146	1	335
公 安	Public Security	650	711	24	10	288	161		228
城 建	City Construction	1307	1418	1	117	177	354	3	766
交通运输	Transportation	57	50	2		8	27	1	12
工 商	Industry and Commerce	149	160	4	16	31	49		60
环 保	Environment	31	27	2	1	6	13		5
林 业	Forestry	82	94	4	19	11	26	1	33
税 务	Taxes	14	11			3	3		5
卫 生	Sanitary and Hygiene	18	21			5	5		11
其 他	Others	4314	4124	131	296	886	1159	10	1642

注：结案中含上年旧存。
Note: The statistics of ended cases include statistics of last year.

主要统计指标解释

社会福利事业单位 指集中收养社会孤老、残、幼的机构,包括由民政部门管理的社会福利院、儿童福利院、精神病人福利院和城镇集体举办的福利院及农村集体举办的敬老院以及优抚医院和具有收养能力的社区服务中心等。该指标主要反映我国在社会福利性单位投入的水平。

社会福利事业单位收养人数 包括民政部门管理和城镇、农村集体举办的社会福利事业单位中收养的老人、少年儿童、缺乏生活自理能力的残疾人员和精神病人。该指标主要反映收养性社会福利单位的收养能力。

社会福利企业单位 指以安置城镇有一定劳动能力的盲、聋、哑和肢体残疾人员就业为目的,享受国家减免税待遇的国有或集体企业。包括福利工厂、福利商业和服务业、假肢厂和安置农场等单位。该指标主要反映我国对残疾人照顾的特殊政策。

粗离婚率 指当年离婚对数占年平均人口的比重,计算公式为:

$$\text{粗离婚率}=\frac{\text{当年离婚对数}}{\text{年平均人口数}}\times 1000‰$$

基本养老保险

1.(参保)职工人数:指报告期末按照国家法律、法规和有关政策规定参加基本养老保险并在社保经办机构已建立缴费记录档案的职工人数,包括中断缴费但未终止养老保险关系的职工人数,不包括只登记未建立缴费记录档案的人数。

2.(参保)离退休人员人数:指报告期末参加基本养老保险的离休、退休和退职人员的人数。

3.基本养老保险基金收入:指根据国家有关规定,由纳入基本养老保险范围的缴费单位和个人按国家规定的缴费基数和缴费比例缴纳的养老保险基金,以及通过其他方式取得的形成基金来源的收入。包括单位和职工个人缴纳的基本养老保险费、基本养老保险基金利息收入、上级补助收入、下级上解收入、转移收入、财政补贴和其他收入。

4.基本养老保险基金支出:指按照国家政策规定的开支范围和开支标准从养老保险基金中支付给参加基本养老保险的离休、通休、退职人员个人的养老金、丧葬抚恤补助,以及由于保险关系转移、上下级之间调剂资金等原因而发生的支出。包括离休金、退休金、退职金、各种补贴、医疗费、死亡丧葬补助费、抚恤救济费、社会保险经办机构管理费、补助下级支出、上解上级支出、转移支出、其他支出等。

5.基本养老保险基金累计结余:指截止报告期末基本养老保险基金收支相抵后的累计余额。

离休、退休、退职人员 指正式办理了离休、退休、退职手续,并享受相应的离休、退休、退职待遇的人员。

基本医疗保险

1.参保人数:指报告期末按国家有关规定参加基本医疗保险的人数。包括参加保险的职工人数和退休人员人数。

2.基金收入:指根据国家有关规定,由纳入基本医疗保险范围的缴费单位和个人,按国家规定的缴费基数和缴费比例缴纳的基金,以及通过其他方式取得的形成基金来源的款项,包括:单位缴纳的社会统筹基金收入、个人缴纳的个人账户基金收入、财政补贴收入、利息收入、其他收入。

3.基金支出:指按照国家政策规定的开支范围和开支标准从社会统筹基金中支付给参加基本医疗保险的职工和退休人员的医疗保险待遇支出,和从个人帐户基金中支付给参加基本医疗保险的职工和退休人员的医疗费用支出,以及其他支出。包括:住院医疗费用支出、门急诊医疗费用支出、个人账户基金支出、其他支出。

4.基金累计结余:指截止报告期末基本医疗保险的社会统筹和个人帐户基金累计结余金额。包括银行存款、财政专户、债券投资和其他。

失业保险

1.参保人数:指报告期末按照国家法律、法规和有关政策规定参加了失业保险的城镇企业事业单位的职工及地方政府规定参加失业保险的其他人员的人数。

2.失业保险基金收入:指按照规定从企业、事业及其他单位筹集的失业保险费及其他并入失业保险基金收入的总额。包括单位和个人缴纳的失业保险费、失业保险基金利息收入、上级补助收入、下级上解收入、转移收入、财政补贴和其他收入。

3.失业保险基金支出:指报告期内为保障失业人员和下岗职工基本生活、促进其再就业等支出的基金总额。包括失业救济金、医疗费、死亡丧葬补助费、抚恤救济费、转业训练费支出、失业保险经办机构管理费、补助下级支出、上解上级支出、转移支出和其他支出。

4.基金累计结余:指截止报告期末失业保险基金收支相抵后的累计余额。

工伤保险

1.参加保险人数: 指报告期末依据国家有关规定参加工伤保险的职工人数。

2.享受保险待遇人数: 指劳动者因工负伤致残、死亡或因患职业病致残,根据有关规定享受工伤保险待遇职工或供养直系亲属人数。包括伤残人数、职业病人数、因工死亡人数、供养直系亲属人数。

3.基金收入: 指根据国家有关规定,由参加工伤保险的单位按国家规定的缴费基数和缴费比例缴纳的工伤保险基金,以及通过其他形式取得的形成基金来源的款项。包括:单位缴纳的社会统筹基金收入、财政补贴收入、利息收入、其他收入。

4.基金支出: 指按照国家政策规定的开支范围和开支标准从工伤保险基金中支付给参加工伤保险的人员及供养直系亲属工伤保险待遇支出及其他支出。包括工伤医疗费、伤残补助金、工亡补助金、护理费、丧葬补助费、工伤预防费用、职业康复费用和其他支出。

5.基金累计结余: 指截止报告期末工伤保险基金累计结余金额。包括银行存款、财政专户、债券投资和其他。

生育保险

1.参保人数: 指报告期末依据有关规定参加生育保险的职工人数。

2.基金收入: 指根据国家有关规定,由参加生育保险的单位按照国家规定的缴费基数和缴费比例缴纳的生育保险基金,以及通过其他方式取得的形成基金来源的款项,包括:单位缴纳的基金收入、利息收入和其他收入。

3.基金支出: 指按照国家政策规定的开支范围和开支标准,从生育保险基金中支付给参加生育保险的职工,因妊娠、分娩和计划生育手术而享受的待遇及其他支出。包括:生育津贴、医疗费用支出及其他支出。

4.基金累计结余: 指截止报告期末生育保险基金累计结余金额。包括银行存款、财政专户、债券投资和其他。

离休、退休、退职人员保险福利费用 指离休、退休、退职人员实际得到的生活费用总额,包括从社会保险经办机构和单位得到的费用。

1.离休金:指按规定支付给离休人员的生活费用。

2.退休金:指按规定支付给退休人员的生活费用。

3.退职生活费:指按规定支付给退职人员的生活费用。

4.医疗卫生费:指单位直接支付给离休、退休、退职人员的医疗费、住院费以及住院伙食补助等费用。

5.其他:指离休金、退休金、退职生活费和医疗卫生费以外的其他保险福利费用,如丧葬抚恤救济费、生活补贴、物价补贴、冬季取暖补贴等。

律师 指依法取得律师执业证书,担任法律顾问,民事(刑事、行政)案件代理人、刑事案件辩护人、办理非诉讼业务,解答法律询问,代写法律事务文书等,为社会提供法律服务的人员。

公证人员 指在公证处工作的人员总称,包括公证处主任、副主任、公证员、公证员助理(助理公证员)和其他从事辅助性工作的人员。

公证文书 指公证处根据当事人申请,依照事实和法律,按照法定程序制作的,具有法律效力的司法证明文书。根据公证书用途和使用地,公证书分为国内公证书、国内经济公证书、涉外民事公证书、涉外经济公证书四类。

调解员 指在人民调解委员会担负调解民间纠纷工作的人员,包括调解委员会的委员和调解小组的调解员。该指标主要反映从事人民调解工作的人员数量。

调解民间纠纷 指调解委员会按照法律规定,根据自愿原则,用说服教育的方法调解民间发生的有关民事权利和义务争执的件数,包括调解成功数和调解未成功数。该指标主要反映人民调解委员会的工作量。

立案 指人民检察院对受理的报案、控告、举报或自首及自行发现的犯罪线索、犯罪嫌疑人进行初步调查后，认为存在职务犯罪事实和应追究刑事责任，并决定作为刑事案件进行侦查的诉讼活动，是追究犯罪的开始。该指标主要反映人民检察院依法将职务犯罪线索作为刑事案件进行侦查的诉讼活动。

大案 指贪污、贿赂案数额在5万元以上，挪用公款案数额在10万元以上，集体私分、巨额财产来源不明、隐瞒境外存款案数额在50万元以上以及按照《人民检察院直接受理的渎职、侵权重、特大案件标准(试行)》认定的案件。该指标主要反映人民检察院立案查办的职务犯罪案件中经济损失大、社会危害严重的案件。

要案 指县、处级以上干部的犯罪案件。该指标主要反映国家工作人员中县、处级以上干部因职务犯罪被人民检察院依法立案侦查的情况。

决定逮捕 指人民检察院对直接受理、自行侦查的案件，认为需要逮捕犯罪嫌疑人时，依据法律做出的逮捕决定。该指标主要反映人民检察院对直接受理的案件行使决定逮捕权的情况。

批准逮捕 指人民检察院对公安机关、国家安全机关、监狱管理机关提出逮捕的犯罪嫌疑人进行审查，根据事实，依法做出逮捕决定。该指标主要反映人民检察院对提请逮捕机关提请逮捕犯罪嫌疑人进行审查后依法做出批准逮捕决定的情况。

决定起诉 指人民检察院对公安机关、国家安全机关、监狱管理机关和检察机关内设机构反贪污贿赂部门等移送起诉的案件进行审查，根据事实，做出提起公诉的案件。该指标主要反映人民检察院对各种刑事案件向人民法院提起公诉的情况。

申诉 指经检察机关信访部门审查处理后，移送到检察机关申诉部门的申诉案件，包括不服检察机关处理决定和不服法院刑事判决和裁定的申诉的案件。

受理劳动争议案件数 指劳动争议仲裁委员会根据国家有关规定，对劳动争议当事人的申请予以审查，符合受理条件而正式立案、准备处理的劳动争议案件数。

Explanatory Notes on Main Statistical Indicators

Social Welfare Institutions refer to institutions taking care of old people without children, handicapped people and orphans. They include social welfare institutions run by civil affairs departments, children welfare institutions, social welfare institutions for mental patients, collective-owned old people's homes in rural areas, convalescent homes and community service centers with the capacity of receiving those people. This indicator reflects the input in social welfare institutions.

Number of People Taken in by Social Welfare Institutions refers to the number of old people, children, totally dependent handicapped people and mental patients taken in by social welfare institutions run by civil affairs departments and those run by collective units in urban and rural areas. This indicator reflects the capacity of social welfare institutions.

Social Welfare Enterprises are collective owned enterprises which employ the blind, deaf-mute, and other handicapped people who are able to work in cities and towns and enjoy exemption from state taxes, including welfare plants, welfare commercial services, artificial limb plants and farms, etc. This indicator reflects the preferential policies toward disabled persons.

Crude Divorce Rate refers to proportion of divorced people to the annual average population for the reference year, the formula is:

Crude Divorce rate= number of couples divorced for the reference year/annual average population x 1000 per thousand

Basic Medical Care Insurance:

1. Number of people participating in the insurance programme refers to people participating in the basic medical care insurance programme according to related regulations by the end of reference period, including number of staff and workers and retirees participating in this insurance programme.

2. Revenue of insurance programme refer to payments made by employers and individuals participating in medical care insurance programs in accordance with the basis and proportion stipulated in state regulations, and income from other sources that become source of medical insurance fund, including income of social comprehensive funds paid by employers, income from individual accounts, government

financial subsidies, interest income and other income.

3. Expenses of insurance programme refer to payment made from social comprehensive funds to those retired and resigned people covered in basic medical care insurance within the scope and standards of expenditure according to related national policies, and medical care payment made from individual accounts to staff and workers and retirees, and other expenses, including medical expenses of hospital inpatients, medical expenses for outpatients and emergency patients, payment from individual accounts and other expenditure.

4. Balance of basic medical care insurance refer to the balance of medical care insurance of social comprehensive funds and individual accounts at the end of the reference period, including bank savings, special fiscal accounts, investment in bonds and others.

Unemployment Insurance

1. Number of people covered refers to staff and workers in urban enterprises or institutions who have participated in unemployment insurance programme in line relevant policies and regulations, and other people who have participated according to local government regulations, by the end of reference period.

2. Revenue of unemployment insurance refer to payments made by employers and individuals participating in unemployment insurance programme in accordance with relevant regulations and other income contributed to this programme, including unemployment insurance premium made by employers and individuals, interest income, subsidies from higher level agencies, income as transfer from subordinate agencies, transferred income, government financial subsidies and other income.

3. Expenses of unemployment insurance refer to total expenses during the reference period to guarantee the basic livelihood of unemployed people and laid-off staff and workers and to encourage their re-employment. Included are unemployment relief, medical fees, funeral subsidies, compensation pension, training expenses, management fees for unemployment insurance agencies, subsidies to lower level agencies, expenses as transfer to higher level agencies, transferred expenditure and other expenditure.

4. Balance of unemployment insurance refer to the balance of unemployment revenue deducting unemployment expenses at the end of the reference period.

Work Injury Insurance

1. Number of people covered refers to staff and workers who have participated in work injury insurance programme in line with relevant national regulations.

2. Number of beneficiaries refers to staff and workers and their direct dependents who can, in line with relevant regulations, benefit from work injury insurance, as a result of work injury leading to disability or death of the staff/worker, or occupational disease leading to disability. Included in this category are number of injured and disabled people, number of people with occupational diseases, number of deaths at work places, and number of direct dependents.

3. Revenue of work injury insurance refer to payments made by employers participating in work injury insurance programs in accordance with the basis and proportion stipulated in state regulations, and income from other sources that become source of work injury insurance fund, including income of social comprehensive funds paid by employers, government financial subsidies, interest income and other income.

4. Expenses of work injury insurance refer to payments made from work injury insurance funds to those who participated in the work injury insurance programme and their direct dependents within the scope and standards of expenditure according to related national policies, and other expenditure, including medical fees for work injury, injury and disability subsidies, death subsidies, nursing fees, funeral subsidies, injury prevention fees, rehabilitation fees for occupational diseases and other expenditure.

5. Balance of work injury insurance refer to the balance of the work injury funds at the end of the reference period, including bank savings, special fiscal account, investment in bonds and others.

Maternity Insurance

1. Number of people covered refers to staff and workers who have participated in maternity insurance programme according to relevant regulation at the end of the reporting period.

2. Revenue of maternity insurance refers to payments made by employers participating in maternity insurance programs in accordance with the basis and proportion stipulated in state regulations, and income from other sources that become source of maternity insurance fund, including income of funds paid by employers, interest income and other income.

3. Expenses of maternity insurance refer to payments made from maternity insurance funds to staff and workers who participated in maternity insurance programme within the scope and standards of expenditure according to related national policies, expenses paid for pregnancy, child delivery or surgeries related to family planning, and other expenditure, including allowance for child bearing, medical fees and other expenditure.

4. Balance of the maternity insurance refers to the balance of the maternity insurance funds at the end of reference period, including bank savings, special fiscal account, investment in funds and others.

Insurance and Welfare Funds for Retirees refer to the total payment for living expenses actually received by retirees, including payment received from social insurance management agencies and units.

1. Pensions for retired veteran cadres refer to living expenses paid to retired veteran cadres according to related regulations.

2. Pensions for retirement refer to living expenses paid to retired staff and workers according to related regulations.

3. Living allowances for resigned staff and workers refer to living expenses paid to resigned staff and workers according to related regulation.

4. Medical care expenses refer to medical fees, hospitalization cost and per diem subsidies during hospitalizations paid by employers directly to retirees.

5. Others refer to insurance and welfare payments other than the above–mentioned payments, including funeral subsidies, living allowances, price subsidies and heating subsidies during winter.

Lawyers are certified legal workers according to law, and who are employed by legal counseling firms to act as legal advisers, agents in criminal or civil lawsuits, or defenders in criminal lawsuits, or to handle non–litigious legal affairs, to advise on matters of law or to write legal papers for others, and provide service to the public.

Notary Personnel refers to people working for notary offices including: directors, deputy director, notaries, assistant notaries, and other people providing assistance.

Notary Documents refer to the judicatory notary documents drawn up by the request of the party and are in accordance with facts and laws and following certain legal proceedings. According to usage and locality, the notary documents are divided into following 4 types: domestic notary documents, domestic economic notary documents, foreign–related civil notary documents and foreign–related economic notary documents.

Mediators refer to workers on peoples mediation committees responsible for mediating in civil disputes and cases of slight infraction of the law. They include members of the mediation committees and mediators of mediation groups. This indicator reflects the number of people engaged in meditation.

Mediation of Civil Disputes refers to number of cases made by mediation committees in mediating in civil disputes concerning civil rights and duties through persuasion and education in accordance with the provisions of law on a voluntary basis, so as to solve disputes by helping the parties involved come to an agreement and understanding, including those unsuccessful ones. This indicator reflects the workload of the mediation committees.

Acceptance of Case refers to the decision made by the people's procuratorate office on reported cases, prosecution, impeachment, surrender, self–found criminal clues or suspects after initial investigation to confirm the act of crime and to start legal proceedings of the case as criminal case.

Large Cases refer to cases involving a corruption or bribery of over 50,000 yuan, or a misappropriation of over 100,000 yuan. Cases of collectively illegal possession of public funds, unstated sources of large properties, or disguised overseas savings deposits involving 500,000 yuan, or a case that has been defined by the "Standard on Serious and Large Cases of Misconduct and Tortious that Directly Ac–

cepted by People's Procurators Office (trial)". This indicator mainly reflects number of accepted cases of job-related criminals that caused serious economic losses or extremely harmful to the society.

Key Cases refer to cases committed by government officials with a ranking of division director or county administrator. This indicator mainly reflects the recorded and spied on cases by the people's procurators offices toward government official with a ranking of division director or county administrator.

Decision on Arrest refers to decision made by people's procurators office, in accordance with laws, to arrest the suspect(s) in the cases that are accepted and to be investigated by procurators office. This indicator mainly reflects the implementation of the decision on arrest by people's procurators office.

Approval for Arrest refers to the decision made by people's procurators office, in accordance with laws and relevant facts, to approve the arrest of the suspect(s) that is proposed by the public security departments, state security departments or authority of prisons. This indicator reflects approved arrests made by people's procurators office that are proposed by related departments.

Decision on Prosecution refers to the decision made by people's procurators office, in accordance with laws and relevant facts, to institute proceedings to the people's court against the suspect(s) of criminal cases handed over by the public security departments, state security departments or authority of prisons, or by the anti-corruption departments within the procurators office. This indicator reflects the condition of the prosecutions made by people's procurators office toward the people's court.

Appeals refer to cases transferred to the appeal departments of procurator's offices after initial review by departments dealing with complaint letters and calls of the public. Included are appeals against decisions made by procurator's offices and appeals against court rules and verdicts.

Number of Labor Dispute Cases Accepted refers to the number of cases of labor dispute submitted that, after being reviewed by the labor dispute arbitration committees in line with the relevant national regulations, are accepted and registered for treatment.

Basic Pension Insurance

1.Number of staff and workers covered refer to staff and workers participating in basic pension insurance programme in line with national laws, regulations and related policies by the end of reference period, who have already had payment records in social security management agencies, including those who interrupt payment without terminating the insurance programme. Those who have registered in the programme with no payment records are not included.

2. Number of retirees participating in basic pension insurance programme refer to number of retirees participating in basic pension insurance programme by the end of reference period.

3. Revenue of basic pension insurance refer to payments made by employers and individuals participating in pension insurance programs in accordance with the basis and proportion stipulated in state regulations, and income from other sources that become source of pension insurance fund, including the premium paid by employers and staff and works, interest income, subsidies from higher level agencies, income as transfer from subordinate agencies, transferred income, government financial subsidies and other income.

4. Expenses of basic pension insurance refer to payment made to those retired and resigned people covered in pension insurance program in terms of pension or compensation within the scope and standards of expenditure according to related national policies, and expenditure occurred due to shift of the insurance relationship or adjustment of funds among agencies, including pension for resigned people, pension for retired people, pension for people quitting jobs, various subsidies, medical fees, funeral subsidies, compensation pension, management fees for social security agencies, expenses on subsidies to lower subordinates, expenses as transfer to agencies at higher level, transferred expenditure and other expenditure.

5. Balance of basic pension insurance refers to the balance of basic pension insurance at the end of the reference period after deducting expenses from revenue.

Retired or Resigned Personnel refers to people who have formally completed formalities for their retirement or quitting work and enjoy the corresponding retirement treatments.

21 开发区主要经济指标

Major Economic Indicators of Development Zone

21-1 湖北省开发区经济发展基本情况(2016)
BASIC INDICATORS OF ECONOMIC DEVELOPMENT OF DEVELOPMAENT ZONE IN HUBEI PROVINCE(2016)

指 标	Item		2015	2016	增幅(%) Percentage of Increase (%)
基本情况	**Basic condition**				
开发区批准规划面积	(平方公里)Floor Areas Approved in Development Zone	(sq.km.)	5396.74	5649.30	4.7
开发区实际占地面积	(平方公里)Actual Land Areas of Development Zone	(sq.km.)	2320.12	2552.67	10.0
企业个数	(个)Number of Enterprises	(unit)	127636	167696	31.4
其中:工业企业	(个)#Those Belong to Industrial Enterprises	(unit)	31657	37311	17.9
其中:规模以上	(个) #Enterprises above Designated Scale	(unit)	10182	10921	7.3
高新技术企业	(个)High and New Technological Enterprises	(unit)	3241	4029	24.3
外商投资企业	(个)Foreign Invested Enterprises	(unit)	1692	1914	13.1
从业人员	(万人)Population of Employment	(10 000 persons)	419.46	465.66	11.0
其中:工业企业	(万人)#Those Belong to Industrial Enterprises	(10 000 persons)	302.97	326.37	7.7
其中:规模以上	(万人) #Those Engaged in Enterprises above Designated Scale	(10 000 persons)	236.59	252.62	6.8
主要经济指标	**Major Economic Indicators**				
规模以上工业总产值	(亿元)Total Output Value of Enterprises above Designated Scale	(100 million Yuan)	31871.30	35531.78	11.5
规模以上工业增加值	(亿元)Value-added of Enterprises above Designated Scale	(100 million Yuan)	9056.32	9660.41	6.7
其中:高新技术产业	(亿元)#Value-added of High and New Technological Enterprises	(100 million Yuan)	3415.13	3915.29	14.6
规模以上工业主营业务收入	(亿元)Total Income From Major Business of Enterprises above Designated Scale	(100 million Yuan)	29592.00	32764.66	10.7
固定资产投资总额	(亿元)Total Value of Investment in Fixed Assets	(100 million Yuan)	13567.22	14712.03	8.4
其中:基础设施建设投资	(亿元)#Infrastructure Investment	(100 million Yuan)	2681.75	3186.39	18.8
施工项目个数	(个)Number of Projects under Construction	(unit)	10626	10433	-1.8
其中:亿元以上项目	(个)#the Value of the Projects is Worth More Than 100 million Yuan	(unit)	4519	4742	4.9
新开工项目	(个)Newly Opened Projects	(unit)	5880	6037	2.7
外商投资项目	(个)Foreign Invested Projects	(unit)	314	332	5.7
省外内资项目	(个)Foreign-funded Projects	(unit)	3090	3691	19.4
开发区税收总额	(亿元)Total Tax Revenue of Development Zone	(100 million Yuan)	1628.76	1657.25	1.7
招商引资总额	(亿元)The Total Investment	(100 million yuan)	9937.41	10911.56	9.8
其中:外商投资金额	(亿美元)#Total Value of Foreign Investment	(100 million dollars)	51.96	55.16	6.2
出口总额	(亿美元)Total Value of Export	(100 million dollars)	208.35	203.13	-2.5

21-2 湖北省131家开发区主要指标(2016)

开发区名称	Name of Development Zone	实际开发面积(平方公里) Actual Land Areas of Development Zone (sq. km)	
		2015	2016
湖北省	**Hubei Province**	**2320.12**	**2552.67**
武汉市	**Wuhan**	**482.75**	**531.6**
武汉江岸经济开发区	Wuhan Jiang'an Economic Development Zone	3.31	3.31
武汉江汉经济开发区	Wuhan Jianghan Economic Development Zone	0.7	0.7
武汉硚口经济开发区	Wuhan Qiaokou Economic Development Zone	1.14	1.14
武汉汉阳经济开发区	Wuhan Hanyang Economic Development Zone	12	12
武汉武昌经济开发区	Wuhan Wuchang Economic Development Zone	2.34	2.34
武汉青山经济开发区	Wuhan Qingshan Economic Development Zone	10	10
武汉洪山经济开发区	Wuhan Hongshan Economic Development Zone	0.27	0.27
武汉临空港经济技术开发区	Wuhan Linkonggang Economic and Technology Development Zone	125.49	139.26
武汉汉南经济开发区	Wuhan Hannan Economic Development Zone	15.13	16.74
武汉蔡甸经济开发区	Wuhan Caidian Economic Development Zone	44.5	53.3
武汉江夏经济开发区	Wuhan Jiangxia Economic Development Zone	108	110
武汉盘龙城经济开发区	Wuhan Panlongcheng Economic Development Zone	20	20
武汉阳逻经济开发区	Wuhan Yangluo Economic Development Zone	31.85	33
武汉经济技术开发区	Wuhan Economic and Technology Development Zone	39.7	
武汉东湖新技术产业开发区	Wuhan East Lake New Technology Industrial Development Zone	68.32	77.54
黄石市	**Huangshi**	**154.67**	**158.36**
湖北黄石港工业园区	Hubei Huangshi Port Industrial Park	2.2	2.2
湖北黄石新港工业园区	Hubei Huangshi New Port Industrial Park	15.3	15.6
湖北西塞山工业园区	Hubei Xisaishan Industrial Park	15.06	16
湖北下陆长乐山工业园区	Hubei Xialu Changleshan Industrial Park	12.6	12.7
黄石经济技术开发区	Huangshi Economic and Technology Development Zone	55	55
湖北阳新经济开发区	Hubei Yangxin Economic Development Zone	15	15
湖北大冶经济开发区	Hubei Daye Economic Development Zone	32.51	34.86
大冶灵成工业园	Daye Lingcheng Industrial Park	7	7
十堰市	**Shiyan**	**88.46**	**88.61**
十堰经济技术开发区	Shiyan Economic and Technology Development Zone	40	40
湖北郧阳区经济开发区	Hubei Yunyang County Economic Development Zone	19.13	19.28
湖北郧西工业园区	Hubei West Yun Industrial Park	1.53	1.53
湖北竹山经济开发区	Hubei Zhushan Economic Development Zone	10	10
湖北竹溪工业园区	Hubei Zhuxi Industrial Park	2.4	2.4
湖北房县工业园区	Hubei Fang County Industrial Park	4.2	4.2
湖北丹江口经济开发区	Hubei Danjiangkou Economic Development Zone	11.2	11.2
宜昌市	**Yichang**	**181.35**	**190.58**
湖北西陵经济开发区	Hubei Xiling Economic Development Zone	4	4
湖北伍家岗工业园区	Hubei Wujiagang Industrial Park	4	4
湖北点军工业园区	Hubei Dianjun Industrial Park	5.4	5.4
湖北夷陵经济开发区	Hubei Yiling Economic Development Zone	28	28
湖北远安工业园区	Hubei Yuan'an Industrial Park	18	19
湖北兴山经济开发区	Hubei Xingshan Economic Development Zone	2.64	3.3
湖北秭归经济开发区	Hubei Zigui Economic Development Zone	6	6
湖北长阳经济开发区	Hubei Changyang Economic Development Zone	2.8	3.08
湖北五峰工业园区	Hubei Wufeng Industrial Park	2.3	2.3
湖北五峰民族工业园	Hubei Wufeng National Industrial Park	0.87	0.92
宜昌高新技术产业开发区	Yichang High-tech Industrial Development Zone	77.5	79.6
湖北宜都工业园区	Hubei Yidu Industrial Park	12.25	17.41
湖北当阳经济开发区	Hubei Dangyang Economic Development Zone	26	26
湖北枝江经济开发区	Hubei Zhijiang Economic Development Zone	29.57	33.8
枝江安福寺工业园	Zhijiang Anfu Temple Industrial Park	1.86	1.89

MAIN INDICATORS OF 131 DEVELOPMENT ZONE IN HUBEI(2016)

企业个数(个) Number of Enterprises (unit)		其中:规模以上工业企业(个) Among which, Industrial Enterprises above Designated Size (unit)		高新技术企业(个) Number of High and New Technological Enterprises (unit)		从业人员(万人) Population of Employment (10 000 persons)	
2015	2016	2015	2016	2015	2016	2015	2016
127636	**167696**	**10182**	**10921**	**3241**	**4029**	**419.46**	**465.66**
71023	**97043**	**1581**	**1660**	**1401**	**1718**	**106.28**	**118.56**
242	242	15	14	7	7	0.90	0.90
399	401	11	11	3	3	2.36	1.89
408	445	27	24	9	10	4.00	4.20
921	921	68	68	25	25	3.89	3.89
216	164	16	14	11	10	1.85	1.74
323	341	99	91	15	15	3.68	2.38
157	158	13	14	18	19	0.87	0.92
29629	37712	273	271	62	102	29.04	31.15
493	487	136	139	13	13	3.70	3.84
479	1495	85	128	18	39	3.30	3.90
738	738	168	168	53	53	6.20	6.30
673	691	41	40		11	5.04	5.10
147	175	85	90	15	18	2.90	2.45
216	230	216	230	89		11.70	11.90
35982	48596	683	745	1063	1391	45.28	47.34
8281	**8835**	**487**	**561**	**145**	**159**	**27.16**	**27.86**
43	45	12	14	12	12	0.43	0.43
33	36	13	11	2	2	0.21	0.22
338	290	72	66	10	10	3.75	3.02
163	165	23	24	7	7	2.01	1.92
5608	6168	180	203	56	64	9.67	10.83
417	426	63	65	12	12	3.42	3.43
1612	1633	187	206	39	45	6.32	6.65
67	72	33	35	7	7	1.35	1.36
5347	**5969**	**617**	**642**	**130**	**150**	**19.78**	**21.88**
3957	4518	233	247	78	86	10.20	11.05
251	267	95	103	17	22	2.93	3.17
53	53	30	26	3	4	0.28	0.26
199	215	28	29	6	6	0.62	0.63
105	108	35	35	3	6	1.80	1.90
159	179	63	65	11	11	0.98	1.89
623	629	133	137	12	15	2.97	2.98
7397	**9421**	**1030**	**1092**	**320**	**363**	**30.61**	**32.53**
546	743	11	11	9	9	0.86	1.19
92	93	32	26	11	15	1.50	1.40
18	18	16	16	9	9	0.32	0.32
1120	1288	150	157	25	28	5.23	5.89
181	198	94	108	18	21	3.27	3.21
49	55	19	22	3	6	1.01	1.28
223	229	75	74	10	12	2.03	2.05
112	129	49	52	13	14	1.28	1.75
300	307	20	20	5	5	0.75	0.76
14	25	9	10	1	2	0.50	0.53
3485	5040	201	220	149	169	8.10	8.30
358	388	204	214	46	51	3.62	3.67
964	978	175	181	39	43	5.84	5.92
1125	1188	177	186	20	27	6.98	6.98
59	66	32	33	3	5	1.22	1.21

21-2 续表 1 continued

开发区名称	Name of Development Zone	实际开发面积(平方公里) Actual Land Areas of Development Zone (sq. km)	
		2015	2016
襄阳市	**Xianyang**	**211.6**	**255.2**
襄阳高新技术产业开发区	Xiangyang High-tech Industrial Development Zone	52.0	75.0
襄阳鱼梁州经济开发区	Xiangyang Yuliangzhou Economic Development Zone	2.0	2.0
襄阳经济技术开发区	Xiangyang Economic Development Zone	76.0	78.0
湖北襄城经济开发区	Hubei Xiangcheng Economic Development Zone	16.0	16.0
湖北樊城经济开发区	Hubei Fancheng Economic Development Zone	8.1	8.8
湖北襄州经济开发区	Hubei Xiangzhou Economic Development Zone	24.6	24.6
襄州双沟工业园	Xiangyang Industrial Park	3.0	5.6
湖北南漳经济开发区	Hubei Nanzhang Economic Development Zone	21.2	21.2
湖北谷城经济开发区	Hubei Gucheng Economic Development Zone	20.0	20.0
谷城石花经济开发区	Gucheng Shihua Economic Development Zone	10.0	10.0
湖北保康经济开发区	Hubei Baokang Economic Development Zone	10.5	11.6
湖北老河口经济开发区	Hubei Laohekou Economic Development Zone	29.0	30.0
湖北枣阳经济开发区	Hubei Zaoyang Economic Development Zone	6.5	6.5
枣阳吴店工业园	Zaoyang Wudian Industrial Park	3.9	3.9
湖北宜城经济开发区	Hubei Yicheng Economic Development Zone	16.0	20.0
鄂州市	**E'zhou**	**65.4**	**70.2**
湖北鄂州花湖经济开发区	Hubei E'Zhou Huahu Economic Development Zone	14.0	15.0
鄂州葛店经济技术开发区	E'Zhou Gedian Economic and Technology Development Zone	30.4	32.2
湖北鄂州经济开发区	Hubei E'Zhou Economic Development Zone	21.0	23.0
荆门市	**Jingmen**	**120.7**	**167.5**
湖北东宝工业园区	Hubei Dongbao Industrial Park	15.5	17.2
荆门高新技术产业开发区	Hubei Jingmen High-tech Industrial Development Zone	38.3	39.7
湖北荆门化工循环产业园	Hubei Jingmen Chemical Recycling Development Zone	13.0	13.0
湖北京山经济开发区	Hubei Jingshan Economic Development Zone	23.5	24.6
湖北屈家岭经济开发区	Hubei Qujialing Economic Development Zone	7.0	7.0
湖北沙洋经济开发区	Hubei Shayang Economic Development Zone	31.5	32.0
湖北钟祥经济开发区	Hubei Zhongxiang Economic Development Zone	22.0	24.0
钟祥胡集经济开发区	Zhongxiang Huji Economic Development Zone	10.0	10.0
孝感市	**Xiaogan**	**210.0**	**214.3**
孝感高新技术产业开发区	Xiaogan high-tech Industrial Development Zone	48.5	48.5
湖北孝南经济开发区	Hubei Xiaonan Economic Development Zone	35.5	36.5
湖北孝昌经济开发区	Hubei Xiaochang Economic Development Zone	12.0	12.0
湖北大悟经济开发区	Hubei Dawu Economic Development Zone	17.3	17.3
湖北云梦经济开发区	Hubei Yunmeng Economic Development Zone	17.6	19.3
湖北应城经济开发区	Hubei Yingcheng Economic Development Zone	21.0	21.0
湖北安陆经济开发区	Hubei Anlu Economic Development Zone	36.6	36.6
湖北汉川经济开发区	Hubei Hanchuan Economic Development Zone	21.5	23.2
荆州市	**Jingzhou**	**249.8**	**258.5**
湖北沙市经济开发区	Hubei Shashi Economic Development Zone	38.0	38.0
湖北荆州城南经济开发区	Jingzhou Chengnan Economic Development Zone	14.1	14.4
荆州经济技术开发区	Jingzhou Economic and Technology Development Zone	55.7	98.2
湖北公安经济开发区	Hubei Gong'an Economic Development Zone	4.0	4.6
湖北监利经济开发区	Hubei Jianli Economic Development Zone	51.1	52.9
湖北江陵经济开发区	Hubei Jiangling Economic Development Zone	14.8	14.8
湖北石首经济开发区	Hubei Shishou Economic Development Zone	34.2	34.2
湖北洪湖经济开发区	Hubei Honghu Economic Development Zone	15.9	20.0
洪湖府场经济开发区	Honghu Fuchang Economic Development Zone	16.0	17.0
湖北松滋经济开发区	Hubei Songzi Economic Development Zone	6.0	7.0
黄冈市	**Huanggang**	**242.5**	**285.8**
黄冈高新技术产业开发区	Hubei Huanggang Economic Development Zone	226.1	247.9

企业个数(个) Number of Enterprises (unit)		其中:规模以上工业企业(个) Among which, Industrial Enterprises above Designated Size (unit)		高新技术企业(个) Number of High and New Technological Enterprises (unit)		从业人员(万人) Population of Employment (10 000 persons)	
2015	2016	2015	2016	2015	2016	2015	2016
12554	**16482**	**1268**	**1349**	**347**	**457**	**53.44**	**67.69**
9225	10949	351	372	181	212	15.90	17.00
50	100					0.12	0.15
912	1125	155	163	35	36	10.79	10.93
256	261	40	40	7	7	2.60	2.61
372	381	122	124	26	20	4.26	4.37
602	641	125	126	42	44	8.37	8.56
346	417	19	20	3	5	3.50	4.30
120	144	87	100	7	11	1.69	2.02
1534	1541	112	113	25	27	7.28	7.30
285	288	51	54	14	18	2.98	3.03
51	61	32	37	9	10	1.50	1.70
453	554	195	208	26	35	4.32	4.67
537	601	157	173	45	50	4.38	5.04
337	387	73	84	5	6	3.08	3.54
151	157	84	86	9	12	3.02	3.40
3449	3923	418	437	68	85	11.86	12.25
365	381	53	48	13	11	1.47	1.63
2766	3212	283	303	44	52	9.25	9.42
318	330	82	86	11	22	1.14	1.20
1578	**1867**	**781**	**857**	**150**	**232**	**22.09**	**22.98**
165	199	92	97	12	12	3.29	3.31
2137	2412	364	425	76	141	8.96	10.52
57	54	29	31	10	13	0.84	1.02
393	398	125	129	19	19	3.52	3.63
51	53	19	21	1	3	0.20	0.20
181	212	83	94	17	19	3.00	3.50
336	357	128	136	19	26	6.46	6.85
76	82	36	37	7	8	1.92	1.95
3971	**5908**	**936**	**973**	**150**	**201**	**28.01**	**29.51**
2208	3708	508	531	107	135	11.30	11.80
381	410	145	157	26	26	5.18	5.33
258	283	37	31	6	14	2.25	2.29
61	68	27	27	5	5	1.50	1.50
302	321	135	138	17	26	8.22	8.31
165	375	139	142	18	18	3.41	3.42
359	366	65	67	12	17	4.33	4.36
1085	1483	299	317	20	30	8.63	9.56
3627	**6591**	**865**	**948**	**105**	**129**	**38.06**	**46.19**
193	209	95	101	5	7	3.41	3.56
805	815	140	155	6	12	6.89	7.25
1456	4629	152	306	38	66	9.46	17.98
111	114	58	58	7	12	0.92	1.00
98	115	90	105	4	5	1.73	1.87
116	123	43	48	7	7	1.01	1.06
83	87	77	80	7	10	1.53	1.54
215	218	54	55	8	8	2.84	2.89
361	362	50	52	7	7	3.68	3.89
189	211	106	122	16	19	6.59	7.56
3043	**3668**	**693**	**775**	**167**	**218**	**26.37**	**28.36**
2730	2758	574	667	139	165	22.99	24.26

21-2 续表 2 continued

开发区名称	Name of Development Zone	实际开发面积(平方公里) Actual Land Areas of Development Zone (sq. km)	
		2015	2016
湖北黄州火车站经济开发区	Hubei Huangzhou Railway Station Economic Development Zone	8.5	9.0
黄州工业园	Huangzhou Industrial Park	2.3	2.3
湖北龙感湖工业园区	Hubei Longganhu Industrial Park	8.5	8.7
湖北团风经济开发区	Hubei Tuanfeng Economic Development Zone	8.5	8.5
湖北红安经济开发区	Hubei Hong'an Economic Development Zone	35.0	36.0
湖北罗田经济开发区	Hubei Luotian Economic Development Zone	10.0	12.0
湖北英山经济开发区	Hubei Yingshan Economic Development Zone	16.9	17.2
湖北浠水经济开发区	Hubei Xishui Economic Development Zone	28.0	30.1
湖北蕲春李时珍医药工业园区	Hubei Qichun Li Shizhen Pharmaceutical Industrial Park	20.0	22.0
蕲春经济开发区	Qichun Economic Development Zone	18.0	18.0
湖北黄梅经济开发区	Hubei Huangmei Economic Development Zone	26.8	28.5
湖北麻城经济开发区	Hubei Macheng Economic Development Zone	35.0	35.0
湖北武穴经济开发区	Hubei Wuxue Economic Development Zone	14.9	14.9
咸宁市	**Xianning**	**104.0**	**117.3**
湖北咸安经济开发区	Hubei Xian'an Economic Development Zone	10.9	11.0
湖北嘉鱼经济开发区	Hubei Jiayu Economic Development Zone	15.0	15.5
湖北通城经济开发区	Hubei Tongcheng Economic Development Zone	6.0	15.8
湖北崇阳工业园区	Hubei Chongyang Industrial Park	9.2	8.4
湖北通山经济开发区	Hubei Tongshan Economic Development Zone	19.3	19.8
咸宁高新技术产业开发区	Xianing high-tech Industrial Development Znoe	16.6	17.9
湖北赤壁经济开发区	Hubei Chibi Economic Development Zone	19.1	21.0
湖北赤壁蒲纺工业园区	Hubei Chibi Puqi Textile Industrial Park	8.0	8.0
随州市	**Suizhou**	**60.4**	**61.0**
随州高新技术产业开发区	Suizhou high-tech Industrial Development Znoe	60.4	61.0
湖北曾都经济开发区	Hubei Zengdu Economic Development Zone	20.0	20.0
湖北随县经济开发区	Hubei Sui County Economic Development Zone	4.8	4.8
湖北广水经济开发区	Hubei Guangshui Economic Development Zone	9.6	10.2
恩施自治州	**Enshi Autonomous Prefecture**	**53.5**	**54.9**
湖北恩施经济开发区	Hubei Enshi Economic Development Zone	14.7	14.7
湖北恩施州经济开发区	Hubei Enshi Prefecture Economic Development Zone	5.1	5.1
湖北利川经济开发区	Hubei Lichuan Economic Development Zone	5.0	5.0
湖北建始工业园区	Hubei Jianshi Industrial Park	4.2	4.4
湖北巴东经济开发区	Hubei Badong Economic Development Zone	6.0	6.5
湖北宣恩工业园区	Hubei Xuan'en Industrial Park	2.5	2.7
湖北咸丰工业园区	Hubei Xianfeng Industrial Park	8.5	9.1
湖北来凤经济开发区	Hubei Laifeng Economic Development Zone	5.5	5.5
湖北鹤峰经济开发区	Hubei Hefeng Economic Development Zone	2.0	2.0
仙桃市	**Xiantao**	**30.8**	**31.2**
仙桃高新技术产业开发区	Xiantao high-tech Industrial Development Znoe	30.8	31.2
仙桃彭场工业园	Xiantao Pengchang Industrial Park	6.5	6.7
潜江市	**Qianjiang**	**26.4**	**26.4**
湖北潜江经济开发区	Hubei Qianjiang Economic Development Zone	7.0	7.0
潜江张金经济开发区	Qianjiang Zhangjin Economic Development Zone	2.4	2.4
潜江园林经济开发区	Qianjiang Yuanlin Economic Development Zone	17.0	17.0
天门市	**Tianmen**	**35.8**	**39.1**
湖北天门经济开发区	Hubei Tianmen Economic Development Zone	35.8	39.1
神农架盘水生态产业园区		2.0	2.0

企业个数(个) Number of Enterprises (unit)		其中:规模以上工业企业(个) Among which, Industrial Enterprises above Designated Size (unit)		高新技术企业(个) Number of High and New Technological Enterprises (unit)		从业人员(万人) Population of Employment (10 000 persons)	
2015	2016	2015	2016	2015	2016	2015	2016
47	48	13	13	6	6	0.27	0.54
27	27	13	13	7	7	0.32	0.35
120	125	31	32	4	4	1.24	1.30
85	86	31	34	8	8	1.02	1.04
416	451	106	119	18	25	3.00	3.71
95	130	40	45	19	30	0.85	1.10
98	98	33	31	21	19	1.69	1.70
526	538	68	80	8	19	3.60	3.80
165	235	34	41	6	7	1.71	1.84
128	171	30	39	3	4	1.78	1.86
218	235	68	72	12	13	3.19	3.59
156	164	75	79	32	33	2.67	2.21
265	274	105	107	13	16	2.76	2.77
1066	**1140**	**564**	**608**	**84**	**113**	**12.29**	**13.24**
172	179	89	95	14	16	1.74	1.89
145	145	137	138	15	19	1.82	1.93
88	89	57	58	6	6	2.95	3.01
126	133	61	69	6	8	1.56	1.62
67	91	35	38	7	7	0.83	0.86
827	868	448	483	68	98	9.36	10.18
123	125	102	106	15	21	0.65	1.05
46	48	20	18	3		0.54	0.58
1852	**2176**	**220**	**232**	**65**	**74**	**9.60**	**9.96**
1852	2176	220	232	65	74	9.60	9.96
302	302	71	71	26	26	2.73	2.86
42	45	28	30	7	11	0.51	0.55
252	263	52	61	12	14	1.41	1.55
940	**1012**	**281**	**324**	**22**	**27**	**11.57**	**11.70**
340	350	40	67	10	11	2.22	2.24
42	43	6	9	1	3	1.22	1.22
65	67	25	25	1	2	0.52	0.62
39	41	25	27	3	3	0.62	0.69
178	220	31	35	2	2	1.59	1.61
85	100	29	37	1	2	1.57	1.72
87	90	55	58	3	3	1.50	1.52
77	78	43	43			1.71	1.73
27	23	27	23	1	1	0.62	0.35
1210	**1308**	**265**	**286**	**48**	**63**	**8.41**	**8.72**
1210	1308	265	286	48	63	8.41	8.72
228	224	46	49	8	9	4.51	4.42
1914	**1933**	**52**	**48**	**21**	**20**	**5.55**	5.61
83	80	21	18	13	13	1.21	1.18
125	125	14	13	4	3	2.12	2.12
1706	1728	17	17	4	4	2.22	2.31
356	**392**	**119**	**124**	**16**	**18**	**8.26**	**8.47**
356	392	119	124	16	18	8.26	8.47
28	28	5	5	2	2	0.12	0.15

21-2 续表 3 continued

开发区名称	Name of Development Zone	其中:规模以上工业企业(万人) Among which, Industrial Enterprises above Designated Size (10 000 persons)	
		2015	2016
湖北省	**Hubei Province**	**236.59**	**252.62**
武汉市	**Wuhan**	**53.31**	**54.34**
武汉江岸经济开发区	Wuhan Jiang'an Economic Development Zone	0.30	0.30
武汉江汉经济开发区	Wuhan Jianghan Economic Development Zone	0.64	0.63
武汉硚口经济开发区	Wuhan Qiaokou Economic Development Zone	1.28	1.27
武汉汉阳经济开发区	Wuhan Hanyang Economic Development Zone	2.00	2.00
武汉武昌经济开发区	Wuhan Wuchang Economic Development Zone	0.92	1.12
武汉青山经济开发区	Wuhan Qingshan Economic Development Zone	3.06	1.96
武汉洪山经济开发区	Wuhan Hongshan Economic Development Zone	0.25	0.33
武汉临空港经济技术开发区	Wuhan Linkonggang Economic and Technology Development Zone	5.68	5.66
武汉汉南经济开发区	Wuhan Hannan Economic Development Zone	1.60	1.72
武汉蔡甸经济开发区	Wuhan Caidian Economic Development Zone	1.76	2.50
武汉江夏经济开发区	Wuhan Jiangxia Economic Development Zone	3.53	3.53
武汉盘龙城经济开发区	Wuhan Panlongcheng Economic Development Zone	0.95	0.97
武汉阳逻经济开发区	Wuhan Yangluo Economic Development Zone	2.30	1.80
武汉经济技术开发区	Wuhan Economic and Technology Development Zone	11.70	11.90
武汉东湖新技术产业开发区	Wuhan East Lake New Technology Industrial Development Zone	32.14	33.43
黄石市	**Huangshi**	**13.27**	**13.12**
湖北黄石港工业园区	Hubei Huangshi Port Industrial Park	0.24	0.24
湖北黄石新港工业园区	Hubei Huangshi New Port Industrial Park	0.17	0.17
湖北西塞山工业园区	Hubei Xisaishan Industrial Park	1.50	1.42
湖北下陆长乐山工业园区	Hubei Xialu Changleshan Industrial Park	1.90	1.80
黄石经济技术开发区	Huangshi Economic and Technology Development Zone	4.45	5.44
湖北阳新经济开发区	Hubei Yangxin Economic Development Zone	2.86	2.87
湖北大冶经济开发区	Hubei Daye Economic Development Zone	4.74	4.91
大冶灵成工业园	Daye Lingcheng Industrial Park	0.79	0.80
十堰市	**Shiyan**	**11.69**	**12.33**
十堰经济技术开发区	Shiyan Economic and Technology Development Zone	5.85	6.27
湖北郧阳区经济开发区	Hubei Yun County Economic Development Zone	2.48	2.67
湖北郧西工业园区	Hubei West Yun Industrial Park	0.24	0.21
湖北竹山经济开发区	Hubei Zhushan Economic Development Zone	0.28	0.31
湖北竹溪工业园区	Hubei Zhuxi Industrial Park	0.49	0.50
湖北房县工业园区	Hubei Fang County Industrial Park	0.55	0.57
湖北丹江口经济开发区	Hubei Danjiangkou Economic Development Zone	1.80	1.80
宜昌市	**Yichang**	**22.34**	**23.41**
湖北西陵经济开发区	Hubei Xiling Economic Development Zone	0.15	0.15
湖北伍家岗工业园区	Hubei Wujiagang Industrial Park	0.40	0.40
湖北点军工业园区	Hubei Dianjun Industrial Park	0.30	0.30
湖北夷陵经济开发区	Hubei Yiling Economic Development Zone	3.27	3.66
湖北远安工业园区	Hubei Yuan'an Industrial Park	2.51	2.46
湖北兴山经济开发区	Hubei Xingshan Economic Development Zone	0.62	0.78
湖北秭归经济开发区	Hubei Zigui Economic Development Zone	1.30	1.30
湖北长阳经济开发区	Hubei Changyang Economic Development Zone	1.00	1.16
湖北五峰工业园区	Hubei Wufeng Industrial Park	0.30	0.45
湖北五峰民族工业园	Hubei Wufeng National Industrial Park	0.37	0.39
宜昌高新技术产开发区	Yichang High-tech Industrial Development Zone	6.00	6.50
湖北宜都工业园区	Hubei Yidu Industrial Park	3.22	3.27
湖北当阳经济开发区	Hubei Dangyang Economic Development Zone	4.53	4.65
湖北枝江经济开发区	Hubei Zhijiang Economic Development Zone	4.53	4.62
枝江安福寺工业园	Zhijiang Anfu Temple Industrial Park	1.14	1.13

规模以上工业增加值(亿元) Above-scale Industrial Added Value (100 million Yuan)		规模以上工业主营业务收入(亿元) Scale Industrial Core Business Revenue (100 million Yuan)		固定资产投资总额(亿元) Total Investment In Fixed Assets (100 million Yuan)		施工项目个数(个) Number of Construction Project (unit)	
2015	2016	2015	2016	2015	2016	2015	2016
9056.32	**9660.41**	**29592.00**	**32764.66**	**13567.22**	**14712.03**	**10626**	**10433**
2791.18	**2796.10**	**7830.17**	**8659.38**	**2916.22**	**3014.67**	**1335**	**1222**
9.03	6.00	42.01	31.68	15.35	15.4	2	2
9.88	9.85	37.43	35.05	7.1	9.33	7	8
26.40	29.30	95.15	109.94	12	6.44	7	7
616.44	534.40	826.40	827.40	72	72.72	29	29
47.98	43.56	195.01	162.78		1.53	1	1
29.14	26.55	132.89	124.93	27.16	17.33	18	18
6.49	8.24	24.05	30.01	4	4.1	2	3
355.53	359.70	664.94	710.30	498.53	500.5	186	234
34.30	34.50	119.73	121.40	53.59	96	27	29
203.00	170.90	571.00	458.90	150	163.2	79	80
161.00	203.95	524.42	746.99	362.91	469	136	105
33.88	30.16	120.90	116.26	57.5	28.16	85	80
130.76	103.40	489.55	397.00	245	225	117	67
679.30	684.70	2257.40	2423.69	661.6	535.9	322	
1778.00	2005.00	6512.00	7437.00	749.48	870.06	375	340
444.56	**469.49**	**2057.15**	**2092.03**	**892.93**	**886.08**	**677**	**626**
2.30	2.51	6.50	7.06	4	2.68	13	15
5.56	5.02	17.54	17.32	15.12	20.85	11	10
61.00	54.20	270.00	235.31	58.01	39.84	54	32
107.00	68.00	1053.00	962.00	37	27	18	12
205.98	225.13	1264.90	1316.66	441.96	428.26	285	263
34.56	32.26	101.11	104.44	67	68	49	38
177.60	197.94	509.47	566.78	207.52	235.65	175	178
25.12	32.45	85.72	108.61	62.32	63.8	72	78
432.00	**482.06**	**1462.16**	**1553.32**	**679.33**	**757.62**	**620**	**729**
290.99	332.04	1025.16	1060.17	386.51	456.12	243	274
46.38	49.12	131.72	147.86	61.37	65.17	119	124
4.45	3.87	11.76	11.10	10.78	8.28	16	9
12.38	12.22	34.38	35.34	37.2	42.26	30	37
8.70	9.70	27.64	29.54	19.4	19.5	16	20
15.66	16.48	46.70	47.80	91.65	92.04	129	196
57.07	62.37	184.80	221.51	72.42	74.25	67	69
1059.13	**1147.72**	**3383.06**	**3714.00**	**1543.08**	**1642.92**	**1357**	**1262**
7.15	7.20	22.04	24.17	35.18	35.56	19	30
15.58	17.80	32.50	35.20	0.56	18	6	7
15.32	11.20	40.49	35.15	20.63	45	15	20
248.96	251.14	785.86	856.58	254.2	296.73	210	218
72.79	82.03	244.23	255.39	113.83	118.3	98	90
14.05	17.50	65.92	81.20	13.4	15.6	13	15
34.98	38.97	96.21	108.59	36.55	35.26	62	53
25.69	26.82	70.72	86.29	56.77	60.91	92	64
5.64	6.05	18.89	21.24	30	30.51	55	37
4.13	4.79	15.57	19.60	4.51	5.64	10	20
408.00	450.00	1492.00	1644.00	560	650	404	371
315.45	345.23	912.78	967.28	364.47	380.5	423	387
156.51	173.56	509.10	545.53	242.65	244.2	195	105
197.30	219.15	632.22	777.08	236.8	254.8	143	155
21.01	24.02	70.21	80.63	47.43	47.55	22	16

21-2 续表 4 continued

开发区名称	Name of Development Zone	其中:规模以上工业企业(万人) Among which, Industrial Enterprises above Designated Size (10 000 persons)	
		2015	2016
襄阳市	**Xianyang**	**33.60**	**39.32**
襄阳高新技术产业开发区	Xiangyang High-tech Industrial Development Zone	13.60	14.50
襄阳鱼梁州经济开发区	Xiangyang Yuliangzhou Economic Development Zone		
襄阳经济技术开发区	Xiangyang Economic Development Zone	6.13	6.16
湖北襄城经济开发区	Hubei Xiangcheng Economic Development Zone	1.40	1.40
湖北樊城经济开发区	Hubei Fancheng Economic Development Zone	2.90	2.80
湖北襄州经济开发区	Hubei Xiangzhou Economic Development Zone	4.41	4.46
襄阳工业园	Xiangyang Industrial Park	0.72	0.86
湖北南漳经济开发区	Hubei Nanzhang Economic Development Zone	1.53	1.58
湖北谷城经济开发区	Hubei Gucheng Economic Development Zone	2.60	2.20
谷城石花经济开发区	Gucheng Shihua Economic Development Zone	1.81	1.85
湖北保康经济开发区	Hubei Baokang Economic Development Zone	0.63	0.73
湖北老河口经济开发区	Hubei Laohekou Economic Development Zone	2.41	2.68
湖北枣阳经济开发区	Hubei Zaoyang Economic Development Zone	2.48	2.82
枣阳吴店工业园	Zaoyang Wudian Industrial Park	1.19	1.36
湖北宜城经济开发区	Hubei Yicheng Economic Development Zone	1.85	2.08
鄂州市	**E'zhou**	**4.73**	**4.96**
湖北鄂州花湖经济开发区	Hubei E'Zhou Huahu Economic Development Zone	0.57	0.52
鄂州葛店经济技术开发区	E'Zhou Gedian Economic and Technology Development Zone	3.42	3.72
湖北鄂州经济开发区	Hubei E'Zhou Economic Development Zone	0.74	0.72
荆门市	**Jingmen**	**15.29**	**15.90**
湖北东宝工业园区	Hubei Dongbao Industrial Park	2.40	2.43
荆门高新技术产业开发区	Hubei Jingmen High-tech Industrial Development Zone	8.24	9.72
湖北荆门化工循环产业园	Hubei Jingmen Chemical Recycling Development Zone	0.51	0.63
湖北京山经济开发区	Hubei Jingshan Economic Development Zone	3.05	3.15
湖北屈家岭经济开发区	Hubei Qujialing Economic Development Zone	0.18	0.18
湖北沙洋经济开发区	Hubei Shayang Economic Development Zone	1.90	2.10
湖北钟祥经济开发区	Hubei Zhongxiang Economic Development Zone	4.00	4.20
钟祥胡集经济开发区	Zhongxiang Huji Economic Development Zone	1.42	1.44
孝感市	**Xiaogan**	**17.32**	**18.20**
孝感高新技术产业开发区	Xiaogan high-tech Industrial Development Zone	8.60	9.01
湖北孝南经济开发区	Hubei Xiaonan Economic Development Zone	1.47	1.58
湖北孝昌经济开发区	Hubei Xiaochang Economic Development Zone	1.31	1.34
湖北大悟经济开发区	Hubei Dawu Economic Development Zone	1.00	1.00
湖北云梦经济开发区	Hubei Yunmeng Economic Development Zone	3.15	3.28
湖北应城经济开发区	Hubei Yingcheng Economic Development Zone	2.51	2.52
湖北安陆经济开发区	Hubei Anlu Economic Development Zone	1.32	1.32
湖北汉川经济开发区	Hubei Hanchuan Economic Development Zone	5.09	5.53
荆州市	**Jingzhou**	**13.24**	**16.59**
湖北沙市经济开发区	Hubei Shashi Economic Development Zone	2.44	2.49
湖北荆州城南经济开发区	Jingzhou Chengnan Economic Development Zone	2.10	2.25
荆州经济技术开发区	Jingzhou Economic and Technology Development Zone	3.05	4.83
湖北公安经济开发区	Hubei Gong'an Economic Development Zone	0.54	0.54
湖北监利经济开发区	Hubei Jianli Economic Development Zone	1.71	1.80
湖北江陵经济开发区	Hubei Jiangling Economic Development Zone	0.59	0.60
湖北石首经济开发区	Hubei Shishou Economic Development Zone	1.52	1.54
湖北洪湖经济开发区	Hubei Honghu Economic Development Zone	0.76	0.85
洪湖府场经济开发区	Honghu Fuchang Economic Development Zone	0.53	0.76
湖北松滋经济开发区	Hubei Songzi Economic Development Zone		2.49
黄冈市	**Huanggang**	**14.22**	**15.25**
湖北黄冈经济开发区	Hubei Huanggang Economic Development Zone	12.48	12.59

规模以上工业增加值(亿元) Above-scale Industrial Added Value (100 million Yuan)		规模以上工业主营业务收入(亿元) Scale Industrial Core Business Revenue (100 million Yuan)		固定资产投资总额(亿元) Total Investment In Fixed Assets (100 million Yuan)		施工项目个数(个) Number of Construction Project (unit)	
2015	2016	2015	2016	2015	2016	2015	2016
1146.84	**1205.05**	**4258.00**	**4716.47**	**2000.36**	**2075.77**	**1049**	**930**
769.70	805.80	2280.80	2508.00	801	803.2	344	365
				0.3	0.02	2	1
315.07	328.46	995.63	1015.14	291.7	293.13	108	97
44.00	44.20	94.00	94.00	26	21	15	4
73.00	72.00	227.00	230.00	92	96	81	84
156.42	173.01	488.05	530.10	285.31	301.12	108	115
33.20	42.90	105.20	135.80	45	54.7	11	15
52.81	63.29	151.35	172.00	88.94	110.7	46	62
89.83	101.90	264.84	296.18	116.73	129.92	119	118
82.70	90.80	173.90	194.50	59.64	70.2	47	66
26.20	29.19	49.97	58.13	39.95	48.65	20	28
132.34	138.78	526.85	586.94	208.5	242.46	151	154
155.31	186.36	515.00	581.95	252	320	108	135
56.85	65.38	177.13	203.67	100.5	115.55	48	55
99.45	104.69	356.00	399.29	65.29	63.31	69	52
254.99	**305.56**	**922.83**	**1091.88**	**513.99**	**638.11**	**317**	**352**
26.93	28.76	103.74	104.18	55.2	66.39	29	25
200.05	247.20	726.40	880.50	407	512.7	248	272
28.01	29.60	92.69	107.20	51.79	59.02	40	55
567.87	**646.80**	**2125.34**	**2502.20**	**854**	**1161.57**	**1271**	**1283**
74.72	88.91	305.93	336.21	148.17	171.29	231	238
268.28	345.47	960.26	1222.16	381.72	458.87	426	438
8.95	12.11	29.10	38.12	40.58	51.12	56	50
84.71	93.04	318.59	346.86	122.9	133.5	189	198
5.34	4.85	19.25	17.11	14.97	17.74	23	25
51.47	60.60	182.50	215.50	120.86	137.52	86	95
153.50	173.90	501.40	561.40	140.1	158.83	184	186
38.37	40.55	154.87	163.98	31.79	32.7	51	53
559.55	**618.44**	**1991.26**	**2189.29**	**956.09**	**1130.98**	**628**	**731**
310.00	341.00	1104.00	1214.00	518	606	335	365
45.20	48.50	170.00	183.00	265	320	277	285
10.32	11.02	38.80	40.12	51.4	72.93	50	85
9.64	9.98	28.70	30.10	34.2	62.6	26	32
83.48	87.14	306.37	323.40	197.9	198.3	147	200
120.02	127.30	422.78	422.81	223.6	260.49	294	762
52.30	57.60	124.30	150.40	105	114	96	124
177.29	198.84	695.46	754.67	247.49	275.45	121	125
409.51	**480.11**	**1447.60**	**1584.97**	**813.98**	**816.72**	**1017**	**884**
55.34	66.09	158.78	178.27	148	156	57	55
72.04	69.05	285.19	249.55	89.95	65.61	62	22
72.30	182.14	243.96	661.92	225.24	565.82	372	402
22.58	24.74	78.58	85.41	53.41	56.91	24	27
61.30	66.26	207.20	212.30	36.45	32.2	43	37
19.32	21.17	69.68	82.42	37.41	30.28	56	38
53.51	42.89	201.57	162.83	50.4	30.17	48	37
40.56	46.15	168.75	169.99	50.72	62.01	98	82
16.74	17.53	55.53	58.85	40.58	45.86	115	102
55.70	70.89	178.26	226.57	81.82	94.56	142	168
315.93	**333.47**	**885.68**	**986.04**	**703.55**	**822.49**	**686**	**730**
265.11	297.41	746.02	868.05	642.35	752.06	539	563

21-2　续表 5 continued

开发区名称	Name of Development Zone	其中:规模以上工业企业(万人) Among which, Industrial Enterprises above Designated Size (10 000 persons)	
		2015	2016
湖北黄州火车站经济开发区	Hubei Huangzhou Railway Station Economic Development Zone	0.06	0.16
黄州工业园	Huangzhou Industrial Park	0.23	0.25
湖北龙感湖工业园区	Hubei Longganhu Industrial Park	0.65	0.80
湖北团风经济开发区	Hubei Tuanfeng Economic Development Zone	0.62	0.64
湖北红安经济开发区	Hubei Hong'an Economic Development Zone	1.20	1.50
湖北罗田经济开发区	Hubei Luotian Economic Development Zone	0.73	0.87
湖北英山经济开发区	Hubei Yingshan Economic Development Zone	0.98	0.99
湖北浠水经济开发区	Hubei Xishui Economic Development Zone	1.11	1.23
湖北蕲春李时珍医药工业园区	Hubei Qichun Li Shizhen Pharmaceutical Industrial Park	1.21	1.23
蕲春经济开发区	Qichun Economic Development Zone	1.11	1.23
湖北黄梅经济开发区	Hubei Huangmei Economic Development Zone	2.58	2.61
湖北麻城经济开发区	Hubei Macheng Economic Development Zone	1.34	1.21
湖北武穴经济开发区	Hubei Wuxue Economic Development Zone	1.54	1.55
咸宁市	**Xianning**	**11.04**	**11.96**
湖北咸安经济开发区	Hubei Xian'an Economic Development Zone	1.50	1.61
湖北嘉鱼经济开发区	Hubei Jiayu Economic Development Zone	1.68	1.82
湖北通城经济开发区	Hubei Tongcheng Economic Development Zone	2.90	2.95
湖北崇阳工业园区	Hubei Chongyang Industrial Park	1.25	1.28
湖北通山经济开发区	Hubei Tongshan Economic Development Zone	0.79	0.81
湖北咸宁高新技术产业开发区	Xianning high-tech Industrial Development Znoe	8.50	9.31
湖北赤壁经济开发区	Hubei Chibi Economic Development Zone	0.62	1.01
湖北赤壁蒲纺工业园区	Hubei Chibi Puqi Textile Industrial Park	0.50	0.56
随州市	**Suizhou**	**5.17**	**5.33**
湖北随州高新技术产业开发区	Suizhou high-tech Industrial Development Znoe	5.17	5.33
湖北曾都经济开发区	Hubei Zengdu Economic Development Zone	2.05	2.11
湖北随县经济开发区	Hubei Sui County Economic Development Zone	0.43	0.36
湖北广水经济开发区	Hubei Guangshui Economic Development Zone	0.93	0.99
恩施自治州	**Enshi Autonomous Prefecture**	**6.31**	**6.42**
湖北恩施经济开发区	Hubei Enshi Economic Development Zone	1.02	1.05
湖北恩施州经济开发区	Hubei Enshi Prefecture Economic Development Zone	0.05	0.08
湖北利川经济开发区	Hubei Lichuan Economic Development Zone	0.40	0.42
湖北建始工业园区	Hubei Jianshi Industrial Park	0.56	0.62
湖北巴东经济开发区	Hubei Badong Economic Development Zone	0.33	0.45
湖北宣恩工业园区	Hubei Xuan'en Industrial Park	0.92	1.02
湖北咸丰工业园区	Hubei Xianfeng Industrial Park	0.96	0.98
湖北来凤经济开发区	Hubei Laifeng Economic Development Zone	1.45	1.45
湖北鹤峰经济开发区	Hubei Hefeng Economic Development Zone	0.62	0.35
仙桃市	**Xiantao**	**5.89**	**6.09**
仙桃高新技术产业园区	Xiantao high-tech Industrial Development Znoe	5.89	6.09
仙桃彭场工业园	Xiantao Pengchang Industrial Park	2.97	3.03
潜江市	**Qianjiang**	**2.57**	**2.74**
湖北潜江经济开发区	Hubei Qianjiang Economic Development Zone	0.55	0.67
潜江张金经济开发区	Qianjiang Zhangjin Economic Development Zone	1.10	1.12
潜江园林经济开发区	Qianjiang Yuanlin Economic Development Zone	0.92	0.95
天门市	**Tianmen**	**6.55**	**6.61**
湖北天门经济开发区	Hubei Tianmen Economic Development Zone	6.55	6.61
神农架盘水生态产业园区		0.05	0.05

规模以上工业增加值(亿元) Above-scale Industrial Added Value(100 million Yuan)		规模以上工业主营业务收入(亿元) Scale Industrial Core Business Revenue (100 million Yuan)		固定资产投资总额(亿元) Total Investment In Fixed Assets(100 million Yuan)		施工项目个数(个) Number of Construction Project (unit)	
2015	2016	2015	2016	2015	2016	2015	2016
6.26	3.54	20.99	14.34	8	12.61	7	16
3.31	3.04	9.76	9.16	2	2.2	3	7
11.50	12.70	38.50	42.50	26.14	24.85	39	35
15.03	13.97	48.25	46.03	13.76	9.64	14	13
30.33	33.45	46.02	51.50	101.4	113.7	100	110
15.50	18.35	45.86	56.48	13.1	18.3	42	51
11.72	5.01	17.65	19.01	25.71	27.28	79	81
21.44	23.71	75.90	83.90	80.2	118.1	79	82
32.89	38.48	101.50	121.95	69.24	85.21	55	57
20.98	24.15	69.80	83.96	58.23	69.46	56	58
25.16	27.25	80.38	88.50	95.6	103.9	96	98
38.41	39.09	95.42	114.24	94.06	96.42	23	24
64.67	70.06	174.25	185.56	70.07	84.85	53	50
351.75	**384.88**	**947.24**	**1021.43**	**568.37**	**560.64**	**378**	**400**
46.17	53.12	138.98	158.72	74.02	90.06	68	74
81.01	89.18	233.84	240.66	103.65	115.49	92	58
38.10	39.10	86.70	89.70	19.5	21.3	12	15
15.60	18.10	62.00	57.00	38.6	16	45	34
17.21	19.33	58.03	64.44	18.86	25.97	32	28
309.63	336.15	794.07	864.80	504.9	513.08	291	330
114.85	119.35	229.15	234.47	181.73	183.34	61	75
9.31	11.30	33.14	35.19	6.01	5.59	10	8
181.63	**185.21**	**495.94**	**546.98**	**254.07**	**294.29**	**324**	**339**
181.63	193.31	524.79	574.78	254.07	296.64	324	339
95.34	87.40	225.23	228.93	134.53	158	186	192
27.27	31.63	67.48	75.76	41.95	40.56	21	19
26.16	33.18	74.26	101.77	21.39	31.22	26	25
108.66	**117.11**	**277.53**	**292.75**	**232.43**	**260.16**	**461**	**465**
40.60	43.80	78.50	85.00	106.1	118.83	110	115
0.97	1.03	3.80	3.90	10.55	13.02	25	27
10.77	12.30	26.45	27.77	12	12.45	21	23
10.55	11.90	26.79	30.29	21.84	25.07	44	45
6.92	5.96	22.87	18.86	37.13	39.95	103	97
5.54	7.08	15.49	18.72	10.54	13	42	45
15.48	16.68	51.81	59.86	13.28	14.25	56	54
10.67	11.15	29.17	30.35	17.46	20.9	45	47
7.16	7.21	22.65	18.00	3.53	2.69	15	12
199.86	**218.84**	**725.45**	**802.97**	**258.77**	**273.24**	**143**	**112**
199.86	218.84	725.45	802.97	258.77	273.24	143	112
32.86	35.56	124.21	126.54	29.75	31.52	32	28
104.39	**130.72**	**346.92**	**547.54**	**190.8**	**150.4**	**189**	**182**
42.66	63.87	149.91	338.40	83.8	72.6	63	96
44.00	45.00	138.17	138.38	22	16	21	13
17.73	21.85	58.84	70.76	85	61.8	105	73
128.17	**138.45**	**434.87**	**462.51**	**185.85**	**222.17**	**146**	**158**
128.17	138.45	434.87	462.51	185.85	222.17	146	158
0.3	0.4	0.8	0.9	3.40	4.20	28	28

21-2 续表 6 continued

开发区名称	Name of Development Zone	其中:亿元以上项目(个) Number of Projects above 100 million yuan (unit)	
		2015	2016
湖北省	**Hubei Province**	**4519**	**4742**
武汉市	**Wuhan**	**535**	**608**
武汉江岸经济开发区	Wuhan Jiang'an Economic Development Zone	2	1
武汉江汉经济开发区	Wuhan Jianghan Economic Development Zone	1	1
武汉硚口经济开发区	Wuhan Qiaokou Economic Development Zone	5	6
武汉汉阳经济开发区	Wuhan Hanyang Economic Development Zone	22	22
武汉武昌经济开发区	Wuhan Wuchang Economic Development Zone	1	1
武汉青山经济开发区	Wuhan Qingshan Economic Development Zone	7	2
武汉洪山经济开发区	Wuhan Hongshan Economic Development Zone	1	2
武汉临空港经济技术开发区	Wuhan Linkonggang Economic and Technology Development Zone	154	160
武汉汉南经济开发区	Wuhan Hannan Economic Development Zone	21	9
武汉蔡甸经济开发区	Wuhan Caidian Economic Development Zone	44	35
武汉江夏经济开发区	Wuhan Jiangxia Economic Development Zone	110	89
武汉盘龙城经济开发区	Wuhan Panlongcheng Economic Development Zone	1	1
武汉阳逻经济开发区	Wuhan Yangluo Economic Development Zone	44	43
武汉经济技术开发区	Wuhan Economic and Technology Development Zone	48	
武汉东湖新技术产业开发区	Wuhan East Lake New Technology Industrial Development Zone	122	236
黄石市	**Huangshi**	**276**	**259**
湖北黄石港工业园区	Hubei Huangshi Port Industrial Park	5	4
湖北黄石新港工业园区	Hubei Huangshi New Port Industrial Park	7	6
湖北西塞山工业园区	Hubei Xisaishan Industrial Park	20	22
湖北下陆长乐山工业园区	Hubei Xialu Changleshan Industrial Park	8	4
黄石经济技术开发区	Huangshi Economic and Technology Development Zone	131	115
湖北阳新经济开发区	Hubei Yangxin Economic Development Zone	39	35
湖北大冶经济开发区	Hubei Daye Economic Development Zone	52	63
大冶灵成工业园	Daye Lingcheng Industrial Park	14	10
十堰市	**Shiyan**	**261**	**267**
十堰经济技术开发区	Shiyan Economic and Technology Development Zone	115	132
湖北郧阳区经济开发区	Hubei Yun County Economic Development Zone	49	50
湖北郧西工业园区	Hubei West Yun Industrial Park	4	3
湖北竹山经济开发区	Hubei Zhushan Economic Development Zone	21	22
湖北竹溪工业园区	Hubei Zhuxi Industrial Park	7	6
湖北房县工业园区	Hubei Fang County Industrial Park	38	33
湖北丹江口经济开发区	Hubei Danjiangkou Economic Development Zone	27	21
宜昌市	**Yichang**	**682**	**686**
湖北西陵经济开发区	Hubei Xiling Economic Development Zone	9	7
湖北伍家岗工业园区	Hubei Wujiagang Industrial Park	3	5
湖北点军工业园区	Hubei Dianjun Industrial Park	7	11
湖北夷陵经济开发区	Hubei Yiling Economic Development Zone	165	168
湖北远安工业园区	Hubei Yuan'an Industrial Park	60	55
湖北兴山经济开发区	Hubei Xingshan Economic Development Zone	3	4
湖北秭归经济开发区	Hubei Zigui Economic Development Zone	14	18
湖北长阳经济开发区	Hubei Changyang Economic Development Zone	22	29
湖北五峰工业园区	Hubei Wufeng Industrial Park	9	8
湖北五峰民族工业园	Hubei Wufeng National Industrial Park	2	2
宜昌高新技术产开发区	Yichang High-tech Industrial Development Zone	271	206
湖北宜都工业园区	Hubei Yidu Industrial Park	185	197
湖北当阳经济开发区	Hubei Dangyang Economic Development Zone	130	86
湖北枝江经济开发区	Hubei Zhijiang Economic Development Zone	71	96
枝江安福寺工业园	Zhijiang Anfu Temple Industrial Park	16	16

新开工项目(个) Number of Newly Opened Projects (unit)		开发区税收总额(万元) Total Tax Revenue of Development (10 000 yuan)		外商投资金额(万美元) Total Value of Foreign Investment (10 000 US dollors)		出口总额(万美元) Total Value of Export (10 000 US dollors)	
2015	2016	2015	2016	2015	2016	2015	2016
5880	**6037**	**16287594**	**16572459**	**519597**	**551589**	**2083491**	**2031250**
472	**532**	**8416562**	**8028184**	**269396**	**306841**	**1086261**	**1076671**
	1	30124	13745			1245	
6	6	139900	159400			7490	8567
	1	112716				16172	14927
12	10	330513	365217			512	14016
		43225	37215			1750	728
5	5	981034	47800	1700	520	1703	1669
	2	28360	30262			260	280
120	171	1371248	1606277	36762	43020	42279	35126
23	11	35419	36661	3859	3991	9400	7331
63	22	115869	140619	16167	20826	50028	27721
28	81	431821	510100	19322	22800	24560	22358
50	62	143136	129383			3800	3431
58	32	115775	128701	15500	12214	14537	11400
75		2954799	2947310	27086	31770	160211	100117
107	128	4573618	5168188	149235	171700	752314	829000
405	**437**	**954290**	**948702**	**12693**	**18823**	**140916**	**141293**
5	4	2600	2400			350	320
3	3	16315	11625			350	380
21	20	96100	82012		325	32549	31802
10		76472	62972			14080	14886
155	178	377172	361959	15426	11710	62014	59719
23	26	34127	36147	863	890	17470	17994
135	141	338964	378437	5500	5700	13636	15592
53	65	12540	13150			467	600
330	**351**	**605041**	**658305**	**25562**	**27627**	**63336**	**58827**
116	128	478499	536777	18668	20634	47451	43551
68	69	35805	38927	3902	3981	2904	2985
8	1	4393	1846	500	500		
5	8	14112	14821			3701	4608
8	3	8000	9000	800	800	500	1500
97	126	14551	15209			5000	5320
28	16	49681	41725	1692	1712	3780	863
832	**834**	**956741**	**1066424**	**41479**	**14555**	**107612**	**126217**
10	29	28598	31308			8504	8750
						14526	15242
12	11	6904	8635	396	7500	5190	6900
108	112	112055	115342	12800	13440	1037	1158
60	56	88343	89343	500		9558	8825
4	8	41500	49200	25870		23100	35200
49	38	50597	43587			6867	7757
53	36	15681	16450			6400	7200
31	28	14885	20016			823	1220
8	16	5380	827			323	514
224	194	501044	554093	31025	30015	60042	65000
276	295	342242	406442	4800	6822	29830	34305
128	63	59503	60273	4641	4732	5845	5671
116	124	224986	237172	3846	3768	23425	22399
19	13	6861	7752	238		9644	9711

21-2 续表 7 continued

开发区名称	Name of Development Zone	其中:亿元以上项目(个) Number of Projects above 100 million yuan (unit)	
		2015	2016
襄阳市	**Xianyang**	**685**	**803**
襄阳高新技术产业开发区	Xiangyang High-tech Industrial Development Zone	245	251
襄阳鱼梁州经济开发区	Xiangyang Yuliangzhou Economic Development Zone		
襄阳经济技术开发区	Xiangyang Economic Development Zone	83	73
湖北襄城经济开发区	Hubei Xiangcheng Economic Development Zone	9	4
湖北樊城经济开发区	Hubei Fancheng Economic Development Zone	50	20
湖北襄州经济开发区	Hubei Xiangzhou Economic Development Zone	83	85
襄阳工业园	Xiangyang Industrial Park	11	13
湖北南漳经济开发区	Hubei Nanzhang Economic Development Zone	34	47
湖北谷城经济开发区	Hubei Gucheng Economic Development Zone	89	88
谷城石花经济开发区	Gucheng Shihua Economic Development Zone	12	12
湖北保康经济开发区	Hubei Baokang Economic Development Zone	20	25
湖北老河口经济开发区	Hubei Laohekou Economic Development Zone	73	74
湖北枣阳经济开发区	Hubei Zaoyang Economic Development Zone	82	115
枣阳吴店工业园	Zaoyang Wudian Industrial Park	30	34
湖北宜城经济开发区	Hubei Yicheng Economic Development Zone	37	35
鄂州市	**E'zhou**	**170**	**195**
湖北鄂州花湖经济开发区	Hubei E'Zhou Huahu Economic Development Zone	18	13
鄂州葛店经济技术开发区	E'Zhou Gedian Economic and Technology Development Zone	135	168
湖北鄂州经济开发区	Hubei E'Zhou Economic Development Zone	17	14
荆门市	**Jingmen**	**507**	**519**
湖北东宝工业园区	Hubei Dongbao Industrial Park	79	89
荆门高新技术产业开发区	Hubei Jingmen High-tech Industrial Development Zone	116	124
湖北荆门化工循环产业园	Hubei Jingmen Chemical Recycling Development Zone	37	40
湖北京山经济开发区	Hubei Jingshan Economic Development Zone	87	95
湖北屈家岭经济开发区	Hubei Qujialing Economic Development Zone	13	6
湖北沙洋经济开发区	Hubei Shayang Economic Development Zone	52	66
湖北钟祥经济开发区	Hubei Zhongxiang Economic Development Zone	80	82
钟祥胡集经济开发区	Zhongxiang Huji Economic Development Zone	15	17
孝感市	**Xiaogan**	**274**	**267**
孝感高新技术产业开发区	Xiaogan high-tech Industrial Development Zone	136	150
湖北孝南经济开发区	Hubei Xiaonan Economic Development Zone	72	79
湖北孝昌经济开发区	Hubei Xiaochang Economic Development Zone	10	10
湖北大悟经济开发区	Hubei Dawu Economic Development Zone	16	18
湖北云梦经济开发区	Hubei Yunmeng Economic Development Zone	62	58
湖北应城经济开发区	Hubei Yingcheng Economic Development Zone	31	38
湖北安陆经济开发区	Hubei Anlu Economic Development Zone	66	41
湖北汉川经济开发区	Hubei Hanchuan Economic Development Zone	46	48
荆州市	**Jingzhou**	**315**	**291**
湖北沙市经济开发区	Hubei Shashi Economic Development Zone	35	33
湖北荆州城南经济开发区	Jingzhou Chengnan Economic Development Zone	27	14
荆州经济技术开发区	Jingzhou Economic and Technology Development Zone	36	109
湖北公安经济开发区	Hubei Gong'an Economic Development Zone	24	25
湖北监利经济开发区	Hubei Jianli Economic Development Zone	26	22
湖北江陵经济开发区	Hubei Jiangling Economic Development Zone	46	30
湖北石首经济开发区	Hubei Shishou Economic Development Zone	35	31
湖北洪湖经济开发区	Hubei Honghu Economic Development Zone	38	35
洪湖府场经济开发区	Honghu Fuchang Economic Development Zone	14	11
湖北松滋经济开发区	Hubei Songzi Economic Development Zone	34	40
黄冈市	**Huanggang**	**278**	**276**
湖北黄冈经济开发区	Hubei Huanggang Economic Development Zone	234	219

新开工项目(个) Number of Newly Opened Projects (unit)		开发区税收总额(万元) Total Tax Revenue of Development (10 000 yuan)		外商投资金额(万美元) Total Value of Foreign Investment (10 000 US dollors)		出口总额(万美元) Total Value of Export (10 000 US dollors)	
2015	2016	2015	2016	2015	2016	2015	2016
617	**674**	**1627184**	**1719584**	**53657**	**60030**	**161840**	**124957**
192	216	784431	817137	30120	35000	81820	73107
2	1	1500	2710				
41	36	437517	456016	7416	7532	19623	19686
2	2	79541	87495	1895	2089	1215	1315
55	38	89732	96013	1615	1710	4071	4320
41	43	223131	230104	8767	8812	15620	16993
4	5	11000	6591	29000	32704	3109	3981
35	43	17363	28348			2433	11520
95	92	72495	81217	1614	1762	8801	9385
35	47	50576	56412	125	127	4915	4388
10	15	8905	10558	2030	2645	5597	6709
75	102	68900	78202	6432	7378	31256	18550
75	86	92683	115854	5103	6736	27100	36585
36	41	35120	40388			1436	1651
33	32	62323	68555	2000		18339	18400
227	**283**	**274256**	**305102**	**7500**	**10150**	**11882**	**13982**
20	20	25003	26520		1500	2470	2248
174	211	221524	246929	7500	8650	8512	9114
33	52	27729	31653			900	2620
848	**850**	**452057**	**628527**	**32396**	**37630**	**88149**	**86187**
190	205	49920	51072			1881	2011
294	275	453244	541623	15735	16920	56293	63808
26	29	187380	232147	5000	12400	4142	8123
128	131	77160	84140	8949	9835	15428	17874
7	10	1124	1488	400	498	1530	700
48	60	29028	31025	3890	4838	13500	13756
120	122	56819	60474	8635	9489	10815	12567
17	18	26665	26558			13889	10086
298	**361**	**824614**	**913503**	**27752**	**35858**	**89251**	**87828**
135	141	550565	609204	19521	26778	44825	35874
185	190	196261	225927	3500	3800	8400	8700
8	58	45200	55600			5579	5842
8	10	29500	31400			2128	2460
113	155	106300	121665	5458	5775	15500	21000
25	676	91004	76550	10012	13210	1009	6012
62	65	29023	31020	1100	1100	3260	3352
85	87	170326	186279	7131	7980	33459	40300
663	**545**	**542181**	**529833**	**10927**	**11656**	**77609**	**66171**
44	36	31516	35292			17228	19016
		52000	49800			13550	9855
352	295	222581	269608			25000	37501
19	23	20802	21668			695	2204
32	25	16700	14900	29560	27500	5950	5730
14	5	6576	6996			815	979
11	10	47835	25661			10183	3774
52	45	22132	22615	1367	1456	3088	3125
54	46	19465	21643				
85	97	102574	100120			1100	
378	**409**	**413359**	**452172**	**19795**	**12701**	**44481**	**44706**
271	292	319225	408402	20933	12701	46762	38265

21-2 续表 8 continued

开发区名称	Name of Development Zone	其中:亿元以上项目(个) Number of Projects above 100 million yuan (unit)	
		2015	2016
湖北黄州火车站经济开发区	Hubei Huangzhou Railway Station Economic Development Zone	7	13
黄州工业园	Huangzhou Industrial Park	1	2
湖北龙感湖工业园区	Hubei Longganhu Industrial Park	24	20
湖北团风经济开发区	Hubei Tuanfeng Economic Development Zone	9	6
湖北红安经济开发区	Hubei Hong'an Economic Development Zone	38	43
湖北罗田经济开发区	Hubei Luotian Economic Development Zone	18	25
湖北英山经济开发区	Hubei Yingshan Economic Development Zone	12	12
湖北浠水经济开发区	Hubei Xishui Economic Development Zone	47	29
湖北蕲春李时珍医药工业园区	Hubei Qichun Li Shizhen Pharmaceutical Industrial Park	16	18
蕲春经济开发区	Qichun Economic Development Zone	18	20
湖北黄梅经济开发区	Hubei Huangmei Economic Development Zone	32	35
湖北麻城经济开发区	Hubei Macheng Economic Development Zone	15	13
湖北武穴经济开发区	Hubei Wuxue Economic Development Zone	33	31
咸宁市	**Xianning**	**164**	**184**
湖北咸安经济开发区	Hubei Xian'an Economic Development Zone	19	20
湖北嘉鱼经济开发区	Hubei Jiayu Economic Development Zone	31	49
湖北通城经济开发区	Hubei Tongcheng Economic Development Zone	5	6
湖北崇阳工业园区	Hubei Chongyang Industrial Park	33	11
湖北通山经济开发区	Hubei Tongshan Economic Development Zone	5	4
湖北咸宁经济开发区	Hubei Xianning Economic Development Zone	124	167
湖北赤壁经济开发区	Hubei Chibi Economic Development Zone	30	31
湖北赤壁蒲纺工业园区	Hubei Chibi Puqi Textile Industrial Park	2	2
随州市	**Suizhou**	**74**	**83**
湖北随州经济开发区	Hubei Suizhou Economic Development Zone	74	83
湖北曾都经济开发区	Hubei Zengdu Economic Development Zone	34	35
湖北随县经济开发区	Hubei Sui County Economic Development Zone	11	14
湖北广水经济开发区	Hubei Guangshui Economic Development Zone	4	4
恩施自治州	**Enshi Autonomous Prefecture**	**90**	**103**
湖北恩施经济开发区	Hubei Enshi Economic Development Zone	23	26
湖北恩施州经济开发区	Hubei Enshi Prefecture Economic Development Zone	12	14
湖北利川经济开发区	Hubei Lichuan Economic Development Zone	13	13
湖北建始工业园区	Hubei Jianshi Industrial Park	5	5
湖北巴东经济开发区	Hubei Badong Economic Development Zone	13	24
湖北宣恩工业园区	Hubei Xuan'en Industrial Park	9	8
湖北咸丰工业园区	Hubei Xianfeng Industrial Park	6	7
湖北来凤经济开发区	Hubei Laifeng Economic Development Zone	9	6
湖北鹤峰经济开发区	Hubei Hefeng Economic Development Zone		
仙桃市	**Xiantao**	**100**	**96**
仙桃高新技术产业园区	Hubei Xiantao Economic Development Zone	100	96
仙桃彭场工业园	Xiantao Pengchang Industrial Park	5	6
潜江市	**Qianjiang**	**63**	**56**
湖北潜江经济开发区	Hubei Qianjiang Economic Development Zone	19	25
潜江张金经济开发区	Qianjiang Zhangjin Economic Development Zone	13	5
潜江园林经济开发区	Qianjiang Yuanlin Economic Development Zone	31	26
天门市	**Tianmen**	**43**	**46**
湖北天门经济开发区	Hubei Tianmen Economic Development Zone	43	46
神农架盘水生态产业园区		2	3

新开工项目(个) Number of Newly Opened Projects (unit)		开发区税收总额(万元) Total Tax Revenue of Development (10 000 yuan)		外商投资金额(万美元) Total Value of Foreign Investment (10 000 US dollors)		出口总额(万美元) Total Value of Export (10 000 US dollors)	
2015	2016	2015	2016	2015	2016	2015	2016
7	6	3410	3868			480	310
		6213	6342				
20	8	8572	9293			200	351
6	2	12850	12650			950	800
30	36	72300	85100	3000	3320	283	305
37	46	10491	14321			5018	5771
55	63	21801	20155			295	319
20	40	19860	21520	780	320	7620	8276
37	40	29580	32942	8665		6983	7015
35	37	25061	27168	500		3715	3783
75	81	29800	32100			4500	
13	15	63749	66298			1198	1241
28	17	56858	62441	20	1545	8927	11761
241	**245**	**404802**	**412749**	**2188**	**2995**	**35518**	**27984**
50	53	31386	34995			4654	5022
52	49	19700	27164	550	452	8500	5031
6	7	27869	28798			5324	5789
34	23	1	1			2360	3102
16	12	16100	17500			575	610
186	208	387695	394248	2188	2995	32583	24272
50	52	78355	85431	1095	1098	5024	5037
5	2	1006	1000				
135	**143**	**120531**	**160929**	**5847**	**9776**	**66470**	**72279**
135	143	120531	160929	5847	9776	66470	72279
61	55	34769	38567			18162	20624
12	9	7245	8714			12668	10242
8	10	11800	14200	2910	3200	4400	4900
183	**154**	**288640**	**290027**	**396**	**533**	**19564**	**18338**
21	19	163150	165000			3410	4435
11	12	6300	7000				159
7	10	64176	65708			496	983
31	29	7263	7850			2786	3138
35	13	13734	9460	1		7710	4336
16	14	4325	4541	155	273	1019	506
35	28	13620	14510	240	260	3197	3284
22	25	12422	13068			488	502
5	4	3650	2890			458	995
43	**51**	**203358**	**221037**	**4384**	**1300**	**55508**	**53063**
43	51	203358	221037	4384	1300	55508	53063
7	8	17536	20435			22653	23567
151	**110**	**139906**	**161143**	**4610**		**27457**	**24545**
61	84	30159	33143	1000		5094	7095
14	12	9000	9100	3610		8155	7950
76	14	100747	118900			14208	9500
52	**53**	**61273**	**73240**	**1015**	**1114**	**7637**	**8204**
52	53	61273	73240	1015	1114	7637	8204
5	5	2800	3000				

主要统计指标解释

规划面积:指国土部门核定的开发区规划面积。

实际开发面积:指开发区实际开发并已完成基础设施建设的面积。

企业个数:指报告期末已在工商行政管理机关登记注册、并在开发区管理机构进行统计登记的法人单位数,包括内资企业、港澳台投资企业和外商投资企业。不含个体企业。

工业企业:包括采矿业、制造业、电力、燃气及水的生产和供应业。

规模以上工业企业:是指企业所在地在开发区内的全部年主营收入2000万元及以上的法人工业企业。即无论企业是否在开发区注册,也无论企业隶属何行政级别或部门,只要所在地在开发区的所有规模以上企业都在本制度规定的统计范围以内。反之,所在地不在开发区,尽管其在开发区注册的规模以上企业也不在本制度规定的统计范围之内。

高新技术企业:指生产高新技术产品经省科学技术厅授牌的企业。

外商投资企业:指企业注册登记类型中的中外合资、合作经营企业、外资企业和外商投资股份有限公司之和。(含港、澳、台商投资企业:指企业注册登记类型中的港、澳、台资合资、合作、独资经营企业和股份有限公司之和。)

第三产业:除第一、第二产业以外的其他各业。由于第三产业包括的行业多、范围广,根据我国的实际情况,第三产业可分为两大部分;一是流通部门,二是服务部门。具体又可分为四个层次:

第一层次:流通部门,包括交通运输、仓储及邮电通信业,批发和零售贸易、餐饮业。

第二层次:为生产和生活服务的部门,包括金融、保险业,地质勘查业、水利管理业,房地产业,社会服务业,农、林、牧、渔服务业,交通运输辅助业,综合技术服务业等。

第三层次:为提高科学文化水平和居民素质服务的部门,包括教育、文化艺术及广播电影电视业,卫生、体育和社会福利业,科学研究业等。

第四层次:为社会公共需要服务的部门,包括国家机关、政党机关和社会团体以及军队、警察等。

从业人员:指报告期末在开发区企业、行政和事业单位中工作,取得工资或其他形式的劳动报酬的全部人员数。包括在岗职工,再就业的离退休人员、民办教师及在企业工作的外方人员和港澳台方人员、兼职人员、借用的外单位人员和第二职业者。不包括离开本单位但仍保留劳动关系的职工。

开发区生产总值:即按市场价格计算的国内生产总值的简称。指开发区内所有常住单位在一定时期内生产活动的最终成果。国内生产总值有三种表现形态,即价值形态、收入形态和产品形态。

从价值形态看,它是所有常住单位在一定时期内生产的全部货物和服务价值超过同期投入的全部非固定资产货物和服务价值的差额,即所有常住单位的增加值之和;从收入形态看,它是所有常住单位在一定时期内创造并分配给常住单位和非常住单位的初次分配收入之和;从产品形态看它是最终使用的货物和服务减去进口货物和服务。在实际核算中,国内生产总值的三种表现形态表现为三种计算方法,即生产法、收入法和支出法。三种方法分别从不同的方面反映国内生产总值及其构成。

(1) 生产法是从生产的角度衡量常住单位在一定时期新创造价值的方法。即从生产的全部货物和服务总产品价值中,扣除生产过程中投入的中间货物和服务价值得到增加价值。国民经济各产业部门生产法增加值计算公式如下:

增加值 = 总产出 - 中间投入 将国民经济各产业部门生产法增加值相加,得到生产法GDP。

总产出:指常住单位在一定时期内生产的所有货物和服务的价值,既包括新增价值,也包括转移价值。它反映常住单位生产活动的总规模。总产出按生产者价格计算。

中间投入:指常住单位在一定时期内生产过程中消耗和使用的非固定资产货物和服务的价值。中间投入也称为中间消耗,反映用于生产过程中的转移价值,一般按购买者价格计算。计入中间投入的货物和服务必须具备两个条件,一是与总产出的计算范围保持一致;二是本期一次性使用的。

(2)收入法也称为分配法。按收入法计算国内生产总值是从生产过程创造收入的角度,对常住单位的生产活动成果进行核算。按照这种计算方法,增加值由劳动者报酬、生产税净额、固定资产折旧和营业盈余四个部分组成。计算公式为:增加值=劳动者报酬+生产税净额+固定资产折旧+营业盈余。国民经济各部门的增加值之和等于国内生产总值。

(3)支出法是从最终使用的角度反映国内生产总值最终使用去向的一种方法。最终使用包括货物和服务的最终消费支出、资本形成总额、货物和服务净出口三部分,计算公式为:国内生产总值=最终消费支出+资本形成总额+货物和服务净出口。

按三种方法计算的国内生产总值反映的是同一经济总体在同一时期的生产活动成果,因此,从理论上讲,三种计算方法所得到的结果应该是一致的。但是,在实践中,由于受资料来源的口径范围的限制和计算方法的影响,要保证这三种计算方法所得的结果完全相等几乎是不可能的。

工业总产值(现价):是以货币形式表现的,工业企业在一定时期内生产的工业最终产品或提供工业性劳务活动的总价值量。

工业总产值包括本期生产成品价值、对外加工费收入,在制品半成品期末期初差额价值三部分。

①本期生产成品价值:是指企业本期生产,并在报告期内不再进行加工,经检验、包装入库的全部工业成品(半成品)价值合计,包括企业生产的自制设备及提供给本企业在建工程、其他非工业部门和生活福利部门等单位使用的成品价值,本期生产成品价值按自备原材料生产的产品的数量乘以本期不含增值税(销项税额)的产品实际销售平均单价计算;会计核算中按成本价格转帐的自制设备和自产自用的成品,按成本价格计算生产成品价值。生产成品价值中不包括用定货者来料加工的成品(半成品)价值。

②对外加工费收入:是指企业在报告期内完成的对外承接的工业品加工(包括用定货者来料加工产品)的加工费收入和对外工业修理作业所取得的加工费收入。对外加工费收入按不含增值税(销项税额)的价格计算,可根据会计“产品销售收入”科目的有关资料取得。

对于本企业对内非工业部门提供的加工修理、设备安装的劳务收入,如果企业会计核算基础比较好,能取得这部分资料,而且这部分价值所占比重较大,应包括在对外加工费收入中。

③自制半成品在制品期末期初差额价值:是指企业报告期自制半成品、在制品期末减期初的差额价值,本指标一般可从会计核算资料中取得。如果会计产品成本核算中不计算半成品、在制品的成本,则总产值中也不包括这部分价值,反之则包括。

工业增加值:指工业企业在报告期内以货币形式表现的工业生产活动的最终成果,是企业全部生产活动的总成果扣除了在生产过程中消耗或转移的物质产品和劳务价值后的余额,是企业生产过程中新增加的价值。

计算工业增加值通常采用两种方法。一是“生产法”,二是“收入法”,目前工业统计主要采用“生产法”计算工业增加值。

“生产法”,即从工业生产过程中产品和劳务价值形成的角度入手,剔除生产环节中间投入的价值,从而得到新增价值的方法。公式为:

工业增加值=工业总产值—工业中间投入+本期应交增值税

上述公式中,本期应交增值税的企业为负数时,综合部门汇总时按零处理。

“收入法”,即从工业生产过程中创造的原始收入初次分配的角度,对工业生产活动最终成果进行核算的一种方法,其计算公式为:

工业增加值=固定资产折旧+劳动者报酬+生产税净额+营业盈余

工业中间投入:1. 定义:指企业在报告期内用于工业生产活动所一次性消耗的外购原材料、燃料、动力及其他实物产品和对外支付的服务费用。

2. 计算原则:计算工业中间投入须遵循以下三条原则:(1)必须是从企业外部购入的产品和服务的价值,不包括生产过程中回收的废料以及自制品的价值。(2)必须是本期投入生产,并一次性消耗的产品和服务的价值,不包括固定资产转移价值:(3)中间投入的计算口径必须与总产值的计算口径相一致:即计入工业中间投入的产品和服务价值必须已经计入了工业总产值中。

3. 分类:工业中间投入按企业支付对象可以分为中间物质投入和中间劳务投入。中间物质投入是指生产过程中所消耗的外购原材料、燃料、动力以及其它实物产品和支付给物质生产部门(工业、农业、批发零售贸易业、建筑业、货物运输及邮电业)的服务费用,中间劳务投入指支付给非物质生产部门(如金融、保险、文化教育、科学研究、医疗卫生、行政管理)的服务费用。

工业中间投入按照具体内容分为直接材料、制造费用中的中间投入、管理费用中的中间投入、销售费用中的中间投入和利息支出五大项。

日常统计中计算中间投入是按第二种分类计算的。

4. 计算方法:计算工业中间投入的具体方法可以分为二种。一是正算法,即将制造费用、管理费用、销售费用中属于中间投入的部分分别相加,再加上直接材料和利息支出,得出工业中间投入合计。二是倒算法,即分别用制造费用、管理费用、销售费用合计减去其中属于增加值的项目(大体包括工资、福利费、折旧、劳动保险费、职工待业保险费等),倒算出三项费用中的中间投入,再加上直接材料和利息支出,得出工业中间投入合计。在实算操作过程中,采用倒算法计算比较简便易行。

5. 资料来源:计算中间投入的资料来源,可分别根据企业“产品成本表”、“管理费用”、“财务费用”、“销售费用”明细表归纳整理填报。

高新技术增加值:增加值是指报告期内企业在生产活动中新创造的价值。

高新技术增加值指报告期省科技厅认定的高新技术企业的增加值和非高新技术企业中的高新技术产品的增加值两部分。高新技术产品指高新技术领域的产品。即满足下列条件之一的产品:①首次应用新科学原理生产的最新产品;②首次应用最新工艺生产并使产品质量、成本和劳动效率有显著改进的产品;③技术水平达到90年代国际先进水平的产品。

有两种计算方法:一是“生产法”;二是“收入法”,亦称要素分配法。计算方法为:

(1)按生产法计算的工业增加值=工业总产值—工业中间投入+本期应交增值税;(2)按分配法计算的工业增加值=固定资产折旧+劳动者报酬+生产税净额+营业盈余。

主营业务收入:指企业经常性的、主要业务所产生的收入。不同行业的企业主营业务收入包括的内容不同。工业企业的主营业务收入主要包括销售产品、自制半成品、提供工业性劳务等收入;商品流通企业的主营业务收入主要包括销售商品取得的收入。主营业务收入一般占企业收入的比重较大,对企业的经济效益产生较大的影响。在会计核算中单独设置“主营业务收入”科目核算经常性的、主要业务所产生的收入。

固定资产投资总额:指开发区各单位报告期内500万元以上(含500万元)项目完成的投资额(包括实际完成的建筑安装工程价值,设备、工具、器具的购置费,以及实际发生的其他费用),是以货币表示的建造和购置固定资产活动的工作量以及与此有关的费用总称。

基础设施建设投资:指报告期内开发区基础公用设施:包括供水排水、供气、供热、供电、环卫设施、排污系统、固体废弃物收集和处理系统、电信及道路、桥梁、平整土地等施工建设投资。

施工项目个数:指报告期内曾进行建筑或安装工程施工活动的建设项目个数,包括报告期内新开工项目、报告期以前开工跨入报告期继续施工的项目以及报告期施过工并在报告期内全部建成投产或停缓建的项目个数。

税收总额:指开发区全口径税收收入。包含国税收入、地税收入。主要有增值税、营业税、所得税、城市维护建设税、城镇土地使用税、房产税、印花税、资源税、土地增值税等。

招商引资总额:指报告期内除本行政区划以外的国内外投资者在开发区的投资金额之和。

外商投资金额:指外国企业和经济组织或个人(包括华侨、港澳台胞以及我国在境外注册的企业)按我国有关政策、法规,用现汇、实物、技术等在我国境内开办外商独资企业、与我国境内的企业或经济组织共同举办中外合资经营企业、合作经营企业或合作开发资源的投资(包括外商投资收益的再投资),以及经政府有关部门批准的项目投资总额内企业从境外借入的资金。

省外境内投资额:指报告期内除湖北省以外的国内投资者(不包括港、澳、台)在开发区的投资金额。

出口总额:指实际出口的货物总金额。我国规定出口货物按离岸价格统计。

高新产品出口交货值:指企业生产的交给外贸部门或自营(委托)出口(包括销往香港、澳门、台湾),用外汇价格结算的批量销售,在国内或在边境批量出口等的高新产品价值,还包括外商来样、来料加工、来件装配和补偿贸易等生产的产品价值。

Explanatory Notes on Main Statistical Indicators

Land Area Approved for Development Zone refers to the land area of development zone ratified for program by the state department of territory.

Floor Area of Development Zone refers to the land area of development zone that is practically exploited and occupied.

The Number of Enterprise refers to the number of impersonal entity that has registered at industrial organs and commerce administration at the end of report period and that has been counted and registered. Included in this catogary are domestic—funded enterprises, enterprises with funds from Hong kong,Macao,Taiwan and foreign—funded enterprises. Private enterprises are excluded.

Enterprises of High and New Technology refer to enterprises verified by provincial office of science and technology that produce hi-tech products.

Industrial Enterprises include mining,manufacturing, and manufacturing and supply of power, gas and water.

Industrial enterprises above designated size refer to entity industrial enterprises whose main annual turnover exceeds 5 million in the circle of development zone where enterpriese are located. That is to say,no matter enterprises has registered or not, what department enterprises belong to, all the enterprises whose location are in the development zone are counted which are above designated size. Otherwise, enterprises above designated size whose location is not in the development zone are not counted although they have registered at development zone.

Employees refer to all the workers working in enterprises in development zone,administrative unit and public institution who have got their income or payment of labour in other forms at the end of report period. Included in this category are workers on guard, re—employed laid—off workers and retirees, citizen-managed teachers; foreign workers in enterprises,workers of Hong Kong, Macao and Taiwan, part—time workers, borrowed workers from external enterprises and second—job workers. Workers having left enterprises who reserve labour relations are excluded.

Total turnover of technology, industry and trade refers to the total sum of product sales proceeds, technological gain and goods sales proceeds that are related to our products,other business gain,external—business gain in one year,and the like.

Technological turnover refers to the gain of technology transferrance, technology contract, technology advisory and service, technology share,products of pilotscale experiment and the gain of external-entrusted scientific research.

Technology contract turnover refers to the gain from contract of technology program design,design and contract of technology project.

Technology advisory and service turnover refers to the income from technical intellegence, technilcal information,technical advisory and test analysis provided availing enterprises themselves of human resources,physical resources and data system, and other kinds of technical service.

Revenue of entrusted reserch and development refers to the revenue from reserch and development of new products contracted provided to various social units.

Gross Industrial Output Value (at current price) refers to the total volum of final industrial products produced and industrial services provided in money terms during a given period .

Gross Industrial Output Value consists of 3 components: value of the finished products during the reference period, income from external processing, and value of change in semi-finished products at the end of and at the beginning of the reference period.

①value of the finished products during the reference period refers to the value of all finished(semi-finished) industrial products that are produced during the reference period without the need for further processing, checked for accepatance, packed and put into the warehouse of the enterprise, including the value of own-produced equipment and the value of products provided to the projects under construction of the enterprise, and to other non-industrial or welfare units. Value of finished products during the reference period is calculated by the quantity of products produced using own materials multiplied by the average unit prices at which products are sold(excluding value-added tax). Own-produced equipment and products for own use are value at cost prices as in the case of enterprise accounting. Value of finished products does not include the value of finished products(semi-finished products) that are produced using the materials from the clients who make the ordres.

②**Income from external processing** refers to income from contracted external processing of industrial products(including processing of industrial products using materials from the clients), and the income from industrial repairing work provided to other units. Income from external processing is calculated using information from the item "products sales income" in the enterprise accounting at the prices excluding value-added tax.For income from external services such as processing, repairing and installation of equipment provided to non-industrial units within the enterprise, if the accounting work of the enterprise is good enough to separate it from other records, and the share of such services is significant, it should also be included in the income from external processing.

③**value of change in semi-finished products at the end of and at the beginning of the reference period** refers to the value of change in semi-finished products at the end and at the beginning of the reference period, which generally can be obtained from accounting records of enterprises. If the enterprise accounting excludes the cost of semi-finished products, then it should not be inculded in the gross industrial output value,and vice versa.

Highandnew technology value High and new technology products refer to products in the area of high and new technology, namely any kind of products meeting following standars: ① the latest products using latest scientific principles the first time; ②the products that are produced by the latest technology and have noticeably improved the quality, cost and work efficiency; ③ products whose technical merit has reached advanced international standards of 1990s. High and new technology value refers to 2 components: the value of high and new technology enterprises designated by provincial Science and Technology Office in reference period, and value of high and new technology products of non-high-and-new technology enterprises.

Industrial value added refers to the final results of industrial production enterprises in money terms during the the reference period.

Industrial value added can be usually calculated by two approaches:the production approach,and the income approach.Industrial stastics mainly adopts the production approach to calculate the industrial value added at present.

The production approach is the approach that newly-increased value is gained by eliminating the value indulged in the production link in terms of value formation of products and labor in the process of industrial prodution. The formula is: Industrial value added= total industrial value-industrial intermediate input

+current value added tax receivable

In this formula,when current value added tax receivale is minus, the Integration Department will treat it as zero.

The income approach is an approach that final results of industrial production activities are checked in terms of the primary distribution of original income created in the indusrial production. Here is its formula: Industrial value added=depreciation of fixed assets+remuneration of labourers+net of produce tax+operating surplus

Industrial intermediate input:

1.Definition: It refers to the service cost for purchased raw material,gas,power and other physical products,and external-paid services consumed during the reference period for the industrial production of enterprises.

2.Calculating principles:Calculating industrial intermediate input must follow the three principles:(1)The value must be the value of goods and services that are purchased from outside,exculding the value of reclaimedwaste materials in the production and that of own products.(2) The value must be the value of goods and services that are inputted into production consumed during the reference period,excluding transfer value of fixed assets.(3)The calculating units of the intermediate input must be in correspondence with that of total value, namely the value of products and service reckoned in industrial intermediate input has been reckoned in industrial value.

3.Category: Industrial intermediate input in terms of pay objectcan be classified as intermediate material input and intermediate labor input . Intermediate material input refers to the the purchased raw material, gas,power and other physical products consumed in the production, and the cost of service paid to departments of material production(industry,agriculcuture, wholesales and retail trade,construction goods transportation and post). Intermediate labor input refers to cost of service paid todepartments of nonmaterial production(finance, insurance,cultural education,scientific research,medical health and administration)

Industrial intermediate input in terms of concrete content can be classified into 5 components , namely direct consumption of materials,industrial intermediate input in manufacturing cost, industrial intermediate input in management cost, industrial intermediate input in marketing cost and expenditure on interest.

Intermediate input in common calculating is calculated by the second category.

4.Calculating approaches:the calculating approaches to industrial intermediate input have two approaches. Positive calculating, namely add respectively the manufacuring cost, management cost,sales cost that belong to intermediate input, then add direct material and interest expense.The final result is reconed into the total.Negative calculating, namely manufacturing cost, management cost, sale cost that belong to value–added items(generally included are sallary, welfarism, depreciation,labor insurance, employee's job–waiting insurance,ect)is substracted respectively from the total.The result is the its intermediate input respectively. Then direct material and interest expense are added. The final result is reconed into the total. Negative calculating is easier to carry out in pratical calculating.

5.Information source: The information source in calculating intermediate input can be obtained from product Cost Table, tables of Management Cost, Financial Expense and Sales Cost.

Value added of high and new technology value added refers to the newly created value in the production in the reference period. There are two approaches to calculting, the production approach, and the income approach,also factor distribution approach. The calculation methods are: (1)industrial value added by the production approach=total industrial value–industrial intermediate input+ current value added tax receivable; (2) industrial value added by distribution approach=depreciation of fixed assets+ remuneration of labourers+net of produce tax+operating surplus

Value added of high and new technology refers to the value added of high and new technology enterprises designated by provincial Science and Technology Office in reference period, and value added of high and new technology products of non–high–and–new technology enterprises.

Income from major business refers to the income of regular and major bussiness of enterprises. The content of the income from major business differs from enterprise to enterprise. The income from major business of industrial enterprises mainly includes the income from product sales,own semi–finished products,industrial labor; the income from major business of commodity circulation enterprises mainly includes the incoome from commodity sales.Income from major business generally takes a big share in the income of enterprise, and has a great influence on the economic benefit.The "income from major business" item is set individually to check income from regular and major business in accounting.

Total investment in fixed assets refers to the generic term for operation capacity of building up and purchasing fixed assets in money terms during the reference period and related cost. Total investment in fixed assets in reference period is calculated by actual investment(including value of actual finish constructive installation engineering,purchasing cost of equipment,tools and devices,and other actual cost)

The number of projects under construction:refers to number of projects that has carried out construction or installation engineering in reference period, including the number of newly–opened projects during reference period,projects opened before reference period and constructed over reference period,and projects that have been constructed in reference period and completed or delayed within reference period.

Total tax revenue refers to tax revenue in all units of development zone.Included in this category are national and local tax revenue.They are mainly value added tax, turnover tax, income tax, city maintenance construction tax, use tax of town land, house tax, stamp tax, resource tax, land value increment tax, ect.

Value of foreign investment refers to the investment made by the soley foreign–owned enterprises opened according to the relevant policies and regulations and by means of convertible foreign exchange, physical goods,and technology,ect ; sino–foreign joint venture run by foreign enterprises,ecnomic organizations or individuals(including overseas Chinese,fellow citizens of Hongkong,Macao and Taiwan and Sino–enterprises registered in foreign countries) with Chinese enterprises or Chinese ecnomic organizations. And capital borrow from abroad and within the total value of investment in projects approved by the relevant department of Government.

Total value of export refers to total value of pratical outward cargoes. Our country stipulates that outward cargoes are calculated on FOB basis.

22 “两圈”“长江经济带”主要经济指标

Major Economic Indicators of “Twice” And “Yangtze River Economic Zone”

22-1 武汉城市圈主要经济指标(2016)
MAIN ECONOMIC INDICATORS OF WUHAN URBAN CIRCLE(2016)

指标	Item	土地面积(平方公里) Land Area (sq.km)	常住人口(万人) Total Population (year-end) (10 000 persons)	地区生产总值(亿元) Gross Regional Product(100 million yuan)	第一产业(亿元) Primary Industry (100 million million yuan)	第二产业(亿元) Secondary Industry (100 million yuan)	#工业(亿元) #Industry (100 million yuan)	第三产业(亿元) Tertiary Industry (100 million yuan)	人均地区生产总值(元) Per Capita Gross Regional Prduct (yuan/person)
合计	**Total**	**58052**	**3144.81**	**20147.78**	**1697.96**	**9213.52**	**7757.75**	**9236.30**	**64314**
武汉市	Wuhan Municipality	8494	1076.62	11912.61	390.62	5227.05	4238.78	6294.94	111469
黄石市	Huangshi Municipality	4583	246.55	1305.55	114.07	721.47	638.56	470.01	53033
鄂州市	Ezhou Municipality	1594	106.85	797.82	97.21	434.58	391.48	266.03	74983
孝感市	Xiaogan Municipality	8910	490.43	1576.69	281.52	756.40	668.13	538.77	32236
黄冈市	Huanggang Municipality	17446	632.10	1726.17	395.30	654.05	509.67	676.82	27373
咸宁市	Xianning Municipality	9861	252.60	1107.93	184.34	527.81	473.17	395.78	44027
仙桃市	Xiantiao Municipality	2538	114.80	647.55	87.94	342.94	313.25	216.67	56235
潜江市	Qianjiang Municipality	2004	96.20	602.19	72.21	310.24	306.90	219.74	62728
天门市	Tianmen Municipality	2622	128.66	471.27	74.75	238.98	217.81	157.54	36552

22-1 续表 1 continued

指标	Item	全社会固定资产投资总额(亿元) Investment in Fixed Assets (100 million yuan)	地方公共财政预算收入(亿元) Revenue of Local Governments (100 million yuan)	#各项税收(亿元) #Taxes (100 million yuan)	地方财政支出(亿元) Expenditures of Local Governments (100 million yuan)	农村居民人均可支配收入(元) Annual Per Capita Disposable Income of Rural Households (yuan)	城镇居民人均可支配收入(元) Annual Per Capita Disposable Income of Urban Households (yuan)
合计	**Total**	**15972.18**	**1882.94**	**1447.73**	**3076.55**	**15039**	**32490**
武汉市	Wuhan Municipality	7039.79	1322.10	1091.90	1523.09	19152	39737
黄石市	Huangshi Municipality	1350.83	105.47	67.42	222.53	12925	29906
鄂州市	Ezhou Municipality	853.26	52.91	32.43	100.19	14813	26986
孝感市	Xiaogan Municipality	1899.43	129.23	81.06	355.12	13554	27939
黄冈市	Huanggang Municipality	2041.65	119.52	74.59	452.54	11076	24796
咸宁市	Xianning Municipality	1438.29	83.34	50.01	216.20	12812	25839
仙桃市	Xiantiao Municipality	483.93	29.08	23.22	74.58	15462	26845
潜江市	Qianjiang Municipality	462.32	23.32	11.65	63.54	15113	26985
天门市	Tianmen Municipality	402.68	17.97	15.46	68.77	14107	24475

22-1 续表 2 continued

指标	Item	农林牧渔业总产值(亿元) Gross Output Value of Agriculture (100 million yuan)	粮食产量(万吨) Output of Grain (10 000 tons)	棉花产量(万吨) Output of Cotton (tons)	油料产量(万吨) Output of Oil-bearing Crops (10 000 tons)	工业企业单位数(个) Number of Enterprises (unit)	房屋建筑竣工面积(万平方米) Floor Space Completed of Buildings (10 000 sq.m)	社会消费品零售总额(亿元) Total Retail Sales(100 million yuan)
合计	**Total**	**2865.09**	**974.88**	**8.94**	**154.28**	**8379**	**4628.81**	**9653.67**
武汉市	Wuhan Municipality	669.65	110.01	0.76	18.14	2529	1654.04	5610.59
黄石市	Huangshi Municipality	165.04	57.26	0.26	9.78	762	298.40	649.59
鄂州市	Ezhou Municipality	169.85	31.12	0.41	6.06	525	162.97	298.45
孝感市	Xiaogan Municipality	522.38	206.33	1.50	23.57	1297	1033.06	883.66
黄冈市	Huanggang Municipality	623.55	290.82	2.99	54.43	1460	814.99	973.94
咸宁市	Xianning Municipality	310.21	96.45	0.24	10.80	845	352.45	442.54
仙桃市	Xiantiao Municipality	149.13	72.45	0.80	12.86	400	90.83	297.19
潜江市	Qianjiang Municipality	124.73	47.09	0.45	7.02	263	66.89	208.50
天门市	Tianmen Municipality	130.56	63.35	1.53	11.63	298	155.19	289.21

22-1 续表 3 continued

指标	Item	实际外商直接投资(万美元) Actually Foreign Direct Investments (USD 10 000)	入境旅游者人数(万人次) Number of International Tourists (10 000 person-times)	国际旅游外汇收入(万美元) Foreign Exchange Earnings (USD 10 000)	金融机构人民币存款(亿元) State Bank Deposits (100 million yuan)	金融机构人民币贷款(亿元) State Bank Loans(100 million yuan)
合计	**Total**	**793800**			**31938.01**	**25620.61**
武汉市	Wuhan Municipality	683298			22196.21	20754.87
黄石市	Huangshi Municipality	14569			1542.37	1012.83
鄂州市	Ezhou Municipality	27087			581.54	391.47
孝感市	Xiaogan Municipality	37269			2078.89	1023.43
黄冈市	Huanggang Municipality	12930			2681.42	1160.66
咸宁市	Xianning Municipality	6998			1207.42	721.27
仙桃市	Xiantiao Municipality	621			582.70	222.96
潜江市	Qianjiang Municipality	6339			546.17	179.33
天门市	Tianmen Municipality	4692			521.32	153.77

22-2 鄂西生态文化旅游圈主要经济指标(2016)
MAIN ECONOMIC INDICATORS OF WUHAN URBAN CIRCLE(2016)

指标	Item	土地面积(平方公里) Land Area (sq.km)	常住人口(万人) Total Population (year-end) (10 000 persons)	地区生产总值(亿元) Gross Regional Product(100 million yuan)	第一产业 Primary Industry	第二产业 Secondary Industry	#工业 #Industry	第三产业 Tertiary Industry	人均地区生产总值(元) Per Capita Gross Regional Prduct (yuan/person)
合计	**Total**	**127909**	**2740.19**	**13691.71**	**1894.31**	**7048.29**	**6369.99**	**4749.11**	**50051**
宜昌市	Yichang Municipality	21084	413.00	3709.36	398.89	2122.74	1925.86	1187.73	89978
荆州市	Jingzhou Municipality	14067	569.79	1726.75	382.72	736.39	666.04	607.64	30284
襄阳市	Xiangyang Municipality	19724	563.90	3694.51	430.90	2046.77	1857.31	1216.84	65663
荆门市	Jingmen Municipality	12404	290.13	1521.00	213.15	789.51	734.91	518.34	52470
十堰市	Shiyan Municipality	23680	340.90	1429.15	173.40	681.59	616.87	574.16	42083
随州市	Suizhou Municipality	9636	220.18	852.18	140.54	398.44	351.49	313.20	38801
恩施州	Enshi Prefecture	24061	334.60	735.70	152.52	264.73	213.06	318.45	22050
神农架	Shennongjia	3253	7.69	23.06	2.19	8.12	4.45	12.75	30007

22-2 续表 1 continued

指标	Item	固定资产投资(亿元) Investment in Fixed Assets (100 million yuan)	地方公共财政预算收入(亿元) Revenue of Local Governments (100 million yuan)	#地方税收(亿元) #Taxes (100 million yuan)	地方财政支出(亿元) Expenditures of Local Governments (100 million yuan)
合计	**Total**	**12967.48**	**1049.90**	**654.59**	**2617.75**
宜昌市	Yichang Municipality	3191.15	300.04	176.71	538.63
荆州市	Jingzhou Municipality	2001.67	115.45	76.28	386.82
襄阳市	Xiangyang Municipality	3188.64	320.70	188.67	639.74
荆门市	Jingmen Municipality	1531.46	91.73	62.35	246.76
十堰市	Shiyan Municipality	1323.81	100.27	67.30	322.54
随州市	Suizhou Municipality	974.27	45.55	29.26	146.72
恩施州	Enshi Prefecture	719.40	71.91	51.44	319.46
神农架	Shennongjia	37.08	4.25	2.58	17.08

农村居民人均可支配收入(元) Annual Per Capita Disposable Income of Rural Households (yuan)	城镇居民人均可支配收入(元) Annual Per Capita Disposable Income of Urban Households (yuan)	农林牧渔业产值(现价)(亿元) Gross Output Value of Agriculture (100 million yuan)	粮食产量(万吨) Output of Grain (10 000 tons)	棉花产量(万吨) Output of Cotton (10 000 tons)	油料产量(万吨) Output of Oil-bearing Crops (10 000 tons)	工业企业单位数(个) Number of Enterprises (unit)
12982	**27660**	**3375.72**	**1690.12**	**9.90**	**175.49**	**7917**
14057	29735	687.02	152.93	1.07	23.99	1487
14707	27666	692.78	371.51	5.03	54.67	1271
14762	28794	775.91	500.14	1.82	26.10	1884
15811	28920	378.30	250.73	1.13	38.85	1155
8514	26030	317.13	105.64	0.01	13.91	911
14077	24799	257.67	157.40	0.85	7.23	677
8728	24410	262.71	149.77		10.70	520
8342	23452	4.20	2.00		0.04	12

22-2 续表 2 continued

指标	Item	房地产企业房屋竣工面积合计(万平方米) Floor Space of Building Completed of the Real Enterprises Estate (10 000 sq.m)	商品房销售额(亿元) Total Sale of Commercialized Buildings Sold	社会消费品零售总额(亿元) Total Retail Sales(100 million yuan)
合计	**Total**	**1299.53**	**1061.52**	**5922.36**
宜昌市	Yichang Municipality	245.24	304.78	1240.33
荆州市	Jingzhou Municipality	106.26	107.09	1056.13
襄阳市	Xiangyang Municipality	485.17	280.03	1325.26
荆门市	Jingmen Municipality	188.43	107.90	614.23
十堰市	Shiyan Municipality	142.90	100.56	724.96
随州市	Suizhou Municipality	32.05	45.96	446.10
恩施州	Enshi Prefecture	99.48	115.20	500.39
神农架	Shennongjia	0	0	14.96

实际使用外资(万美元) Actually Foreign Direct Investments (USD 10 000)	进出口总额(亿元)	进口总额(亿元)	出口总额(亿元)	金融机构(含外资)本外币贷款余额(亿元) Financial Institutions Local & Foreign Currency Balance of Loans (100 million yuan)
219086	**610.9**	**85.8**	**525.2**	**8676.90**
34149	176.0	22.6	153.4	2353.41
14360	74.3	9.5	64.8	1185.93
82426	127.7	17.8	109.9	1809.27
37630	70.1	13.2	57.0	872.56
27753	34.4	0.9	33.5	1137.15
12858	92.2	21.8	70.4	527.40
4910	36.1		36.1	771.35
	0.1		0.1	19.83

22-3 长江经济带国民经济主要指标

指标		Item	2012年	
			绝对数 absolute account	占全国比重(%) proportion
人口		**populations**		
年末常住人口	(万人)	Population of Permanent Residents (10 000 persons)	57852	42.9
城镇化率	(%)	Urbanization Rate (%)	51.8	
国民经济核算		**national accounting**		
国内(地区)生产总值	(亿元)	Cross Domestic Product (100 million yuan)	235915	40.9
第一产业	(亿元)	Primary Industry (100 million yuan)	21550	41.1
第二产业	(亿元)	Secondary Industry (100 million yuan)	115745	40.5
第三产业	(亿元)	Tertiary Industry (100 million yuan)	98620	41.3
固定资产投资		**Investment in Fixed Assets**		
全社会固定资产投资	(亿元)	Total Investment in Fixed Assets (100 million yuan)	149248	39.8
财政		**Finance**		
地方一般公共预算收入	(亿元)	General Public Budget Revenue (100 million yuan)	26293	43.0
农业		Agriculture		
主要农产品产品		**Output of Major Farm Products**		
粮食	(万吨)	Grain (10 000 tons)	22369	37.9
油量	(万吨)	Oil-bearing Crops (10 000 tons)	1547	45.0
棉花	(万吨)	Cotton (10 000 tons)	151	22.1
工业		**Industry**		
规模以上工业企业利润总额	(亿元)	Total Profit ofIndustrial Enterprises Above Designated Size (100 million yuan)	23919	38.6
建筑业		**Construction**		
建筑业总产值	(亿元)	Cross Output of Construction Enterprises (100 million yuan)	72710	53.0
国内贸易		**Domestic Trade**		
社会消费品零售总额	(亿元)	Total Retail Sales of Consumer Goods (100 million yuan)	85470	40.6
对外贸易		**foreign trade**		
货物进出口总额	(亿美元)	Total Value of Imports and Exports (100 million USD)	15636	40.4
出口总额	(亿美元)	Total Exports (100 million USD)	9356	45.7
进口总额	(亿美元)	Total Imports (100 million USD)	6279	34.5

注:长江经济带(上海、江苏、浙江、安徽、江西、湖北、湖南、重庆、四川、贵州、云南)合计占全国的比重以全国各地区合计数为100计算。

MAIN INDICATORS OF NATIONAL ECONOMIC AND SOCIAL DEVELOPMENT BY YANGTZE RIVER ECONOMIC ZONE

2013年		2014年		2015年		2016年	
绝对数 absolute account	占全国比重（%） proportion	绝对数 absolute account	占全国比重（%） proportion	绝对数 absolute account	占全国比重（%） proportion	绝对数 absolute account	占全国比重（%） proportion
58160	42.9	58426	42.9	58766	42.9	59140	42.9
53.0		54.2		55.5		56.9	
259525	41.2	284689	41.6	305200	42.2	332906	43.1
23109	40.6	23800	40.8	25324	41.6	26973	42.5
125481	40.9	132488	41.3	135301	42.2	142739	43.2
110935	41.7	128401	42.0	144575	42.4	163194	43.2
179527	40.2	209459	41.4	237631	42.7	265971	44.2
29688	43.0	32918	43.4	37321	45.0	39444	45.2
22483	37.4	23024	37.9	23473	37.8	23125	37.5
1588	45.1	1625	46.3	1645	46.5	1617	44.6
130	20.6	108	17.6	94	16.8	67	12.6
24889	39.6	28213	41.4	29368	44.4	31023	45.1
85136	53.4	96761	54.8	102183	56.5	110446	57.1
96629	40.6	112693	41.4	125342	41.7	139650	42.1
16385	39.4	17568	40.8	16691	42.2	15676	42.5
9871	44.7	10718	45.8	10395	45.7	9574	45.6
6514	33.4	6850	35.1	6296	37.5	6102	38.4

a) National total is as 100 in calculating the sum of Yangtze river economic zone 11 provinces (Shanghai, Jiangsu, Zhejiang, Anhui, Jiangxi, Hunan, Hubei, Chongqing, Sichuan, Guizhou, Yunnan) respectively as percentage of national total.

23 县域经济主要指标

Economy of Cities and Counties

23-1 县市主要经济指标
MAIN ECONOMIC INDICATORS OF COUNTIES

指标名称	Item	地区生产总值(亿元) Gross Regional Product(100 million yuan)		人均地区生产总值(元) Per CapitaGDP (yuan)		固定资产投资(亿元) Investment in Fixed Assets (100 million yuan)	
		2015	2016	2015	2016	2015	2016
蔡甸区	Caidian District	377.59	411.44	84852	88482	348.93	346.15
江夏区	Jiangxia District	637.93	729.23	74027	81515	590.90	502.01
黄陂区	Huangpi District	563.76	627.87	60747	64923	627.22	479.89
新洲区	Xinzhou District	559.78	606.30	64243	67758	502.28	457.30
汉南区	Hannan District	120.67	130.75	92823	99354	94.66	237.94
阳新县	Yangxin County	190.08	205.09	23027	24692	274.25	313.67
大冶市	Daye City	509.98	540.49	56454	59466	645.52	743.48
郧阳区	Yun County	91.25	100.69	16198	17730	160.38	172.81
郧西县	Yunxi County	61.39	65.90	13594	14464	73.21	78.89
竹山县	Zhushan County	79.75	86.96	19294	20854	138.50	149.48
竹溪县	Zhuxi County	66.61	72.81	21408	23195	76.05	82.01
房县	Fang County	71.04	77.64	17980	19468	131.60	123.55
丹江口市	Danjiangkou City	182.04	198.68	45825	49857	188.39	202.46
夷陵区	Yiling District	486.93	541.38	93014	103061	491.03	495.19
远安县	Yuanan County	190.09	202.29	101652	107716	225.11	251.98
兴山县	Xingshan County	95.06	104.75	55639	61150	41.89	50.17
秭归县	Zigui County	110.09	117.96	30454	32559	111.74	112.11
长阳县	Changyang Tujia A.C.	120.46	131.10	31191	33615	86.24	94.41
五峰县	Wufeng Tujia A.C.	60.23	63.13	32046	33174	52.41	57.23
宜都市	Yidu City	501.00	550.54	128626	140911	550.48	574.27
当阳市	Dangyang City	435.04	474.13	92927	101029	425.68	412.52
枝江市	Zhijiang City	429.70	472.43	85768	93960	442.49	462.70
襄州区	Xiangzhou District	550.92	591.69	66177	70523	504.63	524.32
南漳县	Nanzhang County	212.02	231.02	39274	42553	230.61	246.12
谷城县	Gucheng County	290.82	310.24	57668	61071	252.08	279.15
保康县	Baokang County	100.79	109.57	45126	48482	121.73	131.07
老河口市	Laohekou City	293.74	317.53	60565	66304	260.99	204.38
枣阳市	Zaoyang City	527.09	562.41	53228	56371	430.58	459.19
宜城市	Yicheng City	283.66	304.92	54456	58191	221.11	278.37
梁子湖区	Liangzihu District	59.65	65.48	41352	45221	62.25	73.36
华容区	Huarong District	230.29	253.21	95974	103478	361.62	420.78
鄂城区	Echeng District	441.40	482.54	65397	71066	382.34	359.12
东宝区	Dongbao District	284.20	317.24	82616	91161	365.16	246.08
京山县	Jingshan County	307.51	338.68	56059	61355	424.95	341.74
沙洋县	Shayang County	224.68	245.11	39126	42814	174.58	202.42

23-1 续表 1 continued

指标名称	Item	地区生产总值(亿元) Gross Regional Product(100 million yuan)		人均地区生产总值(元) Per CapitaGDP (yuan)		固定资产投资(亿元) Investment in Fixed Assets (100 million yuan)	
		2015	2016	2015	2016	2015	2016
钟祥市	Zhongxiang City	382.46	420.11	41726	45417	453.00	479.02
孝南区	Xiaonan District	268.56	287.74	29196	31050	361.63	391.85
孝昌县	Xiaochang County	104.28	113.27	17514	19362	131.78	146.13
大悟县	Dawu County	118.84	128.05	19175	20547	192.46	207.46
云梦县	Yunmeng County	196.67	213.00	37164	39783	122.53	255.64
应城市	Yingcheng City	239.08	260.34	39907	43081	252.09	267.51
安陆市	Anlu City	172.22	188.07	29786	32314	226.26	242.16
汉川市	Hanchuan City	416.13	454.14	40474	43891	360.61	388.69
荆州区	Jingzhou District	226.99	243.65	39565	42169	288.93	291.80
江陵县	Jiangling County	68.32	74.71	20575	22564	75.52	90.31
公安县	Gongan County	210.00	226.97	23595	25824	249.59	270.65
监利县	Jianli County	229.33	246.55	21341	23120	188.06	205.68
石首市	Shishou City	149.77	152.07	26101	26660	171.68	186.25
洪湖市	Honghu City	196.44	213.10	23003	25136	104.57	168.47
松滋市	Songci City	218.72	243.83	28255	31724	244.80	273.89
黄州区	Huangzhou District	188.69	203.16	50385	52280	283.41	278.54
团风县	Tuanfeng County	75.45	80.65	22087	23431	73.00	76.44
红安县	Hongan County	130.05	140.92	21560	23201	169.06	183.32
罗田县	Luotian County	112.75	121.79	20569	22063	164.66	168.43
英山县	Yingshan County	82.89	88.97	23019	24530	87.00	96.41
浠水县	Xishui County	199.28	217.57	22657	24704	192.39	183.26
蕲春县	Qichun County	193.50	208.65	24965	26740	249.41	229.71
黄梅县	Huangmei County	174.22	188.16	20160	21657	190.79	210.59
麻城市	Macheng City	244.31	266.27	29570	30230	301.37	343.65
武穴市	Wuxue City	240.72	260.78	39907	39783	247.30	271.29
咸安区	Xian'an District	240.34	259.11	46060	49204	334.21	350.84
嘉鱼县	Jiayu County	201.06	213.51	63758	67438	235.83	250.09
通城县	Tongcheng County	108.97	114.95	26656	27766	137.66	146.44
崇阳县	Chongyang County	102.23	108.56	25577	26778	142.23	150.41
通山县	Tongshan County	95.23	101.40	25927	27112	182.18	178.19
赤壁市	Chibi City	341.36	360.22	70362	73604	467.51	362.31
曾都区	Zengdu District	360.91	393.09	61605	62021	390.65	398.96
随县	Sui Country	178.13	193.28	22423	24190	257.40	278.82
广水市	Guangshui City	246.22	265.24	32200	34492	278.33	296.49
恩施市	Enshi City	171.39	187.86	22338	24293	157.78	174.14
利川市	Lichuan City	98.86	107.27	14962	16107	102.89	110.21
建始县	Jianshi County	77.78	85.79	18702	20504	81.65	88.61
巴东县	Badong County	88.85	96.21	20921	22526	91.74	99.99
宣恩县	Xuanen County	55.01	60.23	18200	19786	40.51	44.67
咸丰县	Xianfeng County	66.20	73.20	21741	23875	57.47	62.88
来凤县	Laifeng County	57.86	62.97	23592	25494	62.02	67.67
鹤峰县	Hefeng County	47.72	51.98	23653	25581	45.56	49.02
仙桃市	Xiantiao City	597.61	647.55	51786	56407	445.50	483.93
潜江市	Qianjiang City	557.57	602.19	58310	62598	435.52	462.32
天门市	Tianmen City	440.10	471.27	34069	36629	373.41	402.68

23-1 续表 3 continued

指标名称	Item	社会消费品零售总额(亿元) Total Retail Sales (100 million yuan)		财政总收入(亿元) Total Fiscal Revenue (100 million yuan)		地方一般公共财政预算收入(亿元) Revenue of Local Governments (100 million yuan)		*税收(亿元) Taxes (100 million yuan)	
		2015	2016	2015	2016	2015	2016	2015	2016
蔡甸区	Caidian District	98.05	109.22	46.19	49.67	30.62	34.38	18.25	22.03
江夏区	Jiangxia District	173.60	193.92	99.41	107.72	70.19	82.57	52.89	44.19
黄陂区	Huangpi District	223.83	249.57	64.52	73.73	48.32	55.16	31.61	35.26
新洲区	Xinzhou District	158.47	177.97	49.50	57.44	32.82	38.66	22.40	27.29
汉南区	Hannan District	21.85	24.23	24.01	28.97	14.58	17.15	13.22	16.00
阳新县	Yangxin County	103.95	114.97	18.08	18.92	12.58	13.84	7.56	7.41
大冶市	Daye City	184.76	207.30	71.73	64.33	45.18	48.82	31.05	26.84
郧阳区	Yun County	61.66	69.62	10.67	12.64	7.07	8.12	5.05	5.93
郧西县	Yunxi County	41.40	46.37	4.66	5.01	3.43	3.72	2.35	2.31
竹山县	Zhushan County	42.73	48.03	7.17	7.42	5.22	5.45	3.56	3.37
竹溪县	Zhuxi County	30.32	33.99	5.89	5.99	4.35	4.36	2.95	2.75
房　县	Fang County	45.85	51.49	6.18	6.93	4.64	5.10	3.07	3.31
丹江口市	Danjiangkou City	69.13	78.11	19.46	18.20	13.21	12.95	8.80	8.12
夷陵区	Yiling District	111.71	126.12	57.65	47.23	42.36	34.01	25.42	20.43
远安县	Yuanan County	40.12	45.01	17.02	13.33	14.69	11.09	8.80	6.65
兴山县	Xingshan County	28.53	32.13	12.72	11.08	9.50	8.27	6.08	4.96
秭归县	Zigui County	38.40	43.35	11.63	9.36	9.84	7.29	6.03	4.38
长阳县	Changyang Tujia A.C.	43.25	48.79	10.73	9.21	9.11	7.55	5.49	4.61
五峰县	Wufeng Tujia A.C.	19.19	21.53	4.62	4.31	3.64	3.24	2.25	1.95
宜都市	Yidu City	98.79	111.73	50.29	44.29	44.97	38.53	27.39	24.07
当阳市	Dangyang City	120.53	136.68	39.19	33.52	31.29	25.40	19.85	15.47
枝江市	Zhijiang City	119.07	132.88	38.05	35.31	31.68	28.59	20.45	17.58
襄州区	Xiangzhou District	159.85	181.58	38.58	35.40	33.55	29.77	21.44	17.89
南漳县	Nanzhang County	89.34	100.60	16.38	16.67	14.12	13.64	9.83	9.46
谷城县	Gucheng County	93.90	106.21	25.39	23.70	21.77	19.80	13.65	11.33
保康县	Baokang County	43.40	49.17	13.64	12.20	11.51	10.30	6.94	6.18
老河口市	Laohekou City	107.76	121.13	31.16	32.55	28.60	28.23	17.29	17.70
枣阳市	Zaoyang City	171.33	192.23	39.34	36.86	35.76	32.96	21.54	19.81
宜城市	Yicheng City	93.18	105.29	28.98	25.04	25.97	23.90	14.19	12.40
梁子湖区	Liangzihu District	18.06	20.10	3.54	4.73	2.79	3.63	1.91	2.77
华容区	Huarong District	66.61	75.41	7.58	7.89	5.88	5.79	4.04	3.71
鄂城区	Echeng District	173.45	192.53	16.24	17.61	12.21	13.06	8.07	8.54
东宝区	Dongbao District	161.78	183.62	27.26	16.33	20.05	14.64	9.22	8.07
京山县	Jingshan County	142.93	161.94	18.14	18.65	14.79	16.30	9.78	9.37
沙洋县	Shayang County	74.92	84.51	8.40	10.16	6.70	7.71	4.65	5.42
钟祥市	Zhongxiang City	169.42	191.78	22.35	24.84	17.58	19.48	11.03	12.46
孝南区	Xiaonan District	149.06	165.60	26.89	28.57	19.24	19.54	12.83	12.28
孝昌县	Xiaochang County	56.54	63.33	11.49	12.63	8.90	9.22	5.35	5.29
大悟县	Dawu County	74.79	83.76	13.29	13.99	8.81	9.49	5.31	5.70
云梦县	Yunmeng County	100.89	113.30	16.59	17.64	12.75	13.21	8.21	8.06

23-1 续表 3 continued

指标名称	Item	社会消费品零售总额(亿元) Total Retail Sales (100 million yuan)		财政总收入(亿元) Total Fiscal Revenue (100 million yuan)		地方一般公共财政预算收入(亿元) Revenue of Local Governments (100 million yuan)		#税收(亿元) Taxes (100 million yuan)	
		2015	2016	2015	2016	2015	2016	2015	2016
应城市	Yingcheng City	124.65	140.86	21.48	22.32	15.82	16.56	10.31	10.74
安陆市	Anlu City	99.47	111.70	13.36	14.55	10.27	10.76	7.20	7.65
汉川市	Hanchuan City	188.50	209.61	29.60	32.67	20.26	21.47	14.63	15.70
荆州区	Jingzhou District	136.85	152.99	22.02	22.79	14.41	14.95	12.32	12.30
江陵县	Jiangling County	40.13	44.62	4.26	5.45	3.02	3.58	1.90	2.47
公安县	Gongan County	127.27	143.69	14.21	15.69	10.30	11.24	7.03	7.39
监利县	Jianli County	132.39	148.27	9.78	10.24	7.32	7.77	5.56	5.41
石首市	Shishou City	91.75	103.59	11.95	10.35	7.34	6.67	5.27	4.79
洪湖市	Honghu City	100.37	120.25	10.61	11.40	8.03	8.39	5.80	5.38
松滋市	Songci City	109.36	123.80	21.51	25.39	12.66	16.56	8.42	10.18
黄州区	Huangzhou District	117.59	130.29	18.53	8.76	12.70	14.16	9.66	4.08
团风县	Tuanfeng County	31.25	34.47	6.65	7.67	4.98	5.29	3.35	3.32
红安县	Hongan County	61.72	69.55	23.83	24.09	13.11	14.71	9.28	10.01
罗田县	Luotian County	60.99	67.58	8.37	9.74	6.29	6.80	4.19	4.26
英山县	Yingshan County	32.75	36.62	5.17	6.09	3.93	4.53	2.78	2.95
浠水县	Xishui County	118.35	133.50	11.45	11.07	8.65	8.67	5.69	4.83
蕲春县	Qichun County	107.16	119.69	15.40	17.28	11.56	12.20	7.20	7.38
黄梅县	Huangmei County	114.31	127.57	12.98	14.09	10.19	10.60	6.52	6.54
麻城市	Macheng City	124.57	141.01	19.86	21.66	14.99	16.04	9.84	9.98
武穴市	Wuxue City	115.79	129.80	19.80	21.89	15.24	16.69	9.70	10.18
咸安区	Xian'an District	105.41	116.48	19.57	11.71	14.42	15.95	6.41	4.99
嘉鱼县	Jiayu County	51.72	58.03	11.32	12.29	9.35	9.81	6.12	5.90
通城县	Tongcheng County	52.65	58.76	8.41	8.82	6.04	6.71	3.63	4.03
崇阳县	Chongyang County	50.00	55.75	7.60	8.56	6.19	6.81	3.88	4.10
通山县	Tongshan County	86.96	96.96	7.19	7.72	5.90	5.97	3.67	3.44
赤壁市	Chibi City	149.16	168.85	23.87	24.41	17.02	17.11	10.86	9.40
曾都区	Zengdu District	179.89	200.94	22.92	20.35	16.96	14.23	13.12	10.29
随　县	Sui Country	115.77	130.01	8.00	10.47	5.20	7.76	3.61	4.32
广水市	Guangshui City	103.55	114.73	20.82	21.22	10.60	11.19	6.97	7.17
恩施市	Enshi City	139.93	157.56	27.01	28.15	21.44	20.47	17.51	16.42
利川市	Lichuan City	79.04	88.29	15.97	16.55	9.74	9.82	7.05	6.50
建始县	Jianshi County	49.78	55.75	8.90	9.22	5.15	5.52	4.01	3.99
巴东县	Badong County	50.63	56.46	8.17	8.50	5.86	5.91	4.31	4.28
宣恩县	Xuanen County	34.00	38.32	4.20	4.73	2.98	3.29	2.48	2.36
咸丰县	Xianfeng County	36.56	41.24	6.14	6.66	3.68	3.95	2.65	2.85
来凤县	Laifeng County	32.29	36.22	7.35	7.51	3.73	3.85	3.01	2.94
鹤峰县	Hefeng County	26.03	29.20	4.58	4.55	3.03	3.33	2.34	2.33
仙桃市	Xiantiao City	266.17	297.31	41.89	44.41	27.69	29.08	22.07	23.22
潜江市	Qianjiang City	186.14	208.47	33.97	35.09	22.85	23.32	15.45	15.46
天门市	Tianmen City	258.90	289.19	25.24	24.28	19.59	17.97	13.67	11.65

23-1 续表 4 continued

指标名称	Item	外贸出口(万美元) Total Exports (USD 10 000)		城镇常住居民人均可支配收入(元) Annual Per CapitaDisposable Income of Urban(yuan)		农村常住居民人均可支配收入(元) Annual Per CapitaDisposable Income of RuralHouseholds(yuan)	
		2015	2016	2015	2016	2015	2016
蔡 甸 区	Caidian District	51555	41003	27060	29360	16502	17748
江 夏 区	Jiangxia District	24560	19434	26716	29174	16641	17972
黄 陂 区	Huangpi District	18163	21923	26562	28979	16228	17559
新 洲 区	Xinzhou District	20037	16418	24798	27037	15894	17046
汉 南 区	Hannan District		7263	26946	29177	16653	18040
阳 新 县	Yangxin County	32108	19089	19960	21946	9267	10050
大 冶 市	Daye City	46659	54124	30848	33341	15861	16987
郧 阳 区	Yun County	7461	5323	21867	23704	7783	8507
郧 西 县	Yunxi County	2417	2144	20853	22500	7509	8220
竹 山 县	Zhushan County	3927	4607	20549	22242	7628	8353
竹 溪 县	Zhuxi County	2149	1185	20076	21746	7550	8279
房 县	Fang County	4758	5265	21622	23432	7592	8304
丹江口市	Danjiangkou City	4072	3268	22827	24719	8553	9367
夷 陵 区	Yiling District	10110	11655	28202	30757	15793	17149
远 安 县	Yuanan County	13425	12258	25817	28164	14715	15892
兴 山 县	Xingshan County	44684	30736	22478	24486	9610	10365
秭 归 县	Zigui County	6926	5572	21810	23725	8062	8825
长 阳 县	Changyang Tujia A.C.	6410	7185	22525	24493	8148	8839
五 峰 县	Wufeng Tujia A.C.	1065	1259	20508	22368	7880	8642
宜 都 市	Yidu City	43281	39625	28651	31195	16449	17789
当 阳 市	Dangyang City	11958	11435	27068	29641	16512	17791
枝 江 市	Zhijiang City	31088	22984	25955	28456	16697	17936
襄 州 区	Xiangzhou District	40954	41945	24330	26598	14808	16008
南 漳 县	Nanzhang County	12159	13991	24265	26599	12350	13394
谷 城 县	Gucheng County	18668	13539	24710	27231	12651	13720
保 康 县	Baokang County	5597	6276	21710	23827	9165	9973
老河口市	Laohekou City	33815	15285	26301	28905	14607	15805
枣 阳 市	Zaoyang City	27184	8440	27040	29676	14280	15487
宜 城 市	Yicheng City	22442	14519	24367	26760	14430	15613
梁子湖区	Liangzihu District	201	166	18930	20684	10563	11351
华 容 区	Huarong District	8287	8883	22284	24161	14476	15500
鄂 城 区	Echeng District	14451	14376	25936	28270	14959	16049
东 宝 区	Dongbao District	8700	9982	28756	31086	14872	15980
京 山 县	Jingshan County	20572	23255	25780	27892	14731	15829
沙 洋 县	Shayang County	14003	5791	25576	27678	14469	15546

23-1 续表 5 continued

指标名称	Item	外贸出口(万美元) Total Exports (USD 10 000) 2015	2016	城镇常住居民人均可支配收入(元) Annual Per CapitaDisposable Income of Urban(yuan) 2015	2016	农村常住居民人均可支配收入(元) Annual Per CapitaDisposable Income of RuralHouseholds(yuan) 2015	2016
钟祥市	Zhongxiang City	25035	23616	25821	27940	15106	16230
孝南区	Xiaonan District	18156	11937	27580	29927	14420	15455
孝昌县	Xiaochang County	4792	5787	22567	24404	8540	9180
大悟县	Dawu County	2131	2371	22803	24655	8742	9401
云梦县	Yunmeng County	15904	17973	26083	28342	14931	15988
应城市	Yingcheng City	10354	6116	26483	28755	15177	16227
安陆市	Anlu City	7173	7941	25364	27530	12796	13667
汉川市	Hanchuan City	38376	40593	26131	28420	14664	15724
荆州区	Jingzhou District	7096	5967	28397	30925	15431	16500
江陵县	Jiangling County	963	1033	22652	24700	12244	13120
公安县	Gongan County	7414	10335	24155	26390	14410	15445
监利县	Jianli County	4887	5613	22579	24610	13327	14263
石首市	Shishou City	9626	3716	23850	25940	13600	14570
洪湖市	Honghu City	1828	2446	23630	25740	13400	14350
松滋市	Songci City	16003	16269	24255	26490	13850	14875
黄州区	Huangzhou District	6477	7342	25538	28174	12573	13643
团风县	Tuanfeng County	1276	1427	20699	22717	9428	10244
红安县	Hongan County	1680	1853	21202	23104	8826	9537
罗田县	Luotian County	5662	4345	21027	22959	8493	9139
英山县	Yingshan County	1697	2243	20502	22308	9072	9774
浠水县	Xishui County	6044	6679	22172	24238	10899	11708
蕲春县	Qichun County	9768	10901	21848	24018	10341	11252
黄梅县	Huangmei County	4527	5622	22733	25038	11413	12367
麻城市	Macheng City	5079	2753	23279	25504	9841	10651
武穴市	Wuxue City	15417	16990	24003	26526	12011	12963
咸安区	Xian'an District	12749	6413	25896	28537	13243	14185
嘉鱼县	Jiayu County	8843	4992	23245	25802	13760	14742
通城县	Tongcheng County	3907	4659	22375	24554	11679	12544
崇阳县	Chongyang County	2393	3083	21131	23198	11247	12089
通山县	Tongshan County	1270	1404	19654	21584	8851	9516
赤壁市	Chibi City	9968	5478	24248	26656	13616	14583
曾都区	Zengdu District	64659	60618	24985	27171	13785	14912
随县	Sui Country	45128	38800	20733	22593	13109	14168
广水市	Guangshui City	7973	7572	22581	24569	12877	13926
恩施市	Enshi City	14109	16681	24226	26559	8274	9037
利川市	Lichuan City	8475	9597	22108	24409	7839	8607
建始县	Jianshi County	4819	4895	20767	22867	7920	8689
巴东县	Badong County	7711	8031	21058	23219	7893	8628
宣恩县	Xuanen County	3219	2331	20606	22784	7805	8550
咸丰县	Xianfeng County	5505	6352	20775	22844	7856	8613
来凤县	Laifeng County	2696	1294	21388	23408	7794	8542
鹤峰县	Hefeng County	5933	5106	21118	23122	8372	9159
仙桃市	Xiantiao City	68922	59891	24641	26845	14422	15462
潜江市	Qianjiang City	29353	24156	24721	26985	14076	15113
天门市	Tianmen City	10472	10004	22618	24475	13178	14107

23-1 续表 6 continued

指标名称	Item	农业总产值(亿元) Total Value ofAgricultural Output(100 million yuan)		农产品加工业产值(亿元) Value of Agricultural Product Processing(100 million yuan)		常用耕地面积(千公顷) Area of Cultivated Land (1000 hectare)		粮食产量(万吨) Output of Grain (10 000 tons)	
		2015	2016	2015	2016	2015	2016	2015	2016
蔡甸区	Caidian District	67.69	77.17	218.77	233.48	24.13	23.96	13.31	11.29
江夏区	Jiangxia District	153.77	165.42	113.25	118.60	35.69	34.97	29.21	24.91
黄陂区	Huangpi District	190.21	208.26	213.44	221.96	52.35	52.16	46.05	40.40
新洲区	Xinzhou District	138.83	140.96	125.40	140.84	50.35	49.88	32.40	28.31
汉南区	Hannan District	23.22	26.54	55.38	58.37	10.05	7.25	3.40	2.85
阳新县	Yangxin County	81.00	85.35	50.02	55.09	52.11	52.11	35.44	31.07
大冶市	Daye City	69.93	72.31	177.94	203.58	35.61	36.79	29.40	25.24
郧阳区	Yun County	45.51	50.70	54.78	66.60	35.69	35.69	23.23	21.03
郧西县	Yunxi County	43.33	46.92	6.31	5.65	26.83	26.96	19.50	17.65
竹山县	Zhushan County	43.29	49.24	19.20	21.69	32.87	34.19	22.98	20.68
竹溪县	Zhuxi County	44.99	48.48	15.26	19.61	28.92	30.39	23.57	21.12
房　县	Fang County	49.27	56.12	32.53	35.92	27.62	27.46	15.40	13.70
丹江口市	Danjiangkou City	52.55	56.64	82.93	99.94	21.16	21.40	12.40	10.94
夷陵区	Yiling District	92.90	106.03	637.78	711.30	33.70	33.66	21.87	19.36
远安县	Yuanan County	30.35	34.80	71.90	88.95	11.99	12.11	10.47	9.45
兴山县	Xingshan County	20.12	22.24	18.48	21.59	16.21	16.56	6.03	5.50
秭归县	Zigui County	37.83	41.97	61.19	69.71	24.10	25.00	9.28	8.45
长阳县	Changyang Tujia A.C.	59.57	65.97	55.30	61.26	40.65	40.65	11.45	10.25
五峰县	Wufeng Tujia A.C.	34.28	37.57	24.71	25.86	20.41	20.41	8.91	8.05
宜都市	Yidu City	71.31	79.75	279.48	326.92	15.73	15.74	11.64	10.35
当阳市	Dangyang City	128.65	141.33	302.26	344.92	55.79	55.81	54.73	48.84
枝江市	Zhijiang City	124.92	138.20	435.62	510.23	45.60	45.60	35.46	31.81
襄州区	Xiangzhou District	170.27	182.93	281.88	325.79	110.69	110.67	136.46	133.85
南漳县	Nanzhang County	76.41	81.86	124.43	135.96	41.13	46.67	45.17	44.59
谷城县	Gucheng County	60.04	67.13	241.46	276.29	28.53	28.53	28.05	27.82
保康县	Baokang County	36.30	36.76	35.67	41.98	22.61	22.46	14.58	14.40
老河口市	Laohekou City	75.24	81.18	302.08	324.24	40.61	40.75	37.42	37.12
枣阳市	Zaoyang City	165.18	178.14	383.52	472.42	110.91	110.88	136.81	135.84
宜城市	Yicheng City	90.76	94.86	363.03	403.99	62.88	62.88	69.75	69.49
梁子湖区	Liangzihu District	43.50	54.06	7.70	7.70	15.16	14.28	10.44	9.69
华容区	Huarong District	45.99	48.01	155.91	129.54	16.07	13.54	11.05	9.78
鄂城区	Echeng District	60.34	67.79	44.44	43.72	15.74	13.03	12.65	11.66
东宝区	Dongbao District	28.23	29.27	66.74	79.60	20.63	20.59	17.41	15.94
京山县	Jingshan County	95.45	100.48	471.68	511.32	69.61	70.02	74.94	69.04
沙洋县	Shayang County	100.75	101.99	227.99	228.87	78.45	78.48	85.59	75.19

23-1 续表 7 continued

指标名称	Item	农业总产值(亿元) Total Value ofAgricultural Output(100 million yuan)		农产品加工业产值(亿元) Value of Agricultural Product Processing(100 million yuan)		常用耕地面积(千公顷) Area of Cultivated Land (1000 hectare)		粮食产量(万吨) Output of Grain (10 000 tons)	
		2015	2016	2015	2016	2015	2016	2015	2016
钟祥市	Zhongxiang City	119.53	124.56	368.00	425.45	84.55	84.18	90.82	82.05
孝南区	Xiaonan District	54.77	59.70	149.46	156.51	34.10	34.10	22.15	18.89
孝昌县	Xiaochang County	54.74	59.25	20.88	18.89	32.72	33.41	27.50	25.60
大悟县	Dawu County	55.88	61.39	25.92	30.21	36.61	36.56	29.35	26.64
云梦县	Yunmeng County	61.62	64.72	114.77	194.58	25.53	25.53	22.53	20.35
应城市	Yingcheng City	80.17	88.29	127.02	136.71	38.59	38.55	37.32	31.89
安陆市	Anlu City	61.98	68.11	157.14	186.93	33.62	33.62	35.10	32.44
汉川市	Hanchuan City	106.51	119.73	644.87	701.74	65.73	65.73	56.63	50.14
荆州区	Jingzhou District	66.13	70.37	172.34	180.81	34.98	35.04	23.11	21.07
江陵县	Jiangling County	36.23	39.36	66.24	77.25	37.99	38.15	29.64	27.09
公安县	Gongan County	103.24	111.96	162.54	187.99	80.38	80.38	69.88	63.25
监利县	Jianli County	160.31	175.30	230.19	241.28	137.69	137.69	146.20	131.97
石首市	Shishou City	60.23	66.57	100.87	109.52	41.70	41.66	23.69	21.50
洪湖市	Honghu City	114.00	127.12	175.69	201.20	64.19	64.19	73.40	65.95
松滋市	Songci City	64.38	72.36	203.80	217.05	59.64	59.63	37.00	33.55
黄州区	Huangzhou District	22.30	23.39	61.68	83.78	10.71	10.68	5.82	5.12
团风县	Tuanfeng County	24.50	25.69	24.82	28.11	17.61	18.18	13.51	11.79
红安县	Hongan County	38.61	40.42	58.84	52.87	37.53	38.53	23.65	20.49
罗田县	Luotian County	42.04	43.95	26.72	29.83	26.35	26.35	25.98	22.74
英山县	Yingshan County	48.56	51.33	37.67	40.91	17.27	17.25	14.50	12.80
浠水县	Xishui County	94.02	98.53	89.27	71.37	44.86	44.95	51.62	45.07
蕲春县	Qichun County	71.90	75.25	128.51	132.28	40.95	40.95	53.67	48.32
黄梅县	Huangmei County	72.34	75.94	117.25	117.94	54.63	54.63	50.31	42.69
麻城市	Macheng City	91.42	95.67	127.00	81.70	58.05	58.07	56.14	48.86
武穴市	Wuxue City	78.32	83.43	87.61	87.14	38.66	38.48	33.66	29.81
咸安区	Xian'an District	48.30	49.34	226.43	247.42	35.22	34.59	19.59	16.96
嘉鱼县	Jiayu County	72.90	74.64	213.03	227.05	31.76	34.03	18.72	16.78
通城县	Tongcheng County	38.85	39.85	28.95	30.20	21.28	21.26	19.09	16.86
崇阳县	Chongyang County	41.38	42.29	15.56	18.70	22.87	23.16	20.68	18.34
通山县	Tongshan County	28.06	29.93	52.33	41.64	23.27	23.14	9.11	8.15
赤壁市	Chibi City	71.66	74.16	231.38	212.97	32.97	33.78	22.25	19.36
曾都区	Zengdu District	45.90	48.11	177.57	167.71	25.99	25.99	26.69	25.92
随县	Sui Country	115.61	121.78	167.62	186.95	78.33	78.85	93.74	90.20
广水市	Guangshui City	82.85	87.78	183.43	166.16	39.07	39.30	42.99	41.28
恩施市	Enshi City	44.26	46.60	85.49	98.10	46.48	46.27	23.72	21.76
利川市	Lichuan City	53.12	55.73	34.94	35.04	57.94	57.30	37.28	33.28
建始县	Jianshi County	31.85	33.33	16.50	18.38	34.27	34.27	23.66	21.09
巴东县	Badong County	29.83	31.42	24.77	24.65	36.32	36.32	22.96	20.55
宣恩县	Xuanen County	25.98	27.25	21.25	24.15	24.80	24.83	13.70	12.15
咸丰县	Xianfeng County	24.38	27.47	26.91	28.88	27.78	28.83	23.61	21.04
来凤县	Laifeng County	20.09	22.04	17.69	17.87	17.01	16.98	13.08	11.55
鹤峰县	Hefeng County	17.88	18.86	38.98	46.14	15.77	16.25	9.38	8.35
仙桃市	Xiantiao City	147.49	149.13	480.40	454.80	90.33	90.33	83.71	72.45
潜江市	Qianjiang City	119.24	124.73	512.53	504.17	72.19	72.64	53.49	47.09
天门市	Tianmen City	129.98	130.66	361.43	377.13	109.93	109.81	75.30	63.35

23-1 续表 8 continued

指标名称	Item	棉花产量(吨) Output of Cotton Cotton (ton)		油料产量(万吨) Output of Oil-bearing Crops(10 000 tons)		肉类产量(万吨) Output of Meat (10 000 tons)	
		2015	2016	2015	2016	2015	2016
蔡甸区	Caidian District	4144	2004	1.54	1.16	1.38	1.44
江夏区	Jiangxia District	160	292	4.05	4.09	8.08	8.24
黄陂区	Huangpi District	2510	2070	6.50	6.45	8.35	8.59
新洲区	Xinzhou District	8233	2713	5.48	5.57	3.24	3.01
汉南区	Hannan District	812	257	0.13	0.10	1.57	1.66
阳新县	Yangxin County	2099	1291	4.85	5.01	4.14	4.09
大冶市	Daye City	1960	1262	4.37	4.50	4.44	4.30
郧阳区	Yun County	48	47	1.90	1.90	5.34	5.29
郧西县	Yunxi County			1.64	1.57	2.58	2.52
竹山县	Zhushan County			4.35	4.70	2.21	2.15
竹溪县	Zhuxi County			2.61	2.64	2.63	2.56
房县	Fang County	32		1.72	1.86	2.85	2.79
丹江口市	Danjiangkou City	27	45	1.07	1.16	2.51	2.45
夷陵区	Yiling District	8	6	3.06	3.09	7.54	7.33
远安县	Yuanan County			1.39	1.43	2.44	2.46
兴山县	Xingshan County			0.84	0.85	2.91	2.77
秭归县	Zigui County			1.42	1.46	5.07	5.06
长阳县	Changyang Tujia A.C.			1.33	1.39	7.60	6.81
五峰县	Wufeng Tujia A.C.			0.52	0.52	2.97	3.03
宜都市	Yidu City	28	28	2.17	2.15	6.72	6.82
当阳市	Dangyang City	4733	3564	7.55	7.42	9.16	8.68
枝江市	Zhijiang City	11400	7083	5.58	5.35	9.12	8.99
襄州区	Xiangzhou District	8270	4714	7.57	9.31	14.53	13.56
南漳县	Nanzhang County	138	92	0.99	1.08	10.48	10.45
谷城县	Gucheng County			1.46	1.48	6.28	5.73
保康县	Baokang County			1.08	1.10	3.06	3.12
老河口市	Laohekou City	4220	2986	2.12	2.09	6.34	6.97
枣阳市	Zaoyang City	5849	3640	1.49	1.68	12.47	11.70
宜城市	Yicheng City	6600	6328	7.28	7.30	8.98	9.14
梁子湖区	Liangzihu District	416	650	1.72	1.73	2.79	2.76
华容区	Huarong District	1891	1390	2.12	2.17	2.79	1.87
鄂城区	Echeng District	1593	2060	2.33	2.16	2.80	4.60
东宝区	Dongbao District	909	531	3.25	2.99	4.58	4.02
京山县	Jingshan County	3690	1878	5.35	4.78	9.49	9.35
沙洋县	Shayang County	3347	1754	13.69	14.27	9.14	8.98

23-1 续表9 continued

指标名称	Item	棉花产量(吨) Output of Cotton Cotton (ton)		油料产量(万吨) Output of Oil-bearing Crops(10 000 tons)		肉类产量(万吨) Output of Meat (10 000 tons)	
		2015	2016	2015	2016	2015	2016
钟祥市	Zhongxiang City	13022	6839	13.21	12.48	10.31	11.22
孝南区	Xiaonan District	3721	2255	3.02	3.18	2.41	2.42
孝昌县	Xiaochang County	1039	810	3.79	3.79	4.58	4.27
大悟县	Dawu County	216	165	5.94	5.90	4.19	3.76
云梦县	Yunmeng County	2018	1484	2.12	2.24	3.56	3.43
应城市	Yingcheng City	2516	1780	3.19	3.10	3.77	3.67
安陆市	Anlu City	750	580	2.02	2.06	8.94	8.40
汉川市	Hanchuan City	13218	7850	3.70	3.17	5.62	5.62
荆州区	Jingzhou District	5292	2350	4.54	3.55	2.82	2.67
江陵县	Jiangling County	5202	3572	7.57	7.27	2.76	2.60
公安县	Gongan County	24509	15355	11.80	10.52	6.09	5.75
监利县	Jianli County	13040	9723	11.94	11.35	8.02	7.82
石首市	Shishou City	11950	8842	7.45	6.05	4.86	4.58
洪湖市	Honghu City	5468	3022	8.58	8.28	3.59	3.39
松滋市	Songci City	7979	6538	7.14	6.88	9.74	9.21
黄州区	Huangzhou District	4508	3588	0.64	0.75	0.70	0.65
团风县	Tuanfeng County	2466	2683	2.37	2.31	1.19	1.14
红安县	Hongan County	818	951	9.73	11.19	5.33	5.76
罗田县	Luotian County	280	211	2.73	2.80	2.74	2.59
英山县	Yingshan County	399	279	1.82	1.87	1.90	1.79
浠水县	Xishui County	6028	6948	8.04	7.89	7.19	6.96
蕲春县	Qichun County	3564	2531	5.78	5.51	7.02	6.91
黄梅县	Huangmei County	6886	4910	6.82	6.64	5.16	4.76
麻城市	Macheng City	5689	4059	10.04	10.08	9.85	9.71
武穴市	Wuxue City	6301	3611	7.69	5.37	7.79	6.16
咸安区	Xian'an District	226	171	4.43	4.44	4.82	4.63
嘉鱼县	Jiayu County	658	500	1.16	1.17	1.55	1.44
通城县	Tongcheng County	282	256	0.56	0.61	5.85	5.66
崇阳县	Chongyang County	532	420	1.20	1.20	5.47	5.36
通山县	Tongshan County			0.55	0.60	1.92	1.86
赤壁市	Chibi City	1087	1100	2.73	2.78	2.40	2.33
曾都区	Zengdu District	1550	1523	0.79	0.90	5.71	5.64
随　县	Sui Country	4050	4405	2.43	2.50	9.31	9.10
广水市	Guangshui City	2356	2522	3.76	3.83	6.43	6.31
恩施市	Enshi City	13	11	1.85	1.86	9.16	8.70
利川市	Lichuan City			1.31	1.37	6.92	6.77
建始县	Jianshi County			1.60	1.63	6.33	6.08
巴东县	Badong County			2.19	2.27	6.85	6.42
宣恩县	Xuanen County			0.56	0.51	5.11	4.93
咸丰县	Xianfeng County			1.76	1.85	5.67	5.11
来凤县	Laifeng County			0.75	0.77	2.55	2.49
鹤峰县	Hofeng County			0.48	0.43	2.16	2.09
仙桃市	Xiantiao City	17567	8002	14.26	12.86	8.54	7.55
潜江市	Qianjiang City	14018	4528	10.22	7.02	8.69	8.93
天门市	Tianmen City	23438	15309	11.73	11.63	8.03	9.07

附录 全国分省主要指标

Major Indicators by Region

附录1-1 分地区行政区划

DIVISONS OF ADMINISTRATIVE AREAS IN CHINA

单位:个 (unit)

省级区划名称	provinces, Autonomous Regions and Municipalities	地级 Number of Regions at Prefecture Level	#地级市 Cities at Prefecture Level	县级 Number of Regions at County Level	#市辖区 Districts under the Jurisdiction of Cities	#县级市 Cities at County Level	#县 Counties	#自治县 Autponomous Counties
全 国	**National Total**	**334**	**293**	**2851**	**954**	**360**	**1366**	**117**
北 京 市	Beijing			16	16			
天 津 市	Tianjin			16	16			
河 北 省	Hebei	11	11	168	47	19	96	6
山 西 省	Shanxi	11	11	119	23	11	85	
内蒙古自治区	Inner Mongolia	12	9	103	23	11	17	
辽 宁 省	Liaoning	14	14	100	59	16	17	8
吉 林 省	Jilin	9	8	60	21	20	16	3
黑龙江省	Heilongjiang	13	12	128	65	19	43	1
上 海 市	Shanghai			16	16			
江 苏 省	Jiangsu	13	13	96	55	21	20	
浙 江 省	Zhejiang	11	11	89	36	19	33	1
安 徽 省	Anhui	16	16	105	44	6	55	
福 建 省	Fujian	9	9	85	28	13	44	
江 西 省	Jiangxi	11	11	100	24	11	65	
山 东 省	Shangdong	17	17	137	54	27	56	
河 南 省	Henan	17	17	158	52	21	85	
湖 北 省	**Hubei**	**13**	**12**	**103**	**39**	**24**	**37**	**2**
湖 南 省	Hunan	14	13	122	35	16	64	7
广 东 省	Guangdong	21	21	121	64	20	34	3
广西壮族自治区	Guangxi	14	14	111	40	7	52	12
海 南 省	Hainan	4	4	23	8	5	4	6
重 庆 市	Chongqing			38	26		8	4
四 川 省	Sichuan	21	18	183	52	16	111	4
贵 州 省	Guizhou	9	6	88	15	7	54	11
云 南 省	Yunnan	16	8	129	16	15	69	29
西藏自治区	Tibet	7	5	74	6		68	
陕 西 省	Shaanxi	10	10	107	29	3	75	
甘 肃 省	Gansu	14	12	86	17	4	58	7
青 海 省	Qinghai	8	2	43	6	3	27	7
宁夏回族自治区	Ningxia	5	5	22	9	2	11	
新疆自治区	Xinjiang	14	4	105	13	24	62	6
香港特别行政区	Hong Kong Special Administrative Region							
澳门特别行政区	Macao Special Administrative Region							
台 湾 省	Taiwan							

注:本部分为国家反馈快报数。

a)Data of this section is from the national feedback letters.

续表 附录1-1 coutinued

单位:个 (unit)

省级区划名称	provinces,Autonomous Regions and Municipalities	乡镇级 Number of Regions at Townships Level	#镇数 towns	#乡数 Towns	#民族乡 National Townships	#街道办事处 Street Communities
全 国	**National Total**	**39862**	**20883**	**10872**	**989**	**8105**
北京市	Beijing	331	143	38	5	150
天津市	Tianjin	245	124	3	1	118
河北省	Hebei	2255	1107	845	49	302
山西省	Shanxi	1398	564	632		202
内蒙古自治区	Inner Mongolia	1014	503	272	18	239
辽宁省	Liaoning	1531	642	212	56	677
吉林省	Jilin	910	428	182	28	300
黑龙江省	Heilongjiang	1197	521	365	52	311
上海市	Shanghai	214	107	2		105
江苏省	Jiangsu	1287	763	69	1	455
浙江省	Zhejiang	1378	655	274	14	449
安徽省	Anhui	1488	953	289	9	246
福建省	Fujian	1105	638	288	19	179
江西省	Jiangxi	1555	824	579	8	152
山东省	Shangdong	1826	1106	73		647
河南省	Henan	2435	1120	682	12	633
湖北省	**Hubei**	**1234**	**759**	**168**	**10**	**307**
湖南省	Hunan	1929	1135	401	83	393
广东省	Guangdong	1600	1128	11	7	461
广西壮族自治区	Guangxi	1246	788	330	59	128
海南省	Hainan	218	175	21		22
重庆市	Chongqing	1028	622	190	14	216
四川省	Sichuan	4633	2105	2182	98	346
贵州省	Guizhou	1379	832	326	193	221
云南省	Yunnan	1389	681	545	140	163
西藏自治区	Tibet	697	140	545	9	12
陕西省	Shaanxi	1295	988	23		284
甘肃省	Gansu	1352	741	487	34	124
青海省	Qinghai	399	140	225	28	34
宁夏回族自治区	Ningxia	237	102	90		45
新疆自治区	Xinjiang	1057	349	523	42	184
香港特别行政区	Hong Kong Special Administrative Region					
澳门特别行政区	Macao Special Administrative Region					
台湾省	Taiwan					

注:乡镇级总数包含河北省、新疆维吾尔族自治区的各一个区公所。

a)Number of regions at townships level include one district office of Hebei and Xinjiang separately.

附录1-2 分地区按三次产业分法人单位数(2015)

REGIONS BY THE NUMBER OF UNITS THREE INDUSTRIES CORPORATE UNITS(2015)

单位:个 (unit)

地区	Region	法人单位数 Corporate Units	第一产业 Primary Industry	第二产业 Secondary Industry	第三产业 Tertiary Industry
全 国	**National Total**	**15729199**	**1005230**	**3544975**	**11178994**
北 京	Beijing	704629	9026	54574	641029
天 津	Tianjin	320203	7189	69642	243372
河 北	Hebei	630137	46867	158127	425143
山 西	Shanxi	382169	72135	48137	261897
内蒙古	Inner Mongolia	231915	28738	32509	170668
辽 宁	Liaoning	552428	21438	131216	399774
吉 林	Jilin	181344	13469	35804	132071
黑龙江	Heilongjiang	225311	21844	38344	165123
上 海	Shanghai	448591	6364	98622	343605
江 苏	Jiangsu	1551446	28699	513278	1009469
浙 江	Zhejiang	1346362	59534	465537	821291
安 徽	Anhui	564967	51418	124592	388957
福 建	Fujian	664420	37796	164644	461980
江 西	Jiangxi	385517	35623	83082	266812
山 东	Shangdong	1269898	52579	299597	917722
河 南	Henan	763210	45044	158960	559206
湖 北	**Hubei**	**678384**	**47658**	**122743**	**507983**
湖 南	Hunan	467954	25373	86309	356272
广 东	Guangdong	1397022	27876	414032	955114
广 西	Guangxi	402587	56320	48303	297964
海 南	Hainan	76095	10167	9312	56616
重 庆	Chongqing	454877	76130	72358	306389
四 川	Sichuan	490038	35213	81407	373418
贵 州	Guizhou	265382	44992	51081	169309
云 南	Yunnan	372760	54454	47273	271033
西 藏	Tibet	26512	570	3745	22197
陕 西	Shaanxi	358073	26498	62615	268960
甘 肃	Gansu	196182	30093	25018	141071
青 海	Qinghai	58654	10705	8282	39667
宁 夏	Ningxia	65679	8796	9604	47279
新 疆	Xinjiang	196453	12622	26228	157603

附录1-3 分地区按行业分法人单位数(2015)
REGION NUMBER OF CORPORATE UNITS BY SECTOR(2015)

单位:个 (unit)

地 区	Region	法人单位数 Corporate Units	#农、林、牧、渔业 Agriculture, Forestry, Animal husbandry, Fishery	#采矿业 Mining Industry	#制造业 Manufacturing	#电力、热力、燃气及水的生产和供应业 Electricity, Gas and Water Production and Supply	#建筑业 Construction	批发和零售业 Wholesale and Retail Trades
全国总计	**National Total**	**15729199**	**1204724**	**103426**	**2801143**	**87486**	**574128**	**4199026**
北 京	Beijing	704629	9551	124	34144	659	20087	206521
天 津	Tianjin	320203	7908	142	54114	655	15517	98551
河 北	Hebei	630137	58834	6547	126557	2747	23139	165475
山 西	Shanxi	382169	78524	6410	27601	2183	12500	94250
内蒙古	Inner Mongolia	231915	37307	5186	18575	2325	6801	55958
辽 宁	Liaoning	552428	32287	6117	97001	2419	27161	155775
吉 林	Jilin	181344	21479	1477	26010	1551	6992	40125
黑龙江	Heilongjiang	225311	32838	2064	27666	1626	7402	49972
上 海	Shanghai	448591	6737	1	82529	191	16781	153401
江 苏	Jiangsu	1551446	44605	759	434394	3389	76873	466828
浙 江	Zhejiang	1346362	64569	1339	423211	4856	37693	374162
安 徽	Anhui	564967	67845	2616	92414	3183	27029	136555
福 建	Fujian	664420	41418	3241	132615	7073	22420	193733
江 西	Jiangxi	385517	40974	4168	60422	4532	14359	80263
山 东	Shangdong	1269898	69181	3726	235765	3734	58283	403965
河 南	Henan	763210	57527	6487	127691	2892	22488	172392
湖 北	**Hubei**	**678384**	**57476**	**4740**	**83366**	**3968**	**31367**	**183287**
湖 南	Hunan	467954	35753	6836	62180	5419	12226	97477
广 东	Guangdong	1397022	37250	3979	365811	10013	36124	391401
广 西	Guangxi	402587	61108	3443	31491	2885	10729	106962
海 南	Hainan	76095	11045	350	3450	422	5151	15881
重 庆	Chongqing	454877	80942	2654	55432	2294	12375	125316
四 川	Sichuan	490038	40698	4959	57055	6135	13673	80348
贵 州	Guizhou	265382	46519	7361	33898	2125	7913	47828
云 南	Yunnan	372760	59970	6690	23311	2882	14632	99551
西 藏	Tibet	26512	617	230	1178	164	2201	2471
陕 西	Shaanxi	358073	29688	4663	38398	2493	18887	87319
甘 肃	Gansu	196182	32849	2308	16692	1774	4529	36704
青 海	Qinghai	58654	11249	1001	4575	621	2143	9654
宁 夏	Ningxia	65679	10336	779	6510	500	1889	16248
新 疆	Xinjiang	196453	17640	3029	17087	1776	4764	50653

附录1–3　续表1 continued

单位:个 (unit)

地区	Region	*交通运输、仓储和邮政业 Traffic, Transport, Storage and Postal Industry	*住宿和餐饮业 Accommodation and Catering Services	*信息传输、软件和信息技术服务业 Information Transmission, Software and Computer Services	金融业 Financial Intermediation	*房地产业 Real Estate	*租赁和商务服务业 Leasing and Business Services
全国总计	**National Total**	**378705**	**274283**	**387842**	**109711**	**466100**	**1440572**
北　京	Beijing	14754	17141	47988	5117	18833	150385
天　津	Tianjin	15560	4658	12589	4218	8472	36907
河　北	Hebei	14280	6000	8114	4687	18376	40060
山　西	Shanxi	8635	5056	5915	2375	9678	24183
内蒙古	Inner Mongolia	6403	3428	3208	2488	7150	16216
辽　宁	Liaoning	16442	8333	14937	4078	19375	48462
吉　林	Jilin	4643	2109	3214	1524	5623	11703
黑龙江	Heilongjiang	5782	2661	4164	2215	7108	14050
上　海	Shanghai	15963	13238	15863	2258	16553	59133
江　苏	Jiangsu	40424	16420	41381	6908	40553	142838
浙　江	Zhejiang	22591	19122	36445	8005	29342	120967
安　徽	Anhui	15307	9009	13734	4478	17223	52265
福　建	Fujian	15702	10556	16932	4432	16047	62383
江　西	Jiangxi	12533	4920	6905	3467	10783	33561
山　东	Shangdong	33779	17774	25610	6952	32596	101010
河　南	Henan	14402	14547	11964	4159	22377	45465
湖　北	**Hubei**	**18409**	**13308**	**19146**	**4114**	**22570**	**68232**
湖　南	Hunan	7907	9786	8401	2996	13880	30928
广　东	Guangdong	35068	24390	38168	9547	54716	165240
广　西	Guangxi	8512	5172	6486	2972	13475	35285
海　南	Hainan	1631	1908	1541	562	6642	8321
重　庆	Chongqing	7840	21802	11706	3478	12134	36399
四　川	Sichuan	10788	10241	7850	3338	14505	33398
贵　州	Guizhou	4392	8149	3042	2163	8751	17043
云　南	Yunnan	6720	8134	9055	3516	10950	31253
西　藏	Tibet	335	602	175	106	229	1160
陕　西	Shaanxi	7908	8371	7021	2810	12816	21989
甘　肃	Gansu	3361	3544	1756	2221	4978	9350
青　海	Qinghai	1033	1179	767	414	1634	3685
宁　夏	Ningxia	1455	979	869	1798	1707	4206
新　疆	Xinjiang	6146	1746	2896	2315	7024	14495

附录1-3 续表2 continued

单位:个 (unit)

地区	Region	#科学研究和技术服务 Research and Technical Service	#水利、环境和公共设施管理业 Water, Environment and Public Facilities Management	#居民服务、修理和其他服务业 Resident Services、Repair and Other Services	#教育 Education	#卫生和社会工作 Health and Social Work	#文化、体育和娱乐业 Culture, Sports and Entertainment	#公共管理、社会保障和社会组织 Public Management、Social Security and Social Organization
全国总计	**National Total**	**661022**	**108069**	**298958**	**461451**	**271571**	**297274**	**1603708**
北京	Beijing	92262	4170	19774	11339	4002	30574	17204
天津	Tianjin	28149	1904	9070	4307	1758	4821	10903
河北	Hebei	19522	4269	10454	20754	9919	8614	81789
山西	Shanxi	9640	3072	9963	10826	5760	7360	58238
内蒙古	Inner Mongolia	6910	2502	4661	7189	5063	3722	36823
辽宁	Liaoning	23503	4430	10606	14632	12871	9416	44583
吉林	Jilin	6006	1675	3622	6392	3923	3186	30090
黑龙江	Heilongjiang	8349	1860	3199	8067	5866	4464	35958
上海	Shanghai	21533	2068	12568	5945	3325	7315	13189
江苏	Jiangsu	65696	9159	26282	21802	17487	20741	74907
浙江	Zhejiang	43731	7155	17458	23549	8873	21070	82224
安徽	Anhui	20225	4301	10042	16224	9301	13372	49844
福建	Fujian	21860	4419	11346	16785	8362	11493	63603
江西	Jiangxi	9574	3018	7082	14760	10167	6586	57443
山东	Shangdong	59213	6534	22923	25908	18964	15590	128391
河南	Henan	36961	6094	11089	44940	38881	17609	105245
湖北	**Hubei**	**30688**	**6110**	**15665**	**20637**	**12415**	**12279**	**70607**
湖南	Hunan	16851	4441	10065	21891	16082	14899	89936
广东	Guangdong	46376	7237	23892	40628	11399	18220	77563
广西	Guangxi	15433	3496	6487	21541	6059	7962	53089
海南	Hainan	2342	568	1381	3653	1194	1798	8255
重庆	Chongqing	10497	2552	12848	11938	5972	9173	29525
四川	Sichuan	19315	4290	7714	26097	18357	15893	115384
贵州	Guizhou	5710	1904	6403	12180	4955	4616	40430
云南	Yunnan	12532	2965	9186	10956	5575	7768	47114
西藏	Tibet	539	82	210	1042	457	512	14202
陕西	Shaanxi	12392	3668	6999	16022	14703	7052	54874
甘肃	Gansu	4874	1507	2723	10503	4241	4818	47450
青海	Qinghai	1775	595	947	1929	1155	1183	13115
宁夏	Ningxia	1529	494	1131	1900	955	1268	11126
新疆	Xinjiang	7035	1530	3168	7115	3530	3900	40604

附录1-4 分地区年末常住人口
POPULATION AT YEAR-END BY REGIONS

单位：万人 (10 000 persons)

地 区	Region	2010	2011	2012	2013	2014	2015	2016
全 国	**National Total**	**134091**	**134735**	**135404**	**136072**	**136782**	**137462**	**138271**
北 京	Beijing	1962	2019	2069	2115	2152	2171	2173
天 津	Tianjin	1299	1355	1413	1472	1517	1547	1562
河 北	Hebei	7194	7241	7288	7333	7384	7425	7470
山 西	Shanxi	3574	3593	3611	3630	3648	3664	3682
内蒙古	Inner Mongolia	2472	2482	2490	2498	2505	2511	2520
辽 宁	Liaoning	4375	4383	4389	4390	4391	4382	4378
吉 林	Jilin	2747	2749	2750	2751	2752	2753	2733
黑龙江	Heilongjiang	3833	3834	3834	3835	3833	3812	3799
上 海	Shanghai	2303	2347	2380	2415	2426	2415	2420
江 苏	Jiangsu	7869	7899	7920	7939	7960	7976	7999
浙 江	Zhejiang	5447	5463	5477	5498	5508	5539	5590
安 徽	Anhui	5957	5968	5988	6030	6083	6144	6196
福 建	Fujian	3693	3720	3748	3774	3806	3839	3874
江 西	Jiangxi	4462	4488	4504	4522	4542	4566	4592
山 东	Shangdong	9588	9637	9685	9733	9789	9847	9947
河 南	Henan	9405	9388	9406	9413	9436	9480	9532
湖 北	**Hubei**	**5728**	**5758**	**5779**	**5799**	**5816**	**5852**	**5885**
湖 南	Hunan	6570	6596	6639	6691	6737	6783	6822
广 东	Guangdong	10441	10505	10594	10644	10724	10849	10999
广 西	Guangxi	4610	4645	4682	4719	4754	4796	4838
海 南	Hainan	869	877	887	895	903	911	917
重 庆	Chongqing	2885	2919	2945	2970	2991	3017	3048
四 川	Sichuan	8045	8050	8076	8107	8140	8204	8262
贵 州	Guizhou	3479	3469	3484	3502	3508	3530	3555
云 南	Yunnan	4602	4631	4659	4687	4714	4742	4771
西 藏	Tibet	300	303	308	312	318	324	331
陕 西	Shaanxi	3735	3743	3753	3764	3775	3793	3813
甘 肃	Gansu	2560	2564	2578	2582	2591	2600	2610
青 海	Qinghai	563	568	573	578	583	588	593
宁 夏	Ningxia	633	639	647	654	662	668	675
新 疆	Xinjiang	2185	2209	2233	2264	2298	2360	2398

注：1.全国数据包括中国人民解放军现役军人数，但不包括香港、澳门特别行政区和台湾省数据；分省数据中未包括中国人民解放军现役军人数。
2.2010年数据为第六次全国人口普查初步汇总数。

Notes:a)The number of national data including military personnel, but not including Hong Kong and Macao Special Administrative Region and Taiwan Province; provincial data does not include active duty PLA.
b)2010 years of data for the sixth national census preliminary summary number.

附录1-5 分地区年末城镇人口比重
PROPORTION OF URBAN POPULATIONS AT YEAR-END BY REGION

单位:% (%)

地区	Region	2008	2009	2010	2011	2012	2013	2014	2015	2016
全 国	**National Total**	**46.99**	**48.34**	**49.95**	**51.27**	**52.57**	**53.73**	**54.77**	**56.10**	**57.35**
北 京	Beijing	84.90	85.00	85.96	86.20	86.20	86.30	86.35	86.50	86.50
天 津	Tianjin	77.23	78.01	79.55	80.50	81.55	82.01	82.27	82.64	82.93
河 北	Hebei	41.90	43.74	44.50	45.60	46.80	48.12	49.33	51.33	53.32
山 西	Shanxi	45.11	45.99	48.05	49.68	51.26	52.56	53.79	55.03	56.21
内蒙古	Inner Mongolia	51.71	53.40	55.50	56.62	57.74	58.71	59.51	60.30	61.19
辽 宁	Liaoning	60.05	60.35	62.10	64.05	65.65	66.45	67.05	67.35	67.37
吉 林	Jilin	53.21	53.32	53.35	53.40	53.70	54.20	54.81	55.31	55.97
黑龙江	Heilongjiang	55.40	55.50	55.66	56.50	56.90	57.40	58.01	58.80	59.20
上 海	Shanghai	88.60	88.60	89.30	89.30	89.30	89.60	89.60	87.60	87.90
江 苏	Jiangsu	54.30	55.60	60.58	61.90	63.00	64.11	65.21	66.52	67.72
浙 江	Zhejiang	57.60	57.90	61.62	62.30	63.20	64.00	64.87	65.80	67.00
安 徽	Anhui	40.50	42.10	43.01	44.80	46.50	47.86	49.15	50.50	51.99
福 建	Fujian	53.00	55.10	57.10	58.10	59.60	60.77	61.80	62.60	63.60
江 西	Jiangxi	41.36	43.18	44.06	45.70	47.51	48.87	50.22	51.62	53.10
山 东	Shangdong	47.60	48.32	49.70	50.95	52.43	53.75	55.01	57.01	59.02
河 南	Henan	36.03	37.70	38.50	40.57	42.43	43.80	45.20	46.85	48.50
湖 北	**Hubei**	**45.20**	**46.00**	**49.70**	**51.83**	**53.50**	**54.51**	**55.67**	**56.85**	**58.10**
湖 南	Hunan	42.15	43.20	43.30	45.10	46.65	47.96	49.28	50.89	52.75
广 东	Guangdong	63.37	63.40	66.18	66.50	67.40	67.76	68.00	68.71	69.20
广 西	Guangxi	38.16	39.20	40.00	41.80	43.53	44.81	46.01	47.06	48.08
海 南	Hainan	48.00	49.13	49.80	50.50	51.60	52.74	53.76	55.12	56.78
重 庆	Chongqing	49.99	51.59	53.02	55.02	56.98	58.34	59.60	60.94	62.60
四 川	Sichuan	37.40	38.70	40.18	41.83	43.53	44.90	46.30	47.69	49.21
贵 州	Guizhou	29.11	29.89	33.81	34.96	36.41	37.83	40.01	42.01	44.15
云 南	Yunnan	33.00	34.00	34.70	36.80	39.31	40.48	41.73	43.33	45.03
西 藏	Tibet	21.90	22.30	22.67	22.71	22.75	23.71	25.75	27.74	29.56
陕 西	Shaanxi	42.10	43.50	45.76	47.30	50.02	51.31	52.57	53.92	55.34
甘 肃	Gansu	33.56	34.89	36.12	37.15	38.75	40.13	41.68	43.19	44.69
青 海	Qinghai	40.86	41.90	44.72	46.22	47.44	48.51	49.78	50.30	51.63
宁 夏	Ningxia	44.98	46.10	47.90	49.82	50.67	52.01	53.61	55.23	56.29
新 疆	Xinjiang	39.64	39.85	43.01	43.54	43.98	44.47	46.07	47.23	48.35

注:2010年数据为当年人口普查数据推算数;其余年份数据根据年度人口抽样调查推算。
Note:Data of 2010 are the census yesr estimates; the rest are the estimates from the annual national sample surver of population.

附录1-6　地区生产总值
GROSS DOMESTIC PRODUCT

单位:亿元　　(100 million yuan)

地 区	Region	2010	2011	2012	2013	2014	2015	2016
北 京	Beijing	14113.6	16251.9	17879.4	19800.8	21330.8	23014.6	24899.3
天 津	Tianjin	9224.5	11307.3	12893.9	14442.0	15726.9	16538.2	17885.4
河 北	Hebei	20394.3	24515.8	26575.0	28443.0	29421.2	29806.1	31827.9
山 西	Shanxi	9200.9	11237.6	12112.8	12665.3	12761.5	12766.5	12928.3
内蒙古	Inner Mongolia	11672.0	14359.9	15880.6	16916.5	17770.2	17831.5	18632.6
辽 宁	Liaoning	18457.3	22226.7	24846.4	27213.2	28626.6	28669.0	22037.9
吉 林	Jilin	8667.6	10568.8	11939.2	13046.4	13803.1	14063.1	14886.2
黑龙江	Heilongjiang	10368.6	12582.0	13691.6	14454.9	15039.4	15083.7	15386.1
上 海	Shanghai	17166.0	19195.7	20181.7	21818.2	23567.7	25123.5	27466.2
江 苏	Jiangsu	41425.5	49110.3	54058.2	59753.4	65088.3	70116.4	76086.2
浙 江	Zhejiang	27722.3	32318.9	34665.3	37756.6	40173.0	42886.5	46485.0
安 徽	Anhui	12359.3	15300.7	17212.1	19229.3	20848.7	22005.6	24117.9
福 建	Fujian	14737.1	17560.2	19701.8	21868.5	24055.8	25979.8	28519.2
江 西	Jiangxi	9451.3	11702.8	12948.9	14410.2	15714.6	16723.8	18364.4
山 东	Shangdong	39169.9	45361.9	50013.2	55230.3	59426.6	63002.3	67008.2
河 南	Henan	23092.4	26931.0	29599.3	32191.3	34938.2	37002.2	40160.0
湖 北	**Hubei**	**15967.6**	**19632.3**	**22250.5**	**24791.8**	**27379.2**	**29550.2**	**32297.9**
湖 南	Hunan	16038.0	19669.6	22154.2	24621.7	27037.3	28902.2	31244.7
广 东	Guangdong	46013.1	53210.3	57067.9	62474.8	67809.9	72812.6	79512.1
广 西	Guangxi	9569.9	11720.9	13035.1	14449.9	15672.9	16803.1	18245.1
海 南	Hainan	2064.5	2522.7	2855.5	3177.6	3500.7	3702.8	4044.5
重 庆	Chongqing	7925.6	10011.4	11409.6	12783.3	14262.6	15717.3	17558.8
四 川	Sichuan	17185.5	21026.7	23872.8	26392.1	28536.7	30053.1	32680.5
贵 州	Guizhou	4602.2	5701.8	6852.2	8086.9	9266.4	10502.6	11734.4
云 南	Yunnan	7224.2	8893.1	10309.5	11832.3	12814.6	13619.2	14870.0
西 藏	Tibet	507.5	605.8	701.0	815.7	920.8	1026.4	1150.1
陕 西	Shaanxi	10123.5	12512.3	14453.7	16205.5	17689.9	18021.9	19165.4
甘 肃	Gansu	4120.8	5020.4	5650.2	6330.7	6836.8	6790.3	7152.0
青 海	Qinghai	1350.4	1670.4	1893.5	2122.1	2303.3	2417.1	2572.5
宁 夏	Ningxia	1689.7	2102.2	2341.3	2577.6	2752.1	2911.8	3150.1
新 疆	Xinjiang	5437.5	6610.1	7505.3	8443.8	9273.5	9324.8	9617.2

注:本表按当年价格计算。本表数据为国家统计局最终核实数。
Note:The table at current prices.National Bureau of Statistics data for this table is to verify the final number.

附录1-7 地区生产总值指数
INDICES OF GROSS DOMESTIC PRODUCT

(上年=100) (last year=100)

地 区	Region	2010	2011	2012	2013	2014	2015	2016
北 京	Beijing	110.3	108.1	107.7	107.7	107.3	106.9	106.7
天 津	Tianjin	117.4	116.4	113.8	112.5	110.0	109.3	109.0
河 北	Hebei	112.2	111.3	109.6	108.2	106.5	106.8	106.8
山 西	Shanxi	113.9	113.0	110.1	108.9	104.9	103.1	104.5
内蒙古	Inner Mongolia	115.0	114.3	111.5	109.0	107.8	107.7	107.2
辽 宁	Liaoning	114.2	112.2	109.5	108.7	105.8	103.0	97.5
吉 林	Jilin	113.8	113.8	112.0	108.3	106.5	106.3	106.9
黑龙江	Heilongjiang	112.7	112.3	110.0	108.0	105.6	105.7	106.1
上 海	Shanghai	110.3	108.2	107.5	107.7	107.0	106.9	106.8
江 苏	Jiangsu	112.7	111.0	110.1	109.6	108.7	108.5	107.8
浙 江	Zhejiang	111.9	109.0	108.0	108.2	107.6	108.0	107.5
安 徽	Anhui	114.6	113.5	112.1	110.4	109.2	108.7	108.7
福 建	Fujian	113.9	112.3	111.4	111.0	109.9	109.0	108.4
江 西	Jiangxi	114.0	112.5	111.0	110.1	109.7	109.1	109.0
山 东	Shangdong	112.3	110.9	109.8	109.6	108.7	108.0	107.6
河 南	Henan	112.5	111.9	110.1	109.0	108.9	108.3	108.1
湖 北	**Hubei**	**114.8**	**113.8**	**111.3**	**110.1**	**109.7**	**108.9**	**108.1**
湖 南	Hunan	114.6	112.8	111.3	110.1	109.5	108.5	107.9
广 东	Guangdong	112.4	110.0	108.2	108.5	107.8	108.0	107.5
广 西	Guangxi	114.2	112.3	111.3	110.2	108.5	108.1	107.3
海 南	Hainan	116.0	112.0	109.1	109.9	108.5	107.8	107.5
重 庆	Chongqing	117.1	116.4	113.6	112.3	110.9	111.0	110.7
四 川	Sichuan	115.1	115.0	112.6	110.0	108.5	107.9	107.7
贵 州	Guizhou	112.8	115.0	113.6	112.5	110.8	110.7	110.5
云 南	Yunnan	112.3	113.7	113.0	112.1	108.1	108.7	108.7
西 藏	Tibet	112.3	112.7	111.8	112.1	110.8	111.0	110.0
陕 西	Shaanxi	114.6	113.9	112.9	111.0	109.7	107.9	107.6
甘 肃	Gansu	111.8	112.5	112.6	110.8	108.9	108.1	107.6
青 海	Qinghai	115.3	113.5	112.3	110.8	109.2	108.2	108.0
宁 夏	Ningxia	113.5	112.1	111.5	109.8	108.0	108.0	108.1
新 疆	Xinjiang	110.6	112.0	112.0	111.0	110.0	108.8	107.6

注：本表按不变价格计算。本表数据为国家统计局最终核实数。

Note:At constant prices, this table.National Bureau of Statistics data for this table is to verify the final number.

附录1-8 人均地区生产总值
PER CAPITA GROSS DOMESTIC PRODUCT

单位:元　　本表按当年价格计算(At current price)

地 区	Region	2010	2011	2012	2013	2014	2015	2016
北 京	Beijing	73856	81658	87475	94648	99995	106497	114653
天 津	Tianjin	72994	85213	93173	100105	105231	107960	115053
河 北	Hebei	28668	33969	36584	38909	39984	40255	42736
山 西	Shanxi	26283	31357	33628	34984	35070	34919	35198
内蒙古	Inner Mongolia	47347	57974	63886	67836	71046	71101	74069
辽 宁	Liaoning	42355	50760	56649	61996	65201	65354	50314
吉 林	Jilin	31599	38460	43415	47428	50160	51086	54266
黑龙江	Heilongjiang	27076	32819	35711	37697	39226	39462	40432
上 海	Shanghai	76074	82560	85373	90993	97370	103796	113615
江 苏	Jiangsu	52840	62290	68347	75354	81874	87995	95257
浙 江	Zhejiang	51711	59249	63374	68805	73002	77644	83538
安 徽	Anhui	20888	25659	28792	32001	34425	35997	39092
福 建	Fujian	40025	47377	52763	58145	63472	67966	73951
江 西	Jiangxi	21253	26150	28800	31930	34674	36724	40106
山 东	Shangdong	41106	47335	51768	56885	60879	64168	67706
河 南	Henan	24446	28661	31499	34211	37072	39131	42247
湖 北	**Hubei**	**27906**	**34197**	**38572**	**42826**	**47145**	**50654**	**55038**
湖 南	Hunan	24719	29880	33480	36943	40271	42754	45931
广 东	Guangdong	44736	50807	54095	58833	63469	67503	72787
广 西	Guangxi	20219	25326	27952	30741	33090	35190	37876
海 南	Hainan	23831	28898	32377	35663	38924	40818	44252
重 庆	Chongqing	27596	34500	38914	43223	47850	52321	57902
四 川	Sichuan	21182	26133	29608	32617	35128	36775	39695
贵 州	Guizhou	13119	16413	19710	23151	26437	29847	33127
云 南	Yunnan	15752	19265	22195	25322	27264	28806	31265
西 藏	Tibet	17027	20077	22936	26326	29252	31999	35143
陕 西	Shaanxi	27133	33464	38564	43117	46929	47626	50398
甘 肃	Gansu	16113	19595	21978	24539	26433	26165	27458
青 海	Qinghai	24115	29522	33181	36875	39671	41252	43531
宁 夏	Ningxia	26860	33043	36394	39613	41834	43805	46918
新 疆	Xinjiang	25034	30087	33796	37553	40648	40036	40427

附录1-9　人均地区生产总值指数
PER CAPITA GROSS REGIONAL PRODUCT INDICES

(上年=100)　　(preceding year=100)

地 区	Region	2010	2011	2012	2013	2014	2015	2016
北 京	Beijing	104.8	103.8	104.9	105.2	105.2	105.5	106.2
天 津	Tianjin	111.7	110.9	109.2	108.0	106.2	106.6	107.4
河 北	Hebei	110.6	109.7	108.9	107.5	105.8	106.1	106.1
山 西	Shanxi	111.2	110.4	109.6	108.4	104.4	102.6	104.0
内蒙古	Inner Mongolia	114.4	113.8	111.1	108..7	107.5	107.4	106.8
辽 宁	Liaoning	113.4	111.7	109.3	108.6	105.7	103.1	97.6
吉 林	Jilin	113.6	113.5	111.9	108.3	106.4	106.3	107.3
黑龙江	Heilongjiang	112.6	112.2	110.1	107.9	105.6	106.0	106.5
上 海	Shanghai	106.4	105.0	105.7	106.2	106.0	106.9	106.9
江 苏	Jiangsu	112.0	110.3	109.8	109.3	108.4	108.3	107.5
浙 江	Zhejiang	109.5	107.2	107.7	107.9	107.3	107.6	106.7
安 徽	Anhui	118.8	112.6	111.8	109.9	108.4	107.7	107.7
福 建	Fujian	113.2	111.6	110.5	110.2	109.1	108.0	107.5
江 西	Jiangxi	113.2	111.8	110.4	109.6	109.2	108.5	108.4
山 东	Shangdong	111.3	109.9	109.2	109.0	108.1	107.3	106.7
河 南	Henan	112.6	112.5	110.1	108.9	108.7	107.9	107.5
湖 北	**Hubei**	**114.7**	**113.5**	**110.7**	**109.7**	**109.3**	**108.4**	**107.5**
湖 南	Hunan	112.9	111.2	110.7	109.3	108.7	107.8	107.3
广 东	Guangdong	109.5	108.0	107.4	107.8	107.1	107.0	106.2
广 西	Guangxi	113.9	112.0	110.4	109.4	107.7	107.2	106.3
海 南	Hainan	115.0	111.1	108.0	108.7	107.5	106.9	106.7
重 庆	Chongqing	116.2	115.1	112.4	111.3	110.0	110.1	109.6
四 川	Sichuan	113.7	113.9	112.3	109.6	108.1	107.2	107.0
贵 州	Guizhou	114.7	116.1	113.5	111.9	110.4	110.3	109.8
云 南	Yunnan	111.6	112.9	112.3	111.5	107.5	108.0	108.0
西 藏	Tibet	110.8	111.3	110.4	110.5	109.1	108.9	107.8
陕 西	Shaanxi	114.4	113.7	112.6	110.7	109.4	107.5	107.0
甘 肃	Gansu	111.6	112.3	112.2	110.4	108.6	107.7	107.2
青 海	Qinghai	114.5	112.3	111.3	109.9	108.2	107.2	107.1
宁 夏	Ningxia	112.2	110.8	110.3	108.6	106.8	106.9	107.0
新 疆	Xinjiang	109.3	110.7	110.8	109.6	108.4	106.6	105.3

附录1-10 按三次产业分地区生产总值

GROSS REGIONAL PRODUNCT BY THREE STRATA OF INDUSTRY

单位:亿元 (100 million yuan)

地 区	Region	地区生产总值 Gross Regional Product	第一产业 Rrimary Industry	第二产业 Secondary Industry	第三产业 Tertiary Industry
北 京	Beijing	24899.3	129.6	4774.4	19995.3
天 津	Tianjin	17885.4	220.2	8003.9	9661.3
河 北	Hebei	31827.9	3492.8	15058.5	13276.5
山 西	Shanxi	12928.3	784.6	4926.4	7217.4
内蒙古	Inner Mongolia	18632.6	1628.7	9078.9	7925.1
辽 宁	Liaoning	22037.9	2173.0	8504.8	11360.0
吉 林	Jilin	14886.2	1498.5	7147.2	6240.5
黑龙江	Heilongjiang	15386.1	2670.5	4441.4	8274.3
上 海	Shanghai	27466.2	109.5	7994.3	19362.3
江 苏	Jiangsu	76086.2	4078.5	33855.7	38152.0
浙 江	Zhejiang	46485.0	1966.5	20517.8	24000.6
安 徽	Anhui	24117.9	2567.7	11666.6	9883.6
福 建	Fujian	28519.2	2364.1	13912.7	12242.3
江 西	Jiangxi	18364.4	1904.5	9032.1	7427.8
山 东	Shangdong	67008.2	4929.1	30410.0	31669.0
河 南	Henan	40160.0	4286.3	19055.4	16818.3
湖 北	**Hubei**	**32297.9**	**3499.3**	**14375.1**	**14423.5**
湖 南	Hunan	31244.7	3578.4	13181.0	14485.3
广 东	Guangdong	79512.1	3693.6	34372.5	41446.0
广 西	Guangxi	18245.1	2798.6	8219.9	7226.6
海 南	Hainan	4044.5	970.9	901.7	2171.9
重 庆	Chongqing	17558.8	1303.2	7755.2	8500.4
四 川	Sichuan	32680.5	3924.1	13924.7	14831.7
贵 州	Guizhou	11734.4	1846.5	4636.7	5251.2
云 南	Yunnan	14870.0	2195.0	5799.3	6875.6
西 藏	Tibet	1150.1	105.0	429.9	615.2
陕 西	Shaanxi	19165.4	1693.8	9390.9	8080.7
甘 肃	Gansu	7152.0	973.5	2491.5	3687.0
青 海	Qinghai	2572.5	221.2	1250.0	1101.3
宁 夏	Ningxia	3150.1	240.0	1475.5	1434.6
新 疆	Xinjiang	9617.2	1649.0	3585.2	4383.0

附录1-11 分地区居民消费价格指数
CONSUMER PRICE INDEX BY REGION

(上年=100) (Previous Year = 100)

地 区	Region	2010	2011	2012	2013	2014	2015	2016
全 国	**National Total**	103.3	105.4	102.6	102.6	102.0	101.4	102.0
北 京	Beijing	102.4	105.6	103.3	103.3	101.6	101.8	101.4
天 津	Tianjin	103.5	104.9	102.7	103.1	101.9	101.7	102.1
河 北	Hebei	103.1	105.7	102.6	103.0	101.7	100.9	101.5
山 西	Shanxi	103.0	105.2	102.5	103.1	101.7	100.6	101.1
内蒙古	Inner Mongolia	103.2	105.6	103.1	103.2	101.6	101.1	101.2
辽 宁	Liaoning	103.0	105.2	102.8	102.4	101.7	101.4	101.6
吉 林	Jilin	103.7	105.2	102.5	102.9	102.0	101.7	101.6
黑龙江	Heilongjiang	103.9	105.8	103.2	102.2	101.5	101.1	101.5
上 海	Shanghai	103.1	105.2	102.8	102.3	102.7	102.4	103.2
江 苏	Jiangsu	103.8	105.3	102.6	102.3	102.2	101.7	102.3
浙 江	Zhejiang	103.8	105.4	102.2	102.3	102.1	101.4	101.9
安 徽	Anhui	103.1	105.6	102.3	102.4	101.6	101.3	101.8
福 建	Fujian	103.2	105.3	102.4	102.5	102.0	101.7	101.7
江 西	Jiangxi	103.0	105.2	102.7	102.5	102.3	101.5	102.0
山 东	Shangdong	102.9	105.0	102.1	102.2	101.9	101.2	102.1
河 南	Henan	103.5	105.6	102.5	102.9	101.9	101.3	101.9
湖 北	**Hubei**	**102.9**	**105.8**	**102.9**	**102.8**	**102.0**	**101.5**	**102.2**
湖 南	Hunan	103.1	105.5	102.0	102.5	101.9	101.4	101.9
广 东	Guangdong	103.1	105.3	102.8	102.5	102.3	101.5	102.3
广 西	Guangxi	103.0	105.9	103.2	102.2	102.1	101.5	101.6
海 南	Hainan	104.8	106.1	103.2	102.8	102.4	101.0	102.8
重 庆	Chongqing	103.2	105.3	102.6	102.7	101.8	101.3	101.8
四 川	Sichuan	103.2	105.3	102.5	102.8	101.6	101.5	101.9
贵 州	Guizhou	102.9	105.1	102.7	102.5	102.4	101.8	101.4
云 南	Yunnan	103.7	104.9	102.7	103.1	102.4	101.9	101.5
西 藏	Tibet	102.2	105.0	103.5	103.6	102.9	102.0	102.5
陕 西	Shaanxi	104.0	105.7	102.8	103.0	101.6	101.0	101.3
甘 肃	Gansu	104.1	105.9	102.7	103.2	102.1	101.6	101.3
青 海	Qinghai	105.4	106.1	103.1	103.9	102.8	102.6	101.8
宁 夏	Ningxia	104.1	106.3	102.0	103.4	101.9	101.1	101.5
新 疆	Xinjiang	104.3	105.9	103.8	103.9	102.1	100.6	101.4

附录1-12 分地区全体居民人均收入与支出
REGIONAL PER CAPITA INCOME AND CONSUMPTION EXPENDITURE OF URBAN AND RURAL HOUSEHOLDS

单位：元 (yuan)

地 区	Region	可支配收入 Disposable Income		消费支出 Expenses on Consumption	
		2015	2016	2015	2016
全国总计	**National Total**	21966.2	23821.0	15712.4	17110.7
北 京	Beijing	48458.0	52530.4	33802.8	35415.7
天 津	Tianjin	31291.4	34074.5	24162.5	26129.3
河 北	Hebei	18118.1	19725.4	13030.7	14247.5
山 西	Shanxi	17853.7	19048.9	11729.1	12682.9
内蒙古	Inner Mongolia	22310.1	24126.6	17178.5	18072.3
辽 宁	Liaoning	24575.6	26039.7	17199.8	19852.7
吉 林	Jilin	18683.6	19967.0	13763.9	14772.6
黑龙江	Heilongjiang	18592.7	19838.5	13402.5	14445.8
上 海	Shanghai	49867.2	54031.8	34783.6	37264.6
江 苏	Jiangsu	29538.9	32070.1	20555.6	22129.9
浙 江	Zhejiang	35537.1	38529.0	24116.9	25526.6
安 徽	Anhui	18362.6	19998.1	12840.1	14711.5
福 建	Fujian	25404.4	27607.9	18850.2	20167.5
江 西	Jiangxi	18437.1	20109.6	12403.4	13258.6
山 东	Shangdong	22703.2	24685.3	14578.4	15926.4
河 南	Henan	17124.8	18443.1	11835.1	12712.3
湖 北	**Hubei**	**20025.6**	**21786.6**	**14316.5**	**15888.7**
湖 南	Hunan	19317.5	21114.8	14267.3	15750.5
广 东	Guangdong	27858.9	30295.8	20975.7	23448.4
广 西	Guangxi	16873.4	18305.1	11401.0	12295.2
海 南	Hainan	18979.0	20653.4	13575.0	14275.4
重 庆	Chongqing	20110.1	22034.1	15139.5	16384.8
四 川	Sichuan	17221.0	18808.3	13632.1	14838.5
贵 州	Guizhou	13696.6	15121.1	10413.8	11931.6
云 南	Yunnan	15222.6	16719.9	11005.4	11768.8
西 藏	Tibet	12254.3	13639.2	8245.8	9318.7
陕 西	Shaanxi	17395.0	18873.7	13087.2	13943.0
甘 肃	Gansu	13466.6	14670.3	10950.8	12254.2
青 海	Qinghai	15812.7	17301.8	13611.3	14774.7
宁 夏	Ningxia	17329.1	18832.3	13815.6	14965.4
新 疆	Xinjiang	16859.1	18354.7	12867.4	14066.5

注：本表按当年价格计算。
Note:The table at current prices.

附录1-13 分地区城镇居民人均可支配收入与支出

REGIONAL PER CAPITA INCOME AND CONSUMPTION EXPENDITURE OF URBAN HOUSEHOLDS

单位:元 (yuan)

地 区	Region	可支配收入 Disposable Income		消费支出 Expenses on Consumption	
		2015	2016	2015	2016
全国总计	**National Total**	31194.8	33616.2	21392.4	23078.9
北 京	Beijing	52859.2	57275.3	36642.0	38255.5
天 津	Tianjin	34101.3	37109.6	26229.5	28344.6
河 北	Hebei	26152.2	28249.4	17586.6	19105.9
山 西	Shanxi	25827.7	27352.3	15818.6	16992.8
内蒙古	Inner Mongolia	30594.1	32974.9	21876.5	22744.5
辽 宁	Liaoning	31125.7	32876.1	21556.7	24995.9
吉 林	Jilin	24900.9	26530.4	17972.6	19166.4
黑龙江	Heilongjiang	24202.6	25736.4	17152.1	18145.2
上 海	Shanghai	52961.9	57691.7	36946.1	39856.8
江 苏	Jiangsu	37173.5	40151.6	24966.0	26432.9
浙 江	Zhejiang	43714.5	47237.2	28661.3	30067.7
安 徽	Anhui	26935.8	29156.0	17233.5	19606.2
福 建	Fujian	33275.3	36014.3	23520.2	25005.5
江 西	Jiangxi	26500.1	28673.3	16731.8	17695.6
山 东	Shangdong	31545.3	34012.1	19853.8	21495.3
河 南	Henan	25575.6	27232.9	17154.3	18087.8
湖 北	**Hubei**	**27051.5**	**29385.8**	**18192.3**	**20040.0**
湖 南	Hunan	28838.1	31283.9	19501.4	21420.0
广 东	Guangdong	34757.2	37684.3	25673.1	28613.3
广 西	Guangxi	26415.9	28324.4	16321.2	17268.5
海 南	Hainan	26356.4	28453.5	18448.4	19015.5
重 庆	Chongqing	27238.8	29610.0	19742.3	21030.9
四 川	Sichuan	26205.3	28335.3	19276.8	20659.8
贵 州	Guizhou	24579.6	26742.6	16914.2	19201.7
云 南	Yunnan	26373.2	28610.6	17675.0	18622.4
西 藏	Tibet	25456.6	27802.4	17022.0	19440.5
陕 西	Shaanxi	26420.2	28440.1	18463.9	19368.9
甘 肃	Gansu	23767.1	25693.5	17450.9	19539.2
青 海	Qinghai	24542.3	26757.4	19200.6	20853.2
宁 夏	Ningxia	25186.0	27153.0	18983.9	20364.2
新 疆	Xinjiang	26274.7	28463.4	19414.7	21228.5

注:本表按当年价格计算。
Note:The table at current prices.

附录1-14　分地区农村居民人均可支配收入与支出
REGIONAL PER CAPITA INCOME AND CONSUMPTION EXPENDITURE OF RURAL HOUSEHOLDS

单位:元　　(yuan)

地 区	Region	可支配收入 Disposable Income		消费支出 Expenses on Consumption	
		2015	2016	2015	2016
全国总计	**National Total**	11421.7	12363.4	9222.6	10129.8
北 京	Beijing	20568.7	22309.5	15811.2	17329.0
天 津	Tianjin	18481.6	20075.6	14739.4	15912.1
河 北	Hebei	11050.5	11919.4	9022.8	9798.3
山 西	Shanxi	9453.9	10082.5	7421.2	8028.8
内蒙古	Inner Mongolia	10775.9	11609.0	10637.4	11462.6
辽 宁	Liaoning	12056.9	12880.7	8872.8	9953.1
吉 林	Jilin	11326.2	12122.9	8783.3	9521.4
黑龙江	Heilongjiang	11095.2	11831.9	8391.5	9423.8
上 海	Shanghai	23205.2	25520.4	16152.3	17070.8
江 苏	Jiangsu	16256.7	17605.6	12882.5	14428.2
浙 江	Zhejiang	21125.0	22866.1	16107.7	17358.9
安 徽	Anhui	10820.7	11720.5	8975.2	10287.3
福 建	Fujian	13792.7	14999.2	11960.8	12910.8
江 西	Jiangxi	11139.1	12137.7	8485.6	9128.3
山 东	Shangdong	12930.4	13954.1	8747.6	9518.9
河 南	Henan	10852.9	11696.7	7887.4	8586.6
湖 北	**Hubei**	**11843.9**	**12725.0**	**9803.1**	**10938.3**
湖 南	Hunan	10992.5	11930.4	9690.6	10629.9
广 东	Guangdong	13360.4	14512.2	11103.0	12414.8
广 西	Guangxi	9466.6	10359.5	7582.0	8351.2
海 南	Hainan	10857.6	11842.9	8210.3	8921.2
重 庆	Chongqing	10504.7	11548.8	8937.7	9954.4
四 川	Sichuan	10247.4	11203.1	9250.6	10191.6
贵 州	Guizhou	7386.9	8090.3	6644.9	7533.3
云 南	Yunnan	8242.1	9019.8	6830.1	7330.5
西 藏	Tibet	8243.7	9093.8	5579.7	6070.3
陕 西	Shaanxi	8688.9	9396.4	7900.7	8567.7
甘 肃	Gansu	6936.2	7456.9	6829.8	7487.0
青 海	Qinghai	7933.4	8664.4	8566.5	9222.2
宁 夏	Ningxia	9118.7	9851.6	8414.9	9138.4
新 疆	Xinjiang	9425.1	10183.2	7697.9	8277.0

注:本表按当年价格计算。
Note:The table at current prices.

附录1-15 分地区一般公共预算收入
GENERAL PUBLIC BUDGET REVENUE BY REGION

单位：亿元 (100 million yuan)

地 区	Region	2012	2013	2014	2015	2016
地方总计	**Region Total**	**61078.3**	**69011.2**	**75876.6**	**83002.0**	**87194.8**
北 京	Beijing	3314.9	3661.1	4027.2	4723.9	5081.3
天 津	Tianjin	1760.0	2079.1	2390.4	2667.1	2723.5
河 北	Hebei	2084.3	2295.6	2446.6	2649.2	2850.8
山 西	Shanxi	1516.4	1701.6	1820.6	1642.4	1557.0
内蒙古	Inner Mongolia	1552.7	1721.0	1843.7	1964.5	2016.5
辽 宁	Liaoning	3105.4	3343.8	3192.8	2127.4	2199.3
吉 林	Jilin	1041.3	1157.0	1203.4	1229.4	1263.8
黑龙江	Heilongjiang	1163.2	1277.4	1301.3	1165.9	1148.4
上 海	Shanghai	3743.7	4109.5	4585.6	5519.5	6406.1
江 苏	Jiangsu	5860.7	6568.5	7233.1	8028.6	8121.2
浙 江	Zhejiang	3441.2	3796.9	4122.0	4809.9	5301.8
安 徽	Anhui	1792.7	2075.1	2218.4	2454.3	2672.8
福 建	Fujian	1776.2	2119.4	2362.2	2544.2	2654.8
江 西	Jiangxi	1372.0	1621.2	1881.8	2165.7	2151.4
山 东	Shangdong	4059.4	4559.9	5026.8	5529.3	5860.2
河 南	Henan	2040.3	2415.4	2739.3	3016.1	3153.5
湖 北	**Hubei**	**1823.1**	**2191.2**	**2566.9**	**3005.5**	**3102.0**
湖 南	Hunan	1782.2	2030.9	2262.8	2515.4	2697.9
广 东	Guangdong	6229.2	7081.5	8065.1	9366.8	10346.7
广 西	Guangxi	1166.1	1317.6	1422.3	1515.2	1556.2
海 南	Hainan	409.4	481.0	555.3	627.7	637.5
重 庆	Chongqing	1703.5	1693.2	1922.0	2154.8	2227.9
四 川	Sichuan	2421.3	2784.1	3061.1	3355.4	3389.4
贵 州	Guizhou	1014.1	1206.4	1366.7	1503.4	1561.3
云 南	Yunnan	1338.2	1611.3	1698.1	1808.1	1812.3
西 藏	Tibet	86.6	95.0	124.3	137.1	155.6
陕 西	Shaanxi	1600.7	1748.3	1890.4	2060.0	1833.9
甘 肃	Gansu	520.4	607.3	672.7	743.9	786.8
青 海	Qinghai	186.4	223.9	251.7	267.1	238.4
宁 夏	Ningxia	264.0	308.3	339.9	373.4	387.7
新 疆	Xinjiang	909.0	1128.5	1282.3	1330.9	1299.0

注：本表数据为地方财政本级收入。
Note: a) This table is local financial revenue

附录1-16 分地区一般公共预算支出
GENERAL PUBLIC EXPENDITURE BY REGION

单位:亿元 (100 million yuan)

地 区	Region	2012	2013	2014	2015	2016
地方总计	**Region Total**	**107188.3**	**119740.3**	**129215.5**	**150335.6**	**160437.1**
北 京	Beijing	3685.3	4173.7	4524.7	5737.7	6405.2
天 津	Tianjin	2143.2	2549.2	2884.7	3232.4	3700.6
河 北	Hebei	4079.4	4409.6	4677.3	5632.2	6038.0
山 西	Shanxi	2759.5	3030.1	3085.3	3423.0	3441.7
内蒙古	Inner Mongolia	3426.0	3686.5	3880.0	4253.0	4526.3
辽 宁	Liaoning	4558.6	5197.4	5080.5	4481.6	4582.4
吉 林	Jilin	2471.2	2744.8	2913.2	3217.1	3586.1
黑龙江	Heilongjiang	3171.5	3369.2	3434.2	4020.7	4228.2
上 海	Shanghai	4184.0	4528.6	4923.4	6191.6	6918.9
江 苏	Jiangsu	7027.7	7798.5	8472.4	9687.6	9990.1
浙 江	Zhejiang	4161.9	4730.5	5159.6	6646.0	6976.3
安 徽	Anhui	3961.0	4349.7	4664.1	5239.0	5529.9
福 建	Fujian	2607.5	3068.8	3306.7	4001.6	4287.4
江 西	Jiangxi	3019.2	3470.3	3882.7	4412.5	4619.5
山 东	Shangdong	5904.5	6688.8	7177.3	8250.0	8749.6
河 南	Henan	5006.4	5582.3	6028.7	6799.4	7456.6
湖 北	**Hubei**	**3759.8**	**4371.6**	**4934.1**	**6132.8**	**6453.1**
湖 南	Hunan	4119.0	4690.9	5017.4	5728.7	6337.0
广 东	Guangdong	7387.9	8411.0	9152.6	12827.8	13414.4
广 西	Guangxi	2985.2	3208.7	3479.8	4065.5	4472.5
海 南	Hainan	911.7	1011.2	1099.7	1239.4	1378.4
重 庆	Chongqing	3046.4	3062.3	3304.4	3792.0	4001.9
四 川	Sichuan	5451.0	6220.9	6796.6	7497.5	8011.9
贵 州	Guizhou	2755.7	3082.7	3542.8	3939.5	4261.7
云 南	Yunnan	3572.7	4096.5	4438.0	4712.8	5019.6
西 藏	Tibet	905.3	1014.3	1185.5	1381.5	1585.5
陕 西	Shaanxi	3323.8	3665.1	3962.5	4376.1	4390.6
甘 肃	Gansu	2059.6	2309.6	2541.5	2958.3	3152.7
青 海	Qinghai	1159.0	1228.0	1347.4	1515.2	1522.6
宁 夏	Ningxia	864.4	922.5	1000.5	1138.5	1257.7
新 疆	Xinjiang	2720.1	3067.1	3317.8	3804.9	4140.7

注:本表数据为地方财政本级支出。
Note: a) This table is local financial expenditure.

附录1-17 分地区电力消费量
ELECTRICITY CONSUMPTION BY REGION

单位:亿千瓦时 (10 000 KW/h)

地 区	Region	2010	2011	2012	2013	2014	2015
北 京	Beijing	809.9	821.7	874.3	913.1	937.1	952.7
天 津	Tianjin	645.7	695.2	722.5	774.5	794.4	800.6
河 北	Hebei	2691.5	2984.9	3077.7	3251.2	3314.1	3175.7
山 西	Shanxi	1460.0	1650.4	1765.8	1832.3	1822.6	1737.2
内蒙古	Inner Mongolia	1536.8	1864.1	2016.8	2181.9	2416.7	2542.9
辽 宁	Liaoning	1715.3	1861.5	1899.9	2008.5	2038.7	1984.9
吉 林	Jilin	577.0	630.2	637.0	653.8	667.8	652.0
黑龙江	Heilongjiang	747.8	801.9	827.9	845.2	859.4	869.0
上 海	Shanghai	1295.9	1339.6	1353.4	1410.6	1369.0	1405.5
江 苏	Jiangsu	3864.4	4281.6	4580.9	4956.6	5012.5	5114.7
浙 江	Zhejiang	2820.9	3116.9	3210.6	3453.1	3506.4	3553.9
安 徽	Anhui	1077.9	1221.2	1361.1	1528.1	1585.2	1639.8
福 建	Fujian	1315.1	1515.9	1579.5	1700.7	1855.8	1851.9
江 西	Jiangxi	700.5	835.1	867.7	947.1	1018.5	1087.3
山 东	Shangdong	3298.5	3635.3	3794.6	4083.1	4223.5	5117.0
河 南	Henan	2354.0	2659.1	2747.7	2899.2	2919.6	2879.6
湖 北	**Hubei**	**1330.4**	**1450.8**	**1507.9**	**1629.8**	**1656.5**	**1665.2**
湖 南	Hunan	1171.9	1293.4	1346.5	1423.1	1430.9	1447.6
广 东	Guangdong	4060.1	4399.0	4619.4	4830.1	5235.2	5310.7
广 西	Guangxi	993.2	1112.2	1153.9	1237.7	1308.0	1334.3
海 南	Hainan	159.0	185.3	210.3	232.0	251.9	272.4
重 庆	Chongqing	626.4	717.0	723.5	813.3	867.2	875.4
四 川	Sichuan	1549.0	1751.4	1830.7	1949.0	2014.8	1992.4
贵 州	Guizhou	835.4	944.1	1046.7	1126.3	1173.7	1174.2
云 南	Yunnan	1004.1	1204.1	1315.9	1459.8	1529.4	1438.6
西 藏	Tibet	20.4	23.8	27.8	30.7	34.0	40.5
陕 西	Shaanxi	859.2	982.5	1066.7	1152.2	1226.0	1221.7
甘 肃	Gansu	804.4	923.4	994.6	1073.2	1095.5	1098.7
青 海	Qinghai	465.2	560.7	602.2	676.3	723.2	658.0
宁 夏	Ningxia	546.8	724.5	741.8	811.2	848.8	878.3
新 疆	Xinjiang	662.0	839.1	1151.5	1539.8	1900.2	2160.3

注:本表数据有由中国电力企业联合会提供。
Note: a) This table is provided by the Association of Power Generation Enterprises.

附录1-18 分地区固定资产投资
REGIONAL INVESTMENT IN FIXED ASSET

单位:亿元 (100 million yuan)

地 区	Region	2010	2011	2012	2013	2014	2015	2016
全国总计	**National Total**	**241430.89**	**302396.06**	**364854.15**	**435747.43**	**501264.87**	**551590.04**	**596500.75**
北 京	Beijing	4916.53	5519.84	6064.86	6797.54	6873.44	7446.02	7888.69
天 津	Tianjin	5896.52	7040.68	7913.26	9103.01	10490.37	11814.57	12756.36
河 北	Hebei	12922.66	15780.26	19104.63	22629.77	26147.20	28905.74	31340.07
山 西	Shanxi	5526.60	6837.69	8584.85	10745.35	12035.46	13744.59	13859.35
内蒙古	Inner Mongolia	8687.99	10252.97	11749.77	14072.39	17437.85	13529.15	12893.96
辽 宁	Liaoning	15106.33	17431.46	21535.37	24791.40	24426.83	17640.37	6436.33
吉 林	Jilin	7395.23	7226.65	9262.23	9725.76	11107.94	12508.59	13773.17
黑龙江	Heilongjiang	6292.67	7157.92	9375.44	11121.28	9537.88	9884.28	10432.55
上 海	Shanghai	4630.47	4959.93	5114.64	5644.13	6012.97	6349.39	6751.68
江 苏	Jiangsu	17416.47	26313.46	30473.74	35982.52	41552.75	45905.17	49370.85
浙 江	Zhejiang	8438.08	13651.65	17095.96	20194.07	23554.76	26664.72	29571.00
安 徽	Anhui	10281.29	12007.87	14943.81	18091.21	21256.29	23803.93	26577.37
福 建	Fujian	7385.78	9677.09	12182.52	15045.81	17869.76	20973.98	22927.99
江 西	Jiangxi	7856.94	8753.93	10378.37	12434.95	14646.31	16993.90	19378.69
山 东	Shangdong	18844.41	25907.38	30319.76	35875.86	41599.13	47381.46	52364.49
河 南	Henan	13934.82	16934.32	20558.61	25188.06	30012.28	34951.28	39753.93
湖 北	**Hubei**	**9405.63**	**12195.39**	**15148.71**	**18796.85**	**22441.67**	**26086.42**	**29503.88**
湖 南	Hunan	8617.98	11407.74	13966.26	17225.19	20548.55	24324.17	27688.45
广 东	Guangdong	12599.26	16599.16	18250.13	21795.52	25843.06	29950.48	32947.30
广 西	Guangxi	6383.26	7580.90	9345.18	11383.93	13287.61	15654.95	17652.95
海 南	Hainan	1257.50	1599.14	2064.44	2625.59	3039.46	3355.40	3747.03
重 庆	Chongqing	6170.61	7366.95	8610.37	10290.95	12140.83	14208.15	15931.78
四 川	Sichuan	11061.38	13687.75	16530.31	19755.29	22662.13	24965.56	28229.79
贵 州	Guizhou	2609.36	4026.47	5504.95	7102.78	8778.40	10676.70	12929.17
云 南	Yunnan	5052.61	5932.75	7553.51	9621.83	11073.81	13069.39	15662.49
西 藏	Tibet	404.98	516.31	670.52	876.00	1069.23	1295.68	1596.05
陕 西	Shaanxi	7569.90	9108.98	11705.83	14533.51	16840.27	18231.03	20474.85
甘 肃	Gansu	2808.55	3870.08	5040.03	6407.20	7759.63	8626.60	9534.10
青 海	Qinghai	840.01	1365.91	1808.67	2285.30	2788.91	3144.17	3455.51
宁 夏	Ningxia	1292.80	1589.14	2033.03	2577.79	3093.92	3426.42	3709.04
新 疆	Xinjiang	3065.13	4444.99	5857.98	7371.24	9067.79	10525.42	9983.86
不分地区	Not Classified by Region	6759.14	5651.29	6106.38	5655.37	6268.38	5552.35	5378.02

注:2010年前为城镇固定资产投资口径;2011年起为固定资产投资(不含农户)。

Note: Datas of the table are urban fixed asset investment before 2011, and are investment in fixed assets in 2011.

附录1-19　分地区房地产开发企业(单位)房屋施工、竣工面积和商品房销售面积

REGIONAL REAL ESTATE DEVELOPMENT ENTERPRISES(UNITS) HOUSING CONSTRUCTION, COMPLETION AND SALES OF COMMERCIAL SPACE AREA

单位:万平方米　　　　(10 000 sqm)

地 区	Region	房屋施工面积 Housing Construction Area		房屋竣工面积 Housing Completed Area		商品房销售面积 Sales of Commercial Area	
		2015	2016	2015	2016	2015	2016
全国总计	**National Total**	**735693**	**758975**	**100039**	**106128**	**128495**	**157349**
北 京	Beijing	12993	12976	2631	2370	1554	1659
天 津	Tianjin	10230	9350	2904	2914	1771	2711
河 北	Hebei	30435	30477	4039	4288	5855	6682
山 西	Shanxi	15734	17069	2114	2684	1593	2061
内蒙古	Inner Mongolia	17641	16906	1697	1664	2369	2528
辽 宁	Liaoning	29283	26364	3238	2709	3916	3712
吉 林	Jilin	11566	11797	1287	1352	1492	1919
黑龙江	Heilongjiang	12410	10866	2924	2376	1997	2117
上 海	Shanghai	15095	15111	2647	2551	2431	2706
江 苏	Jiangsu	58118	58762	10297	10074	11414	13962
浙 江	Zhejiang	41687	41610	5893	7925	5985	8637
安 徽	Anhui	34245	35645	5538	5383	6174	8500
福 建	Fujian	30891	31064	3437	3665	4038	4915
江 西	Jiangxi	15294	16427	1908	1636	3478	4692
山 东	Shangdong	57206	59957	8278	8253	9727	11790
河 南	Henan	40994	47360	5390	6299	8556	11306
湖 北	**Hubei**	**28296**	**29880**	**2785**	**3127**	**6245**	**7427**
湖 南	Hunan	28322	30139	3970	4534	6363	8085
广 东	Guangdong	57942	64234	6044	6594	11681	14612
广 西	Guangxi	18608	21135	1675	1735	3523	4215
海 南	Hainan	8317	8937	1069	1675	1052	1509
重 庆	Chongqing	28986	27363	4630	4421	5381	6257
四 川	Sichuan	38981	41532	4546	7050	7671	9300
贵 州	Guizhou	20878	20352	2583	1901	3560	4157
云 南	Yunnan	20722	20593	2547	2115	3145	3640
西 藏	Tibet	381	349	92	32	51	75
陕 西	Shaanxi	20752	22298	1682	2432	2979	3263
甘 肃	Gansu	8586	8933	962	992	1435	1679
青 海	Qinghai	2586	2848	454	387	393	438
宁 夏	Ningxia	7046	7110	1169	1295	839	966
新 疆	Xinjiang	11465	11531	1609	1696	1825	1828

注:商品房销售面积包括期房。

Note:Sales of Commercial, including Forward House.

附录1-20 分地区房地产开发企业(单位)投资和商品房销售额

REGIONAL REAL ESTATE DEVELOPMENT COMPANY(UNITS) OF INVESTMENT AND COMMERCIAL HOUSING SALES

单位:亿元　(100 million yuan)

地区	Region	房地产开发投资额 Real Estate Development Investment		商品房销售额 Commercial Housing Sales		#住宅 #Residential	
		2015	2016	2015	2016	2015	2016
全国总计	**National Total**	**95978.8**	**102580.6**	**87280.8**	**117627.0**	**72769.8**	**99064.2**
北京	Beijing	4177.0	4000.6	3517.6	4561.6	2512.9	2795.8
天津	Tianjin	1871.5	2300.0	1790.0	3478.2	1663.3	3245.6
河北	Hebei	4285.3	4695.6	3371.6	4301.8	2854.2	3710.9
山西	Shanxi	1494.9	1597.4	775.6	1027.1	702.3	900.8
内蒙古	Inner Mongolia	1081.1	1133.5	1052.2	1149.1	766.1	838.1
辽宁	Liaoning	3558.6	2094.8	2255.0	2256.9	1907.6	1988.0
吉林	Jilin	924.2	1016.8	816.9	1029.6	680.3	806.5
黑龙江	Heilongjiang	992.1	864.8	1027.1	1121.0	824.2	903.7
上海	Shanghai	3468.9	3709.0	5093.5	6695.8	4319.9	5233.3
江苏	Jiangsu	8153.7	8956.4	8396.2	12293.0	7374.9	11055.4
浙江	Zhejiang	7111.9	7469.4	6299.5	9605.1	5519.3	8280.8
安徽	Anhui	4424.9	4603.6	3369.4	5035.5	2714.3	4231.6
福建	Fujian	4469.6	4588.8	3585.8	4530.8	2839.8	3793.4
江西	Jiangxi	1520.1	1770.9	1863.7	2678.4	1606.7	2207.2
山东	Shangdong	5892.2	6323.4	5408.0	6902.9	4510.8	6070.5
河南	Henan	4818.9	6179.1	3945.6	5612.9	3300.3	4839.0
湖北	**Hubei**	**4249.2**	**4296.4**	**3661.4**	**4994.1**	**3198.5**	**4383.8**
湖南	Hunan	2613.7	2957.0	2738.9	3751.9	2253.8	3113.6
广东	Guangdong	8538.5	10307.8	11442.8	16214.6	9967.3	14240.3
广西	Guangxi	1909.1	2398.0	1747.8	2207.5	1459.4	1948.2
海南	Hainan	1704.0	1787.6	982.8	1490.2	908.6	1385.3
重庆	Chongqing	3751.3	3725.9	2952.2	3432.0	2244.4	2635.6
四川	Sichuan	4813.0	5282.6	4199.8	5358.9	3269.5	4296.3
贵州	Guizhou	2205.1	2149.0	1571.7	1790.5	1068.1	1269.4
云南	Yunnan	2669.0	2688.3	1666.9	1917.8	1236.8	1411.4
西藏	Tibet	50.0	48.5	21.1	38.1	16.7	34.7
陕西	Shaanxi	2494.3	2736.8	1597.4	1785.2	1381.3	1585.7
甘肃	Gansu	768.1	850.0	704.9	873.5	603.1	712.3
青海	Qinghai	336.0	396.9	206.0	236.4	139.8	172.1
宁夏	Ningxia	633.6	728.2	370.3	409.7	284.0	325.9
新疆	Xinjiang	998.9	923.4	849.2	846.8	641.6	648.9

附录1-21 分地区货物进出口总额
TOTAL VALUE OF IMPORTS AND EXPORTS OF GOODS BY REGION

(按经营单位所在地分)

(Location of Points by Business Units)

单位:亿美元 (100 million US dollors)

地 区	Region	2010	2011	2012	2013	2014	2015	2016
全国总计	**National Total**	**29740.0**	**36418.6**	**38671.2**	**41589.9**	**43015.3**	**39530.3**	**36855.7**
北 京	Beijing	3017.2	3895.6	4081.1	4290.0	4155.2	3194.4	2820.3
天 津	Tianjin	821.0	1033.8	1156.3	1285.0	1338.9	1142.8	1026.5
河 北	Hebei	420.6	536.0	505.6	549.1	598.8	515.1	466.2
山 西	Shanxi	125.8	147.4	150.4	157.9	162.3	146.8	166.4
内蒙古	Inner Mongolia	87.3	119.3	112.6	119.9	145.6	127.3	116.2
辽 宁	Liaoning	807.1	960.4	1040.9	1144.8	1140.0	959.5	865.2
吉 林	Jilin	168.5	220.6	245.6	258.3	263.8	188.8	184.4
黑龙江	Heilongjiang	255.2	385.2	375.9	388.8	389.0	210.1	165.4
上 海	Shanghai	3689.5	4375.5	4365.9	4412.7	4664.0	4492.4	4338.4
江 苏	Jiangsu	4658.0	5395.8	5479.6	5508.0	5635.5	5455.6	5095.3
浙 江	Zhejiang	2535.3	3093.8	3124.0	3357.9	3550.4	3467.8	3365.0
安 徽	Anhui	242.7	313.1	392.8	455.2	491.8	478.4	443.3
福 建	Fujian	1087.8	1435.2	1559.4	1693.2	1774.1	1688.5	1568.5
江 西	Jiangxi	216.2	314.7	334.1	367.5	427.3	424.0	400.8
山 东	Shangdong	1891.6	2358.9	2455.4	2665.3	2769.3	2406.1	2342.1
河 南	Henan	178.3	326.2	517.4	599.6	649.7	737.8	711.9
湖 北	**Hubei**	**259.3**	**335.9**	**319.6**	**363.8**	**430.4**	**455.5**	**393.5**
湖 南	Hunan	146.6	189.4	219.5	251.8	308.3	293.0	262.5
广 东	Guangdong	7849.0	9134.7	9840.2	10915.8	10765.8	10225.0	9555.1
广 西	Guangxi	177.4	233.6	294.8	328.3	405.5	510.9	478.3
海 南	Hainan	86.5	127.6	143.2	149.9	158.6	139.7	113.3
重 庆	Chongqing	124.3	292.1	532.0	686.9	954.3	744.7	627.7
四 川	Sichuan	326.9	477.2	591.4	645.7	702.0	511.9	493.2
贵 州	Guizhou	31.5	48.9	66.3	82.9	107.7	122.2	56.9
云 南	Yunnan	134.3	160.3	210.1	253.0	296.1	244.9	198.9
西 藏	Tibet	8.4	13.6	34.2	33.2	22.5	9.1	7.8
陕 西	Shaanxi	121.0	146.5	148.0	201.3	273.6	305.0	299.2
甘 肃	Gansu	74.0	87.3	89.0	102.4	86.4	79.5	68.8
青 海	Qinghai	7.9	9.2	11.6	14.0	17.2	19.3	15.2
宁 夏	Ningxia	19.6	22.9	22.2	32.2	54.4	37.4	32.7
新 疆	Xinjiang	171.3	228.2	251.7	275.6	276.7	196.7	176.6

附录1-22 分地区货物出口、进口额(2016)
TOTAL VALUE OF IMPORTS AND EXPORTS OF GOODS BY REGION

单位:亿美元 (100 million dollars)

地 区	Region	按经营单位所在地分 Location of Points by Business Units	
		出口额 Exports	进口额 Imports
全国总计	**National Total**	**20981.5**	**15874.2**
北 京	Beijing	518.4	2301.9
天 津	Tianjin	442.9	583.7
河 北	Hebei	305.8	160.5
山 西	Shanxi	99.3	67.1
内蒙古	Inner Mongolia	43.7	72.4
辽 宁	Liaoning	430.7	434.6
吉 林	Jilin	42.1	142.4
黑龙江	Heilongjiang	50.4	114.9
上 海	Shanghai	1834.7	2503.7
江 苏	Jiangsu	3192.7	1902.6
浙 江	Zhejiang	2678.6	686.4
安 徽	Anhui	284.4	158.9
福 建	Fujian	1036.8	531.7
江 西	Jiangxi	298.1	102.6
山 东	Shangdong	1371.6	970.5
河 南	Henan	427.9	284.0
湖 北	**Hubei**	**260.2**	**133.2**
湖 南	Hunan	176.7	85.8
广 东	Guangdong	5988.6	3566.5
广 西	Guangxi	229.6	248.7
海 南	Hainan	21.2	92.1
重 庆	Chongqing	406.9	220.8
四 川	Sichuan	279.3	213.9
贵 州	Guizhou	47.4	9.6
云 南	Yunnan	114.8	84.1
西 藏	Tibet	4.7	3.1
陕 西	Shaanxi	158.3	140.9
甘 肃	Gansu	40.9	27.9
青 海	Qinghai	13.7	1.6
宁 夏	Ningxia	25.0	7.8
新 疆	Xinjiang	156.1	20.5

附录1-23 分地区农林牧渔业总产值及增长速度(2016)
REGIONAL FORESTYR,ANIMAL HUSBANDDRY AND FISHERY OUTPUT VALUE GROWTH RATE

地 区	Region	农林牧渔业总产值(亿元) Forestry, Animal Husbandry Fishery (million)	#农业 #Agriculture	#林业 #Forestry	#牧业 #Livestock	#渔业 #Fishing	农林牧渔业总产值比上年增长 (%) Previous Year (%)
全国总计	**National Total**	**112091.3**	**59287.8**	**4631.6**	**31703.2**	**11602.9**	**3.5**
北 京	Beijing	338.1	145.2	52.2	122.7	9.2	-9.9
天 津	Tianjin	494.4	244.3	8.4	140.9	89.0	3.3
河 北	Hebei	6083.9	3459.4	132.3	1939.2	211.0	3.5
山 西	Shanxi	1534.0	958.1	100.3	376.2	9.9	3.2
内蒙古	Inner Mongolia	2794.2	1415.1	98.6	1202.9	33.0	3.1
辽 宁	Liaoning	4421.8	1859.5	143.7	1575.7	639.6	-2.6
吉 林	Jilin	2724.9	1232.0	107.2	1252.8	43.0	3.2
黑龙江	Heilongjiang	5197.8	2873.9	219.9	1854.8	129.2	5.5
上 海	Shanghai	285.1	148.5	13.2	62.6	50.2	-9.2
江 苏	Jiangsu	7235.1	3714.6	129.3	1331.5	1621.9	0.8
浙 江	Zhejiang	3146.1	1521.2	158.1	434.3	962.0	2.5
安 徽	Anhui	4655.5	2234.1	291.1	1375.7	513.2	3.4
福 建	Fujian	4155.7	1782.0	315.1	681.7	1235.5	3.7
江 西	Jiangxi	3130.3	1446.9	324.6	788.6	458.9	4.1
山 东	Shangdong	9325.9	4641.3	147.5	2540.8	1485.6	4.4
河 南	Henan	7799.7	4577.2	121.3	2611.3	128.3	4.5
湖 北	**Hubei**	**6278.4**	**2921.3**	**203.4**	**1715.2**	**1030.0**	**4.9**
湖 南	Hunan	6081.9	3255.1	321.6	1762.7	396.7	3.6
广 东	Guangdong	6078.4	3134.4	314.7	1221.8	1195.6	2.9
广 西	Guangxi	4591.4	2347.9	323.5	1266.4	464.2	3.3
海 南	Hainan	1470.4	695.6	100.0	267.1	353.8	4.3
重 庆	Chongqing	1968.3	1151.8	73.4	627.4	85.3	4.5
四 川	Sichuan	6831.1	3711.0	219.1	2551.7	223.9	4.0
贵 州	Guizhou	3097.2	1888.6	195.0	797.2	68.7	6.2
云 南	Yunnan	3633.1	1943.6	330.4	1141.8	94.2	5.8
西 藏	Tibet	173.0	52.2	2.4	113.8	0.2	12.6
陕 西	Shaanxi	2985.8	2027.6	85.5	695.9	26.2	4.1
甘 肃	Gansu	1778.0	1274.7	30.8	299.7	2.2	4.2
青 海	Qinghai	338.8	155.5	8.3	165.7	3.3	5.4
宁 夏	Ningxia	493.6	311.9	10.1	131.7	17.0	4.4
新 疆	Xinjiang	2969.7	2163.1	50.3	653.2	22.2	6.0

注:本表绝对数按当年价格计算,增长速度按可比价格计算。

Note:In this table are at current prices, growth rates at constant prices.

附录1-24 分地区主要农产品产量(2016)
OUTPUT OF MAJOR FARM PRODUCTS BY REGION

单位:万吨 (10 000 tons)

地区	Region	粮食 Food	油料 Oil feed	棉花 Cotton	糖料 Sugar	蔬菜 Vegetables	水果 Fruit
全国总计	**National Total**	**61625.0**	**3629.5**	**530.0**	**12340.7**	**79779.7**	**28351.1**
北京	Beijing	53.7	0.6	0.01		183.6	79.0
天津	Tianjin	196.4	1.6	2.3		450.4	61.5
河北	Hebei	3460.2	156.5	30.0	93.1	8193.4	2138.5
山西	Shanxi	1318.5	15.4	1.0	3.3	1294.5	840.8
内蒙古	Inner Mongolia	2780.3	220.0		267.4	1502.3	316.3
辽宁	Liaoning	2100.6	81.3	0.11	9.4	2257.5	802.3
吉林	Jilin	3717.2	82.5		1.4	852.4	241.1
黑龙江	Heilongjiang	6058.5	21.7		11.4	936.8	259.9
上海	Shanghai	99.2	0.9		0.6	334.2	50.6
江苏	Jiangsu	3466.0	131.9	7.4	9.0	5593.9	893.0
浙江	Zhejiang	752.2	29.1	1.7	62.1	1865.1	724.3
安徽	Anhui	3417.4	214.8	18.5	20.4	2774.7	1043.5
福建	Fujian	650.9	31.0	0.01	37.0	1951.6	853.8
江西	Jiangxi	2138.1	122.0	7.3	65.8	1420.2	617.4
山东	Shangdong	4700.7	326.8	54.8	0.02	10327.0	3255.4
河南	Henan	5946.6	619.1	9.8	23.5	7807.6	2871.3
湖北	**Hubei**	**2554.1**	**329.8**	**18.8**	**37.5**	**4001.7**	**1010.4**
湖南	Hunan	2953.2	242.9	12.3	66.2	4196.4	1048.2
广东	Guangdong	1360.2	113.3		1479.3	3569.1	1717.0
广西	Guangxi	1521.3	68.9	0.3	7461.3	2928.8	1882.5
海南	Hainan	177.9	11.2		204.6	579.8	395.4
重庆	Chongqing	1166.0	62.7		9.7	1875.1	408.7
四川	Sichuan	3483.5	311.3	0.9	49.6	4388.6	979.3
贵州	Guizhou	1192.4	103.4	0.1	117.8	1878.5	243.9
云南	Yunnan	1902.9	68.5		1738.4	1968.6	759.1
西藏	Tibet	101.9	6.2			70.7	1.5
陕西	Shaanxi	1228.3	63.8	3.4	0.2	1896.2	2017.8
甘肃	Gansu	1140.6	76.0	2.0	16.6	1951.5	738.0
青海	Qinghai	103.5	30.0		0.1	170.0	4.0
宁夏	Ningxia	370.6	14.7			593.1	305.8
新疆	Xinjiang	1512.3	71.4	359.4	555.0	1966.5	1790.9

注:水果产量含果用瓜。
Note:Fruit production with fruit with a melon.

附录1-24　续表 continued

单位:万吨　(10 000 tons)

地区	Region	肉类 Meat	#猪肉 #Pork	#牛肉 #Beef	#羊肉 #Sheep Meat	奶类 Dairy
全国总计	**National Total**	**8537.8**	**5299.1**	**716.8**	**459.4**	**3712.1**
北 京	Beijing	30.4	21.8	1.4	1.2	45.7
天 津	Tianjin	45.5	29.2	3.5	1.6	68.0
河 北	Hebei	457.7	265.4	54.3	32.4	448.0
山 西	Shanxi	84.4	57.5	5.9	7.4	95.9
内蒙古	Inner Mongolia	258.9	72.1	55.6	99.0	741.3
辽 宁	Liaoning	430.9	219.2	41.6	8.7	144.2
吉 林	Jilin	260.4	130.6	47.1	4.8	53.4
黑龙江	Heilongjiang	231.2	138.2	42.5	12.8	548.6
上 海	Shanghai	17.4	13.5	0.1	0.5	26.0
江 苏	Jiangsu	355.6	216.4	3.1	8.3	59.0
浙 江	Zhejiang	118.1	90.7	1.3	1.9	15.3
安 徽	Anhui	411.4	244.9	16.5	17.3	32.7
福 建	Fujian	225.6	136.0	3.2	2.5	15.9
江 西	Jiangxi	330.9	242.9	14.4	1.3	13.5
山 东	Shangdong	777.5	383.5	67.0	38.4	276.8
河 南	Henan	697.0	450.6	83.0	26.4	336.6
湖 北	**Hubei**	**425.2**	**322.2**	**23.2**	**8.9**	**16.9**
湖 南	Hunan	529.8	434.8	20.4	12.0	10.1
广 东	Guangdong	415.5	264.4	7.1	0.9	13.0
广 西	Guangxi	411.2	249.8	14.7	3.3	9.7
海 南	Hainan	76.3	42.9	2.6	1.1	0.2
重 庆	Chongqing	210.8	151.3	9.2	4.1	5.5
四 川	Sichuan	696.3	494.5	36.9	26.9	62.8
贵 州	Guizhou	199.3	155.0	17.9	4.5	6.4
云 南	Yunnan	375.6	283.7	35.2	15.1	64.1
西 藏	Tibet	27.7	1.5	16.2	8.2	34.7
陕 西	Shaanxi	111.7	85.9	8.0	8.0	189.1
甘 肃	Gansu	97.3	49.0	20.0	21.1	40.7
青 海	Qinghai	36.0	10.5	12.2	12.0	34.2
宁 夏	Ningxia	30.9	7.5	10.4	10.5	139.5
新 疆	Xinjiang	161.0	33.9	42.5	58.3	164.4

附录1-25 分地区规模以上工业企业主要经济指标(2016)
MAIN INDICATORS OF INDUSTRIAL ENTERPRISES ABOVE DESIGNATED SIZE BY REGION

单位:亿元

地 区	Region	主营业务收入 Main Business Income	主营业务成本 Main Business Costs	销售费用 Selling expenses	管理费用 Overhead expenses	财务费用 Finance expenses	利润总额 Total Profit
全国总计	**National Total**	**1151617.5**	**984902.9**	**30648.6**	**43897.4**	**12532.6**	**68803.2**
北 京	Beijing	19413.6	16167.3	1019.8	1023.8	182.6	1549.3
天 津	Tianjin	27835.8	23812.4	665.2	907.2	174.4	1984.9
河 北	Hebei	46729.4	40926.6	859.0	1324.2	522.0	2610.0
山 西	Shanxi	13957.0	11813.2	489.0	752.7	595.7	208.7
内蒙古	Inner Mongolia	19797.9	16537.6	485.1	713.9	419.3	1242.1
辽 宁	Liaoning	23802.0	20203.8	697.9	1148.8	508.1	657.6
吉 林	Jilin	23268.3	19524.1	949.2	1060.5	240.1	1241.8
黑龙江	Heilongjiang	11166.5	9595.0	283.1	561.0	139.6	244.0
上 海	Shanghai	33844.3	27001.5	1317.0	2284.3	117.5	2906.2
江 苏	Jiangsu	157789.5	135424.7	3890.2	5788.0	1218.8	10525.8
浙 江	Zhejiang	65307.6	54908.2	1845.0	3289.7	817.7	4322.7
安 徽	Anhui	41645.9	36471.0	1038.8	1428.3	425.9	2078.9
福 建	Fujian	42124.1	36310.5	1048.1	1480.9	388.5	2643.3
江 西	Jiangxi	35518.7	31181.8	604.0	813.2	203.6	2399.4
山 东	Shangdong	150034.9	131911.3	3051.3	3836.7	1577.0	8643.1
河 南	Henan	79195.7	69430.1	1463.4	1748.1	788.9	5174.1
湖 北	**Hubei**	**45169.9**	**38784.3**	**1322.0**	**1722.4**	**451.5**	**2441.4**
湖 南	Hunan	37686.5	31823.1	1123.8	1616.6	409.2	1620.5
广 东	Guangdong	127363.1	107569.0	4365.7	6364.9	654.2	8025.4
广 西	Guangxi	21978.4	18819.2	509.0	801.2	217.1	1287.7
海 南	Hainan	1660.3	1296.5	71.3	65.8	41.2	103.5
重 庆	Chongqing	22947.6	19510.5	654.2	918.2	215.6	1584.2
四 川	Sichuan	40639.3	34491.7	1249.7	1573.3	624.2	2176.1
贵 州	Guizhou	10654.9	8668.3	347.3	447.6	225.7	658.7
云 南	Yunnan	10342.0	8166.6	290.1	444.2	318.4	309.1
西 藏	Tibet	170.7	129.4	6.7	12.2	4.5	16.5
陕 西	Shaanxi	19776.8	16118.6	522.8	866.9	324.7	1472.4
甘 肃	Gansu	7711.5	6733.9	127.0	264.5	209.7	116.1
青 海	Qinghai	2227.1	1871.4	58.9	89.9	108.6	76.9
宁 夏	Ningxia	3636.1	3066.9	77.3	141.5	138.3	137.7
新 疆	Xinjiang	8222.3	6634.4	216.7	406.9	270.0	345.1

注:本表为快报数(下表同)。
Note:This table for the number of letters (the same below)。

附录1-25 续表 continued

单位:亿元 (100 million yuan)

地 区	Region	亏损企业亏损总额 Total Loss of Enterprises Running under Deficit	流动资产合计 Total Current Assets	应收账款 Account Received	存货 Inventory	产成品 Finished Products	资产总计 Total Assets	负债合计 Total Liability
全国总计	National Total	8173.6	496173.7	125800.2	105241.8	39752.1	1068296.7	596034.0
北 京	Beijing	254.5	16522.0	4298.3	2279.1	802.4	42848.6	19607.3
天 津	Tianjin	220.9	13010.7	3785.2	2844.2	1020.8	24646.8	15244.8
河 北	Hebei	289.3	17502.2	3553.9	4152.2	1496.4	43754.2	24174.9
山 西	Shanxi	438.0	13296.5	2320.6	1931.7	743.6	33194.1	25253.5
内蒙古	Inner Mongolia	430.9	9804.0	1840.8	1479.3	585.4	29677.6	18451.0
辽 宁	Liaoning	636.6	16555.3	3646.9	4054.8	1333.2	35829.1	22628.7
吉 林	Jilin	219.3	8216.2	1470.6	1758.5	736.3	18785.4	9869.3
黑龙江	Heilongjiang	333.6	6086.2	1325.1	1289.9	449.5	14744.8	8360.3
上 海	Shanghai	287.1	23050.2	6977.9	4662.1	1492.0	39258.2	19017.8
江 苏	Jiangsu	603.3	59628.7	19018.8	12598.1	4755.5	114307.6	59709.2
浙 江	Zhejiang	312.8	38603.9	11173.7	8181.4	3312.2	69755.3	38621.5
安 徽	Anhui	106.2	15404.8	4476.3	3361.3	1338.4	32845.4	18648.8
福 建	Fujian	158.9	15952.7	4200.2	3635.0	1443.7	31317.5	16375.3
江 西	Jiangxi	71.8	8969.1	2094.6	2071.4	863.4	21432.7	10366.1
山 东	Shangdong	584.4	47655.6	8957.0	10658.9	4547.2	104715.5	56578.2
河 南	Henan	382.9	26582.9	5745.3	4416.5	1678.4	59165.5	28132.5
湖 北	**Hubei**	**183.9**	**16653.3**	**4234.6**	**3960.1**	**1594.3**	**36640.1**	**19499.2**
湖 南	Hunan	167.4	10830.9	3172.7	2771.9	900.7	24743.2	13057.5
广 东	Guangdong	426.4	61135.6	18500.6	13270.5	4701.4	104720.0	58614.2
广 西	Guangxi	113.4	7418.9	1495.9	1778.4	786.5	15838.8	9742.5
海 南	Hainan	23.4	1010.8	190.7	197.8	79.5	2740.5	1521.6
重 庆	Chongqing	157.9	8905.9	2485.2	1613.6	716.0	19313.4	11809.6
四 川	Sichuan	421.0	16392.1	3968.0	3433.3	1322.3	40163.6	23608.6
贵 州	Guizhou	122.5	5536.3	921.1	1109.1	333.4	13468.9	8603.8
云 南	Yunnan	439.5	6749.5	1100.9	2207.5	527.2	19427.4	12389.2
西 藏	Tibet	14.9	234.2	21.1	26.4	10.2	1076.4	550.9
陕 西	Shaanxi	144.6	9932.8	2060.4	1955.7	829.2	28153.3	15609.5
甘 肃	Gansu	143.2	4186.1	830.8	1339.4	513.9	11883.1	7751.4
青 海	Qinghai	39.0	1668.4	309.5	326.7	116.8	6107.0	4170.8
宁 夏	Ningxia	59.1	2838.2	581.6	747.7	275.1	8477.1	5732.1
新 疆	Xinjiang	387.1	5839.9	1041.9	1129.5	447.1	19265.6	12334.1

附录1-26　分地区主要工业产品产量(2016)
OUTPUT OF MAJOR INDUSTRIAL PRODUCTS BY REGION

地 区	Region	原煤(万吨) Raw Coal (10 000 tons)	原油(万吨) Crude Oil (10 000 tons)	天然气(亿立方米) Natural gas (100 million cu.m)	布(亿米) Cloth (100 million meters)	农用化肥(万吨) Agricultural Fertilizers (10 000 Tons)	水泥(万吨) Cement (10 000 tons)	生铁(万吨) Pig Iron (10 000 tons)	粗钢(万吨) Crude steel (10 000 tons)
全国总计	**National Total**	**341060.4**	**19968.5**	**1368.7**	**906.8**	**7128.6**	**241352.6**	**70073.6**	**80836.6**
北 京	Beijing	317.6		21.7			510.3		
天 津	Tianjin		3273.3	19.7	2.4	13.4	788.6	1660.8	1798.9
河 北	Hebei	6484.3	546.0	7.8	73.9	226.2	9898.6	18398.4	19260.0
山 西	Shanxi	83043.7		43.2	0.7	438.7	3851.5	3641.1	3936.1
内蒙古	Inner Mongolia	84558.9	44.9	0.3		250.2	6298.4	1469.4	1813.2
辽 宁	Liaoning	4169.7	1017.3	5.5	1.6	58.8	4011.0	6033.9	6029.0
吉 林	Jilin	1684.1	610.7	19.8	0.3	15.9	3086.8	847.6	832.0
黑龙江	Heilongjiang	5890.5	3656.0	38.0	0.1	63.5	3381.0	354.0	372.3
上 海	Shanghai		6.5	2.0	1.1	1.8	418.4	1587.2	1709.1
江 苏	Jiangsu	1367.9	166.0	1.3	140.9	210.1	18038.1	7174.1	11080.5
浙 江	Zhejiang				256.9	32.3	10848.0	848.0	1299.6
安 徽	Anhui	12235.6		3.4	16.5	291.7	13584.1	2242.7	2731.3
福 建	Fujian	1383.9			87.1	52.0	8106.0	980.4	1516.8
江 西	Jiangxi	1556.8		0.2	13.6	149.4	9553.3	2082.0	2241.5
山 东	Shangdong	12817.6	2295.3	4.2	127.5	531.4	16156.1	6769.2	7167.1
河 南	Henan	11946.8	315.7	3.3	28.7	542.1	15672.1	2862.9	2849.5
湖 北	**Hubei**	**593.9**	**58.1**	**1.3**	**82.2**	**1164.9**	**11600.5**	**2323.3**	**2948.5**
湖 南	Hunan	2787.2			4.4	109.5	12239.7	1791.4	1827.8
广 东	Guangdong		1556.3	79.2	31.9	69.5	15080.6	1670.2	2283.2
广 西	Guangxi	432.5	47.4	0.2	0.5	94.3	12034.9	1216.4	2109.6
海 南	Hainan		29.4	1.4		51.7	2227.9		27.6
重 庆	Chongqing	2437.0		51.7	5.4	182.0	6790.2	287.8	366.5
四 川	Sichuan	6164.8	10.8	296.9	20.0	531.0	14615.5	1733.2	2007.7
贵 州	Guizhou	16850.6		3.4	0.3	639.7	10798.5	371.4	515.9
云 南	Yunnan	4586.9				279.5	11104.4	1277.2	1417.3
西 藏	Tibet						623.3		
陕 西	Shaanxi	51566.2	3502.4	411.9	8.8	153.4	7264.0	856.0	924.7
甘 肃	Gansu	4254.3	40.4	0.1		32.1	4640.4	494.3	628.4
青 海	Qinghai	787.3	221.0	60.8		552.4	1895.4	96.6	114.9
宁 夏	Ningxia	7069.3	6.2		0.1	55.0	1984.7	154.3	159.2
新 疆	Xinjiang	16073.1	2564.9	291.2	1.8	336.3	4250.2	849.9	868.4

附录1-26 续表 continued

地 区	Region	钢材(万吨) Steel (10 000 tons)	汽车(万辆) Car (10 000)	家用电冰箱(万台) Household Refrigerators (10 000 units)	程控交换机(万线) PBX (10 000 lines)	移动通信手持机(万台) Mobile Handset (10 000 units)	微型计算机设备(万台) Micro-computer Equipment (10 000 units)	发电量(亿千瓦小时) Power generation (Billion kilowatt hours)
全国总计	**National Total**	**113801.2**	**2811.9**	**8481.6**	**1457.7**	**205819.3**	**29008.5**	**61424.9**
北 京	Beijing	162.8	238.0			6923.9	684.1	434.4
天 津	Tianjin	8667.1	52.9	64.3		4973.5		617.5
河 北	Hebei	26150.4	128.6		13.5			2630.6
山 西	Shanxi	4279.0	0.7			2693.4		2535.1
内蒙古	Inner Mongolia	2016.8	2.1					3949.8
辽 宁	Liaoning	5906.3	107.9	145.7	36.6	640.5	0.1	1778.8
吉 林	Jilin	961.4	254.0					760.3
黑龙江	Heilongjiang	332.8	7.6				1.1	900.4
上 海	Shanghai	2080.1	260.8	56.4	75.3	4801.4	3084.0	807.3
江 苏	Jiangsu	13469.7	138.6	869.0	0.7	5352.4	5285.2	4709.4
浙 江	Zhejiang	3760.9	58.1	797.7	218.6	5099.6	182.8	3197.7
安 徽	Anhui	3225.8	139.1	3058.8		141.2	1659.8	2252.7
福 建	Fujian	2859.6	21.8			2568.6	847.4	2007.4
江 西	Jiangxi	2585.0	53.6	98.2		7414.0		1085.4
山 东	Shangdong	9788.2	86.9	883.4		6082.5	23.7	5329.3
河 南	Henan	4667.9	58.5	186.2		25235.8		2652.7
湖 北	**Hubei**	**3563.8**	**243.5**	**392.1**		**6220.7**	**840.3**	**2479.0**
湖 南	Hunan	1998.7	47.7		3.9	22.7	36.1	1385.1
广 东	Guangdong	4113.3	280.1	1553.1	1103.1	95230.2	3344.9	4263.7
广 西	Guangxi	3644.7	245.3			545.7	0.6	1346.5
海 南	Hainan	36.3	6.7					287.7
重 庆	Chongqing	1234.2	266.3	144.2		25500.0	6764.7	701.2
四 川	Sichuan	2837.2	53.0	85.6	0.9	4469.2	5936.5	3273.9
贵 州	Guizhou	526.2	1.6	147.0		1858.5	317.4	1904.0
云 南	Yunnan	1654.7	13.3		5.1	37.0		2692.5
西 藏	Tibet	1.8						54.5
陕 西	Shaanxi	1233.8	42.0			8.5		1757.4
甘 肃	Gansu	665.9	1.2					1214.3
青 海	Qinghai	125.1						553.0
宁 夏	Ningxia	164.1						1144.4
新 疆	Xinjiang	1087.6	2.1					2719.1

附录1-27　分地区建筑业总产值和房屋建筑面积
TOTAL OUTPUT VALUE OF CONSTRUCTION AND THE AREA OF THE BUILDING BY REGION

单位:亿元、万平方米

(billion、10000sq.m)

地 区	Region	总产值 Total Output		施工面积 Floor Space under Construction		竣工面积(万平方米) Floor Space Completed	
		2015	2016	2015	2016	2015	2016
全国总计	**National Total**	**180757.5**	**193566.8**	**1239717.6**	**1264219.9**	**420784.9**	**422375.7**
北 京	Beijing	8436.7	8841.2	59776.7	61097.5	9886.3	10703.5
天 津	Tianjin	4488.9	4891.8	15644.6	17036.2	3547.2	3428.7
河 北	Hebei	5252.6	5517.7	35616.5	34616.1	11613.0	11145.1
山 西	Shanxi	2931.3	3318.5	13943.4	14620.6	3634.4	3353.3
内蒙古	Inner Mongolia	1123.5	1220.8	6974.6	6296.0	3103.1	2538.6
辽 宁	Liaoning	5413.8	3926.7	28937.1	20390.7	10397.9	6852.5
吉 林	Jilin	2216.3	2283.6	12237.2	10634.4	5602.6	5211.4
黑龙江	Heilongjiang	1680.4	1716.6	5524.2	5404.1	2968.1	2747.0
上 海	Shanghai	5652.5	6046.2	36659.8	36019.7	7258.7	7481.2
江 苏	Jiangsu	24785.8	25791.8	215592.0	221493.6	76823.9	74990.3
浙 江	Zhejiang	23980.6	24989.4	201542.2	198401.2	68316.3	68818.5
安 徽	Anhui	5695.9	6047.3	41476.5	40130.0	15553.6	14588.4
福 建	Fujian	7605.8	8531.5	59277.3	62920.7	16631.3	18121.2
江 西	Jiangxi	4602.5	5179.0	28895.4	28446.2	14255.6	14835.8
山 东	Shangdong	9381.7	10087.4	69478.6	72090.6	23657.0	23721.3
河 南	Henan	8047.7	8808.0	53132.5	55784.0	17963.7	19425.8
湖 北	**Hubei**	**10592.9**	**11862.4**	**62204.7**	**72835.1**	**26828.9**	**28613.5**
湖 南	Hunan	6630.8	7304.2	47504.4	50239.0	17390.0	18629.2
广 东	Guangdong	8865.7	9652.3	50461.6	54358.3	14373.4	15661.7
广 西	Guangxi	2953.4	3449.2	23432.0	26531.9	7720.7	7998.0
海 南	Hainan	278.6	307.8	2132.0	2085.4	744.6	652.4
重 庆	Chongqing	6256.9	7035.8	32801.6	32077.1	13542.6	13751.6
四 川	Sichuan	8768.2	9959.7	52795.4	54048.3	20666.8	21084.9
贵 州	Guizhou	1947.7	2363.0	16769.6	19354.6	3195.8	4112.1
云 南	Yunnan	3268.9	3867.2	15437.1	17052.9	6941.1	7102.0
西 藏	Tibet	106.9	111.3	295.4	244.2	173.9	144.0
陕 西	Shaanxi	4752.6	5329.2	23991.2	24528.3	7087.4	6758.9
甘 肃	Gansu	1849.0	1947.2	10757.1	10422.4	4083.1	3915.2
青 海	Qinghai	409.5	410.6	908.7	886.8	350.2	301.9
宁 夏	Ningxia	524.5	511.3	3285.0	2771.3	1226.6	1017.8
新 疆	Xinjiang	2255.7	2258.2	12233.3	11312.6	5247.2	4669.9

附录1-28　分地区建筑业主要效益指标(2016)
MAIN BENEFIT INDICATORS OF CONSTRUCTION INDUSTRY BY REGION

地 区	Region	企业个数(个) Number of Enterprises(unit)	从事建筑业活动的从业人员平均人数(万人)Average number of Employed Persons (ten thousand people)	按建筑业总产值计算的劳动生产率(元/人) Productivity of Labour (Yuan / person)	人均竣工产值(元/人)Per capita Output Value(Yuan / person)	人均施工面积(平方米/人) Per capita Construction Area (M2/ person)	人均竣工面积(平方米/人) Per capita Completion Area (M2/ person)
全国总计	**National Total**	**83017**	**5757.0**	**336227**	**196095**	**219.6**	**73.4**
北 京	Beijing	2858	165.6	533880	261084	368.9	64.6
天 津	Tianjin	1500	99.3	492879	223320	171.6	34.5
河 北	Hebei	2467	145.3	379815	198827	238.3	76.7
山 西	Shanxi	2532	112.3	295590	113886	130.2	29.9
内蒙古	Inner Mongolia	870	41.3	295574	168293	152.4	61.5
辽 宁	Liaoning	5238	130.5	300927	156872	156.3	52.5
吉 林	Jilin	2191	80.1	285207	192547	132.8	65.1
黑龙江	Heilongjiang	1566	67.0	256076	160577	80.6	41.0
上 海	Shanghai	2662	126.5	477994	261710	284.8	59.1
江 苏	Jiangsu	8770	845.8	304925	251471	261.9	88.7
浙 江	Zhejiang	6174	777.3	321476	203687	255.2	88.5
安 徽	Anhui	2929	169.8	356129	196082	236.3	85.9
福 建	Fujian	3608	321.9	265043	155736	195.5	56.3
江 西	Jiangxi	1873	168.4	307509	179792	168.9	88.1
山 东	Shangdong	6013	322.6	312707	166261	223.5	73.5
河 南	Henan	5123	272.6	323100	181254	204.6	71.3
湖 北	**Hubei**	**3368**	**270.6**	**438438**	**234472**	**269.2**	**105.8**
湖 南	Hunan	2067	229.2	318730	199908	219.6	81.3
广 东	Guangdong	4437	230.5	418829	206361	235.9	68.0
广 西	Guangxi	1139	114.1	302337	161429	232.6	70.1
海 南	Hainan	155	8.1	379671	233394	257.3	80.4
重 庆	Chongqing	2577	217.4	323617	166333	147.5	63.3
四 川	Sichuan	3809	324.3	307129	152910	166.7	65.0
贵 州	Guizhou	891	71.4	330753	117688	270.9	57.6
云 南	Yunnan	2544	132.2	292428	159756	128.9	53.7
西 藏	Tibet	173	3.3	335094	198752	73.5	43.4
陕 西	Shaanxi	2114	136.7	389771	166756	179.4	49.4
甘 肃	Gansu	1323	62.9	309498	168592	165.7	62.2
青 海	Qinghai	371	14.5	283457	114084	61.2	20.8
宁 夏	Ningxia	531	19.1	267566	197925	145.0	53.3
新 疆	Xinjiang	1144	76.5	295359	202207	148.0	61.1

附录1-29　各地区社会消费品零售总额
TOTAL RETAIL SALES OF CONSUMER GOODS BY REGION

单位:亿元　　(100 million yuan)

地　区	Region	2010	2011	2012	2013	2014	2015	2016
全国总计	**National Total**	**158008.0**	**187205.8**	**214432.7**	**242842.8**	**271896.1**	**300930.8**	**332316.3**
北　京	Beijing	6340.3	7222.2	8123.5	8872.1	9638.0	10338.0	11005.1
天　津	Tianjin	2860.2	3395.1	3921.4	4470.4	4738.7	5257.3	5635.8
河　北	Hebei	6821.8	8035.5	9254.0	10516.7	11820.5	12990.7	14364.7
山　西	Shanxi	3318.2	3903.4	4506.8	5139.3	5717.9	6033.7	6480.5
内蒙古	Inner Mongolia	3384.0	3991.7	4572.5	5114.2	5657.6	6107.7	6700.8
辽　宁	Liaoning	6887.6	8095.3	9304.2	10581.4	11857.0	12787.2	13414.1
吉　林	Jilin	3504.9	4119.8	4772.9	5426.4	6080.9	6651.9	7310.4
黑龙江	Heilongjiang	4039.2	4750.1	5491.0	6251.2	7015.3	7640.2	8402.5
上　海	Shanghai	6186.6	7185.8	7840.4	8557.0	9303.5	10131.5	10946.6
江　苏	Jiangsu	13606.3	16058.3	18411.1	20878.2	23458.1	25876.8	28707.1
浙　江	Zhejiang	10387.0	12532.8	14199.6	15970.8	17835.3	19784.7	21970.8
安　徽	Anhui	4300.5	5288.2	6142.8	7044.7	7957.0	8908.0	10000.2
福　建	Fujian	5310.0	6276.2	7256.5	8275.3	9346.7	10505.9	11674.5
江　西	Jiangxi	2971.0	3560.5	4123.3	4696.1	5292.6	5925.5	6634.6
山　东	Shangdong	14620.3	17155.5	19651.9	22294.8	25111.5	27761.4	30645.8
河　南	Henan	8004.2	9453.6	10915.6	12426.6	14005.0	15740.4	17618.4
湖　北	**Hubei**	**7014.4**	**8363.3**	**9682.4**	**11035.9**	**12449.3**	**14003.2**	**15649.2**
湖　南	Hunan	5952.6	7209.0	8318.7	9509.5	10723.5	12024.0	13436.5
广　东	Guangdong	17458.4	20297.5	22677.1	25453.9	28471.1	31517.6	34739.1
广　西	Guangxi	3312.0	3908.2	4516.6	5133.1	5772.8	6348.1	7027.3
海　南	Hainan	663.8	822.5	950.2	1090.9	1224.5	1325.1	1453.7
重　庆	Chongqing	3051.1	3782.3	4403.0	5055.8	5710.7	6424.0	7271.4
四　川	Sichuan	6884.8	8290.8	9622.0	11001.0	12393.0	13877.7	15601.9
贵　州	Guizhou	1531.6	1899.9	2266.3	2601.2	2936.9	3283.0	3709.0
云　南	Yunnan	2555.8	3105.9	3597.9	4112.6	4632.9	5103.2	5722.9
西　藏	Tibet	192.4	237.5	277.9	322.2	364.5	408.5	459.4
陕　西	Shaanxi	3257.5	3900.6	4581.6	5245.0	5918.7	6578.1	7367.6
甘　肃	Gansu	1435.5	1772.9	2064.4	2368.8	2668.3	2907.2	3184.4
青　海	Qinghai	351.0	413.4	480.3	549.6	620.8	691.0	767.3
宁　夏	Ningxia	418.5	515.5	590.5	668.5	737.2	789.6	850.1
新　疆	Xinjiang	1386.1	1662.4	1916.1	2179.5	2436.5	2606.0	2825.9

附录1-30 分地区网上零售额(2016)
ONLINE RETAIL SALE BY REGION

地 区	Region	网上零售额(亿元) Online Retail Sales (100 million yuan)	比上年增长(%) Growth Rata(%)	其中：实物商品网上零售额(亿元) Online Retail Sales in Goods (100 million yuan)	比上年增长(%) Growth Rata(%)
全国总计	**National Total**	**51555.7**	**26.2**	**41944.5**	**25.6**
北 京	Beijing	5271.1	17.5	4226.5	17.9
天 津	Tianjin	767.5	27.4	649.0	37.1
河 北	Hebei	972.4	30.6	833.3	34.5
山 西	Shanxi	177.3	15.3	94.3	29.8
内蒙古	Inner Mongolia	145.7	30.7	69.0	60.3
辽 宁	Liaoning	530.6	23.3	370.1	23.7
吉 林	Jilin	204.1	43.1	88.1	37.8
黑龙江	Heilongjiang	206.9	22.3	120.4	34.1
上 海	Shanghai	5107.3	22.5	4704.4	21.9
江 苏	Jiangsu	4739.7	40.1	3995.3	40.4
浙 江	Zhejiang	9335.1	29.9	6798.5	26.7
安 徽	Anhui	895.7	38.5	732.3	44.6
福 建	Fujian	2181.0	15.1	1912.4	13.8
江 西	Jiangxi	427.4	32.4	363.1	29.0
山 东	Shangdong	1722.4	30.8	1504.6	31.6
河 南	Henan	1064.2	47.2	627.6	41.1
湖 北	**Hubei**	**1121.2**	**22.7**	**827.7**	**28.5**
湖 南	Hunan	723.4	11.3	511.0	16.5
广 东	Guangdong	11426.6	23.1	10348.0	20.3
广 西	Guangxi	273.0	8.6	137.8	27.1
海 南	Hainan	143.8	7.0	25.5	20.6
重 庆	Chongqing	539.0	25.6	340.7	36.7
四 川	Sichuan	1523.9	36.1	1140.0	30.7
贵 州	Guizhou	169.8	55.6	73.3	75.4
云 南	Yunnan	245.6	10.0	152.2	28.3
西 藏	Tibet	5.0	18.7	4.0	7.6
陕 西	Shaanxi	1016.8	36.7	913.2	46.2
甘 肃	Gansu	119.9	15.9	27.6	49.9
青 海	Qinghai	9.5	14.2	8.6	20.2
宁 夏	Ningxia	16.6	31.0	13.4	33.5
新 疆	Xinjiang	44.4	-2.6	40.2	-0.3
不分地区	Not Classified by Region	428.8	—	292.5	—

附录1-31 分地区客运量和旅客周转量(2016年)
REGIONAL PASSENGER TRAFFIC AND TURNOVER VOLUME OF PASSENGER TRAFFIC(2016)

地 区	Region	客运量 (万人) Passenger Traffic (10 000 Persons)	#铁路 Railway	#公路 Highway	#水运 Waterway	旅客周转量 (亿人公里) Turnover Volume of Passenger Traffic (100 million person-kms)	#铁路 Railway	#公路 Highway	#水运 Waterway
全国总计	**National Total**	**1900194**	**281405**	**1542759**	**27234**	**31258**	**12579.3**	**10228.7**	**72.3**
北 京	Beijing	61519	13479	48040		268	150.8	117.7	
天 津	Tianjin	18377	4543	13741	93	262	183.5	78.4	0.1
河 北	Hebei	50701	10771	39925	5	1238	993.6	244.2	0.4
山 西	Shanxi	26374	7530	18702	142	361	219.3	141.1	0.1
内蒙古	Inner Mongolia	15735	5388	10347		375	222.2	152.7	
辽 宁	Liaoning	73632	14040	59054	538	936	623.4	306.7	6.0
吉 林	Jilin	34910	7567	27186	156	431	262.3	168.7	0.2
黑龙江	Heilongjiang	39386	10480	28550	355	471	270.6	200.1	0.4
上 海	Shanghai	14416	10609	3402	404	214	98.7	115.0	0.7
江 苏	Jiangsu	133580	17814	113494	2272	1468	686.1	780.0	2.4
浙 江	Zhejiang	105018	18035	83033	3950	1075	604.0	465.1	5.8
安 徽	Anhui	81106	10370	70523	213	1187	695.7	491.3	0.4
福 建	Fujian	51649	10496	39137	2016	593	338.6	251.9	2.7
江 西	Jiangxi	62876	9249	53366	261	971	688.0	282.3	0.3
山 东	Shangdong	63463	12639	48823	2000	1189	704.5	472.4	12.0
河 南	Henan	120528	13825	106415	289	1684	923.1	760.6	0.6
湖 北	**Hubei**	**102990**	**14197**	**88221**	**572**	**1232**	**741.6**	**487.3**	**3.4**
湖 南	Hunan	121760	11518	108627	1615	1501	920.6	577.0	3.2
广 东	Guangdong	130345	25603	102094	2648	1887	797.3	1079.8	10.3
广 西	Guangxi	48699	8388	39750	561	744	351.1	390.1	2.7
海 南	Hainan	13912	2292	9920	1699	120	41.5	75.4	3.5
重 庆	Chongqing	61255	4911	55594	750	506	164.4	336.7	5.1
四 川	Sichuan	123746	11456	109716	2573	942	341.3	597.8	2.4
贵 州	Guizhou	89464	5169	82199	2096	675	226.0	443.1	5.8
云 南	Yunnan	46519	4056	41208	1255	446	123.4	320.0	2.7
西 藏	Tibet	1155	265	889		40	16.0	23.7	
陕 西	Shaanxi	69820	8302	61093	425	756	464.2	290.8	0.7
甘 肃	Gansu	41626	3604	37932	90	613	360.0	253.3	0.2
青 海	Qinghai	5934	994	4873	66	125	77.5	47.5	0.1
宁 夏	Ningxia	8757	659	7910	188	110	45.2	64.4	0.1
新 疆	Xinjiang	32148	3155	28993		458	244.6	213.5	
不分地区	Not Classified by Region	48796				8378			

注:不分地区合计为民航完成数。
Note: The total passenyer traffil not classified by region lefers to thut completed by civil aviation

附录1-32 分地区货运量和货物周转量(2016)
REGIONAL FREIGHT TRAFFIC AND TURNOVER VOLUME OF FREIGHT TRAFFIC(2016)

地区	Region	货运量 (万吨) Freight Traffic (10 000 Persons)	#铁路 Railway	#公路 Highway	#水运 Waterway	货物周转量 (亿吨公里) Turnover Volume of Freight Traffic (100 million person-kms)	#铁路 Railway	#公路 Highway	#水运 Waterway
全国总计	**National Total**	**4386762**	**333186**	**3341259**	**638238**	**186629**	**23792.3**	**61080.1**	**97338.8**
北京	Beijing	20734	762	19972		825	664.1	161.3	
天津	Tianjin	50506	8150	32841	9515	2302	399.8	372.5	1530.0
河北	Hebei	210586	16313	189822	4451	12333	3704.5	7294.6	1333.6
山西	Shanxi	167076	64861	102200	16	3565	2113.3	1452.1	0.1
内蒙古	Inner Mongolia	186726	56113	130613		4342	1918.1	2423.6	
辽宁	Liaoning	207064	16230	177371	13464	12113	900.9	2936.8	8275.8
吉林	Jilin	45060	3944	40777	339	1479	393.1	1084.8	0.6
黑龙江	Heilongjiang	53569	9542	42897	1130	1533	620.5	904.8	7.3
上海	Shanghai	88324	482	39055	48787	19318	10.2	282.0	19025.6
江苏	Jiangsu	202070	5590	117166	79314	7654	288.9	2140.3	5224.6
浙江	Zhejiang	215558	3913	133999	77646	9789	212.0	1626.8	7950.6
安徽	Anhui	364567	9265	244526	110776	10896	719.7	4915.7	5261.0
福建	Fujian	120352	2918	85770	31664	6071	129.4	1094.7	4846.4
江西	Jiangxi	138118	4357	122872	10889	3898	515.0	3147.5	235.3
山东	Shangdong	285386	20574	249752	15060	8884	1225.5	6071.4	1587.4
河南	Henan	206087	10287	184255	11544	7384	1736.4	4838.5	808.6
湖北	**Hubei**	**162460**	**4088**	**122656**	**35716**	**5923**	**735.7**	**2506.9**	**2680.3**
湖南	Hunan	206527	4114	178968	23445	4057	750.8	2686.6	619.5
广东	Guangdong	366839	8380	272826	85633	21802	259.4	3381.9	18160.3
广西	Guangxi	160761	5898	128247	26615	4260	679.0	2248.5	1332.9
海南	Hainan	21786	793	10879	10114	1061	12.1	76.1	972.5
重庆	Chongqing	107966	1928	89390	16648	2968	156.7	935.4	1876.1
四川	Sichuan	160970	6794	146046	8131	2504	716.1	1565.3	222.7
贵州	Guizhou	89526	5635	82237	1654	1482	566.7	873.2	42.4
云南	Yunnan	115505	5372	109487	646	1600	411.8	1173.1	15.2
西藏	Tibet	1971	65	1906		125	30.1	94.5	
陕西	Shaanxi	149046	35459	113363	224	3445	1518.3	1925.8	0.8
甘肃	Gansu	60661	5866	54761	34	2170	1220.3	949.6	0.1
青海	Qinghai	16881	2834	14047		476	239.8	236.0	
宁夏	Ningxia	43260	5839	37421		820	242.4	577.6	
新疆	Xinjiang	71961	6822	65139		1804	701.7	1102.2	
不分地区	Not Classified by Region	88863			14785	19747			15329.0

注：不分地区合计中包括管道运输企业、民航运输企业、中国远洋海运集团有限公司下属海外公司完成数。
Note: The freight ton-kilometers ont classified by iegion refers to civil aviation,pipelines and that completed bycommpanies abroad under the China Ocan shipping(Gronp)company.

中国统计出版社最新图书简目

（仅供参考，以实际出版为准）

统计资料

中国统计年鉴　中国统计摘要　中国发展报告
中国经济普查年鉴　国际统计年鉴　金砖国家联合统计手册
中国-东盟国家统计手册　中国农村统计年鉴　中国县域统计年鉴
中国城市统计年鉴　中国对外直接投资统计公报　中国地区经济监测报告
中国贸易外经统计年鉴　中国零售和餐饮连锁企业统计年鉴　中国商品交易市场统计年鉴
大中型批发零售和住宿餐饮企业统计年鉴　中国农产品价格调查年鉴　中国住户调查年鉴
中国价格统计年鉴　中国能源统计年鉴　全国农产品成本收益资料汇编
中国环境统计年鉴　中国建筑业统计年鉴　国外资源、能源和环境统计资料汇编
中国工业统计年鉴　中国城乡建设统计年鉴　中国县城建设统计年鉴
中国城市建设统计年鉴　中国科技统计年鉴　中国房地产统计年鉴
中国证券期货统计年鉴　中国劳动统计年鉴　中国第三产业统计年鉴
工业企业科技活动资料　中国社会统计年鉴　中国高技术产业统计年鉴
中国人才资源统计报告　中国教育统计年鉴　中国人口和就业统计年鉴
文化及相关产业统计概览　中国文化及相关产业统计年鉴　中国教育经费统计年鉴
中国民族统计年鉴　中国残疾人事业统计年鉴　中国民政统计年鉴
中国乡镇街道行政区域简册　中国基本单位统计年鉴　中国妇女儿童状况统计资料（英）

省级综合统计年鉴系列

北京 天津 河北 山西 内蒙古 辽宁 吉林 黑龙江 上海 江苏 浙江 安徽 福建 江西 山东 河南 湖北 湖南 广东 广西 海南 重庆 四川 贵州 云南 西藏 陕西 甘肃 青海 宁夏 新疆 新疆生产建设兵团

市(县)级综合统计年鉴系列

滨海新区 石家庄 唐山 邯郸 保定 沧州 邢台 廊坊 承德 衡水 秦皇岛 张家口 太原 大同 阳泉 长治 晋城 朔州 晋中 运城 忻州 临汾 吕梁 呼和浩特 呼和浩特新城区 鄂尔多斯 包头 沈阳 大连 长春 吉林 延吉 四平 通化 松原 哈尔滨 齐齐哈尔 黑龙江垦区 上海浦东新区 南京 无锡 徐州 常州 苏州 南通 连云港 淮安 盐城 扬州 镇江 泰州 宿迁 江阴 丹阳 海门 杭州 宁波 温州 嘉兴 湖州 绍兴 金华 衢州 舟山 台州 丽水 合肥 安庆 马鞍山 福州 厦门 宁德 漳州 龙岩 南昌 九江 上饶 新余 抚州 萍乡 赣州 吉安 景德镇 济南 青岛 潍坊 枣庄 日照 滕州 郑州 洛阳 平顶山 三门峡 商丘 信阳 济源 汝州 武汉 十堰 荆州 宜昌 荆门 咸宁 长沙 广州 深圳 惠州 东莞 汕尾 南宁 柳州 桂林 来宾 河池 防城港 海口 三亚 成都 贵阳 黔南 毕节 昆明 西安 咸阳 延安 宝鸡 安康 铜川 汉中 榆林 兰州 庆阳 银川 乌鲁木齐 兵团一师 兵团十师

调查年鉴系列

天津 山西 内蒙古 辽宁 吉林 上海 福建 江西 河南 湖北 湖南 广西 重庆 四川 云南 甘肃 宁夏 新疆

统计方法应用/实用手册

实用SAS统计分析教程　马克威统计分析与数据挖掘应用案例　统计公文知识问答
乡镇统计人员岗位知识培训系列教材：辅助调查员岗位基础知识　乡镇统计人员岗位基础知识
县级统计人员岗位知识培训系列教材：Excel在统计工作中的应用　简明统计分析
地市级统计人员岗位知识培训系列教材：统计报告与演示　Excel在统计工作中的应用

统计通俗读物/统计科普图书

国家统计局核心统计指标变迁　货架上的统计　账本里的统计

重点图书

砥砺奋进的五年——从十八大到十九大　新编英汉汉英统计大词典　中华医学统计百科全书
新常态下的中国服务业：理论与实践　新动能新产业发展报告-2017
挑大学选专业2018—考研择校指南　挑大学选专业2018—高考志愿填报指南

中国统计出版社发行部电话：（010）63376907　63376908　同楫行书店电话：68783171　68783172
地址：北京市丰台区西三环南路甲6号　邮政编码：100073　网址：http://www.zgtjcbs.com